CTURAL
ASIES

BY JO FARB HERNÁNDEZ

PRINCIPAL PHOTOGRAPHY BY FRED SCRUTON

tra.publishing

CONTENTS

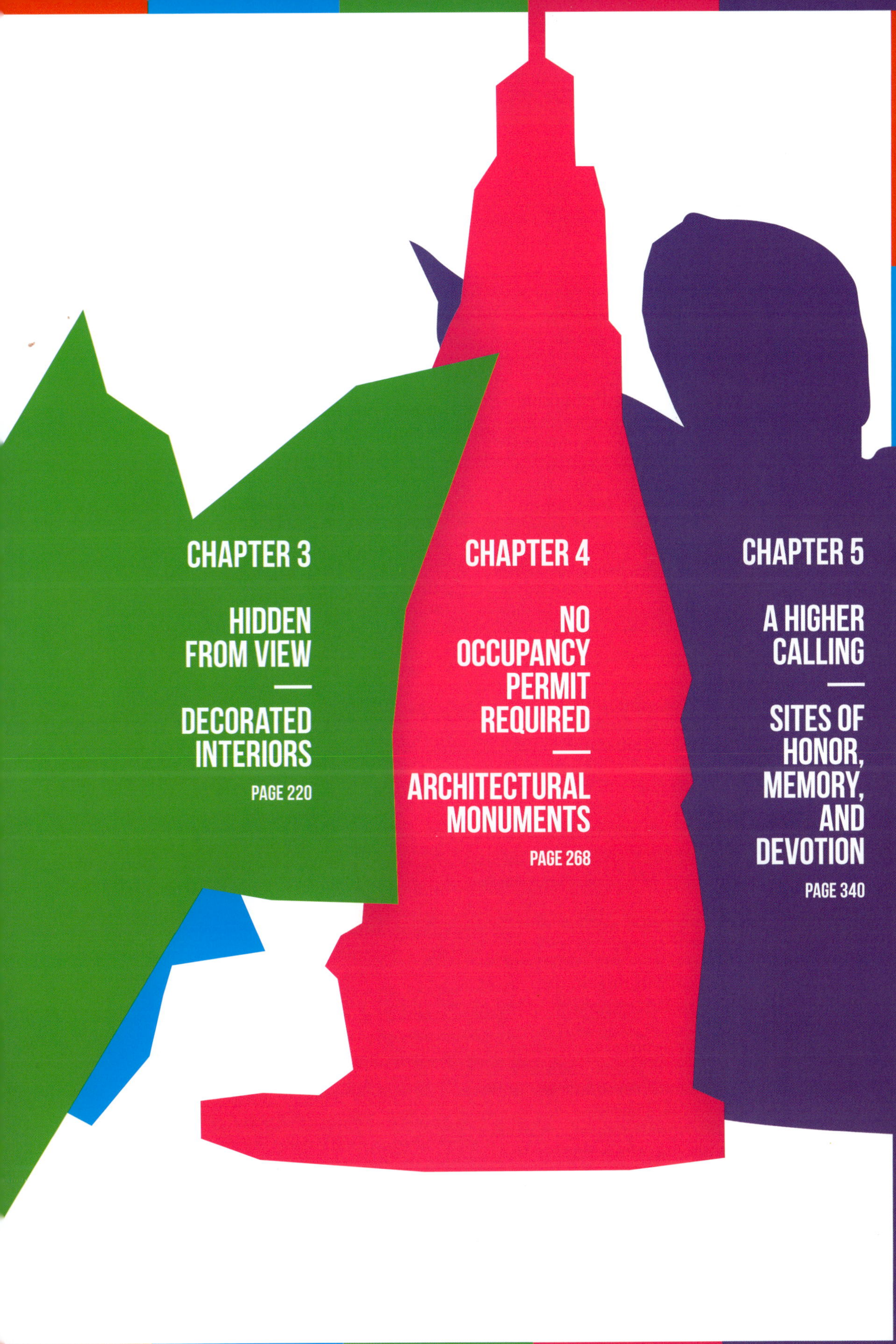

INTRODUCTION

The need for shelter is instinctual, animal.

Even before our prehistoric ancestors left the hollows and caves where they sought shelter—no doubt learning from and mimicking our nonhuman neighbors—they were beginning to alter and decorate their spaces. From these earliest days we began to develop regional norms and protocols, so much so that similar images, techniques, and choices of materials can be recognized among the Paleolithic paintings in caves along Spain's northern coast, for example, or those in the Maros-Pangkep karst of the Indonesian island of Sulawesi. As we evolved, these norms grew more elaborate as we manipulated the resources of our world—the stones, the branches and leaves, the clays—and transformed them into ever more functional dwellings. And these dwellings were not only intended for ourselves and our families, but also for our gods and goddesses.

The shelters we humans built developed in such ways that most of our forms and techniques can be easily identified by our locations. Adobe dwellings in the U.S. Southwest, half-timbered plastered walls in continental Europe, the distinctive roof curves of Asian temples: all are easily distinguished and characterized not only by their appearances and materials but by their histories and, often, by the cultural mythologies, priorities, and worldviews to which they are linked.

In contrast, the architectural spaces introduced in this book reveal more about their individual makers than they do about the larger cultural and historical narratives of the communities in which they are situated. Sacred and secular buildings built from scratch, others whose exterior façades or interior rooms were modified so radically that the bones of the structure have become almost irrelevant if not invisible, and, stretching the genre, monumental sculptures at architectural scale that allow people to walk, climb, or explore within, are examples of what you will find in these pages. These works are unique and incomparable, and often spill over from one classification to another. They respond to neither folk nor mainstream art movements, although they may display techniques or configurations that were learned through academic, occupational, or oral transmission. There are no models for these constructions, no "typical" characteristics, no right or wrong.

While we can track early precursors of such "alt-stream" architecture to follies produced toward the end of the Renaissance, it was not until the 1960s that scholars began to acknowledge the existence of surprising numbers of these curious sites. With increasing attention, growing numbers of photographers and researchers began to identify these discoveries in their hometowns or on their travels, and we all came to realize that these art environments, each unique, are found globally.

We have also realized, over time, that although some members of the public may describe these structures as "outsider art" or "outsider architecture," most of the artist-builders, while self-taught, are not outcasts or recluses disengaged from their communities, nor are they ignorant about the state of their home region, their country, and even the world. In more traditional communities these makers may describe their unpaid labors as a hobby, in sites tied to mainstream religions they may stretch the parameters of sacred architecture, and in more iconoclastic areas they may proudly flaunt the material and intellectual independence that drives their acerbic criticism of the powers-that-be.

In every case, however, while there may be a disconnect with what their community understands this kind of construction to be—a disconnect that, in the most egregious cases, motivates neighbors to call for the site's demolition or renormalization—these creatives are commenting on their own lives, their faith or lack of it, and the state of their universe in a personal way: a way that is the only way they know, a way they choose, and a way in which theirs is the only voice that matters. And they are so enthusiastic—albeit sometimes surprised—about the monumentality of their work that in almost every case they are delighted to tell us about it, often in running commentary that describes all of its intricacies, details of construction, and coded meanings.

Most of these singular constructions are devoid of the intent to profit monetarily from the work. They are developed improvisationally, with neither formalized nor written plans, using an additive process that allows time for learning about techniques and media, accumulation of materials and resources, allocation of working hours, dedication of energy, and reflection about how one creative gesture will inform the next. Some—particularly the sacred spaces—are built with forethought and intentionality, while other sites start as a whimsy, a flower bed, a fountain, and, over years, if not decades, morph into the monumental creations that take our breath away.

Experimental and experiential, with their paeans to love, to faith, to honor, to personal histories and cultural memories—or, in other cases, as a means to air protests and grievances—these idiosyncratic architectural sites straddle a space between the private and the public. With only rare exceptions, artist-built environments are developed on the creators' own properties and are informed by the spatial attributes and social setting of the site itself; nevertheless, despite their personalized location, they present a public face, as most architecture does. While public viewing and response is not typically the initial motivation for beginning work, it frequently becomes an important aspect of the project as construction continues, as a tool to communicate the artist's intent. Over time, any original goal may become instilled with a new and often more outward-looking purpose, as these sites, while not always understood as such, are often conceived by the artist as a gift to the public: to inspire them to slow down and to open their eyes and their hearts to alternative means of communication and expression.

Although governmental regulations increasingly control and restrict every aspect of architectural design and construction, the responses of neighbors, friends, and even family members are often equally as burdensome and difficult to navigate. Whether dissatisfaction with inventive works that breach the conventional aesthetic spectrum is motivated by concerns over property values or embarrassment to the family (or to the neighborhood or town) reputation, such disapproval is powerful and has resulted in the damage or destruction of numerous architectural fantasies. These concerns plague most of the singular works celebrated in this book, and, in fact, numerous significant art environments in our country have already been lost.

The ambivalence with which the public and governmental officials regard these sites is a fundamental factor that often dictates the tenuous nature of their timelines. Rather than being cause to celebrate the creativity of the artists who devote untold hours to bravely building without precedent, these structures are instead regularly subjected to enormous fines and stop-work orders by planning departments, and to vandalism and theft by neighbors or passersby. With the inherent fragility of the often recycled or second-hand building materials contributing to the corrosion caused by weather-related assaults on inadequate construction methods, time and again demolition or collapse is the result. Such economic factors as prospective financial return, with heirs eyeing the comparative values of the aesthetics of the artist's work against the potential of commercial profit from future sale of the property, underscore the fugitive quality of many of these sites. Yet the creativity inherent in dreaming, and the strength to persevere and work to realize those visions, are exceptional talents. Families, the public, and local governments would do well to recognize them as such, and to work more proactively to protect them.

The myriad reasons triggering potential destruction are an important motivation for those of us who study these sites: oftentimes our interviews with the artists and their families, and our photographs and videos of their work, may be the only trace left of their existence after an untimely passing. Consequently, I urge supporters of such singular architecture to involve themselves in political advocacy and activism, if necessary, to encourage local governments to take advantage of these unique constructions and appreciate the distinctive flavor they bring to their communities. Our work, and yours, is critical, because as the sites themselves challenge and expand our social, cultural, and aesthetic norms, they help to open a wider appreciation of the remarkable breadth of human creativity in all its exuberance, and in all its spirited and alternative forms.

ACKNOWLEDGMENTS

Although Fred Scruton and I have individually spent years—decades!—documenting art environments, a project of this magnitude nevertheless could not have been realized without the assistance and counsel of numerous friends and colleagues. Facing the challenge of a tight timetable, we pushed other projects to the side as we supplemented our existing knowledge with new research, buried or long-lost documentation, and additional fieldwork. Along the way we each met new artists and rekindled relationships with those we had worked with earlier, tracked down vintage texts and photographs, and introduced ourselves to researchers who had found some of these sites of interest in years gone by.

The tracks we followed were not always linear, nor were they always fruitful, but they were always intriguing and frequently adventurous, perhaps never so much as when we found ourselves stranded on a snowy New Mexico interstate for 24 hours by a surprise early snowstorm. But the warmth and conviviality with which the artists welcomed us—and our wonder at the monumentality and creativity of their endeavors—is what kept us pushing forward.

To our readers, however, a quick note: please remember that if you choose to visit these sites, most are on private property, and it is important to respect the artist's privacy and seek permission before entering, and certainly before photographing or recording their works in any way.

Our first thanks, of course, go to each of the artists themselves, as well as their partners, family members, and champions. Among these are David Anderson, Matt Arnett, Bill Barksdale, Shelle Barron, Bonnie Bingham, Daniel Bishop, Jenny Cantwell, Hillary Carter-Liggett, John Cary, Tina Cox, Andrew Cunes, Annette Dalzell, Daniel Damonte, Litto Damonte, Alex DeCarli, Katy Emde, Eleanor Every, Charles Fowler, Adrienne Garbini, Kat Gatzke, Lisa Gavon, Pete Gershon, Zack Godshall, Larry Harris, Laura Heller, Larissa Hernández, r.r. jones, Kathryn Kaluzny, Michael Konvicka, Gary LaFleur, Bob Levesque, Tya Every Kottler, Sandy Krause, Keith Larson, Kelly Ludwig, Steven Macias, Nick Malusky, Greg Maynard, Alan E. Mays, Michael McFalls, Jenn Joy Jameson Merchant, Don Meyer, Jacob Neil, Erika Nelson, Shel Neymark, Jane Orleman, Daniel Paul, Steve Plattner, Liz Riedel, Amy Riley, Gloria Dolson Robertson, Nancy Roper, Scott Rubel on behalf of the Glendora Historical Society, Kimberly Sánchez, Lynn Schneider, Cheryl Swanson Scruton, Toni Sherman, Bob Sims, Emily Smith, Itsi Sourelis, Andrew Sturm, Beth Shaw Tripp, David Tripp, Erin Turner, John Turner, Jeff Wack, David Wilson, Amy Wolkins, and Tricia Zigmund.

We are also so appreciative of the following photographers, who provided vintage images of sites that would not otherwise have been able to be illustrated, or that helped us enhance the breadth of the visuals: John Blasdel, Scott Bruno, Tom Chargin, Ted Degener, Katy Emde, Annalise Flynn, Estate of Ron Gasowski, Marissa Gawel, Pete Gershon, Larry Harris, Andrea Hassiba and the Preserve Bottle Village Committee, Vince Hannemann, Sam Hernández, Kirk Huffaker, William Lipke, Kelly Ludwig, J. Miers, JHVE Photo, Susan Moran, Steve Plattner, and Camilo José Vergara. We are further grateful to SPACES (Saving and Preserving Arts and Cultural Environments), now at the Kohler Foundation's Art Preserve, and, in particular, to Annalise Flynn and Brian Rusch; to the Smithsonian American Art Museum and Richard Sorenson; to Pete Gershon and Cody Ledvina of the Orange Show Center for Visionary Art; and to Jeff Wack and the Preserve Bottle Committee, for providing additional images.

This book would not have been able to be produced at all without the vision of Ilona Oppenheim, Publisher and Creative Director of Tra Publishing, and the hard work and creativity of her colleagues Lisa McGuinness, Editorial Director; Jefferson Quintana, Art and Design Director; Morgane Leoni, Designer; Jessica Faroy, Publishing Director; and all members of the Tra team. I also remain so very appreciative of my committed, thoughtful, and dependable copy editor, Lisa V. Comforty, who so deftly and meticulously refined and polished my texts and helped ensure that my delight at the impressive and inspiring works of these remarkable makers would shine through.

Jo Farb Hernández

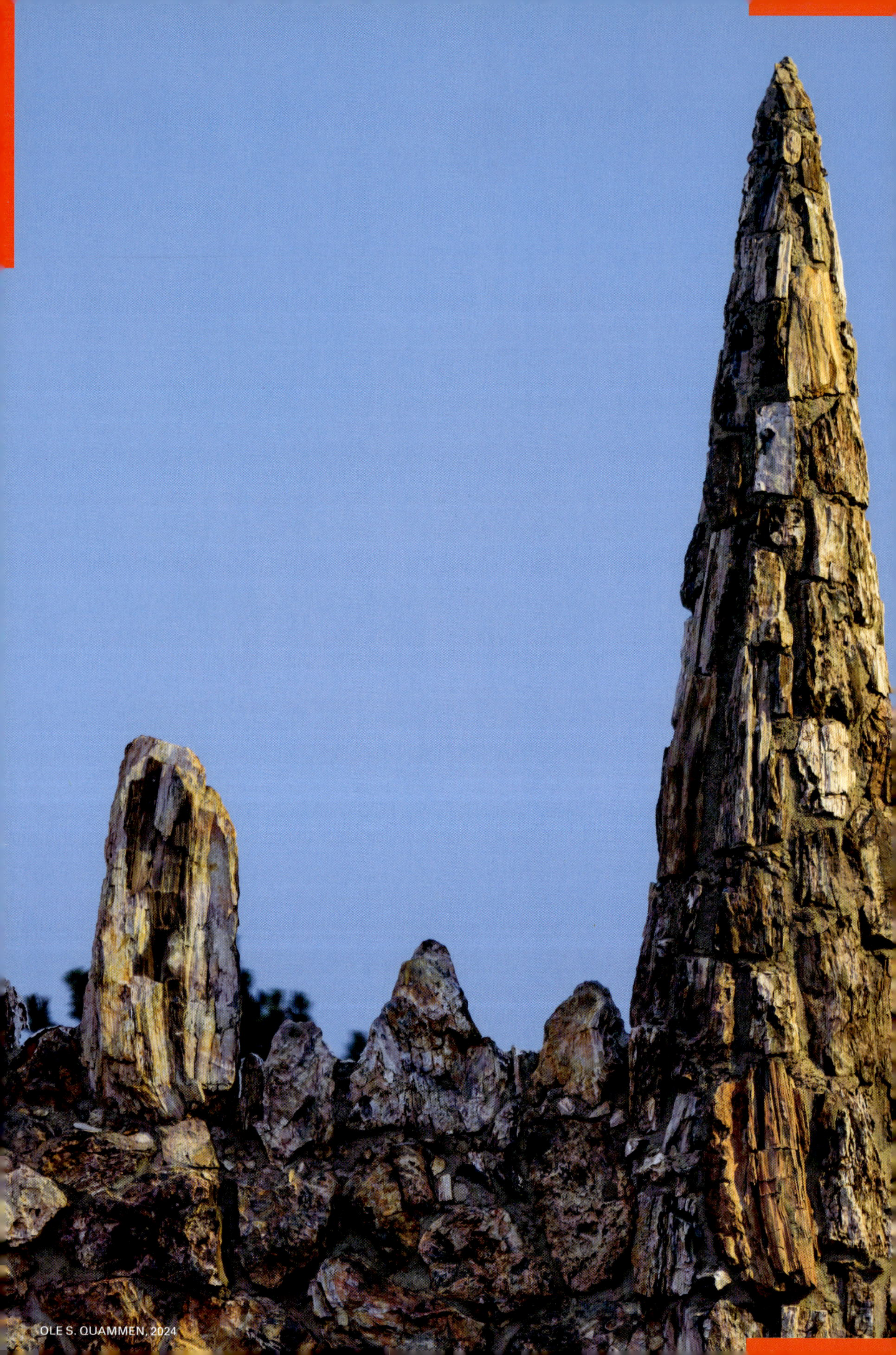

OLE S. QUAMMEN, 2024

CHAPTER 1

BUILT FROM SCRATCH

—

NEW ARCHITECTURE

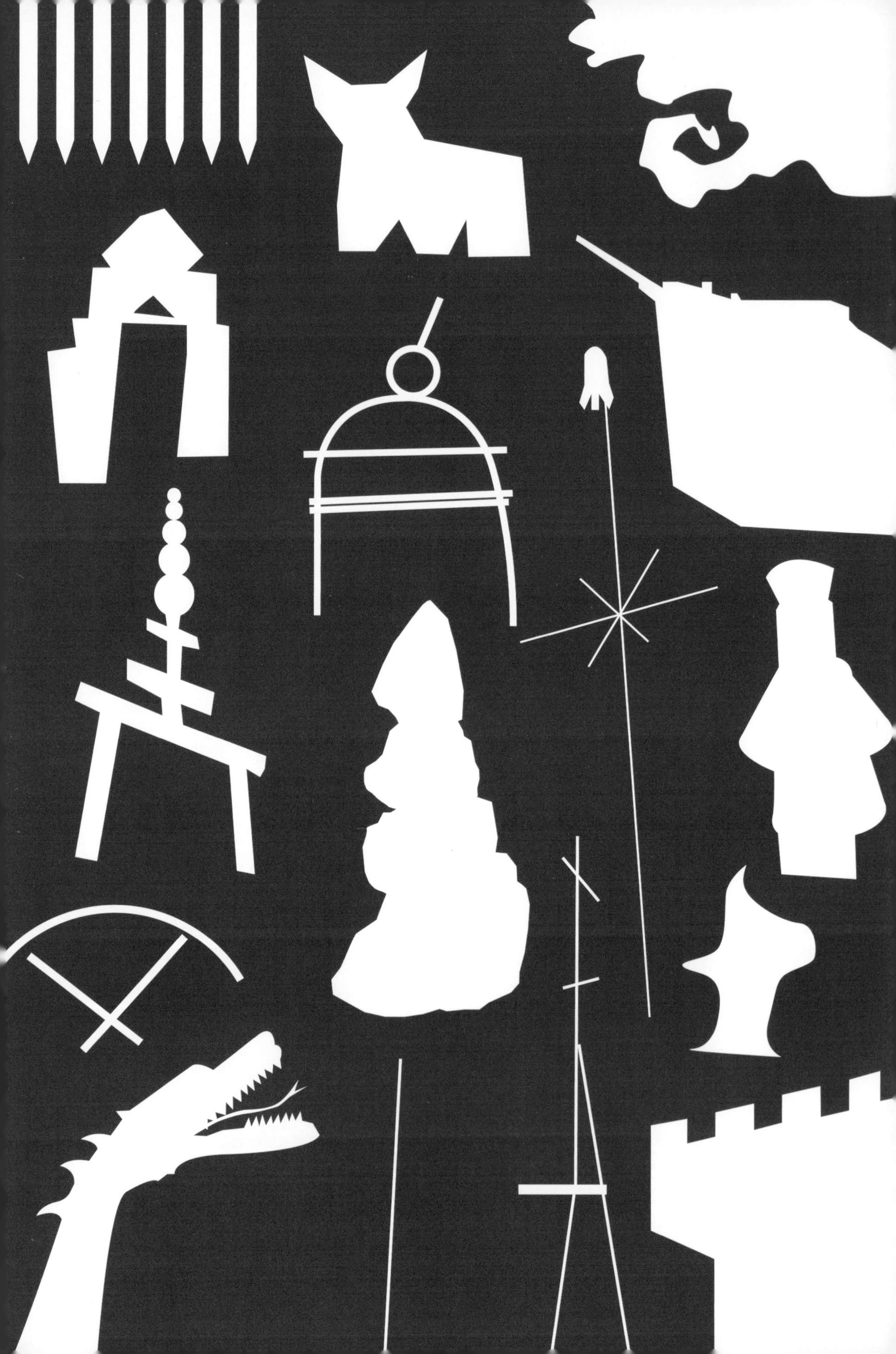

The term "architecture" alludes to engineering, industrial, and technical expertise, and, above all, formal training for its purveyors: the architects. And generally, this is true.

But the builders whose works we celebrate here rarely use that term, nor do they self-identify as architects. Instead, without specialized training, they begin to build with whatever materials they can easily access and afford. There are rarely preliminary sketches, and working drawings, sections, elevations, and schematics are rarer still. The lack of written plans is usually accompanied by a lack of required permits. This may be due not as much to rebellion against the rules of local governments and their zoning laws—although that is common enough—but more because there is seldom the expectation that their construction will become as building-like and elaborate as it turns out to be. In fact, process often overtakes final product as the driving force, and the evolving character of the structure leads to a multilayered, multifaceted outcome in which lack of planning and obsessive intentionality intertwine.

In contrast, not included in this book are homemade buildings that are more standard in appearance, which are better described as vernacular architecture. They represent the conventionally accepted norms of their communities, fulfilling our sixth sense of dimensionality and physicality: protocols of measurement, height, and use of building materials that reflect societal and environmental conditions. Taken as a whole with other similar buildings, they codify the kinds of styles that permit us to characterize them, at least generally, by location and function.

This book's examples of singular architecture give little, if any, hint of the social, cultural, or aesthetic circumstances of neighboring structures. Instead, their builders are inspired by more individualistic concerns. Most importantly, these works reveal the close relationship between builder and building, a relationship that disrupts predictability, bypasses tradition, and is unburdened by conformity.

Untethered to such conventions, these structures frequently push the parameters of what we would normally consider "architecture." They may break through height standards, utilize materials in innovative ways, ignore ease of accessibility and norms such as equal rises for stair treads, and, certainly, disregard any attempt to maintain stylistic consistency among the various components. Generally growing incrementally, they neither demonstrate a static conceptual focus nor visual consistency throughout the process of construction; instead, their hallmark tends to be an often-provocative novelty.

Among these are a series of towers. Most American hand-built towers tend to be one-off structures uniquely considered and without reference to a broader architectural complex. Others may serve only as elevated planters or pedestals, such as works by Mollie Jenson, Herman Rusch, and Grover Cleveland Thompson; as these complement garden ornaments with less architectural framework or intention, they are better considered as landscaping.

Also included in this genre are so-called castles. While continental Europe boasts a dense history of stone-walled fortresses, palaces, and churches, there has been no such architectural tradition in the United States. Our historical fortresses, such as they were, tended to be rings of vertical wooden logs protecting a military or civilian prairie outpost, while our "palaces" were typically governmental offices or museums that often drew their design inspiration from the ceremonial architecture found on the other side of the Atlantic. This same correspondence can frequently be associated with our American houses of worship, as well, whose imposing visual impact affects a connection to formal or sacrosanct European structures even when there is little direct conceptual relevance.

Despite the lack of such locally functional models, the idea of castle remains strong on our shores. Perhaps this has resulted from folktale illustrations in our children's books or Disney films, but we clearly almost viscerally understand this conceptual archetype, as we likewise have a sense of what kinds of architectural elements a castle should include. Home-built castles, therefore, are prominent examples of idiosyncratic architecture built from scratch, although some, like the work of John Medica, Rasmus Petersen, or Ben Hartman are miniature in scale, not allowing for human visitation or the true interaction that we expect from architecture. Conventional castle-like characteristics are also featured in birdhouses such as those fabricated by Samuel Mirelez or Aldobrando Piacenza, and other sites, such as Henry Warren's, while decidedly miniaturized and certainly inspired by architectural idioms, join these others as not true architecture per se.

JIM BISHOP

BISHOP CASTLE

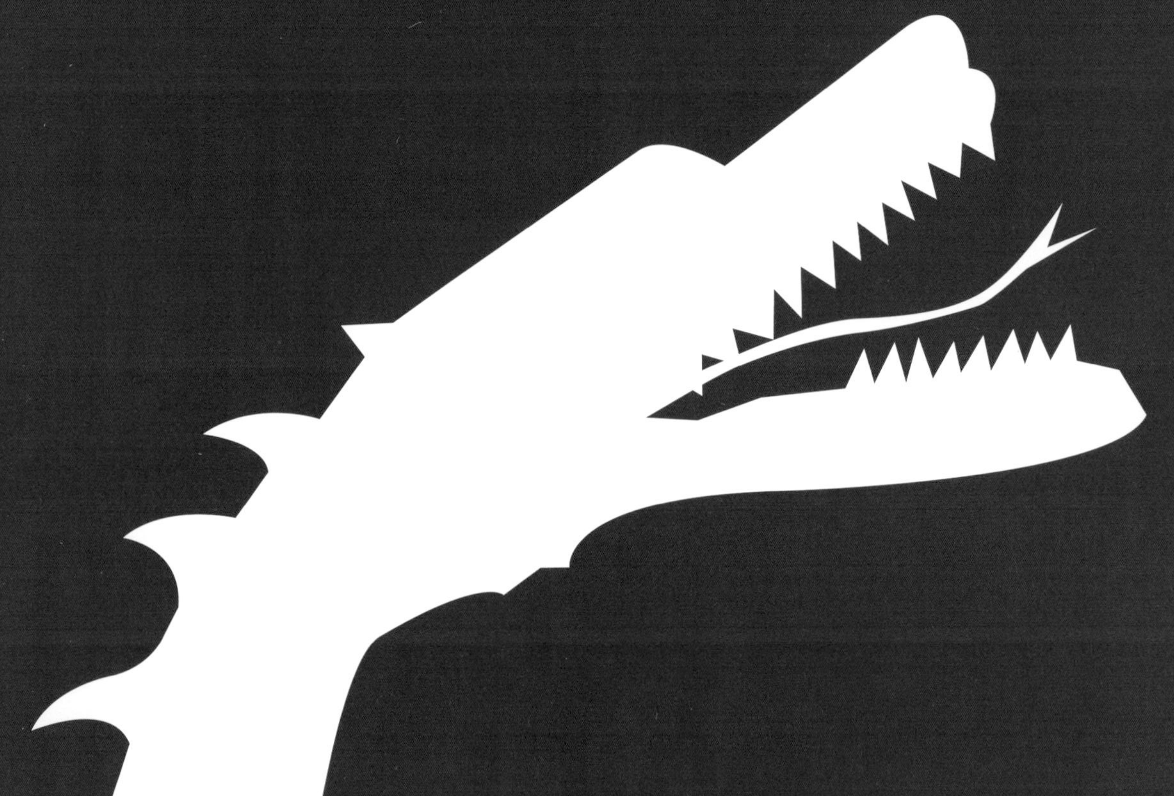

RYE, COLORADO

Bishop Castle is a fine example of this genre. Nevertheless, it—like other castles in the United States—was built less to withstand enemy sieges than to marry the maker's creativity with recognizable elements of the past, sometimes in a playful and capricious way and other times in order to channel and showcase the historical concepts the castles referenced. In many ways *Bishop Castle* also exemplifies the trajectory of these kinds of structures, with prosaically functional elements—in this case, a water tank that, when mounted, suggested the form of a turret or tower to Bishop's friends—evolving to become the fanciful beginnings of a lifetime's work. And, as with other examples of these structures built without reference to blueprints, any sketches served more as fabulist visions or as after-the-fact attempts to appease local planning departments rather than as firm, concrete plans that discouraged any deviation from the design. This lack of a cause-and-effect link underscores the generally impulsive nature of this kind of construction, which was improvised as materials were accumulated and placed.

At age 15, Bishop (1944–2024) had become attracted by a 2.5-acre parcel 9,000 feet above sea level and surrounded on three sides by the San Isabel National Forest, and he persuaded his parents to buy it for him with earnings he had saved from odd jobs and a paper route. Over the next 10 years he and his father camped on the land, clearing and preparing it for the construction of a small family cabin that they intended to build out of the plentiful rocks and stone of the nearby mountains. When not working on the construction, he helped his father in his ornamental welding shop, adding to his developing manual skills. Roughly two years after beginning to build, they installed a recycled 40-foot-tall water holding tank, which Bishop began to sheathe in stones; it was this addition that prompted teasing commentary and questions from neighbors and friends about building a castle.

But this teasing resonated with Bishop, although once he decided to actually build a castle, his father bowed out, and no friends were forthcoming with physical help. As he continued building, his experience in ornamental ironwork came to inform some of the most characteristic components of the *Castle*, as he expanded its use from primarily decorative components to structural ones. Decorative elements include window frames, stair bannisters (particularly notable are the "floating" exterior stairs with their elaborate railings), balconies, and exterior pathways. Singularly impressive are the interior roof trusses and the soaring main central vaulted arch of the church-like *Grand Ballroom*, as well as a spherical open-air structure whose openwork isosceles-triangle walls recall Buckminster Fuller's geodesic domes. A dragon-shaped chimney constructed out of donated stainless-steel hospital trays is another notable metal ornament, which Bishop installed some 80 feet high off of the exterior of the ballroom. He subsequently inserted a donated burner into the figure's throat, repurposed from its original usage powering a hot-air balloon, in order to provide a more "authentic" fire-breathing element.

The curvilinear flourishes of Bishop's ironwork are offset with the more geometric-yet-textural lines of the castle walls and braces. In particular, the splayed buttresses supporting the square tower and the upper levels of the main structure draw the eye upward, in contrast to the more stolid Romanesque-style arches at ground level. Other Gothic characteristics include the large and somewhat asymmetric stained-glass window that lights up the *Grand Ballroom*, a slender 30-foot-high steeple installed on top of the masonry, and the thin pointed arches perforating the exterior walls along the first story. These arches seem to harken back to Islamic styles, while an onion dome graces the top of a round turret. The details add complexity to the design yet somehow do not jeopardize its visual harmony.

Bishop doggedly pushed himself through physical and emotional traumas—among them, diagnoses of cancer and Parkinson's, a breakdown that landed him in a psychiatric ward, the inadvertent death of his four-year-old son, who was crushed by trees that he was clearing, and his wife's death a half-dozen years before his own. By that time, as he turned 80 years old, *Bishop Castle* had risen to roughly 160 feet, the height of a 16-story building, and he estimated that he had used 1.5 million rocks in the course of building this monument to what one person could do if they unwaveringly set their mind to it. Financed with donations (a nonprofit organization facilitates such support), Bishop never charged admission and insisted that the *Castle* be open to welcome the public on a daily basis so that people could appreciate his heartfelt homage to the idea of individual freedom, and his belief that a private act can stand in for, and physically represent, the American Dream.

CASTLE OVERVIEW, 2024

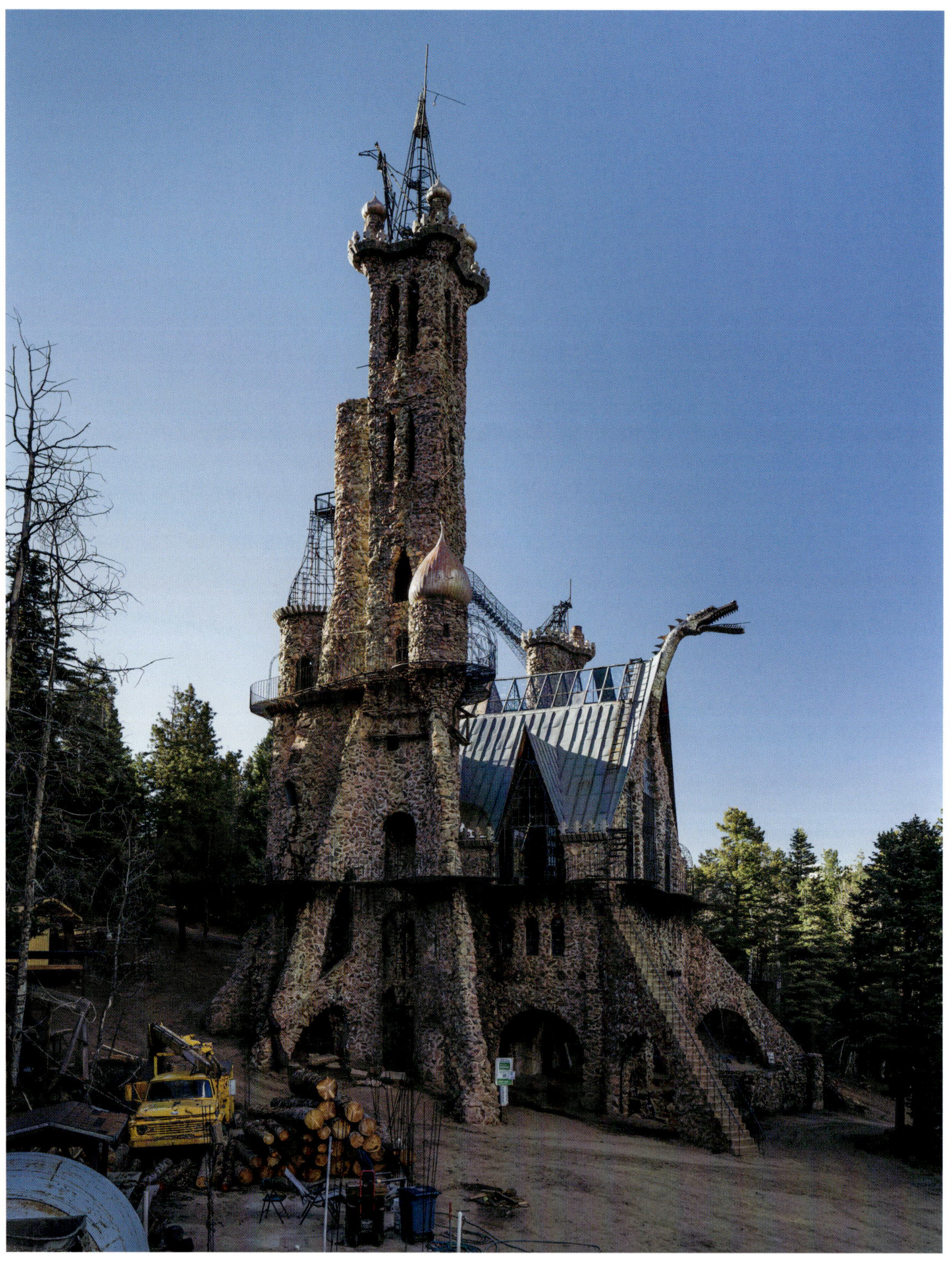

CENTRAL INTERIOR ARCH IN *GRAND BALLROOM*, 2024

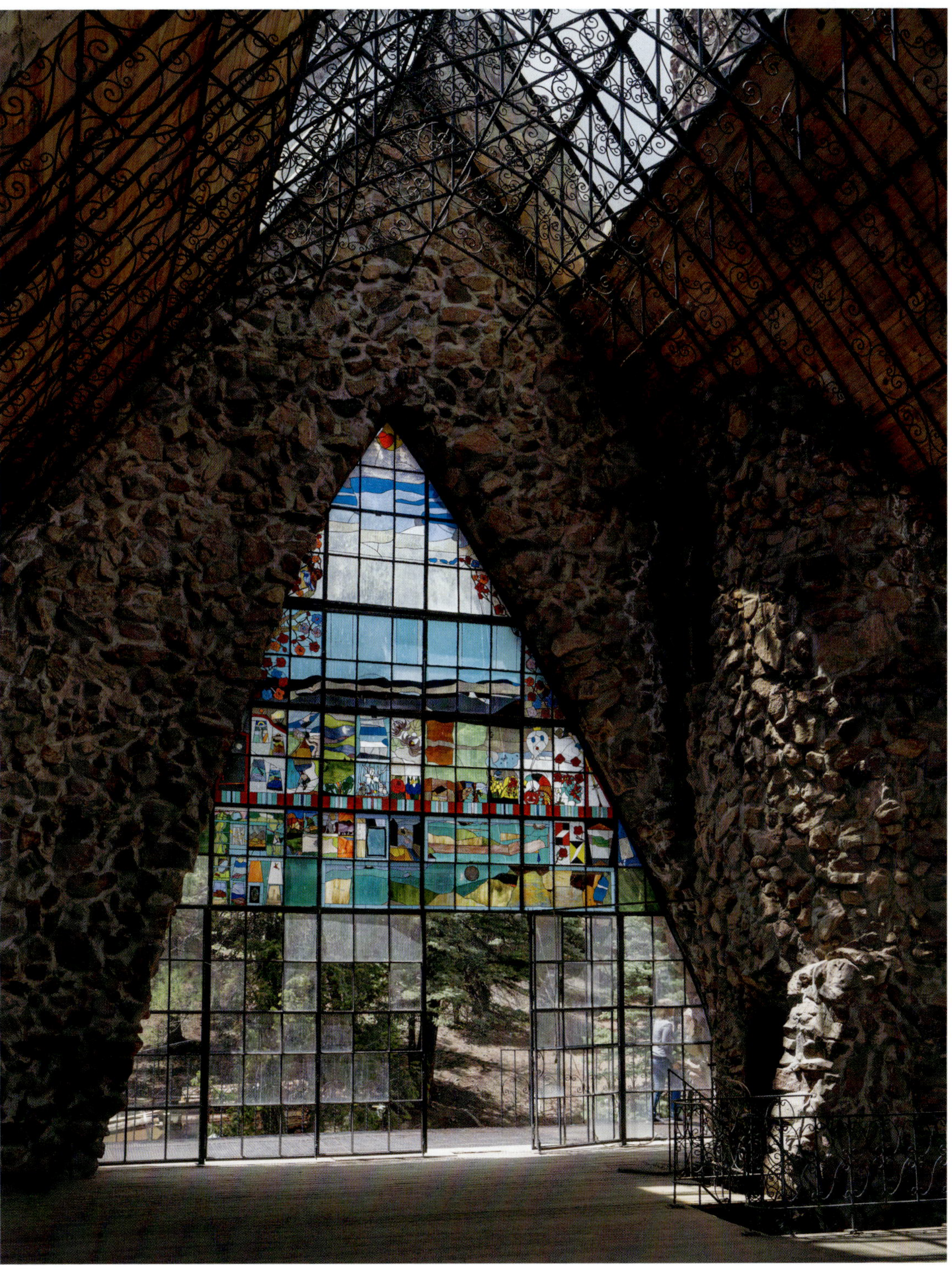

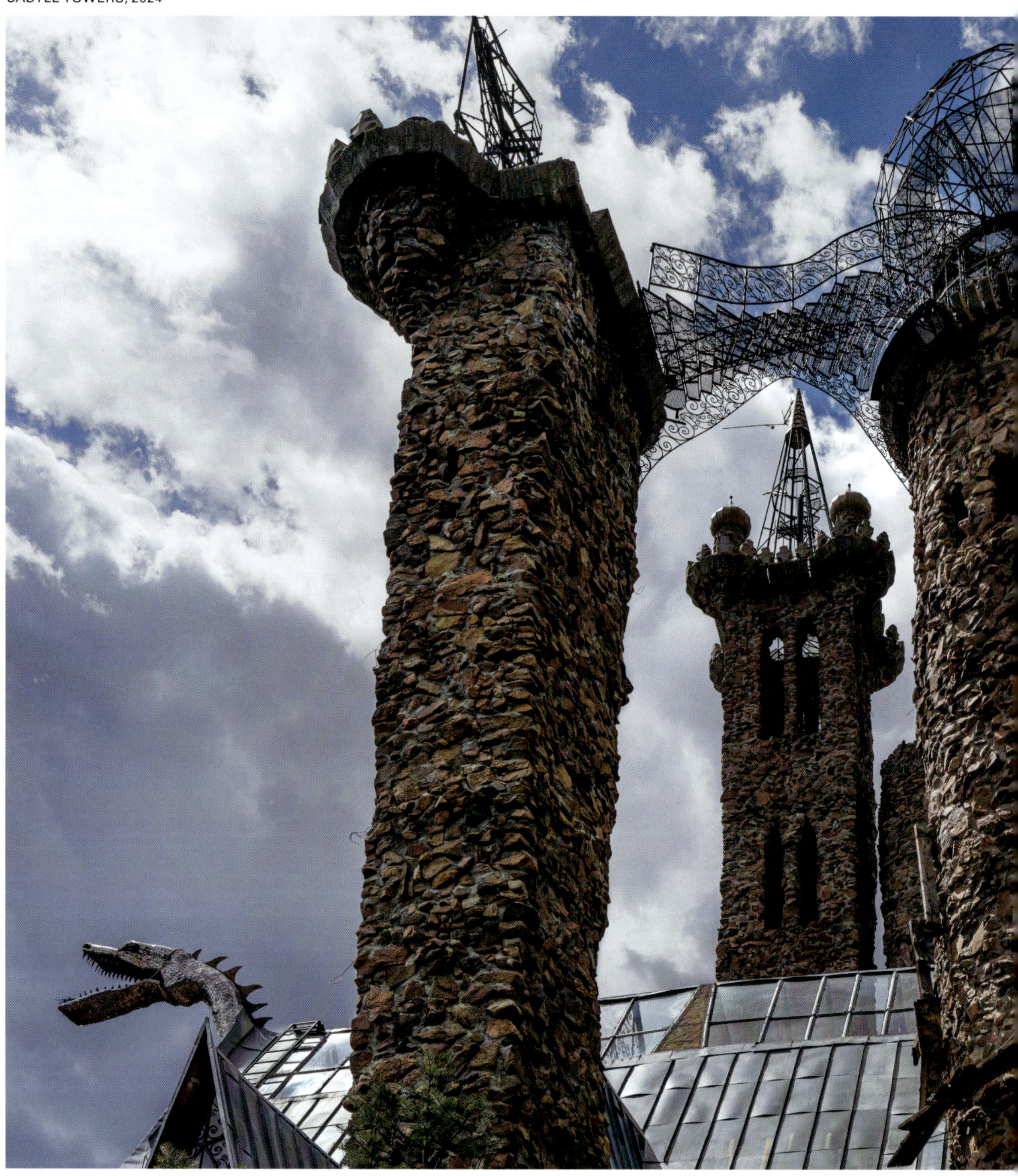

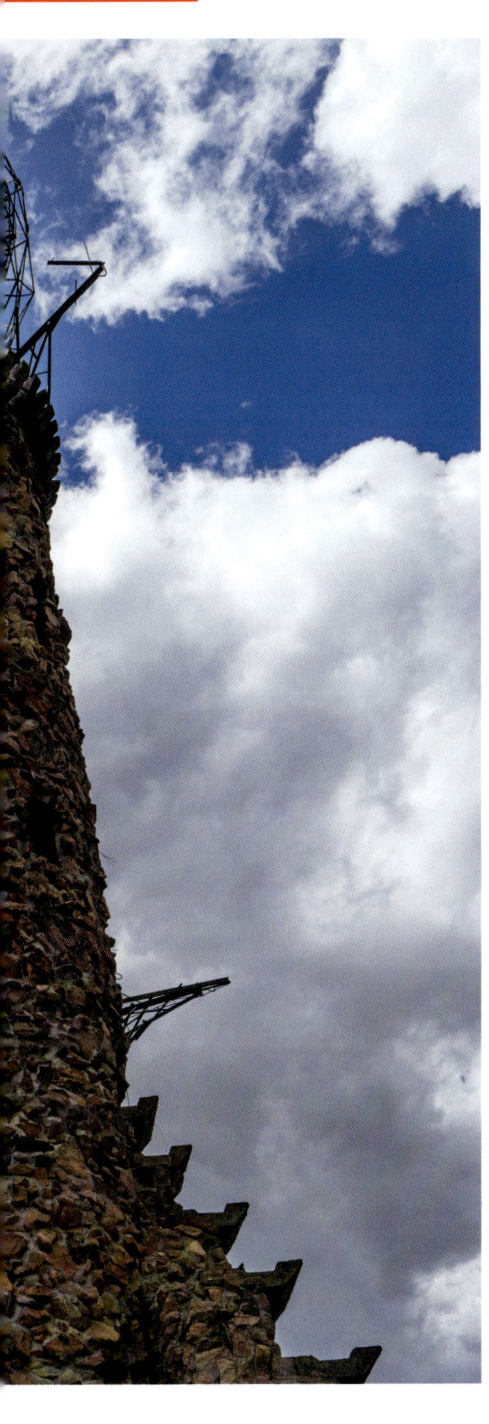

A MONUMENT TO WHAT ONE PERSON CAN DO IF THEY SET THEIR MIND TO IT.

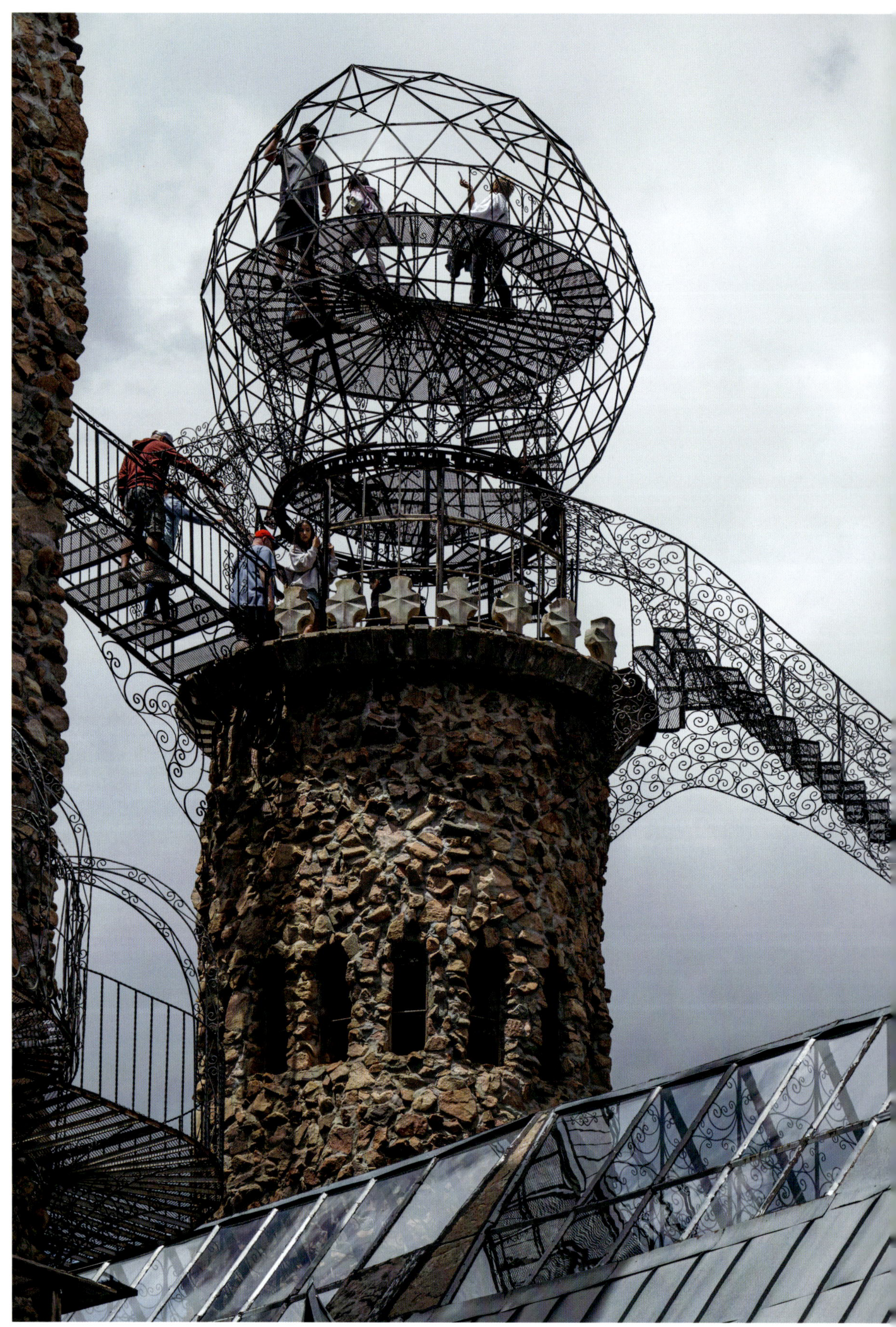

TOWER WITH SPHERICAL OPEN-AIR VISTA POINT AND DRAGON-HEAD CHIMNEY, 2024

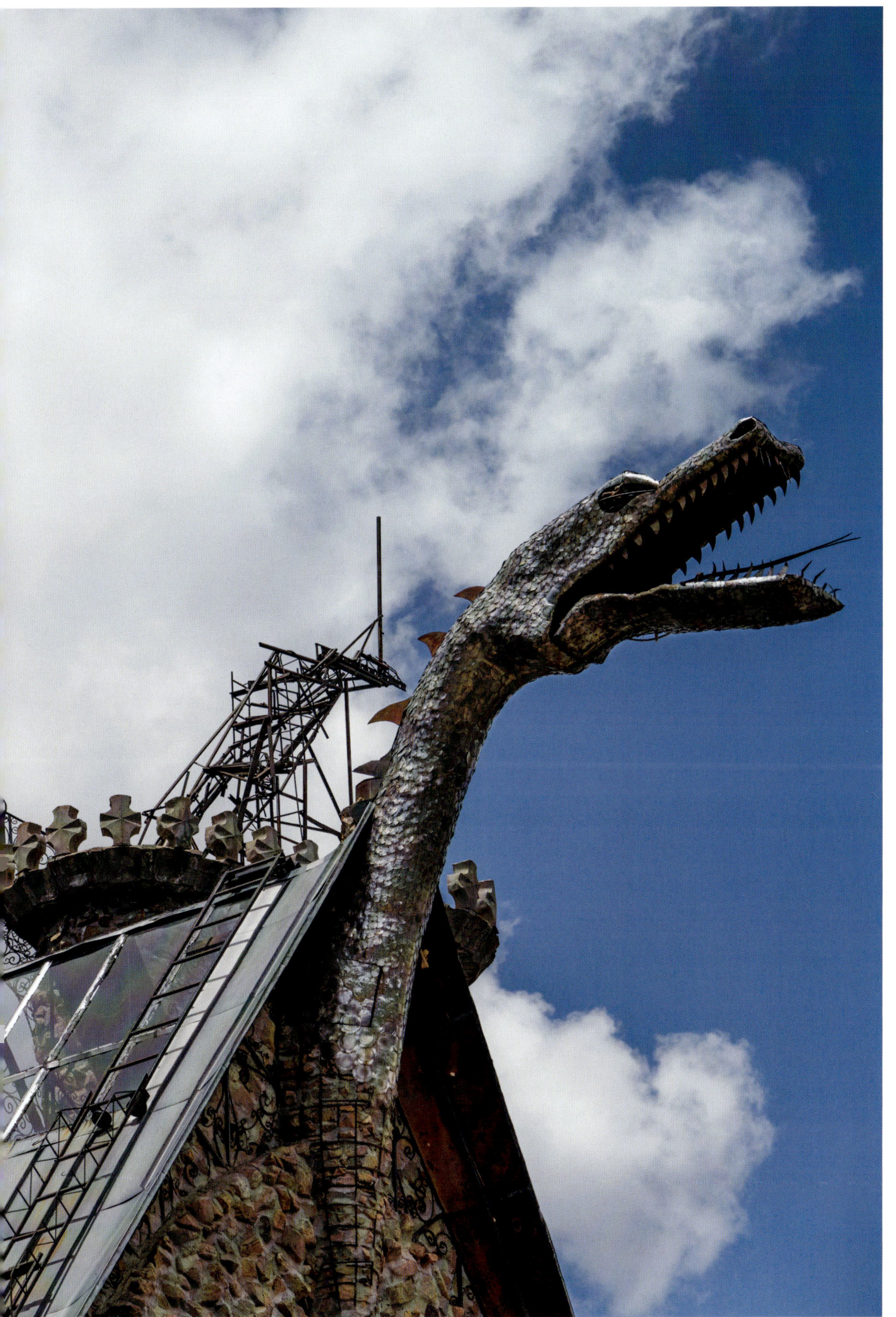

MARTÍN SÁNCHEZ

TÍO'S TACOS CHAPEL

RIVERSIDE, CALIFORNIA

Describing the *Chapel* built by Mexican restaurant owner and operator Martín Sánchez (b. 1966) as constructed of beer bottles, while technically accurate, is also too simplistic. A singular component of Sánchez's elaborate environment in Riverside's urban center, the *Chapel*, like the assorted sculptures and garden ornaments that surround and complement it, is fully composed of recycled objects, all collected, sorted, and installed by this immigrant restaurateur with a modicum of help from his friends and family.

Born to a poor family in Sahuayo in the Mexican state of Michoacán, by age five Sánchez was already shining shoes, washing cars, and running errands. A hard worker with dreams of bettering himself, at age 16 he was smuggled across the border hidden inside of a car, and with no job prospects or place to land, he started selling sacks of oranges streetside in East Los Angeles. After obtaining his green card, he returned to Mexico to marry his girlfriend, and then they moved back to Riverside, where some of her family already lived. He worked at a mobile home factory during the week and rented a cart selling fruits and nuts, and then hot dogs, on weekends. But his profits were minimal, as his clientele preferred Mexican food, so he pivoted and began to sell tacos. With success came more financial independence, so when an existing restaurant became available in downtown Riverside, they rented it, coming up with the name on the spot, using the respectful honorific *Tío* (uncle) that he had been accorded since his youth. He kept saving his money and the landlord, impressed by his drive and his initiative, later helped him to purchase the property, despite his lack of credit.

But he still felt that something was missing: the sense of play that he had not been able to indulge throughout his childhood. During those years, with his family barely having enough money for food, he had had to make his own toys out of pieces of wood, rocks, empty tin cans, cardboard, and whatever else he could find. Remembering this imaginative work—and the skills he had developed as a result—he began again to work creatively, using the backyard of the restaurant to build up a series of "toys." From the beginning of his life in the United States he had been shocked and saddened by how much was thrown away, and he determined to reuse everything he could, from the pork bones, beer bottles, and plastic containers of his restaurant to the family's old shoes and clothing, which he used to dress his characters. So, beginning in 1990, he started amassing these materials without knowing exactly how they would be used, improvising as he continued to collect. The size and number of his constructions grew: the monumental figures of a man and a woman, for example, required some 20- to 30-thousand bottles. This activity brought him joy, lowered his stress level, and, because the building blocks for his creations were all recycled—he only purchased around five percent of his resource materials, such as nails, screws, and cement—it did not greatly impinge on the family's finances.

As the collections grew, but before the structures really began to take shape, a local group of concerned citizens began agitating for everything to be removed and demolished, interpreting his collections as piles of garbage and a public nuisance. For three years Sánchez fought the city's legal action in court, trying to make them understand his vision as he simultaneously assured them that he was actually helping to reduce the community's trash and waste by reusing it in such a creative manner. Supported by another group of citizens, as he continued to build and the whimsy of his work became more apparent, public opinion evolved and the municipal complaint was eventually dropped. The city's attitude change was validated when they asked him to create a public art installation in an alley adjacent to city hall. Known as *Mariposa* (Butterfly) *Alley*, it is not only renowned as an iconic image of downtown but it connects him, in another way, to his Mexican birthplace: when the monarch butterflies leave California in the winter, they fly to Michoacán.

In the middle of the fanciful creatures, fountains, and ornaments, the *Chapel* was a more serious undertaking, albeit one that harmonized with the whole. His wife had wanted a quiet place to pray, so, without discretionary funds to purchase bricks and cement blocks, Sánchez instead built up the basic form of the building, inspired by the shape of the Sanctuary of Guadalupe in their hometown of Sahuayo, and then stabilized the walls with beer and soda bottles that he inserted horizontally in order to let the light stream in with an effect similar to that of stained glass. He added multicolored pews, painted the interior ceiling with Biblical iconography (the angels have the faces of his three daughters), and added two clerestory towers whose peaks are sheathed in the flattened tops of tin cans, as they flank a niche sheltering a statue of the Virgin of Guadalupe. The nave is topped with a semispherical dome covered in colorful ceramic fragments, and the entire site has become a favored background for locally produced videos and films. Having been blessed by the Catholic Church, the *Chapel* periodically hosts weddings, *quinceañeras*, and baptisms.

A second constructed building adjacent to the *Chapel*, an homage to the pyramids of his homeland, also shares the backyard patio space. And the preexisting buildings—both the restaurant itself and also the large Victorian home on the adjacent lot that Sánchez purchased in 2000—have become increasingly adorned with humorous wide-mouthed dragons and figures that ride bicycles, tricycles, and hot wheels; sit on the roof edges; and do handstands. And while there are inlaid names of Abraham Lincoln and Mother Teresa as well as representations of a cowgirl, Popeye, and the droids from *Star Wars*, many of the figures adorning the buildings and those throughout the garden and patio display stereotypical Mexican imagery—skeletons, skinny men with huge sombreros and massive moustaches, mariachis—perhaps chosen by the artist to both tease and reassure their Caucasian clients with familiar motifs. The entirety takes up a full city block, approximately one acre.

With literally mountains of trash generated every day by his restaurant, Sánchez continues to add new and widely varying components, such as a 90-foot-long representation of Mexico's presidential plane and monumental Easter eggs. He describes his work as playing, the product of his inner child, and its manifestation a portrait of himself and his family: what they have used and how they have lived their lives in California. It is an honor for him, he says, to share his work and his dreams with others, and his gratitude for what he has been able to accomplish is inspiring. He does not expect to "finish" this environment until his death.

HE DESCRIBES HIS WORK AS PLAYING, CREATING JOY FROM TRASH.

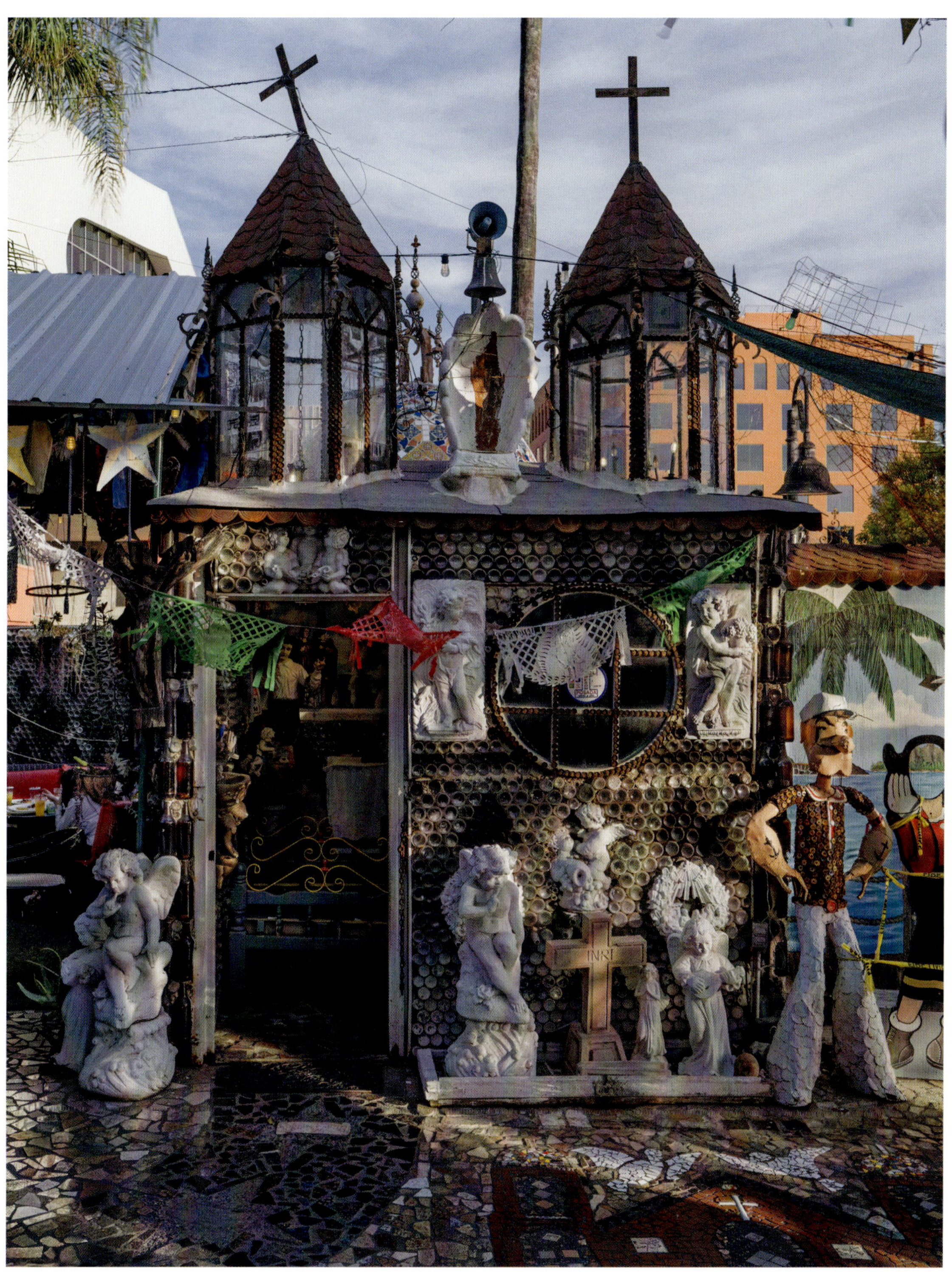

CHAPEL, 2025

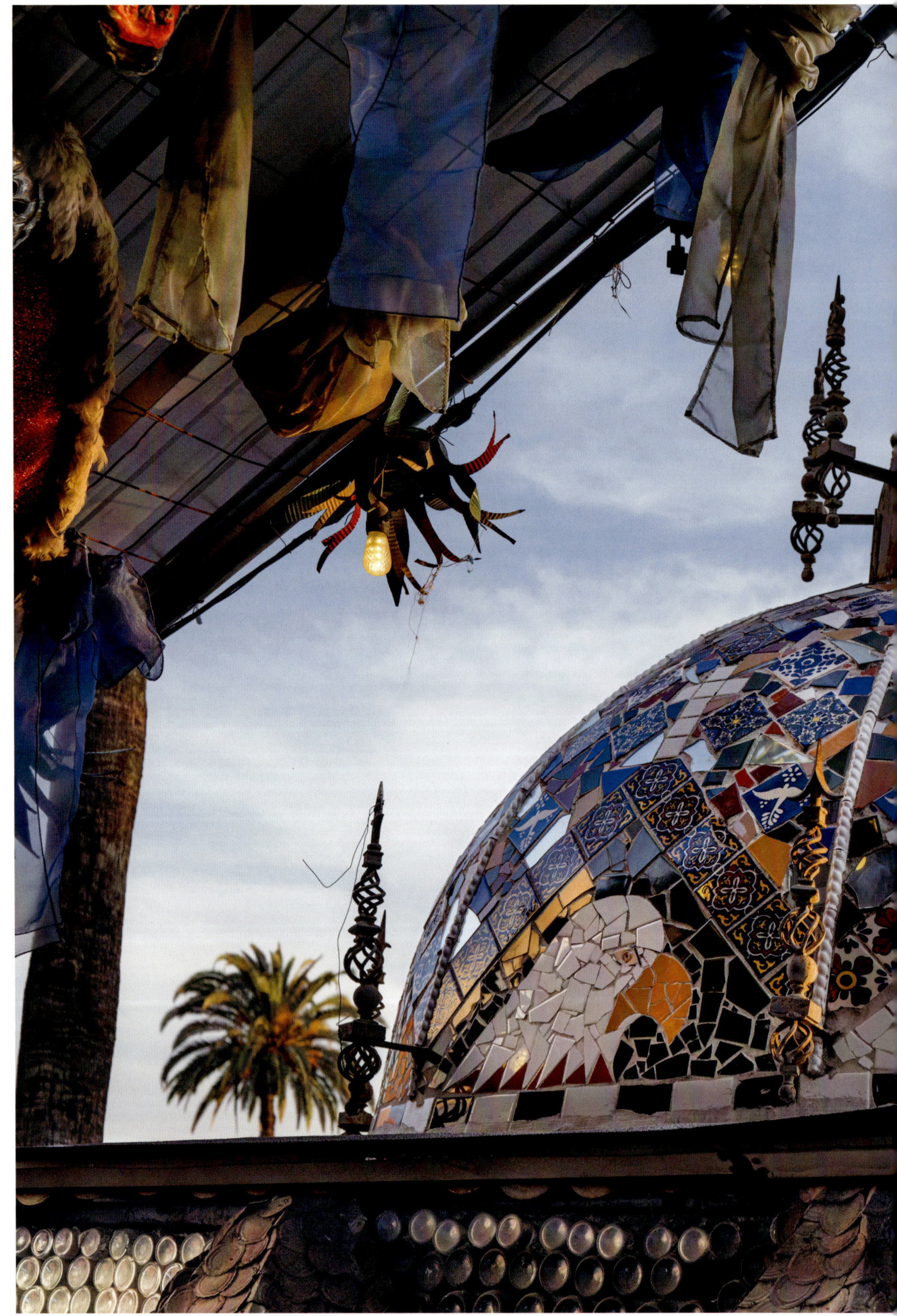

SEMISPHERICAL DOME OVER *CHAPEL* NAVE, 2025

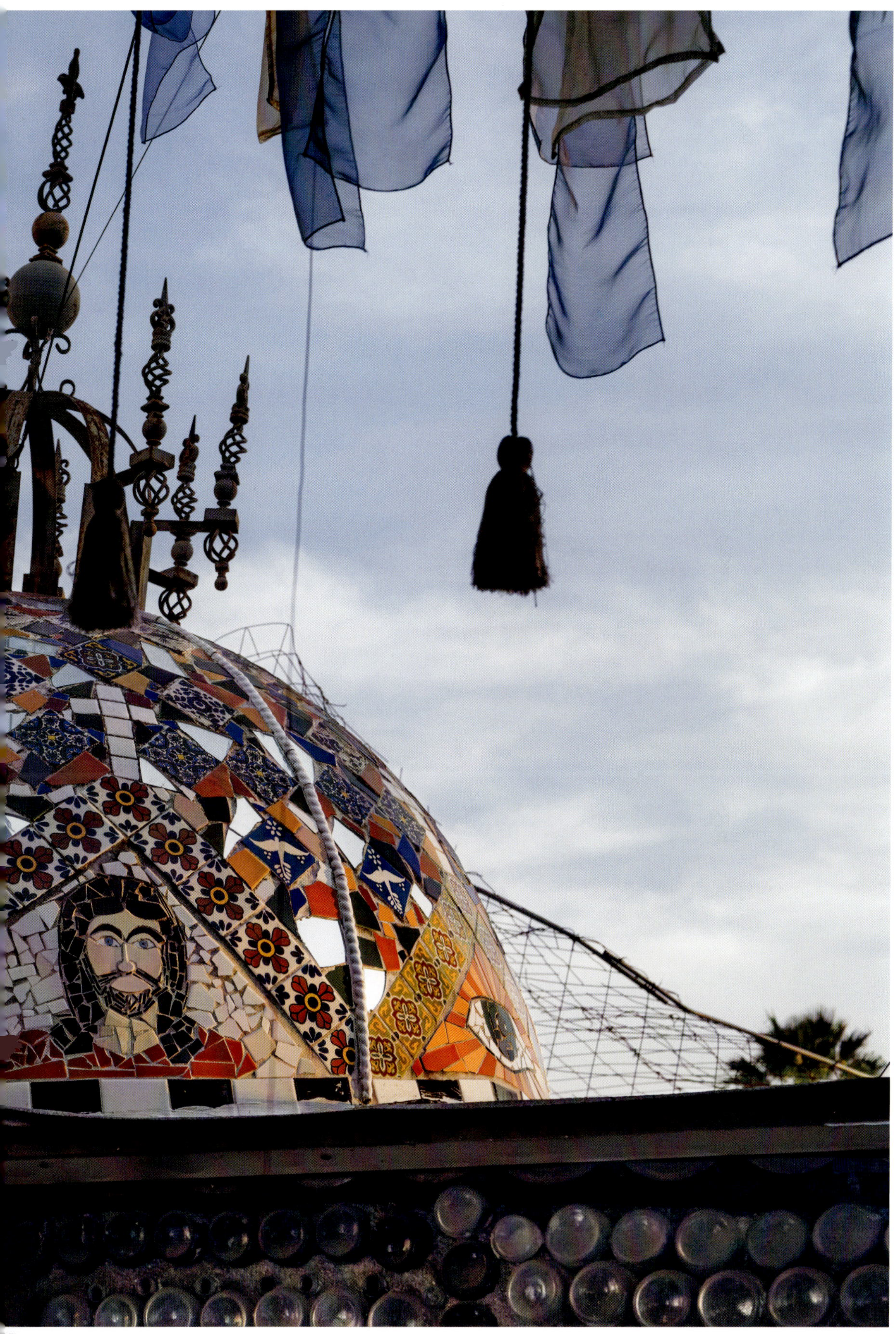

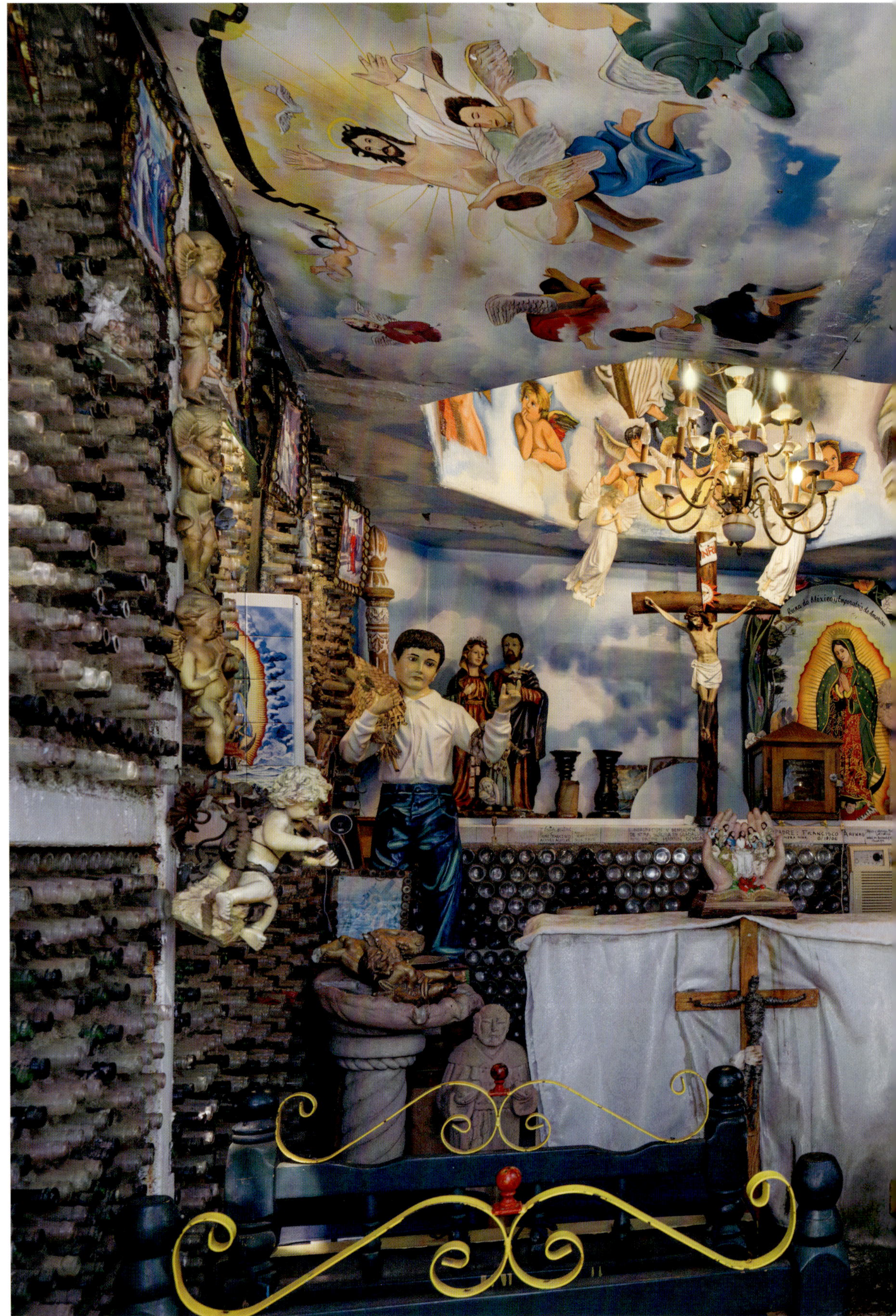

CHAPEL INTERIOR, 2025

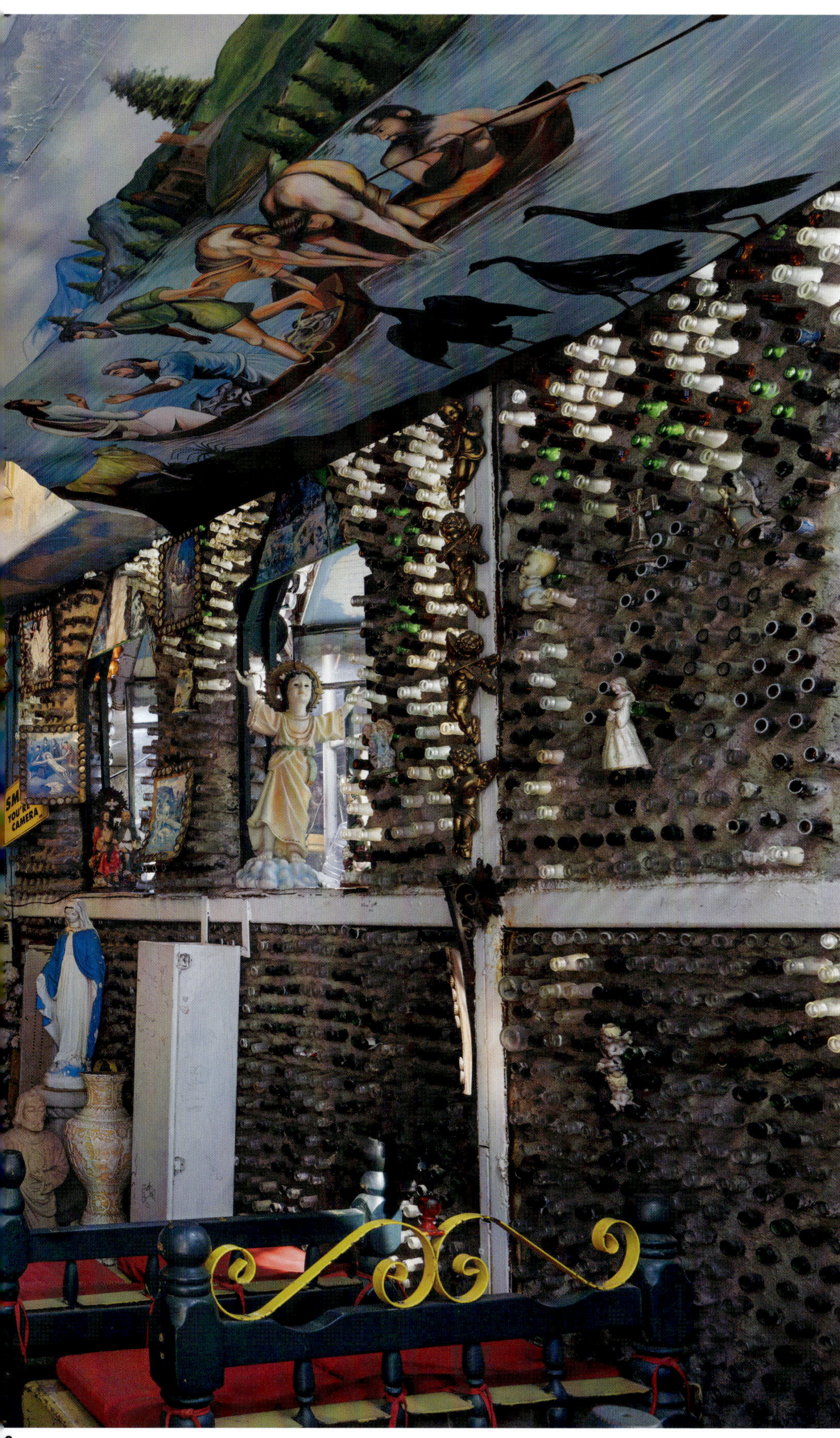

EDWARD LEEDSKALNIN

CORAL CASTLE

HOMESTEAD, FLORIDA

Other castles in the United States are somewhat less formally idiosyncratic than Bishop's (see page 14) but are still remarkable as homemade personalized buildings that reflect the maker's sense of self, interests, and experiences, documenting their individual realities within the broader cultural, historical, social, and, often, religious, setting. The fortifications of Edward Leedskalnin in Florida, Harry Delos Andrews in Ohio (see page 34), and Michael Clarke Rubel in California (see page 38) stretch across the country east to west, each independently inspired by the builder's own set of priorities, intermingled with community considerations and available resources.

Legend holds that Latvian immigrant Leedskalnin (1887–1951) obsessively built for nearly 30 years in order to assuage his grief over being jilted by his fiancée the day prior to their scheduled wedding ("Love Turned to Stone," trumpets a tourist brochure). Hailing from a family of stonemasons, he emigrated to the United States and then traveled widely for some time within the country. But after being diagnosed with tuberculosis, he thought that living in Florida would be good for his health, so he bought two acres outside of Florida City. Taking advantage of the native oolitic limestone (not actually coral, but commonly known as coral rock), the modest beginning of his work—which can only loosely be described as a castle—soon gave way not only to elaborate constructions utilizing 1,100 tons of coral rock in the walls and tower alone, but also to boasts that he was privy to the "secrets of levitation" used to assemble the Egyptian pyramids. He worked alone and only at night, illuminating his workspace with lanterns in order to keep his technique secret. Indeed, it does seem remarkable that he apparently only used handmade pulleys, recycled levers, and hand tools such as wedges, chains, hammers, and chisels to move and install the stones, some of which weigh over 30 tons, particularly since he was only five feet tall and weighed 100 pounds, and the limestone deposits in this part of Florida can reach a thickness of 4,000 feet. He opened his site to the public in 1920.

But after Leedskalnin heard that a subdivision was being planned near his land, he transported as many of his constructions as possible to a new property closer to Miami, and, enlarging it, reopened at this new location in 1940. The *Coral Castle* is now touted as Florida's oldest operating tourist attraction, and it was added to the National Register of Historic Places in 1984 under its original name, *Rock Gate Park*, a reference to the massive stone entrance gate that can be opened with the touch of a finger.

Reflecting the technique of extracting and building with the huge limestone blocks, most of the architectural works on-site are rather ploddingly geometric, with little grace or refinement even among those that seem conceptually capricious, such as one table shaped like a heart and another shaped like the state of Florida. Wall sections surrounding the stone "fortress" are eight feet tall, four feet wide, and three feet thick; dry-stacked without mortar, they were so carefully positioned that no light is visible between the joints. Higher sections can be reached by blocky stone steps, and the whole is complemented with additional tables, rocking chairs, a sundial, a fountain, a throne, and other accoutrements that Leedskalnin believed would enhance the site for tourists (essential because he apparently subsisted thanks to the 10- or 25-cent entrance fees charged to visitors). The largest components are the two-story tower that included his living quarters, erected with blocks weighing four to nine tons each; a 20-foot-high Polaris telescope that aligned with the sun at the solstice; and a 40-foot-high, 28-ton obelisk that measures higher than the standing monoliths of Stonehenge. A sculpture of a crescent moon surrounded by orbiting planets is perhaps the property's most emblematic feature.

Leedskalnin worked on the *Castle* and its grounds until his death. The enigma of how such a slight man was able to move such massive stones has motivated much of the continuing interest in this site, and it still functions as a tourist attraction, now run by the privately owned Coral Castle, Inc. It seems that he initiated some of the rumors about the construction himself, with his allusions to being privy to the secrets of ancient Egyptian pyramid builders, and his interests in electricity and magnetic currents also caused some to hypothesize that he was able to magically harness invisible powers to levitate the stones. Other published accounts suggest that perhaps it was a link to the occult resulting from his masonic background, or perhaps it was alien technology, or perhaps he simply sang to the stones.

TOWER AND GROUNDS, 2022. PHOTO: JHVE PHOTO

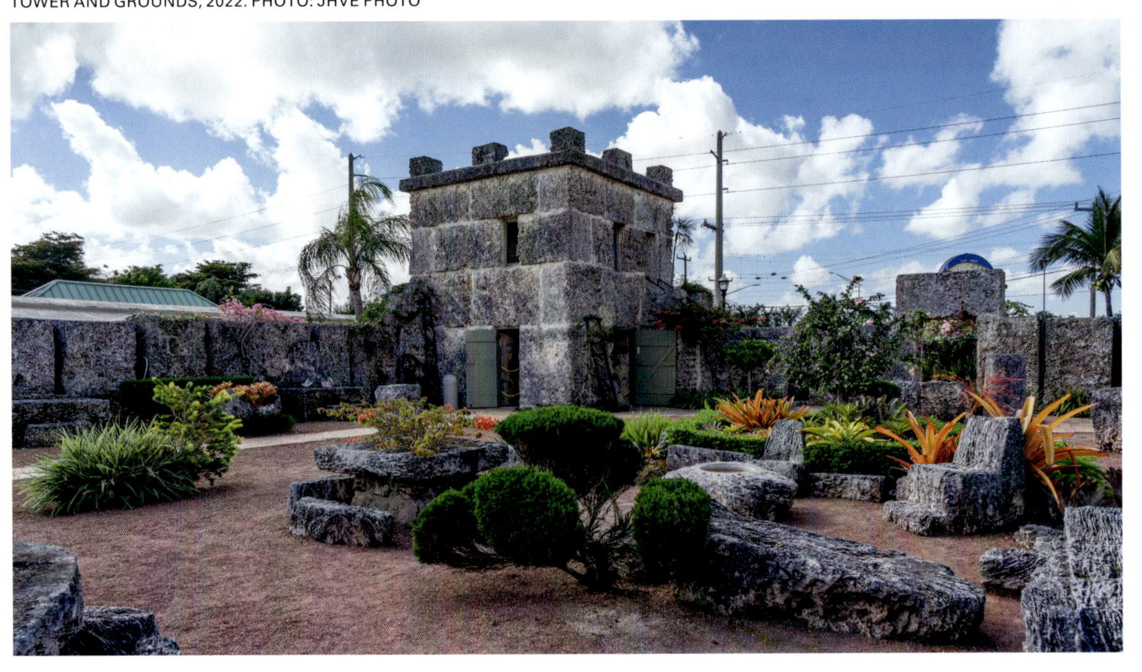

HE IMPLIED
HE WAS PRIVY
TO THE SECRETS OF
ANCIENT EGYPTIAN
PYRAMID BUILDERS.

SITE OVERVIEW, 2009. PHOTO: J. MIERS, JTESLA16 AT WTS WIKIVOYAGE, CREATIVE COMMONS

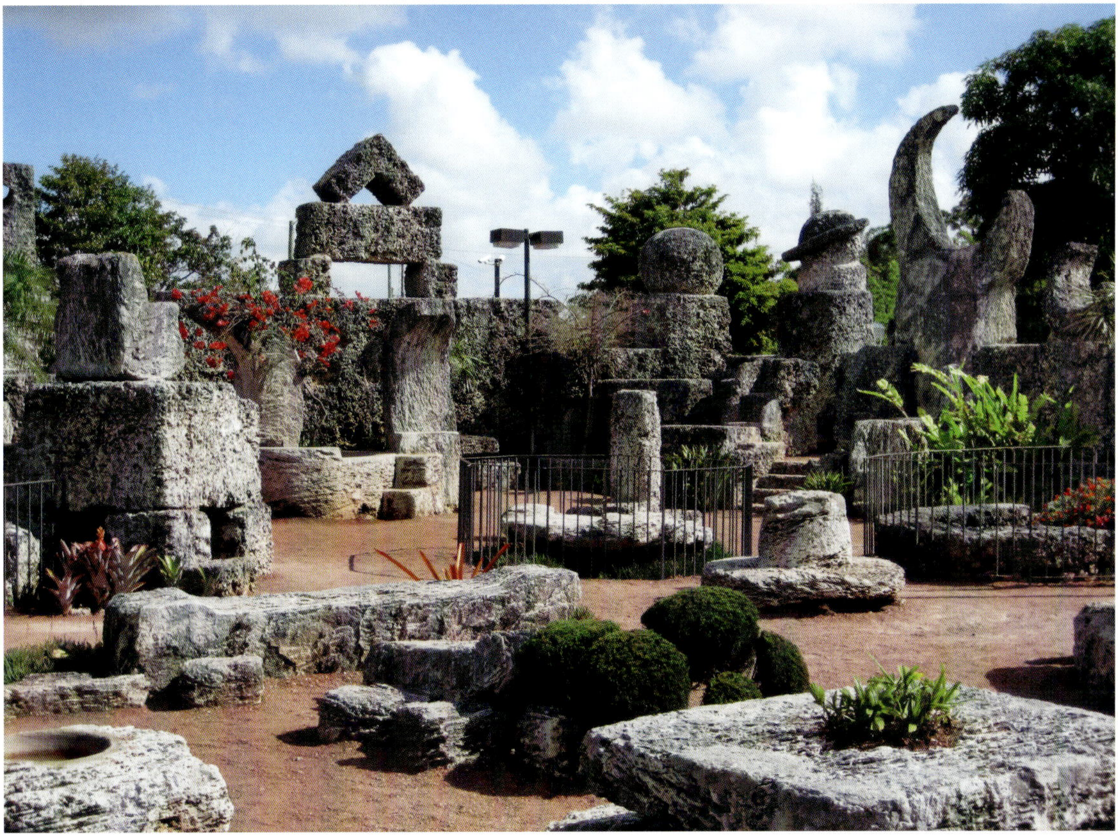

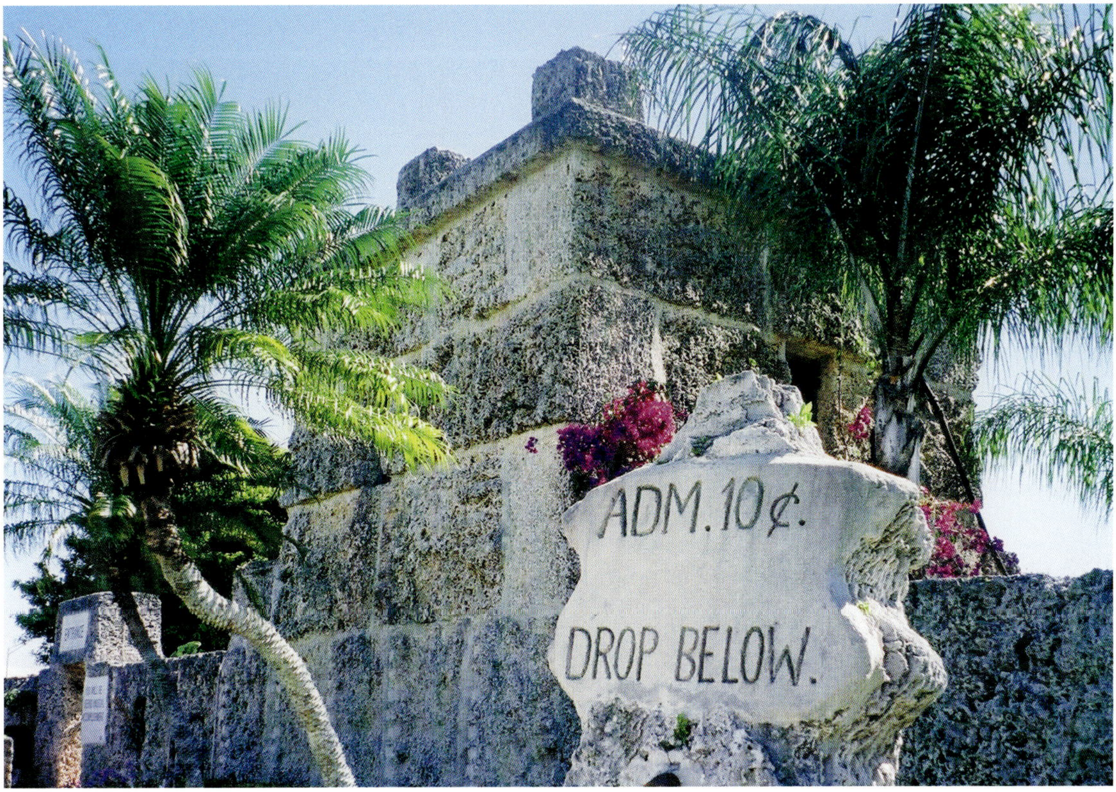

TOWER AND ADMISSION RECEPTACLE, 2005. PHOTO: KELLY LUDWIG

HARRY DELOS ANDREWS

CHATEAU LAROCHE, A.K.A. LOVELAND CASTLE

LOVELAND, OHIO

In contrast to Leedskalnin's rather eccentric rocky ode to his unrequited love (see page 30), the *Chateau Laroche* of Harry Delos Andrews (1890–1981) fits more closely with our mind's-eye images of what a castle should look like, with its crenellations, parapets, watchtowers, and dry moat. The tall, narrow windows represent arrow loops or gun-slits, and a small dungeon is located on the basement level. These manifestations, no doubt, recall Andrews's experiences in Europe after his military service in World War I, when he extended his stay and visited many historical castles and fortresses. (He had studied ancient architecture in college prior to deploying and he continued his studies of medieval architecture and history at Toulouse University after his service, but he was not an architect.)

Returning to Ohio afterward, he became a public school teacher and also taught a weekly Sunday school class. In 1929 he purchased a parcel of property along the banks of the Little Miami River to provide a safe, natural campground for the students in his church classes; in time, this morphed into a youth organization known as the Knights of the Golden Trail (KOGT), whose goal was to raise young men to conscientiously abide by the Ten Commandments. Participants were boys divided by age into groups of Pages (8 to 12 years old), Squires (12 to 17), and Knights (18 or older).

But occasionally the boys' gear would be stolen or damaged if they left it at the campsite, so Andrews decided to build two stone "tents" to protect their belongings. After these were completed, he was inspired to continue building; he laid the foundation in 1929 and placed the cornerstone the following year. Pivoting from his initial idea of merely constructing a shelter for the campers, and with European military and royal fortifications in mind, he determined to construct a castle reflecting those designs, foregrounding his faith in Christianity as the intangible foundation for the *Castle* and adhering to his perception of the noble and chivalrous history of medieval times, with its professed ideals of purity and commitment to goals larger than self.

Building with local field stones and river rocks, Andrews called his 20 x 30′ castle *Chateau Laroche* (the Rock Chateau), although it is also commonly referred to as *Loveland Castle*. But this appellation highlighting the rocks was somewhat deceiving, as the major building modules were actually concrete bricks molded in paper milk cartons, around which the natural materials were later arranged. He molded larger concrete blocks in wooden forms, using tin cans to provide openings, and he formed drainage channels with cans that he laid end-to-end and covered with concrete after their tops and bottoms had been removed. He took advantage of donated materials and the labor of his "Knights," and claimed that he spent only around $125 on materials costs each year.

Work proceeded rather slowly until Andrews's retirement in 1955, when he moved to the site on a year-round basis. He continued working on the *Castle* until his death and bequeathed it to the KOGT organization, which continues to own and operate it. Their website notes that "Any man of high ideas who wish [*sic*] to help save civilization is invited to become a member . . . . [Our] only vows are [to] the Ten Commandments."

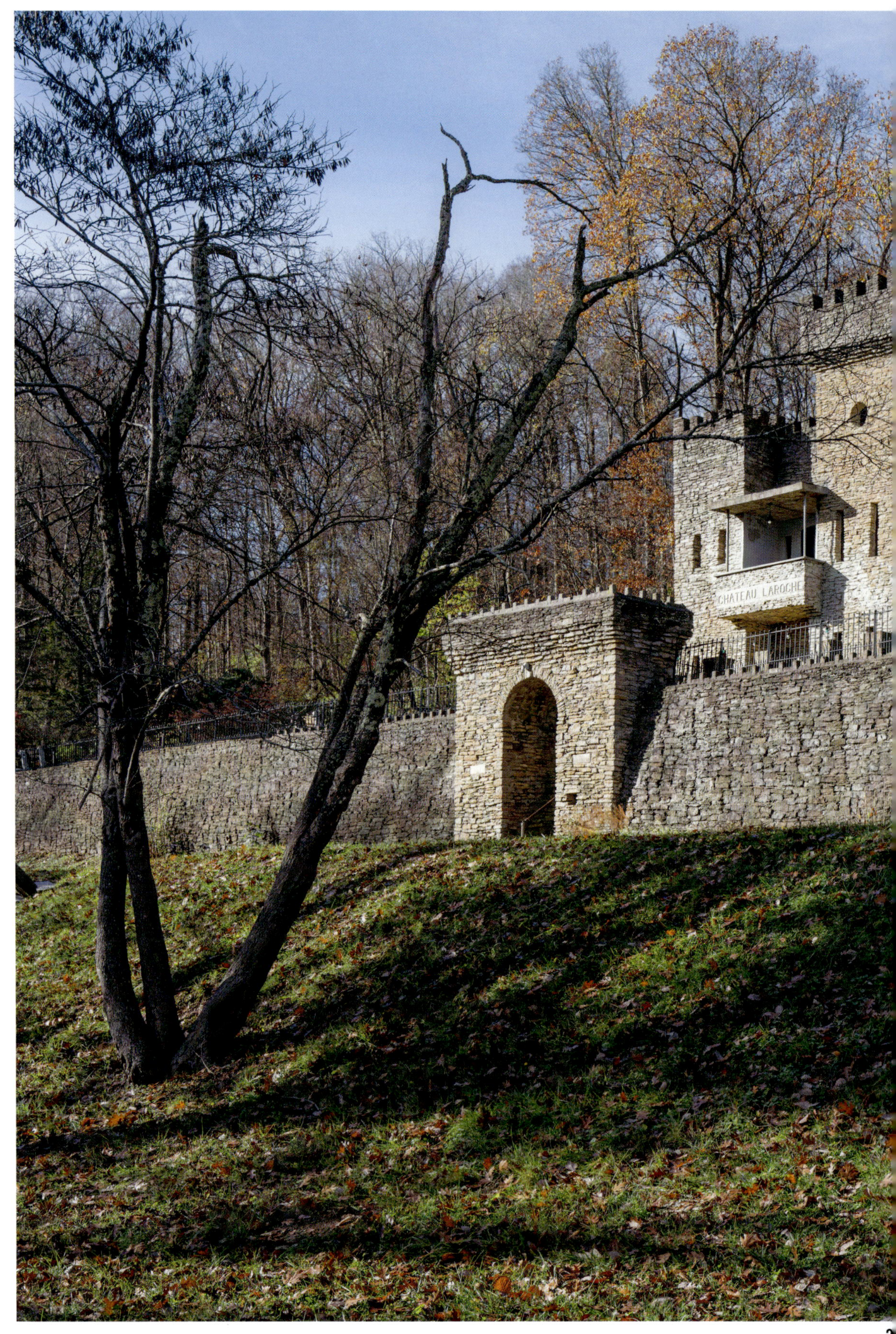
CHATEAU LAROCHE

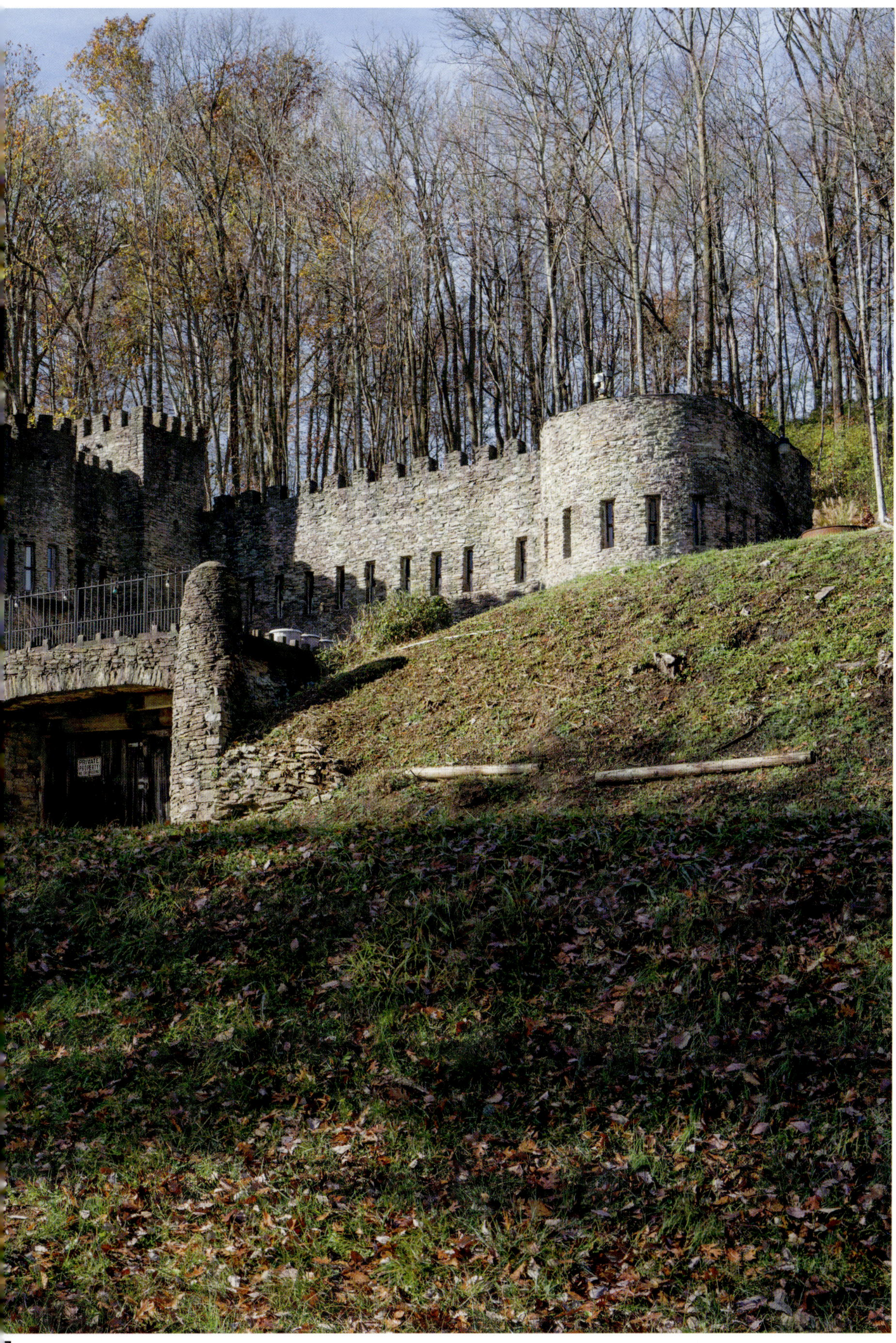

MICHAEL CLARKE RUBEL

RUBEL CASTLE

GLENDORA, CALIFORNIA

In contrast to Bishop (see page 14) and Leedskalnin (see page 30), who built their castles singlehandedly, and Andrews (see page 34), who was occasionally helped by his students and campers, Michael Clarke Rubel (1940–2007) enthusiastically encouraged the involvement of uncounted numbers of friends and neighbors for his site's design, construction, and decoration. Born into a show business family with a tendency for flamboyant gestures, in 1959 Rubel purchased a section of Glendora's old Albourne Citrus Ranch and moved with his mother to the property, which was close to his childhood home. His mother's parties were purportedly the inspiration behind the construction of the *Castle*: he is said to have built the first component, the *Bottle House*, as a refuge in order to escape the raucous frivolity.

He had been fascinated by building forts and castles as a young boy, often making use of objects he rescued from the nearby municipal dump. So he was no stranger to adaptive reuse, and in 1968 he began to focus his efforts on expanding his construction. Utilizing a 124-foot-diameter irrigation reservoir as a foundation, he built up 12-foot walls from river rocks and recycled granite chunks, setting both these structural elements and decorative found-object flourishes in concrete mortar. Stacked, bolted, and welded recycled 10,000-gallon water tanks formed the infrastructure for other components to enhance Rubel's vision for a medieval-style castle, including the 74-foot-high *Clock Tower*. Railroad ties, telephone poles, bed springs, and even a functioning windmill were moved to the site and creatively reused, as were other discarded industrial products that had been dumped as the area's citrus farms declined and those properties were repurposed to provide acres of residential housing. Decades worth of river rocks and stones transported from the San Gabriel Mountains provided a unifying visual aesthetic.

Rubel lived in the *Castle* and worked on enhancing the grounds until just a few years before his death, when he was unable to maintain it, and at that time he donated it to the Glendora Historical Society, which continues to own and operate the property. While enjoying the whimsy of placing post-industrial agricultural castoffs around the site, his focus remained the medieval-style castle. The main gate reflects that sensibility with its latticed grille and heavy timbers, as do the crenellated *Bell* and *Clock Towers*; ancillary buildings remaining from the now-defunct citrus farm complement the entirety with utilitarian and aesthetic features. *Rubel Castle* and its surrounding historic district were added to the National Register of Historic Places in 2013.

HE HAD BEEN FASCINATED BY BUILDING FORTS AND CASTLES AS A YOUNG BOY.

COURTYARD OF *CASTLE* COMPLEX WITH *CENTER TOWER*, 2025

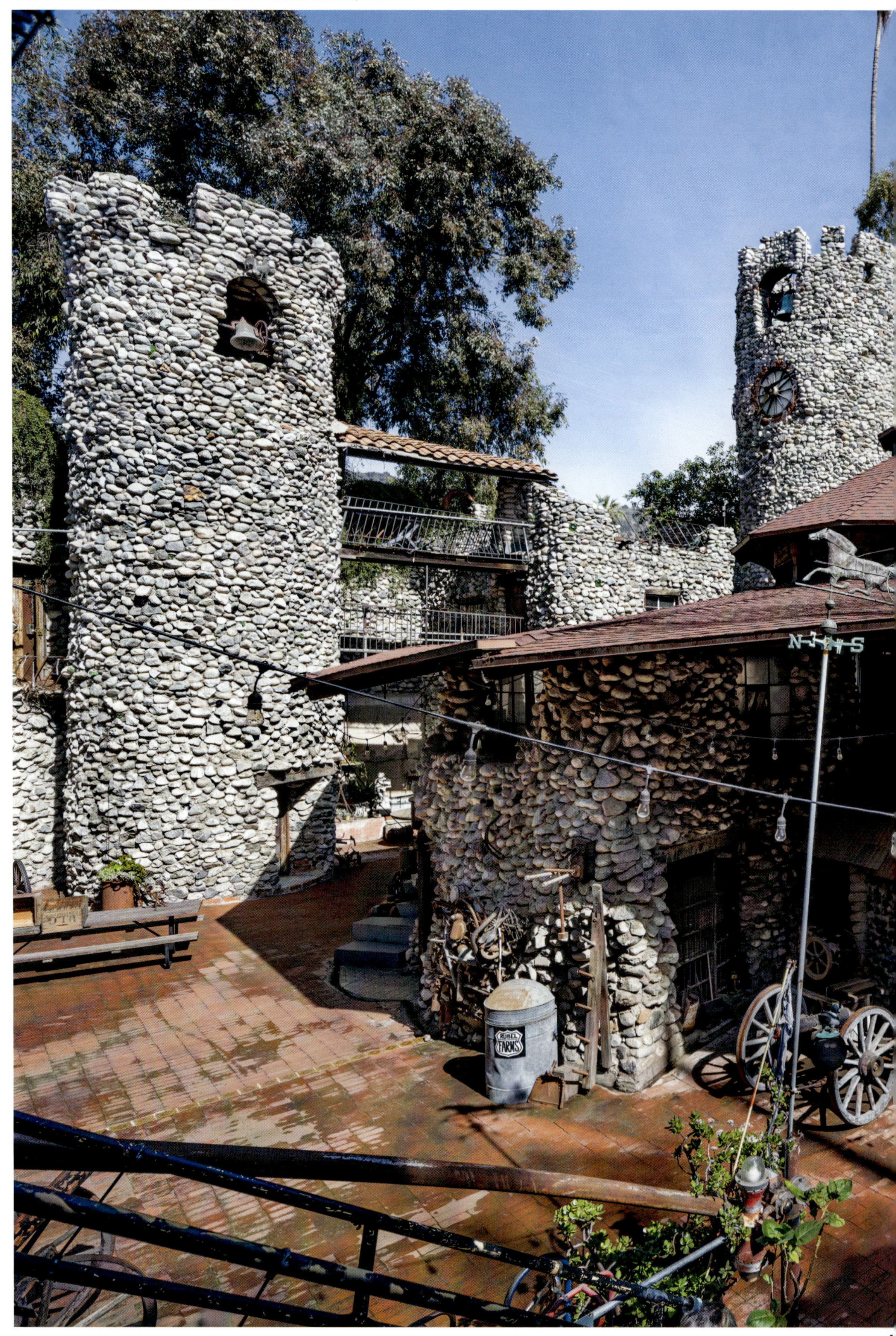

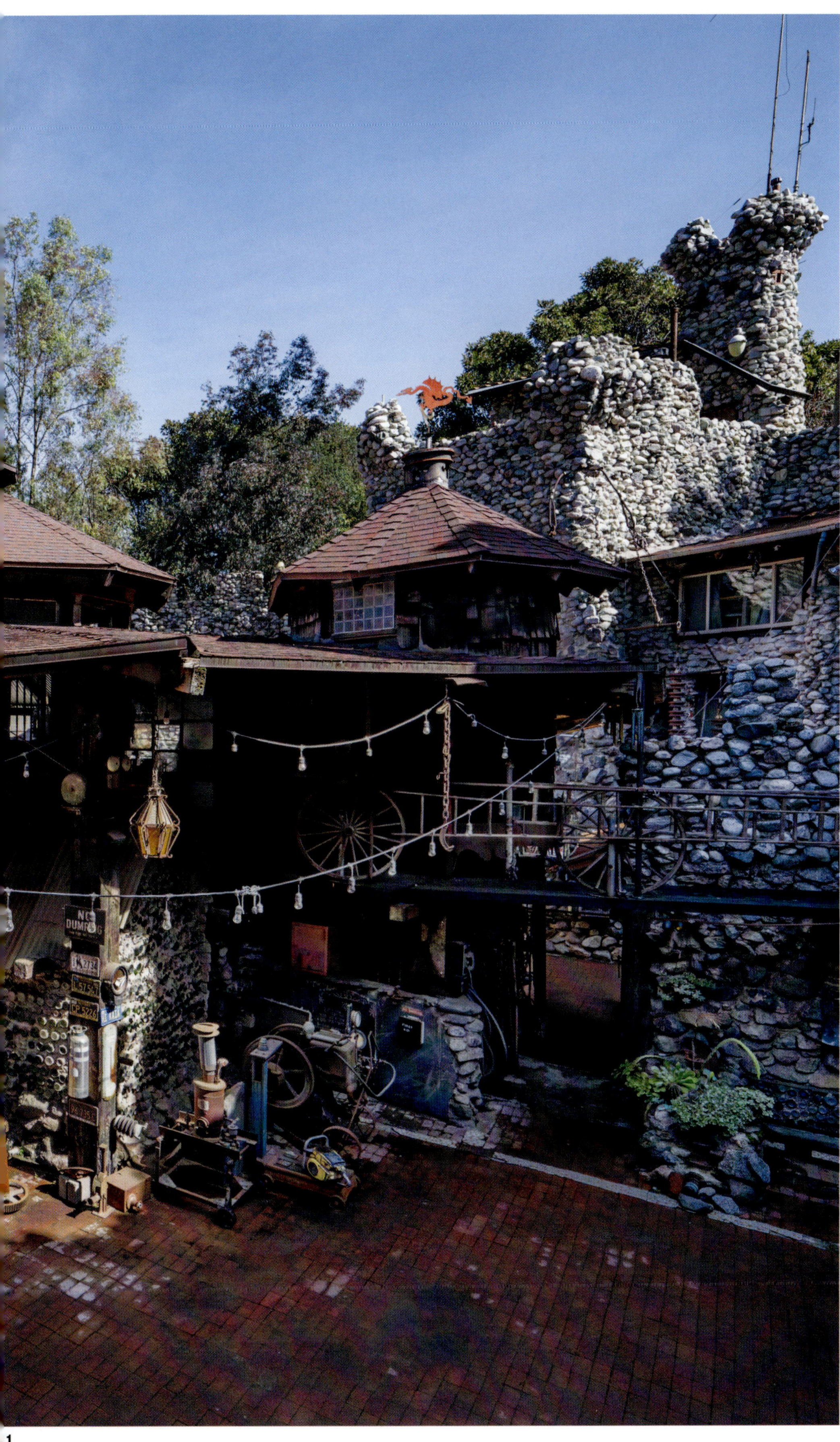
NO
DUMP

FIRE TOWER AND MAIN ENTRANCE INTO *CASTLE* COMPLEX THROUGH ADJUSTABLE PORTCULLIS, 2025

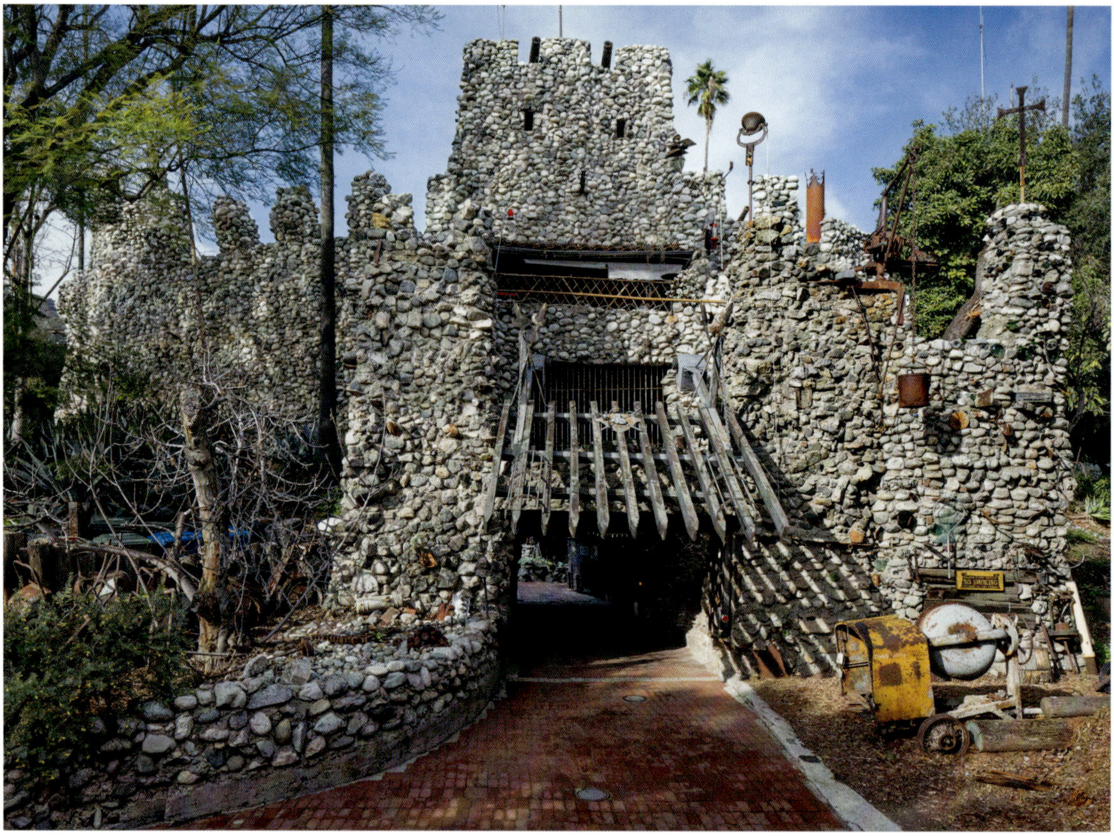

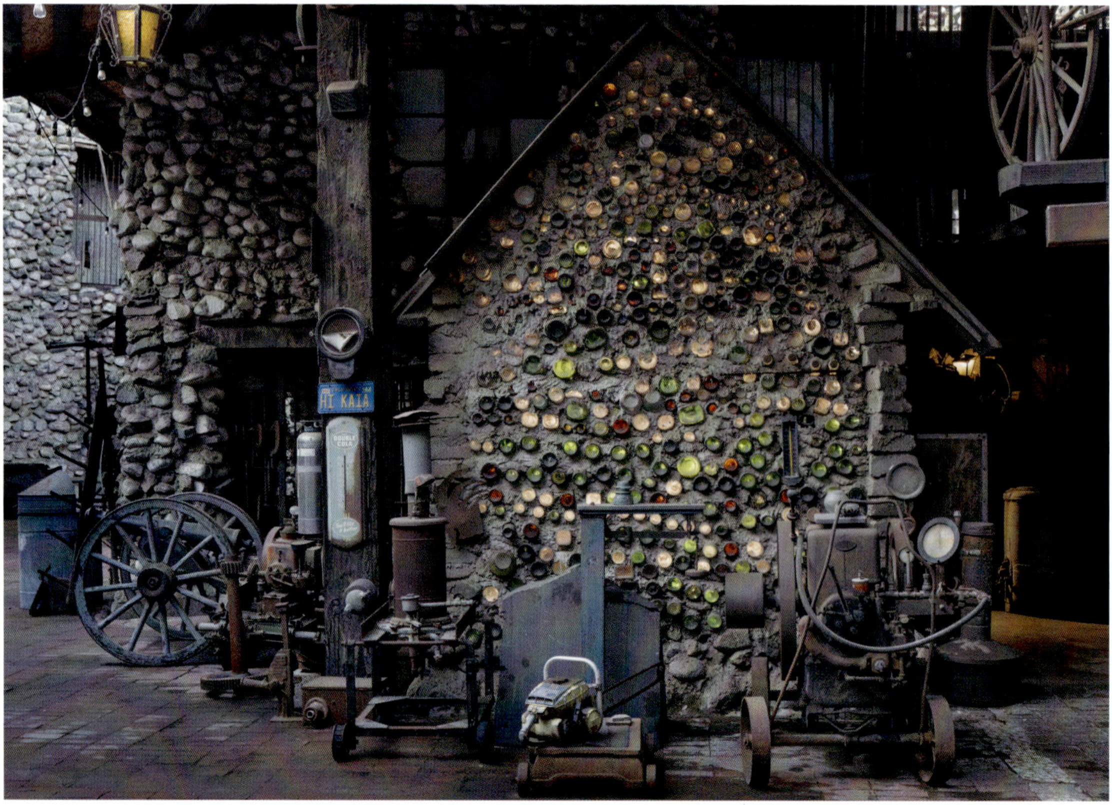

BOTTLE HOUSE AND FOUND OBJECTS WITHIN *CASTLE* COURTYARD, 2025

FIRE TOWER INTERIOR, WITH PAINTING BY EVIE LARRIMORE, 2025

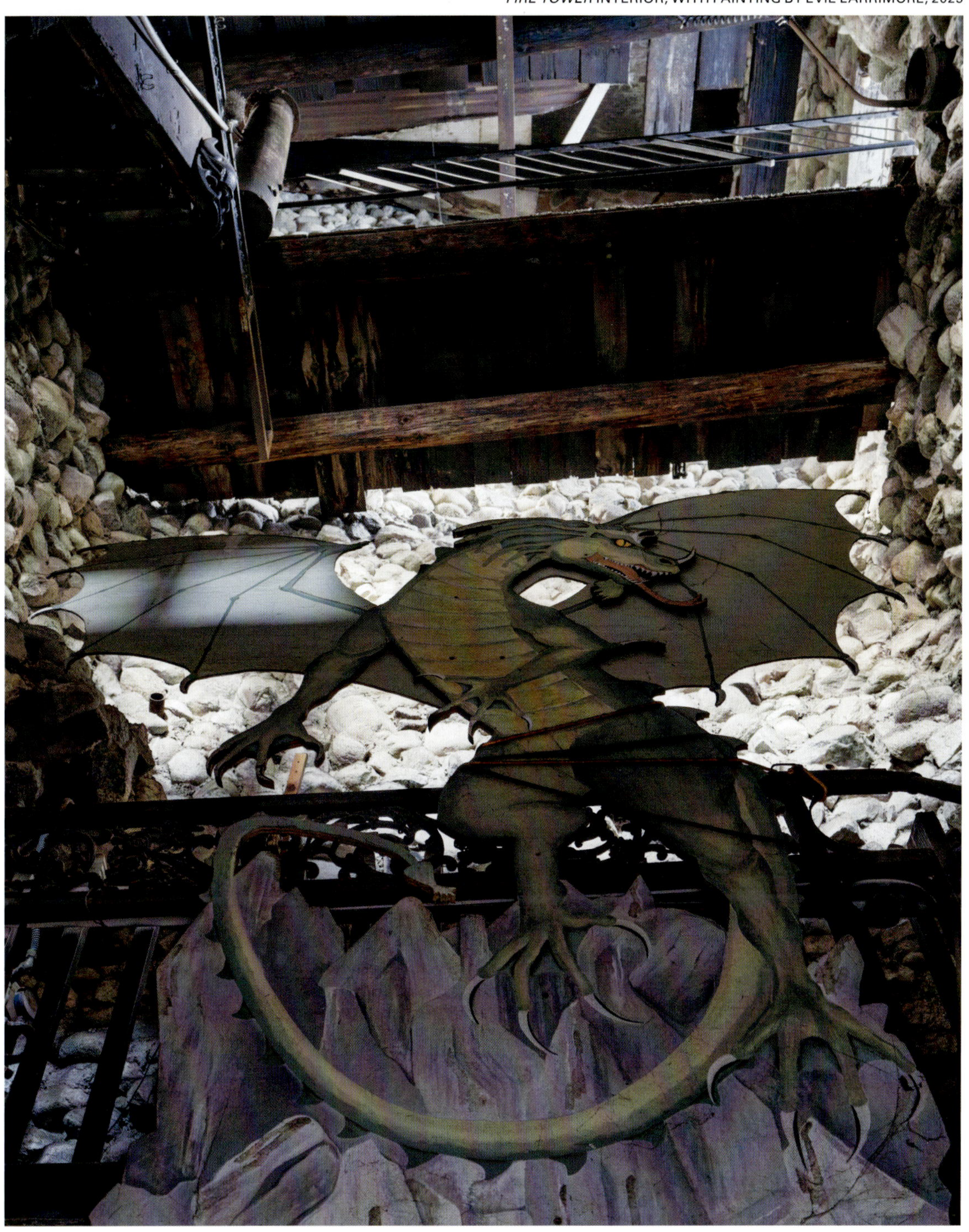

DOMINIC "CANO" ESPINOZA

CANO'S CASTLE

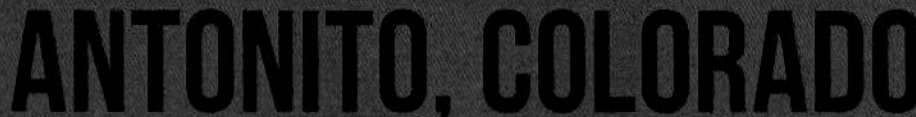
ANTONITO, COLORADO

A castle with an entirely different sensibility rises above the expansive plains of Colorado's San Luis Valley. This impressive edifice, like Andrews's (see page 34), was at least partially inspired by its maker's military deployment, as Espinoza (b. 1948) followed the example of other family members who had served in the armed forces. One of 14 children who was unlikely to find opportunity locally, he enlisted in the Army in 1968 and served two years in Vietnam. While there, he became "fascinated" by the region's Buddhist temples and came to think that perhaps he should erect "something" to honor his own Catholic faith and give thanks for returning safely from his overseas service.

Improving his residence after his homecoming, he augmented his construction skills as he worked improvisationally and took advantage of materials that were cheap or free and easily available. Developing a fire-resistant technique that he would find useful elsewhere, he sheathed the roof with flattened aluminum cans layered like shingles, keeping in mind a 1950s-era courthouse fire that had allegedly destroyed the property records verifying his family's ownership of significant acreage. (In conjunction with an alleged conspiracy by local officials to murder his great uncle, he refers to this appropriation as "the heist.") Despite this precaution, fire broke out and his home burned, suspiciously echoing the earlier blaze. Espinoza is convinced this blaze, too, was a result of arson.

In 1980, moving a short distance away to the town of Antonito to care for his grandparents, he began his next—and, to date, his most consequential—construction project. Beginning as a simple potato cellar for the produce he would glean from neighbors' fields, the two adjacent plots owned by his grandparents at the east end of town slowly became the site of a complex of both residential and devotional/sacred structures. This project finally enabled him to start riffing off of the temples he had admired in Vietnam, as it also was inspired by stories of a builder in Tijuana who collected found objects in a wheelbarrow and then mounded them up to create a singular construction. He has seen so much ugliness, he says, that he was driven to create something special by which he could demonstrate his own distinctiveness and potential.

After erecting an additional story on top of the potato cellar, Espinoza continued to build upward, motivated in part by the admiring comments of visitors. (Despite its relatively isolated location, Antonito is the terminus of a scenic narrow-gauge railroad that brings tourists to town.) He used native volcanic rock as one of his primary building components, and made sure to include many other fire-resistant materials as well, collecting a range of detritus at the dump or soliciting found objects from neighbors, either accepting them as gifts or working off their value in trade. The first floor includes a still-unfinished steam/sweat room, the next three stories are living quarters, and the fifth level is an observatory.

The exterior is liberally sheathed with the cut-off ends of aluminum cans, bicycle reflectors, hubcaps, metal grills, screen doors, and other castoff industrial and commercial scraps. Yet despite the variability and capriciousness of the construction materials he used in both the first tower, which rises some 43 feet high, and the second, a slightly lower spire whose lowest level once served as a stable for his horse, the *Castle* buildings evidence a consistent visual vocabulary, with rhythmic placements of shapes and media: the whole plays off the inherent geometry of the scavenged windowpanes and flattened aluminum shingles. He builds in what he describes as a spiritual "stage" of consciousness, slightly stoned on a daily dose of cannabis that guides him toward self-improvement strategies—eating less meat, staying away from alcohol, and focusing his energy on his architectural creations.

Espinoza recounts how one day he looked up at the two towers and realized that to him they looked like a king and queen, so he began referring to them by these names. As he continued to erect additional structures, he gave them names referencing other chessboard pieces: *Knight*, *Rook*, and *Pawn*. Despite this nomenclature (and his only moderate interest in or knowledge about the game of chess), he refers to the complex as a sanctuary and asserts that these are "Jesus's Castles." Inscribed and sculpted phrases in a mixture of Spanish and English express his devotion to Christ and the Virgin of Guadalupe, and Biblical allusions and imagery—such as an "Egyptian" pyramid of hubcaps affixed to the eastern side of the *Knight*—underscore his devotion.

Indeed, Espinoza frequently notes that God actually built the *Castle*, and he just served as the conduit to bring its physicality to fruition. Furthermore, he asserts he has given the *Castle* buildings to Jesus to occupy, so he himself lives in a house that he is building on the southern of the two adjacent lots, using portable ladders and hanging ropes to move between its levels. While referencing the standard iconography of Catholic (and particularly, Mexican and Mexican-American) beliefs—apparently not perceiving a conflict with his professed self-identification as a Native American and a Spanish Jew—he also uses his installations to comment on certain social ills. For example, he decries the use of alcohol and tobacco and warns against addiction, tribulations he witnessed during his service during the Vietnam War and that he sees locally as well.

The exterior shape of each structure is improvised, based on materials he could find and how he could fit them together. Although he had raced to "finish" the buildings prior to the year 2000 in case some of the theories predicting the collapse of our world as we knew it would have taken place, he daily continues to tweak the design with such additions as a footbridge made of car-tire snow chains strung high up to unite the *King* and *Queen*. These two asymmetrical pinnacles tower over almost every other built structure in town, capturing one's immediate attention not only by their height and idiosyncratic shapes but also as a result of the sun's reflection bouncing off the aluminum cans, hubcaps, and other metal features that have been creatively juxtaposed in a proud declaration of personal faith and community exhortation.

Almost implausibly, for the third time a fire impacted Espinoza's life in the early hours of a January morning in 2022, when his personal residence in the Antonito castle complex burned, although the iconic *King* and *Queen* towers and other buildings were not affected, and he was unhurt. In this case it seemed to be an electrical fire, as the wiring in the residence was probably improvisationally jerry-rigged. He is generally accepted by his neighbors, so it is unlikely that arson was the cause of this blaze, although he believes otherwise. A national crowdfunding campaign helped to provide some financial assistance for rebuilding, and as of this writing, Espinoza is in the process of reconstructing his home.

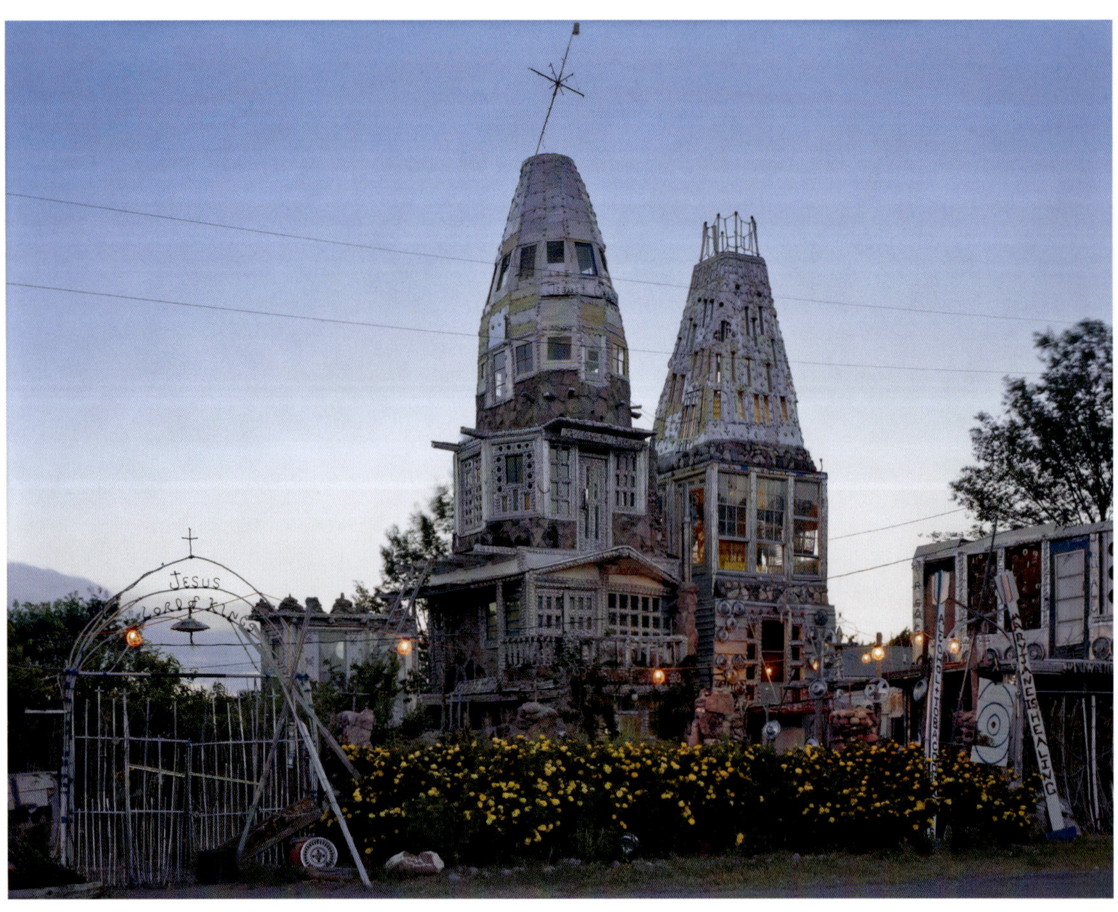

ARCHED ENTRANCE TO PROPERTY, WITH *KING*, *QUEEN*, AND *KNIGHT* (AT FAR RIGHT), 2015

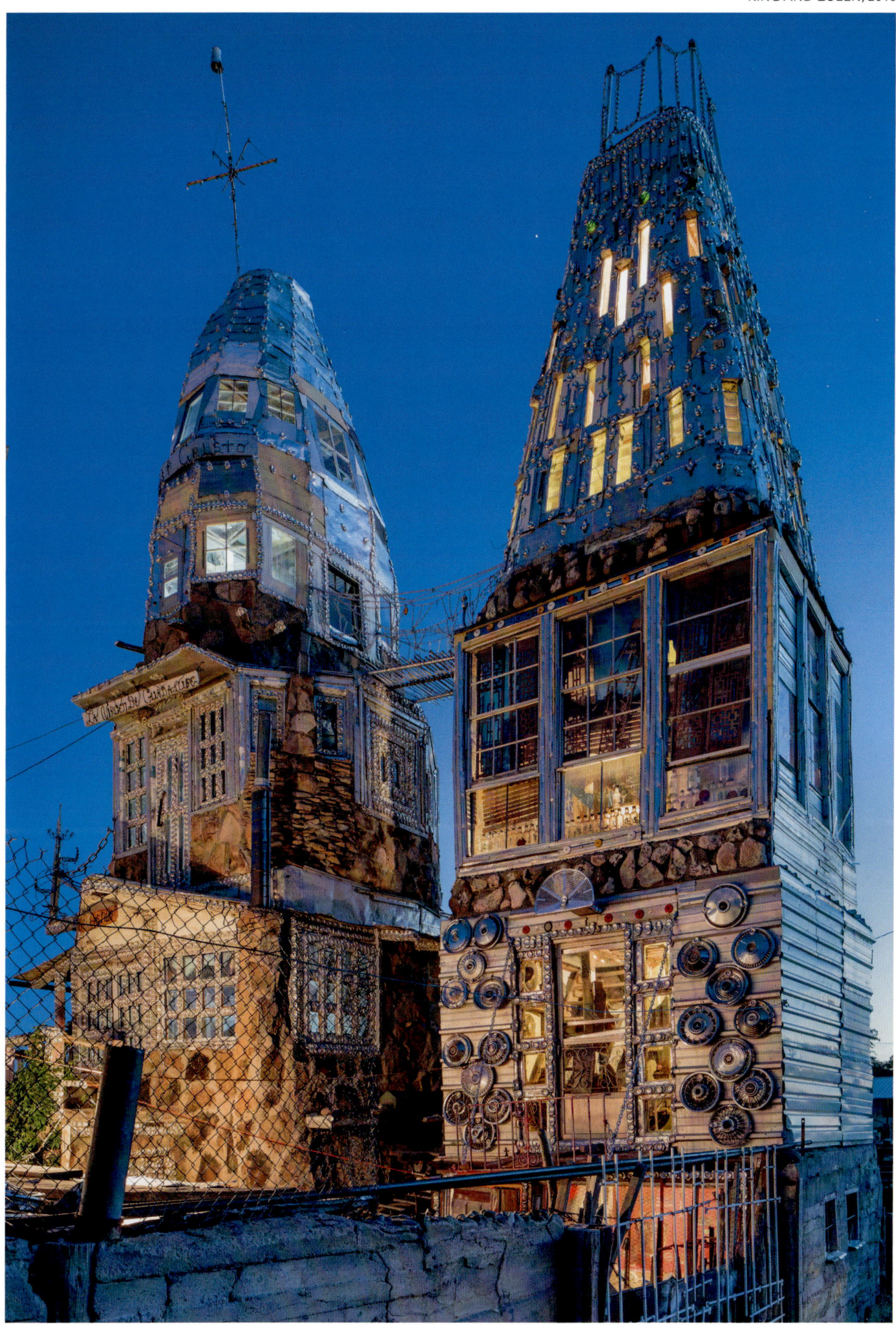

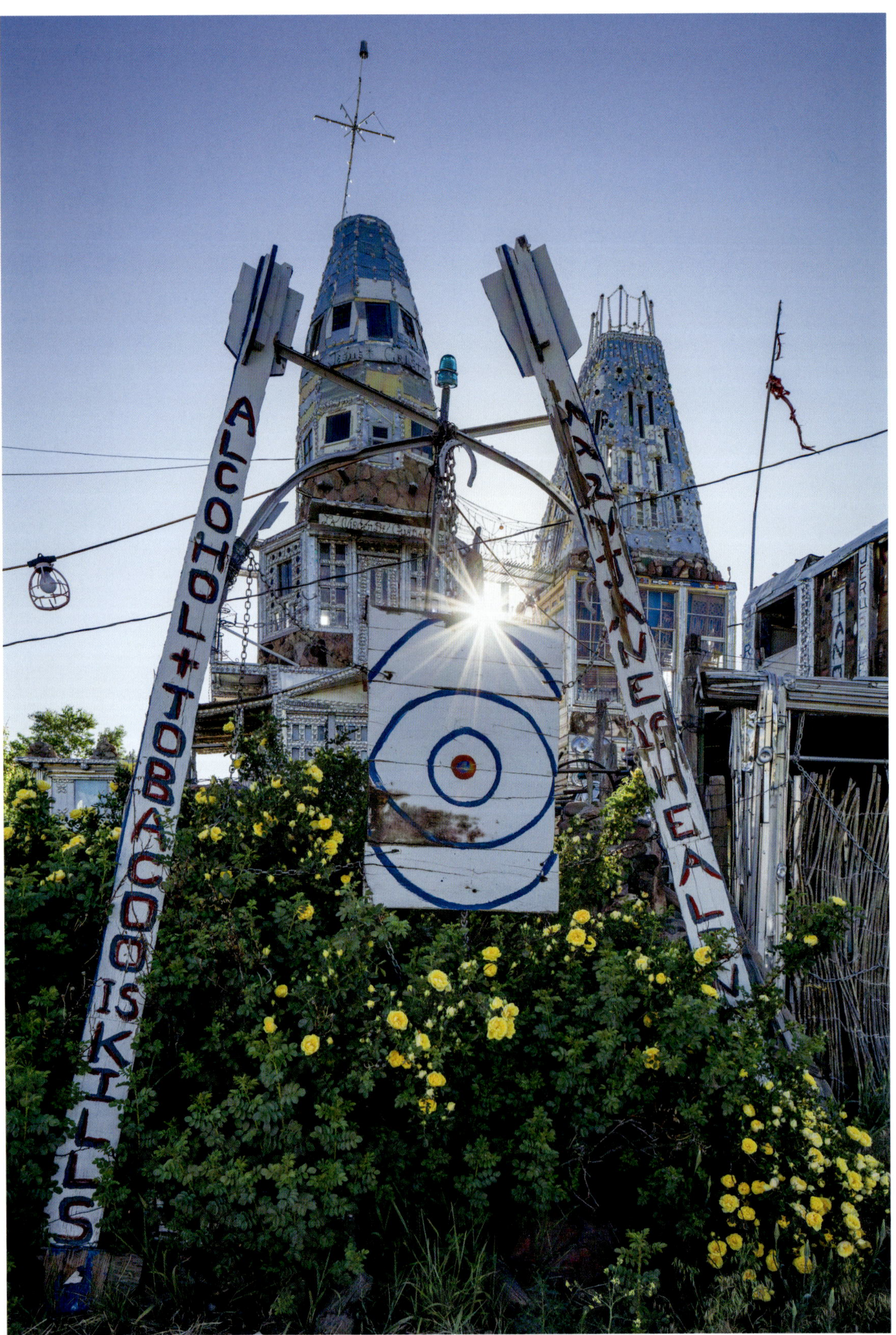

WARNING ABOUT ADDICTION ON GROUNDS IN FRONT OF *JESUS'S CASTLES*, 2016

ESPINOZA'S HOME, 2020

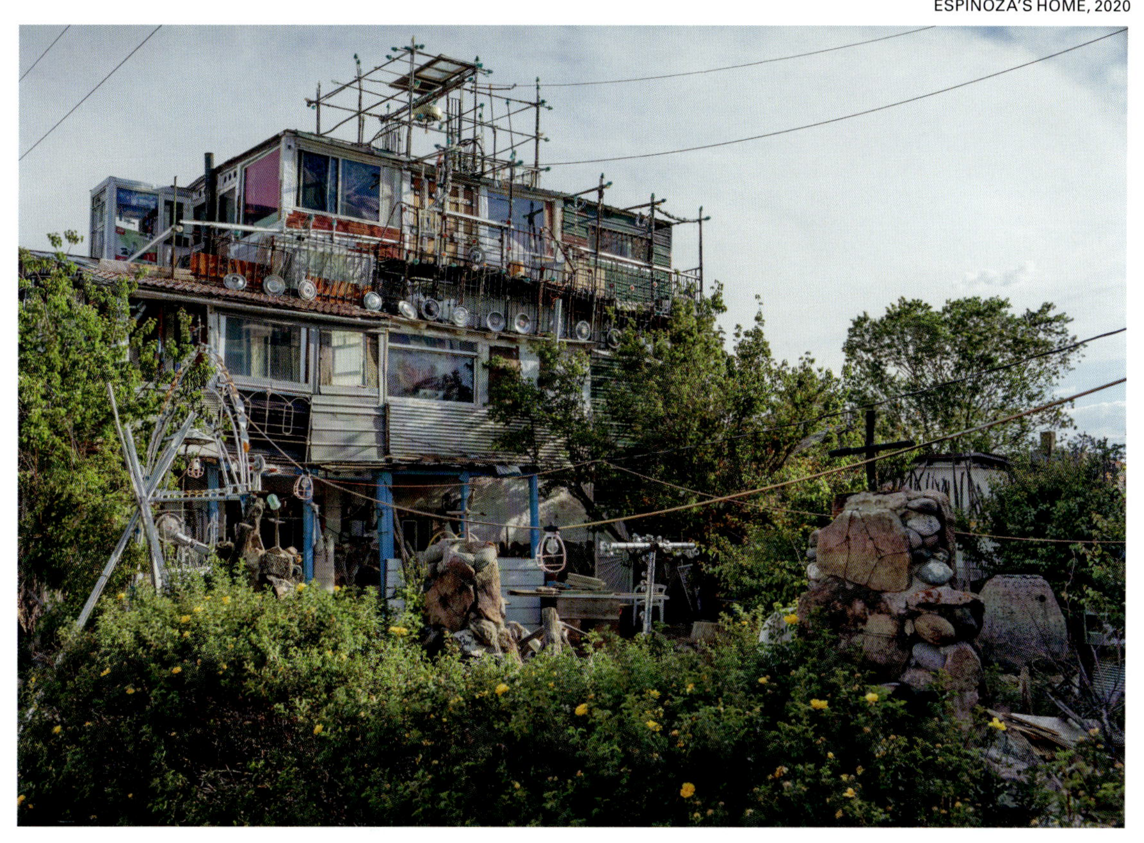

HE BELIEVES THAT GOD ACTUALLY BUILT THE CASTLES, AND HE JUST SERVED AS THE CONDUIT.

ARCHED ENTRANCE AND *CASTLES*, 2015

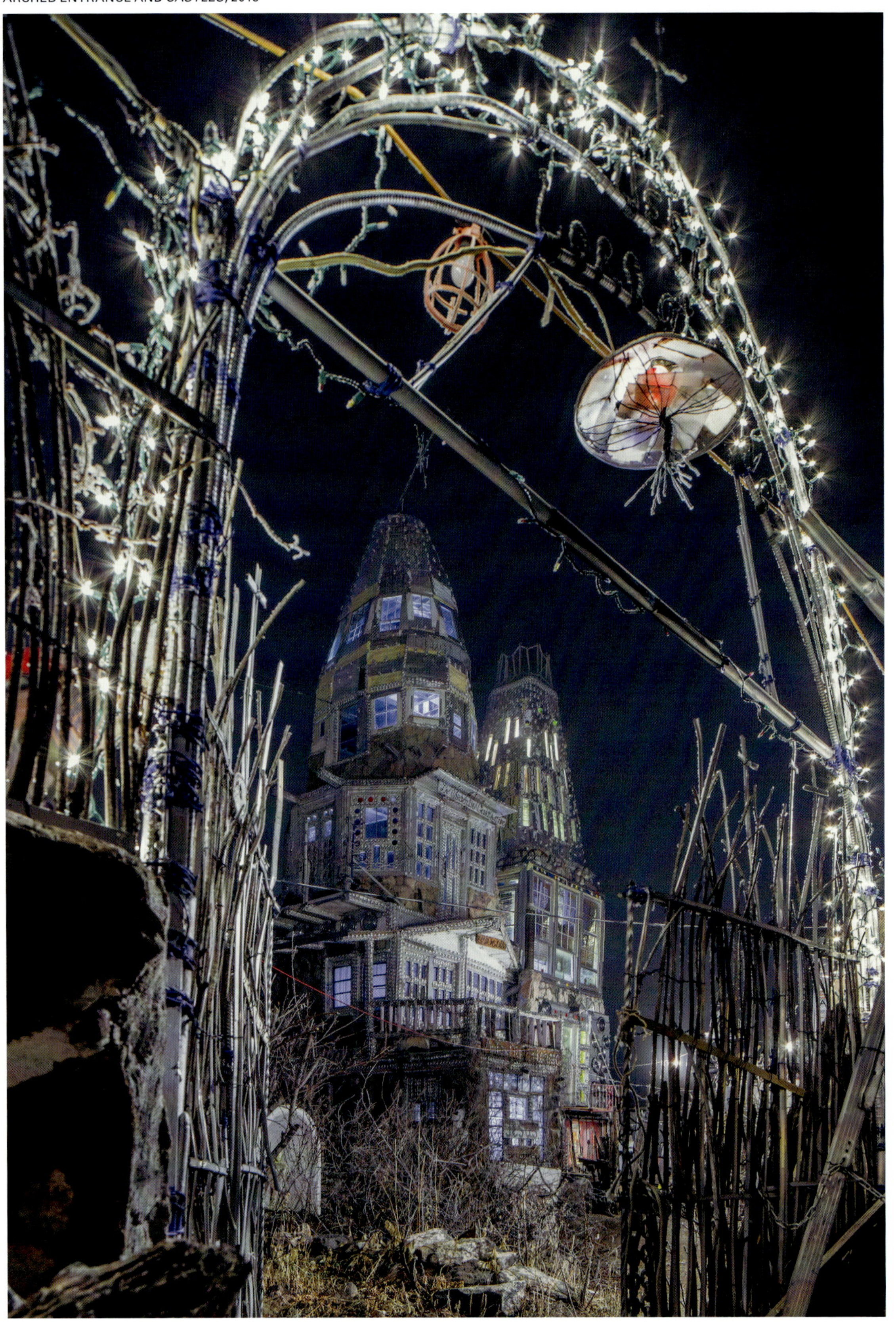

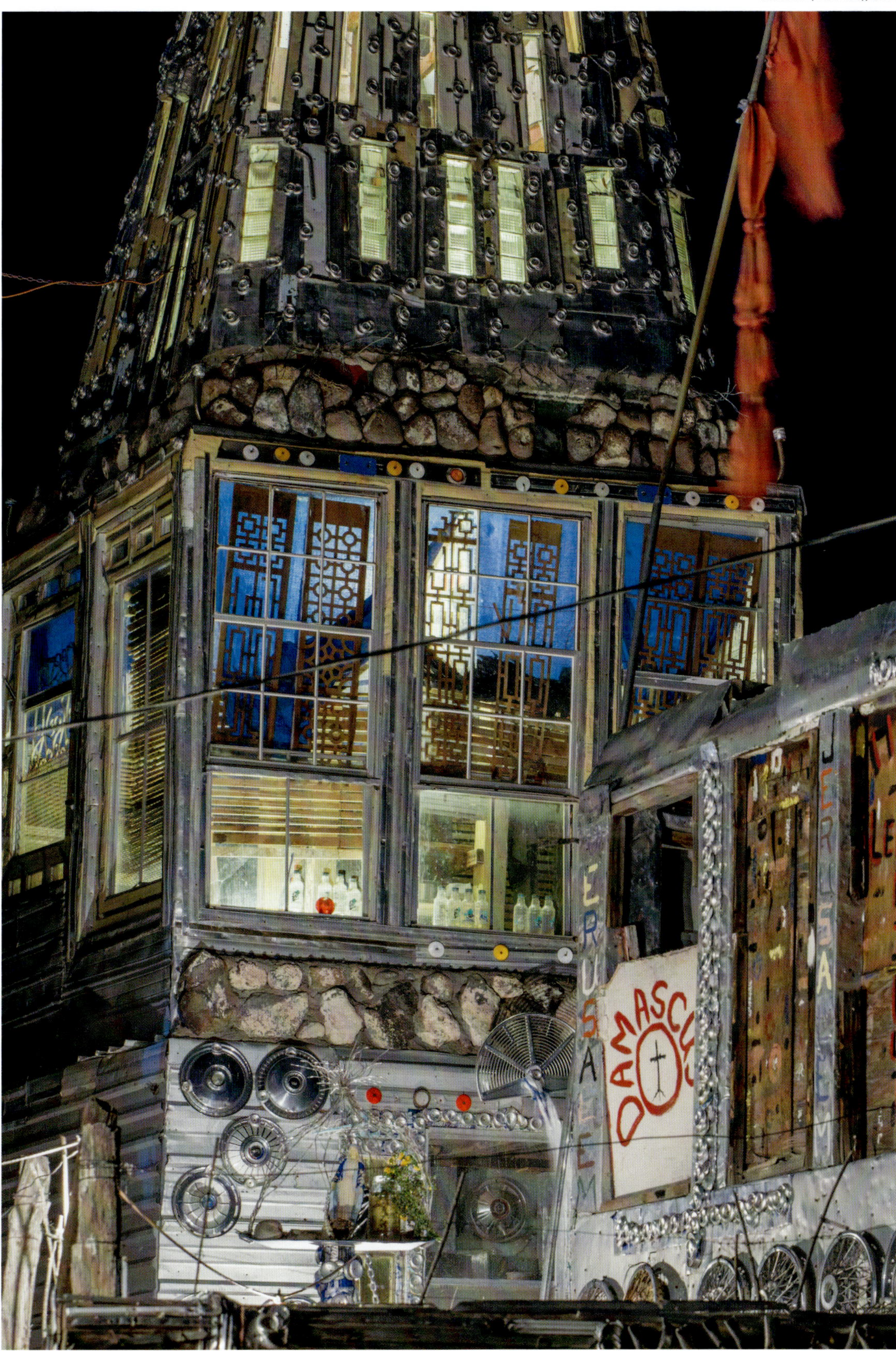
ERUSALEM
DAMASCU
JERUSALEM

FLOYD JESSIE BANKS, JR.

GREENBACK CASTLE

GREENBACK, TENNESSEE

This *Castle* was once conceptualized as a means toward self-aggrandizement and a way to "draw up the ladies," but it has evolved, over time, to serve as a multipurpose structure that codifies the maker's creationist religious beliefs and provides him with the opportunity to spread the word. It also presents "proofs" that validate Banks's (b. 1946) understanding of such scientific phenomena as bird migration, gravity, the extinction of the dinosaurs, the earth's rotation, and, venturing into social science, demographics and the development of a healthy society. While he unashamedly acknowledges his lack of formal education and even the fact that his life experience did not involve formal work in construction or any reliable paying job, his wide-ranging interests motivated him to learn basic building techniques, educate himself about arrowheads and other artifacts utilized by local Native American tribes, and build and oversee roughly a dozen modest rental houses. He is a hard worker and takes pride in repurposing the castoffs of roadbuilding, construction, and personal and industrial detritus to fuel his mission.

Banks began to construct his *Castle* on the outskirts of the small town of Greenback in 1993, a process that was soon aided by the demolition of buildings that had lined the nearby highway: as workers widened the road, they left debris along the sides, and Banks drove over every night in his pickup truck to load up the scraps and transport them to his home, where he cleaned, organized, and ultimately integrated them into the growing structure. He was also assisted by local suppliers who saved him punctured bags of concrete, and by neighbors who donated their own construction remnants and other objects (marbles, shells, stones, tiles, flatware, ceramic figurines, and more) that he used for infrastructure or adornment.

Two 16-foot-high, mostly crenellated walls erected with stones, bricks, and concrete blocks, laid out in an L-shaped form, are the core of the *Castle* construction to date. A large circular tower anchors the intersection of the walls, and six square towers along their length puncture the otherwise rather severe spans of the façades. Some 20 open-air rooms line the interior of the *Castle* walls, some separated by brick archways; others, protected with a roof, shelter Banks's more precious or personal displays.

Around 2003 he began to identify shapes created through his application of concrete as symbolic of religious narratives, or of historical or familial imagery. As he detected increasing numbers of these "pictograph" forms, he asserted that he was not involved in producing them, but simply was unconsciously transmitting their symbolic messages to the material world. He has since come to believe not only that they are specific lessons from God but that his entire *Castle* is a means to convey these principles to the population at large. He now outlines the deciphered images in contrasting paint to emphasize their appearance.

To ensure that this more abstract imagery would be fully comprehended as an integral component of the broader range of his convictions, he has supplemented them with painted concrete-incised plaques to express his insights; at the same time, he uses them to motivate his visitors to reexamine prevailing interpretations and move toward what he believes are the truths about God, the creation of the world, and science. And while planted, painted, lightly sculpted, inlaid, and assembled crosses are signs of his religious tenets and belief in Jesus Christ, there are also composed assemblages of Native American artifacts and bas-relief Egyptian motifs as well as assorted elements linked to a more generic concept of castle, such as an enclosed "dungeon" with implements of torture. Kinder offerings are at hand to complement the more challenging motifs: a bucket of canned foods free for the taking set out for those who are hungry, a pile of second-hand dolls and toys that ask to be taken home by visiting children, and a vegetable garden whose bounty he loves to share. At the same time, while he once was economically relatively comfortable thanks to income from his rental units, he sold those houses off for minimal prices and now asks for donations of spare change from his visitors to help fuel his construction efforts.

Banks is driven by his commitment to completing his *Castle*, as he believes it to be necessary before Christ's Second Coming can be made manifest. He is also anxious for "researchers" to come see it in order to certify his scientific theories. Overcoming mishaps and illnesses, including severe heart ailments, which he interprets as signs of the devil's attempt to impede his progress, he continues to work as much as he is able, welcoming visitors to this clearing in the hills of eastern Tennessee.

CASTLE OVERVIEW WITH CENTRAL TOWER, 2024

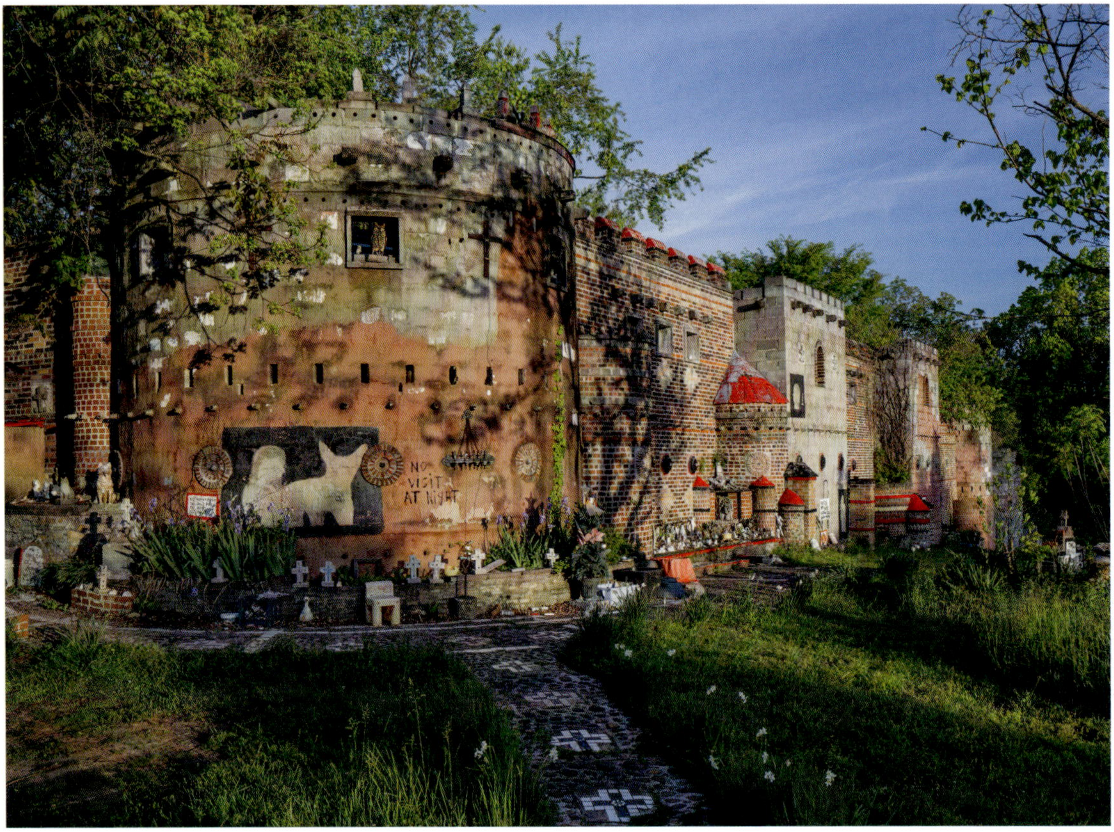

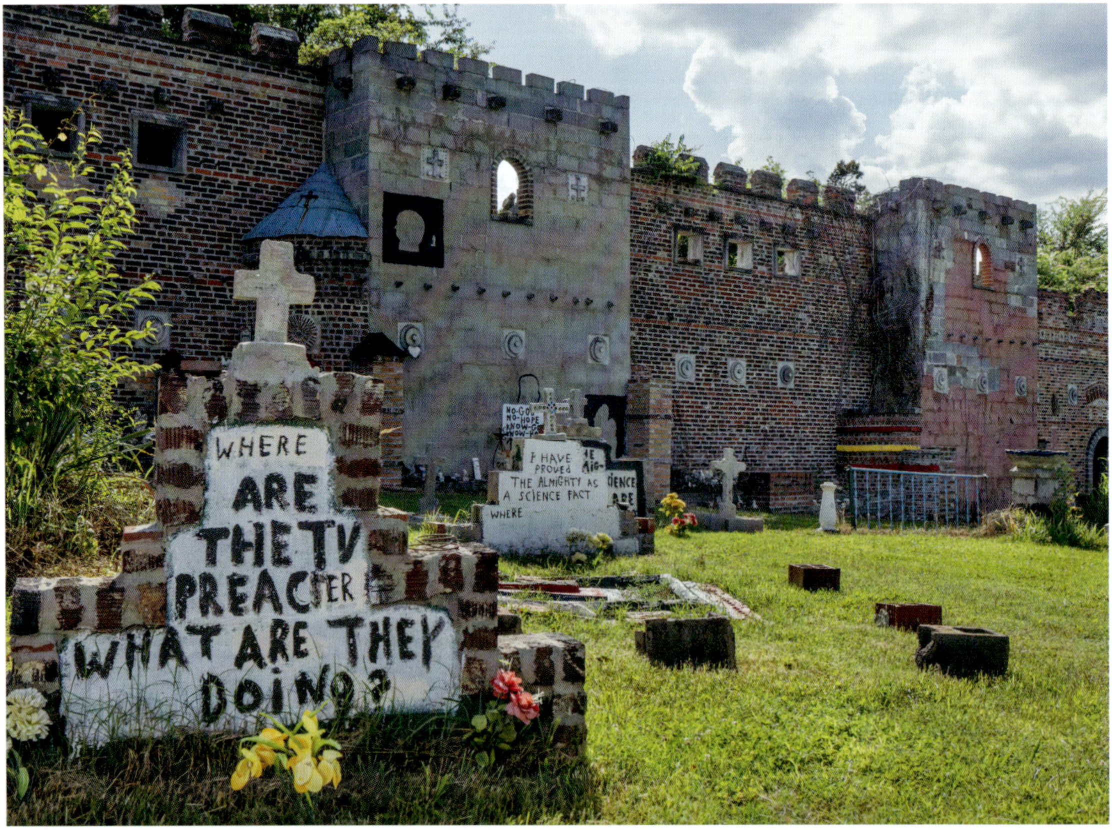

EXTERIOR WALLS WITH INSPIRATIONAL YARD INSTALLATIONS, 2017

HIS CASTLE PRESENTS «PROOFS» THAT VALIDATE HIS UNDERSTANDING OF SCIENTIFIC PHENOMENA.

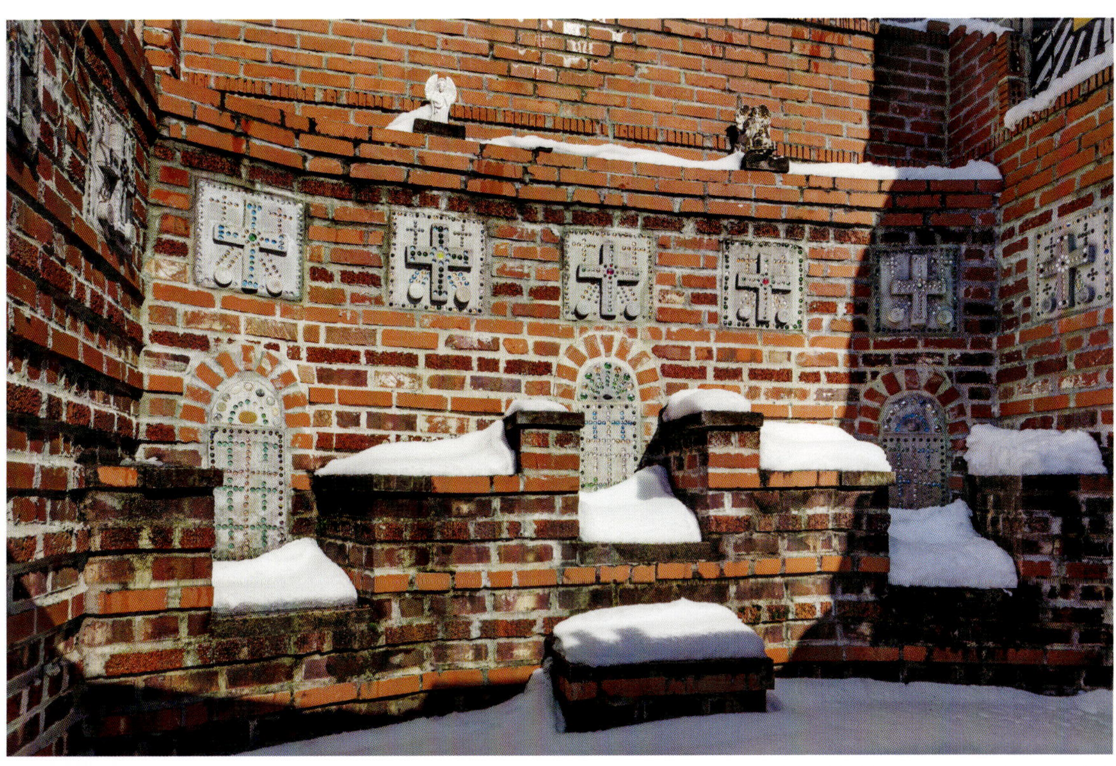

OPEN-AIR *CASTLE* INTERIOR (DETAIL), 2015

FRANK VAN ZANT

THUNDER MOUNTAIN MONUMENT

IMLAY, NEVADA

Van Zant (1921–1989), who later took on the name of Chief Rolling Mountain Thunder, came back from his military service during World War II a changed man. He was born in Okmulgee, Oklahoma, territory that had been settled by members of the Creek Nation beginning in the 1820s, and, despite his Dutch surname, Van Zant asserted that he was a full-blooded member of the Creek tribe, apparently disregarding the modification to his native bloodline from his Caucasian father (or, alternatively, Caucasian mother: there are competing narratives). Upon returning to civilian life, he variously explored theology, law enforcement, and serving as a private investigator.

After he retired in 1968, he set out with his third wife, Ahtrum, looking to find a place to land. Although accounts of why he ended up in Nevada's high desert differ, it is likely that when his truck broke down the couple camped on this spot; at some point the owner of the property came by and offered the barren land to Van Zant for a pittance. He snapped it up.

Thunder Mountain Monument (which is actually located on the flats of Nevada's Great Basin, not on a mountain, and there is, in fact, no local mountain by this name) was built around their one-room, 6 x 9′ travel trailer, as Van Zant gradually covered it with rocks and concrete, adding hallways and stairways, and eventually turned it into a three-story monument. He had earlier seen a house built with walls made from bottles somewhere in the desert and was excited by the challenge of building one, so he created many of the exterior walls with "daub and bottle" construction, allowing their multicolored lights to pour into the interior. A nearby junk yard provided most of the resources for his construction and the rest he scavenged from the desert, using the White man's resources, he would say, to build this monument dedicated to the "Native Peoples of the West." He said that the only thing he ever purchased for his extensive building projects was concrete, and his only tools were his hands and a small trowel.

As he gathered materials he expanded the structure, installing automobile windshields as large windows, using recycled scrap iron and pipe as well as wagon wheels and car hoods for infrastructure, and covering shaped chicken wire with concrete mortar to construct a variety of mostly figurative or anthropomorphic sculptures to adorn the grounds. He used this same technique to ornament the main and ancillary buildings, often using bright colors to enhance their impact. He covered the entire exterior of the *Monument* with bas-relief tableaux that illustrate the injustices, wars against, and betrayals of the Native Americans by the U.S. government, and he ornamented the roof with additional sculptures and interlaced arches, the tallest of which rose 50 feet high, topped with a carved wooden eagle. Ultimately some seven structures and over 200 concrete figures were constructed on the five-acre plot that runs 1,000 feet along the south side frontage of U.S. Highway 80.

Van Zant worked on the *Thunder Mountain Monument* for more than 20 years. With his holistic view of life, spirituality, and artmaking, he spent his time equally engaged with land art, sculpture, painting, and performance as he sought to channel the spirits of his ancestors and the power of the desert environment. As he explored his life journey and looked to reconcile his worldly existence with an expansive spirituality encompassing past and present, he also saw his work as a gift to future generations, helping them to open a path for their own transcendent growth. He welcomed everyone, and during the late 1960s and 1970s the site became a popular hangout for countercultural craftspeople, runaways, dropouts, and hippie "refugees" from the mainstream, particularly as living lightly on the land in the "Indian Way" was so popular at that time. Van Zant, whose spirituality was linked to what he understood as Native American convictions and iconography, enjoyed serving as the adopted patriarch for this ever-changing community of visitors, as he also raised a young brood of his own.

In 1983, he was honored as the State of Nevada's "Artist of the Year." But that same year the three-story hostel house, where most of the visitors stayed, was gutted in a blaze suspected as arson. Later the roof of the underground shelter caved in as well. As Van Zant aged, the other residents drifted away, and he could not keep up with the repairs on the structures. Soon thereafter Ahtrum left him, taking their young children. In 1989, increasingly depressed and infirm after a lifetime spent addicted to cigarettes and caffeine, he wrote a goodbye note that bequeathed the property to his oldest son, Daniel, lay down on a couch inside one of the buildings, and shot himself in the head.

His son, however, was not living nearby, and it took some time for him to claim custody and handle the legal issues pertaining to the property inheritance. In the meantime,

MONUMENT WITH SCULPTURE, 2011. PHOTO: STEVE PLATTNER

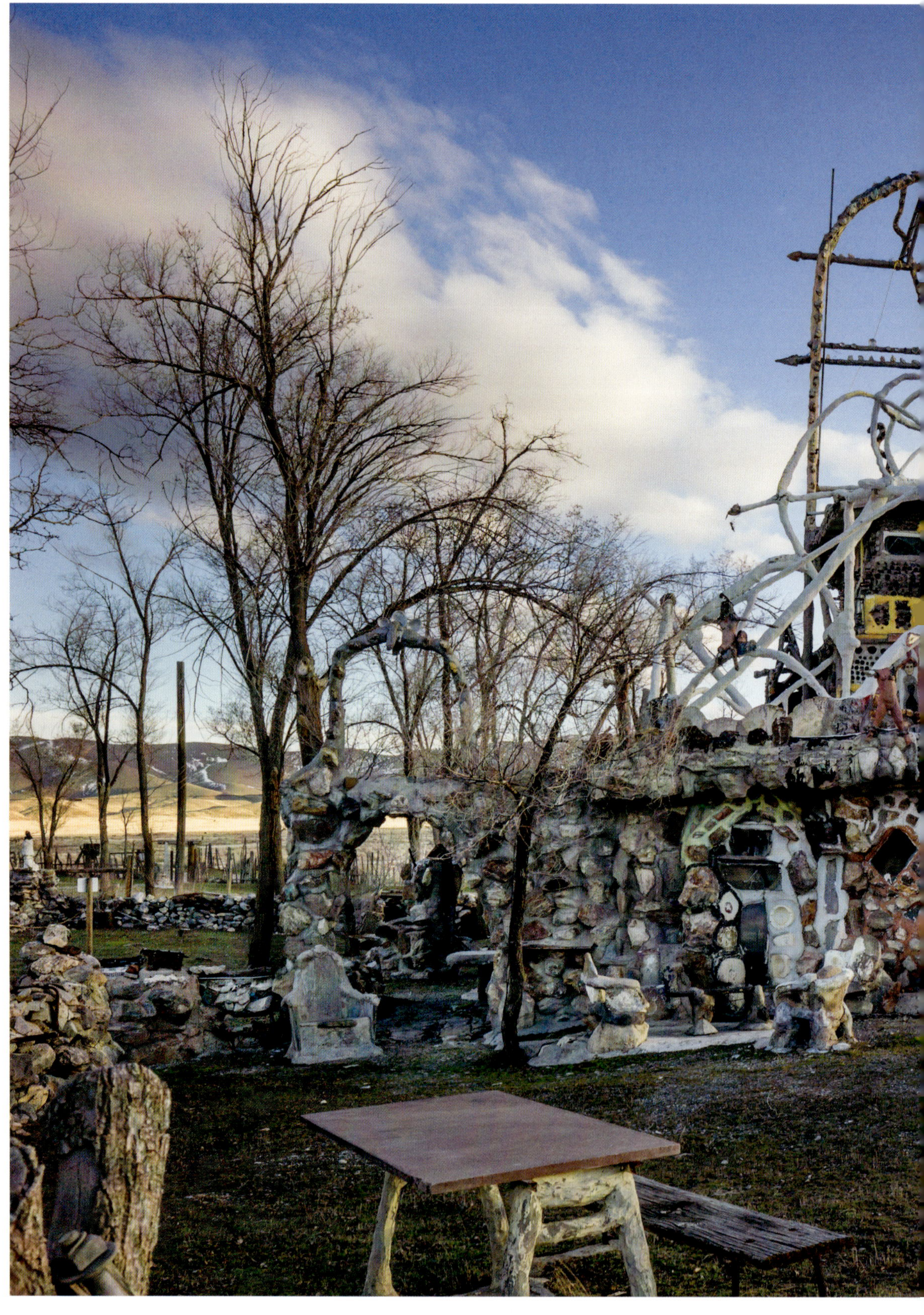

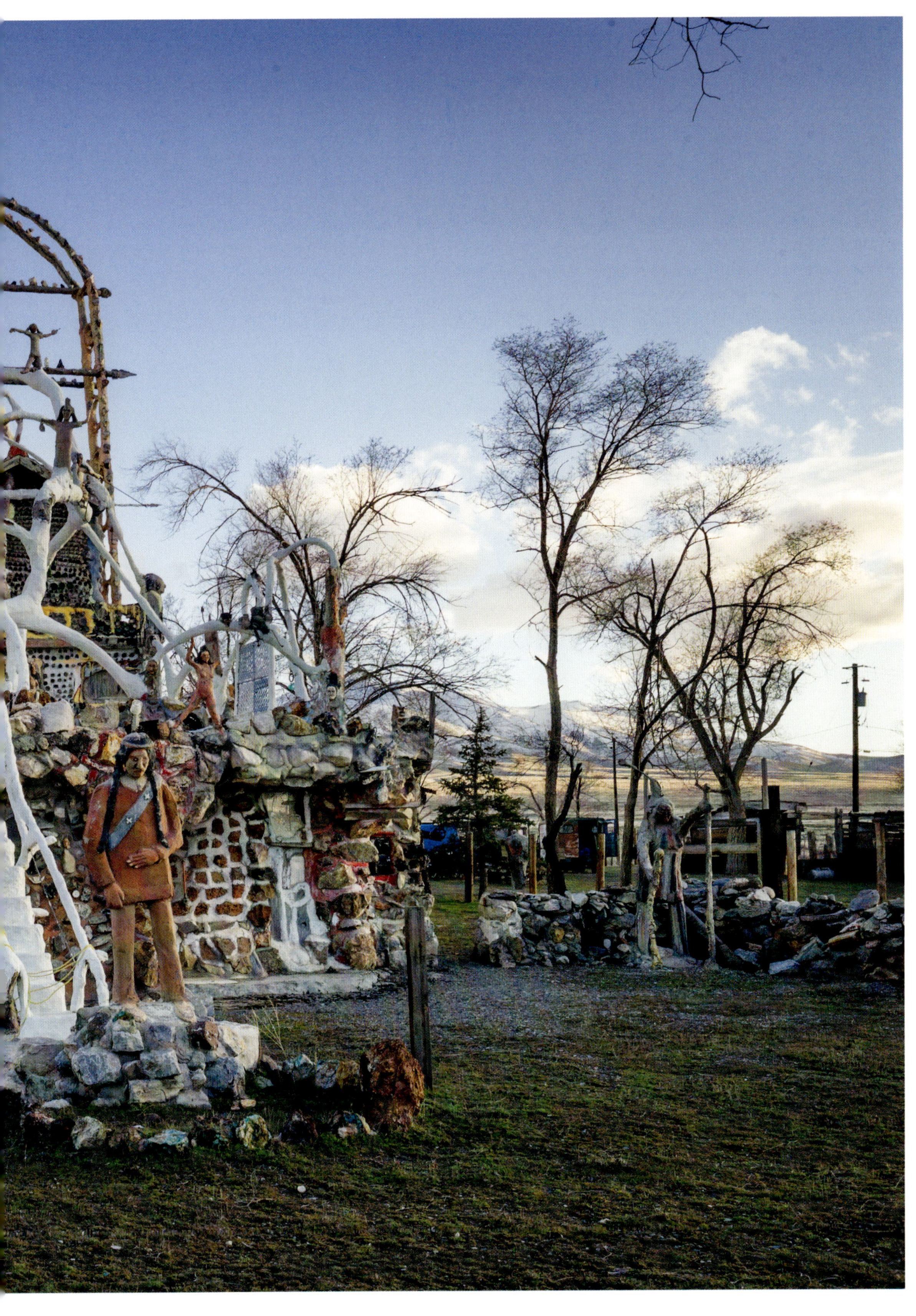

the *Monument* and sculptures continued to deteriorate. In 2002, trying to preserve his father's legacy, Daniel was finally able to begin the cleanup process, hauling away tons of trash—objects his father had collected with the intention of using them as resources for buildings or art. The site had been designated a State of Nevada Historic Site Restoration Project, and in 1992 the *Thunder Mountain Monument* was entered into the State of Nevada's Registry of Historic Sites. But with minimal funding for upkeep and usually no one on-site in this remote location to prevent loss, other buildings have been burned and many sculptures and other installations have been vandalized. This, added to the incremental decline caused by the incessant wind, scorching sun, and widely varying extremes of temperature, has resulted in rather ghostly faded remains of what had once been a vibrant and creative artistic endeavor. His children, grandchildren, and some of the "adopted" family of transient community residents still hope to be able to maintain and preserve his legacy.

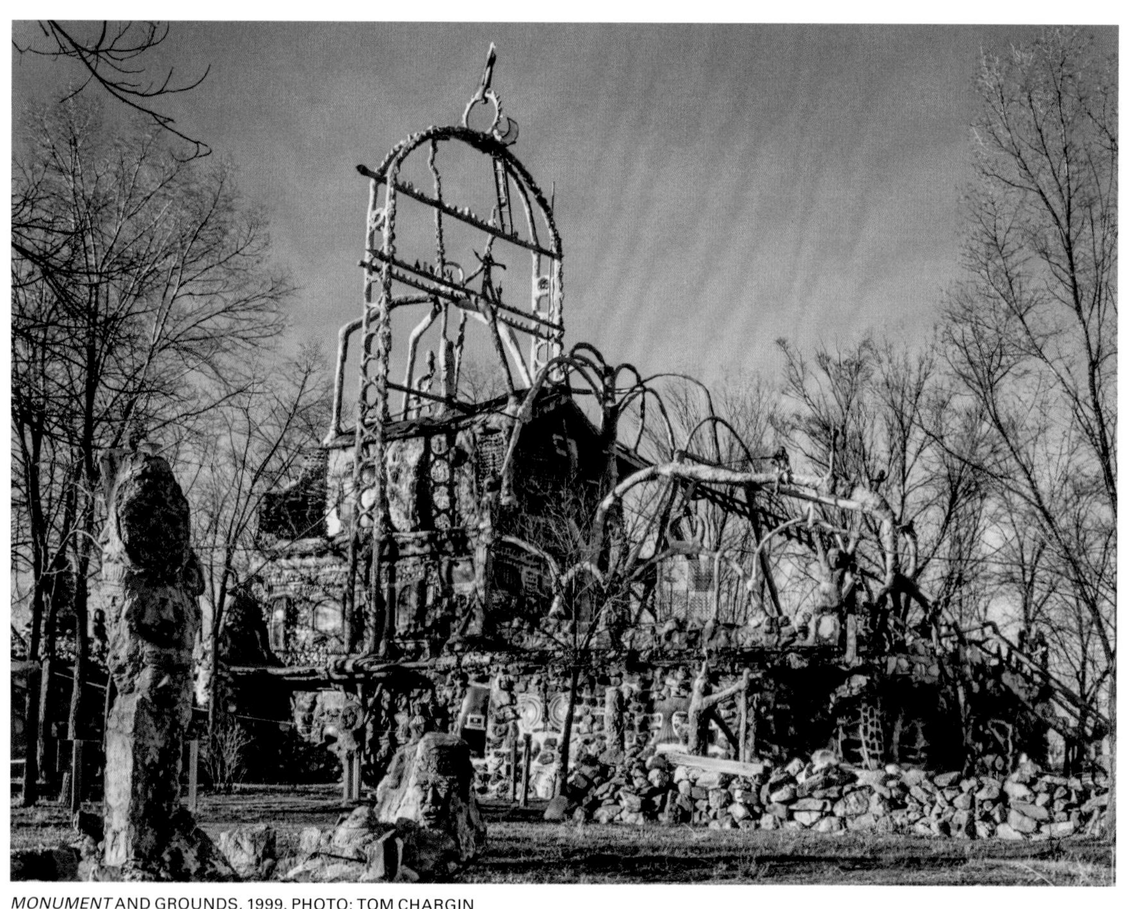

MONUMENT AND GROUNDS, 1999. PHOTO: TOM CHARGIN

HE CHANNELED THE SPIRIT OF HIS NATIVE ANCESTORS AND THE POWER OF THE DESERT.

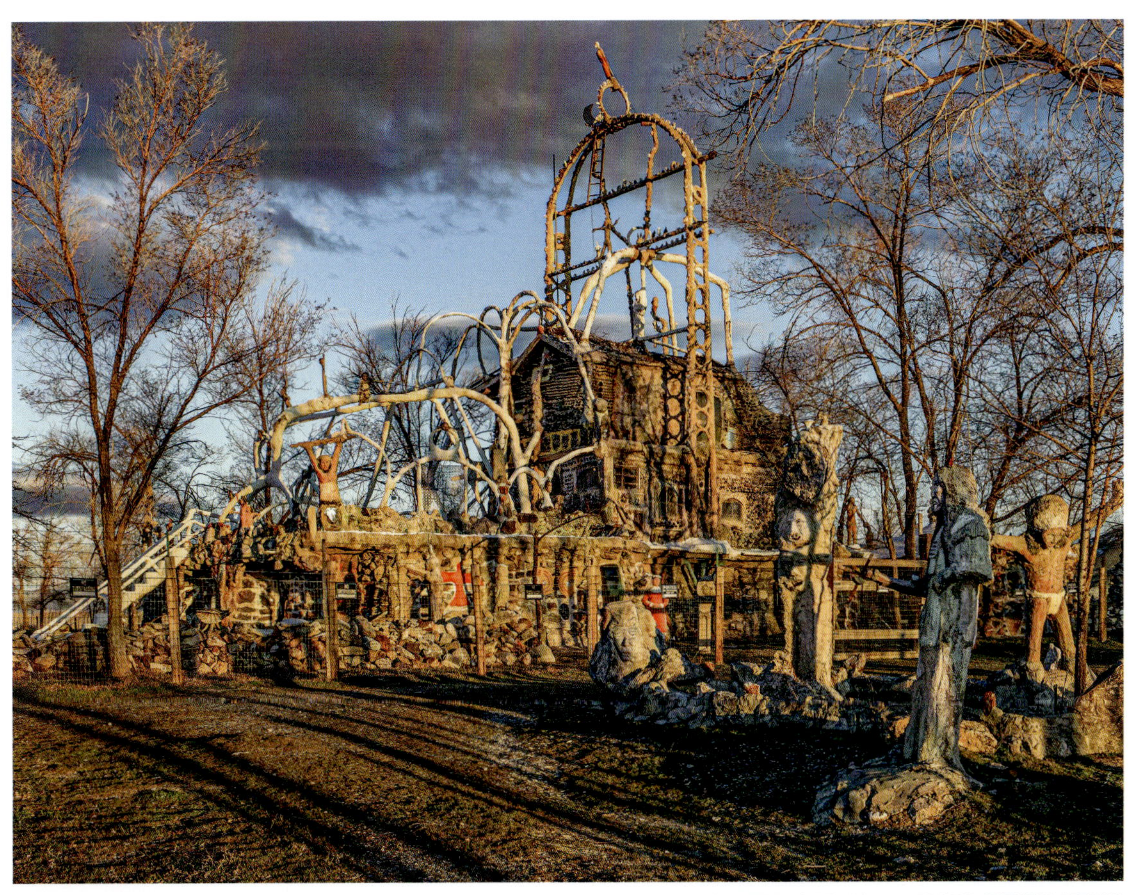

MONUMENT (DETAIL), 2011. PHOTO: STEVE PLATTNER

JONAS PERKINS

VICUNTA

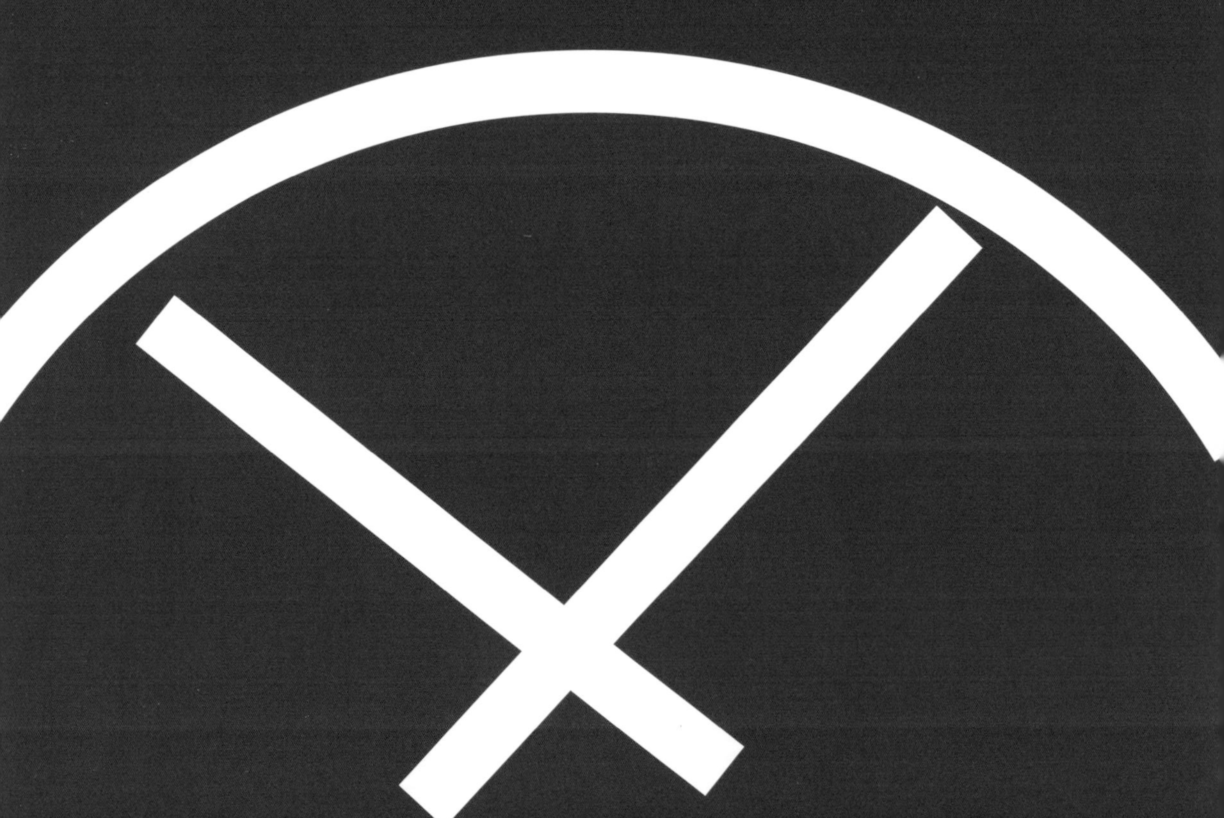

FREDERICKSBURG, TEXAS

Perkins (b. 1947) is perhaps more conscious than most of the sometimes-serendipitous events that mark the journey of a life fully lived. His parents, originally from Alabama and Georgia, had moved north as part of the Great Migration and met and married in Chicago, settling into a predominantly Polish neighborhood in Phoenix, Illinois, a small suburb south of the city. His father was a Pullman Porter and his mother worked at a mental hospital to supplement the family income so that Jonas and his sister could attend a private Catholic school and have the opportunity to negotiate a more fruitful life. But while grateful for their sacrifices, the experience of attending a predominantly White school made him acutely aware of being different, as it caused him to feel as if he had lost his bearings within his Black community. He withdrew from some social interactions and learned quietly, absorbing his academic lessons while pondering the challenges of being caught between two cultures. One day, doodling with a piece of clay, he produced a surprisingly realistic portrait, and realized that perhaps art would be his ticket to a more creative and rewarding existence.

Perkins was accepted into the Art Institute of Chicago to study metal sculpture, but the fit was not right. In the meantime, he worked a variety of jobs to make ends meet—as a newspaper boy, factory hand, brakeman on the railways. On a two-week vacation from his railroad job, he decided to head to the art school in San Miguel de Allende, Mexico, and although he only stayed three weeks at the Instituto, he credits the school with pushing him to see things differently. During his short residency he even taught a class in rubber mold-making.

Having moved back to the South, he serendipitously saw a newspaper ad for land outside of Fredericksburg, in Texas's Hill Country, and in 1978 he purchased a rather isolated 15-acre parcel about 15 miles southeast of town. He had been working out of Houston in a well-paying carving gig but gave it up to move to this new property, living in a tent and learning to survive without running water and electricity. Understanding that this lifestyle change would require him to modify his expectations and his actions, he became a vegetarian (in part to address the challenges of living without refrigeration), and as he honed his technical skills, he simultaneously cultivated his spirituality. For five years he served as a devotee of Hare Krishna, but his guru told him that he did not have to move to their compound and should instead remain on his land: by becoming a great artist he could better serve his deity and the bhakta community.

Perkins began to specialize in modeling unique busts of both living and historical figures. A series of commissions that brought "all kinds" of people into his life helped to break down the social and cultural isolation he had felt at other times, despite the physical remoteness of his back-country life. Ironically, although he had been led in this direction through his involvement with the Hare Krishnas, he became increasingly uncomfortable with how religion separated people: he realized that although people may believe differently, they could still be "holy." The range of his subjects—which included presidents, musicians, social innovators, and local businessmen—corroborated his self-identification as a historian who was inspired to explore different times and places as he forged his own way.

The requirements of making the busts forced him to broaden his technical skills, and he established a basic foundry in his Fredericksburg studio so that he could expand his offerings to those who preferred the durability of bronze. He also began to explore options for constructing a more permanent living situation on the land. Building a new home soon became his obsession.

Motivated to repurpose materials that had previously served other functions—not only as a result of his interest in resource conservation and off-the-grid living but also because it would significantly reduce his costs—he began collecting a wide range of found objects. Satellite dishes became ceilings or roofs, plastic and glass bottles were inserted into frames to form walls, car windshields and pickup camper shells became windows to allow light into interiors, aluminum cans were packed in adobe or sand to provide insulation, molded Styrofoam packing planks and blocks were cut to shape partitions or provide depth for interior and exterior infrastructure. With few exceptions, cement, wood shavings, and expandable foam were his only ongoing expenses: everything else was found or donated.

He began with a bedroom, then a bathroom, then a kitchen, but to date, although their footprints have been determined, nothing has really been finished. This is largely a function of his method of working, which focuses on a more macro approach of enclosing or erecting larger components such as walls, roofs, or windows without immediately addressing more micro concerns such as filling in gaps or apertures to complete and seal them. These cavities and cracks leave the interiors susceptible to leaks and moisture as well as to the accumulation of dirt, while also contributing to a rather haphazard and ad-hoc appearance. Perkins intends to cover all Styrofoam infrastructures with a "papercrete" (paper pulp mixed with concrete) surface and to fill in cracks with expandable foam; these techniques will address surface issues while enhancing the durability of construction, and a final sheathing with mosaic or paint or tiles will wrap up each section.

But things are proceeding relatively slowly. Although he has worked on the house for some 20 years, it easily appears that another 20 will be needed for him to finally achieve his lofty goals (he is age 77 at this writing, and he acknowledges that he will need more help to accomplish some of his plans). But taking his time has enabled him to remain open to ways to utilize the materials he has been collecting; for example, he now inserts aluminum cans for insulation within tires or wooden pallets, which he uses to more rapidly build up walls. And he found that he could use terra cotta roof tiles to round off building corners and serve as a type of molding or wainscoting to seal off wall sections. He is excited about how a newly installed group of recycled windows on the second story—each of a different size and style—will turn that space into a greenhouse so he can grow his own food. Inspired by internet stories of building entire homes inside of a glass superstructure (he particularly commented on the Norwegian home of Margit-Kristine Solibakke Klev), he is conceptualizing his house as a potential biosphere.

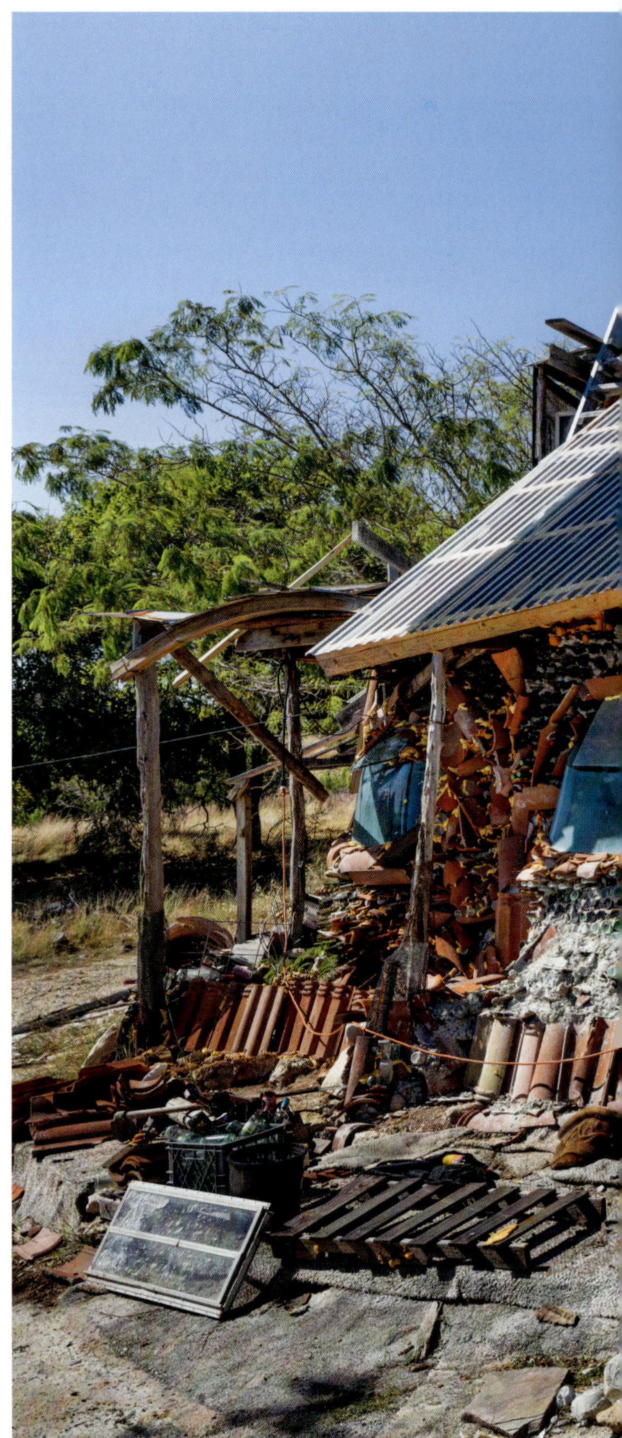

FRONT ENTRANCE WITH BOTTLE-CLAD COLUMNS AND WINDSHIELD WINDOWS, 2024

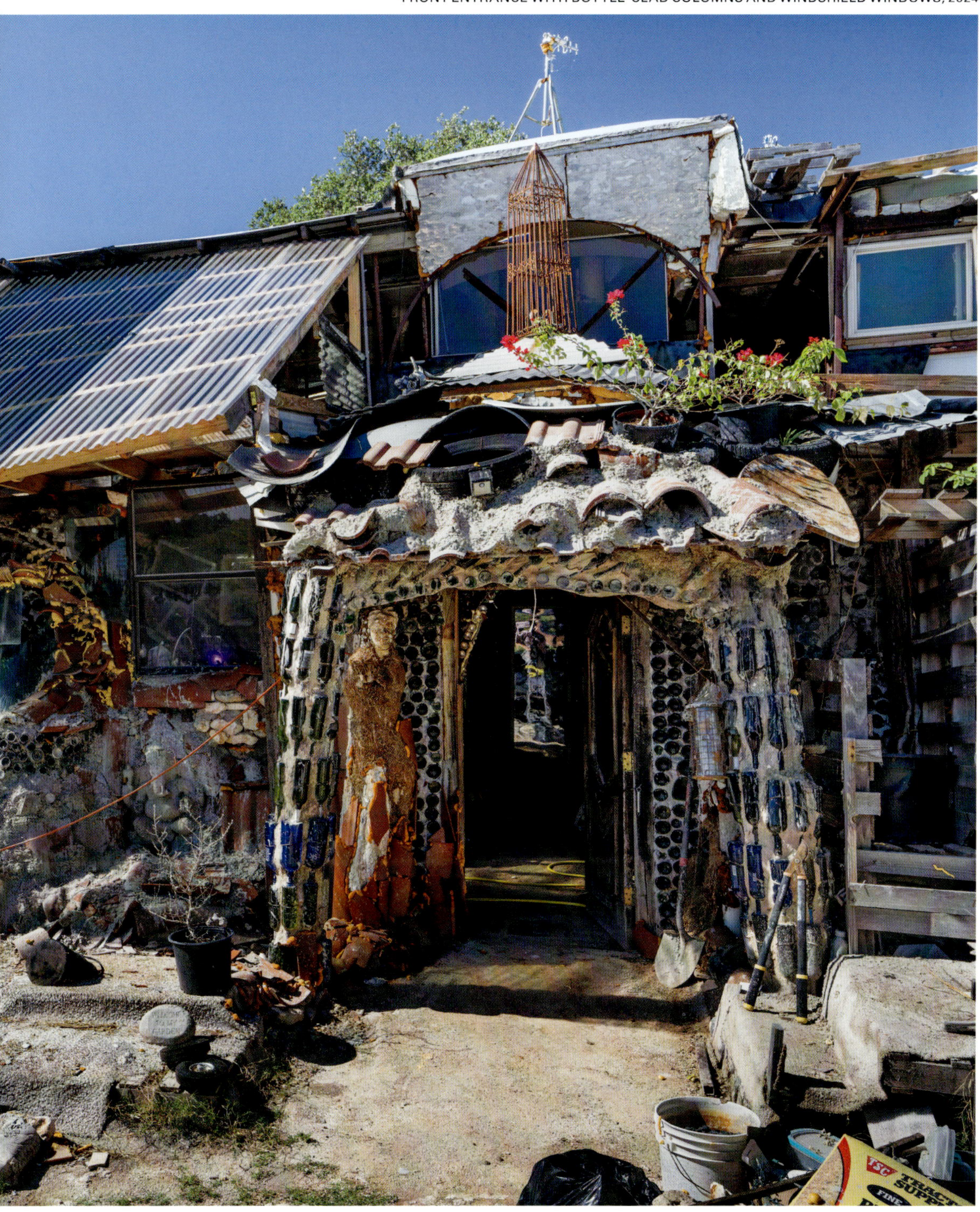

The improvisational manner of construction of Perkins's house seems almost diametrically opposed to the precision with which he carves the busts, which continue to be his main source of income. Each bust is preceded by a series of photographs of the subject from all sides, and the malleability of his clay molds provides him with the flexibility to best capture the appearance and presence of his model. In contrast, he makes no preliminary sketches for the house and addresses many different sections at once, without truly finalizing any of them. His ideas are expansive and innovative: exploring the means of growing food, heating the house, disposing of waste with waterless processes, erecting windmills to provide energy, and, when it is further along, offering a glass of wine and tours to tourists. Yet, again, none of these concepts have been fully realized, as he works on so many different areas at once.

Jonas Perkins encapsulates his approach as "simple living and high thinking." He considers the source of his actions of greater importance than the results and is acutely aware of how off-the-grid technologies were developed. He likewise remains mindful of how he personally landed where he did when he did, having developed the skills to conceive of and accomplish this enormous project. Laboring hard to bring his ideas to fruition, he nevertheless faces his inevitable aging and declining strength with equanimity. He has covered a lot of conceptual and physical ground over the almost eight decades of his life's journey, yet he retains an openness and enthusiasm for different ways of seeing, of thinking, and of living, as he notes the milestones that have marked his days so far.

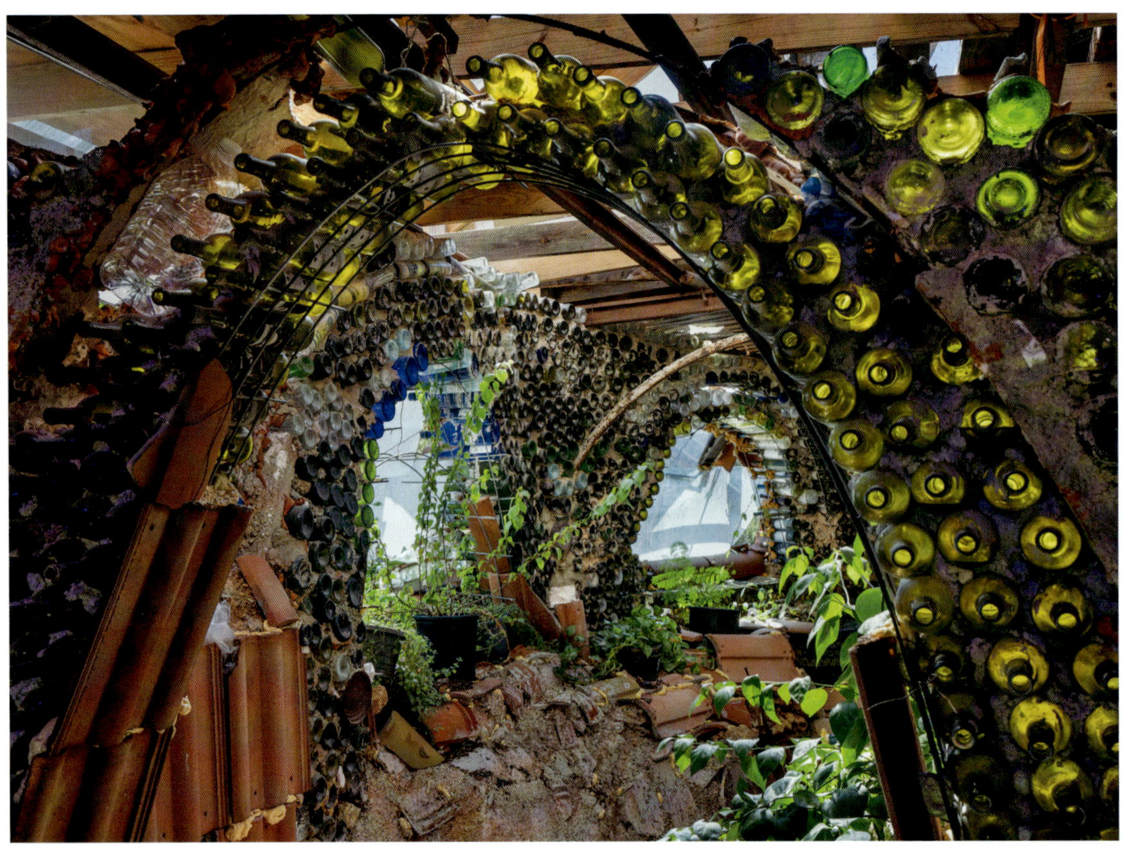

ARCHED ROOM DIVIDER, 2024

INTERIOR ROOM WITH SATELLITE DISH CEILING AND PLASTIC BOTTLE WALLS, 2024

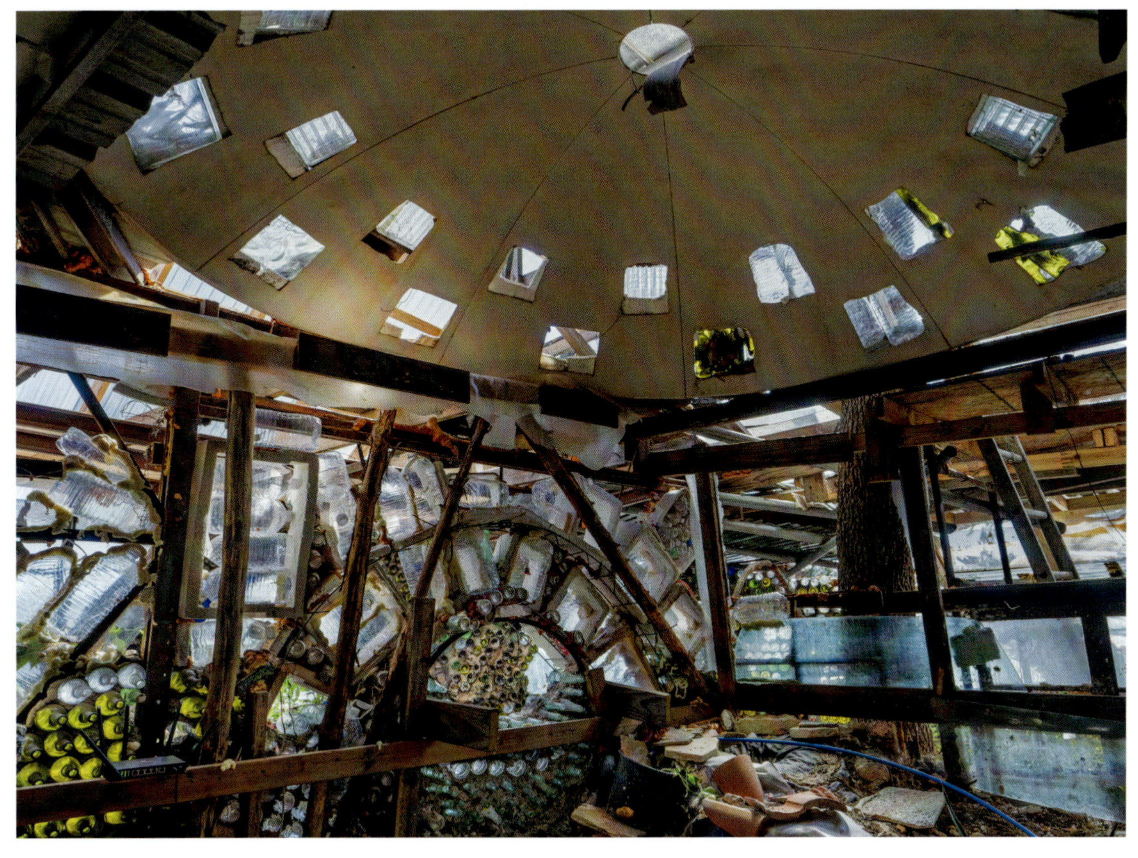

HE SEES HIS HOUSE AS A POTENTIAL BIOSPHERE RESULTING FROM «SIMPLE LIVING AND HIGH THINKING.»

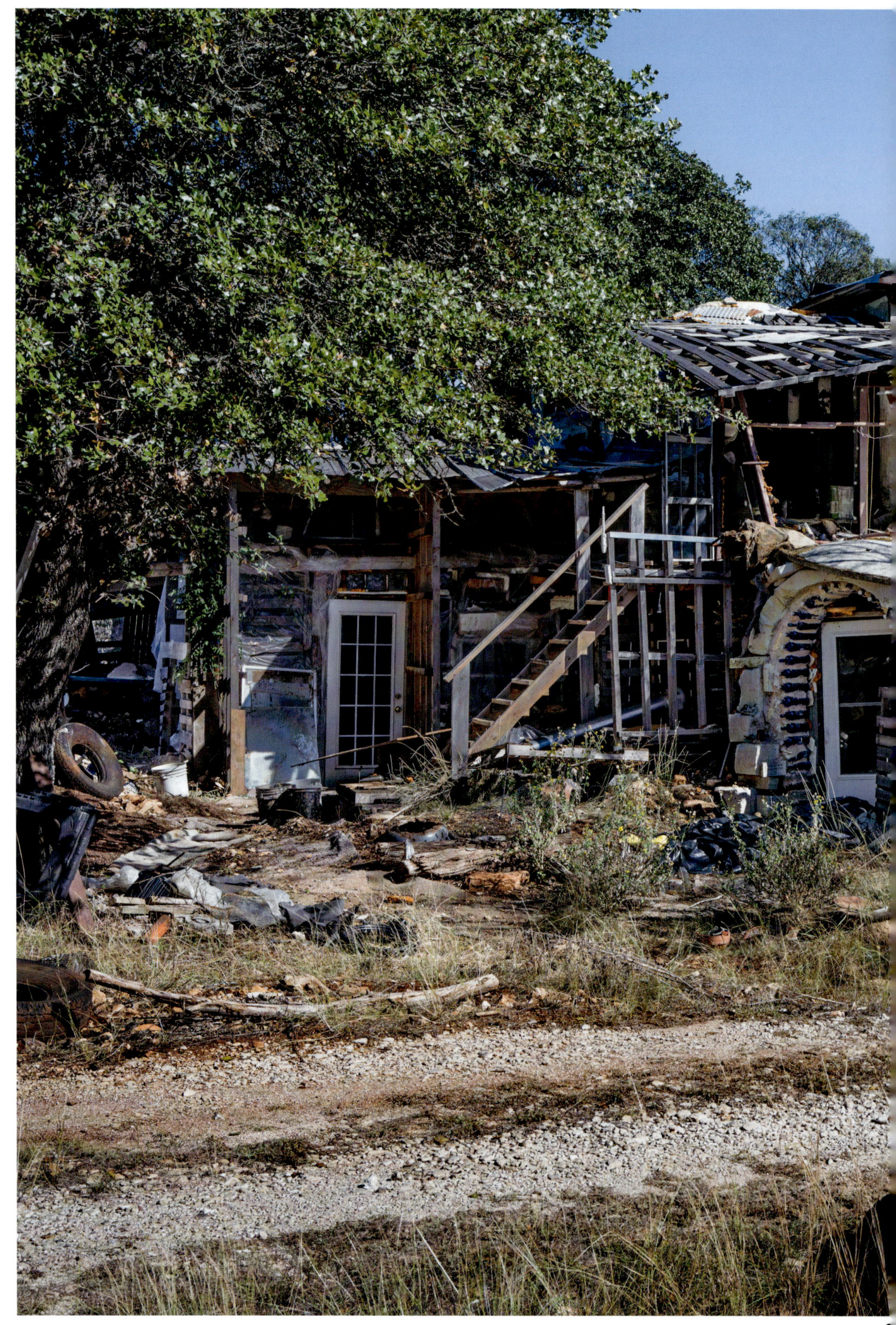

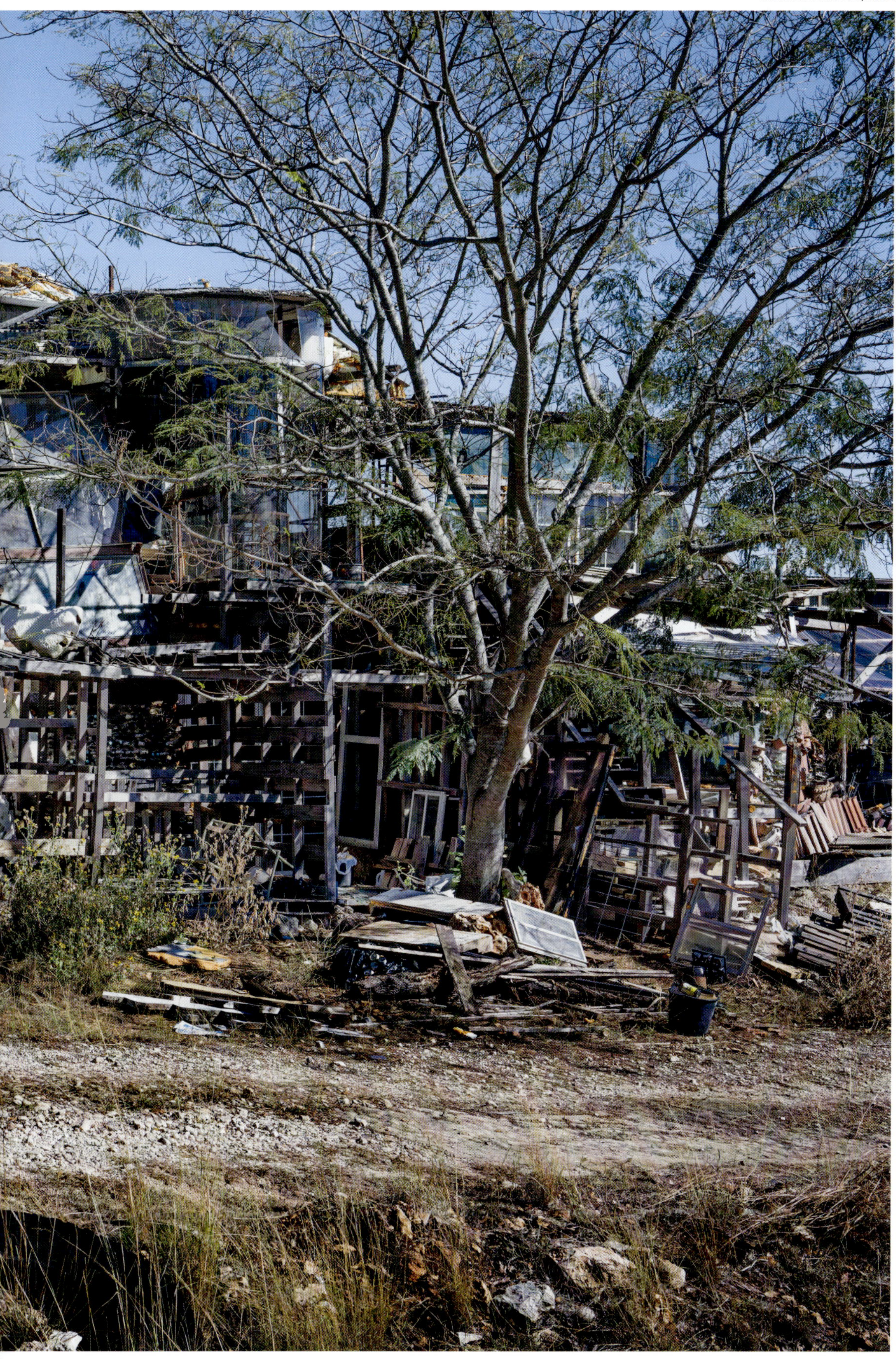

OLE S. QUAMMEN

PETRIFIED WOOD PARK

LEMMON, SOUTH DAKOTA

Quammen (1871–1934) immigrated with his Norwegian family to the United States when he was only one year old. They homesteaded in Minnesota, and as a young man he became variously involved in several different successful business ventures as he ended up in South Dakota, first in the lumber industry and then in oil development. There, he became fascinated by the geological formations of the western Dakotas and developed a personal collection of rocks, petrified wood, and fossils.

So great was his enthusiasm that in 1926 he began to make plans for an elaborate public park to showcase the region's natural treasures, and by 1930 he was ready to break ground: he contracted some 30 to 40 men to realize his ideas, with one crew dedicated to collecting the finest specimens and a second crew tasked with assembling them into various monuments and structures. Having earlier served as mayor of Lemmon, Quammen understood the hardships the local population was suffering during those years of the Great Depression, so addressing these challenges was an integral part of his goal: these men would otherwise have been unemployed. The *Petrified Wood Park*, which covers an entire city block, was dedicated in 1932, and Quammen was elected to the state legislature that same year.

The 4,100 tons (now reduced to 3,200 due to theft and damage) of petrified wood, 100 tons of petrified grasses, 13,000 dinosaur and mastodon bones, and an unspecified number of tons of "cannonball" concretions were all gathered from within a 25-mile radius of Lemmon in North and South Dakota. Some of the procured specimens (which now would be protected and off limits for such usage) were installed individually on this three-acre parcel, while others were assembled into cones, pyramids, and pillars in a variety of sizes. These include 100 conical towers composed of stacked cannonball stones that range from 8 to 32 feet in height and a base diameter of 5 to 10 feet. Together with a wishing well and small rest area, the objects constitute an otherworldly landscape. To enhance ease of access, a road was cut diagonally through the *Park* to enable enthralled visitors from the often-unforested Plains region to drive through a "timberland" with no living trees. (The road has since been replaced by additional petrified formations.) Every monument was laid out in accordance with Quammen's careful designs, and all work was personally supervised by him.

In addition to a waterfall and museum expansion completed in 1989, three buildings constructed of petrified wood were part of Quammen's original design: a circular museum, 50 feet in diameter and ringed with spires, which features exhibits on local geology and history; a gas station to address the needs of the early waves of motoring tourists (later this was turned into the office of the Chamber of Commerce); and a miniature *Castle*, 30 feet high and with a footprint of 24 feet square, which was reportedly assembled from 300 tons of collected materials, including dinosaur bones. It is so named due to its elaborate steeples and spires.

The *Castle's* ground floor level is composed of slabs of petrified grasses and its roof is covered with fossils. A tall, tapered steeple dominates the center, while smaller conical spires adorn each of the four corners; these are more rugged and organically shaped than many others of the *Park's* monuments. Additional upright monoliths surround the center spire and draw the eye upward, increasing the impression of verticality of this otherwise squat one-story structure. The *Castle* entrance is an arched portal protected by a rather formidable iron gate, the walls are cut with rectangular apertures that are each shielded with a petrified lintel, and the whole is ringed with a series of assembled standing monuments as well as smaller individual petrified logs and trunks, some of which feature "dinosaur claw" or teeth marks on their surfaces. To a greater extent than the other buildings on-site, the *Castle* seems more idiosyncratic and mysterious: it would not be out of place in a sinister folktale or as a troll's frightening forest dwelling.

Quammen's daughter gifted the *Park* and its buildings, formations, and embellishments to the town of Lemmon in 1954, and in 1977 it was added to the National Register of Historic Places. During 2000–2001 municipal workers removed and replaced the mortar between the assembled components in order to enhance the stability of the various monuments, and maintenance is ongoing. It is said to be the largest park of petrified wood in the world, and it remains an economic driver for Lemmon and the surrounding area. Admission is free.

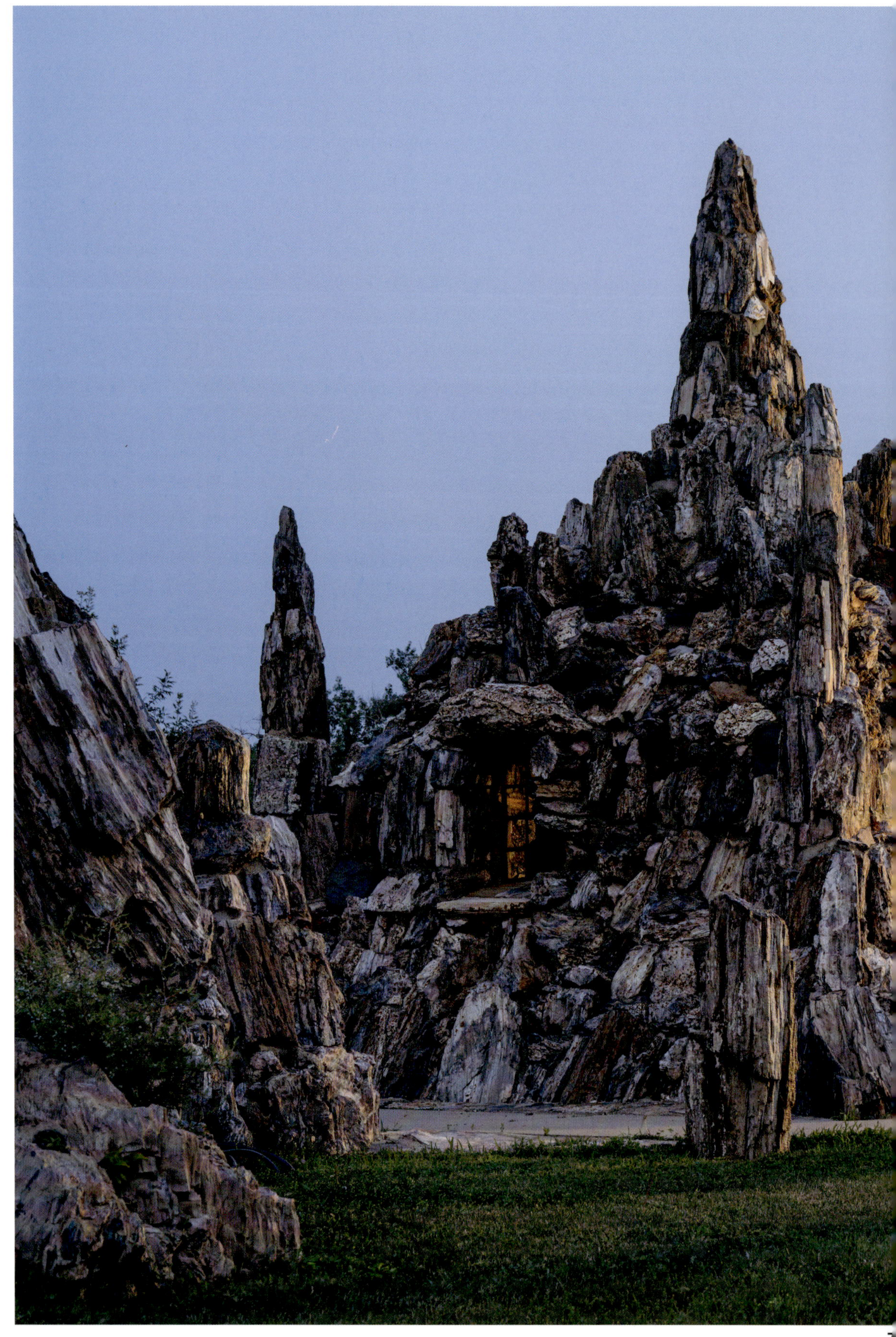

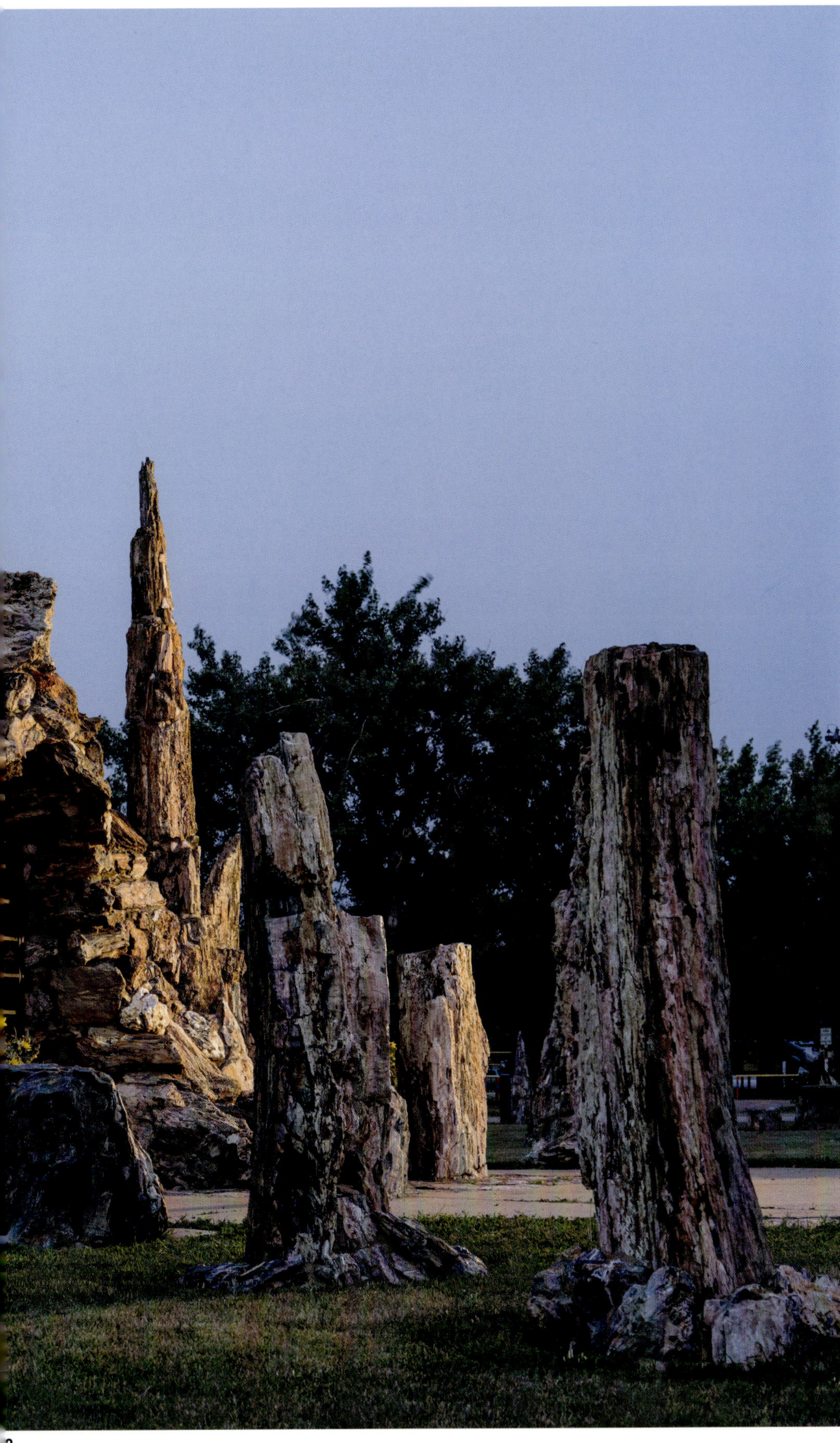

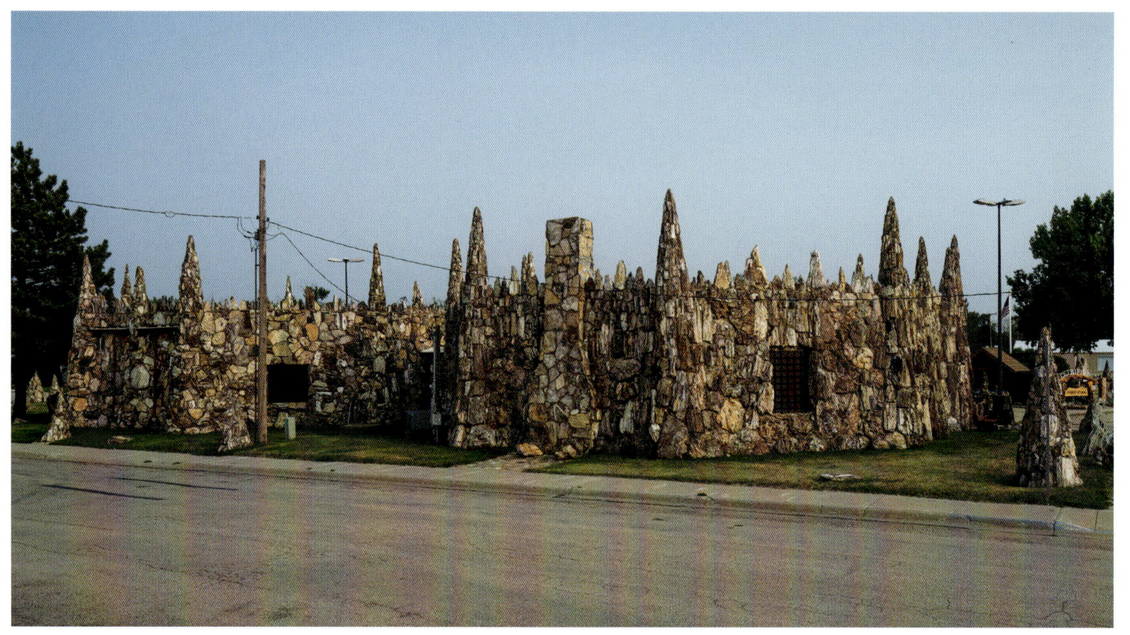

THIS
IS SAID
TO BE THE
LARGEST PARK
OF PETRIFIED WOOD
IN THE WORLD.

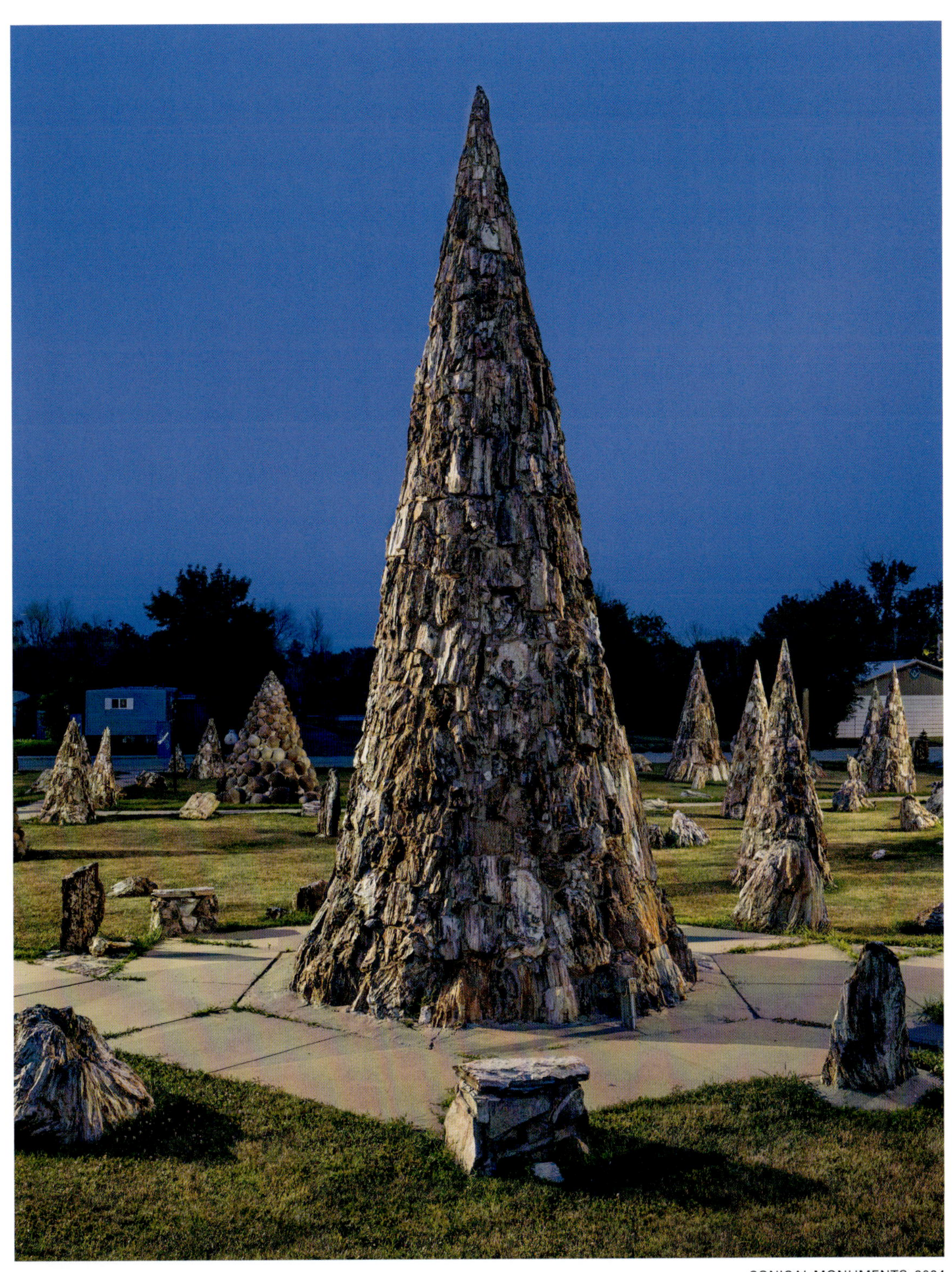

CONICAL MONUMENTS, 2024

STEPHEN SYKES

IN-CURIOSITY

ABERDEEN, MISSISSIPPI

Sykes (ca. 1890–1964), in keeping with the moniker of his handmade building, was a curious man. Born near Aberdeen, he was drafted and served as an Army cook during World War I. By the 1930s, he decided to travel west, and, apparently impressed by the height of the oil rigs he saw on his journey, vowed to return to Mississippi and to someday build his own soaring monument using materials that were easily available and accessible. Not content to help his neighbors farm their cotton, he worked a series of odd jobs, including porter and sidewalk barker for a pawnshop. Therefore, it was not until he retired in 1951 that he was able to begin construction, having moved to a 20-acre parcel located a mile or so north of Aberdeen that he and his four sisters had purchased and named Sykes Ranch. While recalling his earlier inspiration to build, he also noted that his efforts began as a way to fight post-retirement boredom; never having married, he "didn't have anything else to do."

In addition to being curious, Sykes was also a "people person," and he was always happy to discuss his construction project and to give guided tours to any inquisitive passersby (its location on the side of U.S. Highway 45, a major north–south thoroughfare bringing inland residents to the Gulf Coast, ensured many visitors). His belief in his project was so convincing—and he was so appreciative of proffered suggestions and counsel—that soon he was receiving random "gifts" and building materials from folks who had stopped by and wanted to help support his dream. He welcomed them in a ground-level "reception parlor" and "information room," and their interest motivated him to continue to build.

Financed through his veteran's pension and modest income from renting an unused portion of his land, Sykes erected *In-Curiosity* on an infrastructure of wooden poles, tree limbs, and lumber, and ornamented it with a variety of advertising signs and handmade posters (some of which functioned as wall siding), as well as hubcaps, gourds, steer skulls, scrap metal, and a seemingly arbitrary assortment of found objects that he collected or was gifted. The poles were installed unsystematically without always adhering to straight horizontal and vertical sightlines; this resulted in a rather maze-like interior of six staggered and overlapping levels within the 65-foot-tall residence. Nevertheless, it seemed solid and stable thanks to sound construction techniques.

Although in the first couple of years Sykes considered this new construction to be his "summer home," as he added more levels and furnishings he moved in full time. His bedroom was located on one of the highest levels, so he could take advantage of a homemade "air conditioning" unit that consisted of a rooftop periscope-like smokestack that caught any breeze and directed it downward. The kitchen boasted a wood-burning stove, sink, and an ice box that held the weekly groceries sufficient for his modest needs. Other accoutrements included a shower that he rigged up to be fed with rainwater gathered in a rooftop reservoir, although he hauled his drinking water from a nearby well. He had no need for a telephone because he installed a rubber hose that served as an intercom, so visitors on the ground level could speak into a funnel and alert him—six floors up—to their presence. Towering over the whole was a sawmill ventilator, and from that height he could sit and survey the countryside. Not having wired the building for electricity, he relied on coal oil lamps to enable him to see well enough to use his hand tools to work in his shop after dark.

Although Sykes had visions of increasing the height of his home to 100 or 125 feet—an altitude that he believed he would reach if he could obtain some of the newer, higher utility poles—he never achieved that goal. The last published notice of his work was in 1963, and he died the following year. Largely assembled out of perishable materials, Sykes's home began to collapse without him there to maintain it, and it was stripped of its reusable parts before being pulled down. Its final death knell resulted from demolition occasioned by the widening of Highway 45 soon thereafter. There is no remaining trace of *In-curiosity*.

THE 65-FOOT-TALL SKYSCRAPER WAS SUPPORTED BY A MAZE-LIKE INTERIOR OF SIX STAGGERED LEVELS.

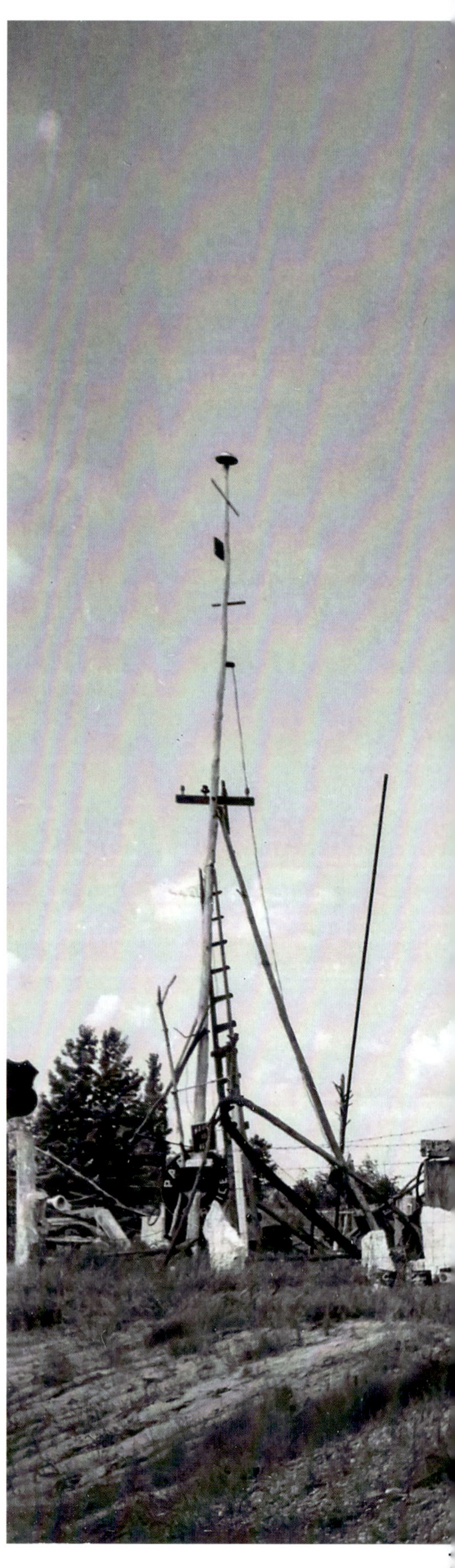

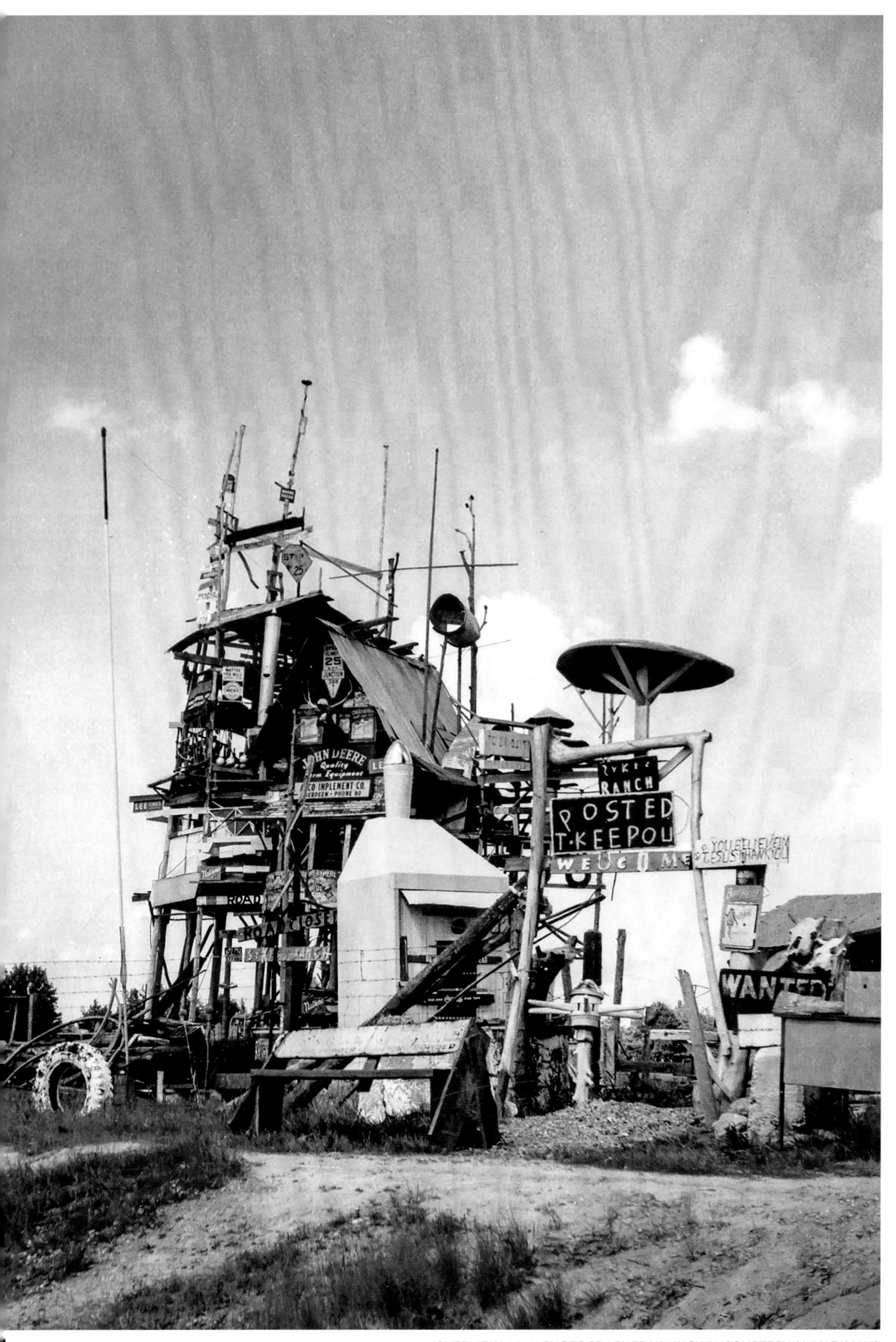

OVERVIEW, 1956. PHOTOGRAPHER UNKNOWN, COURTESY ALAN E. MAYS

ROBERT "RA" PAULETTE

CAVES

EMBUDO, NEW MEXICO

Born in Chicago and raised and educated in northern Indiana, Paulette (b. 1946) served in the Navy during the Vietnam War; upon his return, he traveled around the United States and took odd jobs before settling in northern New Mexico. A self-described late bloomer who did not connect with his vocation of cave digger until age 39, he never finished college, preferring to find his own way and teach himself through a process of trial and error. His palette focused on the solidified and compressed sand dunes in the high desert north of Santa Fe, vestiges of what had once marked the shoreline of an ancient sea.

In contrast to the other builders treated in this book, Paulette created his spaces through a subtractive and extractive process that involved carving out the insides of sandstone rock formations rather than affixing, attaching, and appending components in the more standard additive approach. As the soft sandstone is easily worked, he wielded his scrapers, shovels, and mattocks (a pickax-like tool) with confidence, perhaps incising a line to guide the cut of a volumetric form, but never utilizing drawings of any kind. He pushed his wheelbarrow to the cave site loaded with tools, and packed out the sandy tailings as he tunneled through chambers, formed arched passageways, and opened apertures in ceilings or walls to enable light to flood into the interior.

His first cave, finished in 1987, was dug without permission on public land. Although his intent had been to privately use it as a safe haven (he dubbed this and later excavations "wilderness shrines"), after it was discovered by hikers, increasing uninvited visitation made it clear that solitude in this space would be impossible. He therefore sealed it off, worried that someone would stumble onto it and get hurt.

Over roughly 30 years Paulette partially or fully excavated 13 caves and assisted on three others, all but four of which were commissioned and funded by clients who, not unreasonably, wanted to help direct the scope, scale, and even the aesthetics of the carvings. While he discussed general options with them, his work was directed more by his visceral feeling about the space and how he could open it up and play with the forms. He thought deeply about each one and adamantly rejected the idea that this was a team effort: how the caves developed was, in his mind, not really open to discussion or negotiation. This tended to become a point of contention and frustration for the artist as well as for the owners, who regularly complained that they were exhausting their funds, given that the process always took significantly longer than Paulette had estimated, and that they were not really getting what they wanted. He insisted that he was the only one who could make the final decision about what the caves would look like and when they would be considered complete, but in most instances, he was overruled, and he was forced to pack up his tools before he was ready.

Although each of his caves is different, responding to the physical dimensions of the sandstone outcroppings and to other sedimentary strata that might be present, his characteristic forms immediately identify every one as the product of his hands. Straight edges and geometric forms are generally absent; instead, supple contours and rotund forms undulate around the spaces, sometimes artfully reinforcing the sightlines of height and other times traversing interiors in a more purely ornamental fashion. In some caves he contrasted the sanded interior surfaces with more textural sections revealing fragmented fractures in the cave wall. Elsewhere, terrestrial motifs of monumental flowers, leaves, and hearts were layered in jungle-like profusion, while in still others, rippling abstractions formed dense striations.

They all reveal Paulette's passionate conviction that the caves could not be completely realized without human interaction: he compared them to the fruitlessness of a violin hanging on the wall to be admired instead of being played and used to elicit multisensory responses. He saw his interiors as transformative spaces that uniquely situated their visitors or inhabitants in an extraordinary plane defined by opposing forces: surrounded by earth yet with visual access to sun and sky, cocooned by the intimacy of the cave while dwarfed by soaring walls rising 30 or 40 feet. All of these elements work together to animate the interior, as the movement of the sun through the skylights casts moving shadows on the wall carvings.

While Paulette asserted that he was driven by process, it is clear that the finished spaces also inspired his continuing efforts: interior staircases, seating alcoves, niches, windows, and exterior doors validated his intent to ensure that the effect was practical as well as spiritual (tiled bathrooms, fireplaces, and other accoutrements were sometimes added later by the owners).

CAVE ENTRANCE, 2024

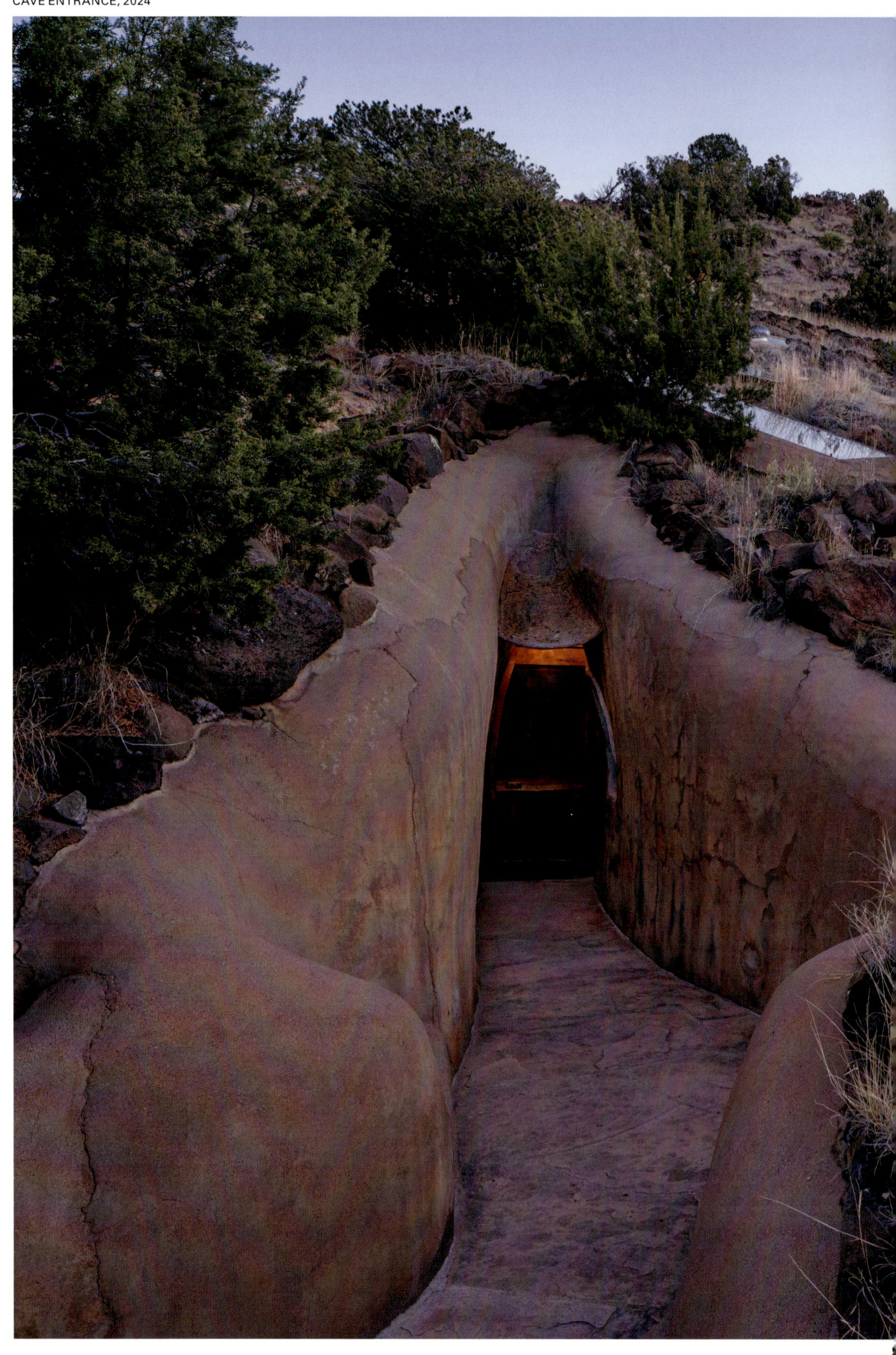

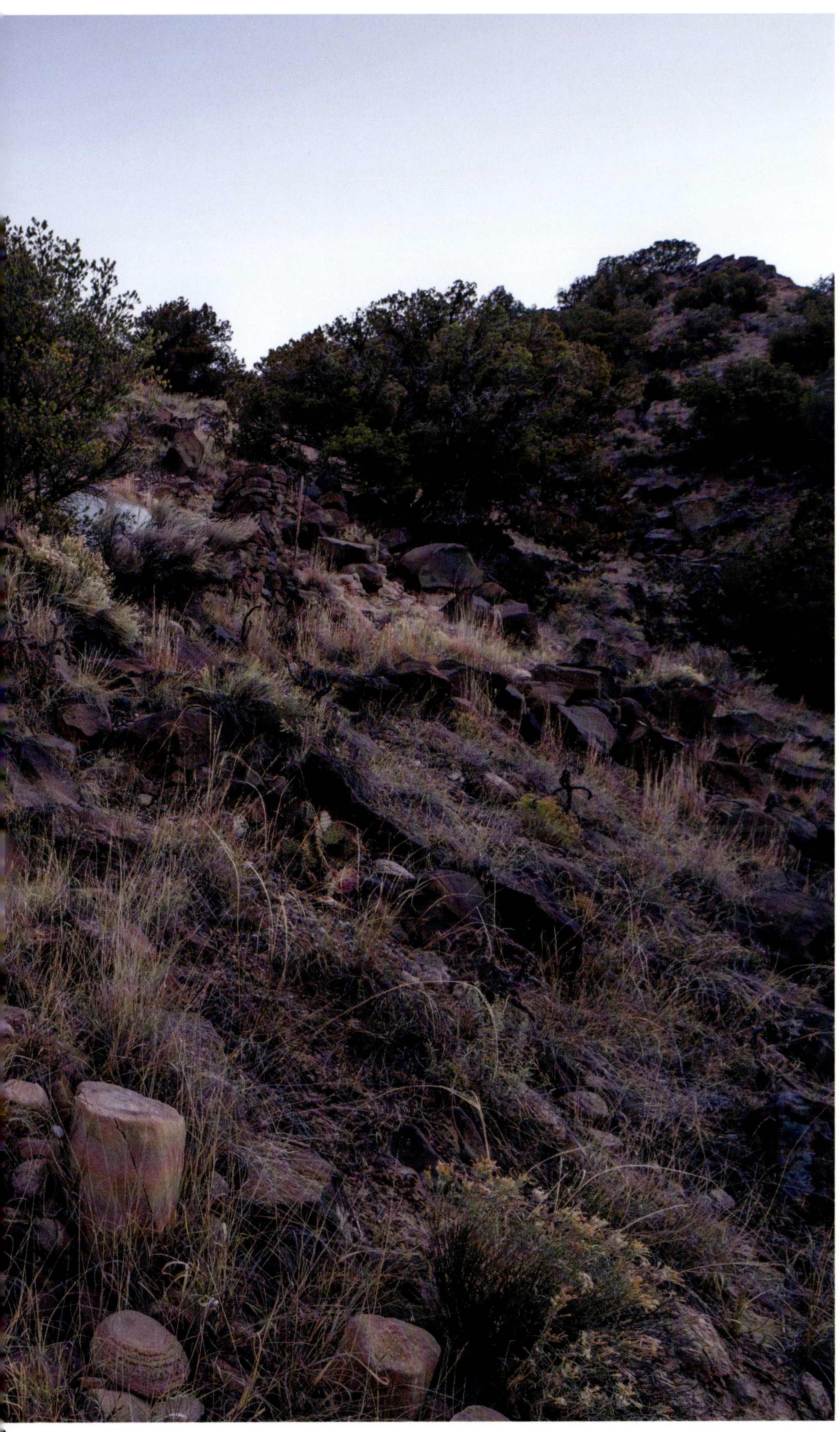

But more transcendent experiences were always encouraged. At least one cave features a hollowed-out, bell-shaped cavity beneath the floor. The cavity is covered with a wooden cap; dancing or walking on it causes it to function as a drum, and the surrounding seats reverberate if one sings, hums, or plays music while sitting there. Slender archways, sometimes ribbed and reminiscent of Gothic cathedrals, connect the different chambers, evidence of Paulette's instinctive understanding that to achieve internal stability and support he needed to avoid carving wider arches. When necessary, he reinforced interior surfaces with rebar or mesh, and he sealed all sandstone surfaces with a nontoxic potassium silicate.

While working, he prophylactically wore a necklace that included a note apologizing to any potential rescuers who might put themselves in danger when recovering his body from a future cave-in: his concern was for others who might visit, rather than for himself. He had at least one close call, when he was working on a personal "magnum opus" and a major chunk of rock dislodged from the ceiling, smashing down onto a built-in bench he had been sitting on moments earlier. (This so damaged the interior of the site—as well as the flow of his creative expression—that he stopped working on this cave and sealed it up.)

After Paulette finished his second "magnum opus" around age 70, he was infected with West Nile virus-induced encephalitis. He moved away as his illness progressed, although he still considers the Embudo area to be his spiritual home, and he may return if he can. Given the potential for injury and the increasing instances of vandalism and carved graffiti that some of the isolated caves had been experiencing, as of this writing the extant sites remain in private hands and there is no further public access.

HIS MEDIUM WAS THE SOLIDIFIED AND COMPRESSED SAND DUNES OF THE HIGH DESERT.

INTERIOR VIEW FROM LIVING ROOM TOWARD ENTRANCE (LEFT) AND BATHROOM (RIGHT), 2024

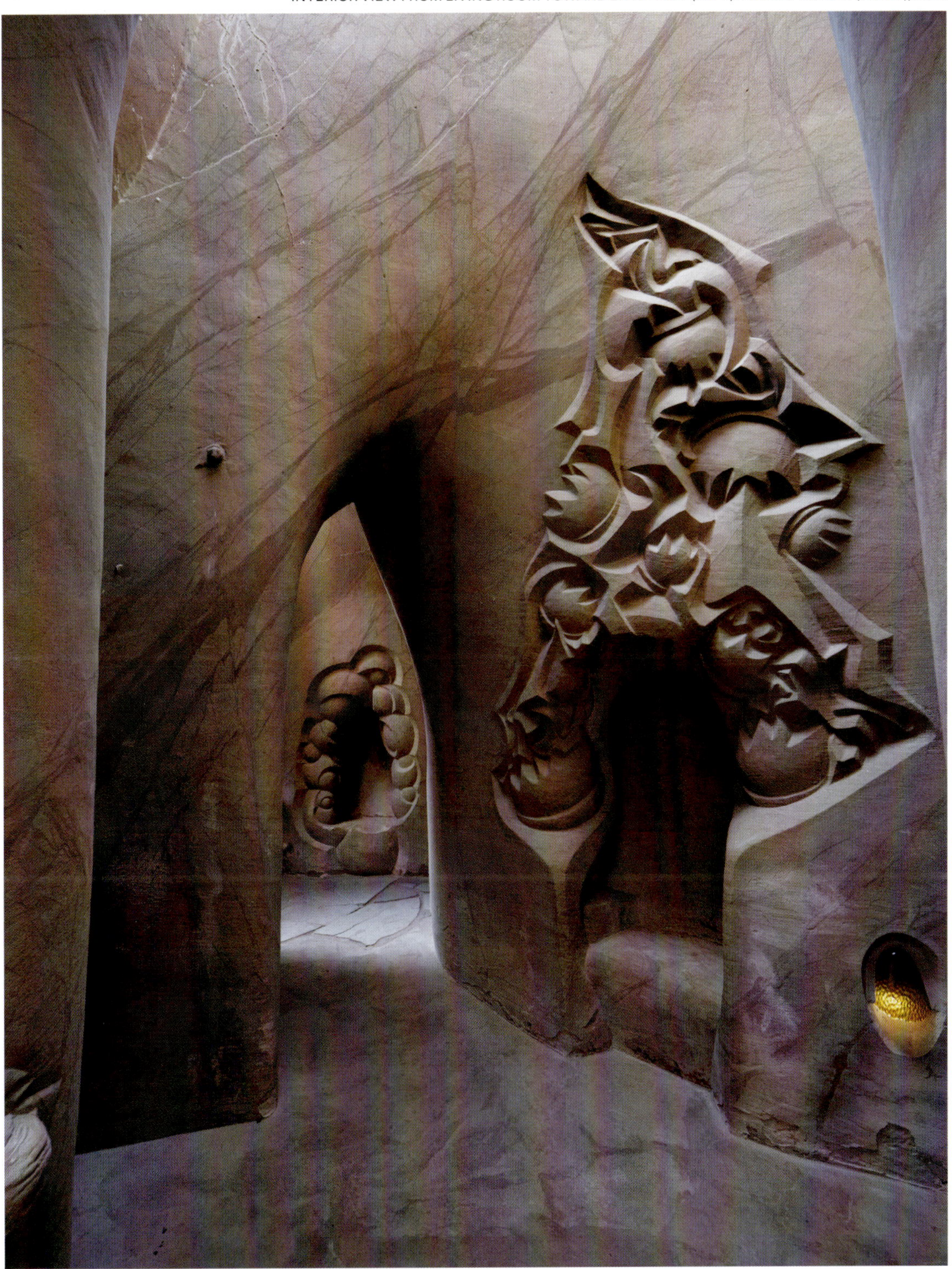

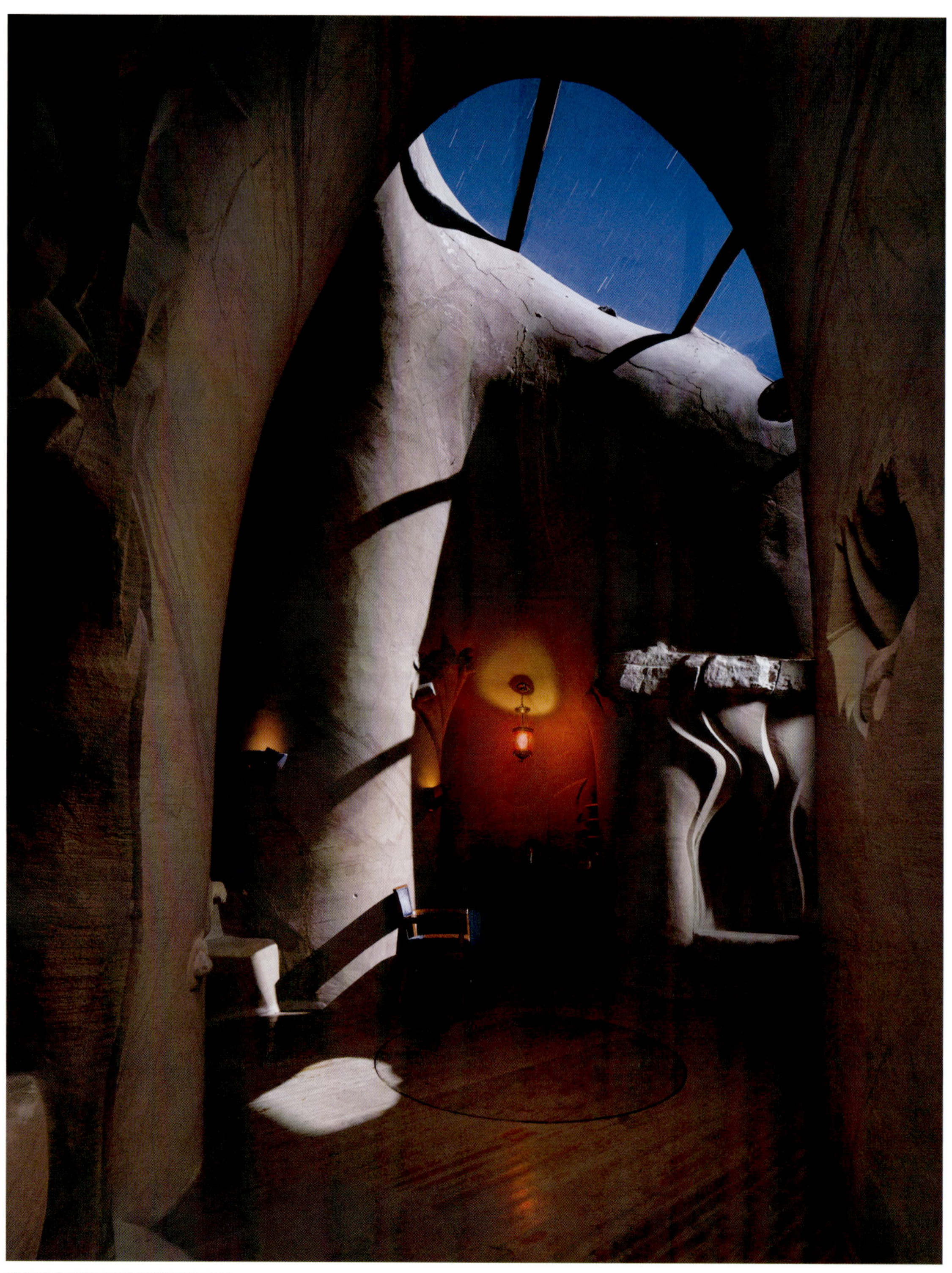

LIVING ROOM AND KITCHEN, 2024

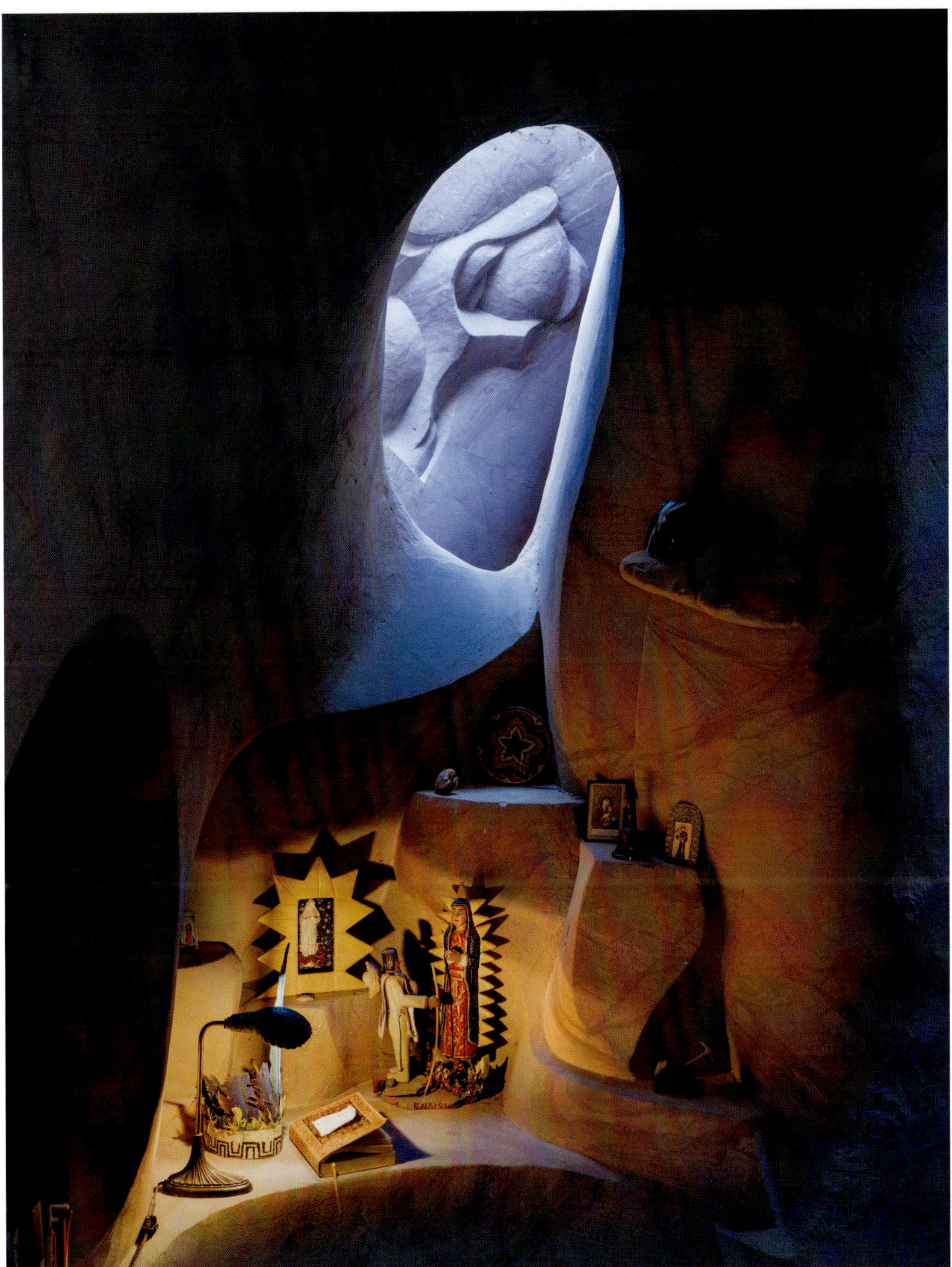

RICHARD "RICKY" BOSCARINO

—

LUNA PARC

SANDYSTON TOWNSHIP, NEW JERSEY

The 8.5-acre compound built by Boscarino (b. 1960) is a textbook example of how an art environment project—even one that became conceptualized as a project that would take a lifetime—has morphed from somewhat low-key home improvements to encompass massive original construction, densely ornamented interiors, and an expansive sculpture garden.

Boscarino is proud of his Italian heritage and, in particular, the generations of carpenters, masons, seamstresses, and other artisans who preceded him. Even as a child he was always making things, and he expressed an early interest in architecture, with a particular focus on the Victorian style. Media-based and technical classes helped him to focus and expand his skills in high school; later he attended the Rhode Island School of Design, spent his senior year abroad studying in Rome, and worked as an apprentice jeweler in New Haven, Connecticut. During this time, he became increasingly interested in film, having made some shorts in high school, so he applied to New York University's film school. He lived in the city one year, making abstract films, and although one won an award at a film festival, school officials advised him that they did not want NYU to become known for that kind of production, so he dropped out. Well acquainted with the mainstream art world, he understood that his work was not, and would not be, welcomed in that rarefied sphere.

He returned to New Jersey, and in 1989, after searching for several years, purchased a small and rather dilapidated 660-square-foot cabin surrounded by overgrown woods. Although it was full of leftover furniture and debris, he could not afford to tear it down and start afresh because he needed somewhere to live. Feeling as if he was on an adventure, the day escrow closed he began cleaning it up and soon had painted the exterior walls in bright colors, attaching "gingerbread" trim that he designed and cut out to ornament the eaves. (Interior renovations took longer, as he blasted out walls and had to rewire all the electricity.) By 1994, as he felt more grounded in the new property and as his collecting habits accelerated, he began to improve and expand the cabin beyond his earlier goal of simply achieving livable shelter. He worked—and works—out of a separate workshop building also located on the property that includes a fully outfitted ceramics studio with an electric kiln. A plasma cutter and welding equipment are set up in an outdoor area.

He began his improvements with the idea of punching out and ornamenting a bathroom, but this relatively modest expansion still required permits. After having his first sketches rejected—they were drawn out on the back of a paper placemat from the local diner—he resubmitted his application with more precise drawings. He had taken a technical drafting class in high school, and his father was a professional draftsman, so he was essentially able, as owner/builder under New Jersey state law, to present the required elevations. Once given approval, it took five years for the bathroom to reach the point that he was satisfied with it, although he continues to augment it as inspiration strikes. It had been a small closet-like space with such questionable plumbing that he had generally preferred to use an exterior outhouse. By the time he had finished the new bathroom, he had expanded it into a 150-square-foot room that was, for a time, the largest in the house.

A spacious riot of color and texture, light streams in through four slender stained-glass windows that he made on-site, setting the glass in a traditional copper foil technique to depict the four stages of life—birth, growth, labor, and death—motifs that are also found elsewhere in the house. Another small window in the bathroom uses a more novel method to affix the glass, employing adhesive and grout instead of copper or lead. Two larger windows also illuminate the space, as does a large translucent skylight set into the ceiling. The saturated colors of the window glass complement the swirling ceramic and stone mosaic designs—the fragments of commercial porcelain tiles following his expressively improvisational scrawled-on chalk lines—on the floor, walls, and organically shaped nest-like enclosure around the large oval bathtub. This enclosure, formed by chicken wire and newspaper, spills out in some sections to form benches, sculptures, and steps that provide easy access into the tub.

The bathroom ceiling is ornamented with Boscarino's collection of metal bedpans; the solid color of the ceiling paint allows for visual breathing room as it both sets off the bedpans and amplifies the impact of mosaic border friezes. Below, the mosaic-covered vertical surfaces echo the ceiling with their own assemblages: attached Fiestaware gravy boats float at a diagonal in one section, while sconces and shelves supporting small sculptures, vessels, and lights adorn others. A shallow vitrine is filled with an

ARTICHOKE PORTICO AND MAIN ENTRANCE, 2024

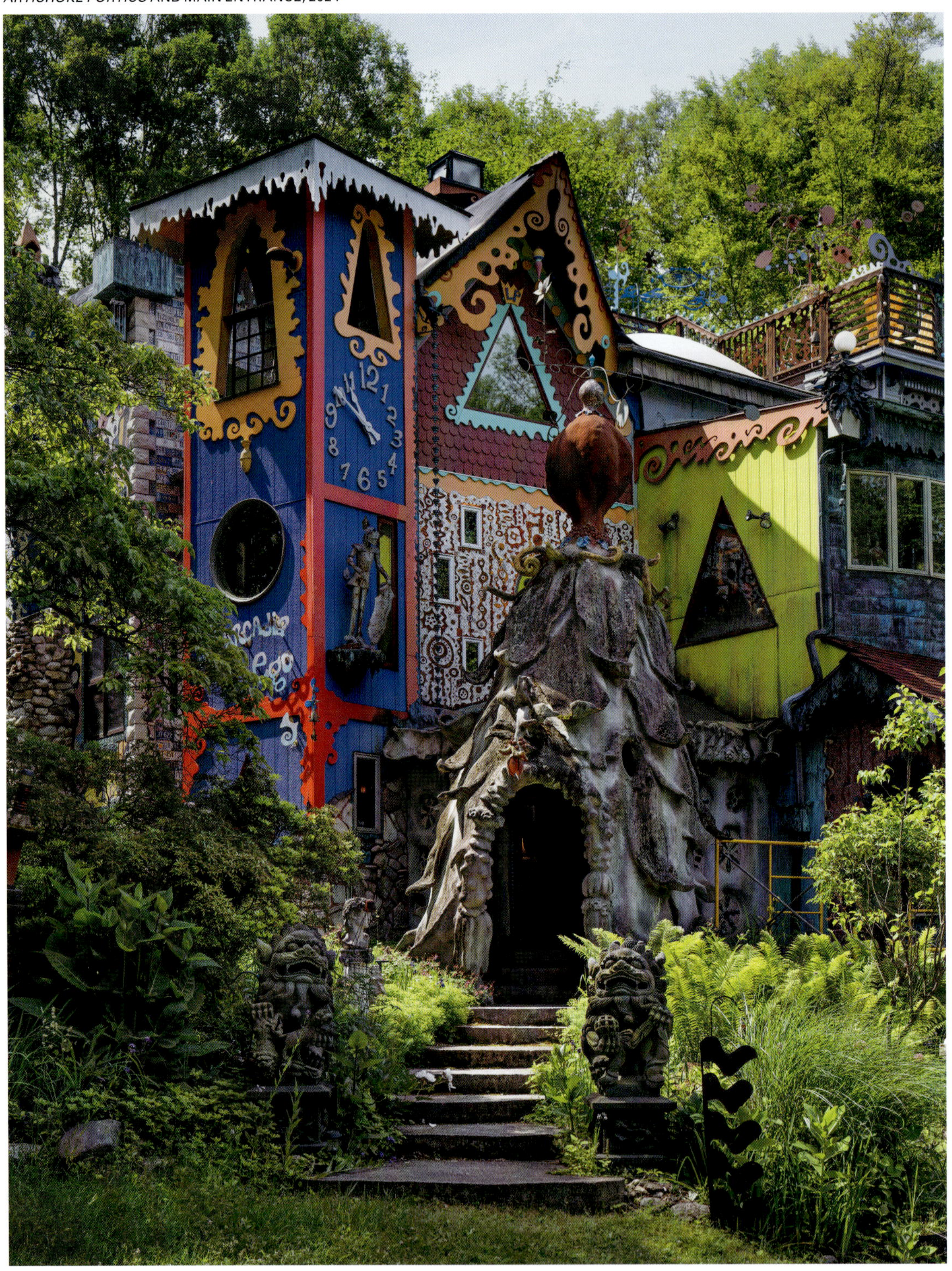

organized display of thirty-plus years' worth of empty toothpaste tubes he purchased for use while traveling. Elsewhere, figural corbels and plastic fruit push into three dimensions. More bedpans are attached to some of the walls in a complement to the ceiling display, emphasizing his belief that bathrooms (and kitchens) lend themselves to fantasy; he calls this room the *Temple to the Body and its Functions*.

After completing the bathroom and already understanding that it had served as an incubator for future concepts and techniques, he took a break and traveled around the world, collecting as he went. Once back home, he targeted the woods adjacent to the cabin and created numerous concrete and mosaic sculptures, many installed in what he called his *Eclectic Garden*. But he was beginning to feel crowded in the small cabin, so in 2005 he broke ground for a contiguous building that would become his own private gallery. He called it the *Museum of the New Alchemy*, so identified to reference how all kinds of diverse materials can be transformed into art (in contrast to the original use of the term alchemy, in which the goal was converting diverse materials into gold): for Boscarino, art was his gold. Conceptualized as a repository for the display of his increasing—and increasingly varied—collections, he continued what he refers to as "major construction" for 20 more years.

As he worked, he began thinking about a broader goal for his labors: developing a property that could function in perpetuity as both a training and residency program for artists and craftspeople. To that end, in 2015—after he was able to purchase the property next door at a very advantageous price—he established the nonprofit Luna Parc Atelier Foundation, Inc. This enabled him to more formally host one or two college-age interns for two to five weeks each summer to help him in his project, paying them a weekly stipend and providing room and board. Although the Foundation does receive occasional grants, most of Boscarino's expenses were historically covered by the sale of his jewelry and ceramics at crafts fairs and on-site or online, although more recently the revenue from workshops and public tours of the property, which he began in 1997–98, has become his primary source of income. At his death, the Foundation will inherit all of his property and art, and the expanded house will function solely as a museum, with a caretaker and student interns living in another building on-site. Although still relatively young, he is mindful of defining and preparing for his legacy in perpetuity.

The new building grew organically, thanks to a sufficient number of new technical drawings that persuaded the municipality to grant him additional construction permits. During the early years he mostly worked alone, only taking advantage of friends and helpers when he needed someone who could "carry the other end of the beam." Not hiring a contractor and doing all the physical labor himself slowed his production, particularly because he was exacting about each component as he adhered to such self-imposed parameters as insisting on distinct media for each exterior façade. But it also enabled him to work in a more improvisational manner and to take his time as he developed the concepts and gathered the materials to work on each section.

The main entrance *Artichoke Portico*, for example, 25 feet tall and made of rebar and galvanized mesh covered with sprayed-on cement prior to being hand-troweled to achieve the desired shape, has been in process for years. (It was the only component of the house that triggered the requirement for a civil engineer to approve his plans.) Boscarino's idea is to eventually cover part of it with ceramic tiles and mosaics referencing the imagery found in the caves of Lascaux, although other sections will be stained. One approaches the *Portico* by six shallow steps that are flanked, at ground level, by two enormous Chinese Fu dog guardian sculptures that had once been owned by a local Tibetan monastery.

Each façade is treated distinctly, with different materials meant to provoke a different response. The southwest side is particularly complex, with inlaid Latin aphorisms, symbols of alchemy, a message in Morse code that references the popular 1965 song "What the World Needs Now Is Love, Sweet Love," and allusions to mathematical "magic squares," all assembled in a striking range of media. The corners are set off with nonstructural blocks of cast concrete affixed to the surface. The need to isolate during the Covid pandemic markedly boosted his output, and he completed the bulk of this façade in 2020–21.

The *Great Chimney* on the east side is also particularly dense with ornamentation. Rising out of a square-sided base faced in field stones found on-site, it took him 10 years to completely sheath its three 22-foot-high sides; among its patterns is a mosaic

EXTERIOR FAÇADE WITH ORIGINAL HOUSE IN FRONT AND *ARTICHOKE PORTICO* AT LEFT, 2024

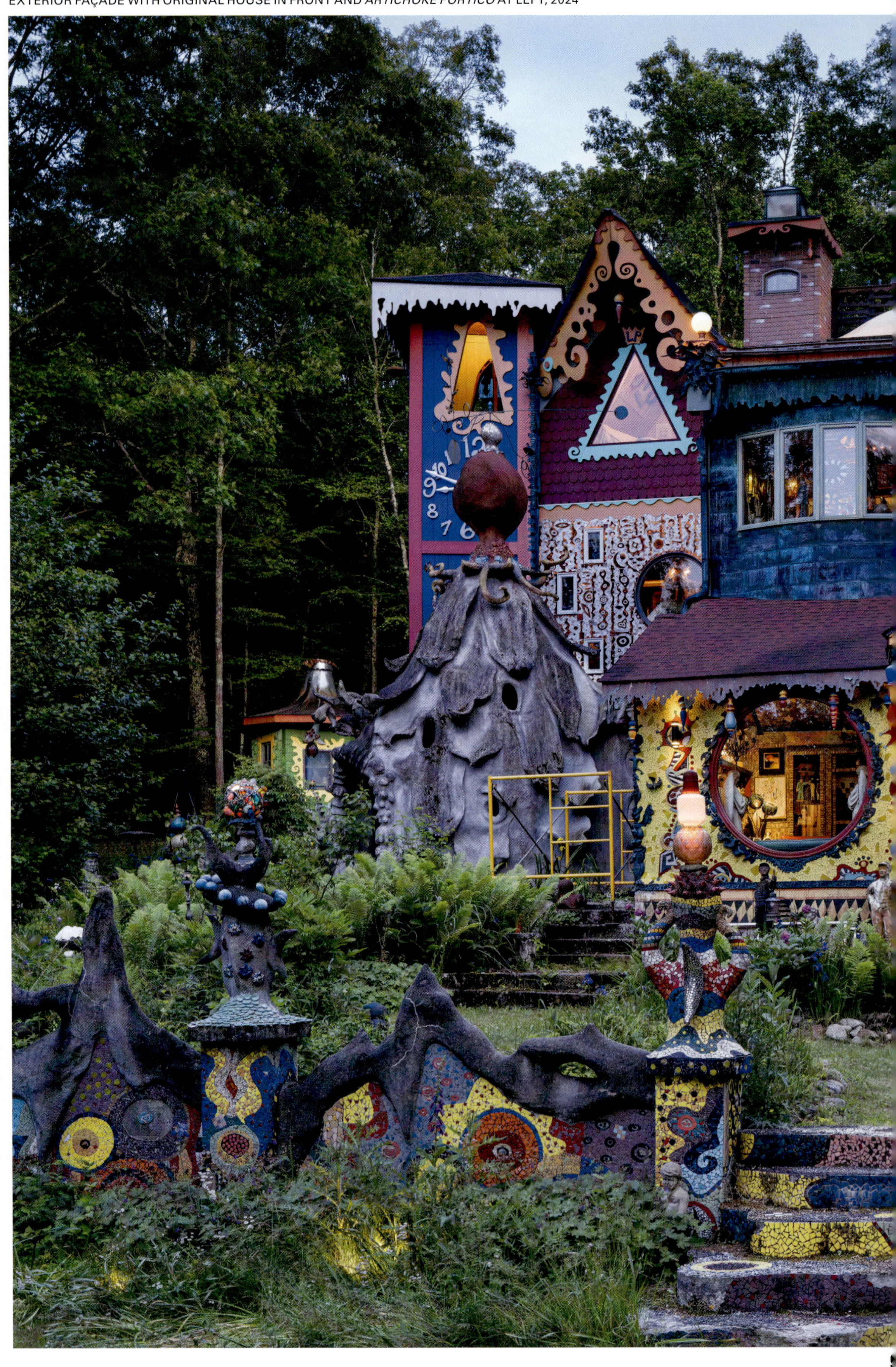

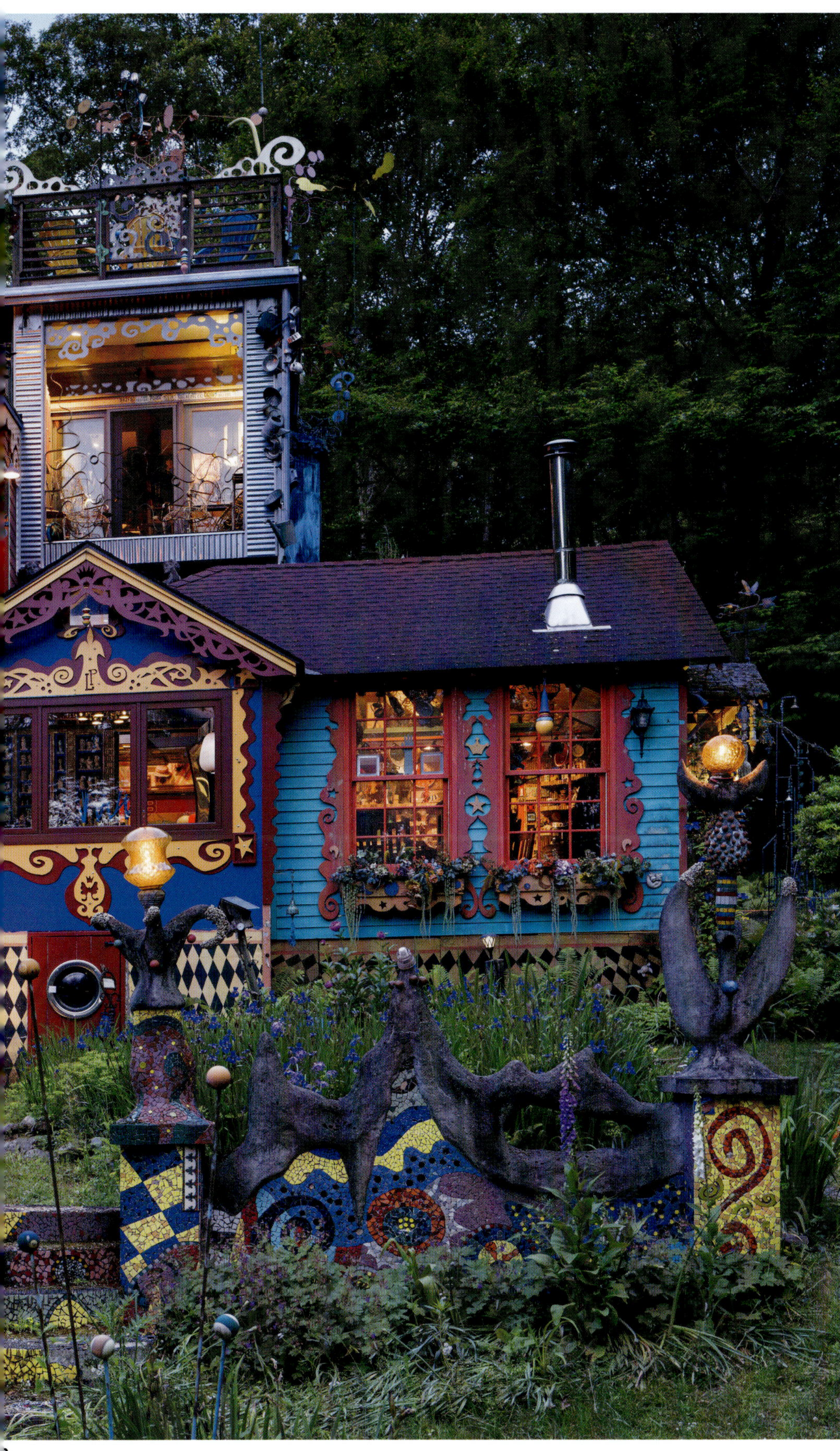

inscription that reads *Sine Limite* (No Limits). The most impactful motif on the chimney is a 10-foot-high bas-relief ceramic-tile skeleton, and adjacent to the chimney is a window adorned with patterns of bones referencing the Crypt of the Capuchin Monks in Rome, accompanied by the Italian phrasing for "As you are now, we once were; as we are now, you shall be." Coptic crosses and other imagery adorn the window lintel. Here, as elsewhere, he first mounts the bas-relief sculptures on the façades and subsequently fits the mosaic fragments in around them.

On interior level three, the *Grand Ballroom*—which is so densely filled with various objects that there is no room for dancing—fulfilled Boscarino's vision of having a large room at the heart of the expanded house that could serve as a classroom and for such public functions as poetry readings and performances. With its 14-foot-high ceiling, a focal point is a 20-foot-long chandelier that spans levels two and three and was assembled by his friend Warren Muller from a variety of primarily wood and metal objects found in the original house and shed or left lying around outside. This central work is complemented by many of Boscarino's small oil-on-board portrait paintings, which he has hung salon-style on the walls; they are interspersed with shallow glassed display cases for some of his collections. A strip of "wood mosaic" floor in front of the found-stone fireplace reads "I Got You, Babe" in Morse code. Behind the *Ballroom* is a more modest room in which a small box has been secreted in the floor; here Boscarino will have his ashes placed and on display for all eternity.

Other interior displays are quirky and amusing. While a group of hats collected in countries all over the world (located in the *Hall of Hats*) may not necessarily surprise, the hanging curtains made from 300 small white circular tabs used to open milk cartons is unexpected, as are bulbous jugs filled with the multicolored tabs used to close plastic bread bags, or a slender vitrine set into the wall that showcases his flashlight collection. His mother's wedding dress is on display, as are a 200-year-old human skeleton that he purchased on eBay from a chiropractor's widow, fragments of the Berlin Wall, numerous animal skulls and antlers, insect specimens, a massive double door he shipped back from China, bird nests found on-site, and taxidermy animals. Mannequins spaced periodically throughout the house sport an array of costumes—among those, that of a U.S.S.R.-era soldier, an American Boy Scout, a drum majorette—and different rooms are designated by their contents, such as the *Asia Room* (which, questionably, includes a collection of Hopi Kachinas), the *Music Room*, the *Weaving/Thread Studio*, and the *Nature Lab*. There is also a *Zen Room*, a *Biblioteca* (Library), a *Gallery*, and a *Cantina*. The levels of the house are reached by his *Grand Staircase*. He envisions developing a database program with every element separately identified with a bar code so that visitors can scan the codes and learn about each object and the story of how it was acquired.

In deference to his neighbors and local laws, Boscarino does not advertise *Luna Parc* with a sign on-site, but his scheduled weekend tours and mosaic or concrete sculpture workshops are nevertheless always fully booked. The more he works on the house, the more ideas he has for ornamenting different aspects of the property, and with the house mostly complete, he has recently turned his attention back to his increasingly dense sculpture garden. The woods also host the as-yet unfinished meditation pavilion he calls the *House of Bottle Blues*, kinetic mobiles, seating areas, illuminated sculptures, weathervanes, shrines, and the *Chapel of the Saints*, which he constructed to honor his grandfather's observation of a miracle curing, and which is accompanied by a fence composed of cast-off crutches. Having expanded the modest one-story cabin into an 11-level, almost 5,000-square-foot palace celebrating color, texture, media, and all of the humanities, he assiduously follows his motto, *Tempus Fugit*—time flies—and tries to take advantage of each day. Boscarino plans to live until the age of 106, thinking that by then he may have been able to accomplish all of his projects.

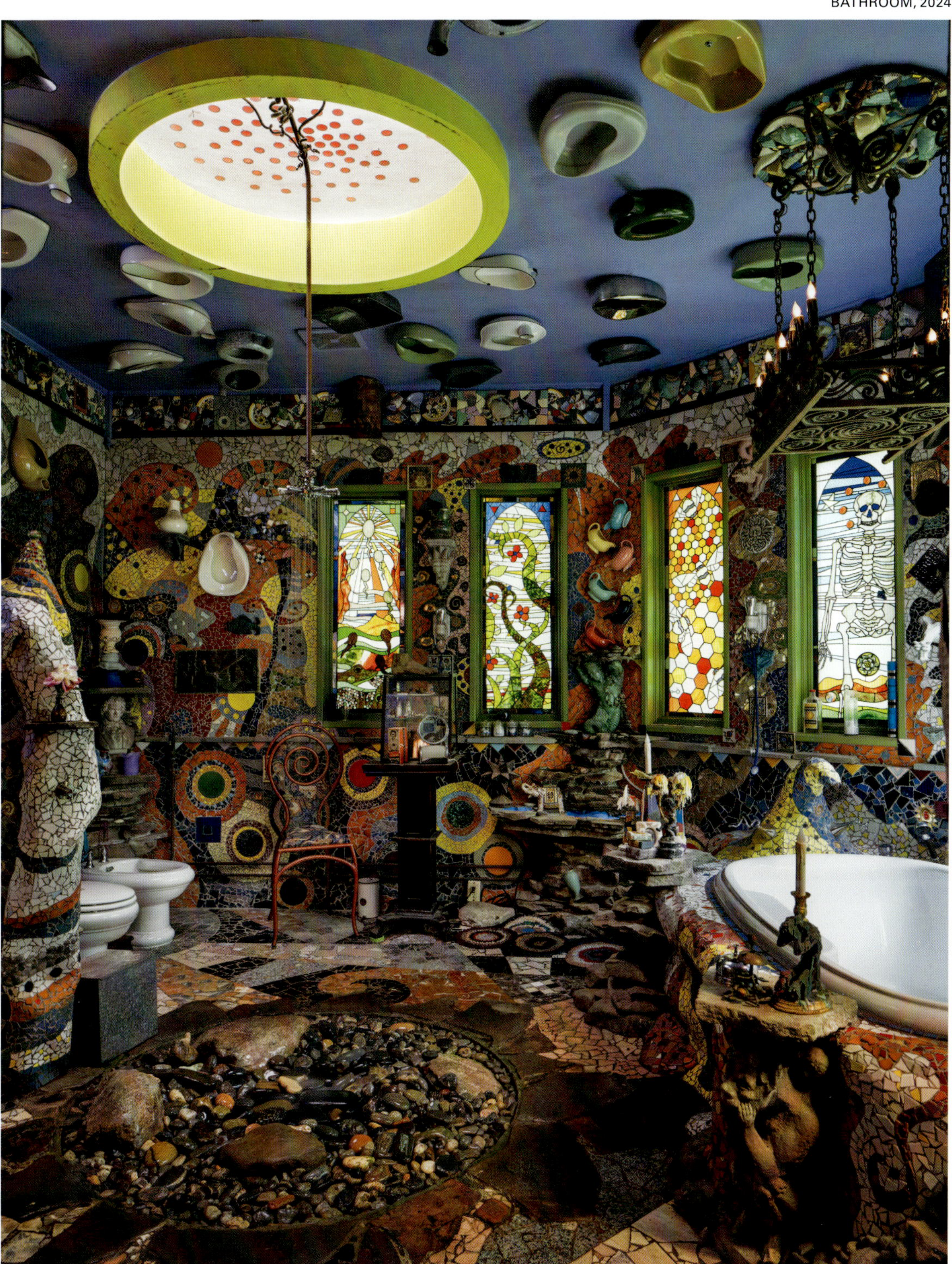

CHAPEL OF THE SAINTS INTERIOR, 2024

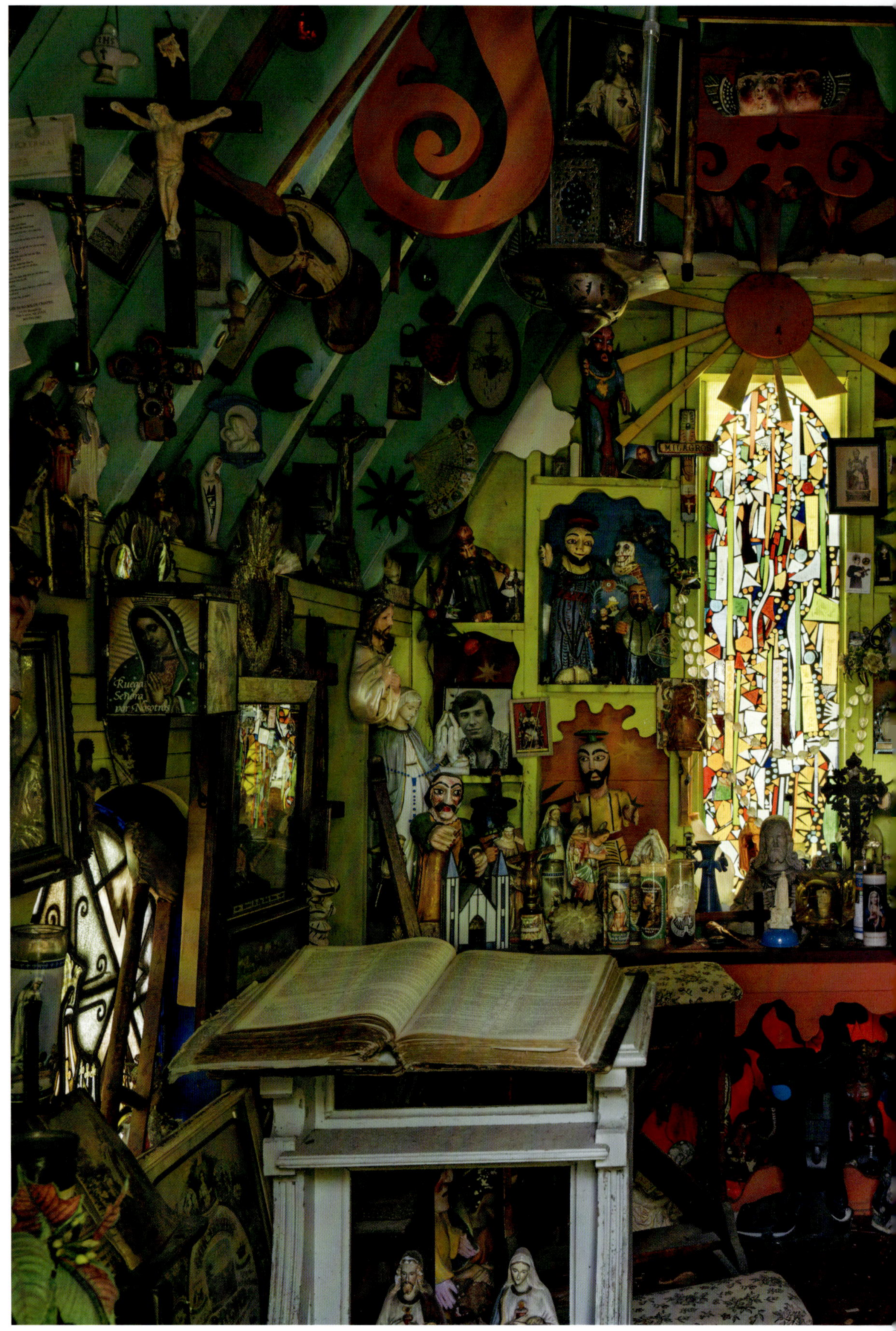

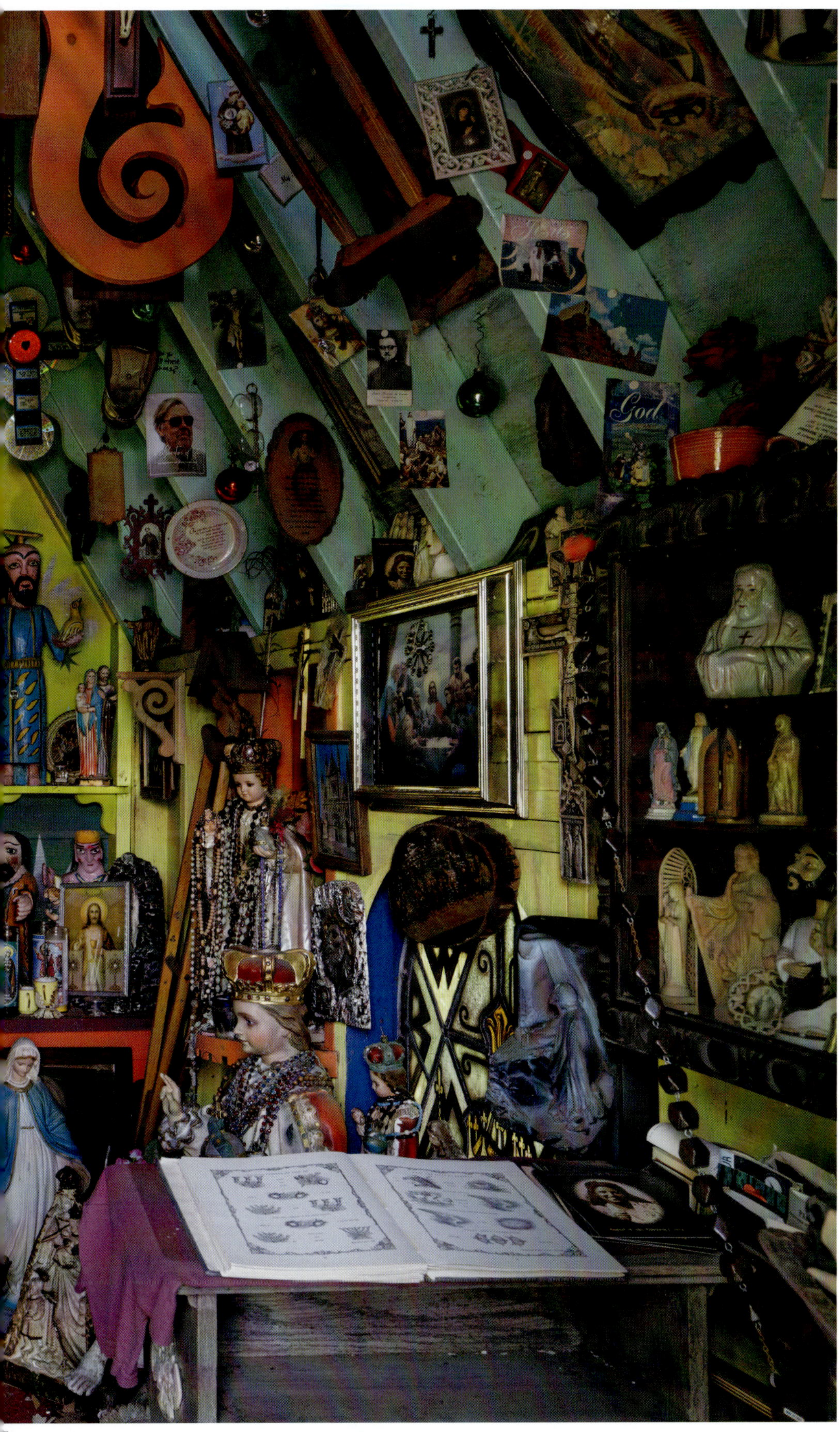
God

KEA TAWANA

ARK

NEWARK, NEW JERSEY

The motif of a seaworthy vessel regularly appears as a metaphor among artists of all periods and styles. It may be a symbol not only of voyage, but also of escape, a means to evade or elude one's circumstances by navigating to a different place, whether it be across time or space. And so, in the 1980s, out of the abandoned rubble of Newark's burned-out and devastated Central Ward, Tawana (1933– or 1940–2016) built an enormous edifice 28 feet high, 86 feet long, and 20 feet abeam, estimated to weigh around 90 tons and shaped like a ship. She identified it as an ark, and it was simultaneously a building, a sculpture, and a watercraft that honored and memorialized the city's ruins. It also provided a dream not only for herself personally—to travel back to Japan in order to lay flowers on the ground where her mother died—but also for the area's mostly poverty-stricken African-American residents, who, as they saw it growing phoenix-like out of the detritus of their demolished homes and stores and churches, fantasized that it might transport them to a different kind of life, to a regeneration of their community, and even to Jerusalem.

Tawana's early history is in dispute. Perhaps most plausible is that she was the middle of three children born to a Japanese mother and an American father—a civil engineer who was in Japan during World War II—and that she escaped the death that claimed her mother and baby sister when the family's home was leveled by an Allied bomb. After the war, she, along with her father and older brother, was repatriated to the United States, traveling in steerage on a large ship that slowly separated her from her home. When they arrived in California, the family was detained in a displaced persons camp with guard towers and barbed-wire enclosures, hardly a welcoming start to their new life. After her father was perhaps inadvertently killed by guards, the children were moved to an orphanage and then to foster care.

The young girl ran away when she was 12 to escape harassment that she believed was a consequence of her half-Japanese heritage. She dressed like a man and took odd jobs then and in years to come in construction, mining, quarrying, lighting, demolition, ironwork, and equipment and amusement-park ride repair, among other trades, as she rode the rails through the South and East. She ended up in Newark around 1953 and built a home on the back of a trailer: as she had no money to buy property or pay rent, she needed to be able to keep on the move. By the early 1960s she had begun to assemble the raw material that she would need to build her vessel, a task made easier after the 1967 Newark uprising thanks to her contract with the city to do demolition and help clean up the debris: the agreement was that she would take the buildings down to ground level and then others would backfill the hole. What she had no personal use for she would either sell or cut into firewood to keep herself warm. She carted countless loads by hand back to a city-owned lot, where she stored them until August 8, 1982, when she was ready to begin construction. As Newark had no laws on the books that regulated the building of arks, she was unable to obtain a building permit.

Tawana studied Coast Guard specifications and consulted nineteenth-century boat-building guidebooks as she built, and she was well served by the range of manual skills she had picked up over the years. Her sketches for the *Ark* featured three masts that would have supported 12,000 square feet of sail, room for four months' worth of food storage and 1,400 gallons of freshwater storage, and a chapel, library, auditorium/lecture hall, museum, greenhouse, laundry, and infirmary, as well as studio spaces for fabricating stained glass and working with metal. She assembled the frame, reinforced the bulkhead with iron, and segregated five watertight compartments to ensure that the *Ark* would float. If anything, it appeared to be overbuilt, with sturdy ribs firmly secured with mortise and tenon joints and a hand-hewn keel. Topped with a 48-star American flag rescued from an old school locker, the *Ark* was not aesthetically graceful, but it appeared powerful and looked as if it would ensure that, as captain, she would never again be forced to stay below deck, as when she left Japan. She said that she was going to christen her construction *Aka Matsu Kaisha* (*Red Pine Company*), perhaps a reference to some of the materials she used.

Tawana started to conceive of the structure as a veritable museum of the city of Newark, not only because it was physically being erected from its demolished constituent remnants, but because, through her collecting, she had amassed historical photographs, books, and other documentary evidence that were important records of people and places now passed. But she also said that she needed to build the *Ark* because nothing on land seemed safe, and she was concerned about being displaced again, this time by developers and urban renewal. Because she could

HER VESSEL WAS A SYMBOL NOT ONLY OF VOYAGE, BUT ALSO OF ESCAPE.

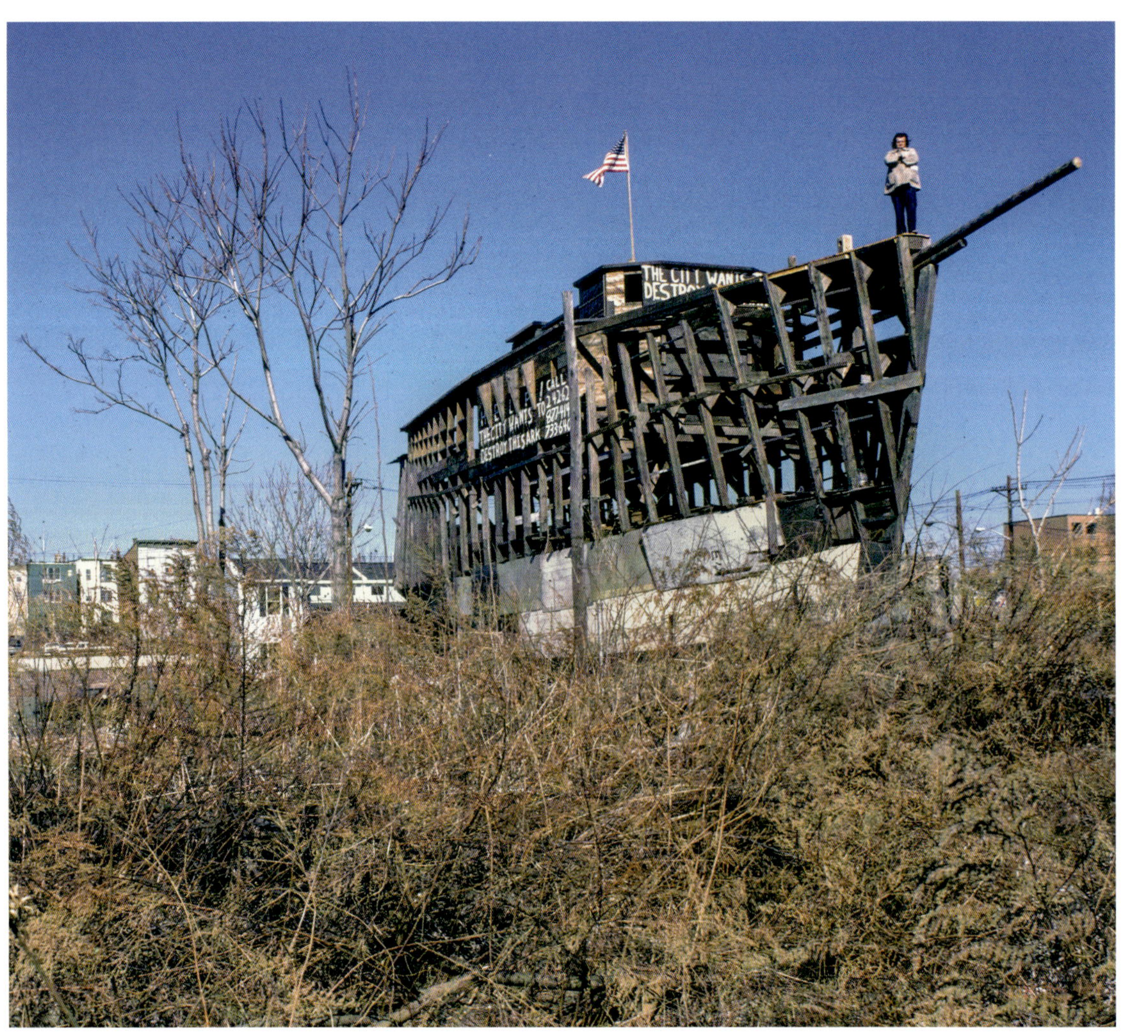

TAWANA ON HER *ARK*, 1987. PHOTO: CAMILO JOSÉ VERGARA

not do anything about those inexorable trends, she would instead choose to "get out of the way" and live at sea.

While she was in the process of cladding the hull, the city sold the lot on which her unauthorized building was rising, and Newark officials mandated that the *Ark* be demolished, because—despite the fact that she and other neighborhood members conceived of it as the spark that might bring new life and hope to the blighted city—it did not conform to zoning regulations. Tawana immediately began publicizing the city's plans, in part by posting signs on the structure's sides that included the phone numbers of the mayor, Chamber of Commerce, and local newspaper. Soon community members as well as out-of-town supporters were inundating City Hall with letters and calls. Her story was carried in the national and international news; the *Ark* was soon the most famous structure in all of Newark.

With the city unwilling to retreat, citing various undisclosed and unidentified structural and safety issues, Tawana engineered a way—via telephone poles and jacks—to roll the *Ark* all by herself off the contested property and over to the parking lot of the Humanity Baptist Church, 25 feet away. (In exchange for their welcome, she would serve as their caretaker.) A pro bono attorney argued her case in court and obtained a temporary restraining order against the city to prevent it from demolishing her construction: her supporters defined the structure as art—as lawyers and community members had defined Sabato Rodia's *Towers* almost three decades earlier (see page 332)—and therefore theoretically exempt from building codes. (Newark never decided if the *Ark* was a building or a ship, so it never clarified which codes might apply. They certainly never considered it to be art.) But when the city began threatening to revoke the Church's nonprofit status and fine it $50 daily as long as the *Ark* was parked there, arguing that it was not germane to the Church's religious purposes, Tawana surrendered. Unable to locate another site to which she could move the structure, rather than watching the city demolish it with bulldozers, she dismantled it herself over a period of several months with crowbars and handsaws. At first, she just removed the upper decks so that it could avoid overhead wires and be moved via city streets to the river, but soon it became clear that this would not be possible. By summer 1988 it was gone.

Although there is no evidence that Tawana's *Ark* would actually have been seaworthy, it appeared to simultaneously serve her as a projected physical means to escape her marginalized and rootless existence and, if she could have actually sailed on it, would have provided her with a means of confronting the trauma of her mother's sudden death: visiting her grave and letting her know that her daughter had turned out worthwhile would hopefully have brought her some peace. It would have been her safe space, as the Biblical Noah's Ark was for its passengers, on which she would have sailed to a new life, away from intimidation, displacement, and harassment. But it was not to be. She stayed in Newark for another year, continuing to tangle with the city as they tried to evict her from her home; at one point Tawana even threatened to shoot police and demolition workers and set herself and her house on fire if they did not back off. But by 1989 she had moved on, and, like Rodia, was subsequently reluctant to discuss her life's work.

Tawana relocated to Port Jervis, New York, and refocused on other things, including writing a proposal to renovate dilapidated buildings in cities such as Newark by hiring the homeless, teaching them construction skills, and then allowing them to move into the buildings they saved, as they would be able to henceforth support themselves with new jobs powered by their new skills. She also designed other projects, including an elaborate plan for a utopian city that would include artist live-work spaces, a senior citizen center, and even a substance abuse recovery ward. In Port Jervis, too, she seemed to find solace in the natural world.

The symbolism of Tawana's early efforts was not lost on a generation of Newark residents, who were well aware of the precarity of their own lives after the 1967 burning of their city, and the memory of her unusual architectural/maritime construction remained widespread. When word came of her passing almost 30 years after the *Ark* had been dismantled, a nonprofit gallery in Newark organized a commemorative exhibition, and innumerable residents or former residents came forward to share their memories of her, of the *Ark* itself, and of the import that her visionary construction had had for their community.

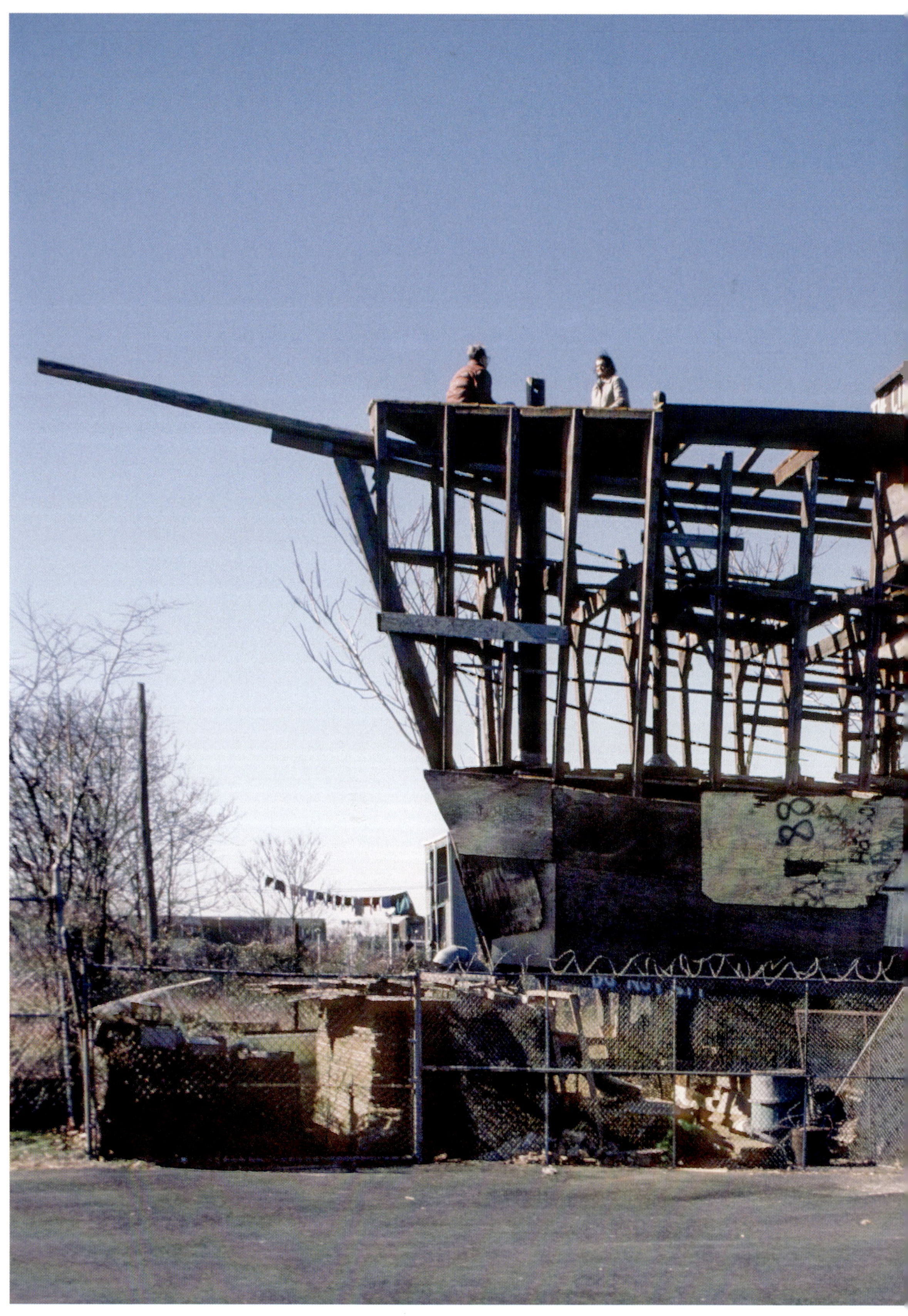

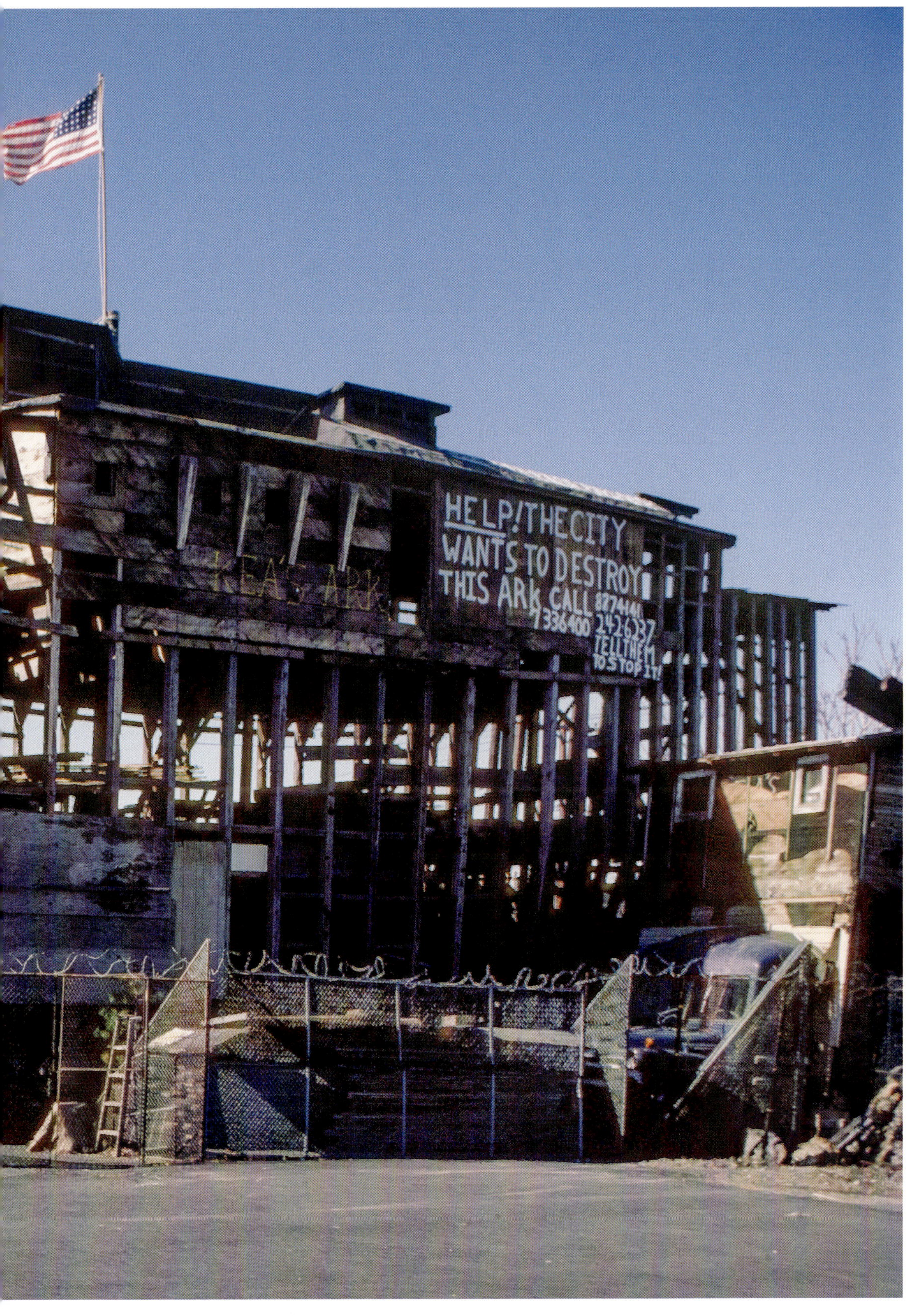
HELP! THE CITY
WANTS TO DESTROY
THIS ARK CALL 8874141
7336400 2426237
TELL THEM
TO STOP IT!

CLARENCE SCHMIDT

HOUSE OF MIRRORS

WOODSTOCK, NEW YORK

The assembled buildings and installations created by plasterer and stonemason Clarence Schmidt (1897–1978) on the side of Ohayo Mountain in New York's Catskill Mountains, near the town of Woodstock, could arguably be identified as the most renowned example of original alternative architecture in the United States. And although most of his constructions have not been extant for over 50 years, they are still widely remembered, referenced, and admired.

After having inherited five acres of land from a cousin, Schmidt began developing the site with little fanfare in the late 1930s while he summered on this mountainous site overlooking the Ashokan Reservoir. His first building, named *Journey's End*, was a simple log cabin constructed with railroad ties that he covered with industrial roofing tar, paint, and varnish to protect the wood and repel insects. He later marbleized the surfaces with other paints and varnishes and ornamented them with glass shards. While he was still working on it (he sold it shortly after its completion), he also began to build up retaining walls on the remaining part of his property, which he constructed from quarried native stones, and he cleared the grounds for a larger home above the terraced plantings.

While the core of Schmidt's new home was similarly birthed as a log cabin built from railroad ties that leaned against a tree for support, by the early 1950s he had begun to expand the house in all directions, with both its shape and footprint determined by the steep topography. By 1967 it had grown into a rather labyrinthine seven-story structure that enclosed a living tree within. Wood-framed sash windows, barely two alike, became a recurrent element that graced almost the entirety of the outward-facing façade on every level; they were sometimes arranged along the existing wall planes but elsewhere they connected adjoining planes at a diagonal. The differently sized panes underscored the asymmetry of the whole, as did the various balconies, ramps, and landings that outlined each of the floors and connected to the planted terraces.

A variety of found objects increasingly adorned both exterior and interior spaces, reaching significant density on a rooftop "garden" and an "alleyway" in front of the main house. Perhaps most striking was the sheathing of various structural and decorative elements of the constructions with aluminum foil to enhance their brilliance and reflectivity. Schmidt later also utilized this technique to wrap the branches of trees and shrubs in what would become his *Silver Forest*. The reflections from the glass windows, foil, and shiny found objects were a consciously recurring and noteworthy emphasis throughout the site and helped to stretch the dimensionality of the house and his other constructions.

This reflectivity as well as the improvisational method with which Schmidt worked and his ad-hoc accumulation and placement of found objects both inspired and channeled some of the major movements of mainstream contemporary art that were being explored at that same time. Pivotal installation artist Allan Kaprow specifically referenced Schmidt's work as the primary motivator behind his own articulated "principle of extension," in which paintings were built up to include three-dimensional sculptural elements and interior sculptures spread out to become complex and nonlinear "happenings" and exterior environments. This dovetailed, on several levels, with the concurrence among art historians that assemblages themselves—and particularly those made of non-art materials sourced from industrial detritus or popular culture—were quintessential examples of Modernism. Such groupings forced viewers to balance their identification of the familiar conventional fragments making up the work with the conceptual leap required to consider the work as a whole unto itself, its constituent elements no longer fulfilling their original purposes but instead included for aesthetic impact alone. Any interconnection between components was similarly prioritized by visual, rather than functional, significance.

The various shrines and garden ornaments along the terraces surrounding Schmidt's house were prime examples of this accumulative aesthetic and displayed some of the same visual choices. But despite the inherent interest of the individual shrines and "garden" areas, most renowned—and most pertinent to this book—was the large *House of Mirrors* itself.

Propped up against the mountain's incline at the rear and supported by piled piers of dry-stacked rocks at the front, the house had around 35 rooms at its most expansive, although not all were habitable in every season (Schmidt would retreat to the "inner sanctum" of the log cabin as winter approached). Nor could all of the different "modules" be entered via straightforward linear access: although generally based on standard frame construction, the organic way he built necessitated circuitous interior routes to connect staircases, hallways, and variously sized chambers. His joinery and carpentry techniques were modest at best, and he often used his walls as foundations for higher levels, so it was not unheard of for weakened modules to loosen and plunge down the mountainside. By the early 1960s Schmidt began to resurface sections of the exterior with rough-sawn planks to which he affixed long thin boards, skewing them so that their angles obscured any of the house's more standard vertical and horizontal architectural lines.

Unlike the Canadian Richard Greaves, a later "anarchitect" who chose to assemble his structures with baling wire and twine instead of nails so that they would continue to shift and, ultimately, lead to the sensation (although not necessarily the reality) of deterioration, Schmidt seems to have evidenced no such conceptual aesthetic, despite certain visual resemblances. The asymmetry of the *House of Mirrors* was linked to the slope of the land and his ad-lib construction as he collected his mostly recycled or found materials, but this was his home, not an artificial folly designed to provide an illusion of imbalance or collapse. Nevertheless, while as a trained mason he undoubtedly understood basic principles of construction, this seemed to be of less priority than his improvisational use of materials as they became available, and his artistic treatment and placement of these finds after he brought them on-site.

Schmidt enlivened his interior spaces with strings of Christmas tree lights and spotlights, bouncing their shimmering illumination off the aluminum foil-sheathed branches, found objects, mirrors, and constructed elements that crowded the space. It is highly unlikely that the electrical components were wired to code, so when a large branch crashed through the house during a storm in January 1968, fire quickly

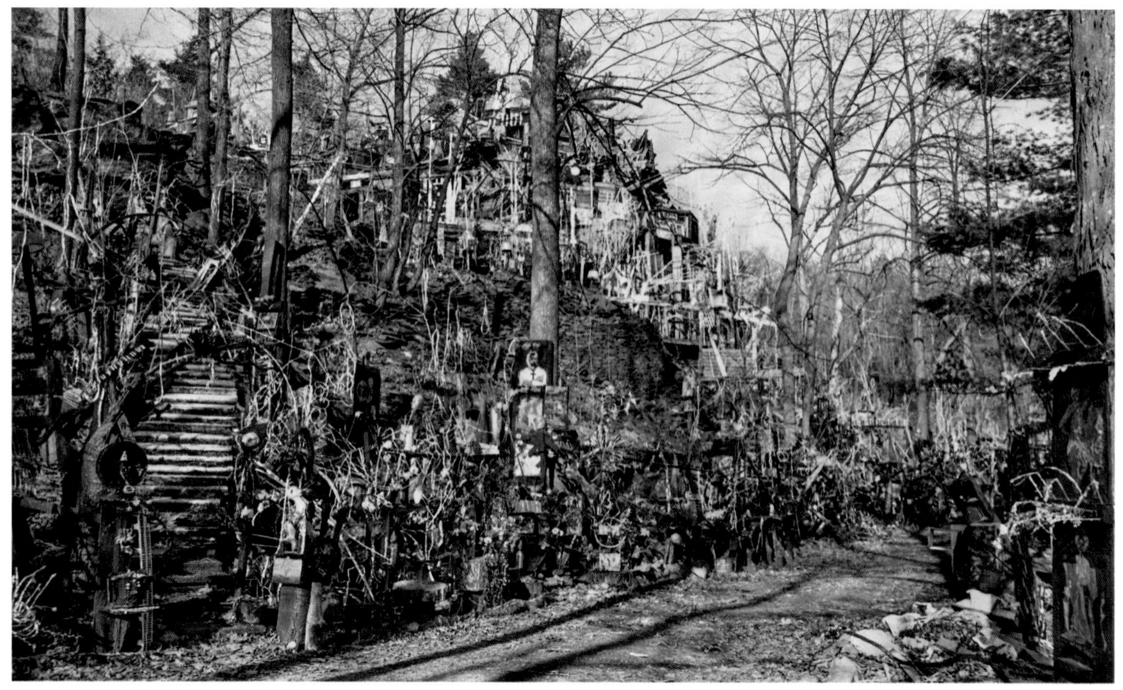

OVERVIEW OF ALLEY AND HOUSE, 1967. PHOTO: WILLIAM LIPKE, COURTESY SPACES ARCHIVES AND JOHN MICHAEL KOHLER ARTS CENTER

TOTEM SHRINES (DETAIL), 1967. PHOTO: GREGG BLASDEL, © SPACES ARCHIVES, COURTESY JOHN MICHAEL KOHLER ARTS CENTER

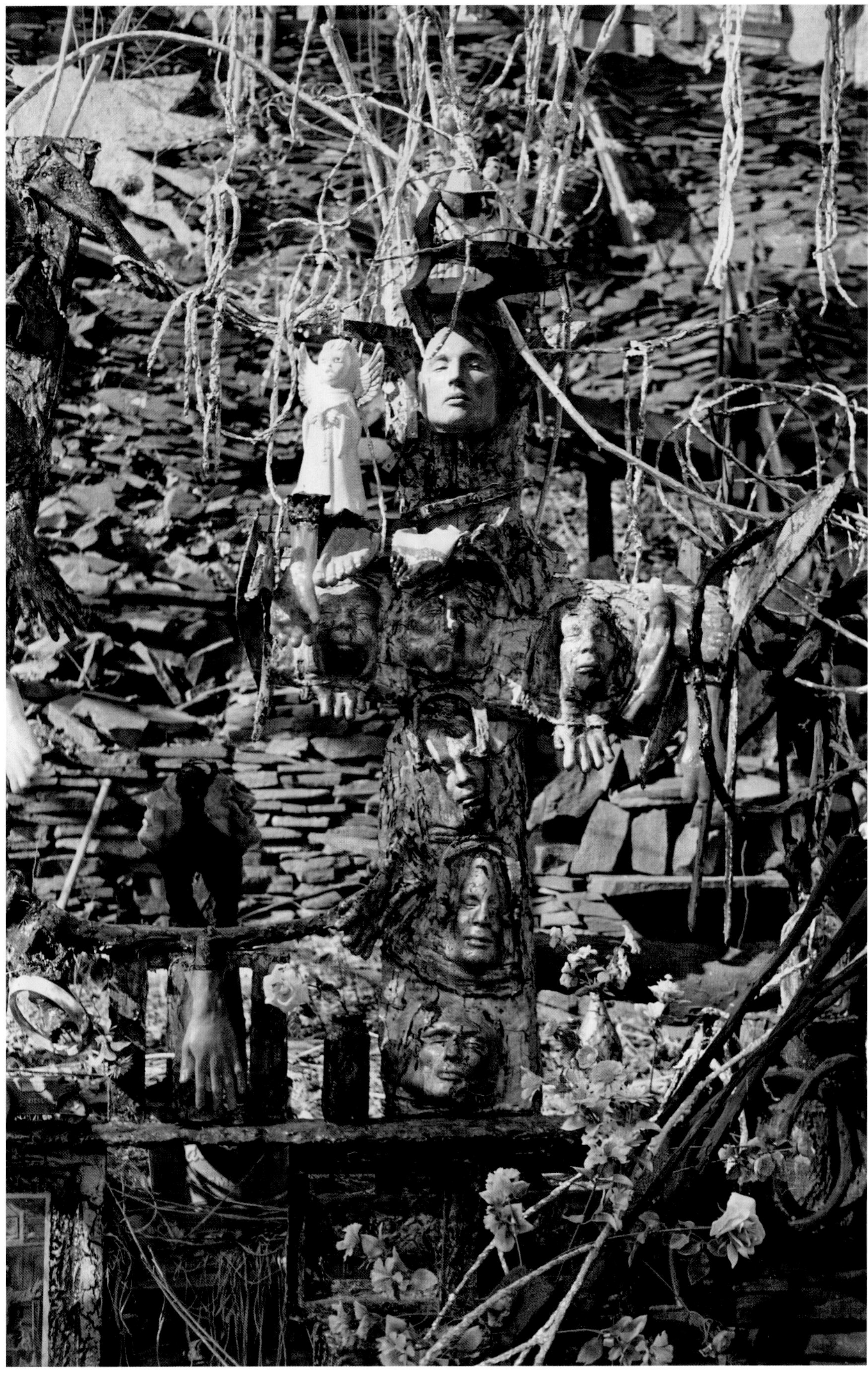

broke out. The tarred surfaces were all flammable, and worse, they had also trapped moisture on the wood surfaces, causing them to decay and rot, so as everything exploded, the conflagration burned hot and long for days, shooting flames into the sky as they off-gassed poisoned plumes of post-industrial products.

Beginning almost immediately to build again, Schmidt's next projects were the aluminum foil-sheathed branches of the *Silver Forest* trees and a new building, *Mark II*, which he began to build over the base of an old Studebaker station wagon backed up to a tree. But he had completed only one sleeping room on top of a wooden platform over the car before this structure, too, caught fire, in December 1971. At this point, Schmidt moved into the town of Woodstock but, with no access to or funds for permanent lodging, he slept in doorways and other temporary shelters until he was sent to a state hospital for physical and mental appraisal. He subsequently lived in two different nursing homes until he died of heart failure, never having returned to the mountain. While some discrete objects had been salvaged from the blazes, invasive vegetation and the temperature swings of this northern clime have erased most evidence of Schmidt's works.

HIS HOME INSPIRED SOME OF THE MAJOR MOVEMENTS OF MAINSTREAM CONTEMPORARY ART.

UPPER LEVELS OF HOUSE, 1967. PHOTO: JOHN BLASDEL, COURTESY SPACES ARCHIVES AND JOHN MICHAEL KOHLER ARTS CENTER

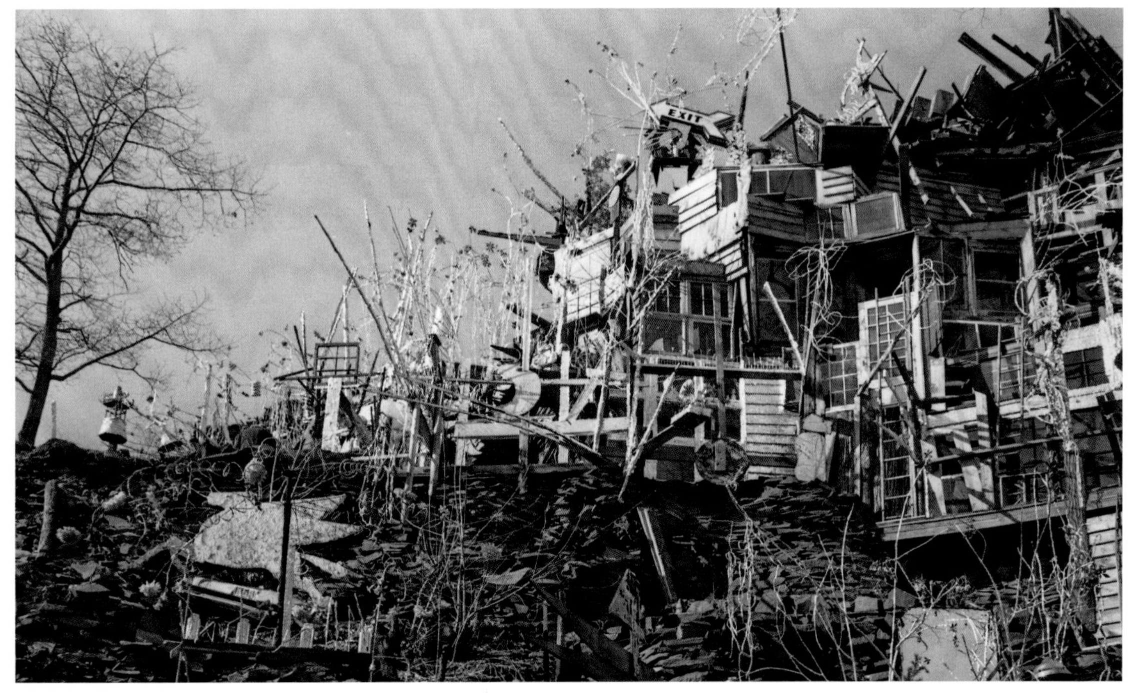

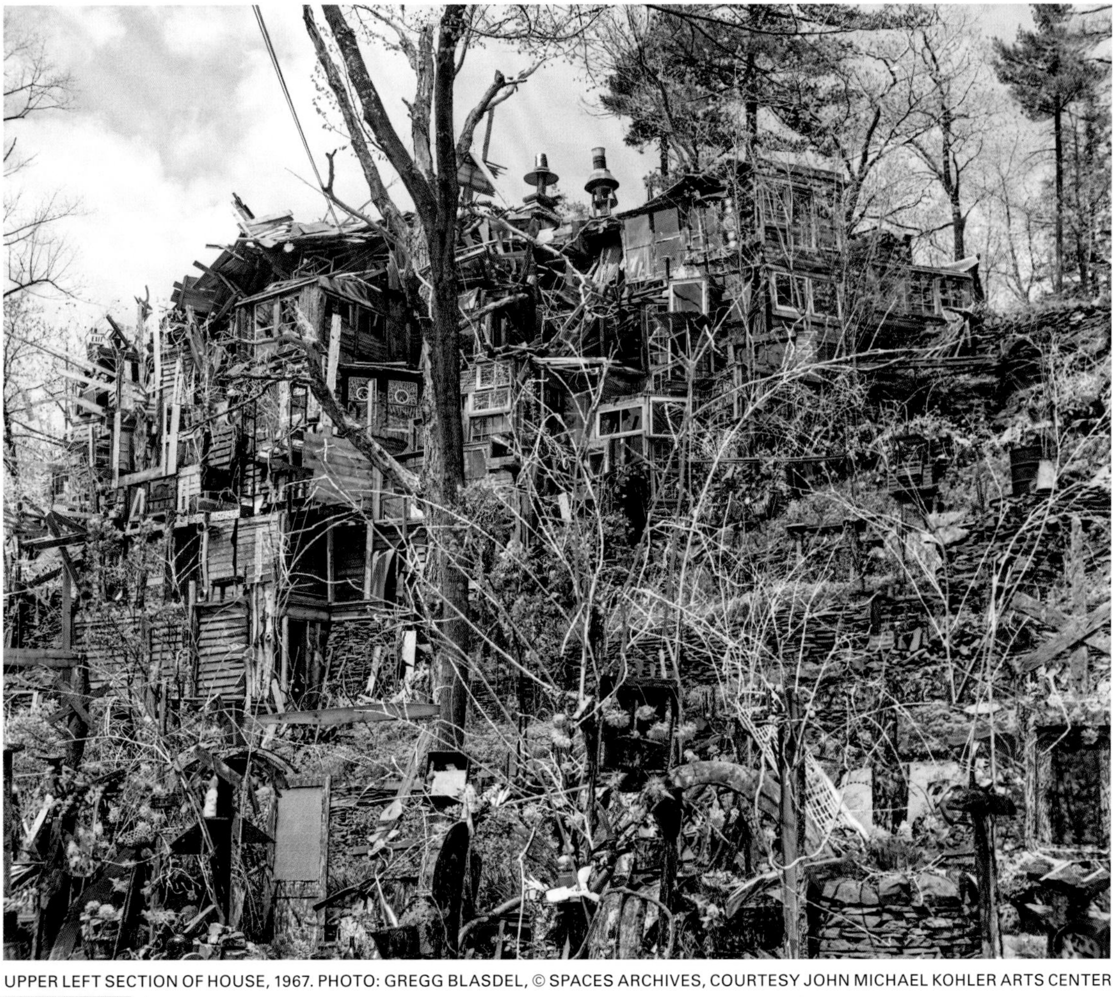

UPPER LEFT SECTION OF HOUSE, 1967. PHOTO: GREGG BLASDEL, © SPACES ARCHIVES, COURTESY JOHN MICHAEL KOHLER ARTS CENTER

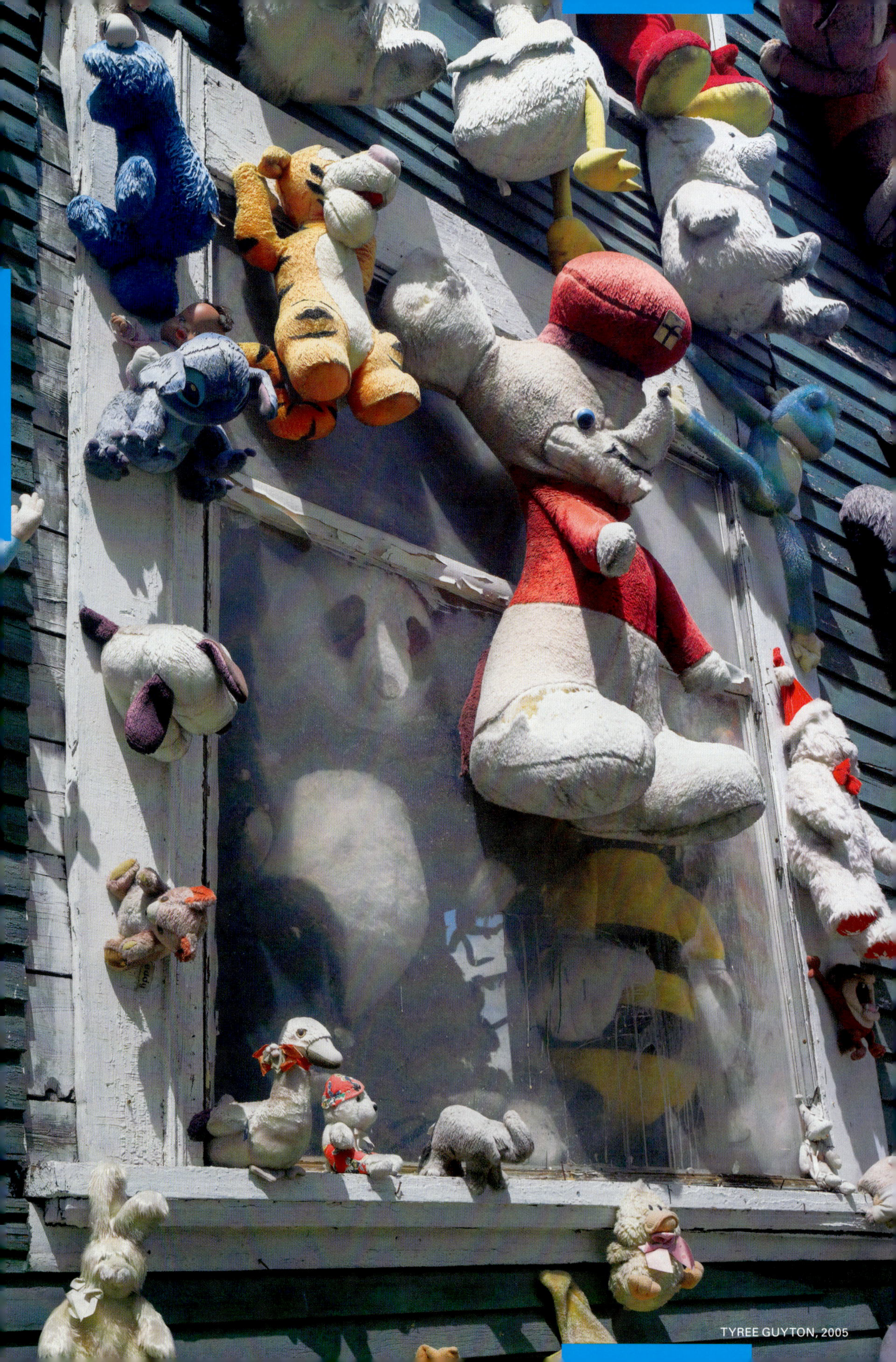

TYREE GUYTON, 2005

CHAPTER 2

FROM CONVENTIONAL TO OFFBEAT

MODIFYING EXISTING BUILDINGS

While many of us actively try to decorate and furnish our homes in ways that reflect our personalities and increase our comfort level, the artists in this category go far beyond hanging pictures or painting walls. In fact, these makers designate all or part of the building itself as their blank canvas. The resulting elaborate environments may be developed on top of anonymous vernacular dwellings, within conventional urban complexes, or as part of secluded rural outposts, but each has been transformed in a way that the original architectural foundation of their efforts becomes practically unrecognizable—if not effaced altogether.

Nevertheless, the process of ornamentation is generally similar in every case: either an idea is born or a special object or a bag of supplies is found or gifted and strikes a chord, and the first tentative steps toward altering and personalizing the living or working space is begun. If the assemblage or fabrication or painting is successful, it motivates further attempts to continue the process: thinking about what might come next encourages the artists to find more resources and to continue exploring their creativity with these new materials in these new ways. As with the unique architectural structures that we sampled in the first chapter, which flourished more elaborately than the builder had originally imagined, creators who convert their conventional spaces and transform them into something radically idiosyncratic also rarely visualize the entirety as they begin.

Because working additively is the easiest way for this kind of adornment to unfurl, the accumulation of raw materials and the maker's own physical stamina and timetable are often the determining factors of how quickly the environment reaches a level of exceptionalism. The unpredictability of the time needed to gather or manufacture potential adornments, or, more rarely, to save up funds to purchase them, does not seem to prejudice the process in any way: artists just tend to pause after they produce or affix or paint or assemble whatever objects they currently have, and return to further development when the availability of materials and energy is again abundant.

These kinds of sites—like those in all of the sections of this book—tend to defy easy categorization. Exterior decoration may move to the interior. Garden ornaments may become complemented by architectural embellishments. Landscaping may lead to built areas of sanctuary or reflection. These kinds of progressions (and their inverses) may result from the makers' evolving thought processes as creation continues and they discover new ways and locations in which to pursue their vision. Such evolution may also be an outcome of the augmented skills and enhanced capacity for more elaborate interventions that accompany their developing work, and/or it may be tied to the physical nature of available resources. Creation brings great satisfaction, if not joy, to the makers, and a desire to share their work with others. But it is also true that here, as we see elsewhere, the transformation of existing structures—while empowering for the author—does not always result in positive response either from neighbors or from the bureaucrats of municipalities or regional governments.

Because a previously manufactured structure serves as the art environment's infrastructure or substructure, it may come as no surprise that these kinds of sites are among the most numerous. Sadly, they are also often the easiest to dismantle, particularly when the embellishment consists of the attachment of discrete objects, such as in Sanford Darling's iconic but no-longer-extant *House of 1000 Paintings* (Santa Barbara, California), or Fred Burns's modest seaside dwelling with its façades covered with strips of painted wood (Belfast, Maine): painted façades can always be painted over. Happily, however, Avery and Doris Sisk's *House of Mugs* (Collettsville, North Carolina) remains celebrated and its 30,000-plus hanging mugs intact. But typically, it is the case here, as in most other art environment categories, that after the creator's passing the site may quickly fall into disrepair or may be demolished so the property can be repurposed for other uses (which is what happened, for example, with Lloyd "Ace" Parsons's *Rainbow House* in Vancouver, Washington, as well as countless others), unless surviving family members or later generations are motivated to continue their elders' passion. Still others, like Art Beal's *Nitt Witt Ridge* (Cambria, California), have passed hand-to-hand, slowly degrading with each new change of ownership.

CHERI PANN AND GONZALO DURÁN

THE MOSAIC TILE HOUSE

VENICE, CALIFORNIA

The modest, drably painted one-story bungalow that Pann (1940-2025) purchased in 1994 was ill-fitted for her extroverted and creative personality. So when she got together with Durán (b. 1943), a paint store employee whom she met while shopping, they jointly embarked on a total reformation of the simple gabled building.

Pann was born in the San Francisco Bay Area, although she grew up in East Los Angeles, where she was involved in theatre as a young girl. In her teens she switched to the visual arts, and she studied printmaking, drawing, and ceramics at several local institutions, ultimately earning her Master of Fine Arts degree. She purchased the small house because it had space in the back of the deep lot for her to build a studio, which she needed to accommodate her large-scale paintings. Durán, too, had a background in the arts. Born in Mexico to a shoemaker who specialized in dance shoes for flamenco and *folklórico* dancers, he took some university-level art classes in Los Angeles but never completed his degree. They built two large and airy studios behind the house, as planned.

Both artists continued to explore discrete works in a variety of media, but the transformation of the nondescript 1940s-era bungalow and its surrounds soon categorically eclipsed those efforts. After completing the studios, although neither had had significant experience in mosaic work, Pann began to make some colorful tiles for the bathroom, and soon she and Durán were altering the house interior by ripping out walls and adding built-in shelving as they covered everything with vibrant, saturated paint colors and the deep and radiant hues of randomly fragmented tiles. Durán also made tiles, primarily in blue and white, which he often illustrated with line paintings, poems, or pithy quotes, and he also assumed primary responsibility for breaking up the tiles Pann made, afterward laying the fragmented shards into various shapes and forms. Neighbors and friends helped out by bringing them their broken or unneeded objects, and in recent years a full-time employee assisted with installation.

The interior astonishes with the pulsating interaction of the intense palette and the textural tiles, as well as with the brightly painted walls and assemblages of broken mirrors, kitchen implements, and many and varied collections. But perhaps the exterior, with its radical three-dimensional accoutrements, is even more compelling. The couple worked by building up vertical or extended shapes with rebar wrapped with tar paper and wire mesh before adding concrete. After letting it set for 24 hours, Durán would apply a ¼-inch layer of thinset mortar onto which he laid the tiles and found objects. Colored grout was added to secure the additions 24 hours later.

Swirling color and humorous touches are everywhere: pergolas and supporting buttresses are scalloped with a fringe of protruding handles of coffee cups and mugs, window sashes are thickened with concrete inlaid with small beads and buttons, a door is screened with hundreds of pieces of flatware or tools, exterior ceramic-tiled walkways shine with dazzling delineated paths enhanced with bas-relief patterns in the shape of sunbursts and mandalas, and a garden area is bordered with a rippling front fence that incorporates a wide range of found natural and fabricated objects. Thrift-store ceramic figurines, plastic toys, wrought-iron findings, rocks and shells, CDs, empty paint cans and lids, strings of bottle caps, cast-concrete garden ornaments, and pots and pans wrestle with each other for space: it is a cacophony of textures, of colors, and of shapes.

The original front roofline of the house was modified with a deep overhang that created an intimate shaded porch. While the top surface remains what is possibly the only unadorned space on the entire property (probably for reasons of weight), the interior ceiling and floor of the porch are fully sheathed in sparkling ceramic-tile fragments, and the supporting posts—interrupted with more slender tiled branches—bulge with extended sculptural motifs. Fronting the porch area is an organically globular sculpture that follows the same linear path as the house and porch. Curiously, its rounded and somewhat ungainly forms recall some of the semibotanical or semi-anthropomorphic ceramics of the Funk movement popular in the San Francisco Bay Area in the 1960s and early 1970s. It terminates close to the home's front door in a rounded archway, a design repeated at the property frontage, where it adjoins a fence constructed with mosaic-sheathed trunks interspersed with slender steel members that mimic plant shapes.

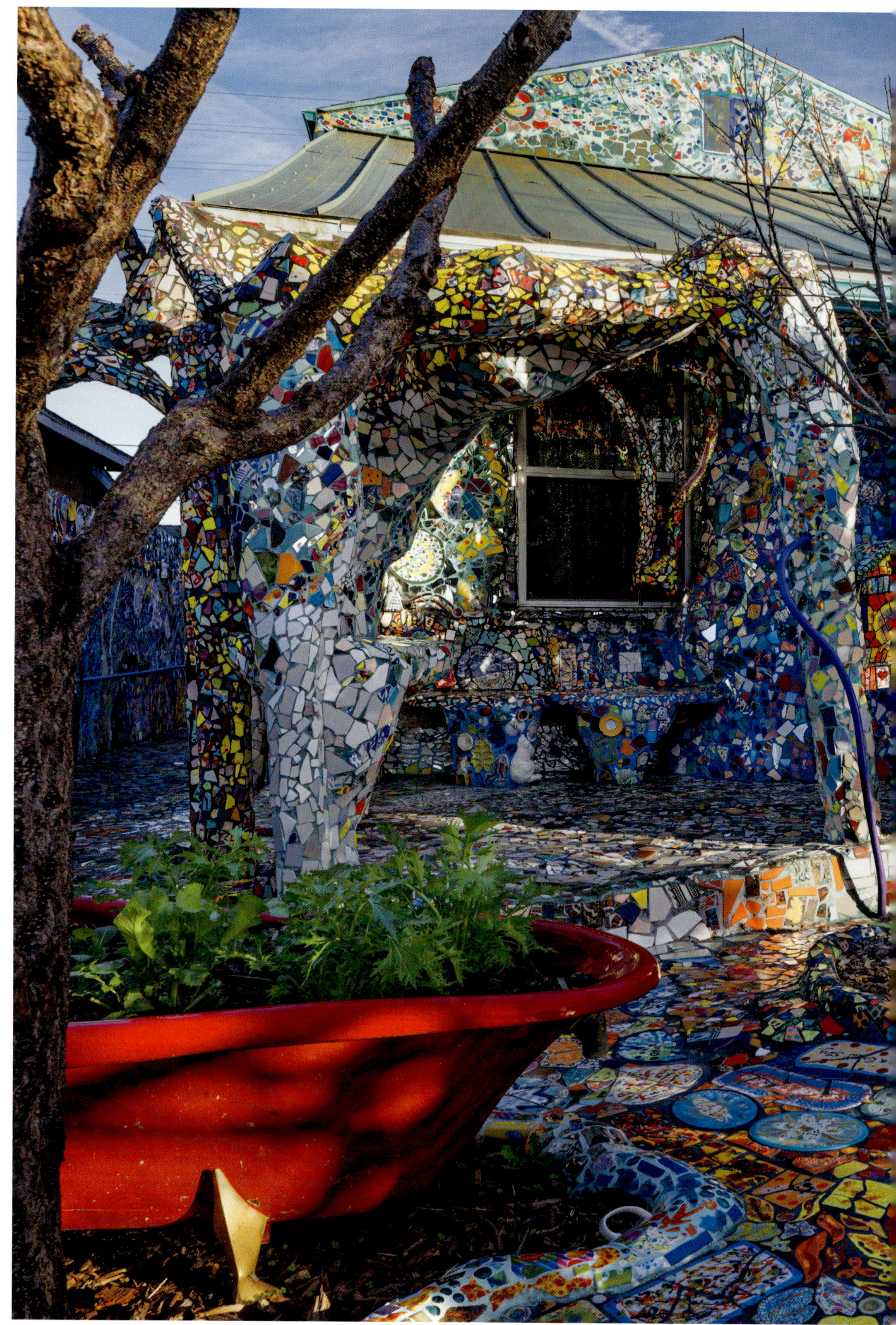

FRONT FAÇADE AND GROUNDS, 2025

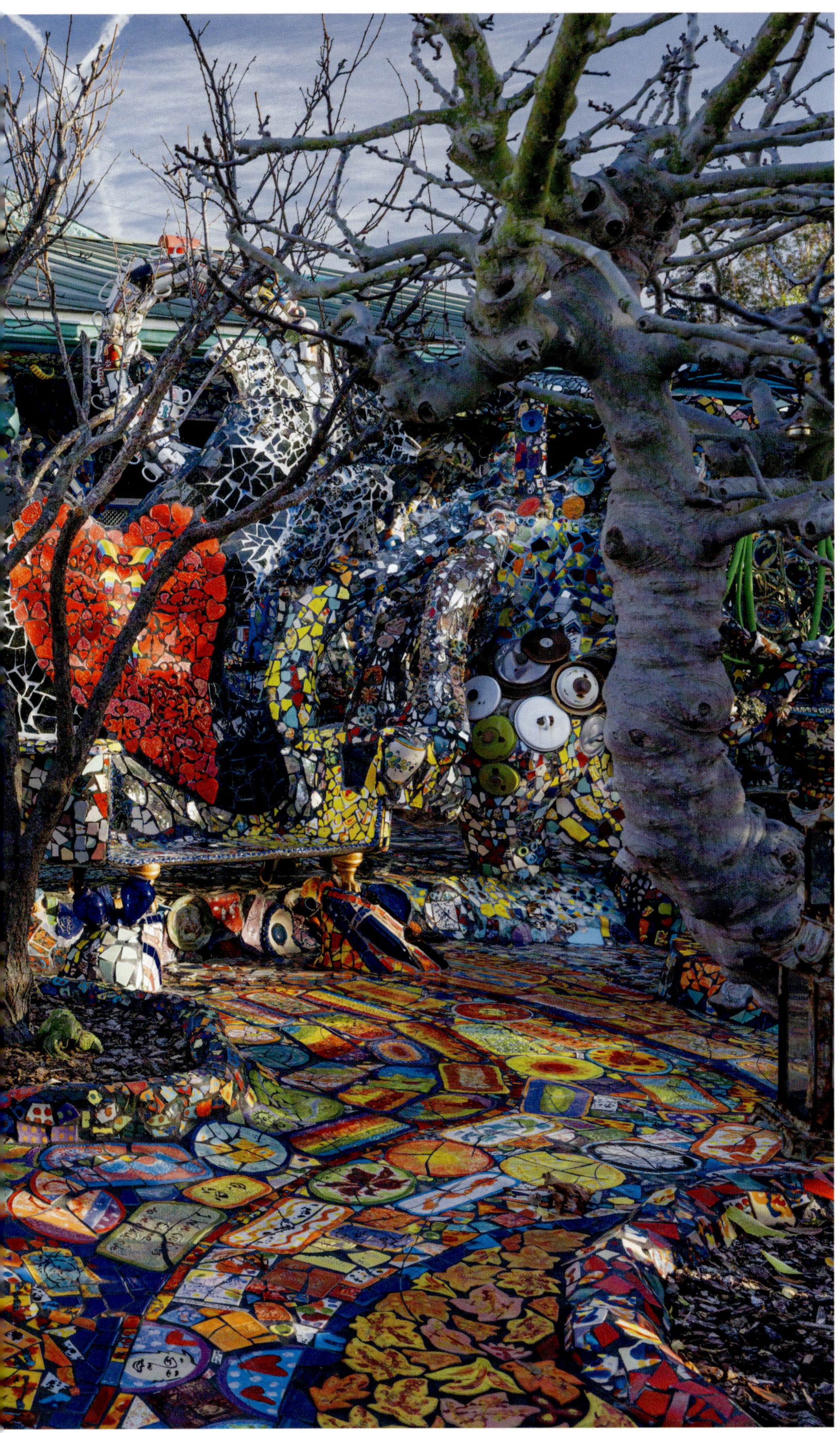

FRONT GROUNDS AND SCULPTED WALL, 2025

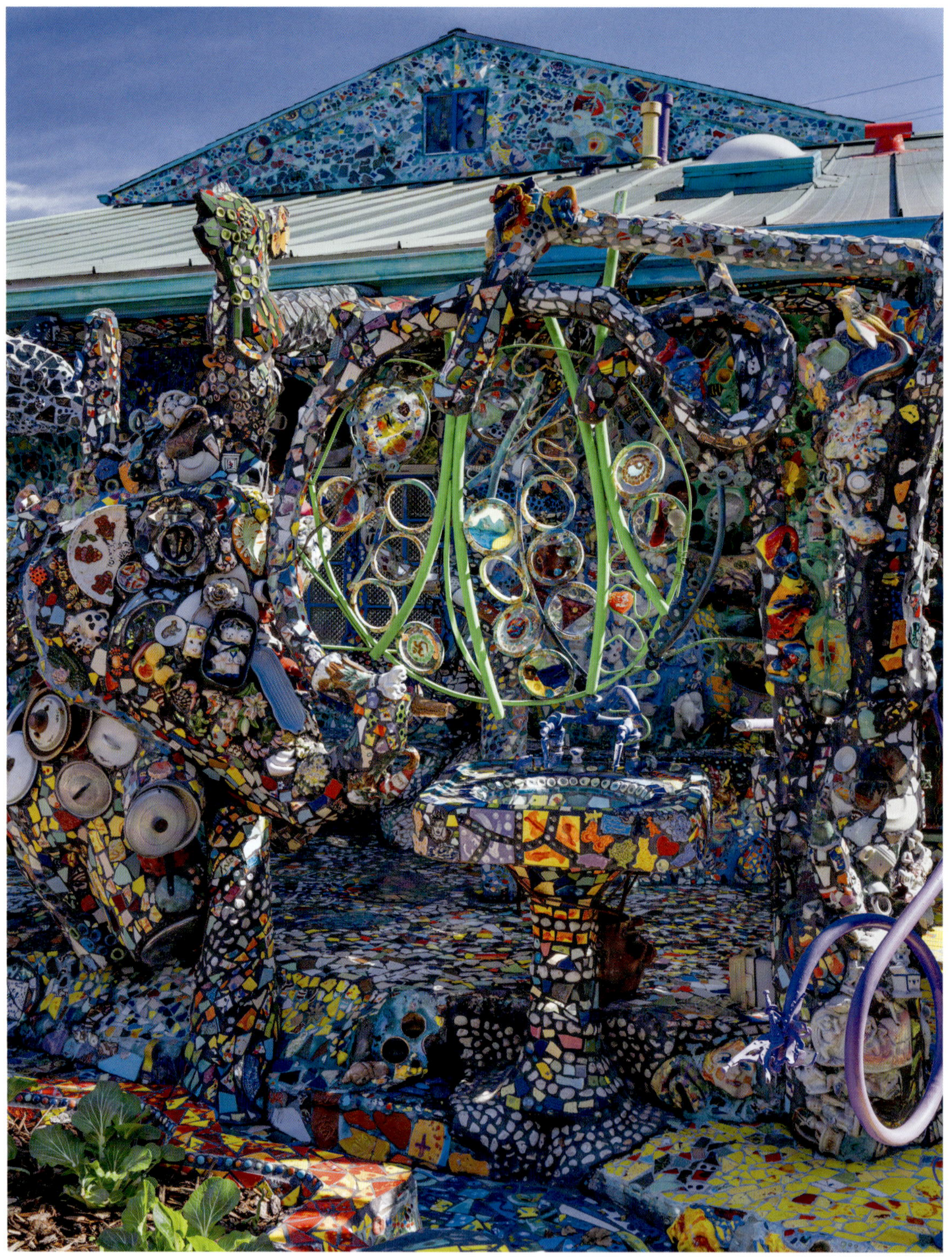

The textural ceilings, walls, and floors of the property are complemented with a series of small sculptures that are similarly tiled in ceramic fragments. A fortune cookie, a standing panda, a dragon, an iguana, a hot tub sheltered with a gazebo supported by arching ribbed structures that Pann said reference Sabato Rodia's *Towers* in Watts (see page 332), and settees and benches (including one that alludes to the caterpillar in *Alice in Wonderland*) share space with citrus trees whose bright fruit orbs nicely complement the space. Since Pann's passing, Durán has continued to make art and to open their spaces to the public on Saturday afternoons for a small fee. They had hoped to have the *Mosaic Tile House* protected in perpetuity, but the means for doing so have not yet been clearly identified.

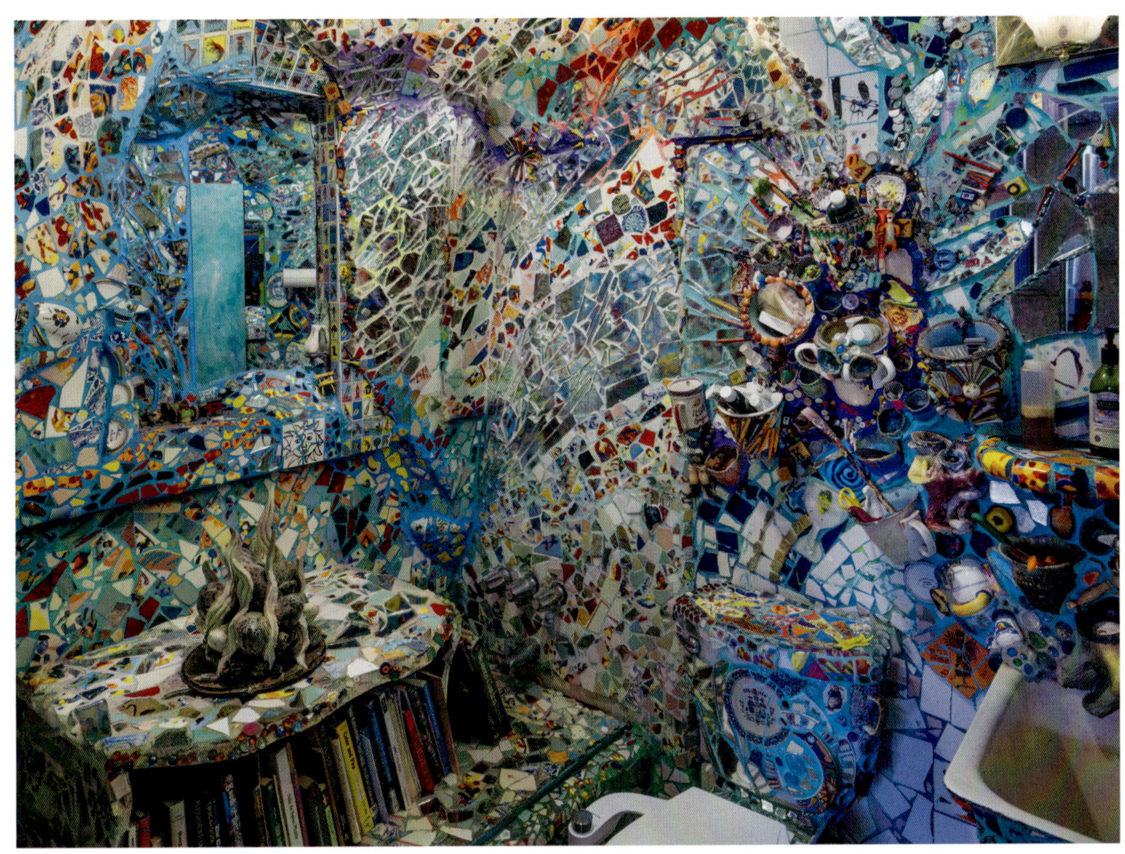

9

BATHROOM, 2025

SWIRLING COLOR AND HUMOROUS TOUCHES CREATE A DAZZLING CACOPHONY OF TEXTURES AND SHAPES.

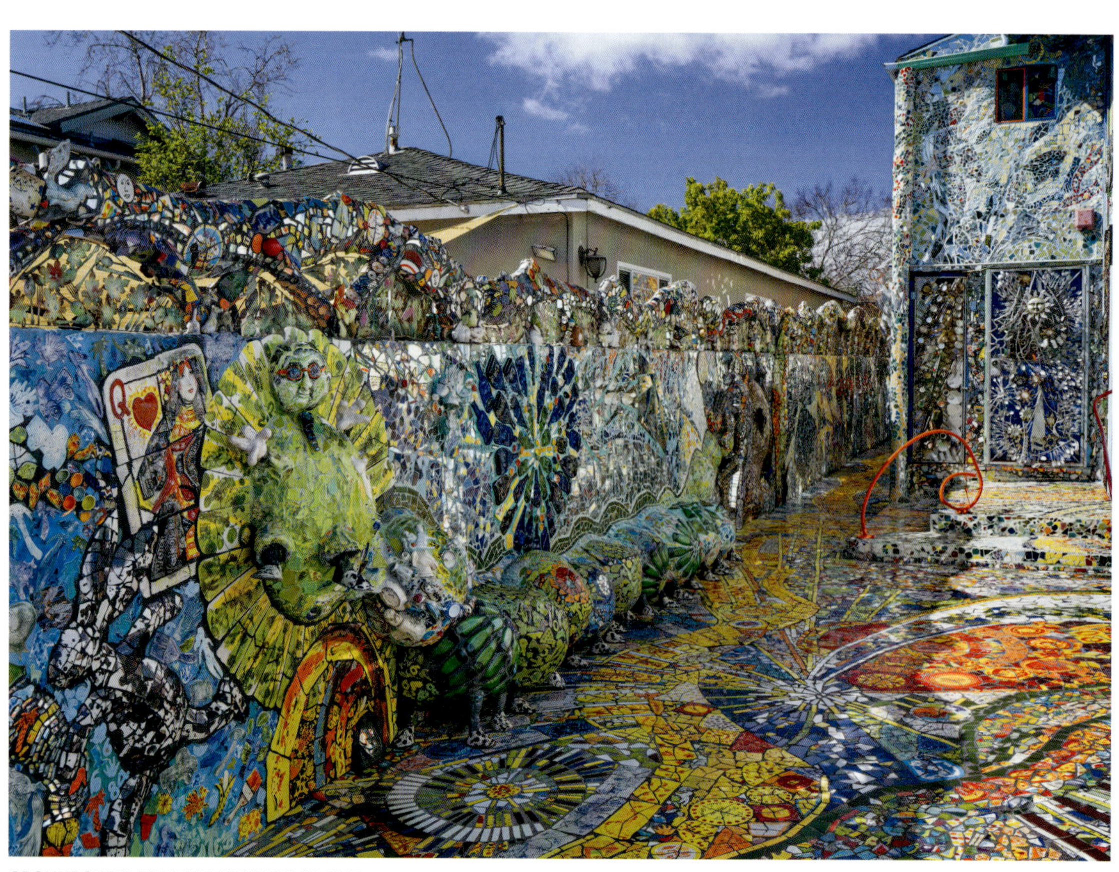

GROUNDS AND REAR FAÇADE (DETAIL), 2025

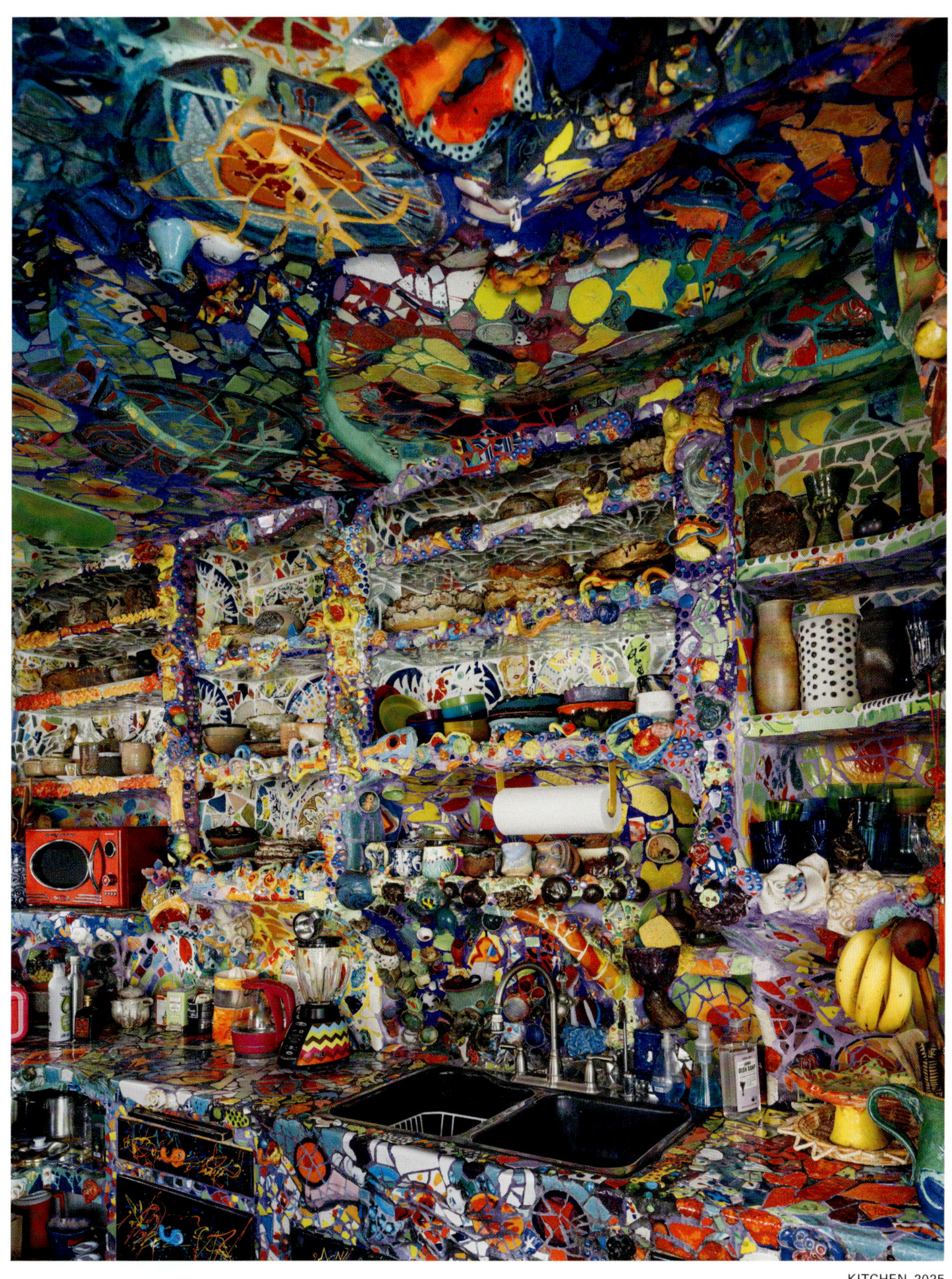

KITCHEN, 2025

GARY BREWER

DECK HOUSE

SAN AUGUSTINE, TEXAS

Towering over a busy intersection at the southeast corner of San Augustine's town square, Brewer's *Deck House* is a startling contrast to the low vernacular brick buildings of the historic commercial center. Main Street America, a nonprofit organization, has deemed San Augustine to be in need of revitalization and has accredited the town to help promote a more resilient economy and strengthen community resources. Enthusiastically welcomed by locals, the Main Street America connection has also contributed to the frustration of those community members who feel Brewer's novel architecture undercuts the ability to resuscitate this declining logging/timber town of less than 2,000 inhabitants.

Brewer (b. 1959) was born about 50 miles southwest in Lufkin, Texas, the third of five children. His father, a draftsman for the telephone company, and his homemaker mother divorced when Brewer was about eight, and afterward he moved with his mother and siblings to San Augustine, where her parents lived. He spent his childhood there, attending the local elementary school, and then bounced between high schools as he moved between his parents. After a couple of years of nine-to-five jobs following graduation, he was hired as a "connector," hanging monumental steel beams and girders that formed the infrastructure of large-scale architectural projects. He worked statewide and often out of town, enjoying the job immensely: he had loved to climb trees as a youth, and he retained a love for high places. He recalled these years as some of the best of his life.

After he married and had a son, he gave up this career and turned to carpentry so he could work closer to home (there were no multistory buildings in San Augustine, nor were any planned for the future). But his partiality to high places did not abate. After his marriage ended, he purchased an inexpensive, rundown home on that downtown intersection, and while he initially targeted the front room for repairs and renovation, he quickly tired of that work and almost immediately turned his attention to building an exterior deck that he fit over and around the original gabled roof of the 1935 home. Enlarging a rear porch (where he would soon install a hot tub), the broad deck provided him some distance from San Augustine's daily life while helping to satiate his passion for high places. But it was not high enough.

Brewer added a second deck 20 feet above the first, but then, after he erected a 20-foot-high 4 x 6" post above a 35-foot-high third deck in preparation for increasing its height even further, the city stepped in, spurred by neighbors' complaints. Some petitioned the fire marshal to declare it too potentially combustible, while others referred to the Main Street project and the visual conventions of the historic downtown to demand its removal. But there were no regulations regarding style or aesthetics on the city's books, nor was there an ordinance restricting height, as one had never before been needed.

Playing catch-up, in December 2019 the city council voted to limit buildings to 35 feet, although variances might be granted after evaluation by a licensed structural engineer and subsequent approval by the city council. Brewer quickly hand-sketched a "blueprint" of his construction and submitted it to a state-registered structural engineer in Lufkin, who approved it with the caveat that the proposed top level be further supported with additional beams, studs, and cross braces. Brewer agreed, and soon, with council approval and payment of a $20 permit fee, he began working on the fourth and final deck, which—given the additional contract work he had as an "essential worker" during the Covid pandemic—took him three more years to complete. Even after it reached its 52- to 57-foot height (the differential resulting from the property's slope), he was not quite done: the council's height ordinance had exempted "uninhabitable" elements (e.g., structural supports for flagpoles), and within about six months he had erected a "crow's nest" 20 feet above the fourth deck, accessible only by climbing up the bearing post and squeezing through a hinged hatch. (He did briefly install a flag there, but later moved it to the front of the highest deck.)

While continuing to avoid most house renovations, Brewer remains enthusiastic about enhancing the decks: he plans to add a cover above the highest deck as protection from the elements, to move a wooden throne he constructed in the same style as his home up from its current placement on the third level, and to add a second hot tub near the fire pit. He also knows he needs to repair the deck floors and some of the older suspended adornments, particularly on the first and second levels, because he fabricated everything out of pine, which is highly susceptible to weathering and decay. (Although cedar is available locally, it is

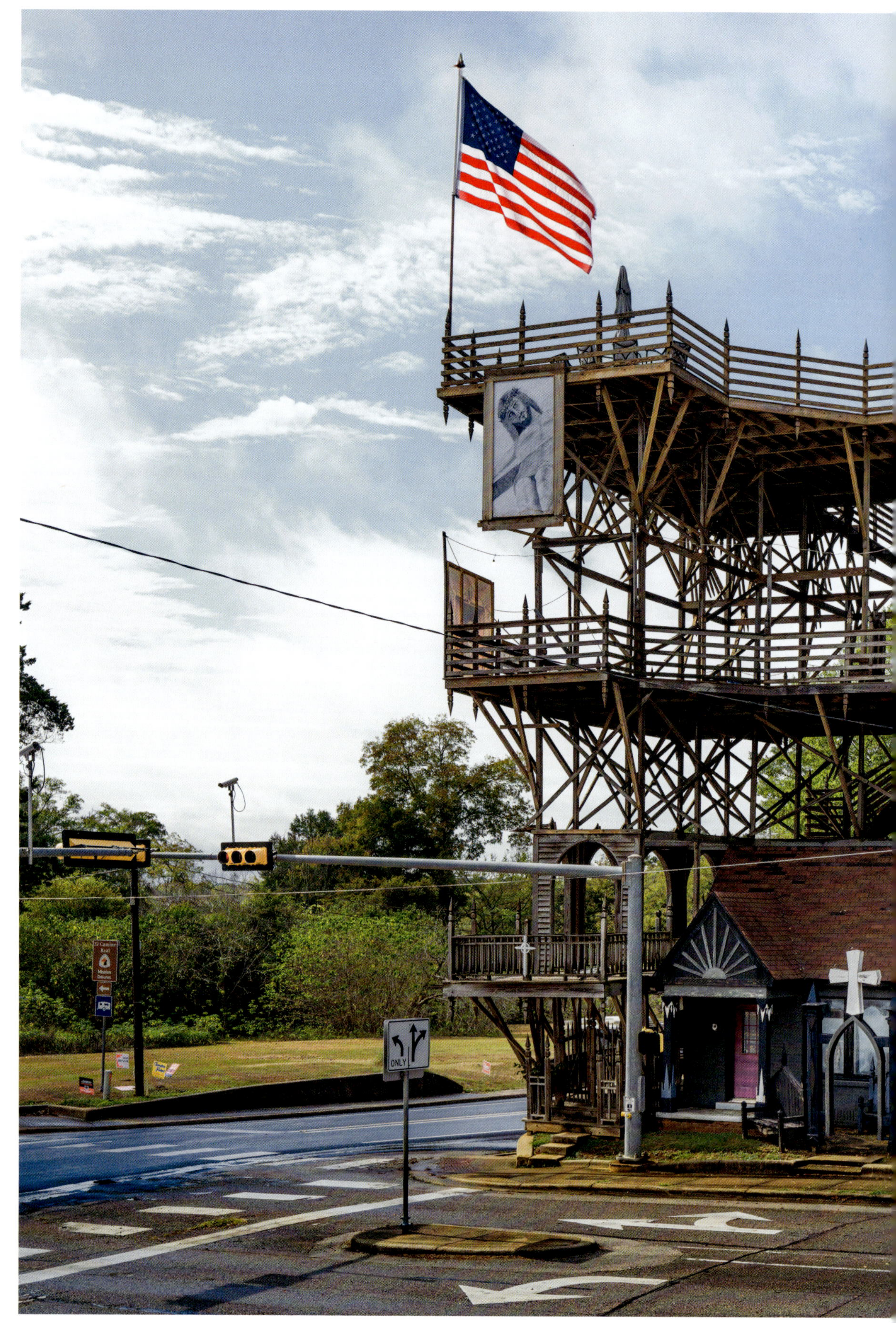

FRONT VIEW (EAST FAÇADE) OF DECKS OVER ORIGINAL HOUSE WITH BREWER ON THE CROW'S NEST, 2024

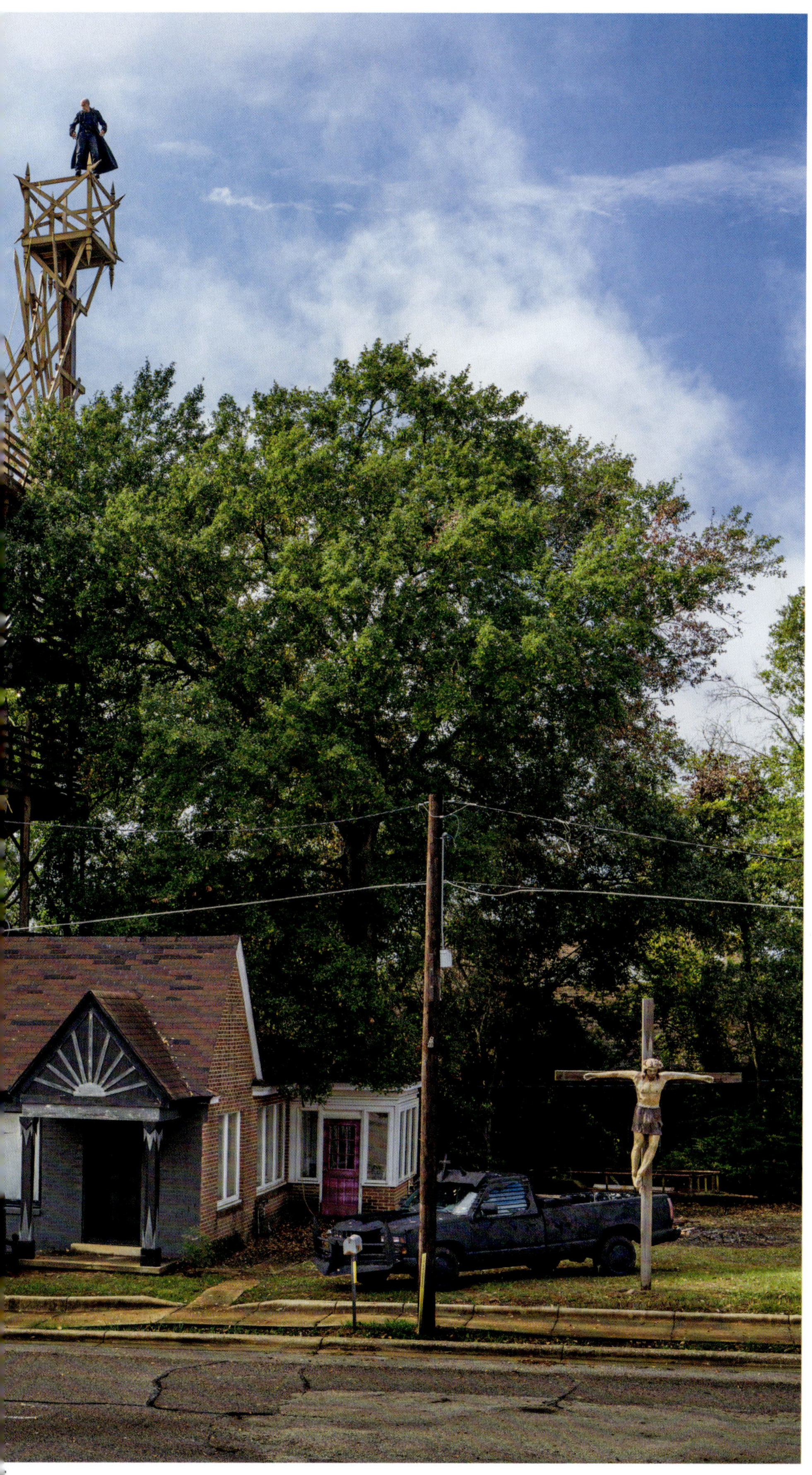

BREWER IN THE CROW'S NEST ABOVE THE HIGHEST DECK LEVEL, 2024

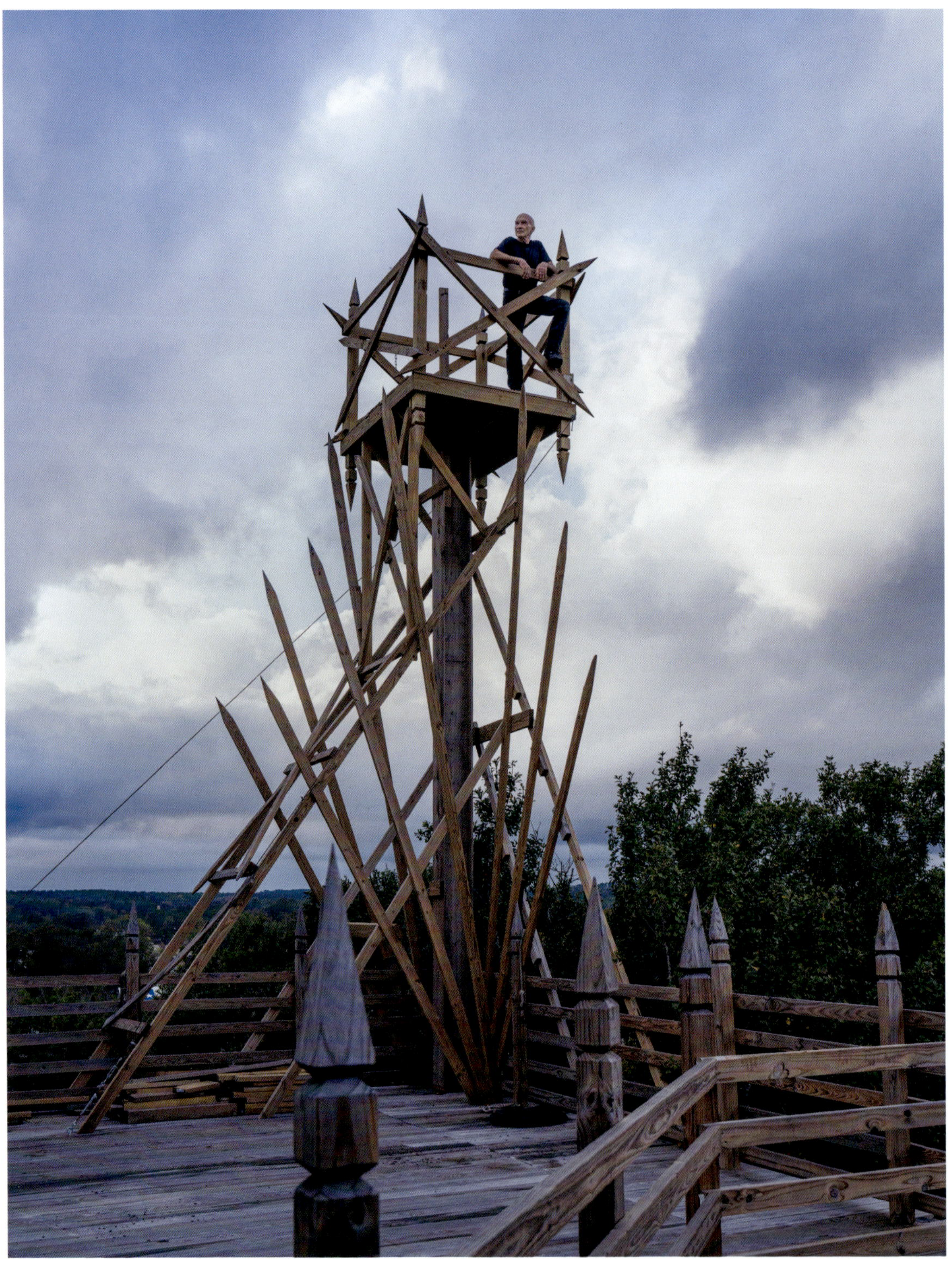

too expensive to be affordable, particularly considering the enormous square footage of the decks and embellishments.)

Brewer's neighbors are concerned not only by the height and monumental impact of the decks, but also by their decoration. The entrance to the first deck is "protected" with piercing spikes hanging from the upper level and by sharp points that terminate each picket. Further, elaborate "projectiles" are installed horizontally at the center top juncture of the four low-Gothic arches that shield the north side, each protruding roughly three feet as if to warn off an attack (or perhaps, he suggests, to deter dragons from alighting on the deck), emphasizing his notion that the building needed fortification in order to potentially withstand an enemy siege.

A high cross, painted white and with similar spiky finials, also ornaments the second level, as does a sculpture of a black panther ready to pounce; other images adorning the deck skirting include advertisements for his Tai Chi classes and carpentry business, as well as a scrawled red sign that reads "I SEE CROSSES," an allusion to *The Sixth Sense* film in which the young protagonist says "I see dead bodies." (Brewer has erected several additional white crosses with barbed finials around town: he notes potential locations and asks the property owners for permission to install them. To date he has not received paid commissions for the crosses, although he is very sought after for his general carpentry business.)

In 2022 Brewer was approached by the owner of a defunct auto parts shop located just south of the *Deck House*, who offered to let him occupy the space if he would maintain it and pay the back taxes and utilities. He used the shop full time for his business for a couple of years, as it is a much more expansive space than the small lower-level area on the north side of the *Deck House* where he and his son had previously worked. With plans to purchase the building, he replaced the shop's original façade with elaborate carvings and bas-relief onlaid motifs, and began to ornament it with columns, spikes, crosses, and even two carved wooden gargoyles. What he identifies as sixteenth-century architecture appeals to him, and he was inspired to decorate this building by online images of castles and, in particular, the portcullis—the slatted vertical closing gates of medieval fortifications. While he ultimately decided against acquiring the property, his modifications will find—or have already found—new locations either on the *Deck House* (where he plans to transfer the balcony and gargoyles) or at a new home he is building in the country (among other components, he is planning to make this the new setting for the massive front doors and Gothic arch-shaped shutters).

While architectural constructions and modifications are Brewer's focus, he has also become rather adept at large-scale graphite drawings, a skill he neglected until after his divorce. He prefers close-cropped faces and busts, mostly images of Christ, self-portraits, and anonymous figures. Hanging from the fourth level on the eastern façade of the *Deck House*, for example, as well as at street level on the north, are good examples of his graphics. On the east is a seven-foot drawing of Christ wearing the crown of thorns, while on the north is a tightly cropped self-portrait of Brewer's face and a bust of *Seventh Jesus*—his seventh portrait of Christ—again wearing the crown of thorns.

The theatricality and semi-aggressive quality of Brewer's work is mirrored in his projected public persona. While he counts "everybody" in town as his friend—and everybody does seem to describe him as amiable, willing to help, and a generally nice guy—those who do not know him personally may be disconcerted by his regular sorties in a long black fitted "Neo" trench coat, white contact lenses, and shaved head. This is not a costume, he insists, just what he wears, and he enjoys striding out forcefully, not meeting people's eyes, his face set in a determined gaze.

This persona is amplified when he drives his customized 1961 Chevy pickup, which is decorated with steel plates bolted to the hood and cutout spikes welded to the bumpers and around the windows. He has worked on the truck for some time, frequently inspired by surplus steel scraps from his commercial work. The "hubcaps" are repurposed trash-can lids, the entire exterior surface of the vehicle is covered with a heavily textured, matte-black, polymer paint for truck bedliners mixed with sawdust, and he carries two loaded semi-automatic rifles in the gunrack above the bench seat. The truck presents as a combination of a Mad Max rig and a Batmobile.

There is a seeming disconnect between Brewer's genuinely genial demeanor as a helpful neighbor, attentive tradesman, and teacher and practitioner of Tai Chi devoted to bringing his body and mind into harmony, and the rather threatening quality of much of his aesthetic. The townspeople object to the black and gray colors he painted the original house, as well as to its black archway surrounded by spiky posts, pointed finials, and projectiles. And the impression given by the rather wicked-looking fanged gargoyles—of bellicosity, torture, and even evil—clearly do little to mollify local concerns. Townspeople have implored him to repaint his house a lighter color and remove the spikes and projectiles, maintaining that they would be fine with his work "as is" if it were out in the country, but its downtown location is exasperating. But Brewer describes the pointed spikes as simple design motifs, and, as a fervent believer, he considers a focus on Christ's suffering essential to attain salvation.

Already competing with (and taller than) the restored, three-story Classical Revival County Courthouse for designation, in the popular imagination, as the most imposing structure in San Augustine, Brewer is unfazed by local criticism of the scale of his architectural explorations or of his aesthetic. He defends his work and is confident that at some future time, not only will the increasing number of out-of-town visitors and journalists appreciate his "progressive" efforts to contribute to the town's revitalization, but the locals will as well. He is spurred on by the motivational phrase "if you build it, they will come," and, in the meantime, he continues his constructions and adornments, sitting on his throne or balancing on the crow's nest 73 feet in the air, getting away from everything without leaving town.

BREWER'S FAITH AND SENSE OF THEATRICALITY COMBINE TO PROTECT AND FORTIFY HIS PASSION FOR HIGH PLACES.

CARPENTER SHOP, FRONT FAÇADE, 2024

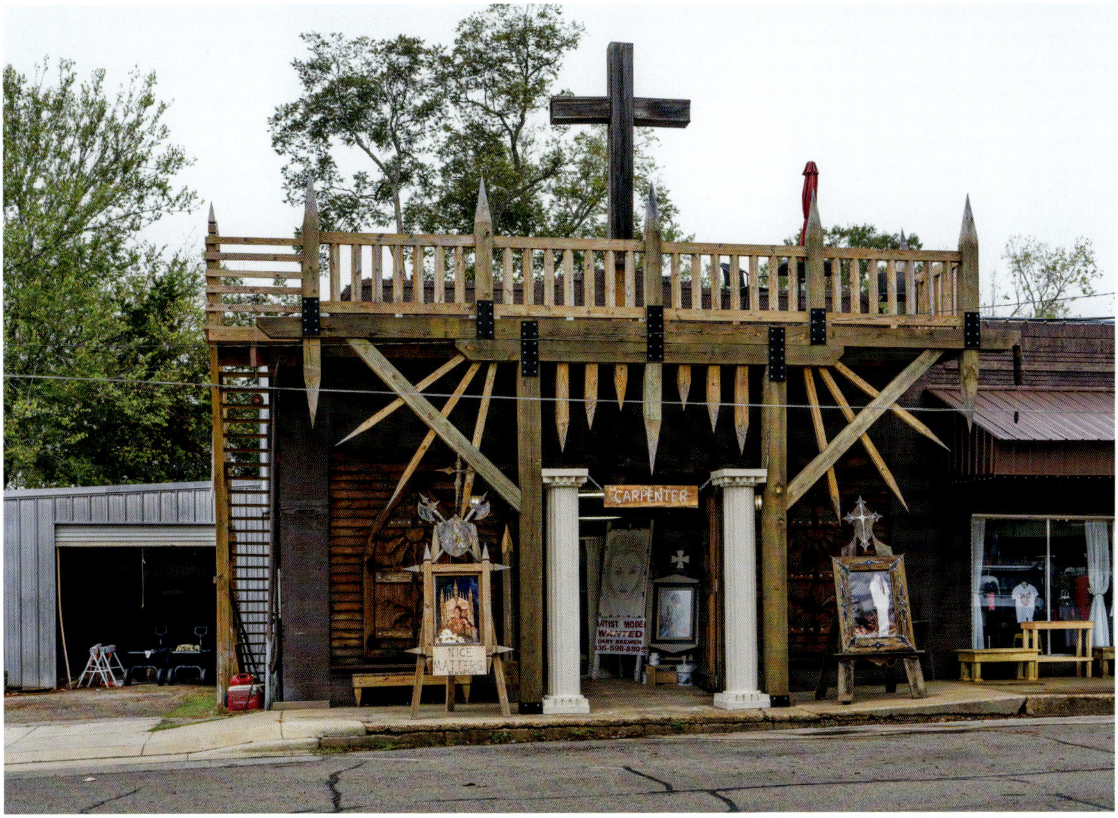

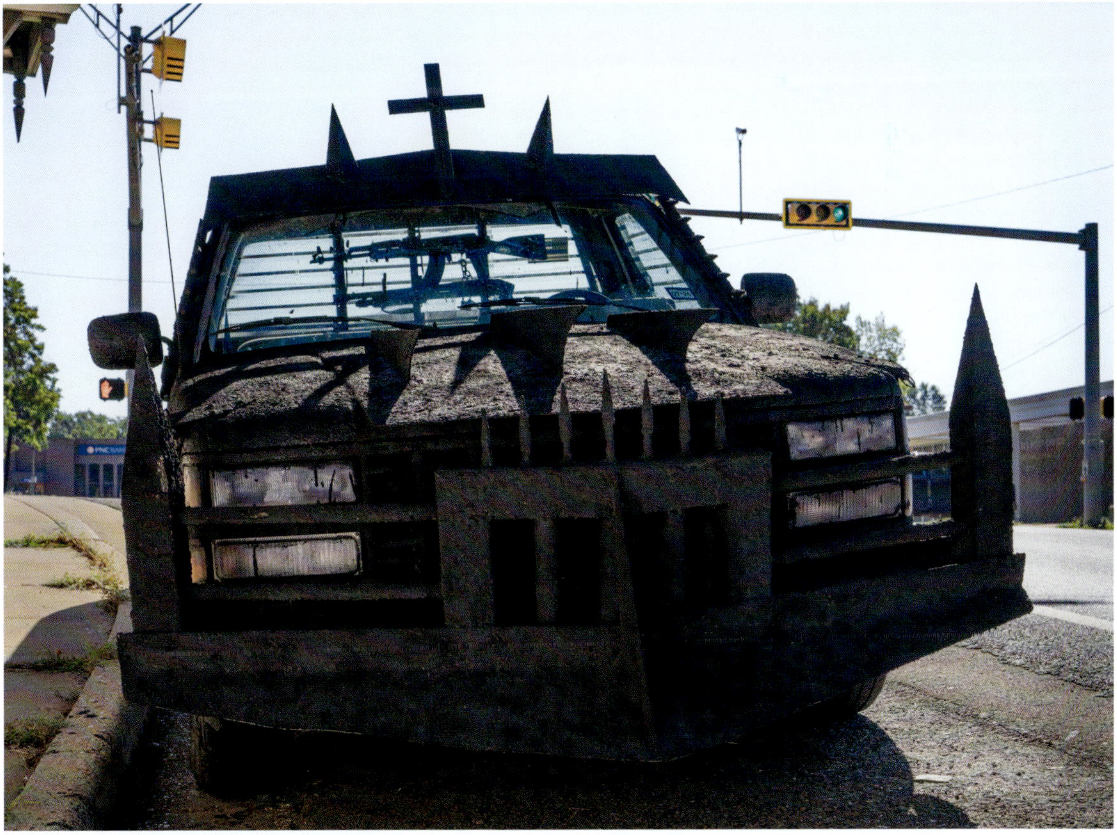

BREWER'S MODIFIED TRUCK, 2025

CLEVELAND TURNER

THE FLOWER MAN'S HOUSE

HOUSTON, TEXAS

It is common for those who fall into the depths of ill-health or addiction to vow to offer thanks with a physical creation if they recover, and to dedicate that promised work to their god. But Turner (1935–2013) chose not to impose his personal vision on others or to direct their responses to his creative expression: rather, he gathered found objects, assembled them, and then left it to his visitors to understand and interpret what he had done. His spiritual commitment did not include conventional religious symbols, perhaps because his overriding objective was to brighten his neighborhood and to bring a smile to faces.

Turner was one of 10 children of a Vicksburg, Mississippi, family; his mother descended from Cajun stock and his father's family had been enslaved people and Sauk Indians. When his mother died when he was only three years old, Cleveland's father remarried, and the family moved to Brandon, Mississippi. With his father working as a Pullman Porter and often away from home, his stepmother raised the brood. After his father was killed in a train collision when Cleveland was 11, a 40-acre parcel and a regular stipend to support the children was provided by the company.

He quit school after second grade, taking advantage of the daytime hours to pick rabbit tobacco and roll cigarettes that he then surreptitiously sold to his classmates as they left school each day. He took other odd jobs and worked on the family farm, learning how to plant and manage crops, and also engaged in semi-legal transactions on the side. Although he earned enough money to buy a car, stringent Jim Crow laws prohibited him from even driving it down Brandon's main street. By 1962 he decided he had had enough, and he planned to travel by bus to California to take a job arranged by one of his relatives. He made it as far as Houston, where he met a friend and spent all his money—even cashing in his bus ticket—to buy alcohol instead.

Stuck in Texas, he continued to drink ever more heavily, losing his apartment and his employment and winding up homeless for around 17 years, surviving thanks to occasional odd jobs that he supplemented by selling recycled bottles and cans for pennies. After one binge left him passed out facedown and near death in the gutter, a motorist called an ambulance and he spent several weeks in the hospital, so far gone that he did not remember his name.

But it was during this stay that he had a vision of a beautiful construction made from junk that rose up to the heavens. Then and there he promised God that if he could stay sober, he would realize this vision.

The hospital staff worked to help him, letting him trade his labor at the hospital for room and board. And then they took him out to the motorist's home so he could thank her; she was so shocked, having thought he was dead, that she offered him a gardening job. Soon several of her neighbors offered him jobs as well, and given his arrangement with the hospital, he was able to save every penny: he was adamant that either he would die with a jar full of money or he would die owning his own home.

The route to this vision was not linear. He rented one house on Sauer Street and began to ornament it with a profusion of plants, flowers, and castoffs, but in the fall of 1988 a pyromaniac neighbor set it on fire. Furious at the devastation, Turner destroyed what remained—toys, dolls, rocks, decorations, tools, and all of his colorful plantings. The Orange Show Foundation staff then helped him find another place on Sampson Street, in Houston's Third Ward, and they worked with him to haul what was salvageable from the Sauer Street home and plant another yard full of flowers. Around this time he also returned to the family farm in Mississippi and brought back some mementos, tools, and animal skulls to complement the materials he had found locally, assembling some and mounting others on the house and all over the yard. The ornamentation was constantly changing, and he knew that he would never be done, because his vision also continued to evolve.

But he ran into trouble on Sampson Street, too. In spring 2000 he was cited by the city's public works department because his voluminous plants and assemblages were encroaching on the sidewalk and street on both sides of the corner lot. These rules sprang from the 1993 Community Urban Rehabilitation and Building (CURB) ordinances that had been intended and used in large part to maintain middle-class standards and values—if not racial divisions. Neighbors and members of the art community rallied to fight the citation, however, and after protracted legal proceedings and a promise that he would henceforth keep his plants and assemblages from blocking public access, Turner and his backers ultimately prevailed.

OVERVIEW OF SAMPSON STREET HOUSE, CA. 1990. PHOTO: LARRY HARRIS

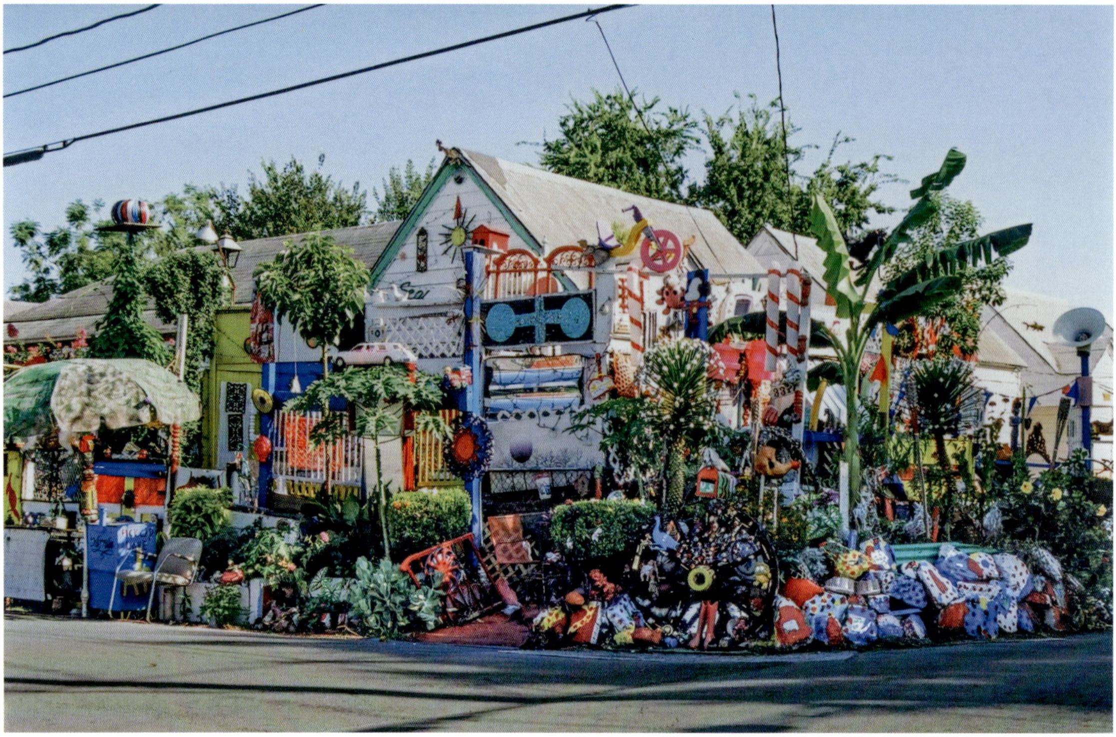

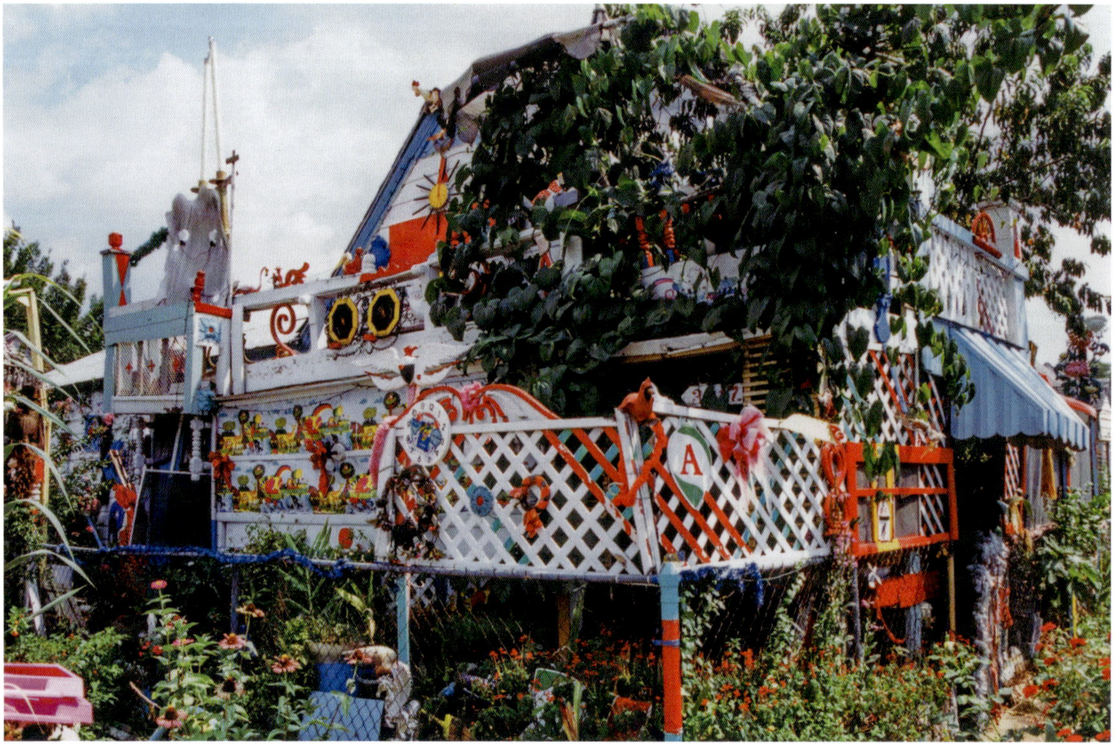

SAMPSON STREET HOUSE (DETAIL), CA. 1990. PHOTO: LARRY HARRIS

Turner's interventions on his rental house had, to a large degree, inspired Project Row Houses, a community organization, to purchase and renovate tax-delinquent houses in Houston's Third Ward area; they anointed him "artist-in-residence," and he decorated at least one additional house for them. But he was still holding on to the dream of owning his own home, and in 2003 he took all of his savings to split the purchase cost of one of Project Row House's properties on Francis Street. He had not understood that they would maintain title so that they would be able to pay his taxes and ensure that municipal codes would be enforced. Frustrated and disillusioned when he found his name was not on the deed, it took much further negotiation for that change to be made and trust to be reestablished.

In the end, Turner, who called himself the Flower Man, was able to recover his energy and begin again to ornament his new Francis Street home with an ever-changing palette of dolls, stuffed animals, pinwheels, Christmas lights, building supplies, and buckets of plastic flowers, all set off by flower beds with colorful blooms, herbs, and shrubs. He painted this house bright yellow and continued his practice of collecting and assembling found objects and flowers that he installed indoors and out. He also constructed a high perimeter fence out of plywood, which he painted with a bright palette and used as a substructure for hanging additional works. This fence ensured him greater privacy and let him retreat somewhat from the exposed setting of the previously decorated homes. Rather than have the foregrounded installations serve as lower-level terraces as they had at the Sampson Street house, Turner's last home was practically hidden behind the ornamented fence. It simultaneously served as a public barrier that enhanced his safety and security, and as a canvas for his creative expressions.

In the five years or so prior to his death, while continuing to modify and enhance his home, Turner deferred structural maintenance, and this left it more susceptible to damage when Hurricane Ike roared through Houston in 2008. While he continued to live there, after his passing it was deemed irreparable, and the house was razed and all installations removed in early 2015.

A VISION INSPIRED HIM TO ASSEMBLE COLORFUL OBJECTS AND FLOWERS TO ORNAMENT HIS HOMES.

ISAIAH ZAGAR

PHILADELPHIA'S MAGIC GARDENS

PHILADELPHIA, PENNSYLVANIA

Although Zagar (b. 1939) received an art degree, it appears that his introduction to the genre of art environments at age 19, when he visited Clarence Schmidt's *House of Mirrors* (see page 104), carried more weight in determining his artistic trajectory than did his academic training. Two years after that visit, 1961's *Art of Assemblage* exhibition at New York's Museum of Modern Art, which included references not only to Schmidt but also to Antoni Gaudí, Sabato Rodia (see page 332), and Ferdinand Cheval, reinforced his interest in agglomerative techniques. Seeing images of this kind of work at such an august institution gave him "permission" to later pursue this art form on his own.

Returning to the United States in 1968 after spending three fulfilling years in the Peace Corps in Peru with his wife Julia (as a conscientious objector, this was an alternative to his military service), they settled in a modest, working-class neighborhood of Philadelphia, full of fixer-upper buildings and cheap rent. It was a stressful era of bitter culture wars and political assassinations, and Zagar suffered a mental health crisis and attempted suicide after ingesting some street drugs to which he reacted badly. His distress was further aggravated as he realized that his traditional landscapes and portraits were not welcomed by the mainstream art world, which at that time was deep in the throes of abstraction and hard edges.

Julia opened an international folk art gallery and the Zagars subsisted through sales and, increasingly, by buying and renovating derelict buildings. Remembering his artistic discoveries from a decade or so earlier as well as the vibrant expressions of Peru's folk artists, Zagar turned to colorful mosaic work to heal. As he mounted his mosaic assemblages on the façades of rundown structures, he, together with other local artists, was instrumental in revitalizing the area around his South Street neighborhood and transforming it into a cultural hub. By 1991, he was focusing his energies on the two vacant lots adjacent to his studio courtyard, having facilitated his access to those lots by pushing over the fence dividing the properties. He covered the façades overlooking those spaces with mosaics, adding textured walls densely layered with found objects of all kinds.

But those vacant parcels did not belong to him, and in 2004 the out-of-town owner, learning about Zagar's "improvements" some 10 years after he had begun ornamenting the spaces, threatened to evict him and demolish his artwork. The community successfully rallied to defend this project, arguing that it had come to define the neighborhood, and the Zagars were able to raise enough money to purchase the property in the name of a nonprofit organization, *Philadelphia's Magic Gardens*, established to preserve Zagar's work on that site and elsewhere in the South Street area. It now includes two indoor galleries and offers an array of community concerts, workshops, and hands-on activities, although the main attraction remains Zagar's mosaic work. *PMG* has been open to the public since 2008.

Already by 2004 he had begun to enhance the open courtyard space, adding hallways and sculptural elements, but by 2008, energized not only by the additional footage afforded by the vacant property but by expressions of community support, he began to form stairways, sculpt organically shaped partitions, scoop out below-grade tunnels, and cover labyrinthine walkways. He paid visual homage to art environment heroes such as Rodia, Robert Tatin, Father Mathias Wernerus (see page 388) and Emery Blagdon (see page 224) as his work blossomed deeper into three dimensions from its mostly bas-relief mosaic beginnings. Philosophical musings and exhortations complement geometric abstractions and representational motifs—including more than one self-portrait of the artist—with a compelling tactility.

The range of materials that make up the adornment is seemingly boundless—international folk art as well as post-industrial remnants, "treasures" rescued from empty factories and vacant lots, commercial tiles as well as those hand-painted by Zagar (glazed and fired in his on-site kiln), bicycle wheels, cast-concrete garden ornaments, ceramic dishes, mirrors and other reflective surfaces, and a wide range of other found objects. While the majority of the fragments are attached in an improvisational manner, some of the larger motifs, such as human figures or faces, are first painted on the background walls so that he can follow the outline as he fills in the corpus with smaller pieces.

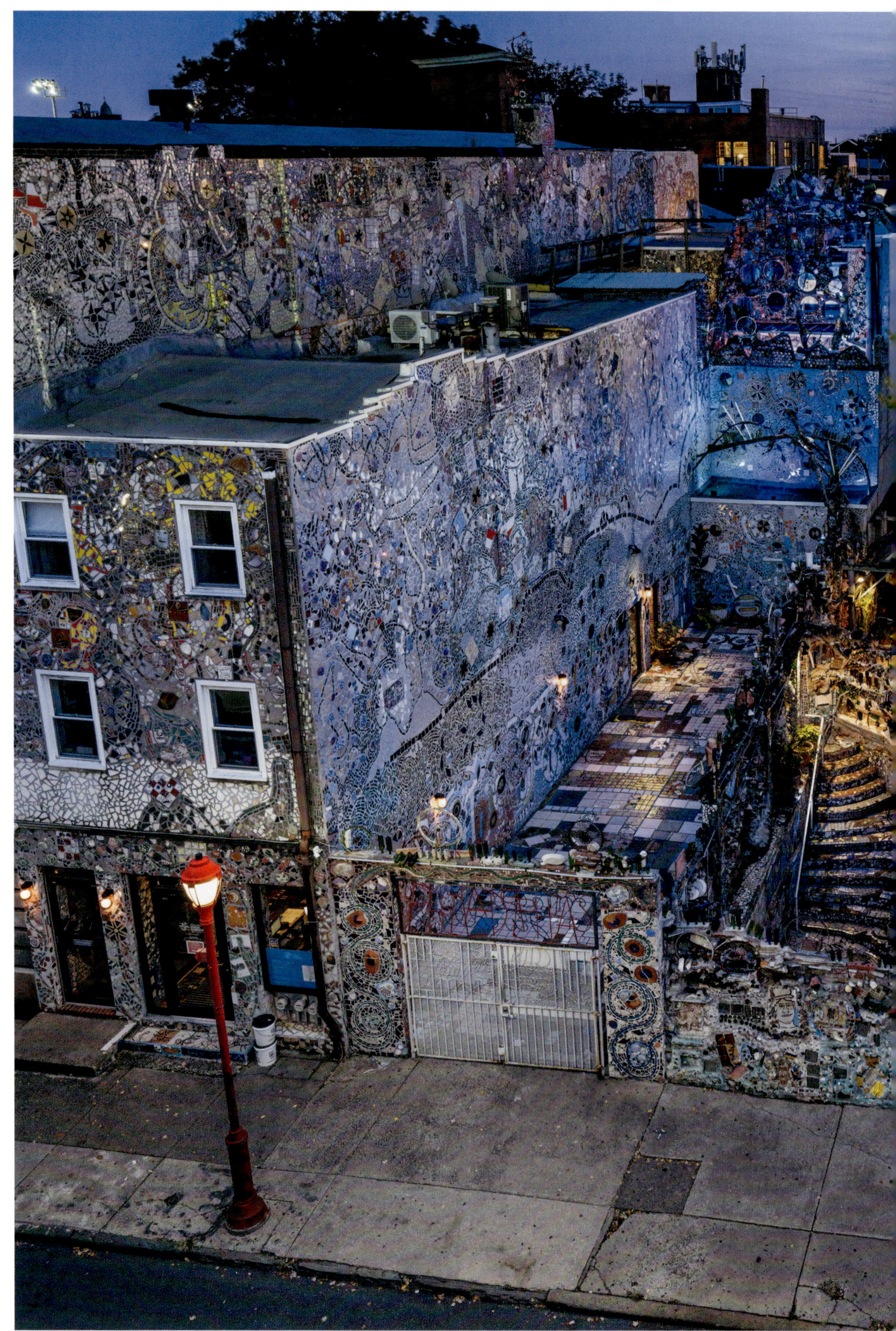

OVERVIEW, *PHILADELPHIA'S MAGIC GARDENS*, 2023

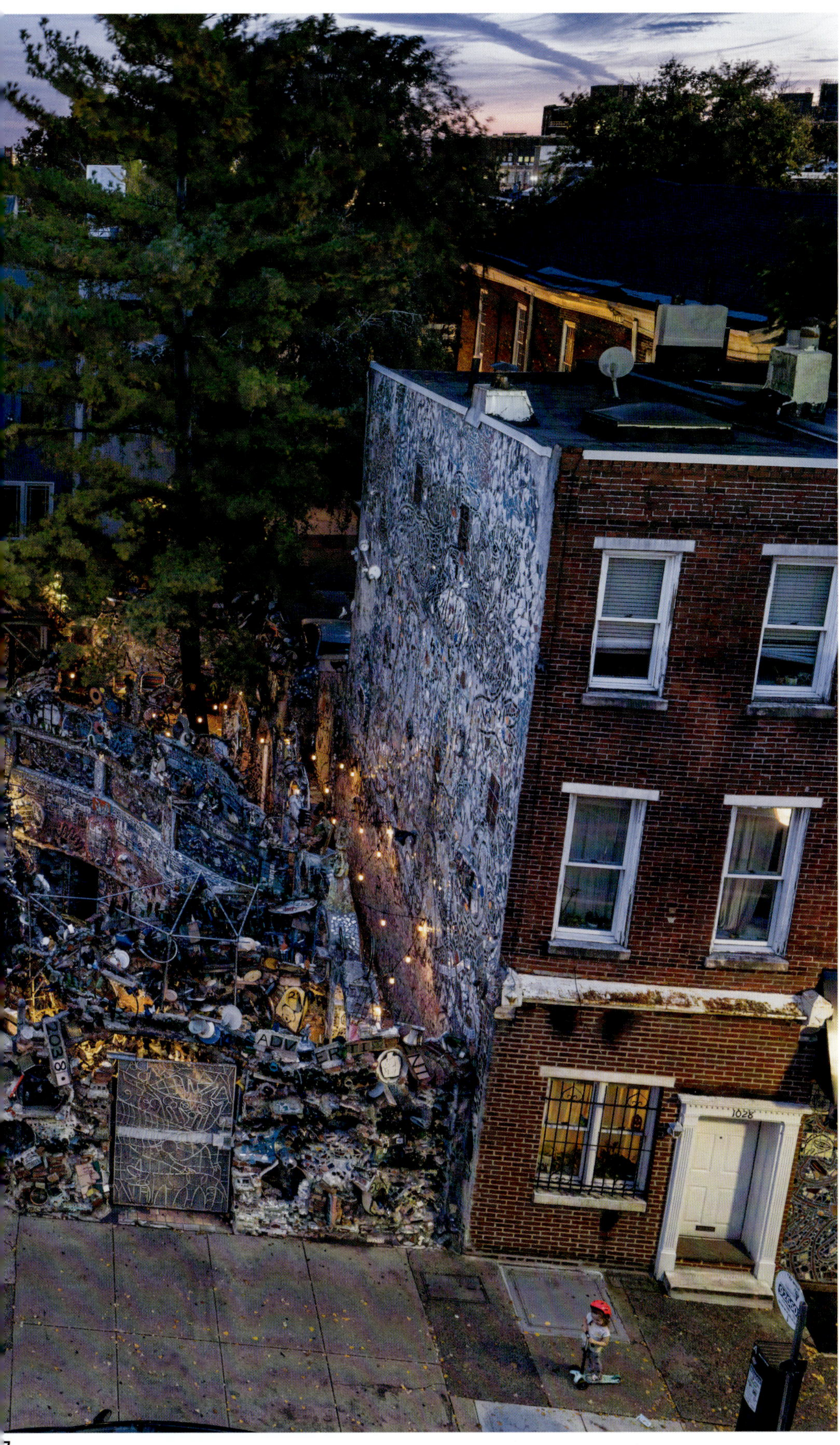
1028

INTERIOR COURTYARD, *PHILADELPHIA'S MAGIC GARDENS*, 2023

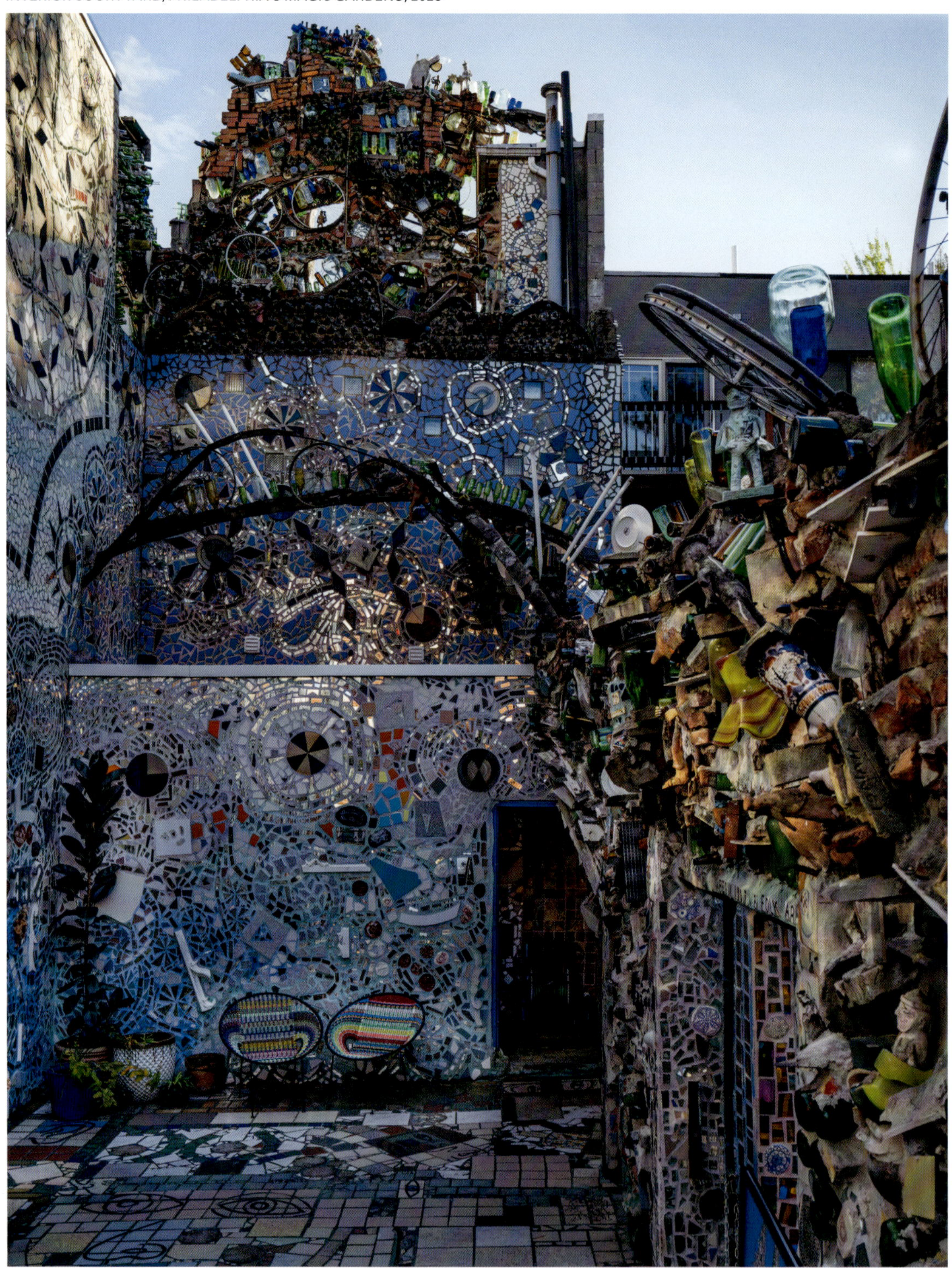

In 2022 an off-site, 7,000-square-foot mosaic known as the *Painted Bride* was destroyed after Zagar and his supporters lost a five-year battle with the new owners (some of the individual elements were able to be salvaged). And in 2023, Zagar was diagnosed with Parkinson's disease, so he is no longer able to work independently. Nevertheless, he continues to support the *PMG* nonprofit however he can, articulating the narratives that he materially realized on the walls and floors of his environment and the numerous public and private façades scattered around town that he has ornamented, donating individual pieces of his artwork and additional adorned properties to be managed and cared for on behalf of the public, and advising on archival and preservation tasks. Giddy with the almost improbable extent of his realized pieces—today his work can be seen in over 200 public murals that cover approximately 50,000 feet, created over five decades—he retains a focus on achieving wider recognition and, finally, making his mark on the broader art world.

COMBINING MOSAICS WITH FOUND OBJECTS PROMOTED HIS PERSONAL HEALING AS IT ALSO REVITALIZED HIS URBAN NEIGHBORHOOD.

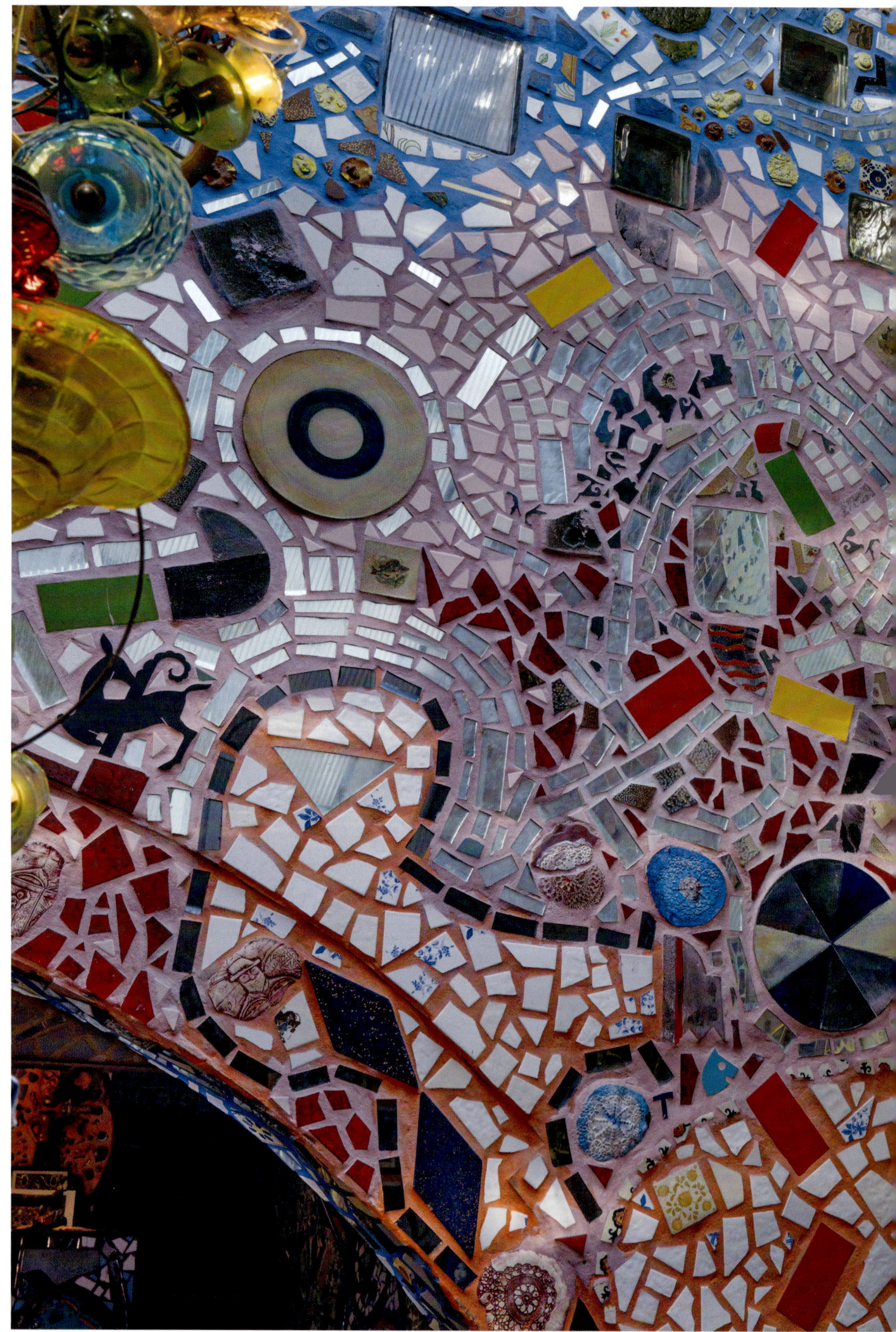

ZAGAR HOME INTERIOR DECORATION, BASEMENT LEVEL (DETAIL), 2023

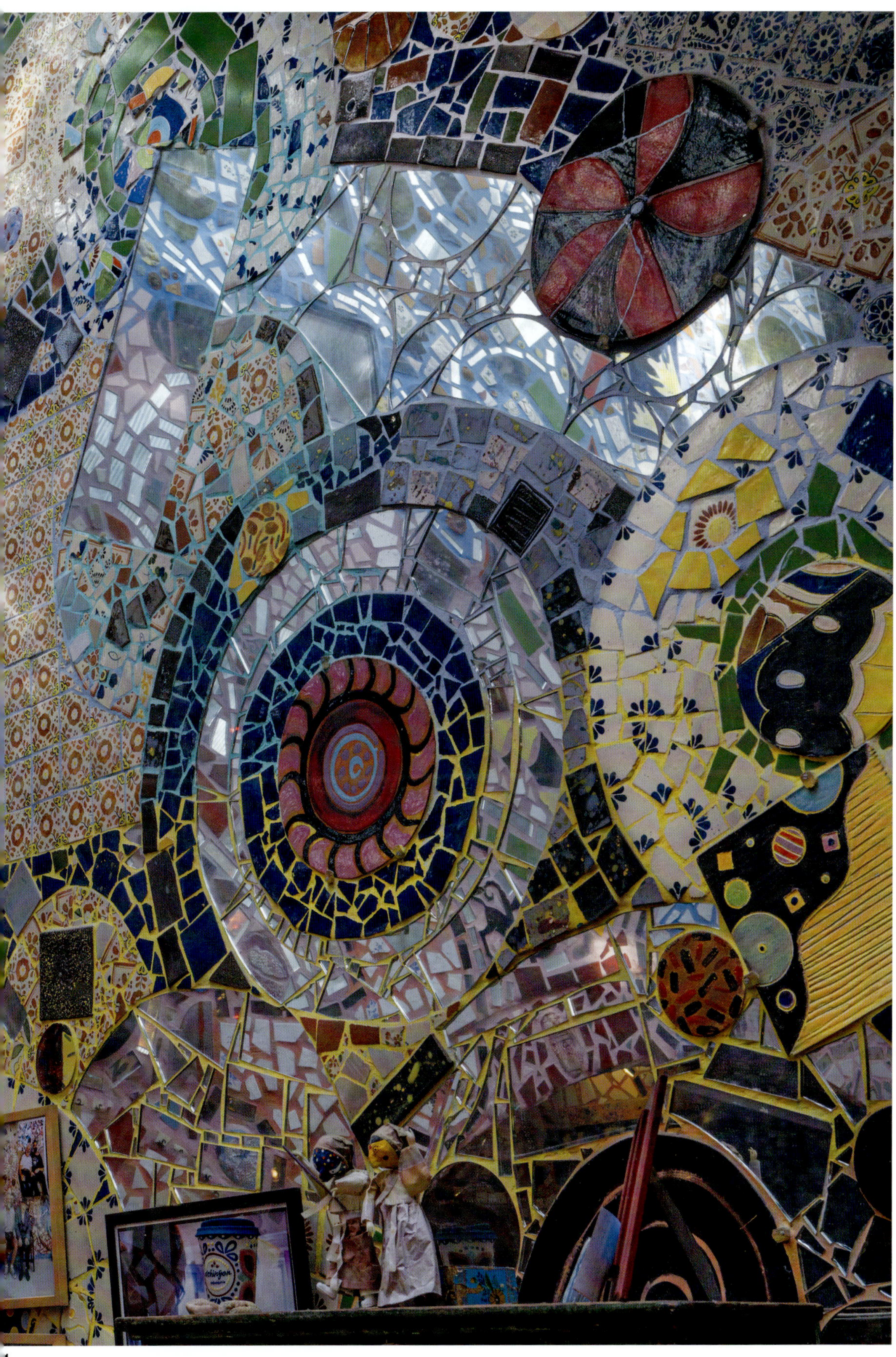

OLAYAMI DABLS

DABLS MBAD AFRICAN BEAD MUSEUM

DETROIT, MICHIGAN

Dabls (b. 1948) tells a story about how, as a young man, he would take dates to explore Detroit neighborhoods settled by different ethnic groups and how captivated he was by the ways they celebrated their cultures through their arts and traditions. Yet he found no equivalent representations in African-American neighborhoods, although African Americans constitute an overwhelming majority in the city.

Born James Lewis in Mississippi, Dabls moved north with his family in the mid-1960s, toward the end of the decades-long Great Migration of Black families from the South. He worked as a draftsman for General Motors for several years, but after injuries sustained during a car accident forced him to shift his focus, he took art therapy classes to assist with his occupational and mental healing. This inspired him to continue to explore his creativity, and he enrolled in painting classes at Wayne State University. But his studies only presented the Western canon, and he chafed at their ethnocentric emphasis. He felt this limitation even as he moved into curatorial work at what is now the Charles H. Wright Museum of African American History, an institution that, while community based and focused on American Black culture, still was structured according to the kinds of organization and interpretation common to museums in the West. So after 10 years he left to start his own museum, which would reach further back in time to link more directly to African identity, culture, and history, doing so in a way that was more profoundly anchored in oral and visual storytelling traditions. Along the way he rechristened himself Olayami Dabls to better reflect his African heritage and to throw off the colonialist legacy of his given name.

Dabls had started to collect African beads in the mid-1980s, and he began to realize that the original communities in which they were found did not consider their primary function to be adornment. Rather, the beads were used as a kind of language: how they were worn and by whom conveyed important information about the wearer. Dabls believed that the beads could be used to connect the African experience—particularly the Middle Passage but also everything growing out of that trauma—to the American experience and, specifically, to create a more profound understanding of the contemporary experience of Black Americans in Detroit.

He obtained the legal right to use the surviving buildings and open spaces of a long city block near the freeway in northwest Detroit, a blighted and mostly vacant property whose earlier derelict structures had been razed but not replaced. In 1998, he opened the *MBAD African Bead Museum* (its name an acronym built from the first names of his four children). Here he displayed and sold a wide variety of African beads as he began to ornament the exterior façade of a large gabled building at the northwestern section of the property. He conceptualized this structure as the *N'Kisi House*, channeling the traditional function of protective spirits (specifically, in this case, containers that serve as vessels for spirits) in order to aid emotional and cultural healing. At the other end of the block, he also ornamented the first level in three century-old townhouses that currently house the bead museum/shop, a gallery, his artist's studio, and his African art collection.

The once debris-filled grounds stretching between the built constructions on either end of the block provided him room to site a series of 18 evocative art installations that metaphorically communicate specific episodes linked to the contentious history of encounters between Africans and Europeans. There are no interpretive plaques here that direct visitors to accept only a singular understanding of his works. Rather, he hopes that the touchable, less-structured displays, accompanied by his compelling oral histories, will elicit personal meaning for each individual. He is optimistic that his efforts will be only the beginning, and will serve as the cultural anchor of what will become "African Town," a counterpart to the Mexican, Polish, Middle Eastern, and other ethnic neighborhoods that had fascinated him in his youth.

Dabls's media of choice for all of his constructions are iron, stone, wood, and mirrors, elements almost universally common, yet, in his hands, specifically associated with African material culture. While all components on-site are integral to his vision, the *N'Kisi House*, which displays the *African Languages Wall* on one façade, is the most architectural. It is sheathed in multiple strata of plywood boards that have been painted, inscribed, and sometimes obscured behind layers of mirrors, wire grates and fencing, wood scraps, paint cans and lids, and tools, among other found objects. In contrast

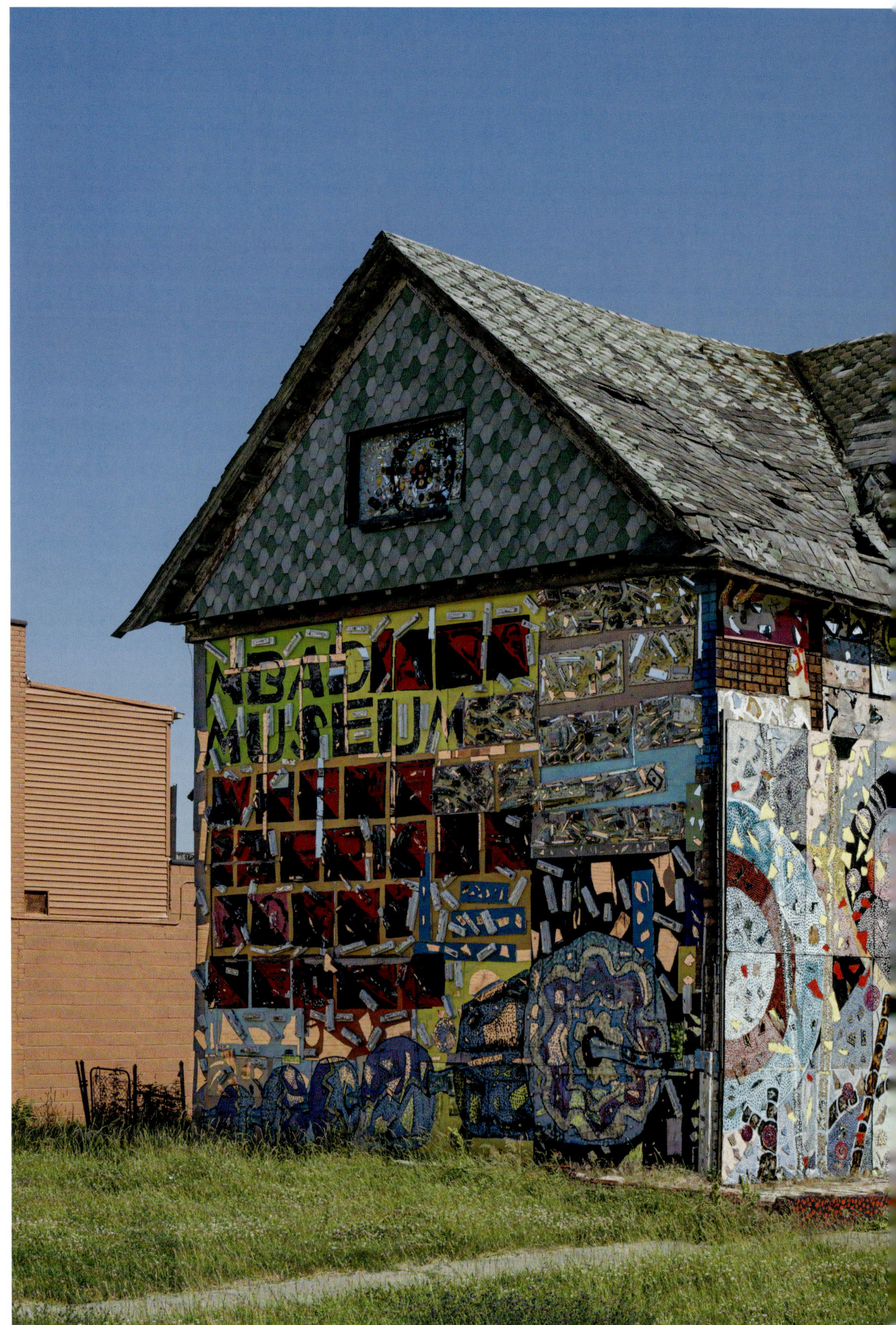

N'KISI HOUSE, 2024

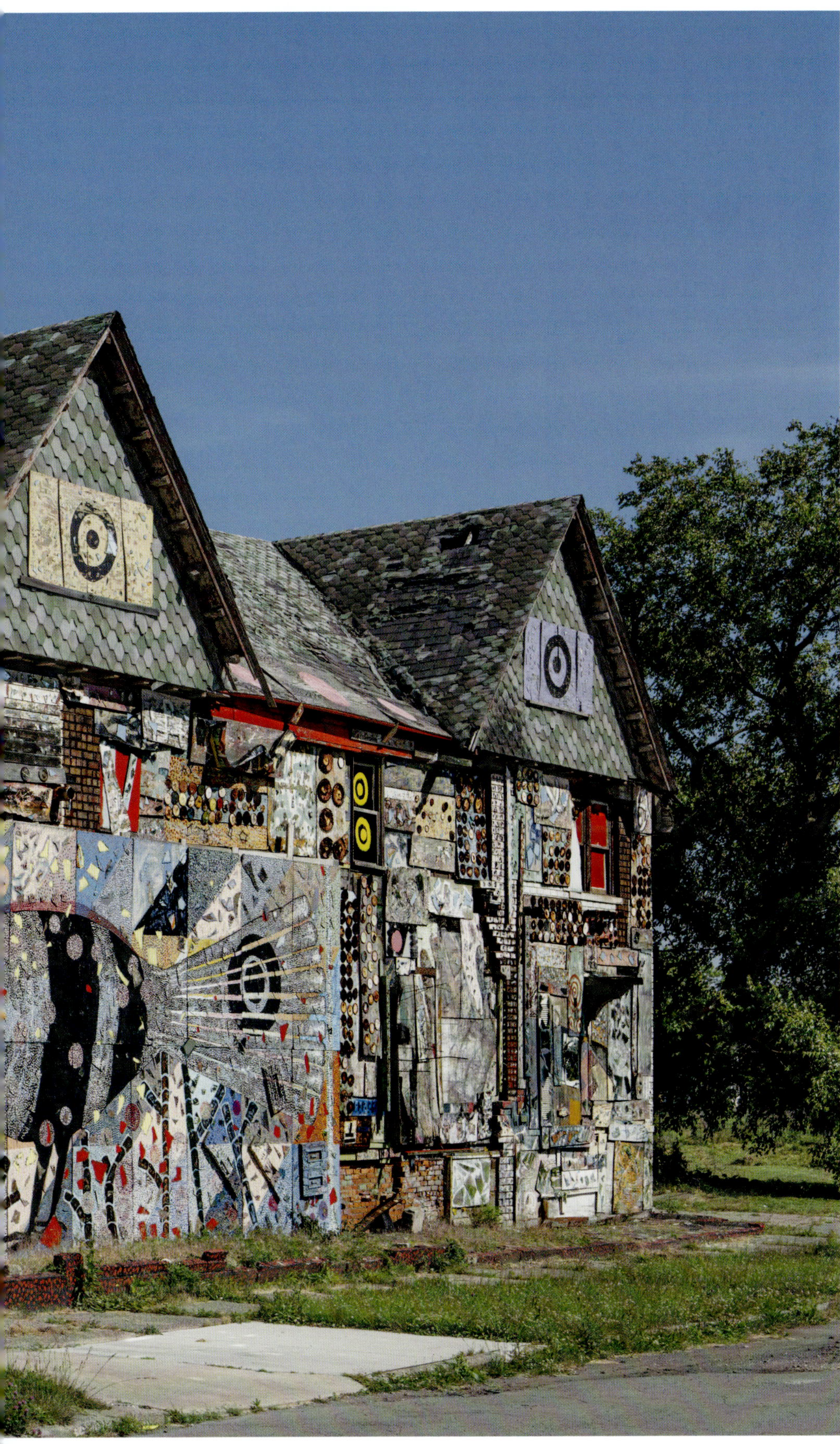

N'KISI HOUSE, FAÇADE DETAIL, 2016. PHOTO: MARISSA GAWEL, COURTESY SPACES ARCHIVES AND JOHN MICHAEL KOHLER ARTS CENTER

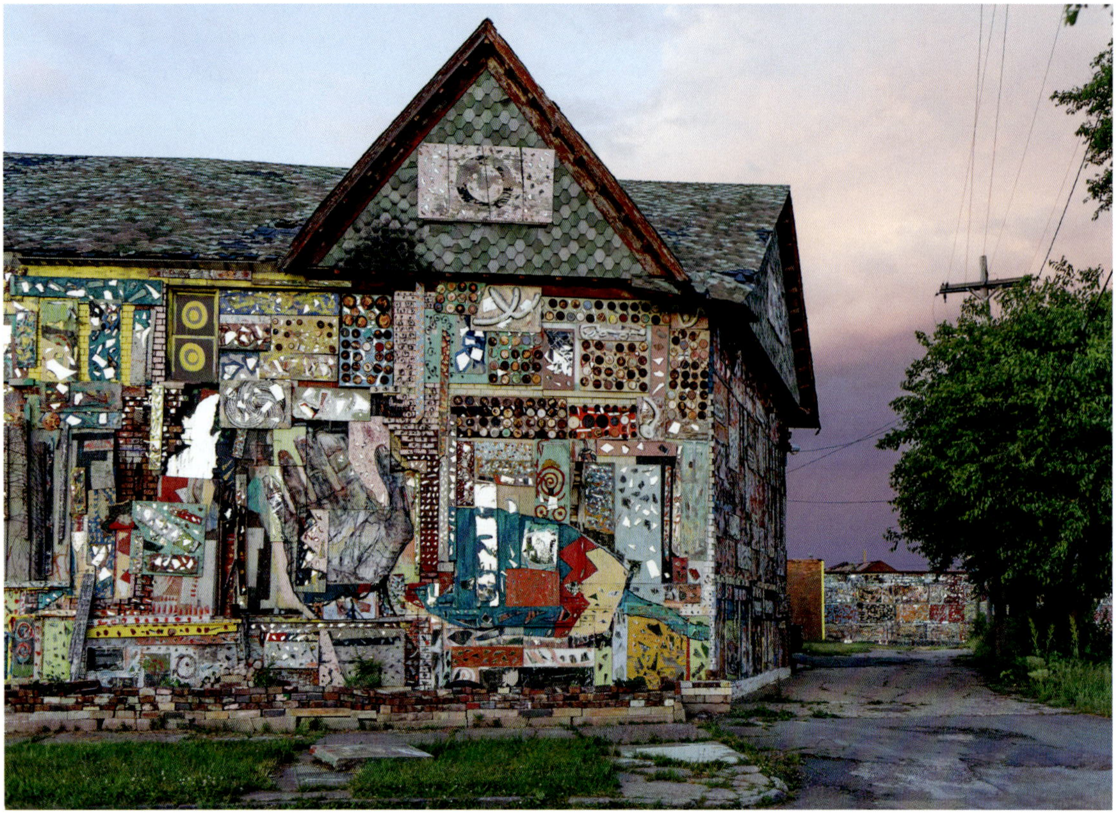

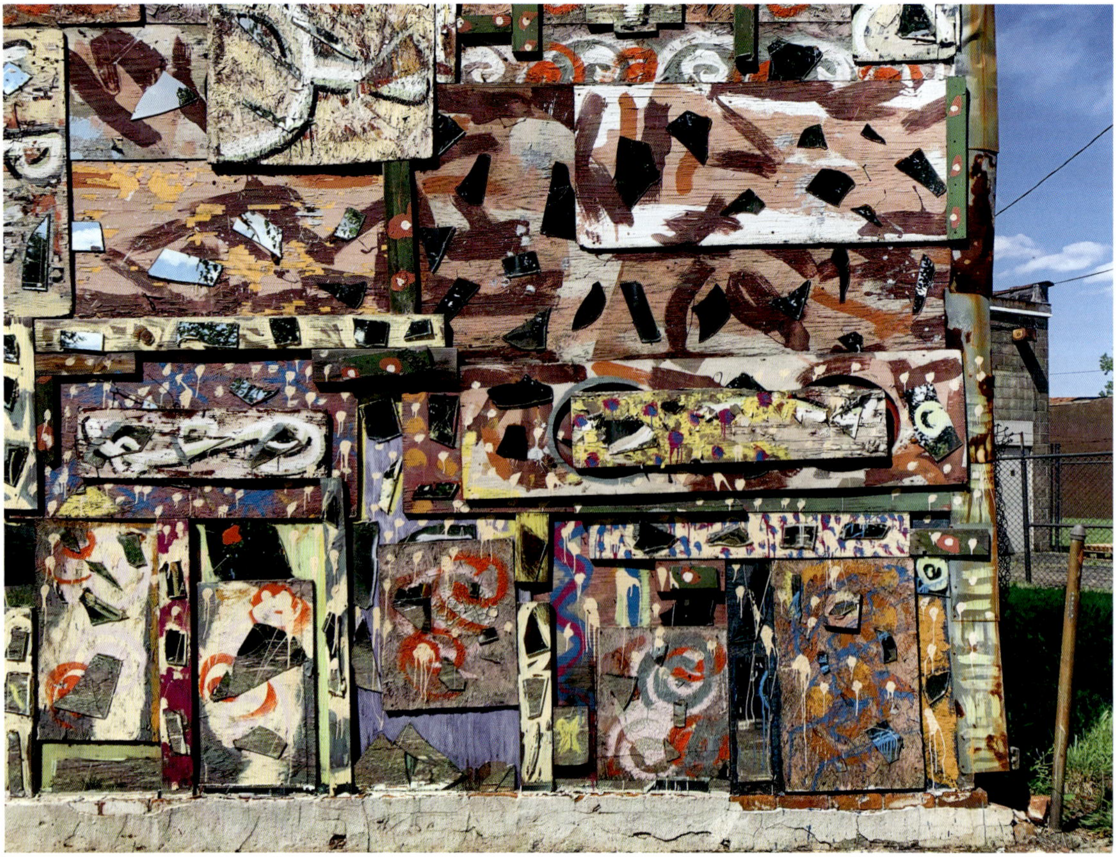

N'KISI HOUSE, FAÇADE DETAIL, 2021. PHOTO: ANNALISE FLYNN, COURTESY SPACES ARCHIVES AND JOHN MICHAEL KOHLER ARTS CENTER

to work like that of Isaiah Zagar (see page 134), where the intrigue is often hidden in tiny mosaic fragments, Dabls's is bigger, bolder, brighter, and more expressionistic. While generally abstract, notes written in calligraphy appear, as do images: of a large hand, a bird, and, of course, strings of beads.

Dabls is raising funds to renovate the townhouses and repair other sections of the property that are degrading so that the museum will be able to provide indoor programming during the winter months, educating visitors through African artifacts and his own interpretation of how they can elicit potent sensory and emotional experiences. In 2019–23 the property was enhanced thanks to a collaboration with the University of Michigan, which enabled the construction of the solar-powered *African Futurist Greenhouse*. Its form was inspired by indigenous architecture, and it has been filled with plants native to Africa that provide food, fibers for weaving or dying, and even, in some instances, seeds that are used for beads. Access to the exterior of the buildings and the sculptural installations is available 24/7.

HIS MULTIFACETED CELEBRATION OF AFRICAN IDENTITY, TRADITIONS, AND HISTORY IS INTENDED TO PROMOTE EMOTIONAL AND CULTURAL HEALING FOR DETROIT'S BLACK AMERICANS.

TYREE GUYTON

THE HEIDELBERG PROJECT

DETROIT, MICHIGAN

Detroit is a city determined to regain its earlier glories, but its notable troubles have left it with desolate reminders of the turmoil it experienced during late 1960s and subsequent decades. Swaths of blighted and scarred neighborhoods floundered for many years, and particularly those that were historically Black even lacked basic civic services. Incongruously, perhaps, the dilapidated homes interspersed between burned-out empty lots and abandoned properties offered a certain leeway for public art installations, as some artists found a freedom to create at an astonishing scale in the most unexpected of contexts. This freedom to create, however, has not been accompanied by freedom from municipal frustrations, demands, penalties, and even destruction.

Guyton (b. 1955) joined the Army as a young man to fulfill his military service, and upon his return he worked for the automotive industry, as did so many others in his East Side neighborhood. Later he left his position at Ford's River Rouge plant in order to attend university-level classes in art, but he dropped out after the administration seemingly discouraged him from continuing.

In the meantime, he was increasingly angered to see the zone around his childhood home on Heidelberg Street awash in illicit drugs, increasing violence, and systemic poverty. As families moved out, illicit drug users and squatters moved in, and Guyton watched his three brothers decline and succumb to homelessness amidst the surrounding urban decay. He felt that he himself was confronted with a choice: he could either pick up a weapon or he could pick up a paintbrush. So, in 1986, encouraged by his then-wife, Karen, and emboldened by his grandfather Sam Mackey, a house painter, they grabbed brooms and painting supplies and began to clean up the accumulated trash.

Helped by area children and motivated by his belief that art could be used to address some of the challenges of racism, the decline of inner-city neighborhoods, and the socio-economic inequities amplified by governmental policies, Guyton began to festoon existing homes with collected detritus and to paint them in bright colors and polka dots. He included existing trees, sidewalks, and even streets in what became an enormous and evolving art environment that he called *The Heidelberg Project*.

Within two years, Guyton and his friends had so transformed the neighborhood that they decided to formally incorporate *The HP* as a nonprofit organization. According to their website, their mission is to "challenge the status quo, create a community for art, and cultivate a unique gathering space for all who seek inspiration outside museum walls. [They seek to be] a catalyst for change, a platform for social justice and a cultural asset for Detroit."

Guyton continued to adorn the various built and natural elements of the neighborhood, which were modified and changed as different people became involved and new concepts were proposed. Working thoughtfully as he took cues from the unpredictable availability of reclaimed objects and the ideas of his always-changing collaborators, he mounted his found materials in three-dimensional assemblages that represented different themes on the different houses. In so doing, he revealed his shared attention to both the original function of the found objects and to their shapes and colors. The apparent whimsy of the installations was also typically code for more serious social and political concerns: the *Clock House*, painted with numerous clock faces and affixed with scrounged timepieces, enabled him to affirm that "it's time for change" or, alternatively, "the time is now" to take action in support of urban revitalization; the *Party Animal House*, covered in innumerable stuffed animals, exhorted viewers to "stop partying and get down to business." Junked cars, appliances, and shopping carts served as infrastructure for installations of smaller objects, such as shoes, vinyl records, signs, and plastic toys. He variously wedged objects together in dense configurations and arranged motifs in a more open fashion, with room to breathe.

As resources became available, the *Heidelberg Project* began to gain not only broad renown but also funding from a variety of foundations and agencies that supported the efforts to revitalize this part of the city through art. Nevertheless, the City of Detroit was a consistent detractor, and repeatedly targeted the work by issuing citations for violations of the municipal planning codes. In both 1991 and 1999 the mayors directed several of the art houses to be bulldozed.

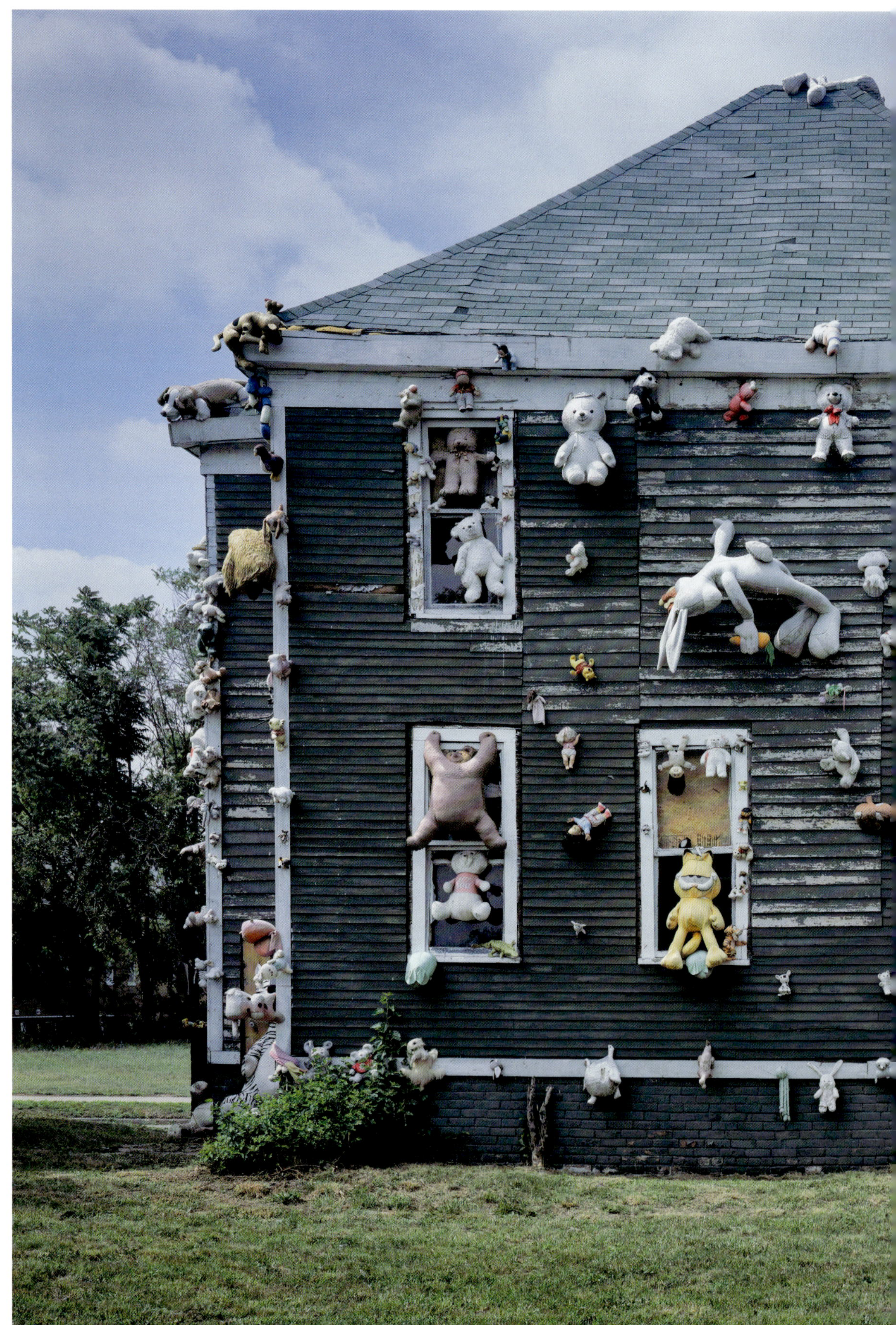

PARTY ANIMAL HOUSE, 2005

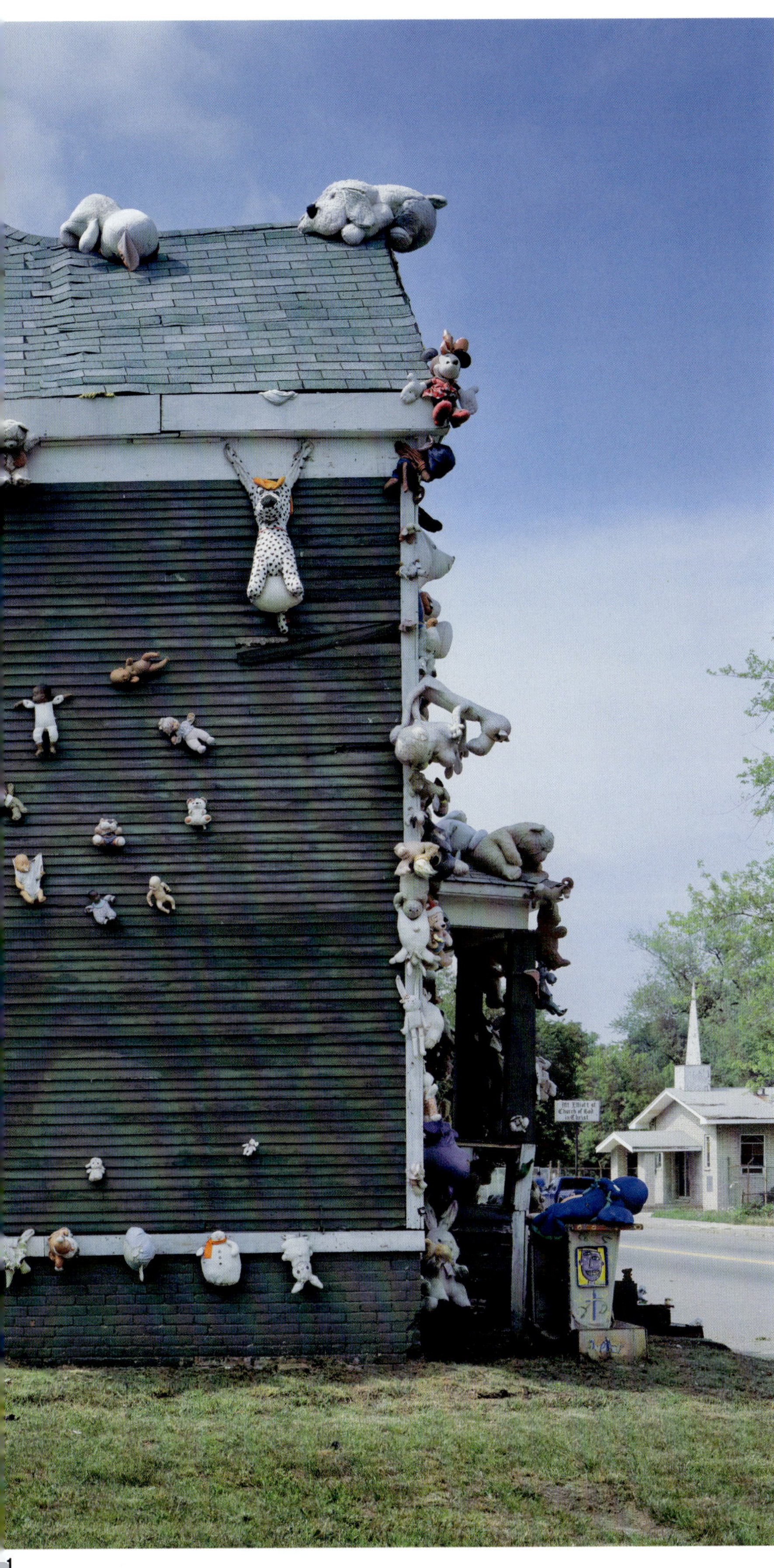
Church of God
in Christ

STUFFED ANIMAL TREE AND FRONT FAÇADE, *POLKA DOT HOUSE*, A.K.A. *DOTTY WOTTY HOUSE*, 2010. PHOTO: RON GASOWSKI, COURTESY SPACES ARCHIVES AND JOHN MICHAEL KOHLER ARTS CENTER

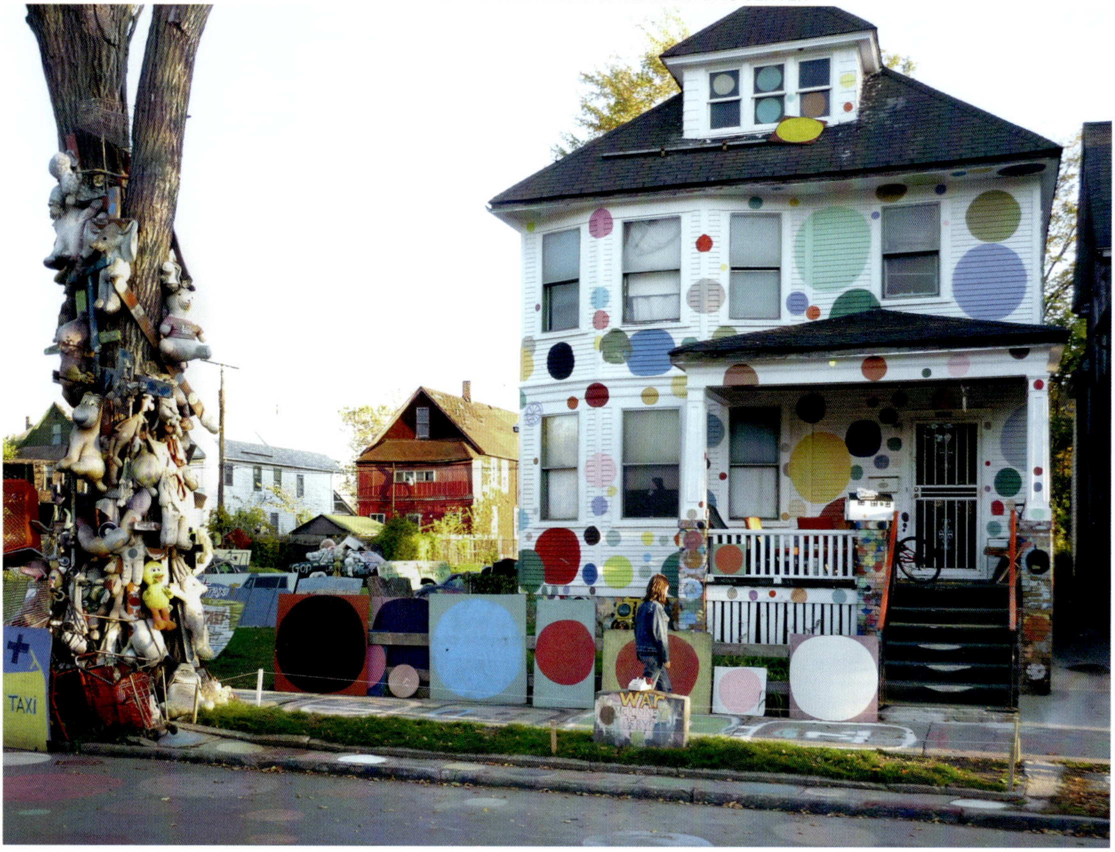

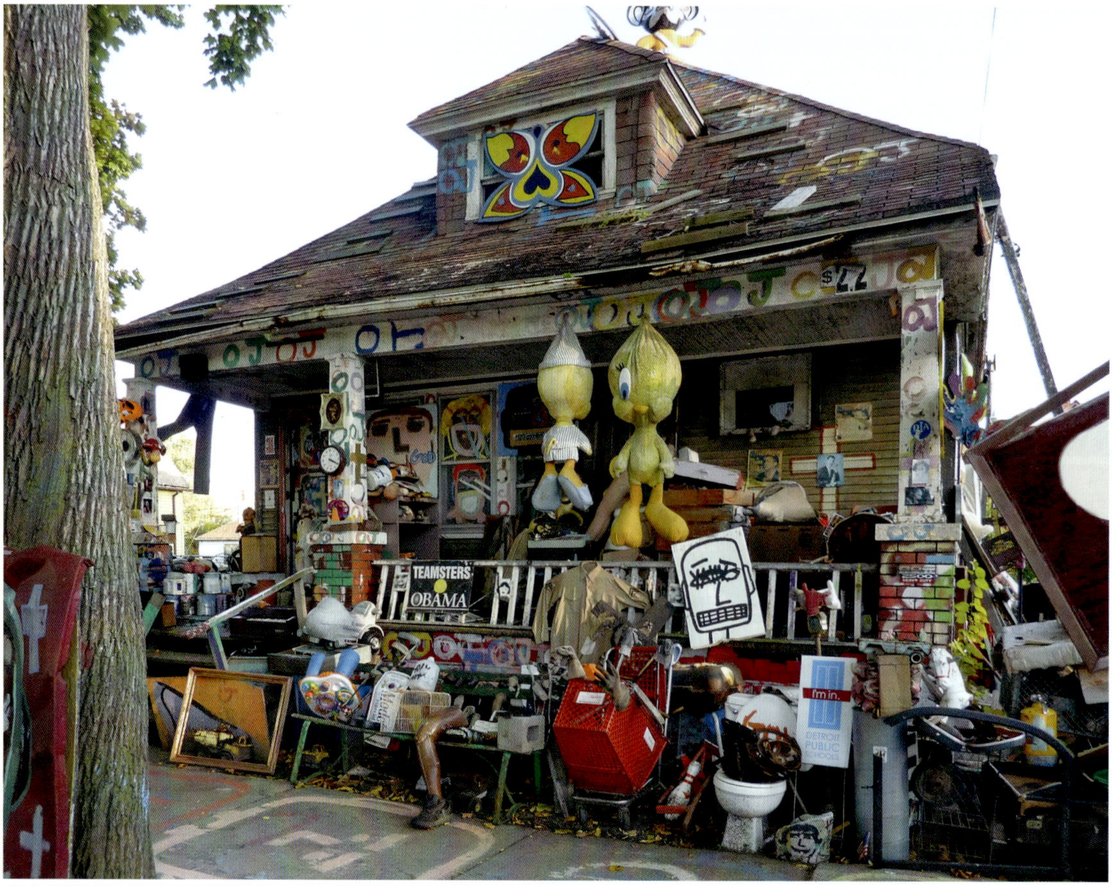

OBSTRUCTION OF JUSTICE HOUSE, 2010. PHOTO: RON GASOWSKI, COURTESY SPACES ARCHIVES AND JOHN MICHAEL KOHLER ARTS CENTER

Yet Guyton and *HP* supporters persevered, extending not only their physical reach on Heidelberg Street and in the larger McDougall-Hunt neighborhood but also through the enhanced visibility brought on by commentary about or photographs of the work in exhibitions, books, and articles. Children's programs and street festivals complemented the found-object installations and sculptures as international awards, documentary films, displays, and on-site programs in museums and schools further broadened its reach. In 2008 *The Heidelberg Project* was one of 16 alternative architectural and artistic practices that represented the United States in the Venice Architectural Biennale.

Despite the increased pride most residents felt about their neighborhood thanks to Guyton's efforts, which were accompanied by a generally diminished rate of crime (drug dealers were not inclined to stick around with so much public visitation and publicity), a dozen arson attacks in 2013–14 damaged several *HP* components. (A federal investigation was initiated, but there was no formal response from the city.) Although only two of the thirty-some original houses remain as of this writing (the *Dotty-Wotty House* and the *Numbers House*), where before the art was displayed primarily on the houses, creative work has expanded further onto the land and trees. Densely packed, the entire two-block-long installation area now functions more as an art park. Many people like it even better this way.

Plans include adding a revenue-generating gallery to their headquarters building, renovating components of the original art environment and Guyton's childhood home, and providing space for artist-in-residence programs and community activities. *The HP* has provided jobs for a modest number of community residents, generated millions of dollars annually for Detroit, and is one of the most visited cultural sites of the city. Nevertheless, the nonprofit suffered some hard times during and subsequent to the Covid pandemic, and certain programs and services had to be limited or suspended.

In contrast to their support of Dabls's projects (see page 142), Detroit has never stepped up to support Guyton's endeavor through the significant funding one might think it deserved as a result of its international fame. *The Heidelberg Project*, however, seems to no longer be under direct threat of the kind of municipal demolition it suffered in 1991 and 1999, and finally, in 2021, the city acknowledged Guyton's work with its Lifetime Achievement Award. He and his supporters have drawn on the threats against and actual damages suffered by *The Heidelberg Project* over almost 40 years to incorporate an ongoing circle of political protest, resistance, and renewal within the artwork, thus reinforcing Guyton's original social-activist intentions for the evolving art environment and his belief that it could serve to help empower his community and transform people's lives.

HIS INSTALLATIONS HELP TO ADDRESS CHALLENGES OF URBAN DECLINE, RACISM, AND INEQUITY.

LOUISE AND AZIZ FARNAM

MOSAIC HOUSE

SANTA MONICA, CALIFORNIA

Louise (b. 1956) and Aziz (b. 1948) Farnam, Iranian Jews, fled to Los Angeles after the Iranian Revolution of 1979. They moved into a standard 1930s-vintage Southern California-style bungalow of 2,500 square feet with five bedrooms and three bathrooms, where they had enough room to raise their six children. When son Ariel's school suggested that the parents take classes in mosaic work so they could produce projects for a school fundraiser, Louise went to the school to learn the basic techniques.

She was immediately enthralled by the process, and after doing some early work adorning low tables with elaborate designs—some of which took up to six months to complete—she began to ornament the exterior façade of the family's house. Landscapes, seascapes, a portrait of the family macaw, and even the famous Hollywood sign have been immortalized on the walls. They show "all of nature," she commented: motifs of apple trees, grapes, rivers, mountains, sky, birds, fish, and other elements of the natural world adorn the home's exterior. Other areas are more abstract, with geometric cuts overriding the more organic broken forms of the fragments used in the representational images. Her enthusiasm for this medium became contagious, and soon her husband, Aziz, joined her in ornamenting the façades.

The mosaic work continues around the side of the house, the retaining wall that surrounds the property, and even the back side of the garage, which faces an alleyway not easily viewable from the street. Found objects were added to wall tiles, floor tiles, and ceramic plates as the couple worked to sheathe all exterior surfaces. Louise estimated that they are covered with over 15 million tile fragments.

In contrast, the interior walls are not themselves ornamented with mosaic but, nevertheless, there is no lack of visual interest within the house. The focal point of the living room is the mirrored fireplace, composed of hundreds—if not thousands—of individually cut forms arranged floor to ceiling. Mosaic-covered table and floor lamps, tables, vases, and picture frames, along with numerous Persian rugs laid end to end, all join into a colorful, almost vibrational display.

The couple continued to ornament the house while also maintaining their import-export, mosaic art, and natural cosmetics businesses. Most of the neighbors are positively inclined toward the ornamentation, and their work has been celebrated on a television program, so the Farnams's enhancements have not been challenged by the city. Much of the work is viewable from the street.

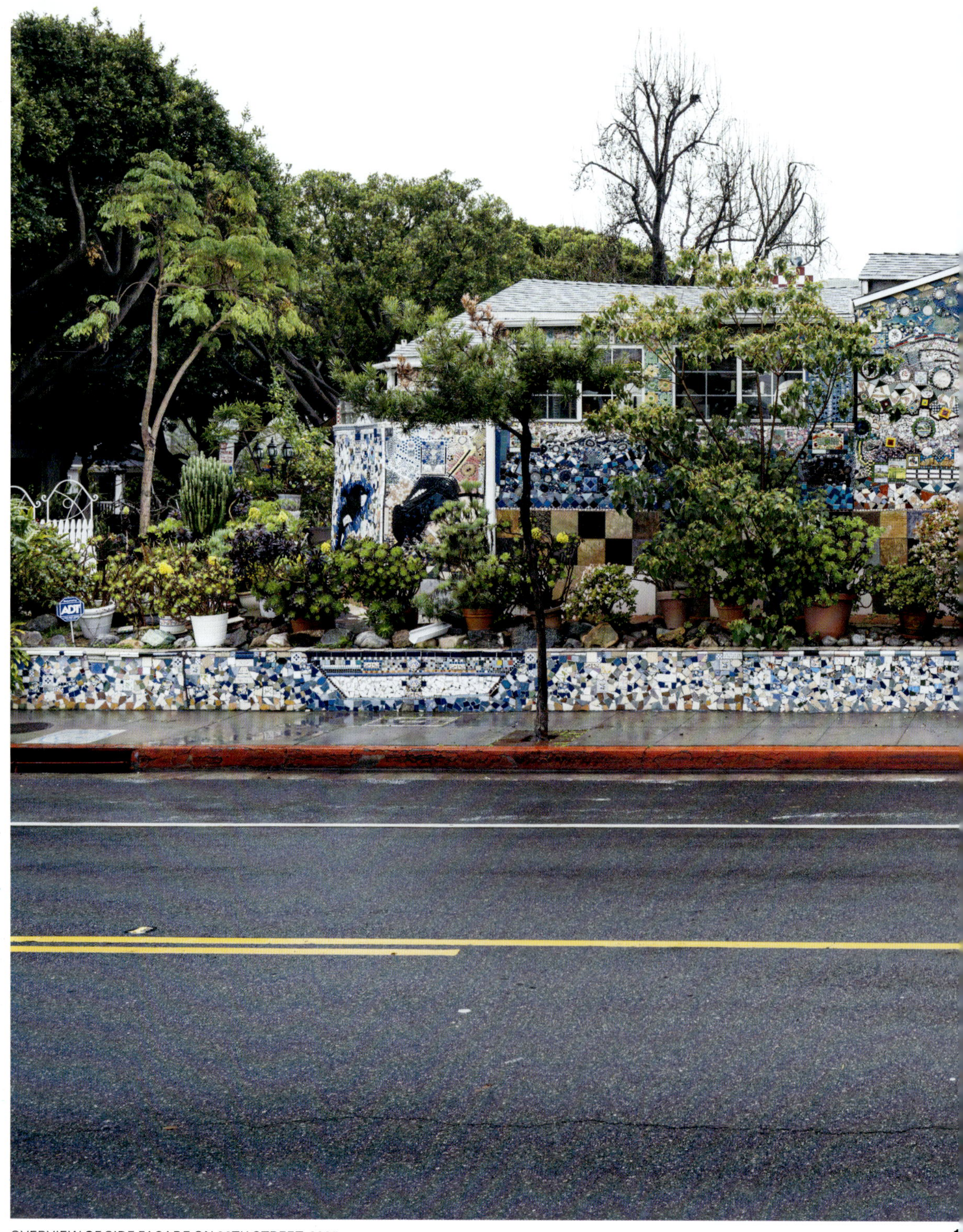

OVERVIEW OF SIDE FAÇADE ON 26TH STREET, 2025

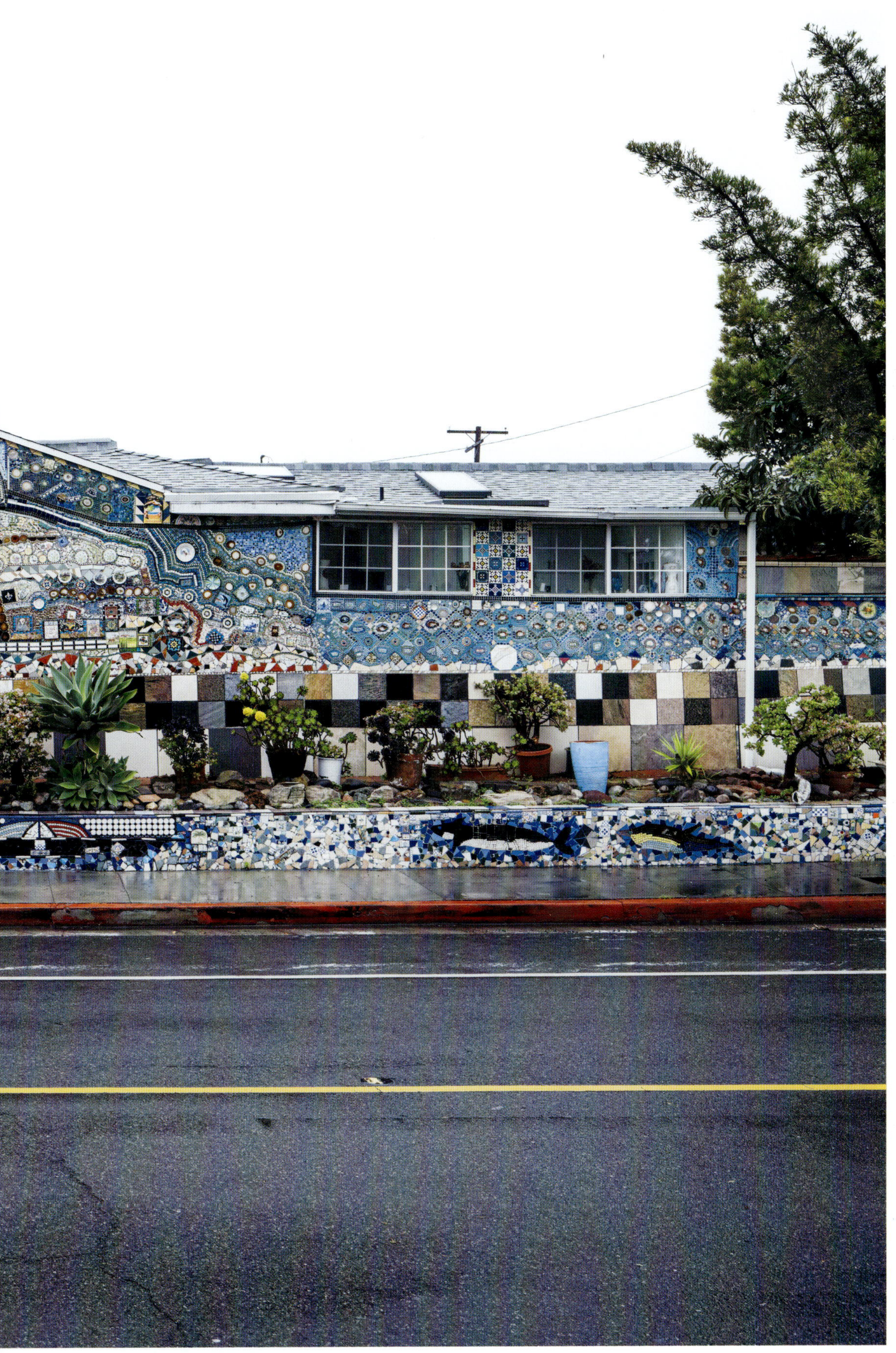

INSET DOOR ON SOUTHWEST CORNER OF FRONT FAÇADE, 2025

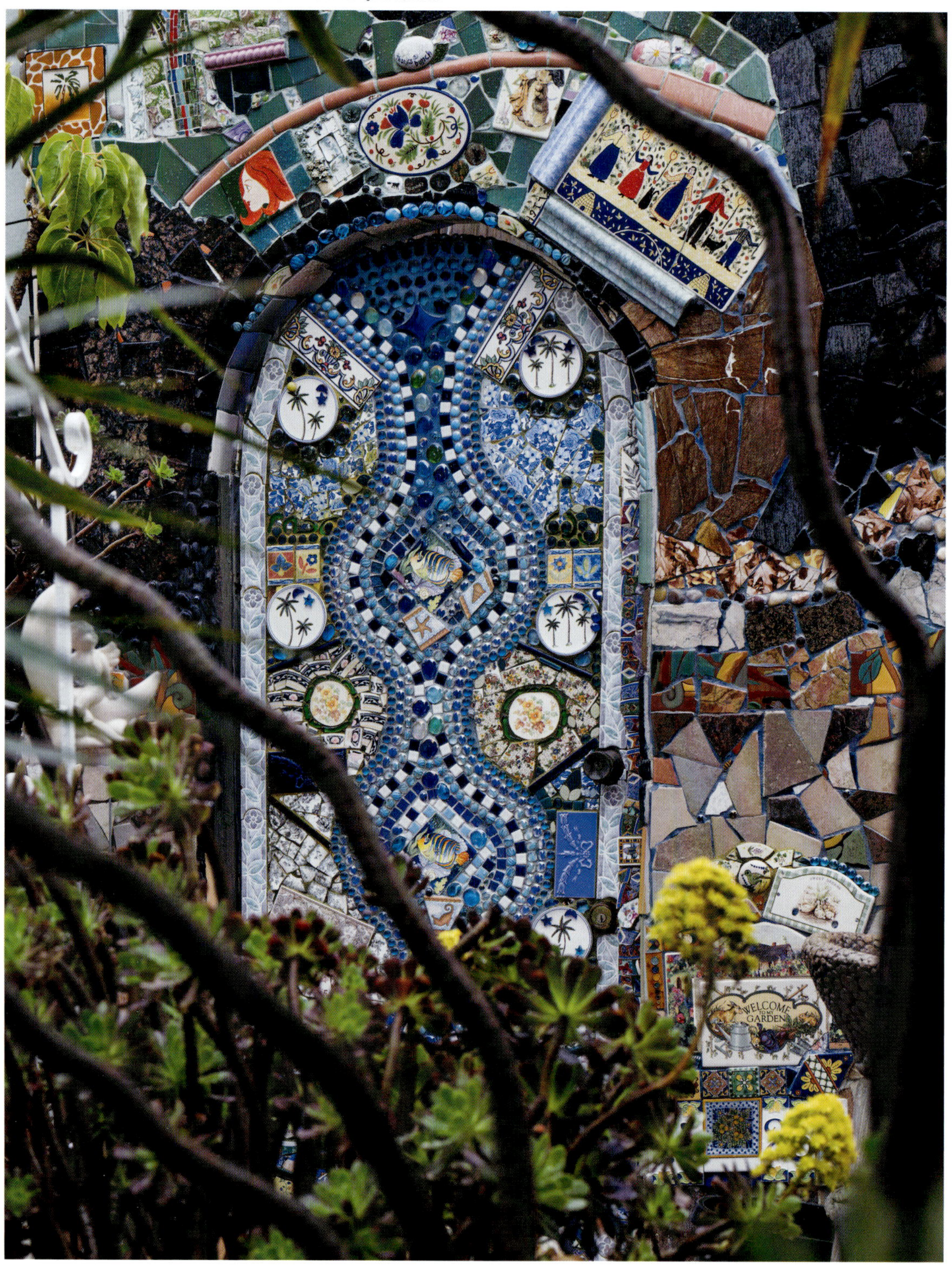

MOSAIC IMAGES OF NATURAL AND GEOMETRIC FORMS—AND EVEN THE FAMOUS HOLLYWOOD SIGN—ORNAMENT THE HOME'S EXTERIOR.

JEFFREY ELERSIC

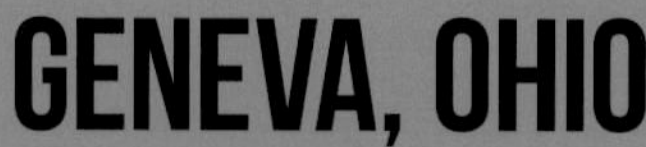

Along with his four brothers and two sisters, Elersic (1954–2024) was born near Johnston, Pennsylvania, but moved with his family to eastern Ohio's Lake County when his father, an operational engineer, could no longer find work. Stressed by his inability to properly support his family, he died at age 47; one of the lessons the younger Elersic took from his father's untimely passing was to avoid taking a fulltime job, so he never held one. Instead, he made his way by doing home remodels for family members, and he described himself as an artist and jack-of-all-trades who could do electrical work, plumbing, and carpentry, and who was able to operate heavy equipment. He had also been licensed as a notary public.

As a child, Elersic modeled small, realistic, figurative ceramic sculptures, and at age 16 he met a woman who inspired him to start creating "fantasy paintings," mostly organic abstractions in bright colors. He painted works in this genre for many years, usually using water-based paints on 16 x 20" papers. He saved a few and gave away many others.

After one of his brothers died in 2001, however, he became a man on a mission. He believed his brother's death had erroneously been ruled an accident, and he took it upon himself to broadcast an alternative narrative. He hoped his opposing conclusion would help to indict, through public opinion, the various local police officers, attorneys, and judges whom he accused of conspiring to cover up what he believed was murder. He also separately believed that he had been robbed of the inheritance due him following the death of his mother in 1994. He spent years researching documents, gathering evidence, and painting the results of his investigations on large, carefully lettered signs that he posted on the front and side façades of his home on the outskirts of Geneva.

Although Elersic decried what he considered to be cover-ups, he repeated again and again that he was grateful for the freedom allowed by America's system, which gave him the opportunity to publicly criticize and berate this very system. He was rigorously peaceful in his protests, taking care to stay within the letter of the law. He took his signs to the county courthouse in Painesville, around 20 miles west, holding them up while wearing a clown costume, and he displayed others on the sides of his cars, raising the ire of public officials because he purchased license plates with the names of some of the judges whom he held responsible. He paid every ticket he was given—daily, if necessary—but he would not be silenced.

Elersic added signs to the house whenever he had the means to buy paint and board. With the amount of time and money he spent painting the signs, he said, he could have painted the entire house three times over. For several years he lived with his sister June, who had a small apartment at the rear of the house. She refused to let him adorn the façade of *her* section with his signs, however, so that section remained unornamented. (After she moved out, he rented that apartment as well as the garage/workshop area.) Elersic was not worried about running out of space, however, as he also painted and repainted vehicles that he owned, including cars and boats. "Give me a mountain," he said, "and that mountain would be covered." The signs were colorful and carefully painted, with some emblazoned on boards in the colors of the American flag, some painted with standard horizontal lettering, and others designed to be read vertically. He often worked on horizontal surfaces so the paint would not drip, marking off the lines for his texts with masking tape. Other issues that he felt deserved his commentary, such as medical marijuana, complemented the signs focusing on his personal legal protests. The total effect was colorful and compelling.

Elersic's signs chronicling his battles with the local "L.E.O.s," (Law Enforcement Officials, as he called them) were occasionally replaced with others or removed so that he could use the plywood for other projects. With the home's location just off the road, his running visual commentary was always easily visible to motorists, but since his passing, the future of the site is unclear.

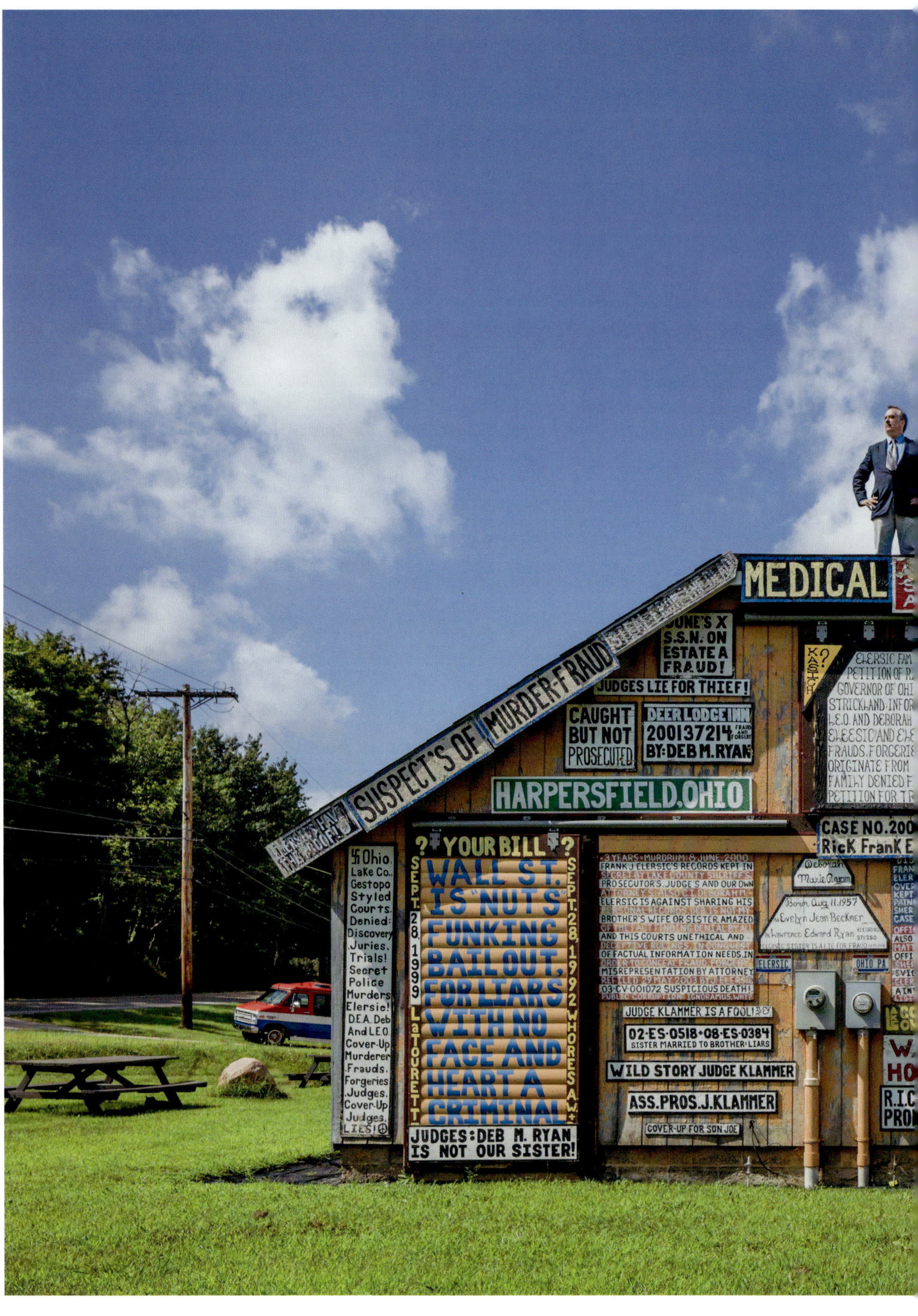

MEDICAL
JUNE'S X S.S.N. ON ESTATE A FRAUD!
JUDGES LIE FOR THIEF!
CAUGHT BUT NOT PROSECUTED
DEER LODGE INN 200137214 BY:DEB M.RYAN
SUSPECT'S OF
MURDER-FRAUD
HARPERSFIELD,OHIO
Ohio Lake Co. Gestopo Styled Courts. Denied: Discovery Juries. Trials! Secret Police Murders Elersic! DEA. Deb And LEO. Cover-Up Murderer Frauds. Forgeries Judges. Cover-Up Judges. LIES!
? YOUR BILL ?
WALL ST. IS "NUTS" FUNKING BAILOUT, FOR LIARS WITH NO FACE AND HEART A CRIMINAL
SEPT. 28, 1999 LaTOURETT
SEPT. 28 1992 WHORES A.W.
JUDGES: DEB M. RYAN IS NOT OUR SISTER!
JUDGE KLAMMER IS A FOOL!
02-ES-0518-08-ES-0384
SISTER MARRIED TO BROTHER-LIARS
WILD STORY JUDGE KLAMMER
ASS.PROS.J.KLAMMER
COVER-UP FOR SON JOE

ELERSIC ABOVE THE SIDE FAÇADE, 2016

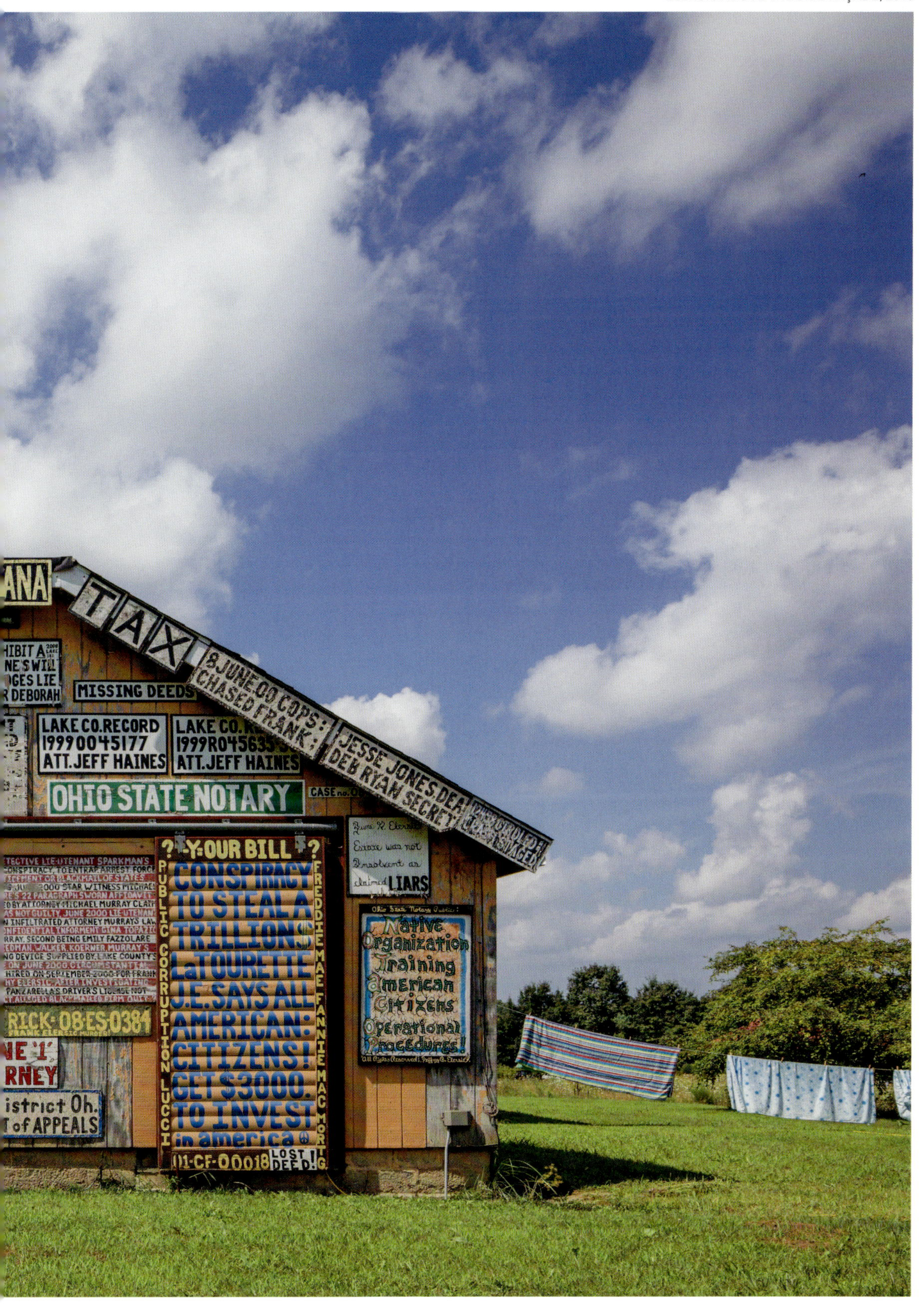

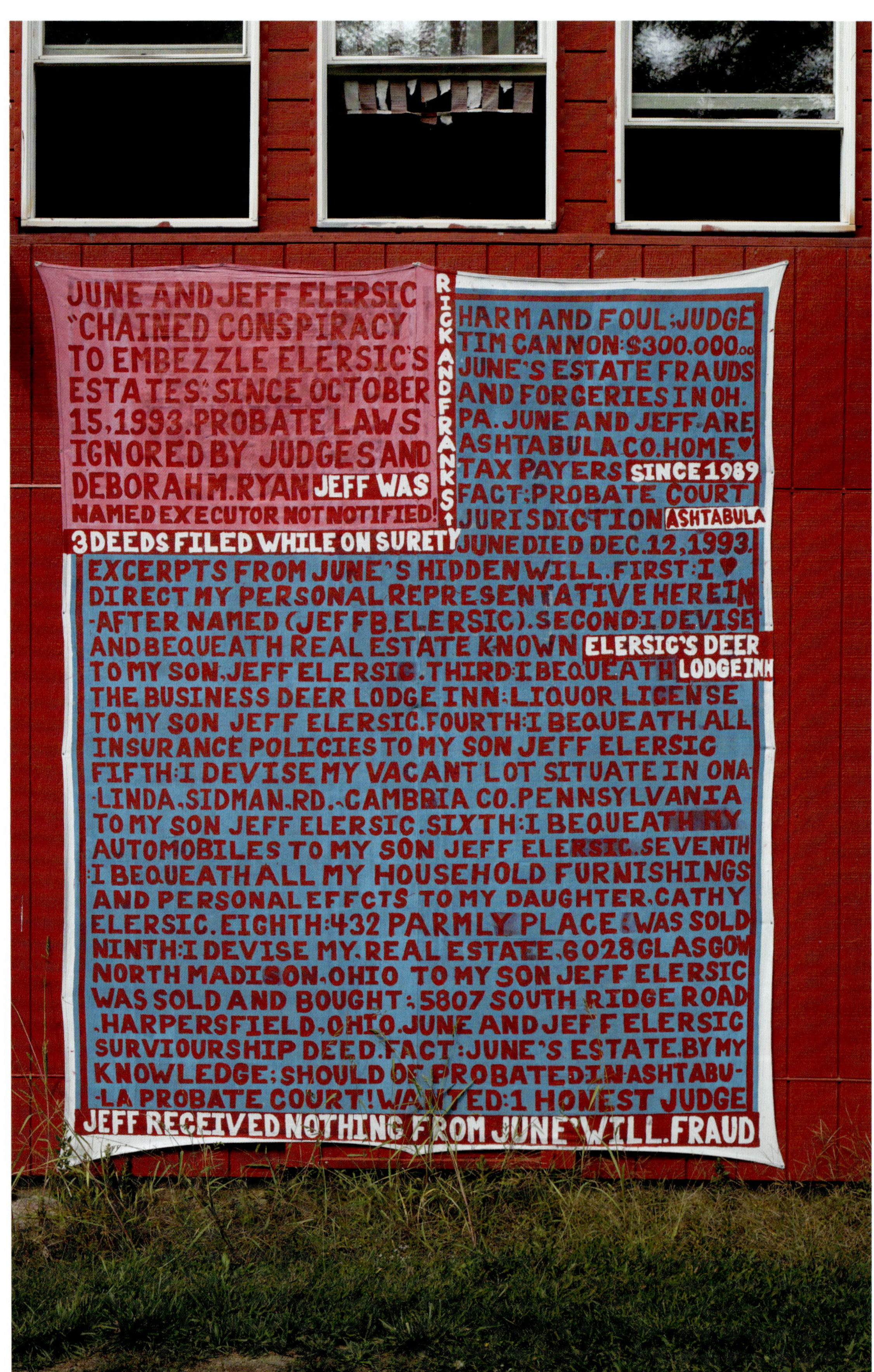

POSTED SIGNAGE (DETAIL), 2022

FRONT AND SIDE FAÇADES, 2016

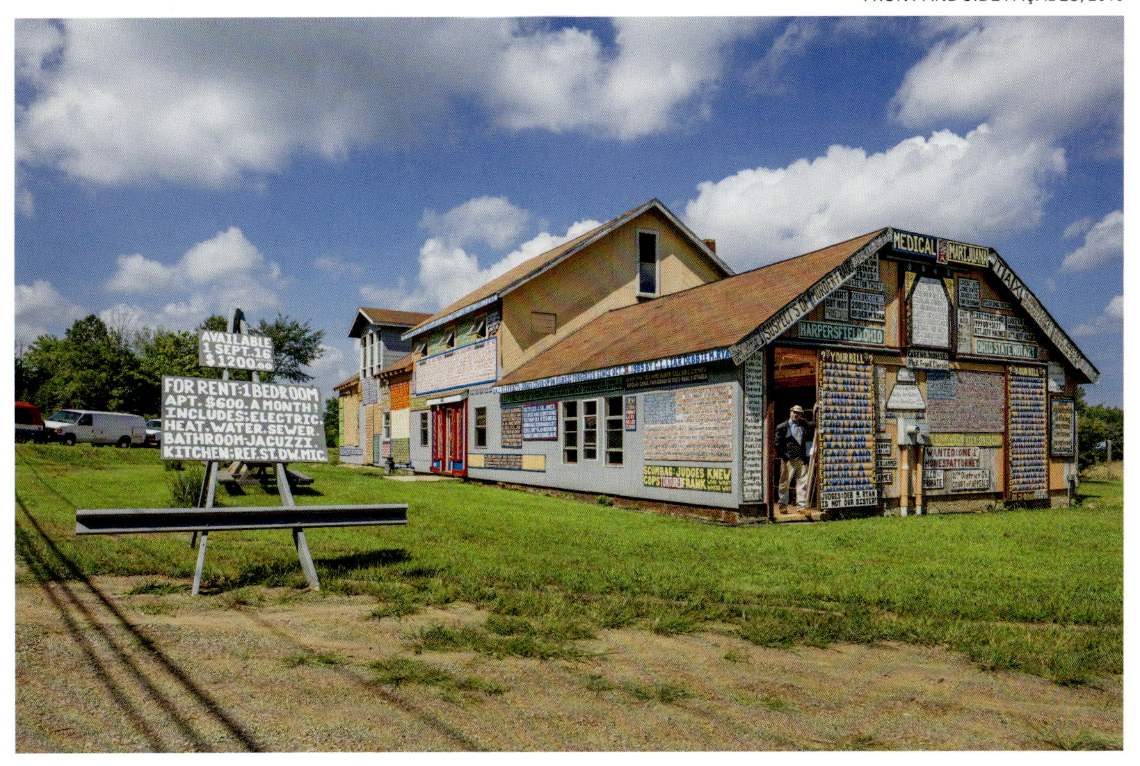

HE USED HIS HOME AND CAR TO BROADCAST HIS CRITIQUES OF ACCEPTED POLITICAL AND LEGAL NARRATIVES.

WILLIAM NORMAN "J" JACKSON

BUTTERFLY HOUSE

PACIFIC GROVE, CALIFORNIA

The history of built architecture is replete with narratives of constructions inspired by or promised in exchange for healing, victory, or accomplishment. And while a modest single-level home may pale in comparison to some of the elaborate stone palaces or cathedrals of Europe, the use of a building to declare love and facilitate therapy follows a similar path of intent and motivation.

Jackson (1937–2020) grew up in Bridgeport, Connecticut, and then served both in the U.S. Army and the Marine Reserves. He relocated to California, and, around 1977, he and his beloved wife Sonja moved into what was then a tiny cottage of less than 900 square feet not far from Monterey Bay. She had been diagnosed with degenerative retinitis pigmentosa at age 18, and the home's small footprint helped her navigate the interior. But the structure was in need of repair, so Jackson, a retired massage therapist and counselor for the local public schools, stripped it down and rebuilt it in 1992, adding another 500 square feet with a two-car garage that he utilized as a workshop, as well as an area for plantings and a new masonry wall fronting the public sidewalk.

Although Sonja's eyesight was worsening, she loved taking short walks around the neighborhood with her seeing-eye dog. Jackson noticed that although she was by then legally blind, she was still able to perceive bright colors. So he constructed a colorful wooden butterfly to mark the two-bedroom home, in homage to Pacific Grove's nickname of Butterfly Town, U.S.A. and the area's monarch grove sanctuary, where thousands of monarch butterflies overwinter each year. He attached his oversized wooden butterfly to the home's front façade, hoping that it would help his wife find her way home as she returned from her walks.

Her response—echoed by neighbors and passersby—was so enthusiastic that Jackson continued to construct approximately 1,000 more butterflies. He even created a "Butterflies of Hope Memorial Wall," adorned with wooden, plastic, and ceramic versions purchased by others in honor or memory of their own loved ones. Braille annotations enable blind visitors to appreciate the installations. Proceeds from these sales and from donations deposited in a jar out front were gifted by the Jacksons to the Blind and Visually Impaired Center of Monterey County.

Despite the increasing numbers of visitors and their positive responses to Jackson's colorful work, the municipality did not celebrate his efforts or take steps to link him to their annual butterfly parade, a slight that he never understood. But he continued to enhance his home with its ever-denser butterfly imagery, each painted differently, and many additionally adorned with mirrors or jeweled beads. Although some friends suggested that perhaps he might consider painting on discrete boards or canvases as a way to generate income, he was never interested in doing so, and he continued to focus on his home. It—along with its bright color palette and its appealing narrative of his love for his wife—were everything to him, and, as he aged, he seemed to finish decorating their home as his own life neared its end.

Sonja continued to live in the house for two years following her husband's death, and she sold the house in December 2022, less than a month before her own passing, on January 1, 2023. The current owners continue to delight in Jackson's vision and maintain the vibrant exterior decorations—including the technicolor night lighting—to entertain the community and celebrate unconventional artistic practices.

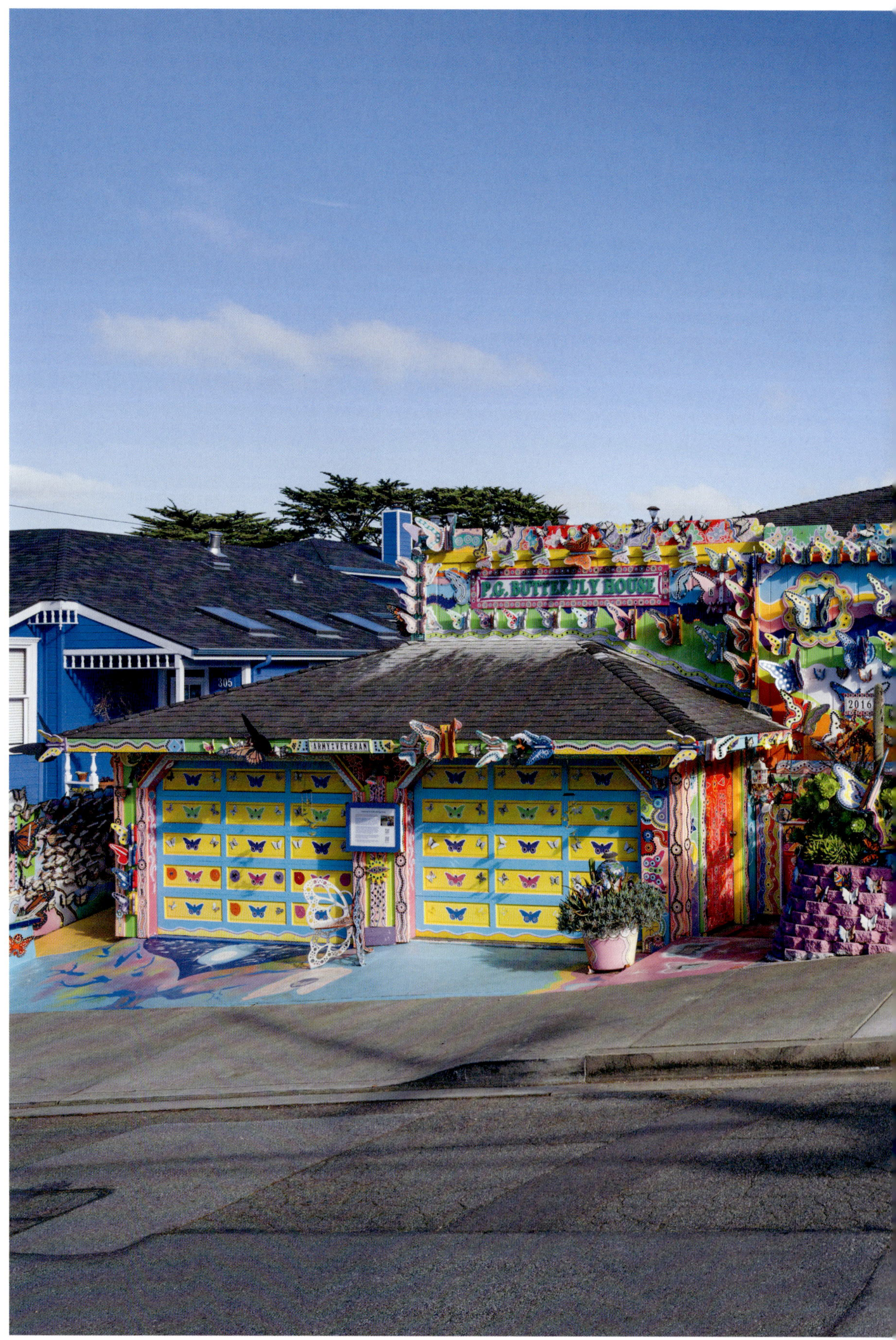

OVERVIEW, FRONT FAÇADE, 2025

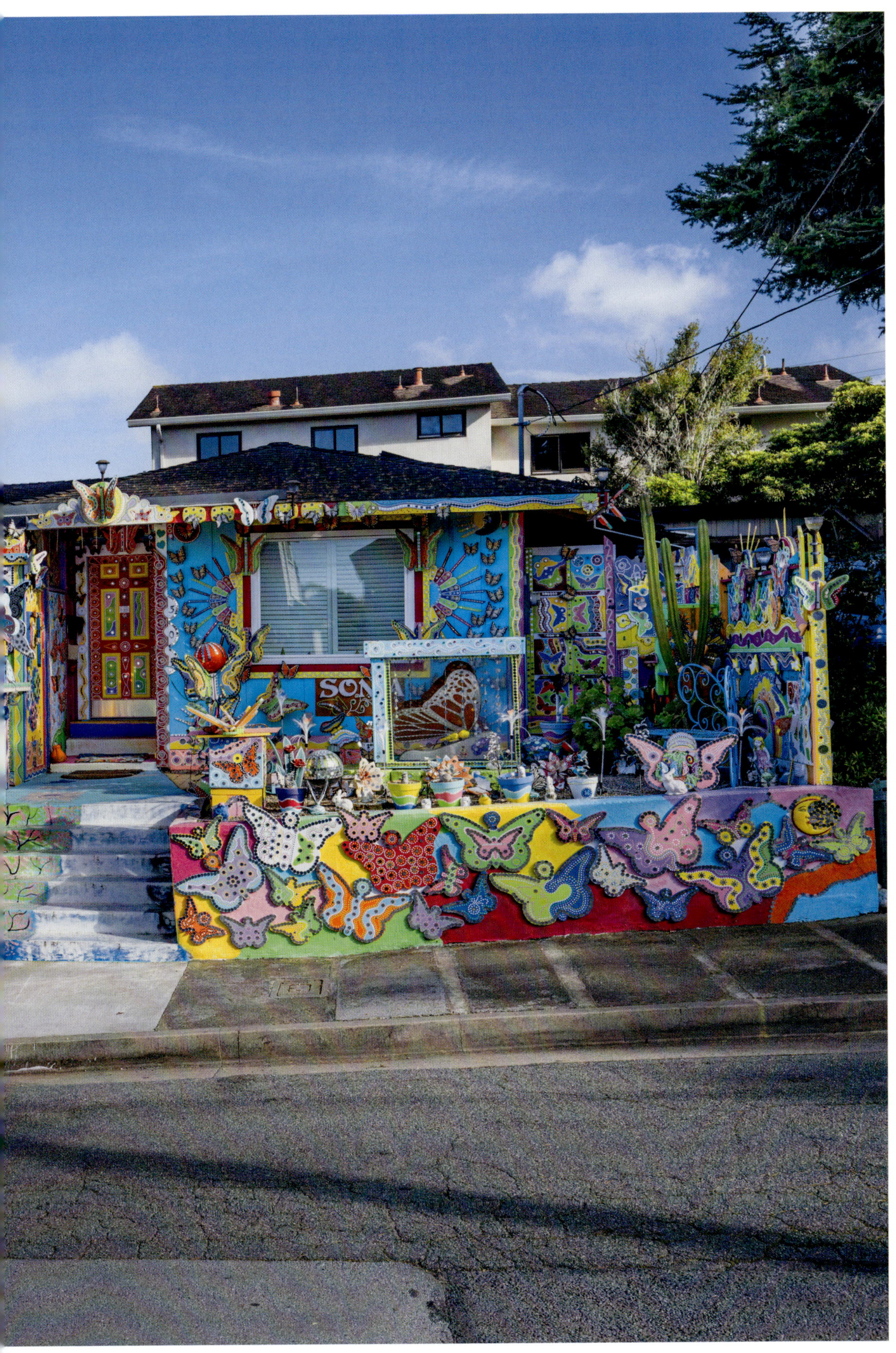

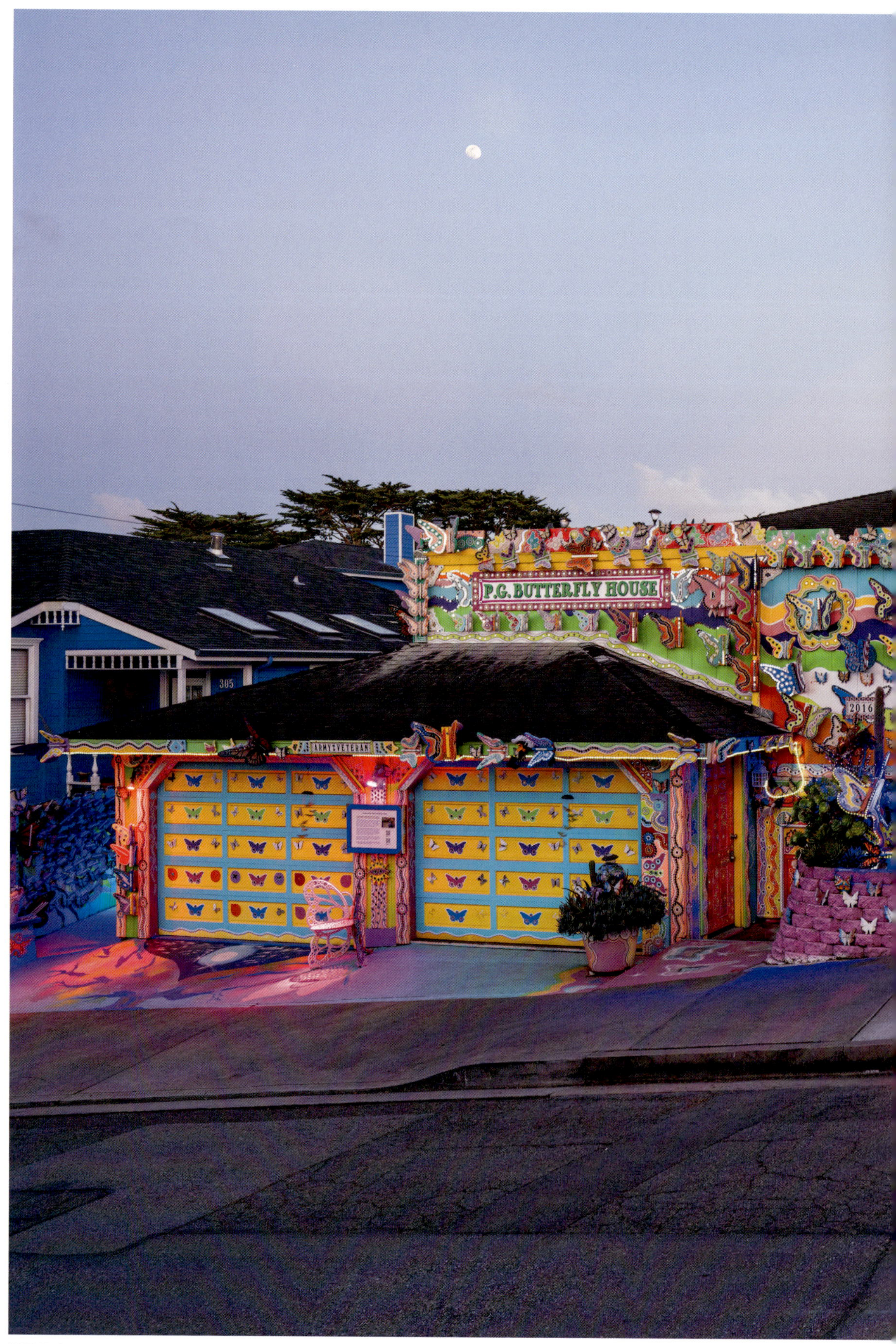

EVENING LIGHTS, FRONT FAÇADE, 2025

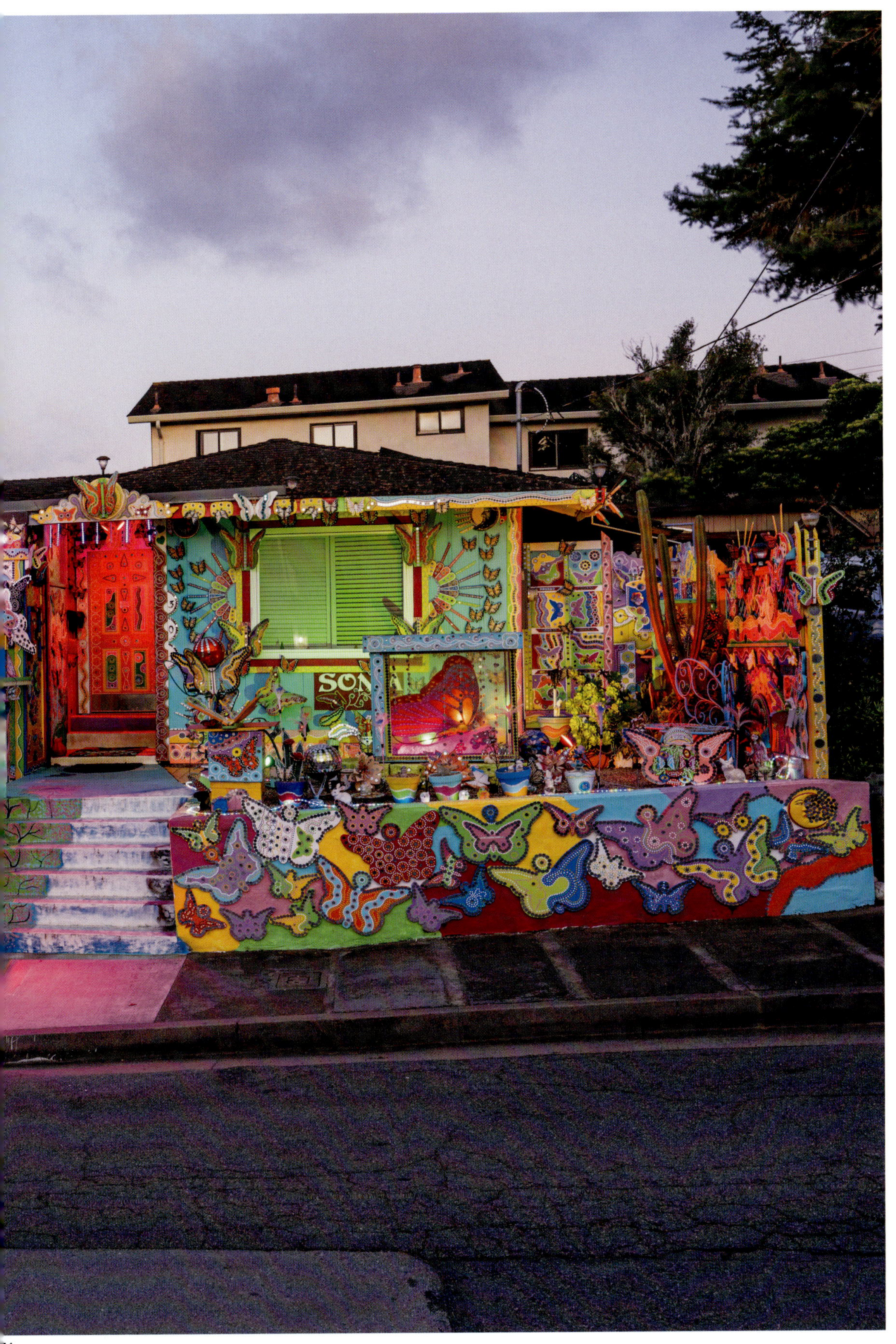

FRONT FAÇADE (DETAIL), 2025

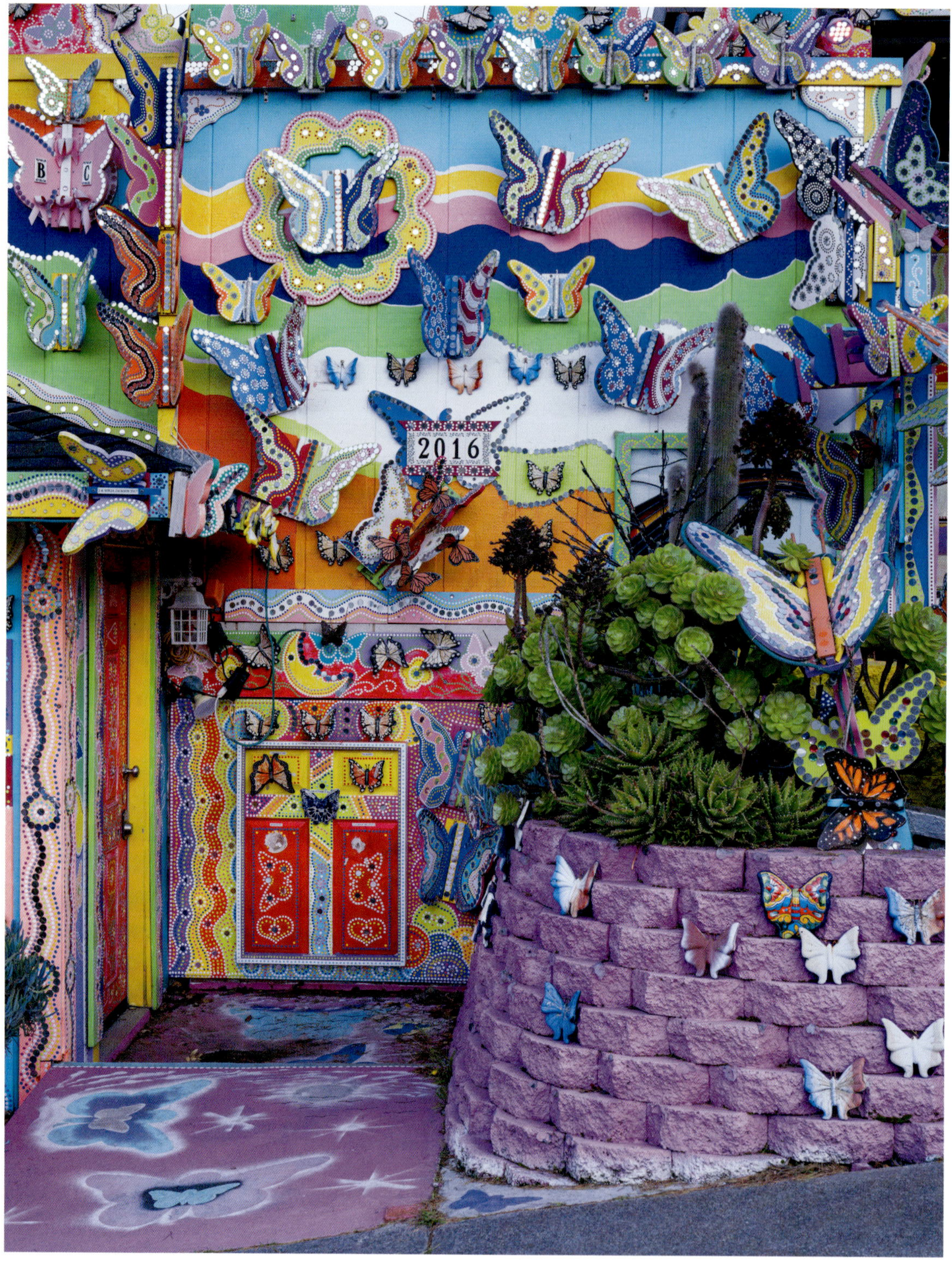

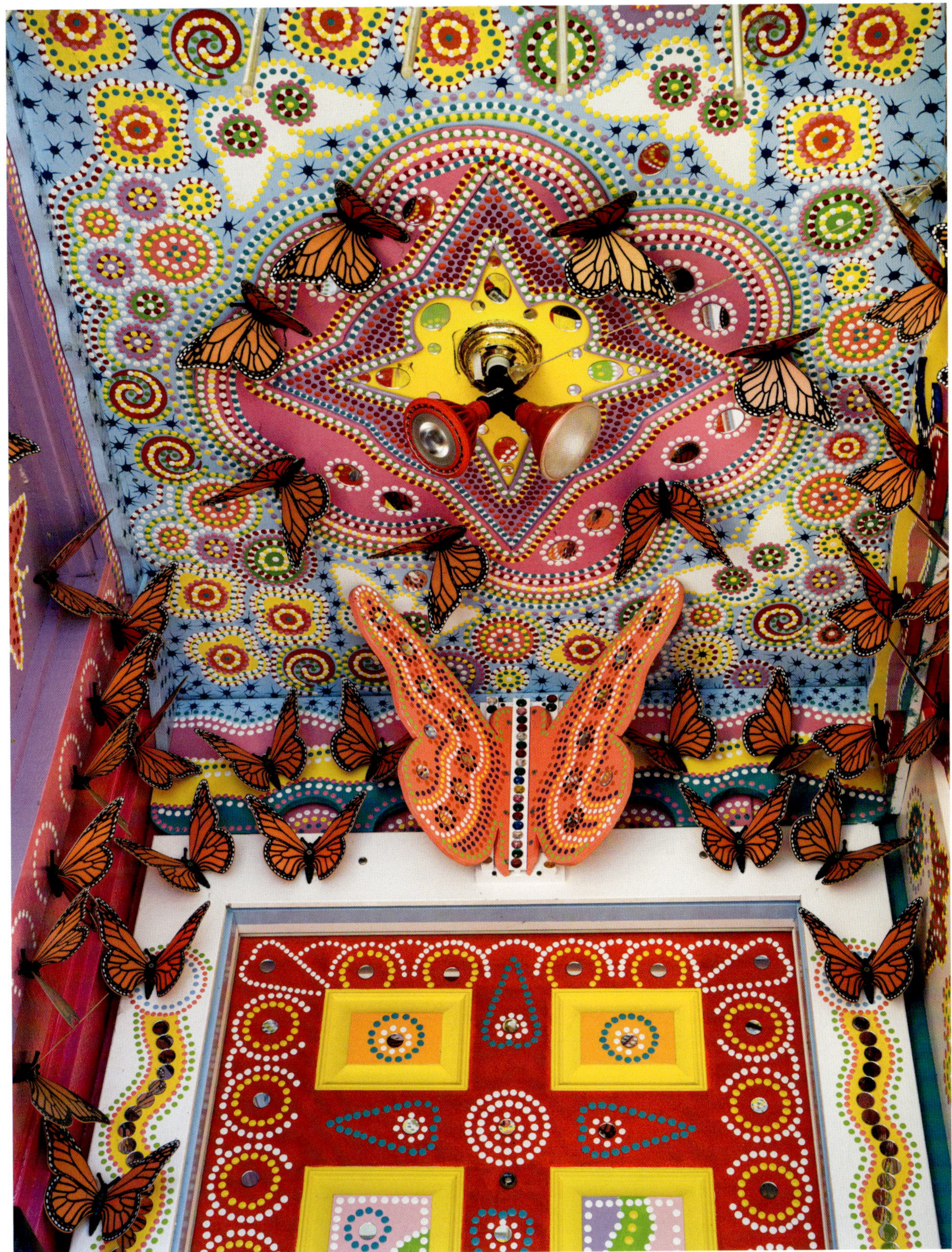

CLARKE BEDFORD

VANADU ART HOUSE AND GARDENS

HYATTSVILLE, MARYLAND

It is certainly not uncommon for museum staff members to try their hand at creating their own artwork, but they rarely use their knowledge of art history, materials, and technique to poke fun at the ecosystem of mainstream art that they daily work to support. Typically, their artistic efforts tend to be sober and serious—indeed, often humorless—expressions that illuminate few paths for public appreciation. But Bedford (b. 1947), who had made art since he was a child, took a lighthearted and often satirical (or perhaps contrarian) approach to his own paintings, photographs, prints, and installations even while he was on staff at the Hirshhorn Museum in Washington, D.C. There, with a background in both science and art as well as conservation technology, he worked from 1980 to 2013 as a skillful conservator of paintings and, earlier on, of three-dimensional mixed media objects as well.

In 2000, after separating from his wife, Bedford moved to a 1918-era bungalow in Hyattsville, and soon afterward he began modifying an old Saab convertible. Other vintage vehicles with radical ornamentation followed, and he turned them all into fully functioning, legally registered, and insured art cars. His most iconic ride was a 1988 Econoline van with the license plate VANADU (alluding to S.T. Coleridge's rather hallucinatory poem *Kubla Khan*, with its unique and bewitching palace in Xanadu). In the early to mid-2000s, he started attaching found objects that he could not fit onto his cars to the perimeter fencing around his property; soon, as the fence filled up, he expanded his efforts to include the yard (which he began calling *Vanadu Gardens*) and, by 2005, he began targeting the façade of the house as well. He likes to look at "stuff," he has explained, so he needs a lot of stuff to look at.

Assembling and layering so many different kinds of objects has helped him construct an environment in which he feels at home. His aesthetics are often drawn from late-nineteenth-century estates that seem to almost capriciously incorporate such diverse styles as Islamic, Japonesque, and Victorian into a singular building; Modernist constructions; Dada; and the decorative arts that celebrate the aesthetic and design of objects primarily created for utilitarian purposes.

Bedford chooses weather-resistant objects, bolting them in place and then aging them with a carburetor cleaner and/or painting them with a uniform palette to obtain a consistent patina that emphasizes his appreciation for the so-called "steampunk" aesthetic of Victorian-age industrial components. He fits together smaller pieces in his on-site studio, and given his skill set and vocational background, he is particularly attentive to the importance of ascertaining that no fragments can easily dislodge, especially on the vehicles, and he uses his considerable technical expertise to ensure that everything has been stabilized. He adds ceramic and glass objects and mosaics rather than paint to provide contrasting color accents; his passion for trawling for antiques in thrift stores, estate sales, and vintage shops helps maintain an abundance of resource materials.

Well aware of the interest in assemblage manifested by mainstream Modernist artists, he densely packs otherwise incompatible shapes, media, and figures together to create a compelling universe of his own that, while hardly symmetrical, evinces a pleasing balance of form and elevation. Spherical hubcaps, wagon wheels, fans, springs, bowls, globes, and balls share space with geometrically hard-edge plinths, finials, pipes, spires, and rods, and are complemented by statues, horns, doll and mannequin parts, old signs, lamp parts, helmets, cages, and musical instruments. All are arranged thoughtfully to balance each other in an unapologetic equilibrium. Delighting in the individual elements, he nevertheless does not divorce them from the entirety of the *Vanadu Art House* environment, which he conceptualizes as a completely "new thing" and a whole unto itself.

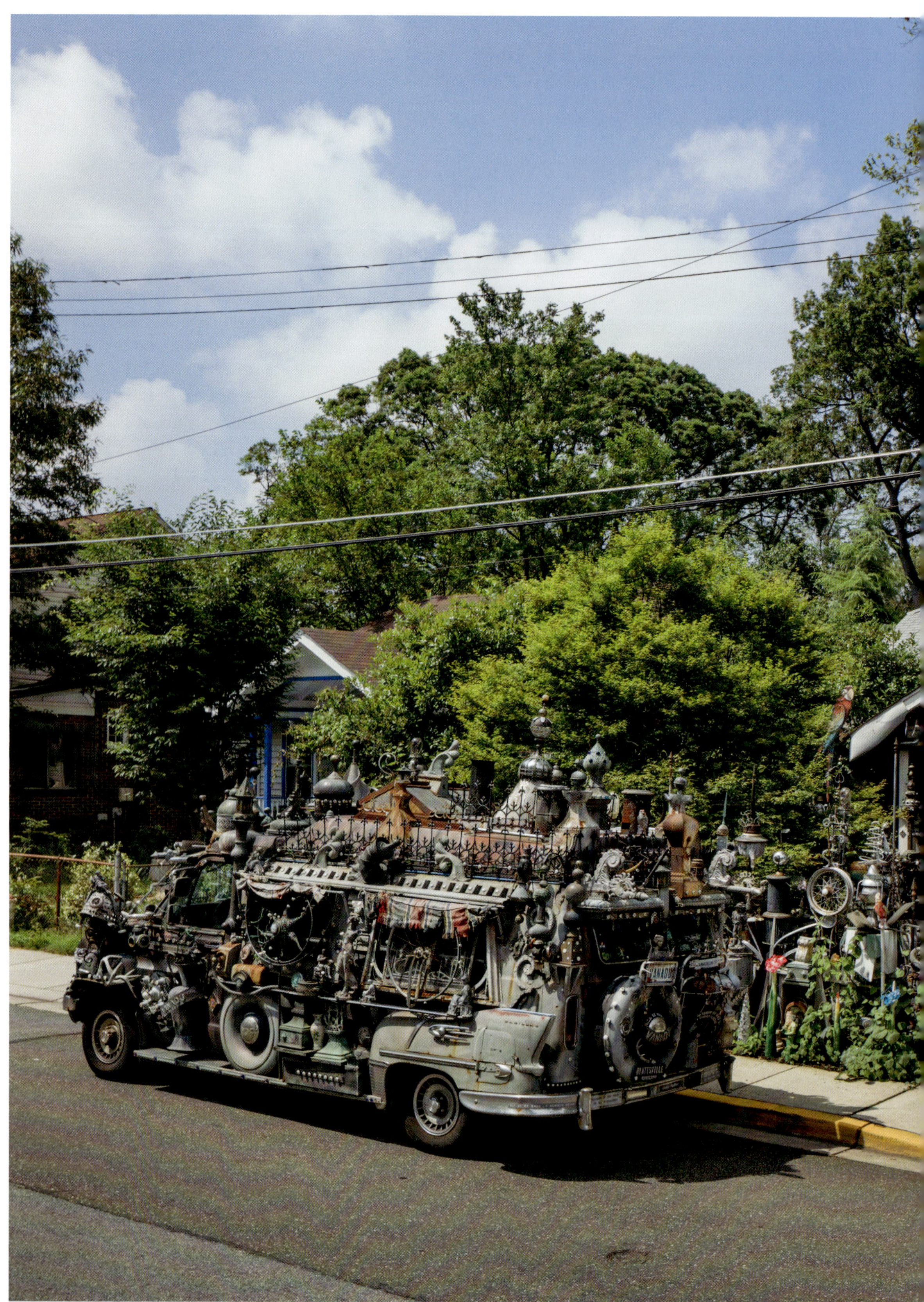

VANADU VAN AND FRONT VIEW OF HOME, 2016

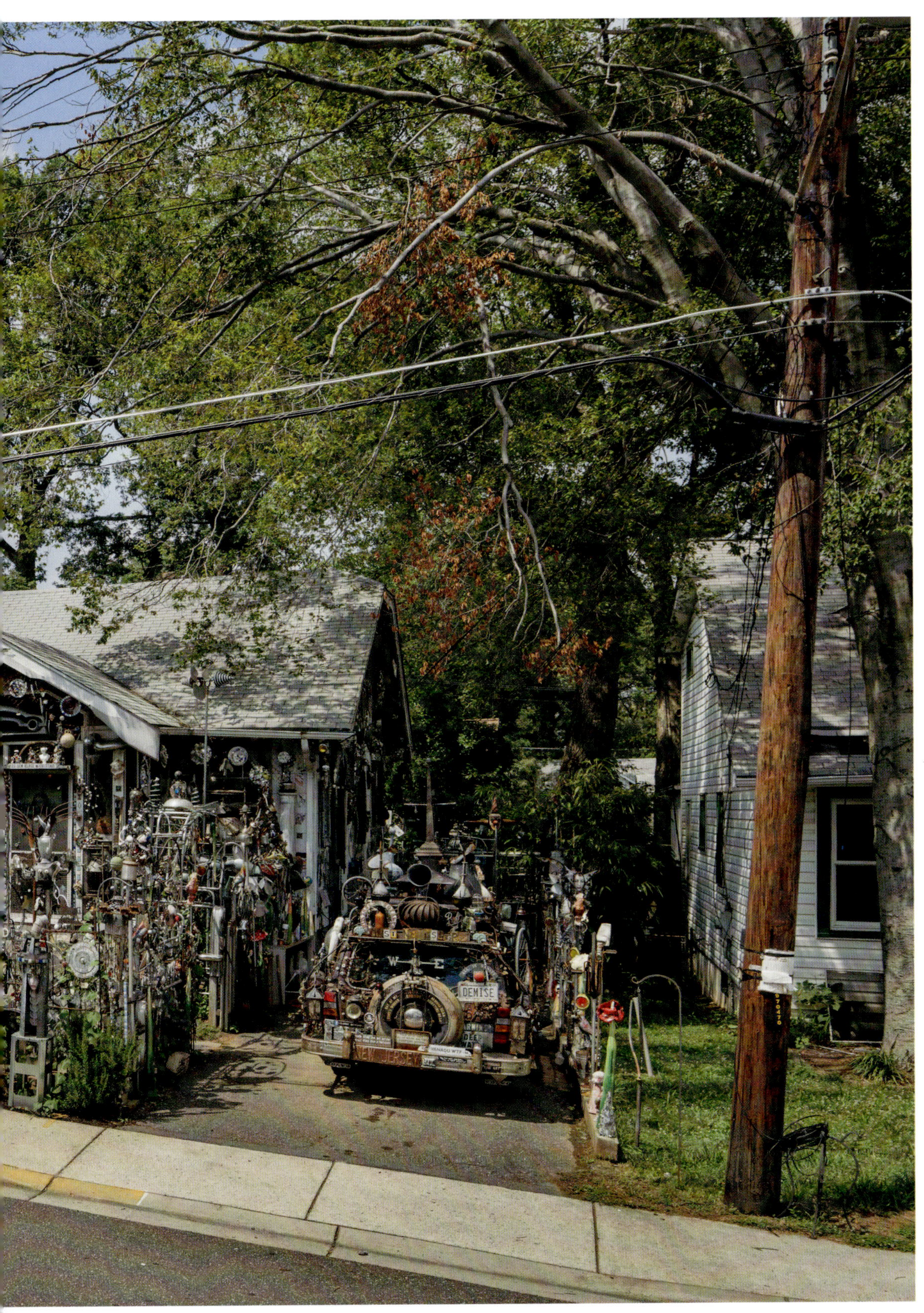
DEMISE
NEW JERSEY

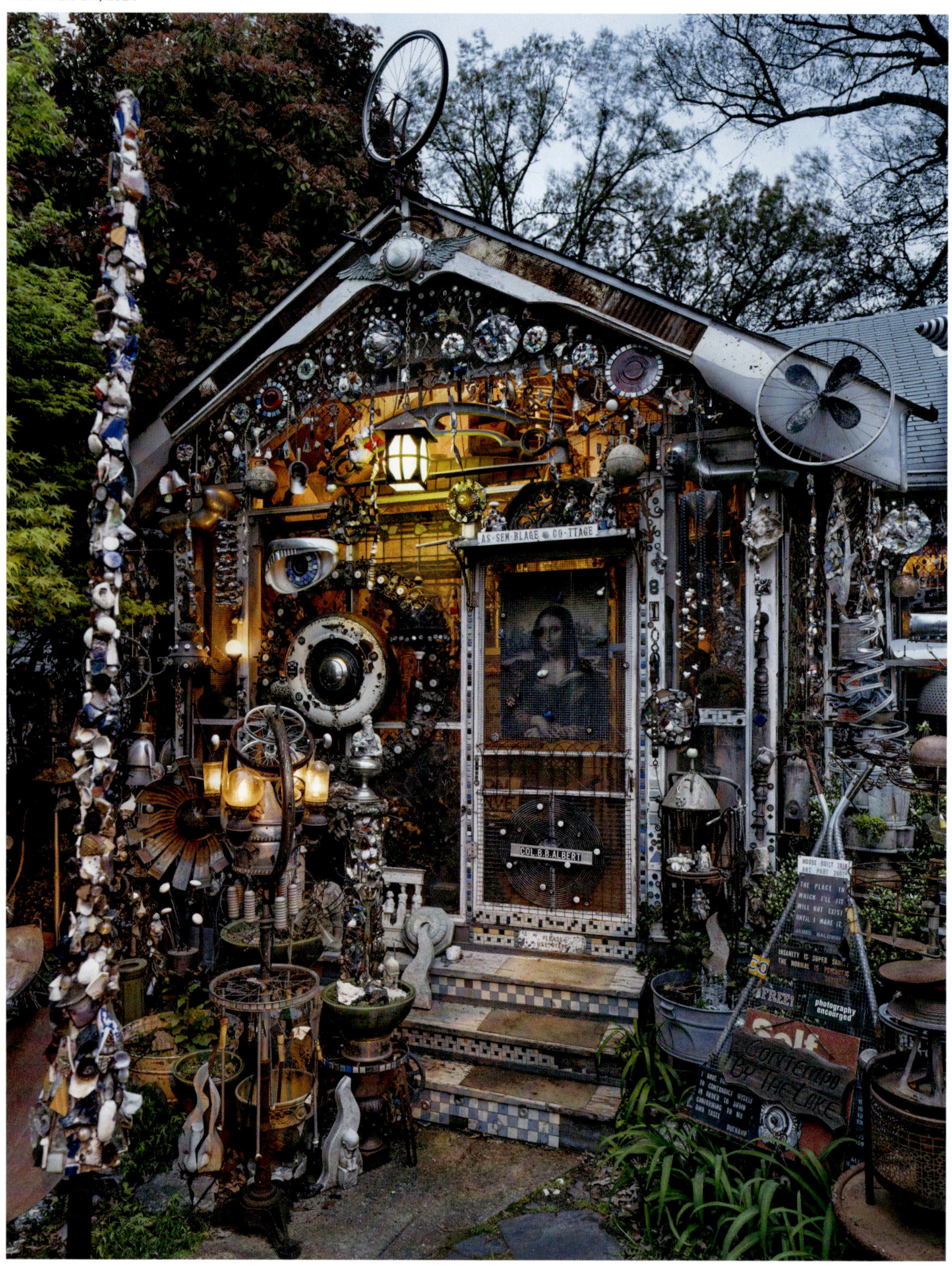
AS-SEM-BLAGE CO-TTAGE
COL.B.B.ALBERT
THE PLACE IN WHICH I'LL FIT WILL NOT EXIST UNTIL I MAKE IT
BALDWIN
INSANITY IS SUPER SANITY THE NORMAL IS PSYCHOTIC
FREE!
photography encourged
I HAVE TO CONTRADICT MYSELF IN ORDER TO AVOID CONFORMING TO MY OWN TASTE
DUCHAMP

VANADU VAN (DETAIL), 2016

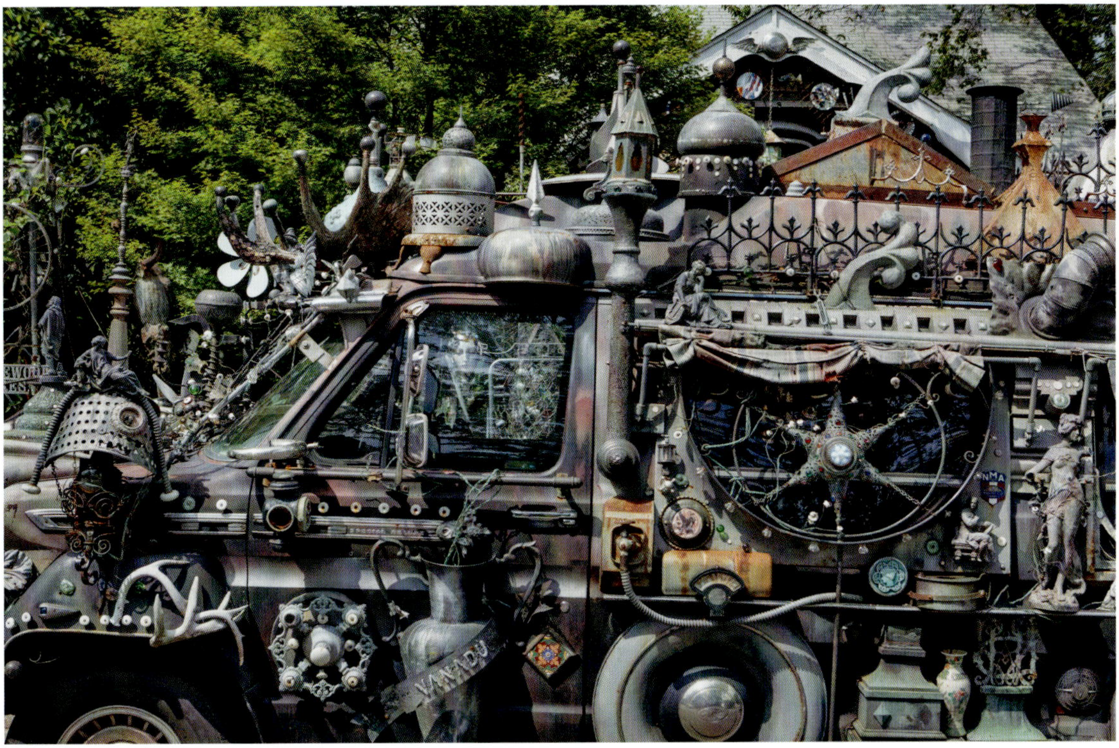

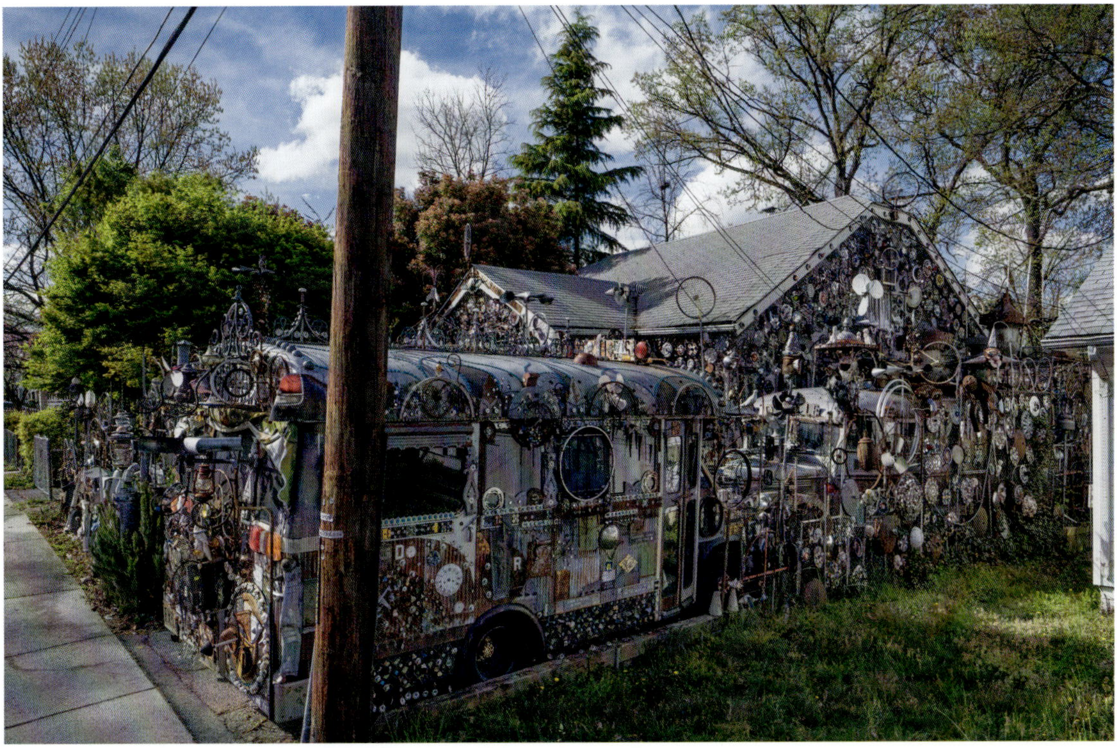

RIGHT VIEW OF HOUSE WITH GMC VANDURA CUTAWAY BUS AND CHEVROLET BUS CAMPER, 2024

LIVING ROOM, 2024

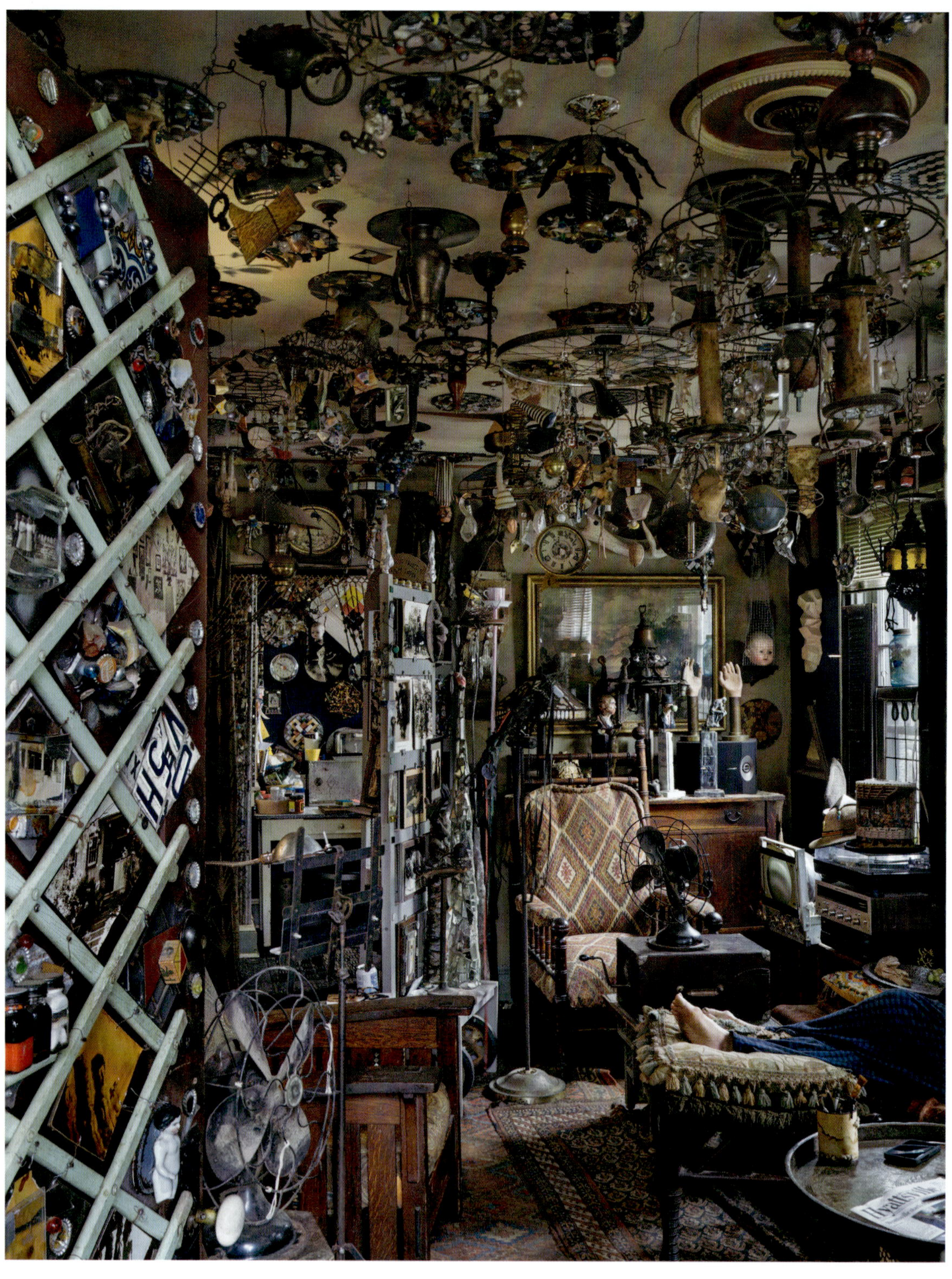

LEFT SIDE OF HOUSE WITH DECORATED PERIMETER FENCE (DETAIL), 2016

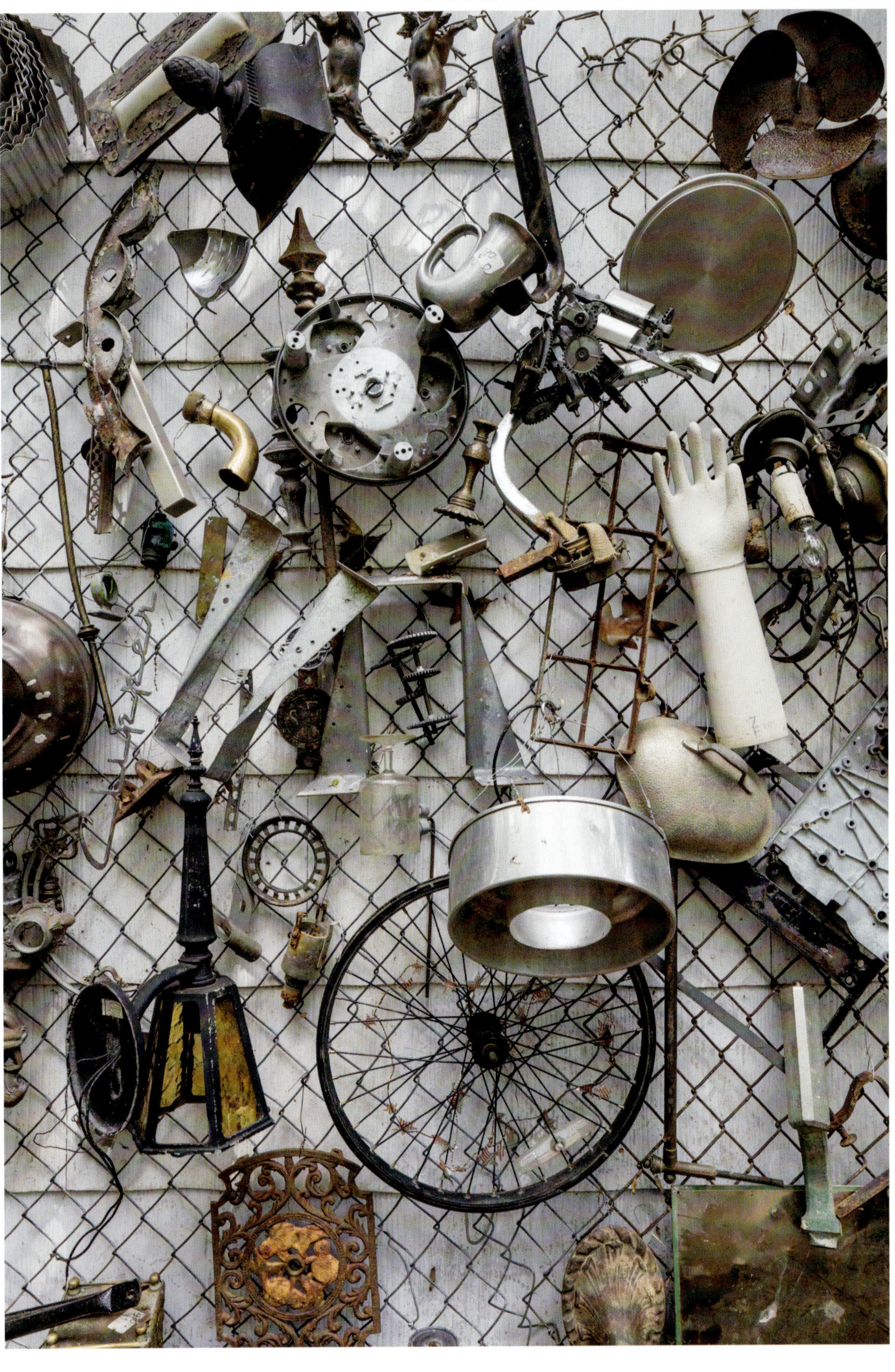

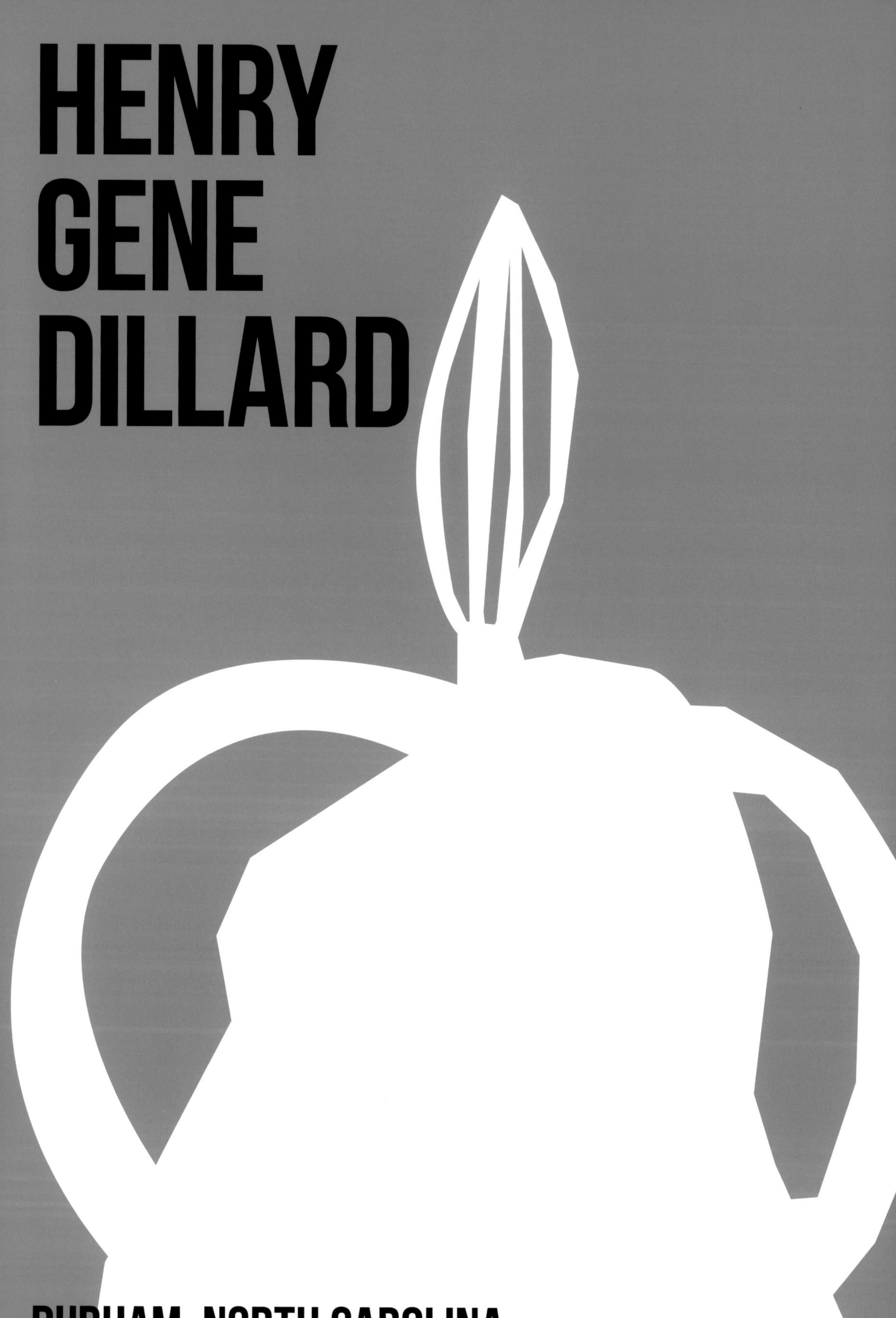
HENRY
GENE
DILLARD
DURHAM, NORTH CAROLINA

Dillard (b. 1955) was raised in the southern California town of Carlsbad, but he moved all the way across the country before he began the constructions that would eventually turn into an elaborate and multifaceted art environment. Family members, most of whom worked in blue-collar jobs or managed their own small businesses, instilled in him a belief that anything was possible as long as you were willing to put in the time and effort to make it happen. He was always a hard worker, and he had a knack for understanding how things were put together, troubleshooting issues if they were not working as they should.

Dillard met his future wife while volunteering for the Catholic Worker community in San José, California, and their first child, a son, was born there. After a few years of marriage, Dillard and his small family followed his wife's mother to Cedartown, Georgia, and then on to Durham, now joined by a baby daughter. He had had some training in refrigeration and so was able to secure a position at a restaurant equipment company; he later moved on to repairing scientific equipment and then biomedical equipment, teaching himself and broadening his knowledge and skills with each step. At the same time that he worked his day jobs, he maintained his own repair business, beginning with small establishments and moving up to contracts with larger institutions. Many of the calls were emergency fixes that required 24/7 availability, a situation that turned out to be detrimental to his marriage.

The couple's midlife divorce caused Dillard to re-evaluate his lifestyle. In 2000 he bought a small clapboard home in Durham's Northgate Park neighborhood and—with a welder that he had acquired in trade from a client—began "messing around" with steel pipes and rebar, which he complemented with discarded metal objects he found at construction sites or collected from his walks along the nearby railroad tracks. Sculpting them into flat forms by using his welder as a glue gun, as he continued installing them in his front yard it was not long before his increased production necessitated the purchase of additional materials to supplement those he could serendipitously find. He focused on arbors, recognizable objects, and often humorous characters, including a Loch Ness-style sea serpent that holds Dillard's mailbox in its mouth. But soon he felt the need for greater change, so in 2003 he closed his business and joined the Peace Corps, spending two years in Honduras building water sanitation systems. Upon his return, he restarted his equipment repair business.

It was around this time that he also started contemplating more radical changes to his ¼-acre lot. Encouraged by his neighbor Ren Smith, a voracious reader who helped introduce him to a range of artworks, he was increasingly intrigued as he learned about the robust modifications manifested in art environments on a global scale, and he began visiting these sites whenever he could. He and Smith took motorcycle trips around the South, but he also visited Ricky Boscarino's *Luna Parc* in New Jersey (see page 88), Rodia's *Towers* in Los Angeles (see page 332), and the *Palais Idéal* in France. He was amazed, inspired, and humbled by what he experienced.

Much like those artist-builders, Dillard did not have a grand plan for his property, but he already had a solid repertoire of skills, a significant understanding of materials, and a robust work ethic instilled by watching family members ply their trades, which he had already applied in his own various jobs and businesses. He also realized that his undiagnosed dyslexia as a youth had probably prepared him for resilience: he was used to making mistakes, so he was not afraid of them, and when he set his mind to do something he focused on its completion until it was successfully accomplished. He believes this is his strongest suit.

Dillard began learning about working with cement through a neighborhood project of making small stepping-stone pavers, which he decorated with old tools, bottle caps, or marbles. Then, after seeing a bottle house on one of his trips, he expanded his own vision about what might be possible in this medium, and in 2006 he erected an undulating bottle wall that culminated with a mosaic-sheathed, 10-foot tower. Soon he added palm trees to the yard; he shaped their trunks by molding concrete inside of bundt-cake pans. By 2007, with Smith's help, he had begun to ornament the sides of the garage by affixing tiles, plates, and fragments of ceramic and mirrors.

OVERVIEW OF ARTIST'S HOME AND YARD, 2025

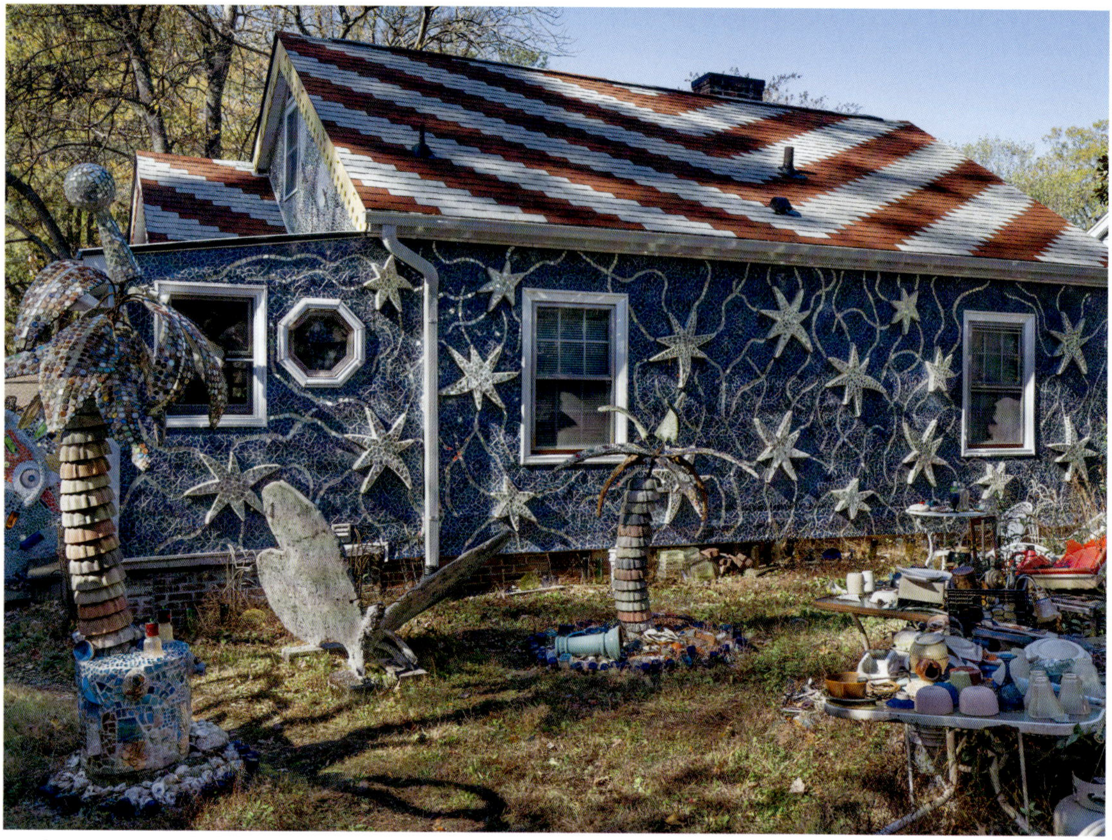

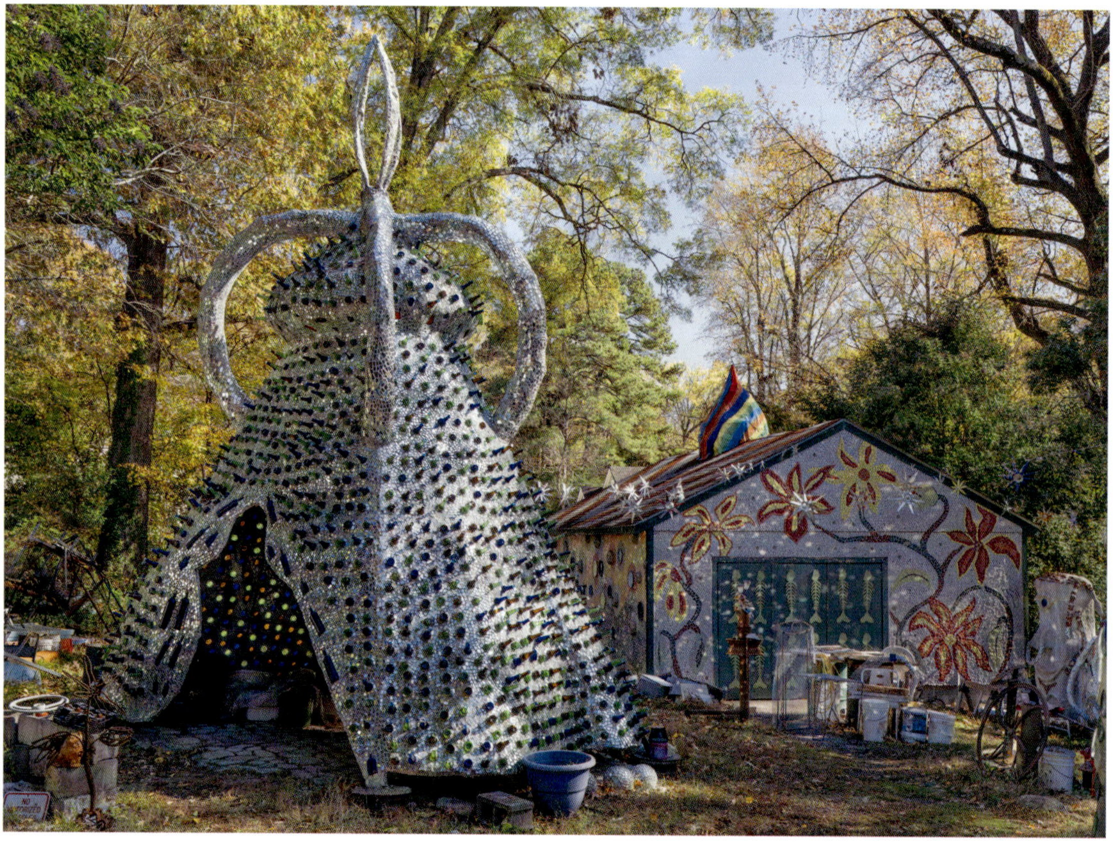

SPACESHIP AT LEFT WITH GARAGE AT REAR, 2025

He treated each side of the garage differently. The eastern (rear) façade features an organically swirling botanical form loosely based on Gustav Klimt's *Tree of Life, Stoclet Frieze*; the north is a polychrome series of rippling wave-like shapes visually intersected by bundt-cake-molded concrete forms and multicolored kitchen plates; and the west showcases a series of fish skeletons affixed to the doors, surrounded by wildly effusive floral motifs. He did not decorate the southern façade, as that side is only 10 inches from the property line, and he would have had to work from his neighbor's back yard, thus potentially bothering the residents. Dillard finished one wall each year through 2008. By the time the ornamentation was completed, he had learned by trial and error how to manipulate the materials to not only realize his visions but to do so in a manner that was technically proficient and that would render his creations durable.

In the meantime, during the winter months he also began to slowly decorate sections of the house interior. He built out recycled plywood valances into rounded door jambs and lintels with colorful mosaic flowers, and raised the living room ceiling to house a skylight, which also provided the opportunity to mosaic the interior walls of the light well with more ceramic flowers and vine-like mirrored tendrils. He further ornamented the ceiling by affixing high-relief mosaic stars and enormous sculpted flower petals to visually anchor drop lights, and he mounted fantastical papier-mâché heads to interior columns.

As Dillard worked on the garage, he naturally began musing about the exterior of the house as well, so in 2008–09 he ripped the vinyl siding off the back side (facing the garage), leaving the thin Styrofoam inner layer that he then covered with chicken wire, screwing it to the house's infrastructure to ensure that his ornamentation would not collapse. He attached high-relief star forms like those on the interior ceilings and then began to surface the rest of the façade with dark blue tile fragments. After seeing his preliminary work, Smith suggested that he connect the stars' points to "trails" of mirror fragments, a restrained design of tendrils that helped to tie the composition together. He added still more leftover stars to the front façade, and tore off most of the rest of the home's vinyl siding, by then intending to mosaic the entire building. (He maintained some of the siding on the southern façade because he suspected that the poorly constructed concrete foundation in that area would not be able to support the weight of the tiles. It also provided a reference to show visitors what the house used to look like). During this period he was still working at his scientific instrument repair job, so he set up exterior lights so he could work on the house after he returned from his job in the evenings.

By 2018 he had added what he now identifies as a bottle-walled *Spaceship* (he originally thought of it as a teepee) to the yard. It is likely that the three-dimensional arms that circle the onion-domed top of that structure inspired Dillard to consider adding more dimensional adornments to the house as well. He rolled up tubes of chicken wire and covered them with concrete, turning them into protruding vines that seemed to grow out of the home's southern façade. He later ornamented them with glass beads that maintained the color palette of the walls from which they emanated. In contrast to the organic abstractions on most of the house exterior (but perhaps more in line with some of his humorous steel sculptures), he added a figurative mosaic of mirror and tile fragments outlining a smiling face sporting a Salvador Dalí mustache on the chimney. The head wears a crown-like headdress topped with mirrored spheres built from beach balls covered with fiberglass. The roof is further enhanced with randomly poured slicks of colorful latex paint that mimic the droppings of a monumental prehistoric bird, an idea that came to him as he was working on the chimney, gazing across his neighbors' homes with their "boring" rooftops.

Taken as a whole, Dillard's art environment is both amusingly creative and subtly extravagant. Bursts of color on walls or freestanding sculptures are mostly muted by a low-key color palette, and the generally human scale of his modifications is not incongruous in this modest residential neighborhood. This is reflected in the public's view of his work: the city was, for a time, interested in the *Spaceship*, thinking that perhaps it was going to be a habitable structure, but Dillard showed them that the walls do not quite reach the ground, and as he can store his tools within, he "officially" identifies it as a tool shed. Likewise, he has rejected the idea of charging admission to the property, saying that his work did not come at much greater cost to him than his own sweat equity, and he is happy to share it. He feels that his neighbors' support has been essential in reinforcing his efforts, but speculates that their support might waver if the site were to generate too much traffic or crowds of onlookers slowing down to gawk from the street.

Dillard does not travel as much as he used to, nor does he spend copious amounts of time online looking at other art environments, yet he continues to change his personal space and is currently building a 4 x 45' long wall that he is decorating with pottery shards. (He had hoped that his work might spark other local unique home modifications and is disappointed that, to date, it has not.) As a repairman, he did not generally receive payment until his task was accomplished, so he learned to finish everything he started, and as a youth with a learning disability, he recognized that he needed to carry on and not be afraid of making mistakes. So he continues to come up with new ideas, always completing each project. While not necessarily defining himself as an artist, he does not deny that his best reward is seeing visitors' smiles as they view what he has built.

DILLARD RELISHES THE PLEASURE VISITORS TAKE IN HIS AMUSINGLY CREATIVE AND SUBTLY EXTRAVAGANT ART ENVIRONMENT.

DIMENSIONAL ADORNMENTS ON HOUSE (DETAIL), 2024. PHOTO: STEVE PLATTNER

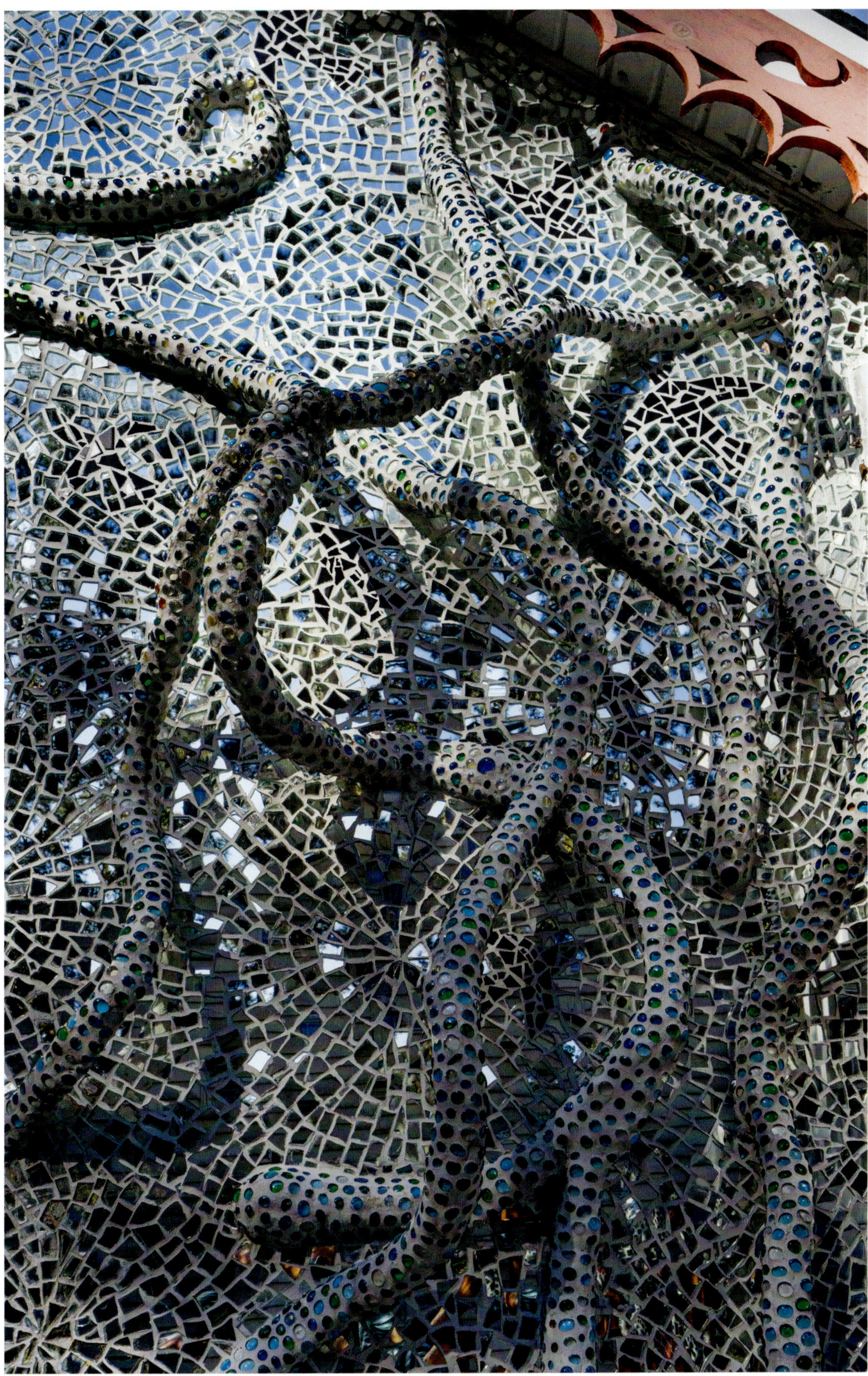

TODD RAMQUIST AND KIARALINDA (A.K.A. THE WHIMZEY TWINS)

WHIMZEYLAND

SAFETY HARBOR, FLORIDA

Kiaralinda (b. 1960) is a native Floridian, born and raised in Clearwater (Kiaralinda is a name she gave herself in 1987). Ramquist (b. 1960) was born in Berwyn, Illinois, and lived there until seventh grade, when he relocated with his parents and siblings to a home four doors down from Kiaralinda's. They met in an art class and from then on they palled around, first in groups and then, by junior or senior year, as a couple. Although they never married, they have been together ever since. Both attended St. Petersburg Junior College (now St. Petersburg College) for two years before transferring to Florida State University and graduating two years later: he, thinking he might attend law school, with a degree in criminal justice and finance, and she with a degree in advertising, already by then knowing that she would spend her life making art.

They spent their first 18 years after graduation producing abstract, reverse-painted Plexiglas artworks, a technique they adapted from her father's display company, but they modified the process with bold color, warping, cutting, and the addition of other media, including wire. They started out to make a living on the art fair circuit, surprising themselves with their immediate success; even today they spend around six months on the road each year, traveling cross-country to sell their wares. They easily transitioned from the Plexiglas-and-wire pieces to their current offerings, aluminum wire twisted into various shapes, names, and words. In contrast to the Plexiglas works, the wire pieces are weatherproof and can be assembled anywhere: all they need are needle-nose pliers.

Kiaralinda's mother passed away soon after their graduation, and in 1985, with her $10,000 bequest, the young couple purchased a 900-square-foot beige bungalow on a standard 50 x 100′ lot in a somewhat forgotten neighborhood of Safety Harbor. Sometimes people are inspired by what is there, but other times people are inspired by what is missing; here they were liberated from the kind of rigid rules they were familiar with in the subdivisions in which they grew up: in this neighborhood there were no rules. Hands-on doers, the couple immediately started to clean and fix up the house, at first not thinking that it would turn into a canvas for their art.

They initially painted the house exterior gray, white, and lavender—the latter color a rebellious take on the more conventional mauve of those years. But by the time the house needed repainting, they chose hot peach, plum, azalea, and teal. Soon they were highlighting every surface—door panels, eaves, window jambs, and each façade—with different colors. Inspired on their travels by the Victorian gingerbread of San Francisco's "Painted Ladies" and the pastel colors of Key West, they constructed their own rickrack and began scavenging for other components they could modify to suit their needs—bed spindles, pieces of balconies, cast-concrete yard art.

Landscaping was needed, too, and a sign at a flea market offering 10 free bowling balls to anyone who asked became the spark to set off different areas of the grounds. But the mostly black balls did not fit with their color scheme, so Kiaralinda painted some, neighborhood kids painted some, and even passersby who wanted to help painted some. To date, between 800 and 1,000 bowling balls have been placed around flower beds or piled into pyramids on the exterior, in addition to around 100 balls that were painted by invitation by artists in and outside of the contemporary art mainstream. They complemented the bowling balls in the yard with artworks they traded with other artists, with luxurious plants that were scavenged or gifted, and with winding walkways covered with bright mosaics.

With such a small home—the interior reduced even further by the installation of their collections—the need for more space became increasingly pressing. So they kept their eyes and ears open: a local restaurant was getting rid of a gazebo, for example, and offered to give it to them if they would remove it quickly, so they cut it into movable pieces, trucked it over to their yard, and rebuilt it for use as a dining area and event space. They did the same for a small clapboard structure that they originally used as a studio (now it functions more as a museum, displaying the painted bowling balls and photographs of artists, musicians, and celebrities holding those balls). These two vernacular structures were incorporated into the *Whimzeyland* compound without the need for permits, and they were decorated and painted according to the couple's vibrant color palette and aesthetic of "more is more."

But they were still running out of space, so they purchased other nearby bungalows—two of which they use as temporary lodging for visiting friends and artists, and others that they use as rentals—and turned yet another into what became the Safety Harbor Arts and Music Center, a nonprofit

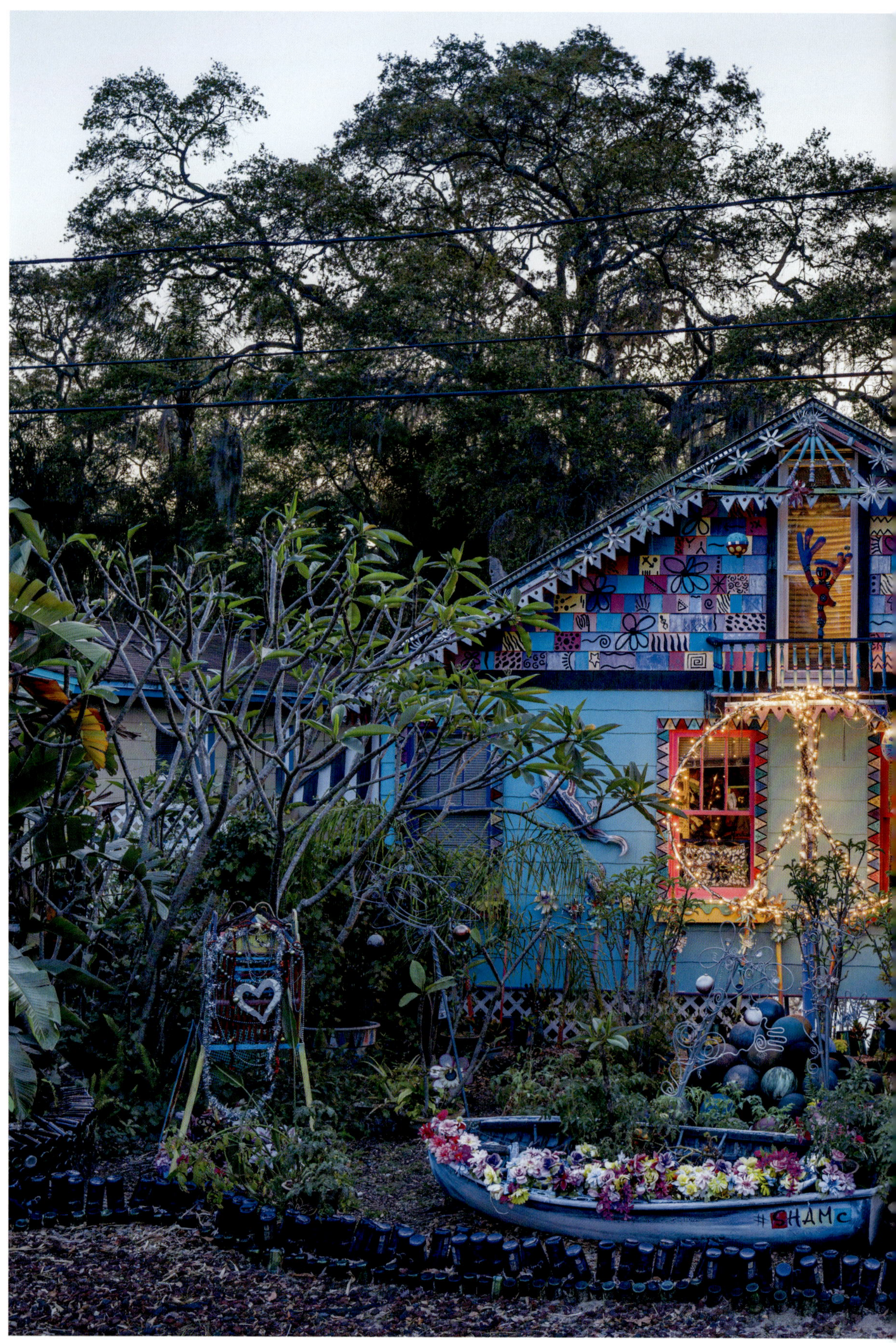

FRONT FAÇADE, 2024

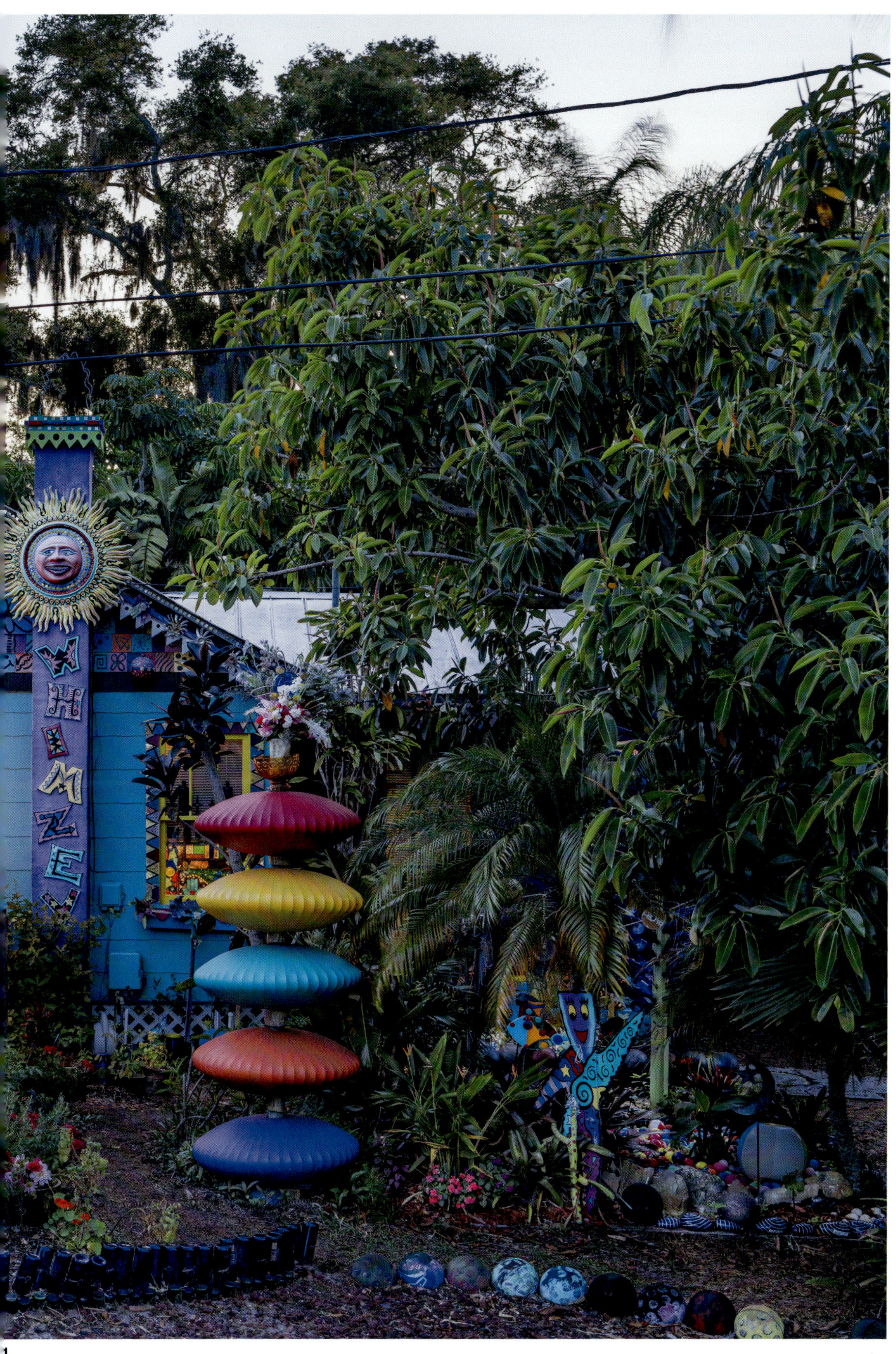
WHIMZEY

cultural center run by volunteers, where people can enjoy concerts, exhibitions, and art workshops, and sign up for more extensive tours of *Whimzeyland*. (A spacious modern structure was later added to the project, thanks to a grant from PepsiCo.)

The intensity and density of the evolving *Whimzeyland* site has been amplified over the years due to the couple's open-ended appreciation of the work of other artists and, in particular, the art environments that they visit on their travels. Their own creations depend on the availability of scavenged resources, which they improvisationally add as they find them, working directly with the materials without plans or preliminary sketches. The entire site organically developed in this way: there was never a "grand plan" for the elaboration of such expansive development. Two art cars and various works of public sculpture also complement their work on-site.

While some makers of art environments have monetized visits to their properties, Ramquist and Kiaralinda steadfastly refuse to consider it, even while sometimes hosting up to 100 people a day in fine weather. They have organized their lives such that their wire sculpture sales and house rentals cover their expenses, and they are dedicated to keeping *Whimzeyland* free and open for people to enjoy. They have had young people come to them and tell them that they became artists thanks to early inspiration they received from their site, and as they themselves continue to make their art their life, they want to spread their connections, their energy, and their passion for creating.

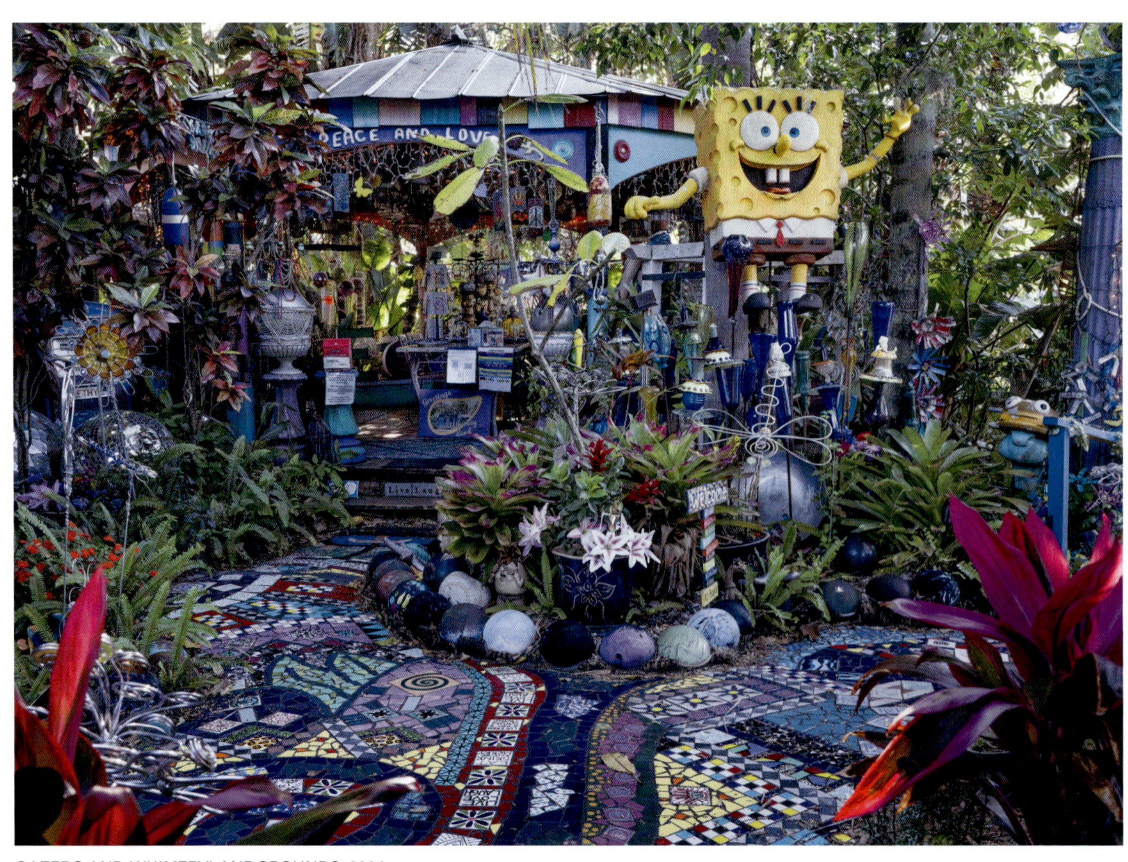

GAZEBO AND *WHIMZEYLAND* GROUNDS, 2024

KITCHEN CEILING IN THE NEARBY *CASA LOCO* [*SIC*], 2024

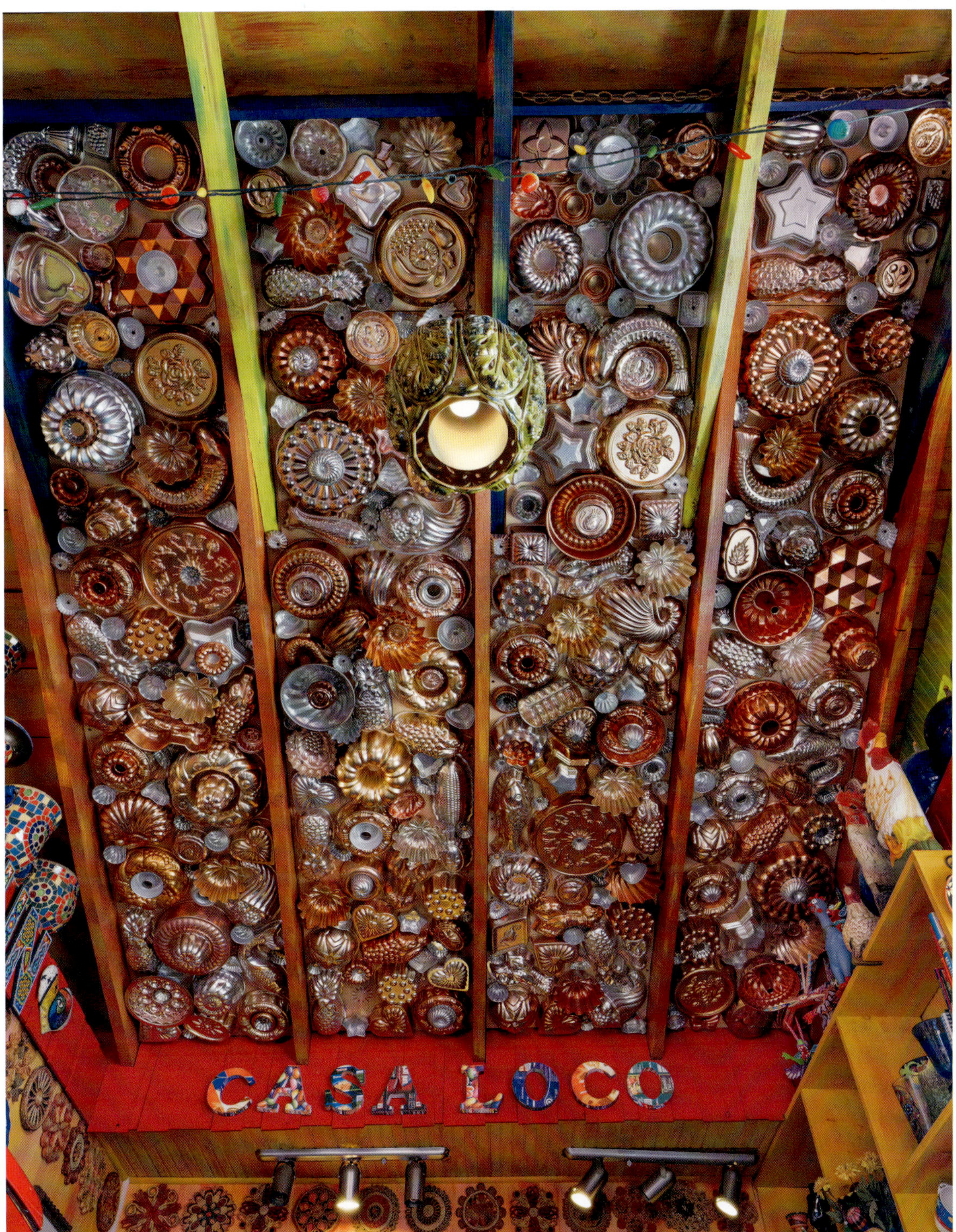

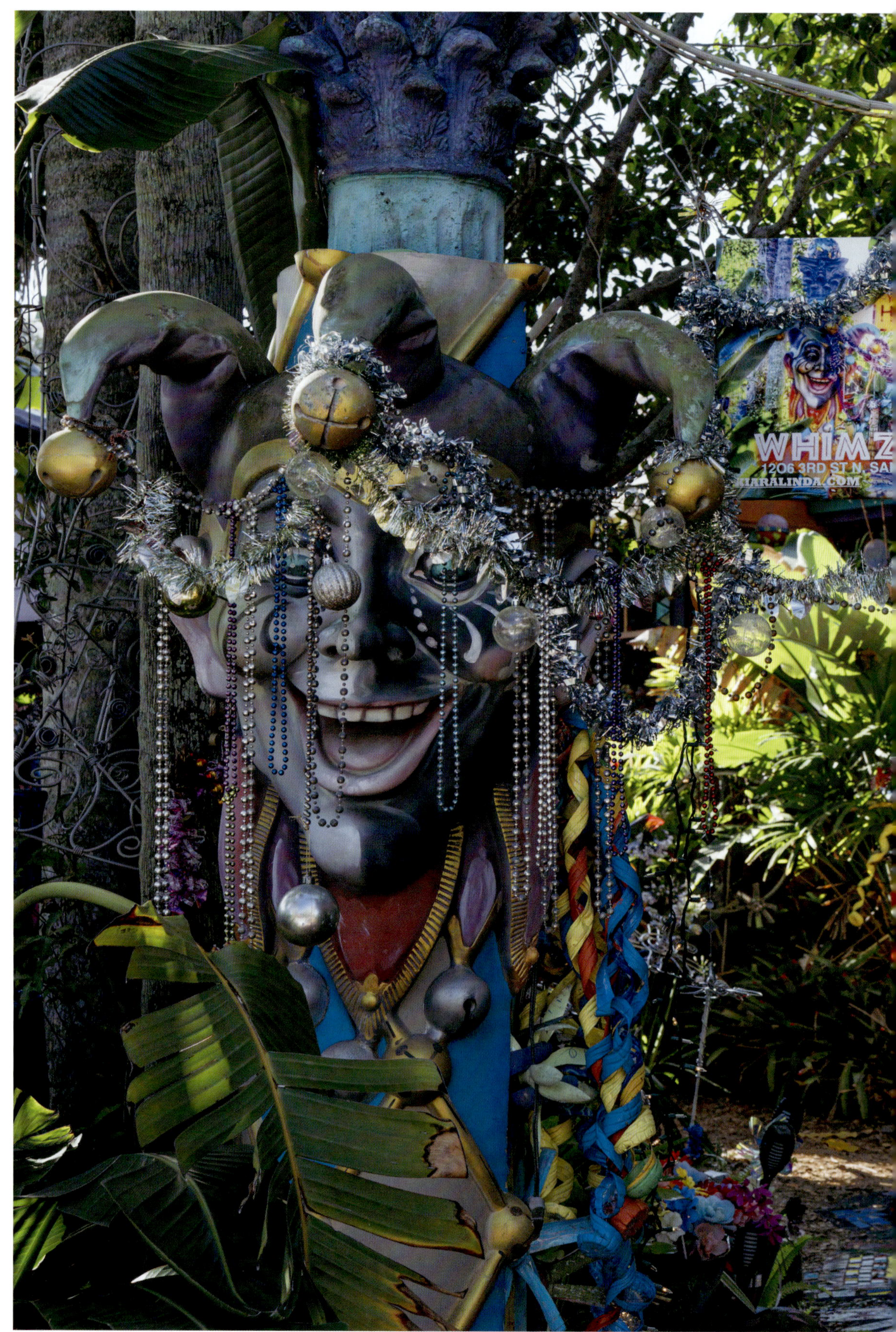

WHIMZEYLAND GROUNDS, 2024

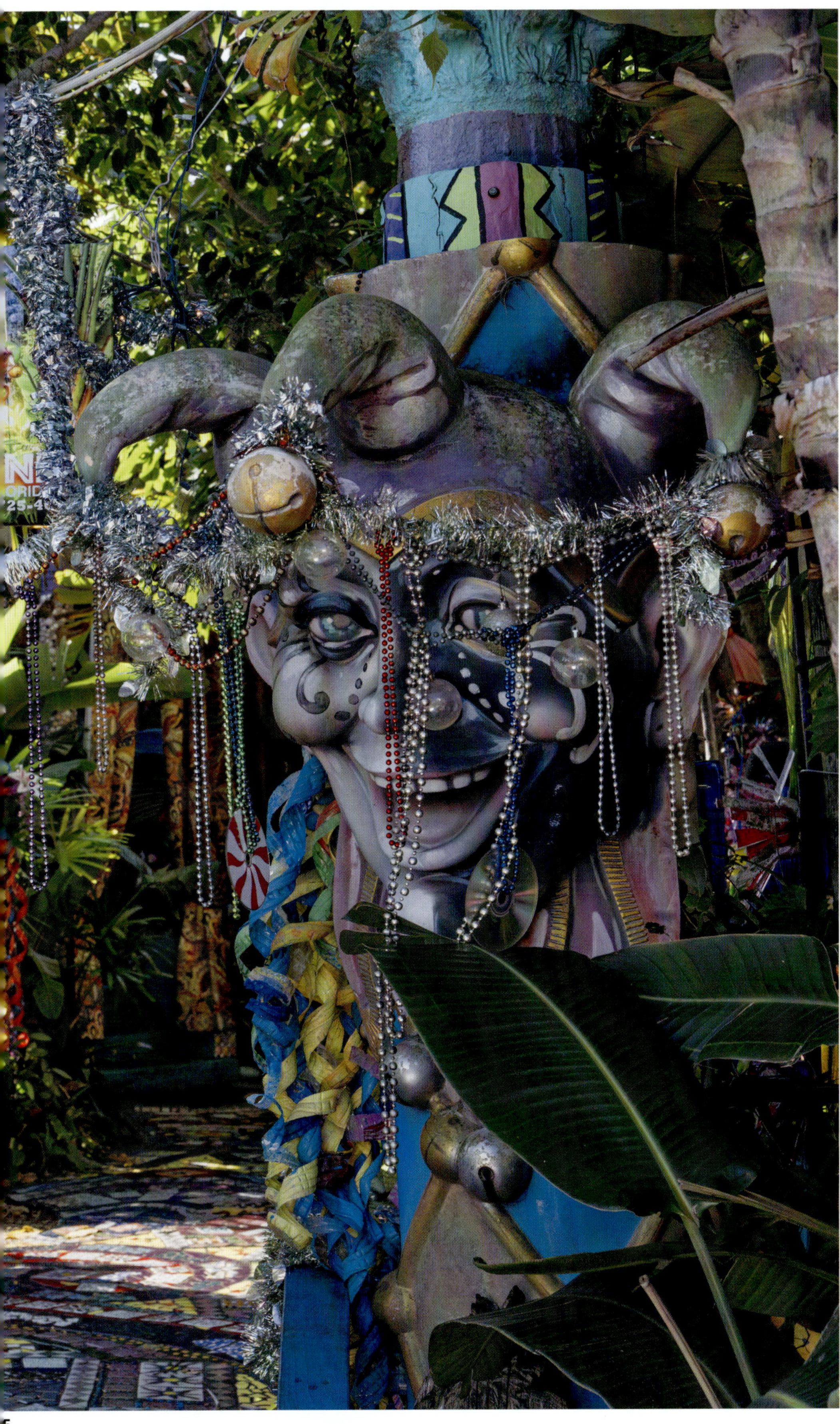

EMANUELE "LITTO" DAMONTE

HUBCAP RANCH

POPE VALLEY, CALIFORNIA

California's Napa Valley, world renowned for the beauty of its rolling hills and the quality of its wineries, hosts literally millions of tourists annually. But most of them miss another local attraction: the decorated lower areas of the Damonte family ranch.

Damonte, known as Litto (1892–1985), immigrated in 1907 from Arenzano, Italy, with his father, a marble mason who had been hired to work on Stanford University's Memorial Chapel. (His mother and siblings joined them later.) Although he had been an altar boy in Italy and, with his life centered around his church, had considered becoming a priest, the younger Damonte instead helped his father lay marble and mosaic floors. He settled in San Francisco and worked in marble and then as a cement contractor and tile setter in both San Francisco and Daly City. Looking for lower taxes, in the interwar years he bought a couple of hundred mostly empty acres outside of the town of Pope Valley in the eastern part of Napa County. After retiring in the early 1940s, he moved full time to the country, managing herds of sheep, pigs, horses, and cows, and constructing several small buildings in the vernacular style.

He also piled up rocks from a nearby cliff alongside the entrance to his driveway, but motorists would turn around at that point and knock the rocks over. To discourage this, he built an entrance barrier out of tires, rocks, a few found objects, and gravel, inlaying them into concrete mortar. In that era, the unpaved country roads were notoriously potholed, and drivers would routinely lose their hubcaps; family legend has it that Damonte began to pick them up and carefully arrange them along the entrance fence in case drivers might return to claim them. But few ever did. (The county road was finally surfaced in 1960.)

Noticing the display, neighbors and friends also brought him hubcaps, and Damonte began to hang them up on the fences and trees, flanking the driveway that provided access into the property and adding others to adorn the sides of the ranch buildings. He complemented them with such other discarded metal objects as pie tins, flattened beer cans, trays, pans for washing and sluicing gold, horseshoes, tractor seats, license plates, and pull tops. Antlers, painted tires, road signs, car parts, toys, wine bottles, abalone shells, ceramic dishes, porcelain toilets, and other found objects rounded out his palette, accompanying scores of wishing wells that he had already created from gravel he hauled from local quarries as well as some 200 birdhouses he built from recycled boxes and crates. Dense interior spaces featured an even more eclectic arrangement of Litto's natural and industrial collections. He was proud of his accomplishments and, amused by the interest, welcomed passing visitors to admire his assemblages. He worked six days a week, 10 to 12 hours a day.

At his death, it was estimated that the self-proclaimed "Hubcap King" had collected around 3,000 hubcaps, representing almost every make and model of American cars as well as a broad sampling of European marques; as of this writing, the latest generation of the Damonte family who lives on the ranch estimates that there are around 5,000 hubcaps on display. It has been said that the U.S. parachute team used the ranch as a landmark, as the reflections off the metal helped them position themselves for their high-altitude jumps.

In 1981, this site, along with nine other California art environments, was nominated as a State Historical Landmark. The State Historical Resources Commission placed a plaque honoring its inclusion as Landmark #939 two years after Damonte's death.

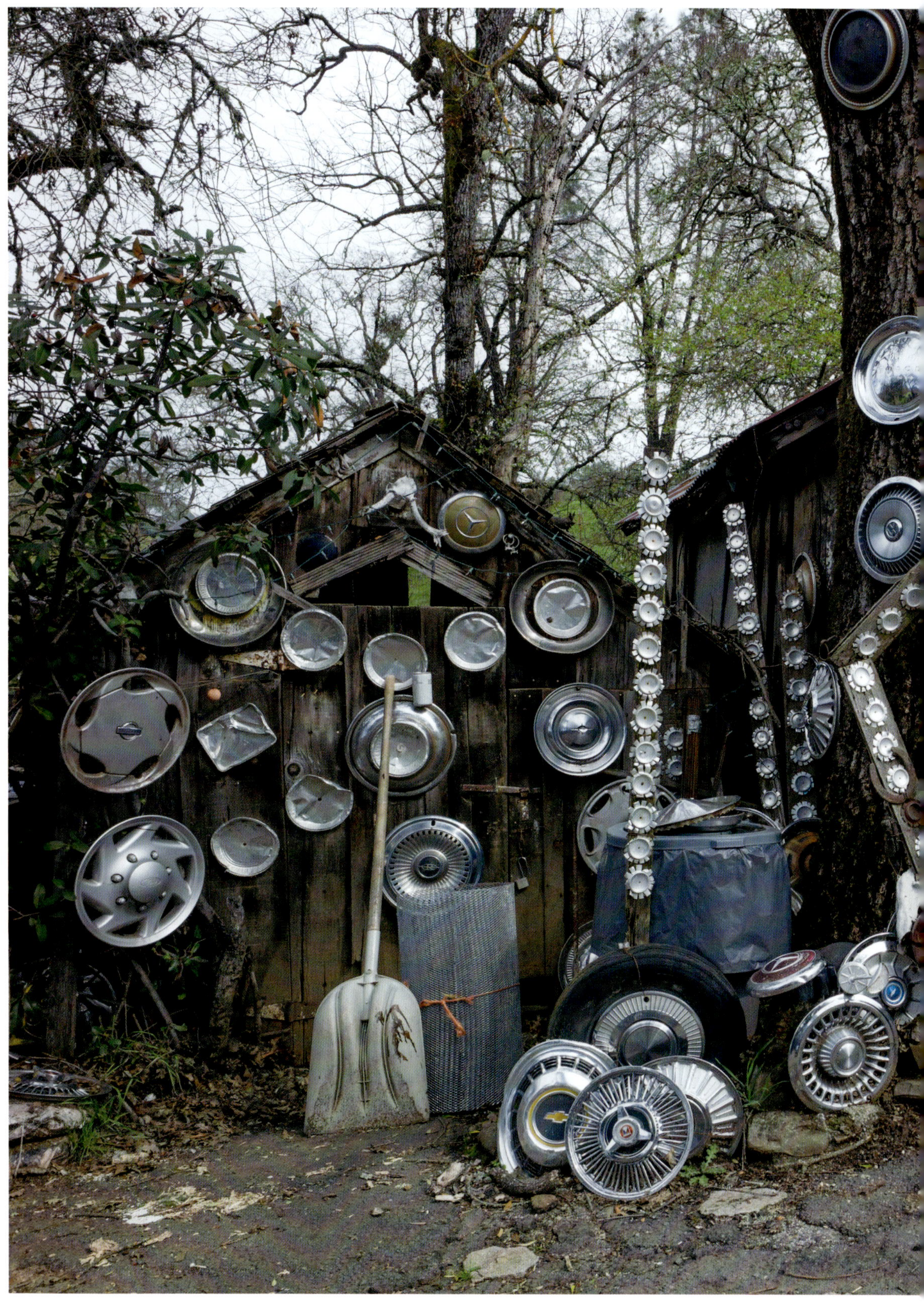

OUTBUILDINGS, *HUBCAP RANCH*, 2010. PHOTO: STEVE PLATTNER

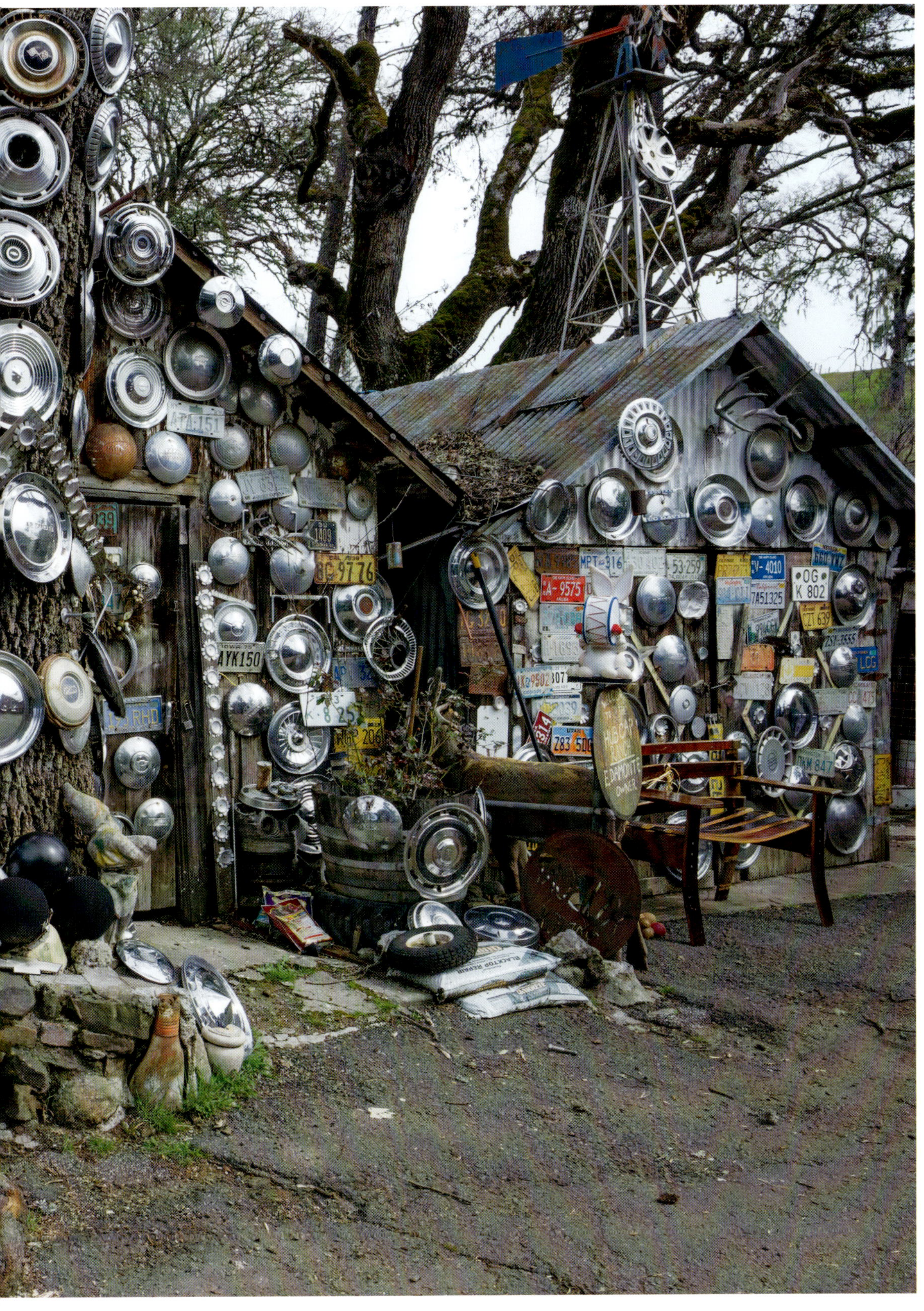

ENTRANCE TO *HUBCAP RANCH*, 2010. PHOTO: STEVE PLATTNER

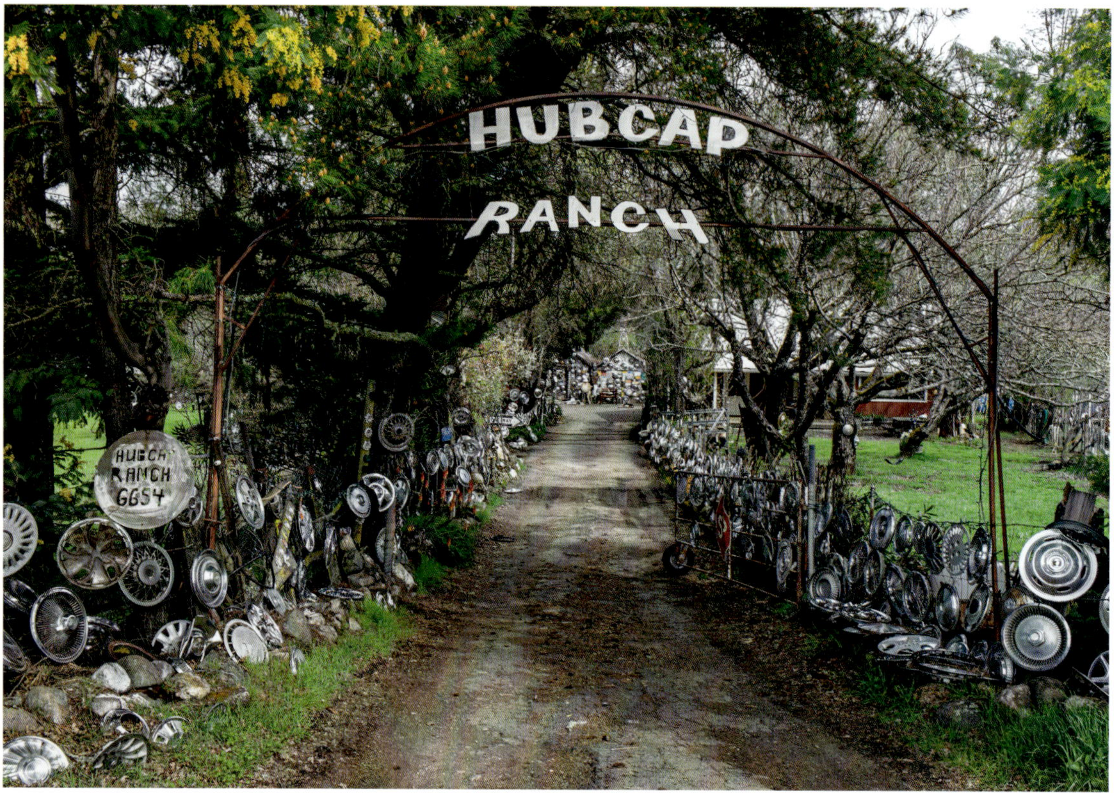

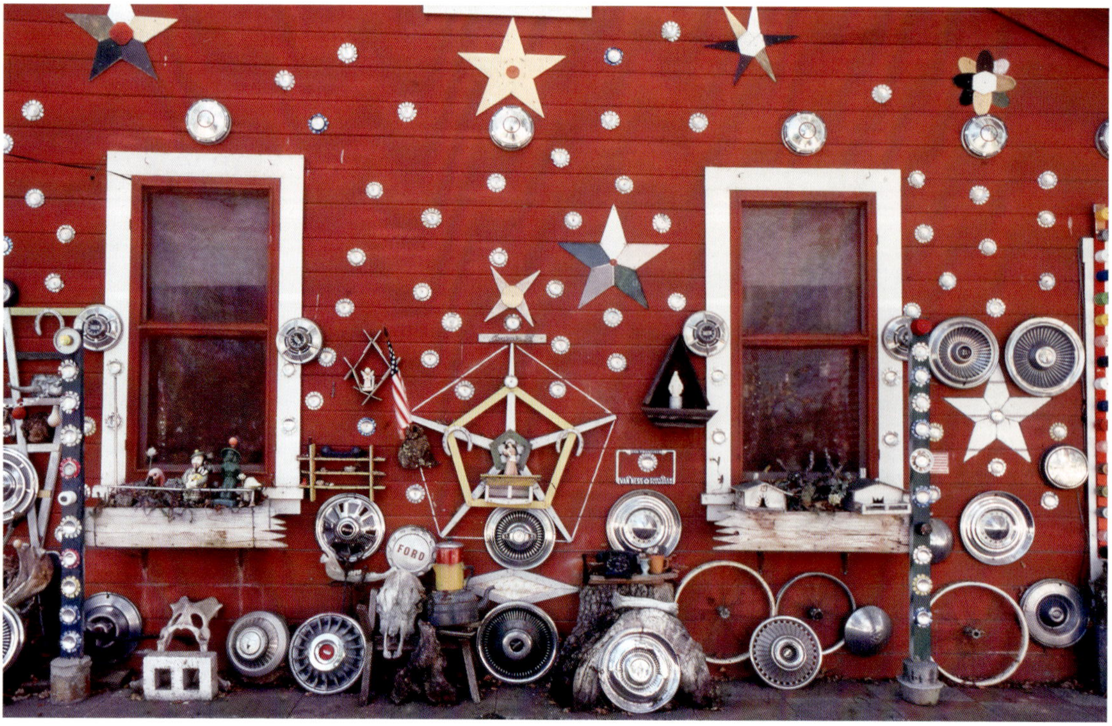

SIDE FAÇADE, DAMONTE HOME, 1977. PHOTO: SEYMOUR ROSEN, © SPACES ARCHIVES, COURTESY JOHN MICHAEL KOHLER ARTS CENTER

REFLECTION OFF THE "HUBCAP KING'S" COLLECTIONS HELPED THE U.S. PARACHUTE TEAM POSITION THEMSELVES FOR HIGH-ALTITUDE JUMPS.

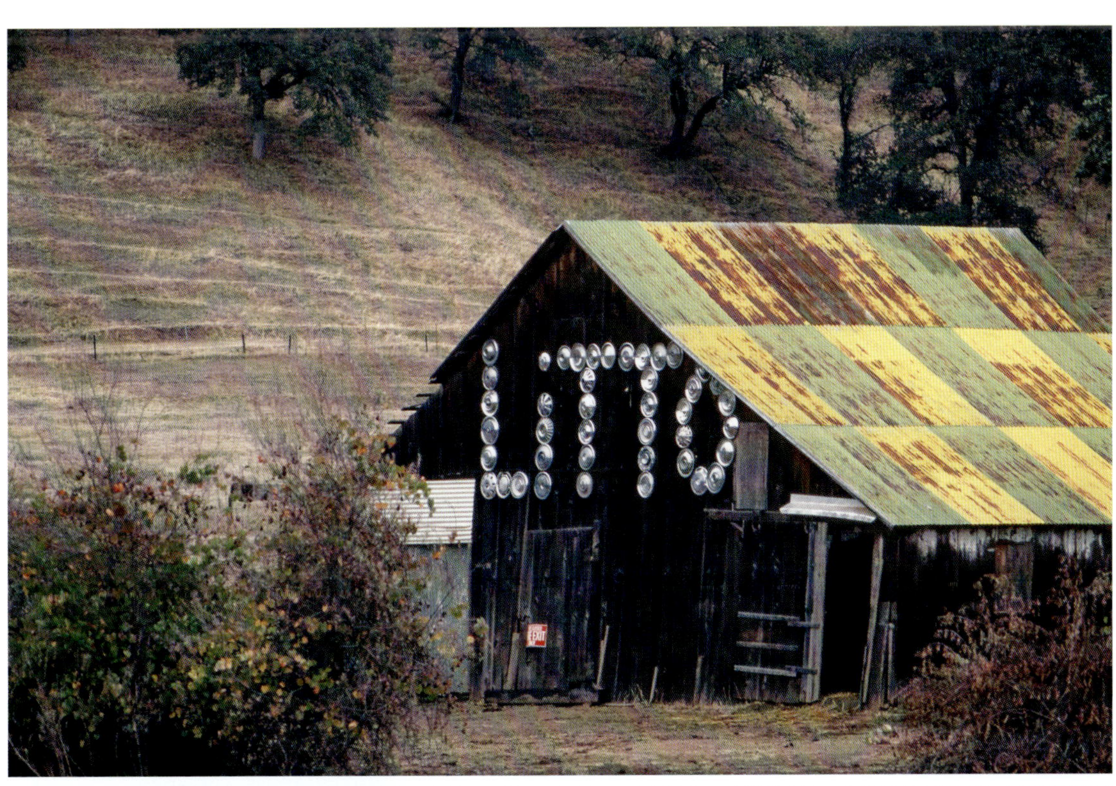

 OUTBUILDING, *HUBCAP RANCH*, 1984. PHOTO: SEYMOUR ROSEN, © SPACES ARCHIVES, COURTESY JOHN MICHAEL KOHLER ARTS CENTER

CHRIS DONG VO

FLOWER HOUSE

CLEVELAND, OHIO

When he was a teenager, Vo (1964–2021) fled Ho Chi Minh City as a refugee in order to escape the communist regime under which he had lived until that time. He found his way to Ohio, and in 2011 purchased a typical ranch-style home on Cleveland's West Side, near the border with Lakewood. Little by little, he began adding decorations: hundreds of plastic flowers—from which came the public moniker for his home—but also figurative, animal, and religious sculptures as well as lights, arranged stones, and garden ornaments.

For Vo, this house represented America and the freedom and equal opportunity he had dreamt of. He also explicitly noted that he was decorating the house to honor those who, like his nephew, lost their lives trying to escape communism, as it was likewise a nod to Vietnamese traditions that considered the decoration of one's property an accepted sign of one's prosperity. As news of his intent grew, anonymous members of the public began to drop off additional objects for the house. He interpreted these donations as an effort to increase America's beauty and to vaunt her celebrated welcome of immigrants.

Complementing his after-hours adornment of his home environment, Vo worked as a hair stylist, devoting his career to making individuals beautiful, as well. Around 2006, ballroom dance instructor and performer Nick Malusky moved in and supported Vo's efforts as he continued to embellish the house and property. However, several of their neighbors were not pleased with the decorations, and called for the city council to force their removal, citing, in particular, their concern that some of the artificial flowers and decorations were installed at a level that interfered with sightlines on the corner stop. (There had been no records of any accidents at this intersection attributable to this supposed obstruction.) Vo responded to the articulated concerns by removing decorations in that area, but charged that the complaints had more to do with the fact that he and Malusky were gay life-partners, rather than the home's decorations. There are no municipal laws that address an overabundance of decorations in Cleveland.

Although one of the neighbors who had objected so vociferously about the decorations later apologized, the negative publicity the house received attracted more bad actors. Unexpectedly, Malusky received an email from a reality television show, offering to "improve" the *Flower House* in exchange for letting them film the property and broadcast it on their program. The producers required a 30-day moveout to allow them time to do their work and so they could broadcast the surprising reveal, but when Vo next saw the property, all of his decorations had been stolen or destroyed. Personal items, housewares, and furniture were also missing, and the promised construction projects had not been completed. The reality show staff filmed how upset he was, defaming his character by stating he had "lost touch with reality" and inferring that he was crazy. Although Vo did not give them permission to air the segment, they did so anyway, causing him to lose family, friends, and clients.

While a crowdfunding campaign attempted to raise funds to resurrect the environment, it never recovered its earlier splendor. And then the day after Christmas, 2021, Vo was found savagely beaten, stabbed, strangled, and shot in his home's garage. Two members of the local gay community with prior criminal convictions, acquaintances of Vo's who had set him up for a robbery, were ultimately found guilty of homicide and each was sentenced to life imprisonment. Vo's ashes were shipped back to Vietnam so he could be buried near his parents. Sadly, there is no surviving trace of the *Flower House*.

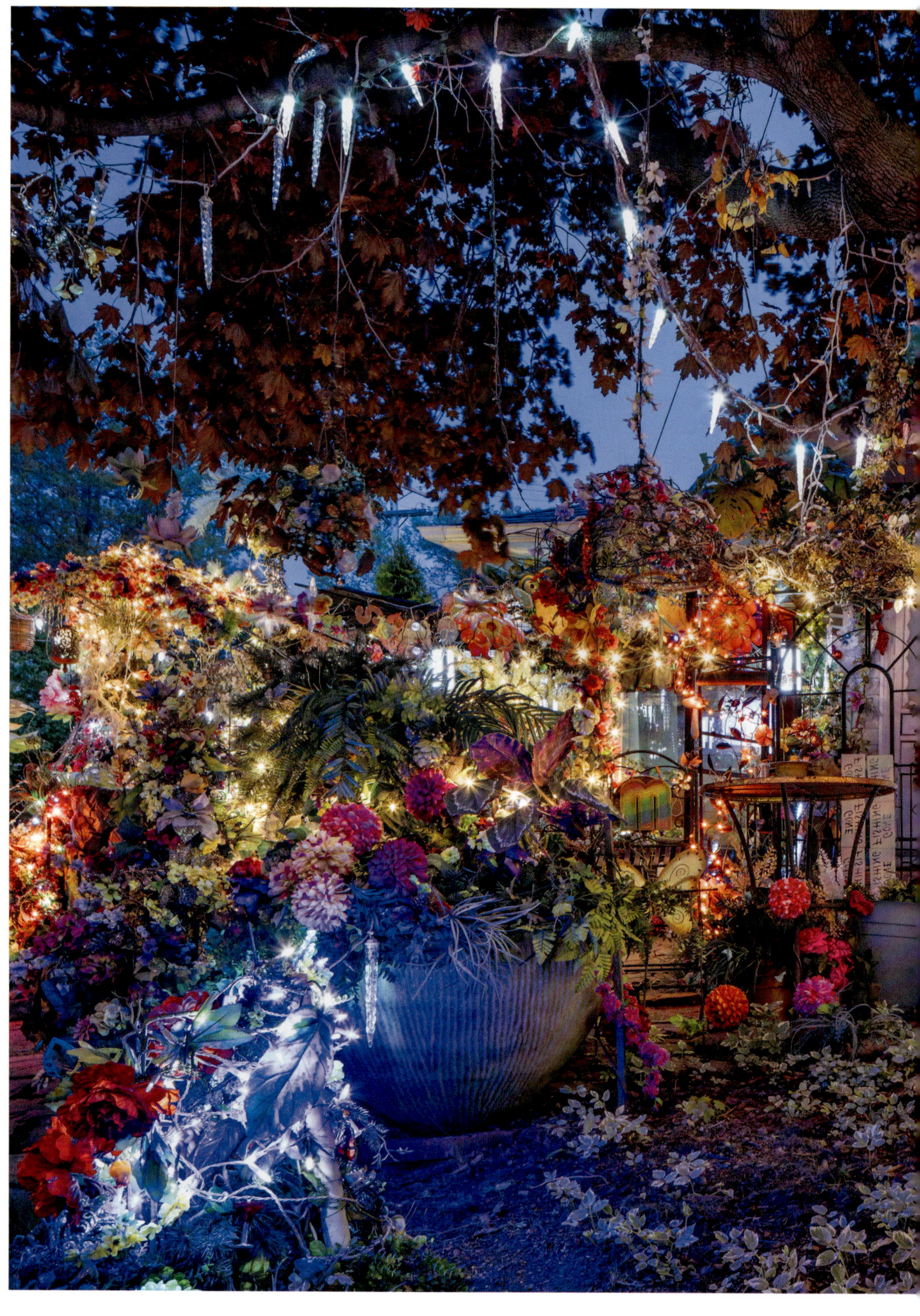

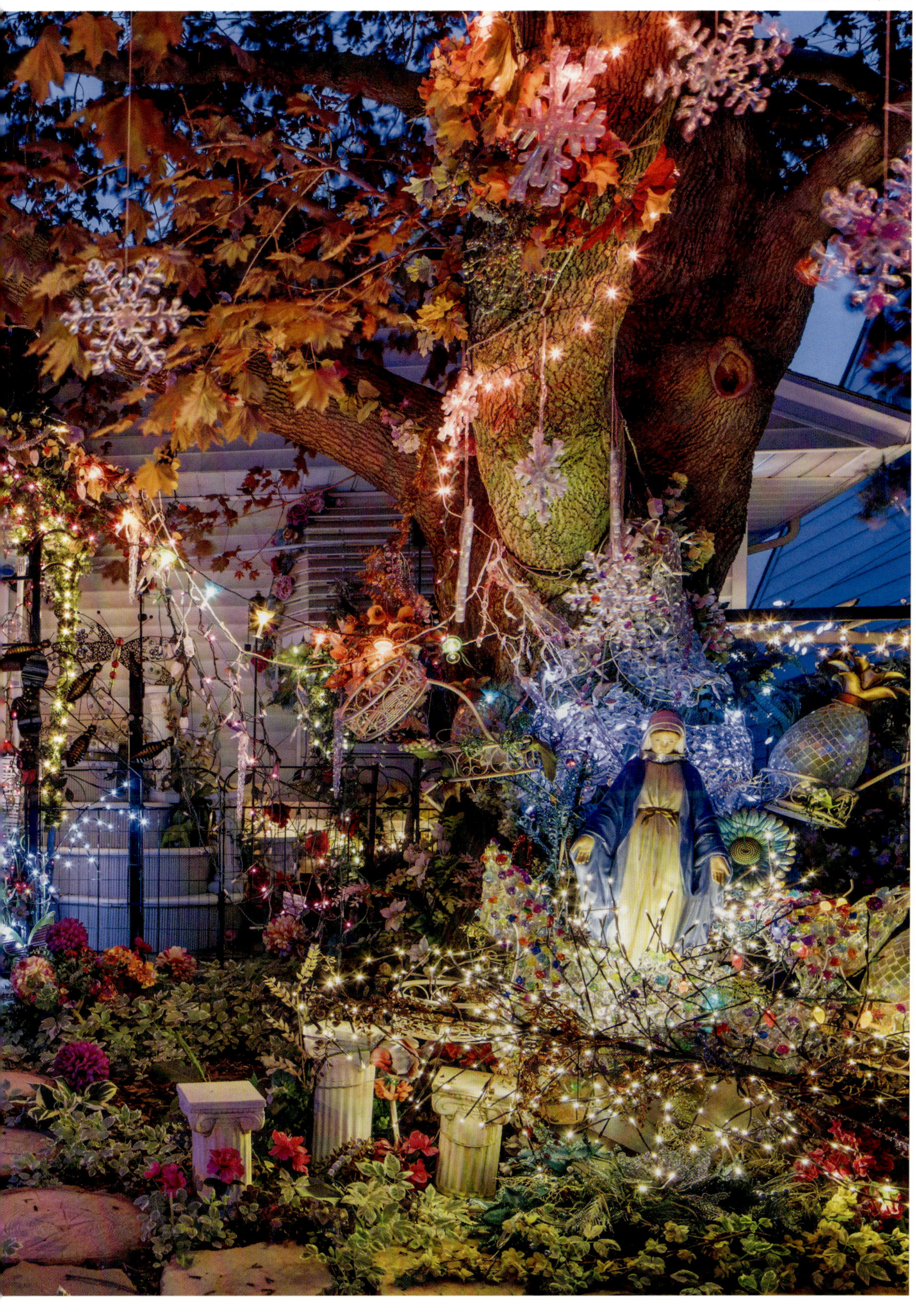

OVERVIEW OF *FLOWER HOUSE* AND GROUNDS, 2016

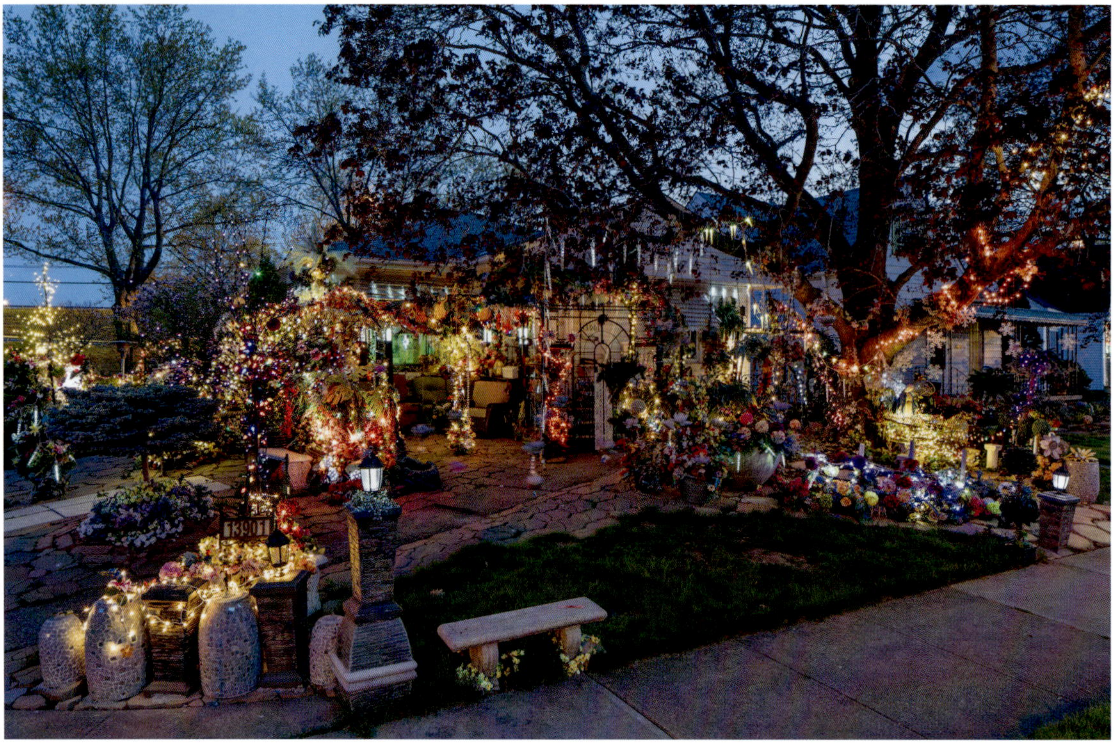

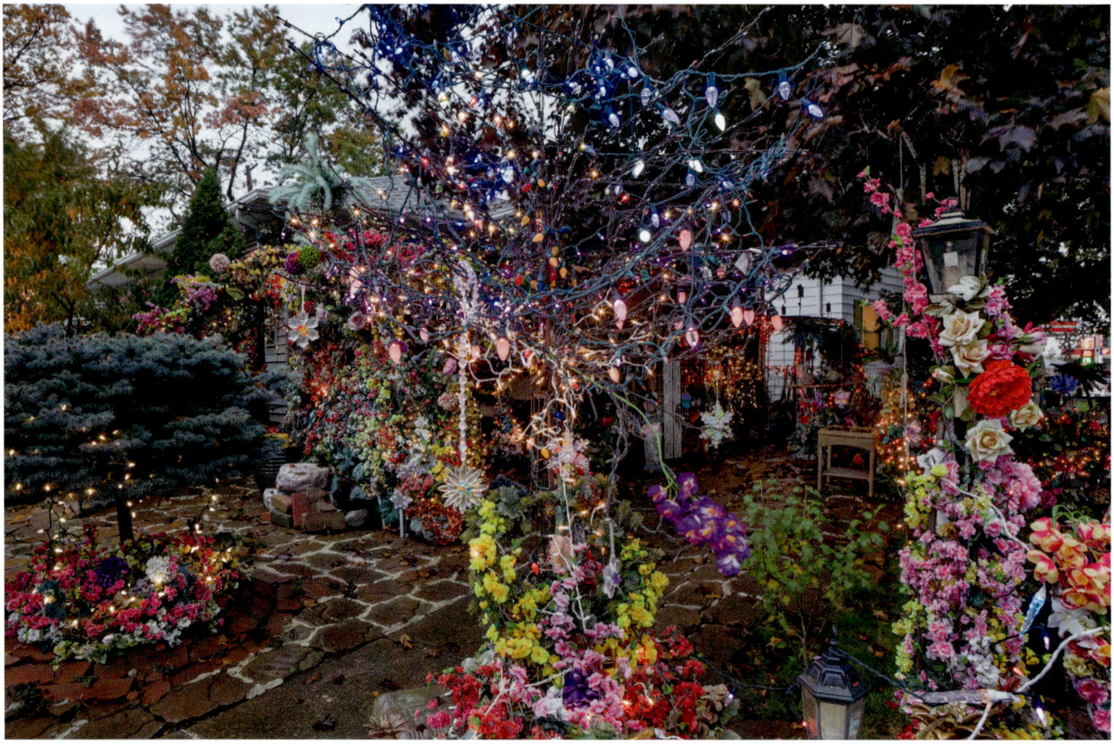

FLOWER HOUSE GROUNDS, 2017

THE HOUSE REPRESENTED AMERICAN FREEDOM AND THE EQUAL OPPORTUNITY THIS VIETNAMESE IMMIGRANT HAD DREAMT OF.

CASIMIRO "CASEY" T. MÁRQUEZ

CASA DE COLORES (HOUSE OF COLORS)

LAS VEGAS, NEW MEXICO

A former auto body repairman and house painter, Márquez (1930–2010) was handy with a spray-paint can and knowledgeable about the use of color. Around 1985 he turned his hand to ornamenting a small and ramshackle one-story home at the end of a cul-de-sac, and while the general infrastructure of the modest building, with its single-gable corrugated metal roof and adobe/plaster/plywood/rock walls would not normally occasion a second glance, the painted and affixed ornamentation was striking and immediately attracted attention.

The primary colors of red and blue featured predominantly on the exterior. There were also many polka dots, some made larger through outlining in contrasting colors, and certain sections of the walls were gridded off, promoting a sense of greater cohesion and rhythm. Triangles and almost Aboriginal patterning of lozenges, stripes, snakes, and random abstractions communicated an impression similar to that of a patchwork quilt—distinct yet complementary sections, evincing a direct elemental approach without preciousness or awkwardness.

He assembled a front perimeter fence from various materials and painted it with his characteristic polka dots, angled lines, and stripes, and later he mounted large plastic rocking horses on top. Laundry lines with metallic mylar fringe were strung across the enclosed dirt yard in front of the house, and he hung larger stuffed animals and toys from the lines "to bring out the kid" in himself. But his exterior ornamentations weathered poorly in New Mexico's hot summers and snowy winters.

Márquez stayed mostly indoors during the winter, busily decorating the interior with multicolored polka dots and other abstractions on the walls, ceilings, and floors. Representational framed prints, drawings, and religious posters punctuated the designs he painted on the walls, as did more stuffed animals rescued from visits to the local thrift store. A large geometric abstraction of concentric circles in contrasting red, white, and blue connected by carefully drawn sunburst lines, almost Symbolist in its impact, was the central point of reference for the kitchen floor. Smaller images with similarly painted lines—horizontal, vertical, and at 45-degree angles—were outlined as if framed, not only on the kitchen walls but elsewhere on the property as well. His bed frame was also festooned with polka dots, complemented by the bedspread, which featured a patriotic commercial print of stars and anchors in red, white, and blue.

Local artist Michael Baca, whose wife Yvonne had helped Márquez as a caregiver as he aged, began adding his own images to exterior walls. Discrete and generally figurative, they contrasted markedly with the abstractions, but Márquez seemed not to mind. Many were reminiscent of conventional graffiti motifs of aliens, spaceships, animals, and mushrooms, but he also painted a resplendent polychrome Virgin of Guadalupe basking in her rays. Following Márquez's death, other local graffiti artists added their own touches to the built environment, identifying the site as a "Bear Cave." But the enclosure became overgrown, with no organization to the random deteriorating objects that once had presumably been intended to augment the home's decoration. As the artworks further degraded, the yard became a storage area for neighbors' vehicles as well.

Although Márquez's painted decorations tended toward geometric abstractions, he complemented these designs by identifying the property with his name, the moniker of the house, and its location, as well as with text warning trespassers away with his tongue-in-cheek sign "*Mi Casa No Es Su Casa* (My House Is Not Your House)," a notice that was painted and repainted numerous times. A humble dwelling without running water, the infrastructure itself was fragile, and the decorations even more so. The stuffed animals became moldy, the paint peeled off the walls, the found objects once so joyfully fastened to the walls became detached. In its current state, this art environment can no longer be considered extant.

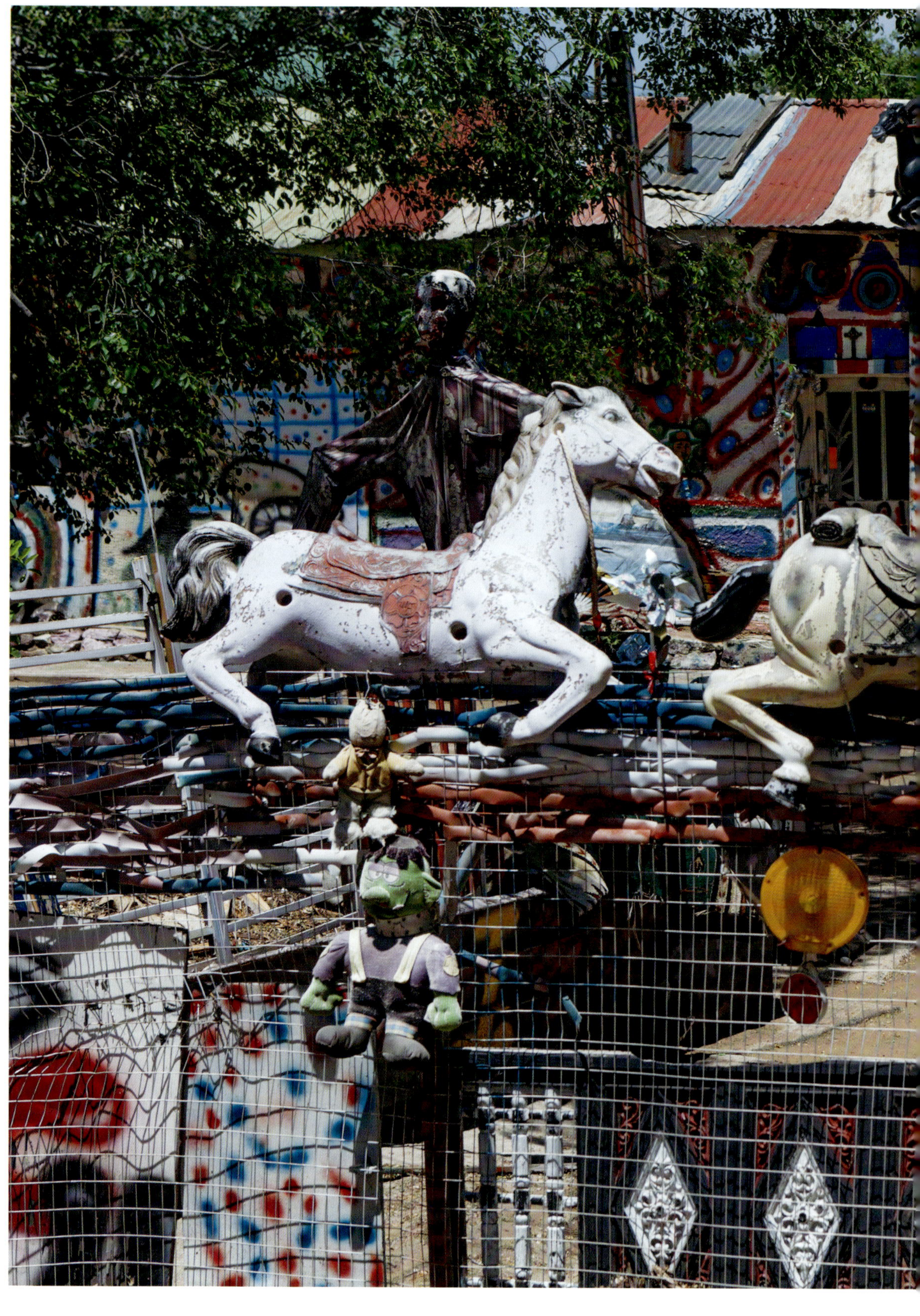

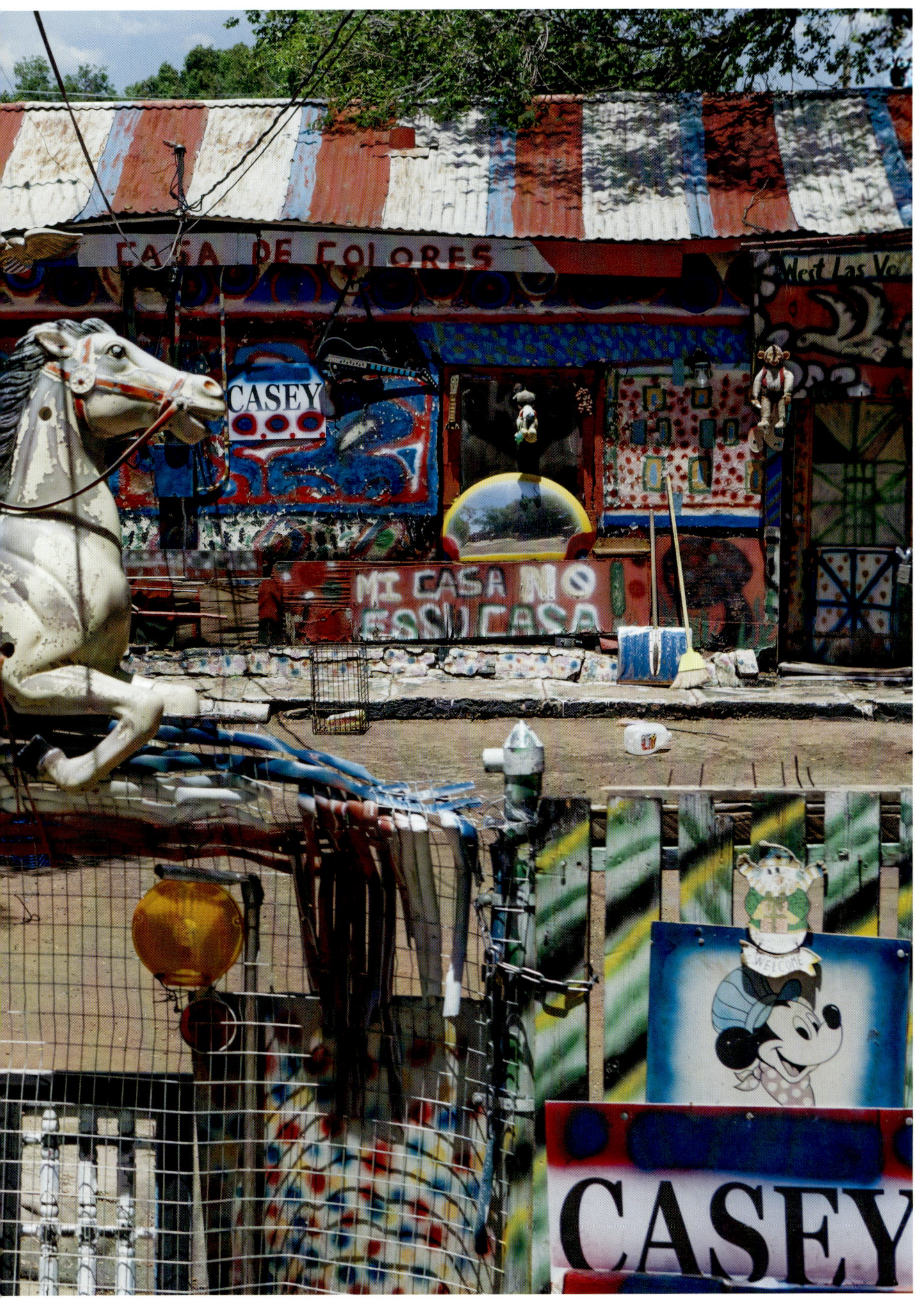
CASA DE COLORES
CASEY
MI CASA NO
ES SU CASA
CASEY

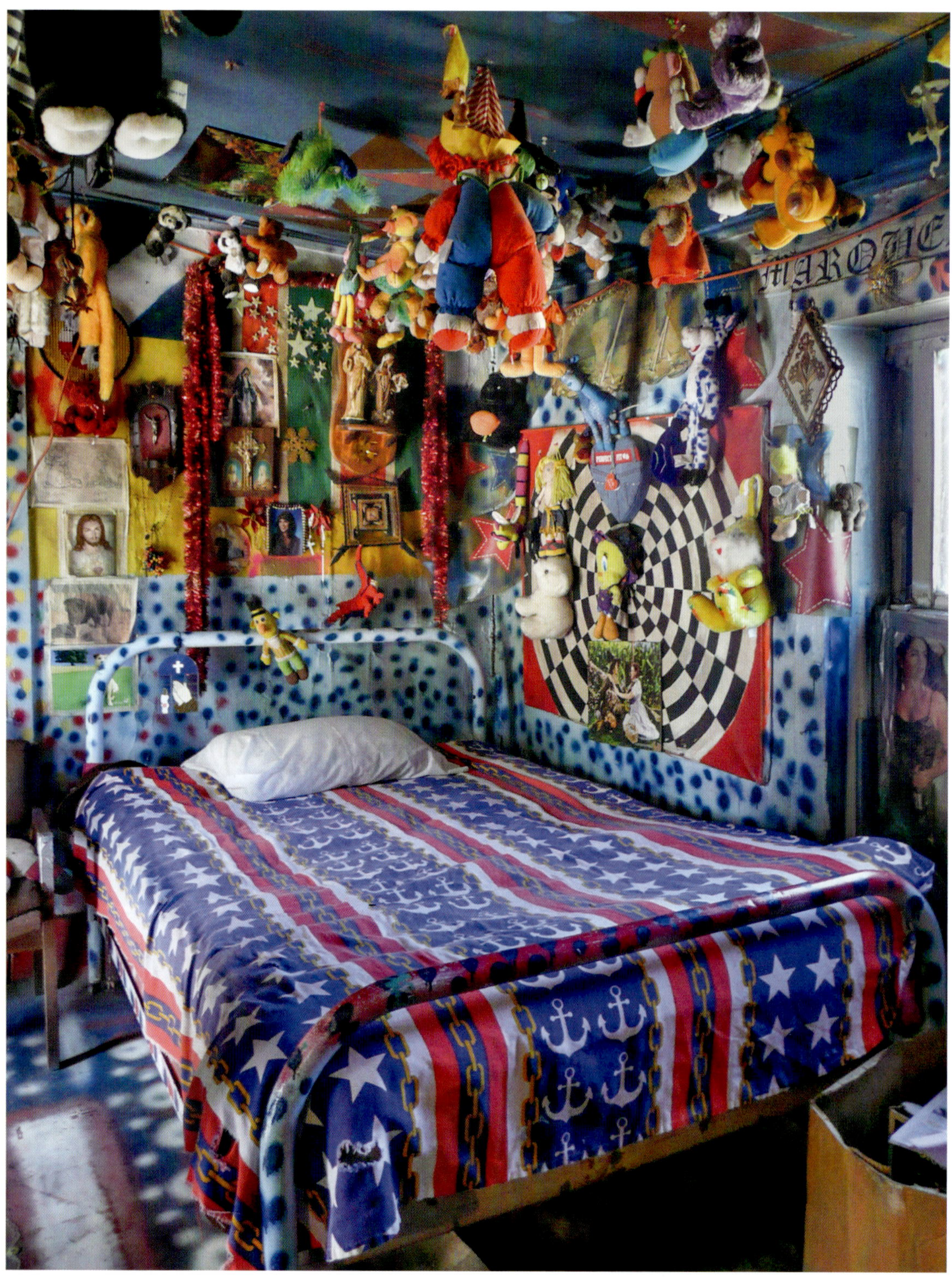

BEDROOM, 2008. PHOTO: KELLY LUDWIG

HOME EXTERIOR, 2008. PHOTO: KELLY LUDWIG

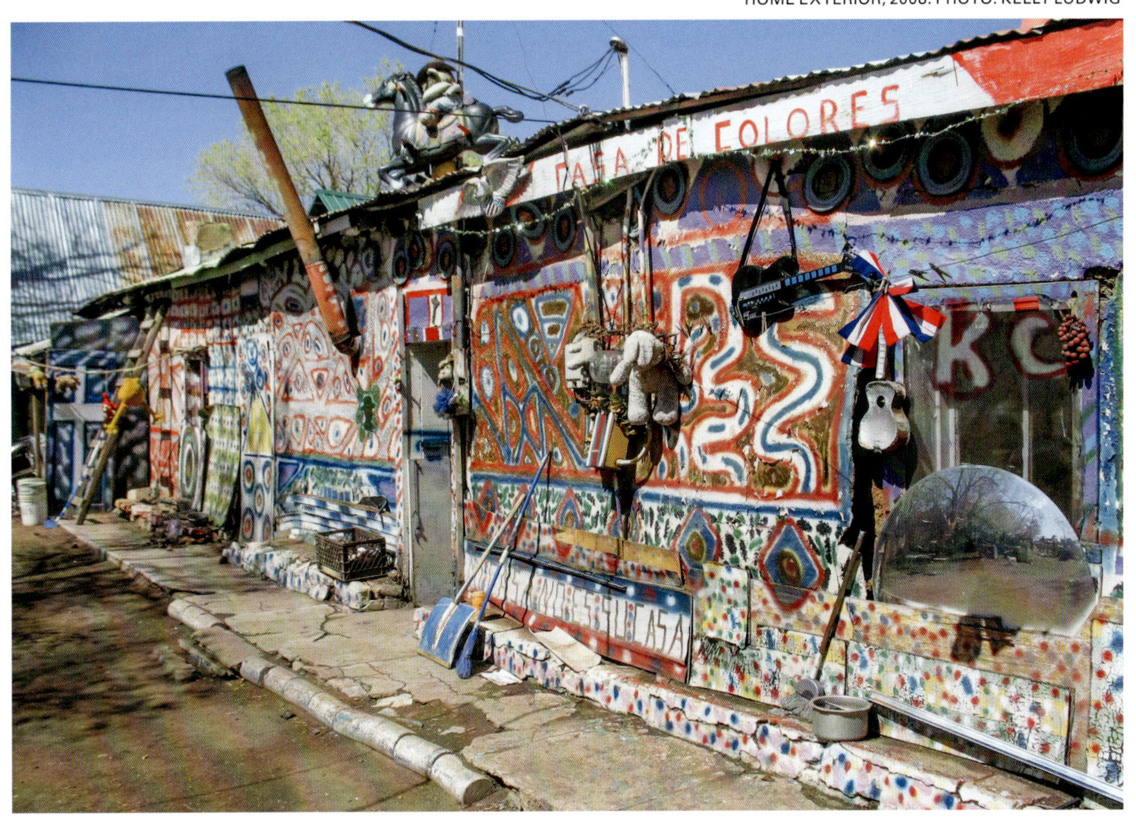

PAINTED GEOMETRIC ABSTRACTIONS AND POLKA DOTS COMPLEMENTED FOUND OBJECTS TO BRING OUT "THE KID" IN THE ARTIST.

JOHN MILKOVISCH

BEER CAN HOUSE

HOUSTON, TEXAS

It is relatively common for builders of art environments to begin their labors in order to address a seemingly routine problem that, once resolved, leads to continuing creative displays around the property. Milkovisch (1912–1988) wanted to enhance his 1939 bungalow and its 1/10-acre lot in Houston's West End, originally built by his father as a rental property, by constructing a rear patio that would be sheltered from the sun, a place where he and his wife could sit outside after work and on weekends to share a beer and a laugh. After paying off the house's mortgage in 1968, they purchased a metal canopy and underneath he installed and decorated a concrete stepping-stone floor. He ornamented the spaces between the painted stones by inserting samples of his collection of multicolored marbles, enhanced with brass fragments, into the wet concrete. Later he added a similarly ornamented curved walkway between the patio and driveway and the home's backdoor. He had no need for restraint when it came to marbles, as he had earlier purchased all remaining stock from a store that was going out of business, lugging them home in a wheelbarrow. (He had also earlier used marbles to adorn a rear property-line fence, but it was destroyed in a 1983 hurricane.)

Milkovisch, an upholsterer who worked for the Texas and Louisiana Line Railroad (later renamed the Southern Pacific Transportation Company) and whose academic education had terminated after eighth grade, continued to expand his ornamented concrete designs in the front and back of the house through at least 1973, sheathing all of the grounds with concrete decorated with stones, shells, and fragments of glass and ceramic: his explanation was that he was trying to avoid gardening and he didn't like mowing the lawn. He complemented the flat paved surfaces with embellished planters and flower beds, as well as small, three-dimensional sculptures and various garden ornaments. Within two or three years he had also perfected several techniques to utilize some of the thousands of aluminum beer cans that he had been accumulating over the past 17 years; as a young man during the Depression, he hated waste, and although he was not initially sure how he would utilize the cans, he knew they would serve him well. Learning as he worked, he developed ways to link the different parts together (pull tabs, bottoms, tops, rims, and sides), and also to adapt to changes in their manufacturing over time. (An example of this kind of change was a new, environmentally conscious modification of the old formula for plastic six-pack holders that made it easier for the holders to break down, a change that—unfortunately for Milkovisch—also decreased their usefulness for long-term display.)

By 1978 he had hung a curtain of can tops from the eaves along the entire southern façade of the house in order to shade that side from the strong Texas sun. And then by the following year, the other eaves were similarly ornamented, the hanging elements producing a gentle and rather mesmerizing sound as they moved with the wind, complementing its visual interest. By 1980–81, after the installation of the can-top garlands, he proceeded to create sheets of flattened cans and can tops that he assembled on 2 x 4′ panels and attached like siding on top of the wooden house façades and even over some of the windows, another effort to further reduce the sun's force. (His dislike for mowing the lawn was equaled by his aversion to recurrent painting of the house's wooden siding.)

Milkovisch drank various brands of beer (although his favorite, he quipped, was always the one that was on sale), and fabricated the can sheathing based on their designs and coloration. If he found that certain colors turned out to be more light sensitive and thus faded more quickly, he soon stopped using them in order to maintain his color fields the way he had intended. He perceptively alternated can components to showcase their different textures and how they reflected light. Too, although the shading and reflecting functions of the cans and their component parts may have been the initial motivation, he clearly enjoyed the metallic jingling noise of the curtains dangling off the eaves, and the appeals they made to the senses of touch and hearing.

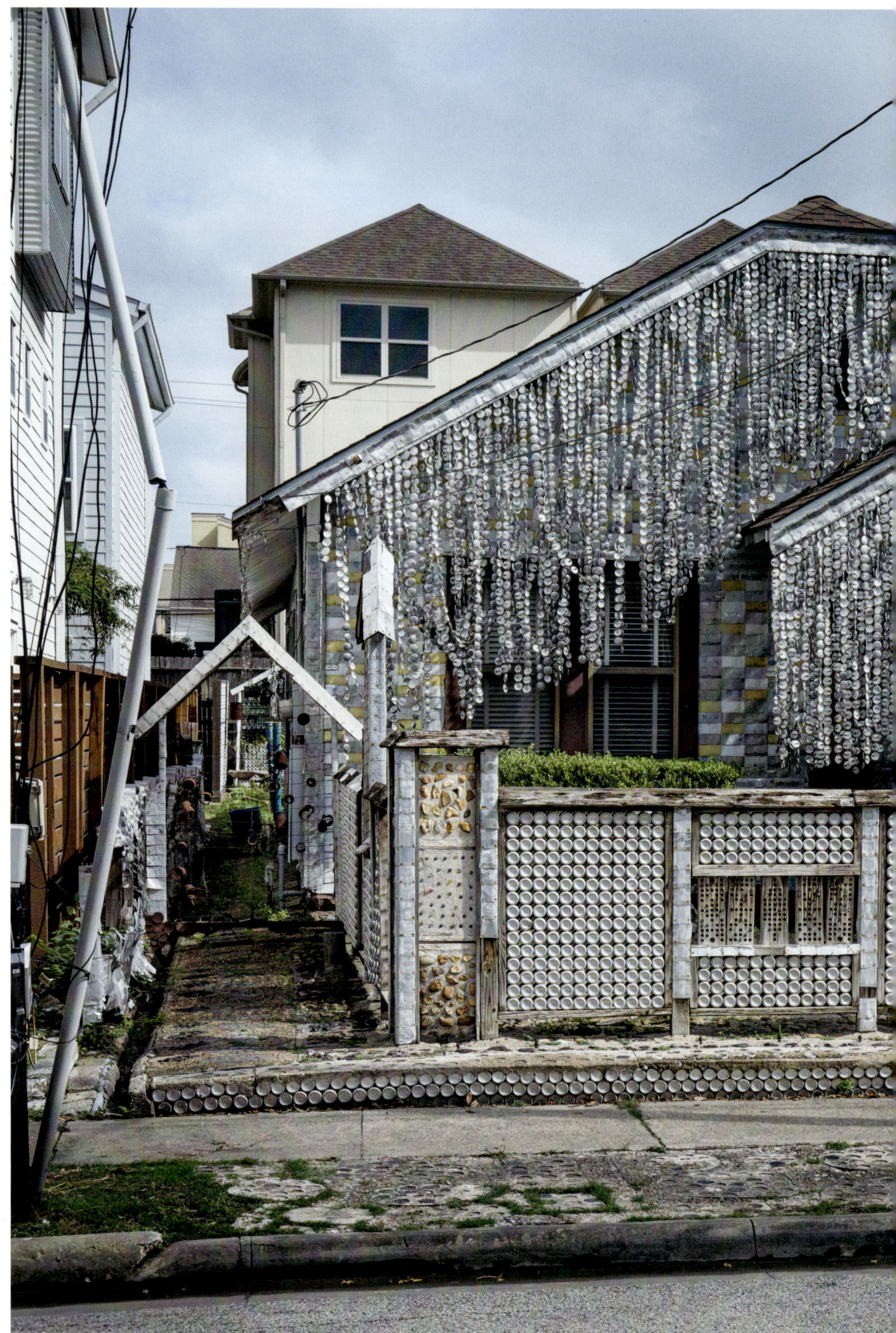

FRONT FAÇADE AND NORTH WALKWAY, 2024

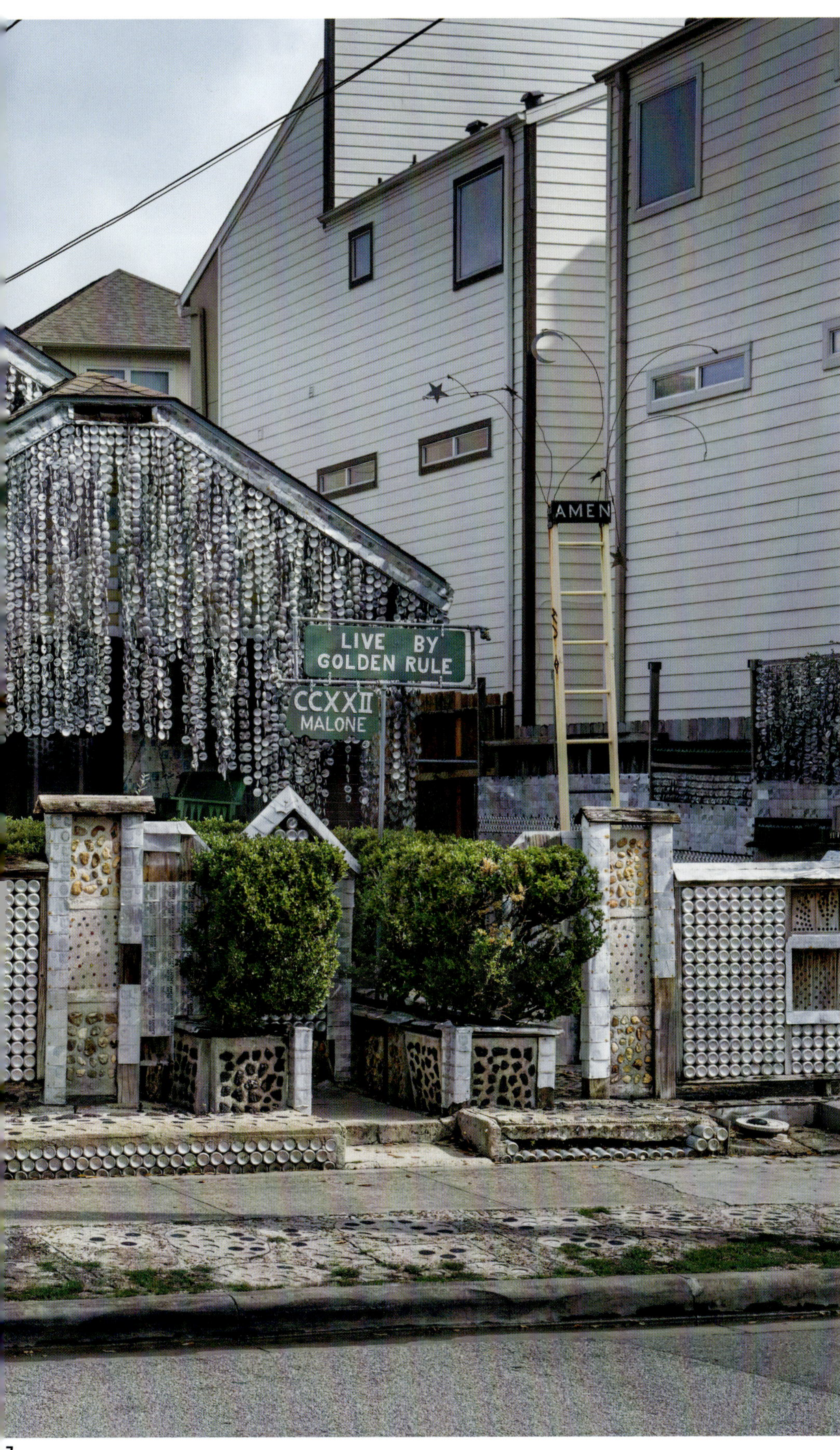
AMEN
LIVE BY
GOLDEN RULE
CCXXII
MALONE

Milkovisch continued to work on the house until he had a stroke in 1987, and he passed away the following year. Although an initial estimate from *Ripley's Believe it or Not* counted around 50,000 cans, subsequent tallies by conservators put the total (including fences, window coverings, and all other manifestations) closer to 30,000. Located in a residential neighborhood and maintaining the same scale and gabled lines as many of the older homes on the street, it is now encircled by three-story townhomes. Nevertheless, the house remains surprisingly unassuming and unpretentious, yet dazzling: simply one man's efforts to shade and embellish his home while making innovative use of the discarded remains of his daily consumption of his favorite beverage.

In 2001, the Orange Show Center for Visionary Art purchased the *Beer Can House* from the family, incorporating its management with *The Orange Show* environment and their annual Art Car parade. Following three years of fact-finding, research, and consulting on preservation technologies, the nonprofit organization spent the next three years restoring it, a process that included reproduction of some of the original artwork that had been lost or significantly degraded over the years. The interior has now been converted into a mini-museum showcasing Milkovisch's work bench, tools, favored beer labels, photographs, and selected original components, such as portions of the exterior curtain walls. It has been open to the public most weekends since conservation was completed in 2008, and by prior appointment. In 2025 it was added to the list of Historic Artists' Homes and Studios maintained by the National Trust for Historic Preservation.

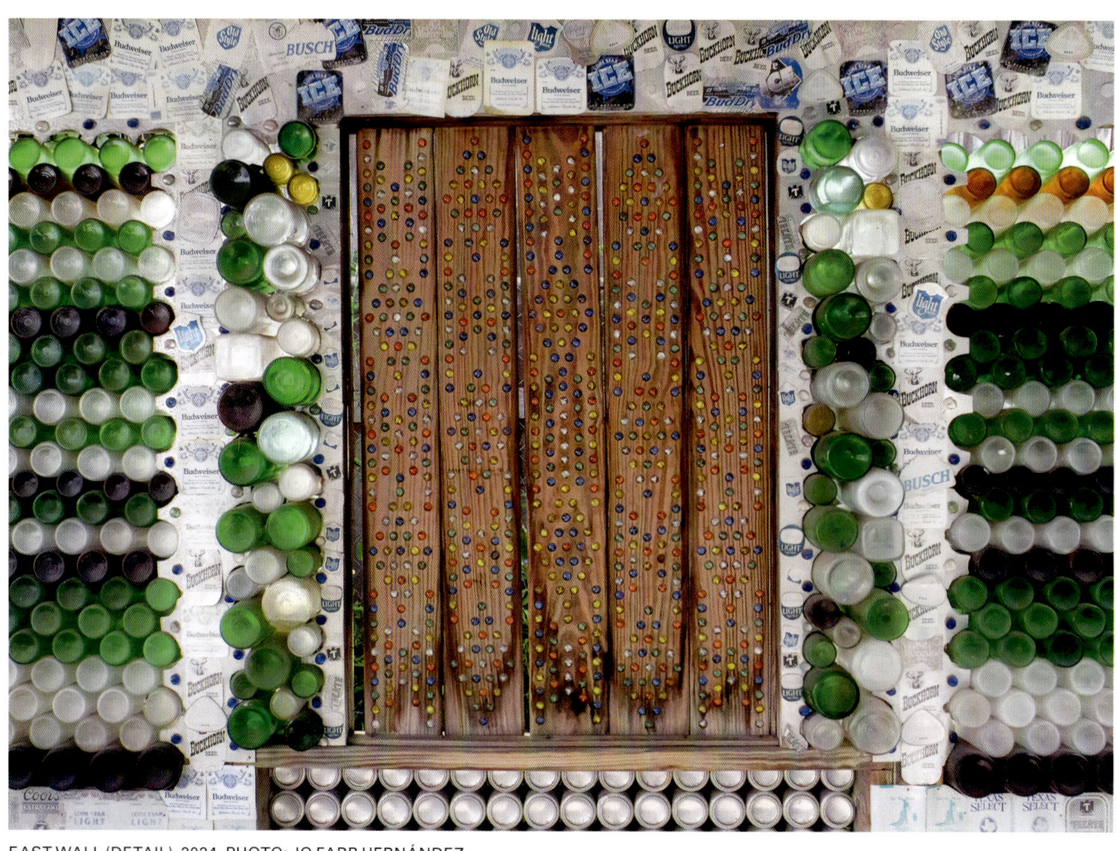

EAST WALL (DETAIL), 2024. PHOTO: JO FARB HERNÁNDEZ

DECORATIVE FLOURISHES AND SCULPTURES HELPED THE ARTIST AVOID MOWING THE LAWN AND PAINTING THE HOUSE.

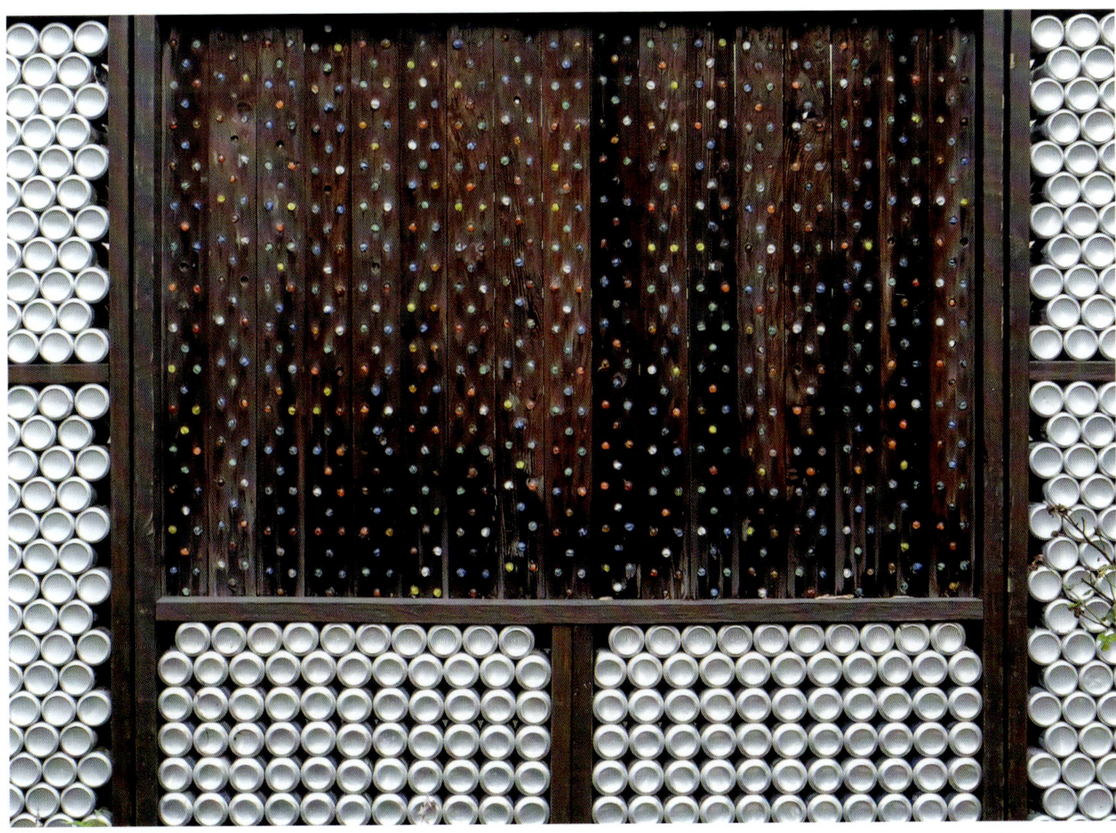

NORTH FENCE (DETAIL), 2024. PHOTO: JO FARB HERNÁNDEZ

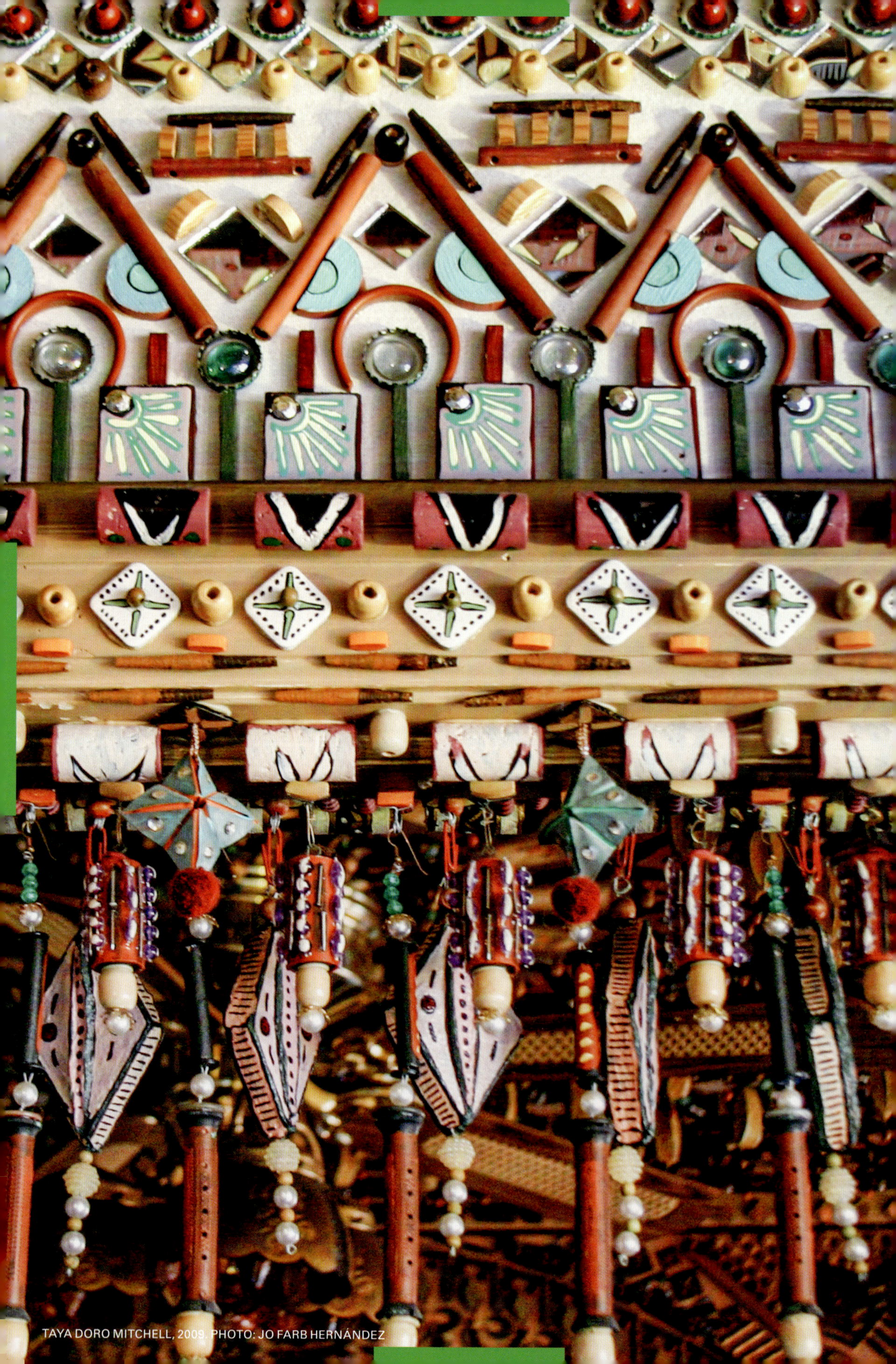

TAYA DORO MITCHELL, 2009. PHOTO: JO FARB HERNÁNDEZ

CHAPTER 3

HIDDEN FROM VIEW

—

DECORATED INTERIORS

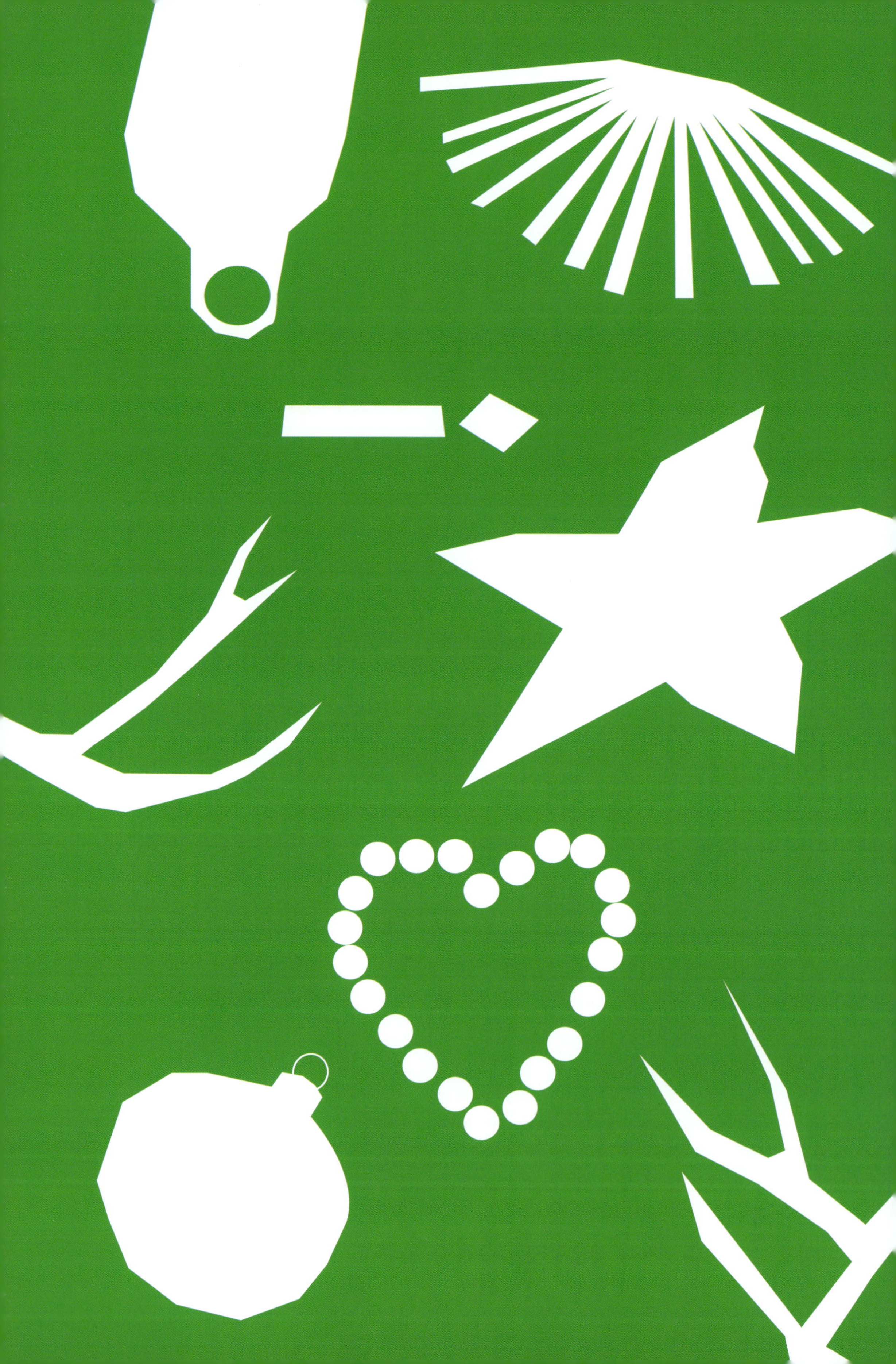

As we've seen, the lines between types of art environments are quite permeable and easily blur and shift. Many sites feature decorations on both interior and exterior, and while in some cases the evolution of the adornment moved outside from inside, in others the reverse was true. In a smaller number of cases the decorative elements appear solely within the building's interior and are generally not visible to the public. This may have been a function of trying to maintain privacy, or of boundary-setting negotiations with a disapproving spouse or partner, or simply of the ease of working with the materials chosen to express one's creativity. While sometimes surprised at a potential viewer's interest, these makers, in general, are nevertheless happy to share their work and are proud of what they have done.

The line between a display of discrete works of art and that display becoming the art itself is also sometimes permeable. Some artists begin by simply hanging their own paintings on interior walls so they can continue to view and evaluate them, mining them to inform their future pieces. And while salon-style installations may by themselves be overwhelming to a casual visitor, they rarely cross that line from "exhibit space" to "art environment." Among those whose interior spaces blur the line are Brenda Davis of Prattville, Alabama; Wille Jordan of Erie, Pennsylvania; Ron Mann of Clio, Michigan; Robert Morgan of Lexington, Kentucky; and Mary Paulsen of Lockwood's Folly, North Carolina. More rarely, we find those in-between kinds of situations when an artist is commissioned to adorn the interior of a business, such as the *Tabernacle Bar* in Buffalo, New York, which has been covered in paintings by Jeremy Twiss. Still other makers display not their own work but their collections or samples of their hobbies, and often these, too, will cross the line and become works of art themselves. Examples of these sites are Amad Samaan's *Lawndale Market* in Detroit, Karl Virag and his *Decoupage House* in Galveston, and Frieda Warther and the *Button House* in Dover, Ohio. As with so much in this field, all boundaries are decidedly porous.

EMERY BLAGDON

HEALING MACHINES

GARFIELD TABLE, NEBRASKA

Perhaps the most extraordinary example of art environments within this category was hidden within a weather-worn outbuilding on a plateau surrounded by the Sandhills of northcentral Nebraska.

Blagdon (1907–1986) was born in the town of Callaway on land homesteaded by his maternal grandfather. He was not a particularly engaged student and left school partway through his eighth-grade year. As a young man he was hired by a local rancher and a local sawmill but soon left to seek his fortune, riding the rails to the West Coast and working a series of low-paying jobs to cover his minimal expenses. After over a decade away, he returned home in the late 1920s or early 1930s when he learned that his mother had terminal cancer. He helped on the farm and cared for his parents but became profoundly distressed as he watched his mother suffer and, later, as he saw his father progress through mourning her death, self-imposed social isolation, and his own cancer diagnosis.

After his father's death, one of his sisters moved with her husband and children into the family home. The young Blagdon continued to live there, too, until 1955, when he moved out to a bachelor-uncle's 160-acre farm after inheriting the house and property. He began almost immediately to make it his own: among other changes, he painted concentric circles in contrasting colors spreading out from around the central ceiling light in the kitchen, a motif that he would widely employ later in his paintings on wood. Although he had never been interested in farming—he leased his newly acquired farmland to a brother, although he did grow a bountiful vegetable garden—like farm children everywhere, Blagdon had learned how to problem-solve, to fix and repair, and to work with a variety of hand tools to manipulate a range of materials. He had also become renowned locally for his mechanical abilities and was always available to help fix a niece's bicycle or a neighbor's tractor.

And so, in his spare time, he had the skill to create small assemblages out of what he found available: wire; household staples such as aluminum foil, cardboard, hairpins, and masking tape; magnets; and found pieces of wood and local stones. Bits and pieces of farm implements, televisions, engines, and other devices or appliances that he could deconstruct in order to reuse their components also made their way into his forms, and he threaded pill bottles, corncobs, and spent rifle shells through the wires. Over a period of approximately 30 years, working mainly with hand-held, needle-nose pliers, his assemblages became increasingly complex.

As cancer not only took his parents but also all but one of his five siblings (he was the oldest of the six), he navigated his emotional pain through a sad passage that augmented his interest in alternative therapies for combatting what was at that time understood as a death sentence: he wanted to try to tackle human helplessness in the face of such suffering. He was particularly intrigued with the possibility of channeling the power of electricity, which had been touted as a curative treatment for a variety of ailments since the late nineteenth century, above all when used in conjunction with certain plants, minerals, and salts.

At the pharmacy in the nearby town of North Platte, he inquired about purchasing specialized pharmaceutical herbs and minerals, believing that if these substances were fortified with electricity and routed through his assemblages, they could cure a variety of illnesses. He wired little glass vials and baby food containers filled with his purchases into the core of some of his fabricated metal components and hung them from the frames of others. He considered himself an inventor, not an artist, and with his focus on scientific experimentation and medical challenges, he came to identify the purpose of his work, which he called his "pretties," as *Healing Machines*.

Blagdon used the smaller shed of a reconstructed dirt-floor outbuilding behind his house as a dedicated workshop, while the adjacent larger and higher room behind—which he kept safely padlocked—became increasingly crowded with his mixed-media assemblages, many of which had expanded into constructions that reached several feet in length, width, or diameter. He added texture and color with beads, ribbons, and painted glass vials, and produced sound as the small metal tubes and aluminum can cutouts jostled each other: the way he suspended the lightweight pieces from nails pounded into interior studs and ceiling joists had enhanced their kinetic possibilities. He festooned the display with strings of Christmas tree lights and brightly painted bulbs, as well as with a series of bold two-dimensional abstractions painted on scavenged wood, which he often placed in stacks or arranged around the building's interior perimeter. Understanding that paint and pigments were composed of natural

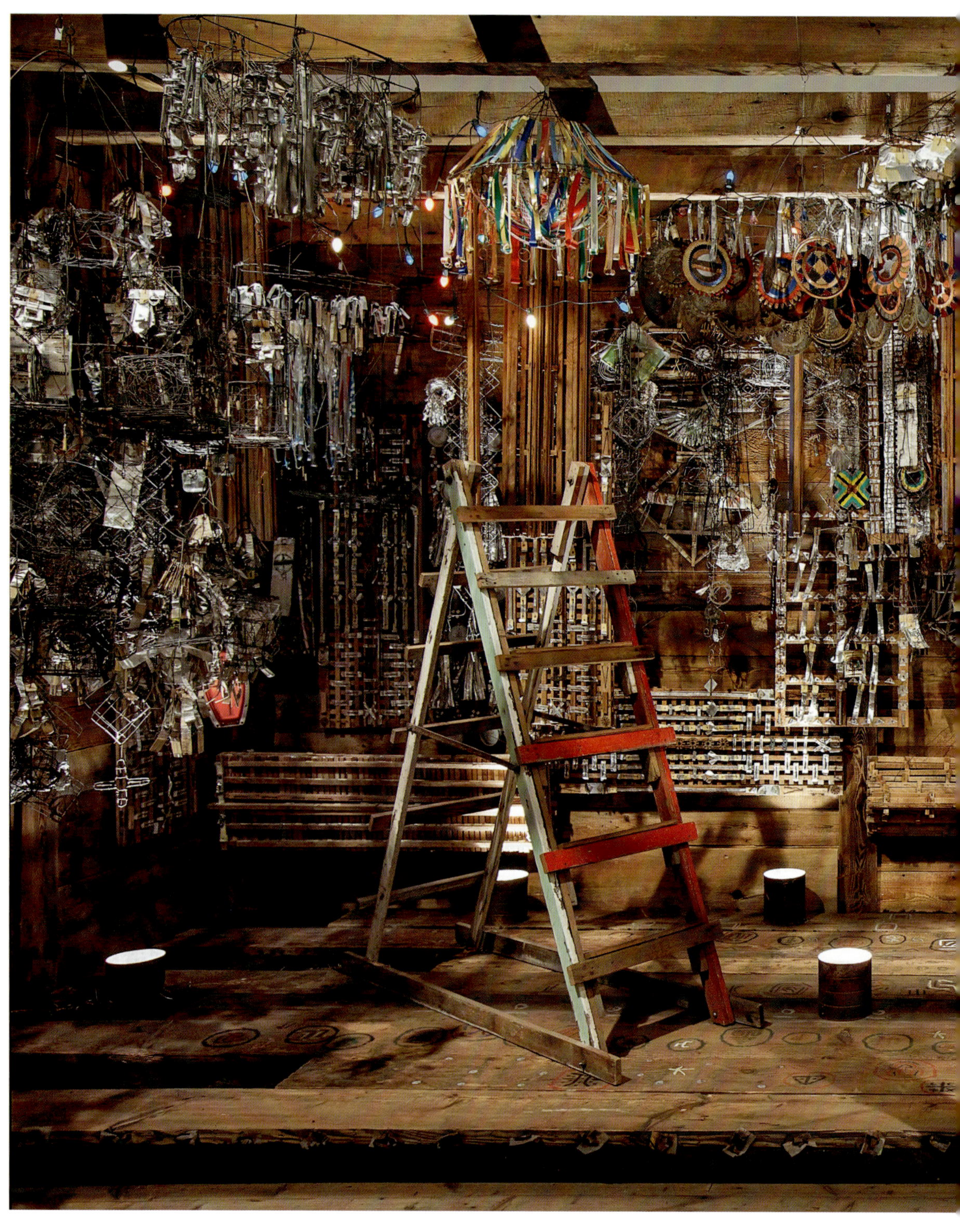

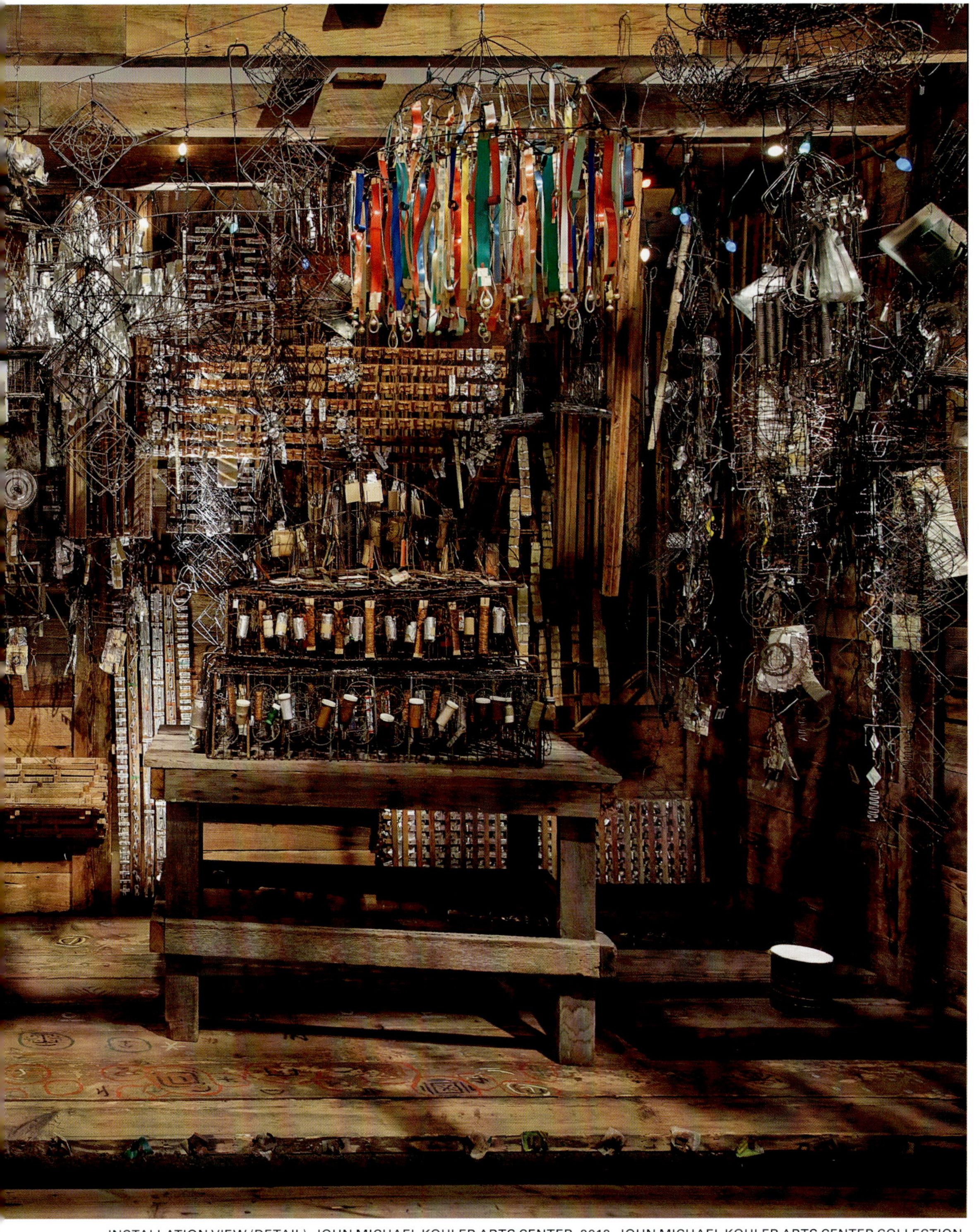

INSTALLATION VIEW (DETAIL), JOHN MICHAEL KOHLER ARTS CENTER, 2012. JOHN MICHAEL KOHLER ARTS CENTER COLLECTION, GIFT OF KOHLER FOUNDATION INC. PHOTO: COURTESY JOHN MICHAEL KOHLER ARTS CENTER

INSTALLATION VIEW (DETAIL), ART PRESERVE OF THE JOHN MICHAEL KOHLER ARTS CENTER, 2021. JOHN MICHAEL KOHLER ARTS CENTER COLLECTION, GIFT OF KOHLER FOUNDATION INC. PHOTO: RICH MACIEJEWSKI, COURTESY JOHN MICHAEL KOHLER ARTS CENTER

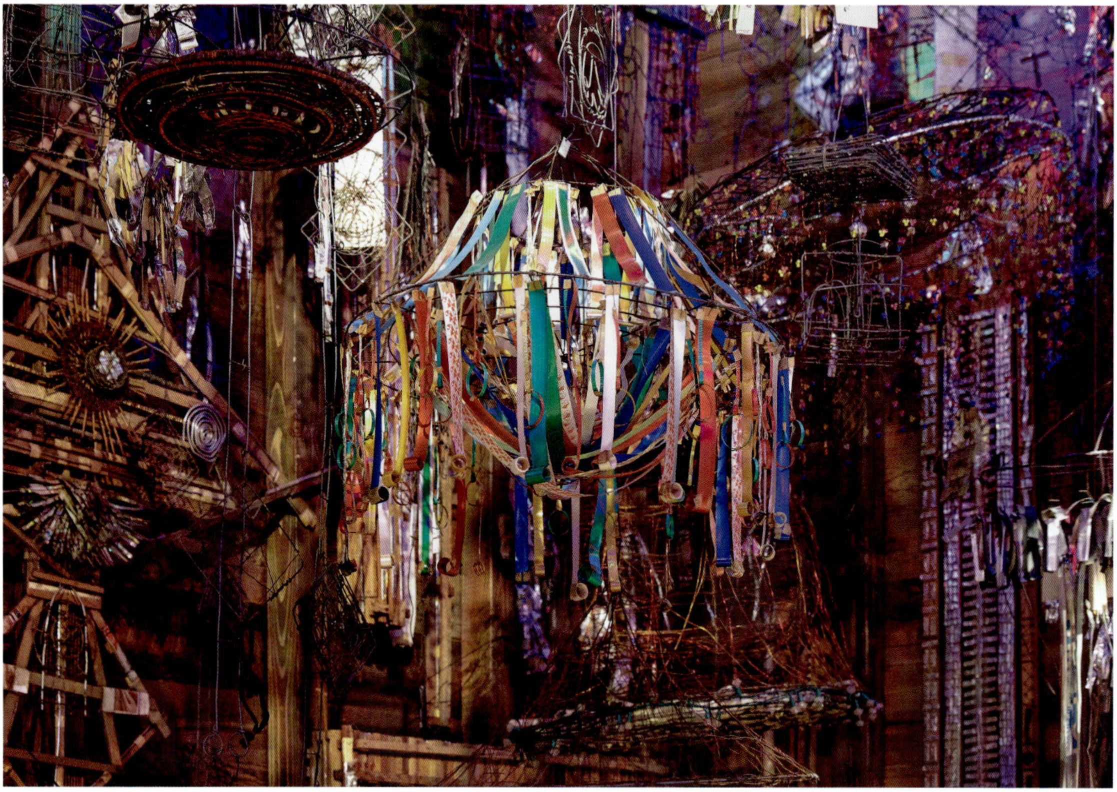

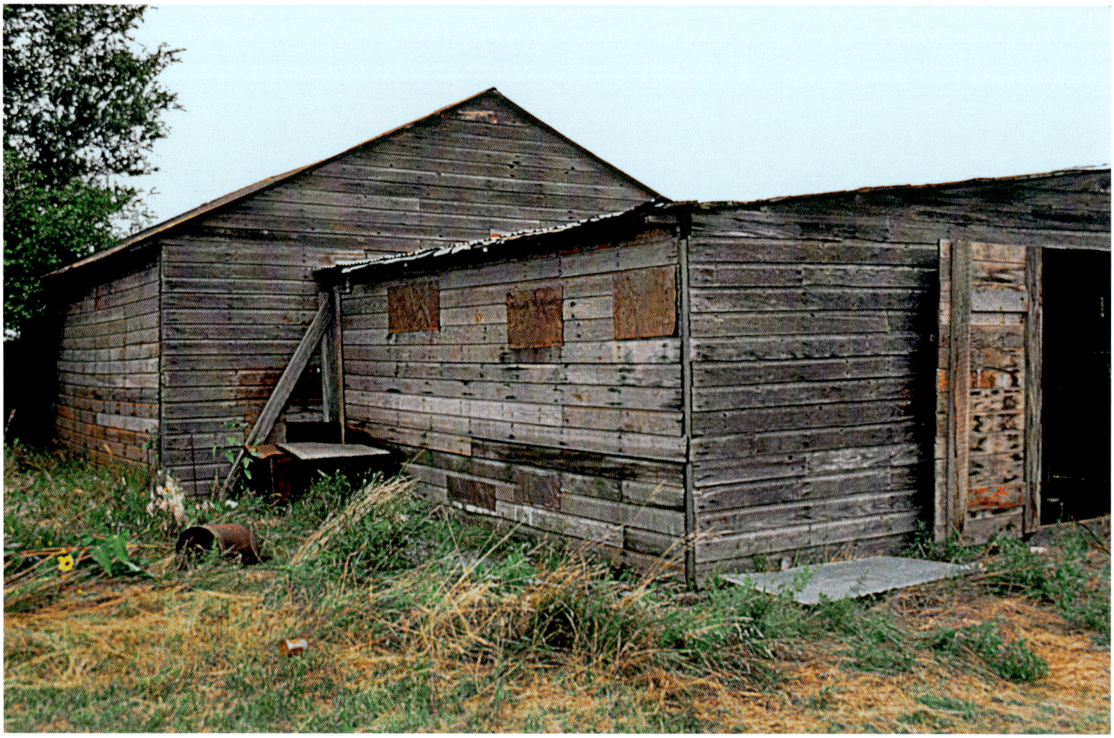

OUTBUILDING CONTAINING THE *HEALING MACHINES*, 1986. PHOTO: DAN R. DRYDEN, JOHN MICHAEL KOHLER ARTS CENTER COLLECTION, GIFT OF KOHLER FOUNDATION INC. PHOTO: COURTESY JOHN MICHAEL KOHLER ARTS CENTER

minerals, he considered his paintings an integral part of his built environment. Although not all were openly visible, these geometric and often seemingly symbolic or diagrammatic abstractions confidently expressed his understanding of energy flow via an alternative medium.

Approximately 100 paintings and 600 works of hanging or freestanding sculptures and wire assemblages featured reiterative and generally symmetrical forms that magnified what he considered each one's distinctive energy field. Blagdon also believed that each, in turn, would influence the next, multiplying the effects of every individual object. Consequently, every one of his two- and three-dimensional works was conscientiously and precisely installed to make a unique contribution as it likewise enhanced the whole. The reflections of the colored lights off of the gently moving metal components augmented the impact of the entire environment as they both intensified and amplified the sensation of its size. While each object was distinct and created separately, he conceived of the totality as a single installation that would help him achieve his goal of addressing physical afflictions. This was not an abstract concept for him: indeed, he viscerally felt the force emanated by his pretties in his own body and would freely share access to his work with neighbors, who would visit seeking a cure for their own physical ailments. He did not know why it worked, he confessed, but he was certain it did.

Although Blagdon never stopped believing in the ambient power of his constructions, despite his decades-long efforts his *Machines* did not work as effectively as he had hoped, and he, too, died of cancer (he had been ill for at least 10 years but had refused to see a doctor, relying solely on his *Healing Machines* as treatment). But his work had already influenced numerous people, among them Don Dryden, the pharmacist who sold the minerals and medicinal herbs that Blagdon wired into his assemblages. Inspired by Blagdon's path, Dryden had sold the family pharmacy and moved to New York to follow his own dream of becoming a sound engineer.

Serendipitously, Dryden had returned to his hometown for a high school reunion when he was alerted to an auction of Blagdon's assets (Blagdon had no will and never married or had children, and so his property passed to the state). Dryden and his friend Don Christensen pooled their funds and purchased the entire collection of assemblages and paintings, and spent 18 years numbering, photographing, and cataloguing the work. In 2004 it was purchased in its entirety by the Kohler Foundation and, following conservation, was gifted to the John Michael Kohler Arts Center in Sheboygan, Wisconsin, where it is now on display at its Arts Preserve. Although far from the rolling prairies of Nebraska's Sandhills, it is now protected and esteemed.

HE DIDN'T KNOW WHY HIS HEALING MACHINES WORKED, HE CONFESSED, BUT HE BELIEVED THEY DID.

TAYA DORO MITCHELL

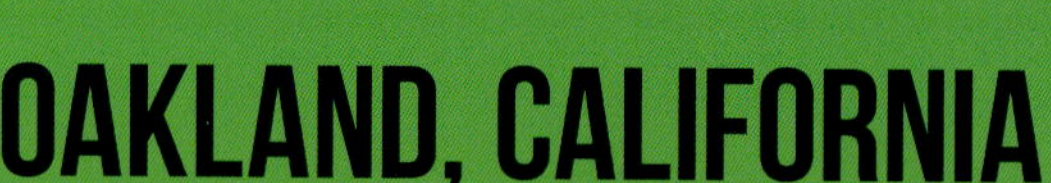

This art environment, secreted within a nondescript, white clapboard house on a busy street corner in a semimarginal neighborhood, was also linked to sickness and healing, yet in a way different from Blagdon's explorations into curative therapy (see page 224). In contrast, the work of Doro Mitchell (b. 1935) was the means by which she kept watch over her ill husband while concurrently indulging her artistic ambitions and bringing herself a measure of tranquility.

Born in the small village of Heemstede in the Netherlands, she had a difficult childhood, having been raised by a strictly controlling, moralizing mother and a mostly absent father. When she was about age 13, Doro's mother withdrew her from school, feeling that by then she had had sufficient education. Her mother steered her daughters to become seamstresses, the sole occupation that she felt would be open to them as lower-class women during a period that was still extremely class-conscious. Doro internalized her mother's constant harping to "move her hands" and to always be doing something, a propensity she retained all her life.

During the 1950s young women could rarely leave the family home without first marrying, but Doro knew that by age 18 she would no longer be subject to her mother's authoritarian dictates. She planned for that day years in advance and joined a family service organization that trained young girls to help mothers and children in difficult circumstances. She was able to travel there by bicycle, and it was tuition-free: this granted her first steps toward personal freedom. Yet this organization was run almost as strictly as a convent. The teachers wore religious habits, and the not-quite-concealed intent was to entice the indigent girls into dedicating their lives to the organization as quasi-nuns, taking a vow of poverty, obedience, and chastity. Doro complied and remained with them for over a dozen years, choosing to dedicate herself to nursing.

Yet as she became a professional psychiatric nurse in the mid-1960s, her school was not immune from intrusions of the worldwide social and cultural revolutions. Nuns were doffing their habits, priests were leaving the Church, and many of Doro's friends were moving away from the organization's sheltering, stifling cloister. Doro was no different. She was even able to arrange to go to the United States, where she easily found a job at a local hospital, and in her off hours she made little pieces of jewelry that were sold in the hospital's gift shop. People admired her handiwork and began to call her an artist long before she began to self-identify as such.

In 1971, finally realizing that it was up to her to make her own decisions and direct her own life, she impulsively moved to the San Francisco Bay Area. The cultural upheaval of that time was a dramatic shock to her authoritarian upbringing and voluntary confinement: everything that she had been told was bad—including sex and drugs—were now being heralded as good. A 36-year-old virgin, she felt she needed to do some "catching up," which included sex with multiple boyfriends and using fairly significant amounts of cannabis.

Yet she had still never lived on her own, never spent a day without doing what someone else had told her to do, and never felt that she was defining her own way. So, in 1973, approaching age 40, she decided to go to art school. She graduated with a Bachelor of Fine Arts degree in painting from the San Francisco Art Institute, but, not having produced a comprehensive portfolio, she was not accepted into any master's programs. She found and purchased that little white clapboard house in Oakland, and for the first time, she was really on her own.

One day she called a friend, but after speaking with the man on the other end for several minutes, she realized that she must have misdialed, and that it was not her friend at all. Yet she had had an enjoyable conversation with this new acquaintance. John Mitchell, an African American 14 years older and recently a widower, called her back, and despite his family's opposition, they dated and later married. He was always quiet, and as she wanted to work on her art—mostly freestanding sculptures and small paintings—they were a rather reclusive pair, which suited them both. But after about 10 years of marriage, he began to exhibit the early stages of Alzheimer's disease. Given her background, she wanted to nurse him herself rather than place him in an institution, but as his disease progressed, she realized that she could not leave him alone.

In October 1989 the deadly Loma Prieta earthquake rocked the San Francisco Bay Area. Doro Mitchell's house sustained several large cracks in the walls, so she installed mirrors in the hallway to cover them, as she also realized that they would make the narrow corridor seem more spacious and would help lighten the space. But once the mirrors were up, she felt they were too austere and needed frames. She chose to make her own, slicing, cutting, painting, and gluing on ornamental elements that fanned out from the simple geometrical mirror shapes in grand, Baroque style. She moved on from the "frames" to covering all of the walls and ceiling of the hallway: she loved the effect, which made her feel as if she were living inside of a jewelry box.

In the meantime, her husband's disease was worsening, and he had become bedbound. As she cared for him at home, she began transforming the walls of his sickroom, too: in this way she could watch him constantly, he would not be alone, and he could watch her. Her obsessive creation of this intricate artwork was calming for both of them.

Literally hundreds of thousands—perhaps millions—of tiny objects came to adorn the interior walls and ceilings of the little house. The textural quality of the surfaces was mesmerizing, with multitiered strata and elegantly symmetrical design development. Dividing up the spaces into smaller areas—a rectangle here, an archway there—she glued the pieces on, one by one, without any preconceptualization of design or even choice of media. She haunted thrift stores and flea markets, constantly on the lookout for old frames and sewing accessories she could cut and paint or glue, as well as pen tops, bottle caps, beads, buttons, barrettes, earrings, clothespins, and other items.

Her early training as a seamstress served her well, as her artistic eye for pattern and her sense of craft brought an intricate, tapestry-like aesthetic to her work. She kept all of the small tools she needed at hand—drills, scissors, coping and jeweler's saws, glue guns—as she gathered shapes and colors and volumes to encrust the walls and ceilings with a multilayered accumulation of found and modified objects pulsating with textures and intensity and movement.

Following her husband's death, Doro Mitchell continued to work on the walls of her home. Then in 2009 she purchased some property in New Mexico and moved there, yet again dramatically changing her life. Her Oakland house was purchased by a nonprofit organization that provided art classes for children, and for several years it seemed as if the environment would be preserved. By 2018, however, it was put on the market again, and it was purchased by an investment firm whose intention was to flip it in the speculative local real estate market. Despite the obvious quality of the artwork that lined the walls—and the Bay Area's reputation as sensitive to and supportive of culture in all its forms—this firm believed that the property would be more saleable if Doro Mitchell's creations were removed. They stripped the home of all its decorations.

Doro Mitchell continued to express herself creatively in New Mexico, adorning the walls of her new home a bit, but not nearly as extensively as the original Oakland masterpiece. Her husband had been sick for a long time, yet as she adorned the walls of his sickroom, she helped to diminish his suffering as she healed herself as well. Unfortunately, none of her original environment has been preserved.

GUEST BEDROOM, 2009. PHOTO: JO FARB HERNÁNDEZ

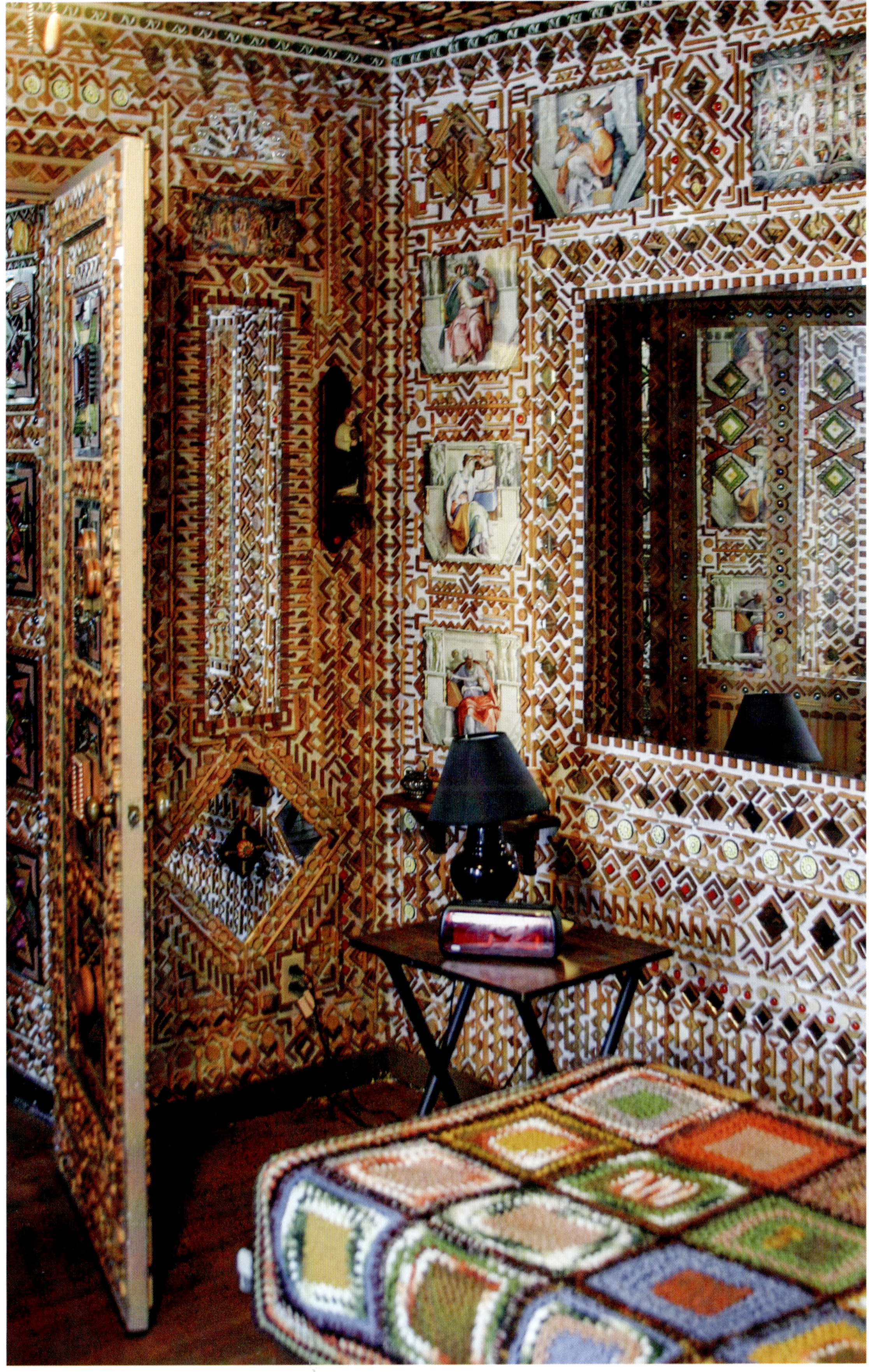

CENTER MEDALLION ON LIVING ROOM CEILING, 2009. PHOTO: JO FARB HERNÁNDEZ

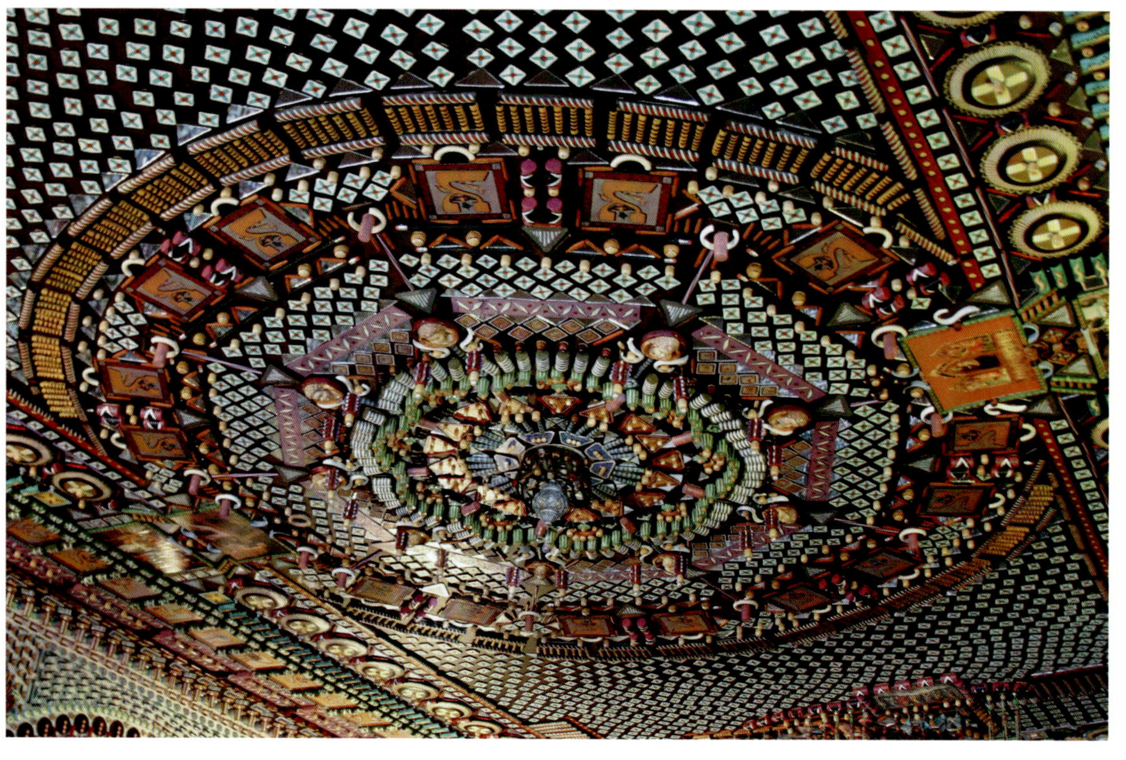

WHILE CARING FOR HER ILL HUSBAND, SHE TRANSFORMED THE INSIDE OF THEIR HOME INTO A DAZZLING JEWEL BOX.

LIVING ROOM WALL, 2009. PHOTO: JO FARB HERNÁNDEZ

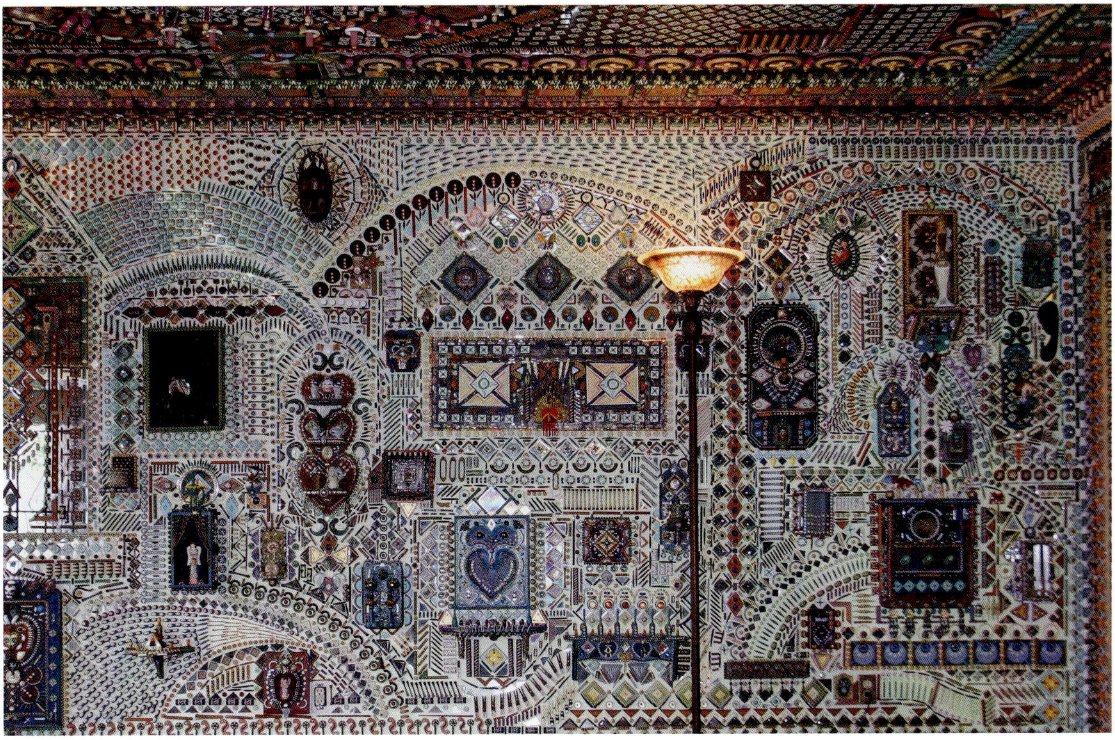

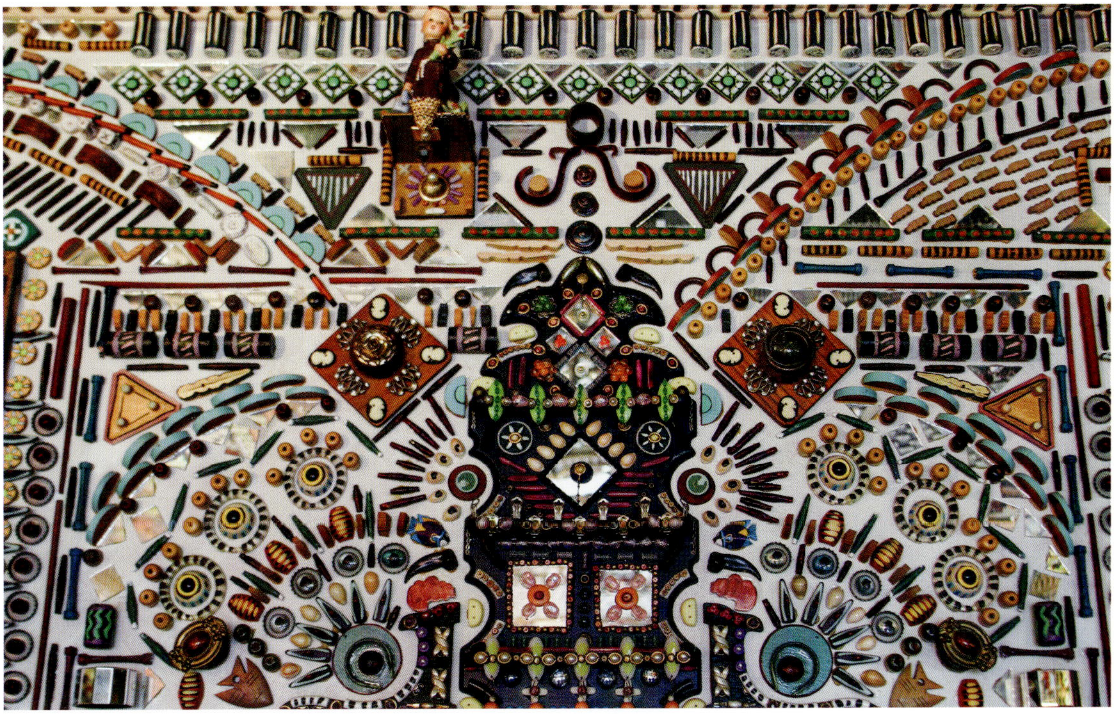

LIVING ROOM WALL (DETAIL), 2009. PHOTO: JO FARB HERNÁNDEZ

LOY ALLEN BOWLIN

BEAUTIFUL HOLY JEWEL HOME

MCCOMB, MISSISSIPPI

A small Mississippi town was the original location of another modest white clapboard bungalow that hid a marvel of color and texture, although Bowlin (1909–1995) was not as retiring or unassuming as Taya Doro Mitchell (see page 230). In fact, inspired by the 1975 Glen Campbell song, he came to style himself as the "Original Rhinestone Cowboy," driving around town wearing adorned hats and flashy Western-style polyester suits (one for each day of the week) that he painted and ornamented with glitter. His vehicle of choice was a wildly embellished 1967 Cadillac with longhorns on the hood. He rounded off his look with eyeglasses bedecked with paint and baubles, as well as dazzling rhinestones that he had inserted into his dentures by the local dentist, the two front teeth rimmed in gold.

This extravagant new identity seems to have been a reaction to an intensifying series of traumas and difficulties throughout his life: his early upbringing as one of 12 children in a poor family, a difficult marriage fractured by the death of two of their three children, a hardscrabble life in a house without electricity or running water, and increasing mental distress that was finally treated with a brief institutionalization and electroshock therapy. As he aged, divorced and retired from a succession of low-level jobs (collecting and selling scrap metal, working as a used-car salesman and part-time mechanic, and engaging in subsistence-level agriculture), his sense of self was threatened. So, bored, lonely, and depressed, he sought to reinvent himself. Wearing his glittery costumes, he would dance, tell jokes, and play the harmonica in shopping malls and public spaces, making new friends in the process and earning a few dollars. He billed himself as "The World's Most Famous Entertainer."

By the late-1970s or early 1980s, less spry than he had been, he reduced his public performances and began to decorate his home in the manner he thought commensurate with such a glitzy persona. While Bowlin made some efforts to publicize his work with a modicum of embellishment on the home's exterior, hoping to attract fans to come to him, the interior was truly the capstone of this environment. He supplemented intricate geometric arrangements of paper cutouts, tinted foil, and collaged illustrations with bright paints, glitter, rhinestones, and tinsel garlands onto the walls and ceilings, often—for ease of working—first attaching them to stiff sheets of poster board or construction paper before nailing or tacking them up. The ornamented boards were complementary yet were each distinct, somewhat like a patchwork quilt that features different patterns in a similar color palette. Diamonds, circles, sunbursts, crosses, and more random polyhedrons abutted each other, sometimes gridded off with rectangles or separated by borders of stripes or polka dots, everything set off with glitter and foil. He hung multicolored, glass Christmas-tree ornaments off the ceiling; directly painted dots and patterns on his furniture, window frames, and doors; and installed rose-colored wall-to-wall carpeting and red vinyl window shades. A local sign painter made him a placard to hang from the eaves over his front porch, identifying the humble dwelling as "The Beautiful Holy Jewel Home of the Original Rhinestone Cowboy."

He told some visitors that the designs came to him in his dreams, others that he was influenced by the stained glass in local churches, and to still others he confessed that during his electroshock therapy comparable patterns would manifest themselves behind his closed eyelids. The preponderance of patchwork quilts in the southern United States, the old patterned carpeting that underlay his later crimson upgrade, and the design on the linoleum floor of his kitchen may have been other design sources, some of which were perhaps unconsciously assimilated. But he took these conventional motifs—and/or the imagery from his dreams or medical treatments—and assembled them all in a way that was unique and transformative.

After his death, the *Beautiful Holy Jewel Home* faced demolition. Houston artist and collector Katy Emde learned of the threat and, horrified at the possibility of destruction, purchased the house with all its contents, agreeing to the stipulation that everything would be removed from the property. She and a friend photographed and videotaped the entirety, mapping and cataloguing the location of each piece before carefully dismantling everything so that it could be later reassembled. She moved the components into temporary storage in Houston, where selections were later displayed at the time of a Folk Art Society of America conference. There, Leslie Umberger, then senior curator at the John Michael Kohler Arts Center, saw it and, learning that it needed a permanent home, recommended it to the Kohler Foundation for acquisition. They acquired it in 1998 and set to work to more fully examine and conserve each

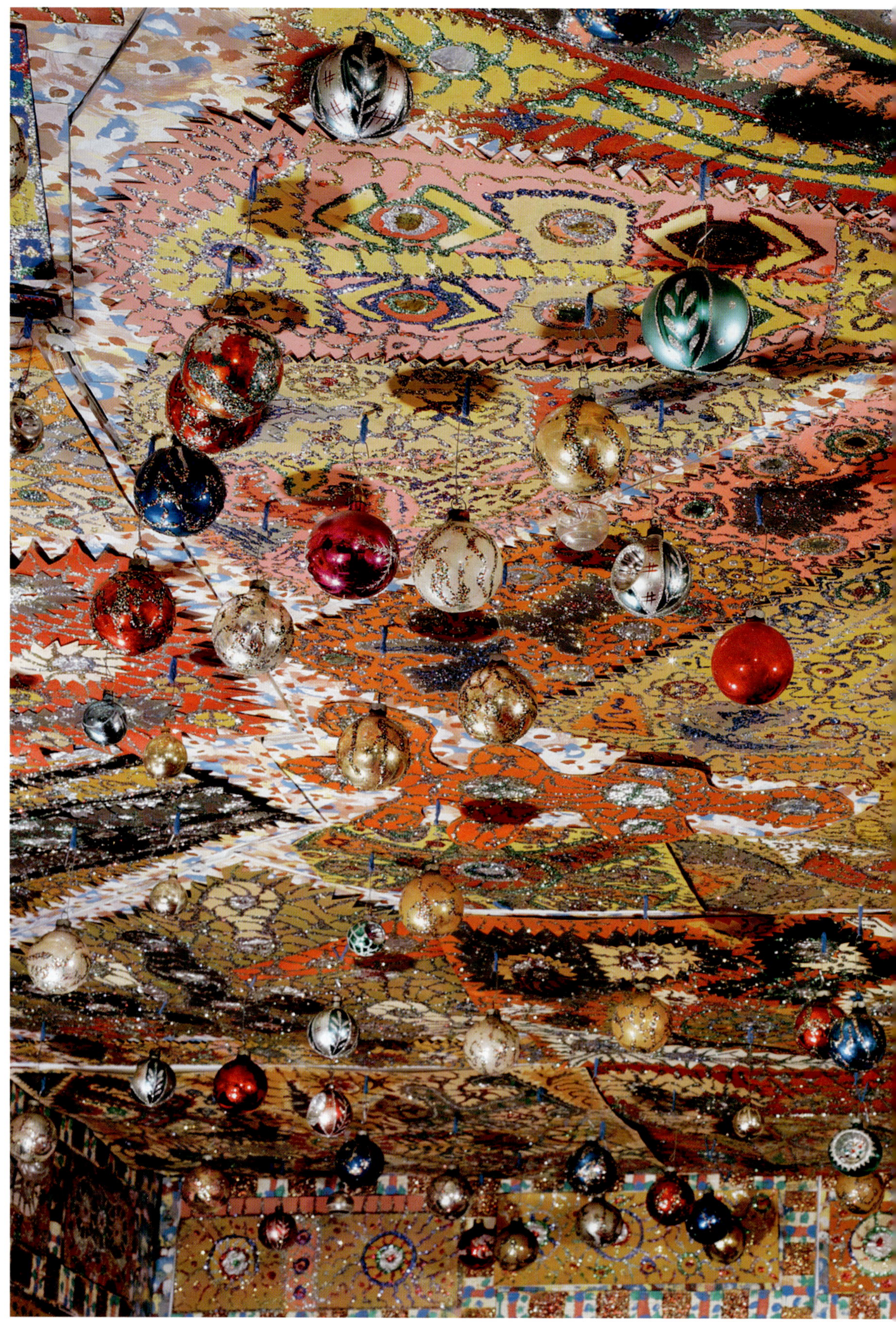

LIVING ROOM CEILING (INSTALLATION DETAIL). JOHN MICHAEL KOHLER ARTS CENTER COLLECTION, GIFT OF KOHLER FOUNDATION INC., 2006. PHOTO: COURTESY JOHN MICHAEL KOHLER ARTS CENTER

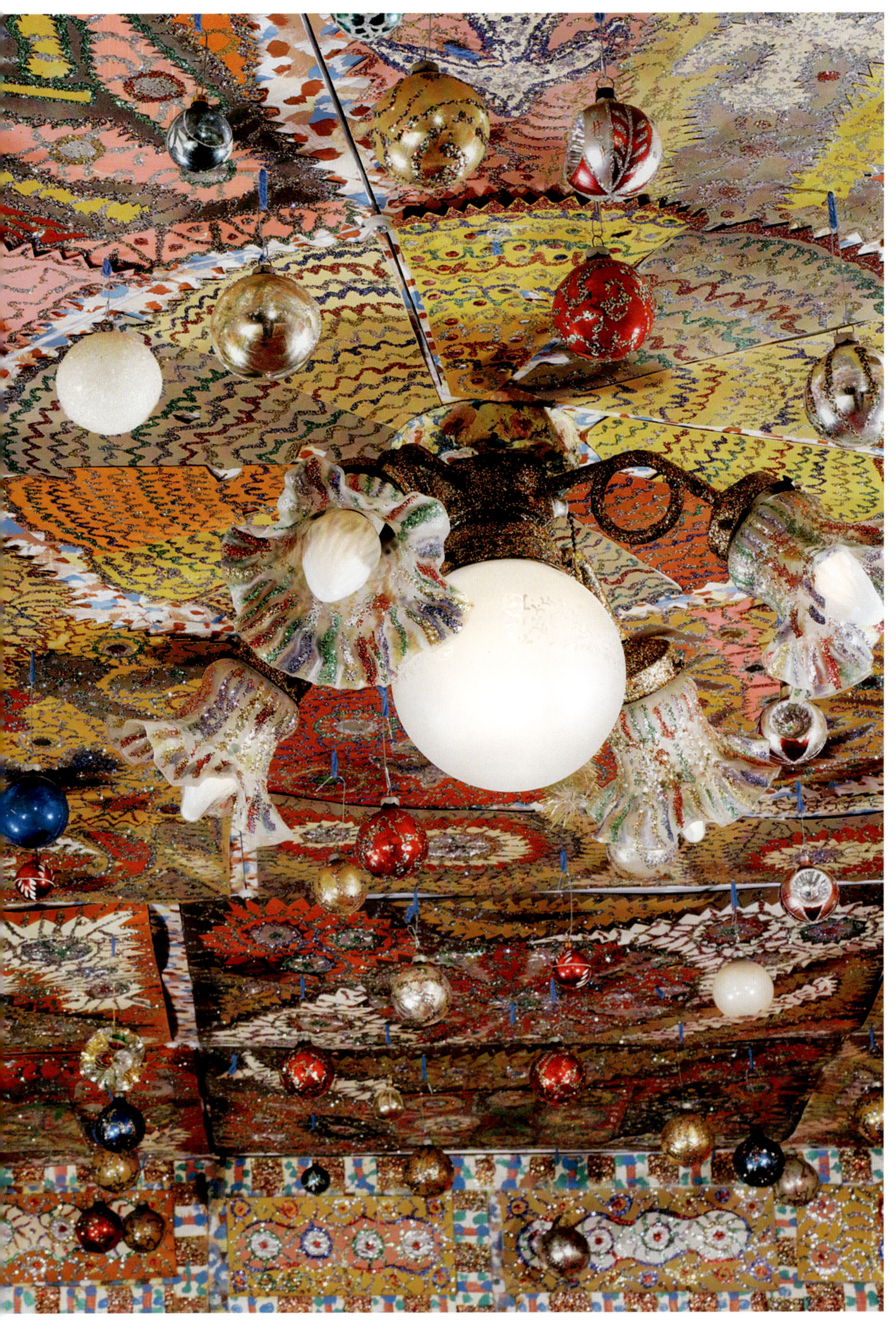

EXTERIOR FAÇADE, *BEAUTIFUL HOLY JEWEL HOME*, 1997. PHOTO: KATY EMDE

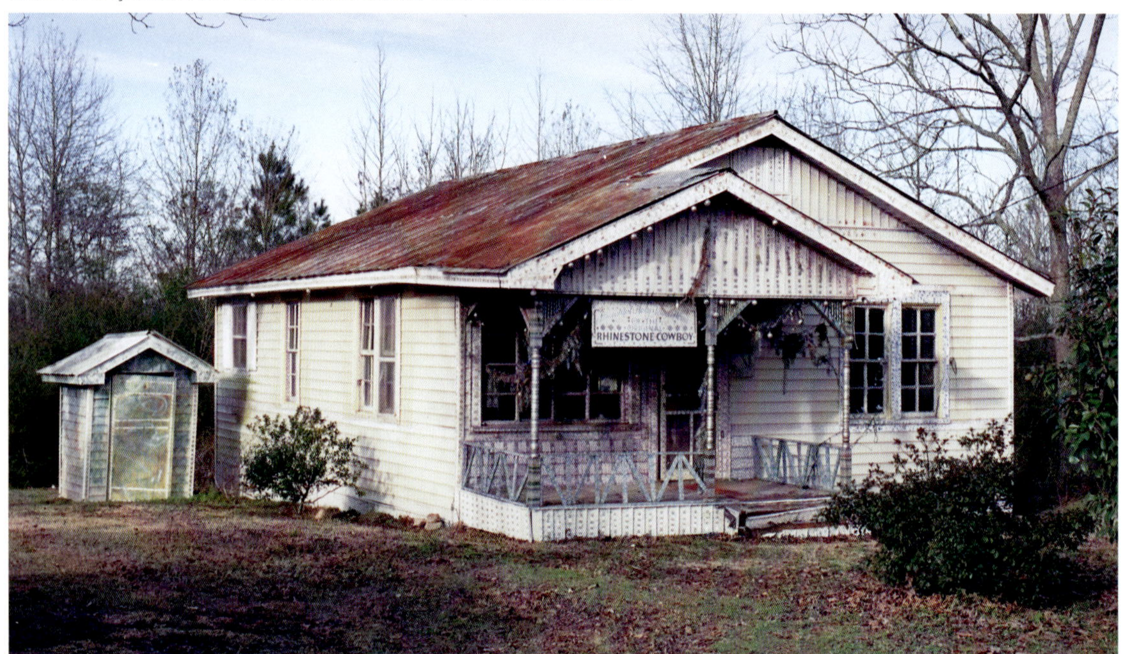

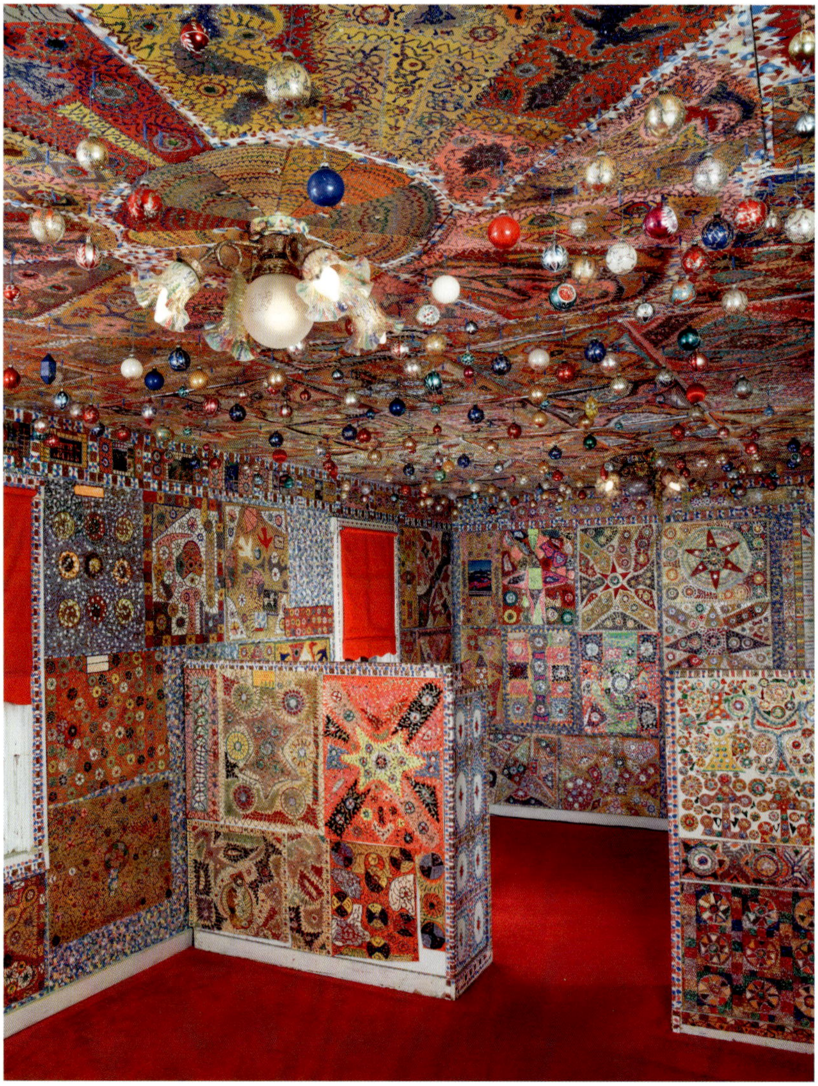

LIVING ROOM (INSTALLATION DETAIL), JOHN MICHAEL KOHLER ARTS CENTER COLLECTION, GIFT OF KOHLER FOUNDATION INC., 2004 PHOTO: COURTESY JOHN MICHAEL KOHLER ARTS CENTER

element of the work, a project that lasted four years. While stabilizing colors and replacing deteriorating boards, glues, and glitter, they remounted the whole within a modern modular framework that allows for easier transportation and reinstallation. It is now on display at the Art Center's Art Preserve in Sheboygan, Wisconsin.

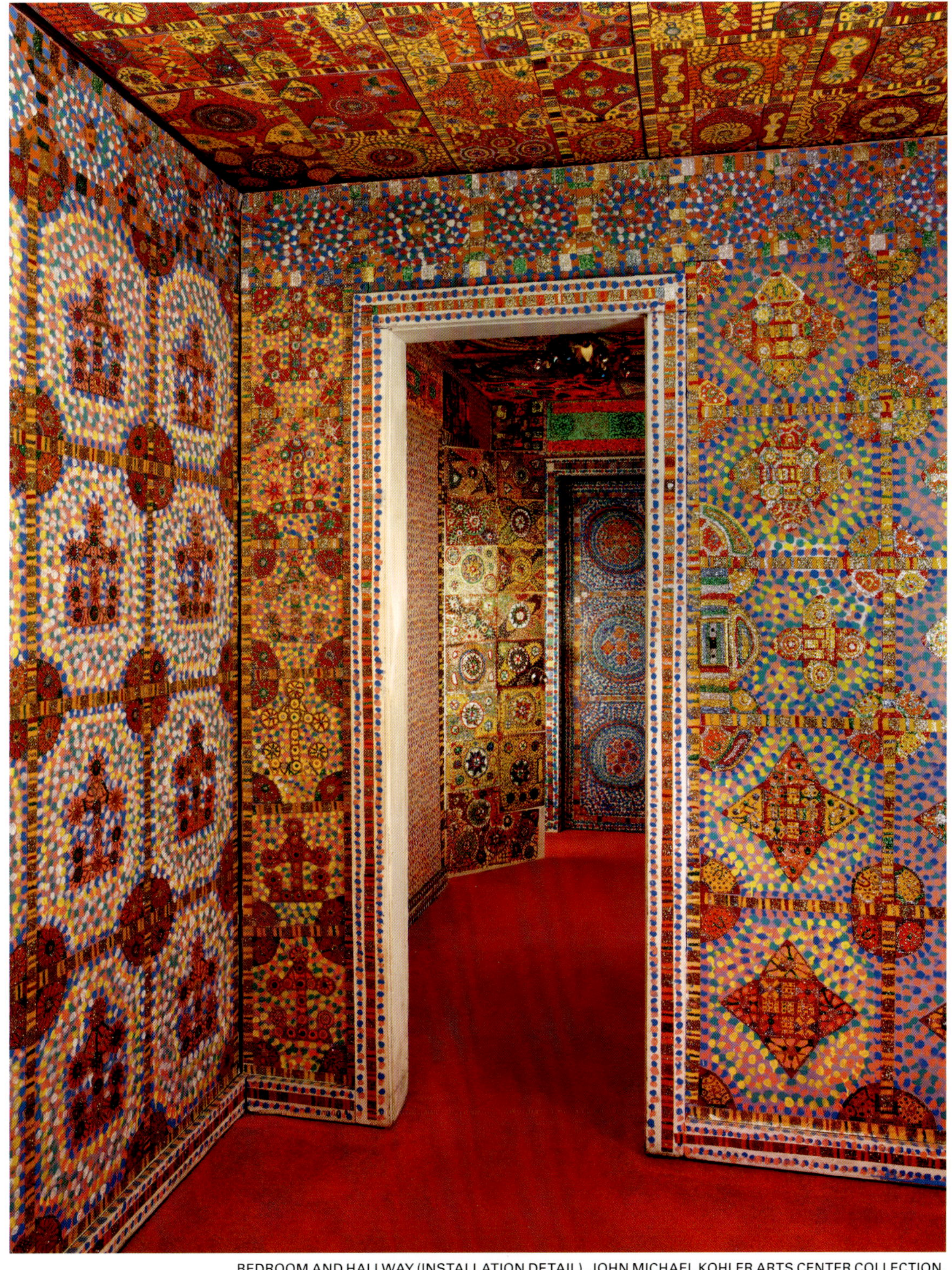

BEDROOM AND HALLWAY (INSTALLATION DETAIL). JOHN MICHAEL KOHLER ARTS CENTER COLLECTION, GIFT OF KOHLER FOUNDATION INC., 2006. PHOTO: COURTESY JOHN MICHAEL KOHLER ARTS CENTER

JAMES C. PHILLIPS

JIM'S HORN HOUSE

THREE FORKS, MONTANA

In contrast to the displays of other artists that feature a wide range of materials and incongruous positionings, Phillips (1948–2023) concentrated his interior decorations on a single genre: antlers. But far from being repetitious or monotonous, his innovative displays amaze with texture and density, and the subtlety of the colors emphasizes the sophistication of the installation.

In 1958, at 10 years old, Phillips found his first set of antlers—which are naturally shed and grow back each year with no harm to the animals—a short walk from his parents' homemade trailer. He carried them home, then found more antlers a few days later and walked those back as well. Throughout his life, his manner of working stayed the same—he never purchased antlers (although he occasionally traded out from his own collection to obtain more unusual specimens), and he packed every one of the sheds and racks of deer, moose, antelope, and elk out of the mountains himself, stacked and intertwined so he could carry them out on foot, without a horse, dog, or any motorized vehicle. He occasionally sold them, however, and during the 1980s he unloaded 600 brown elk and 1,500 deer sheds to put his three daughters through college. He confessed later that he regretted losing the antlers—although he was happy to have been able to help pay for his daughters' education.

Phillips may have gotten the collecting bug from his mother's aunt, a collector of Native American artifacts and arrowheads, fossils and agates. He frequently accompanied her on her collecting trips, and credits her with not only teaching him a love of hunting for the object, but also with the ability to read history in the woods and the artifacts, and the patience to take the time to evaluate and treasure each find. He would never walk outdoors without scanning the ground for the ivory tips of antlers, and he learned, by observation and practice, where the most likely treasure spots would be. He never used binoculars or scopes, relying instead on his intuition, and he would gather antlers that had been bleached by the sun as well as those that had been newly shed. His only concern was that the points be intact.

Beginning in 1969, Phillips kept meticulous records about his antlers, noting type, size, and where they were collected. The count at his death was more than 16,000 (he also journaled information about his garden and other daily events and activities). He had originally stored most of the antlers in a shed or, sometimes, outside, mounting them in stacks or arches up to 16 feet, the height limited by the size of his ladder. He created these forms by intertwining the antlers and wiring them together, and he would leave these assemblages up for several years before dismantling them and reusing the antlers to create another form.

However, he came to feel that these kinds of displays were insufficient in terms of viewing and appreciating the differences in color, size, and shape of each shed or rack, and he wanted to enhance the ability to more easily decipher the narrative behind the animal and its life. So he decided to arrange them in a separate space, and he built a 30 x 64' pole barn from lumber recycled from the demolition of an old grocery store on Main Street, allocating the tongue-and-groove flooring for tabletops in order to augment his display space. Images of the rising and setting suns on the long east and west walls include elements of local petrified wood, and embedded in the complementary rock work are different types of calcite that Phillips recovered from the local talc mine where he worked. The rock work also features elk antler burrs (the base of the antler that is naturally shed each year) that were either too chewed or decayed to display separately. Among other images are two Egyptian-style dog heads (north wall) and two arrowhead shapes (south wall), although they later became mostly hidden by the antlers. The display tables and poles also reveal special designs, and even the walking path through the interior is local sandstone laid out in a pattern, hauled in one pickup load at a time.

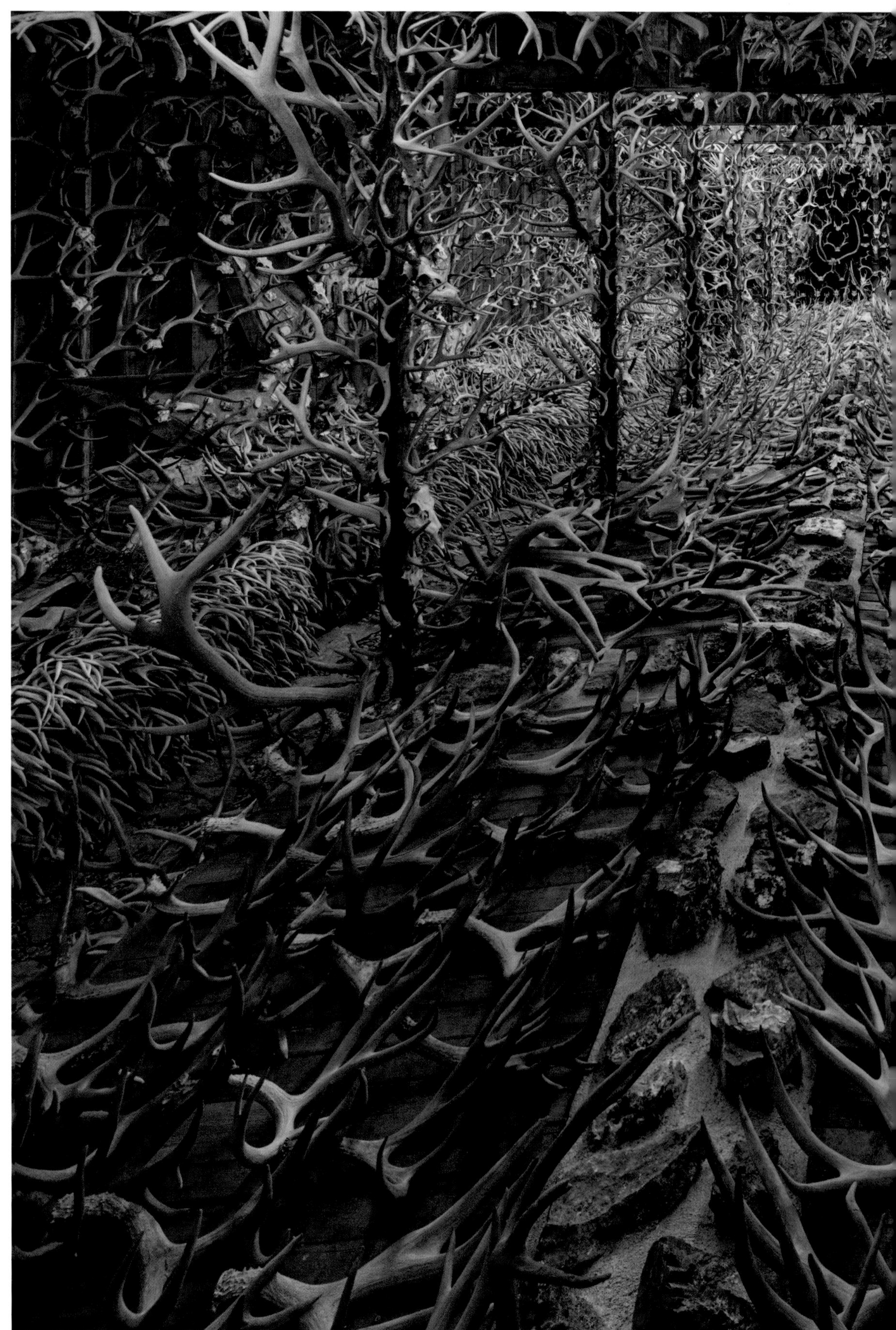

CENTRAL BAY, 2023

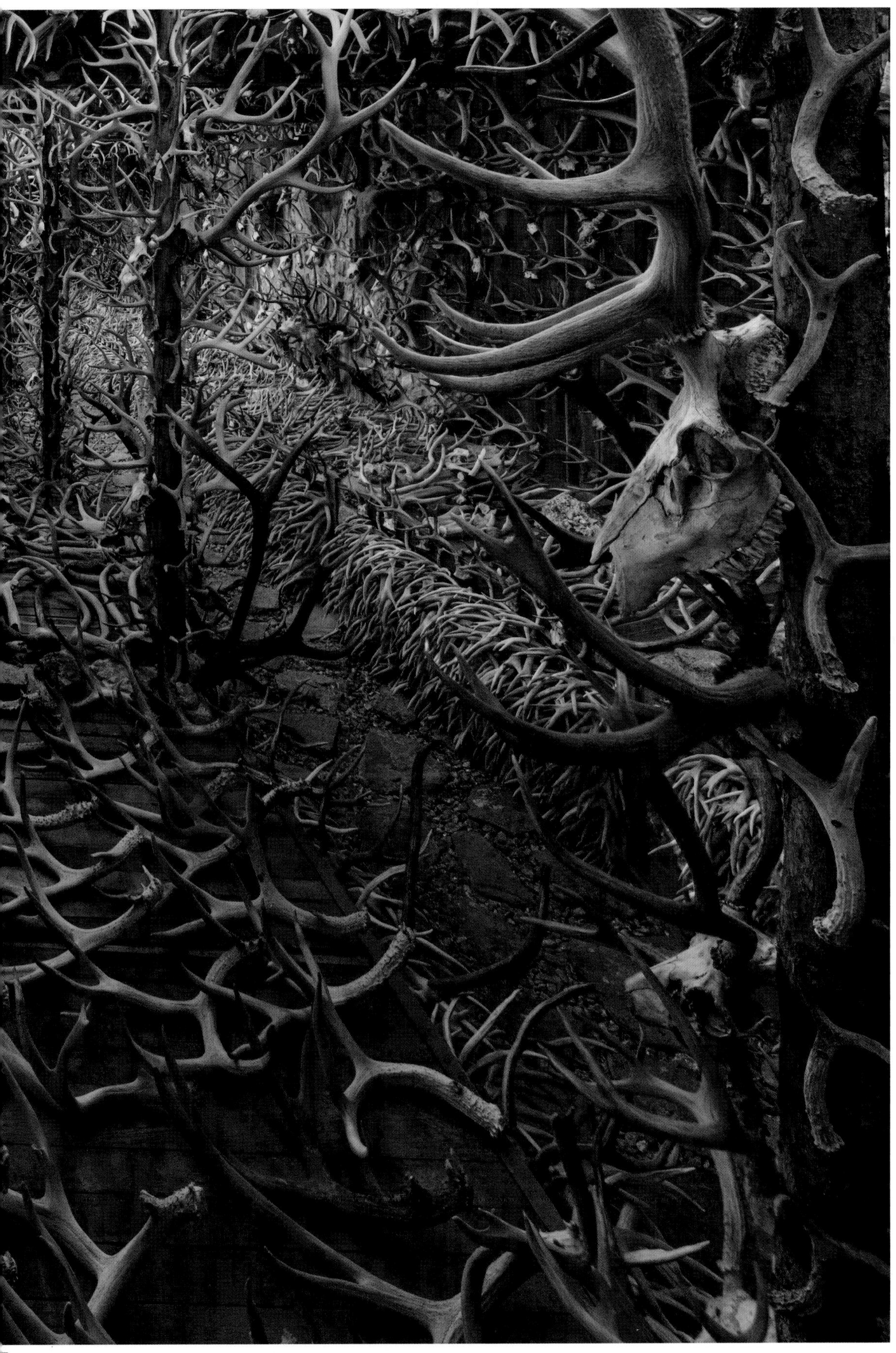

While it took Phillips two years to complete the interior of the building, he installed the antlers in a matter of months. He arranged them in patterns according to color and size, as he had envisioned, in compositions that helped him explore the history that each antler revealed about the life of the animal: whether it might have been injured or died from old age, and how such factors as disease, nutrition, and the animal's level of maturation would impact the form. He was particularly interested in what he termed "oddities": antlers that had been lying in the woods so long that a tree branch or trunk had grown around them, inverted antlers, racks where the pedicle had been bent forward, specimens where another buck's antler was lodged in a competitor's skull, or those with asymmetrical points—in general, those that did not correspond to what we might consider "normal." The impact of the interior of this building is extraordinary, with antlers stacked on the floors, ceilings, poles, and walls. The curving, twisting forms, stretching out in all directions, create a powerful sensation of movement. One cannot help being astonished by the complexity and delicate beauty of the installation.

Known as the "Antler Man," Phillips was always delighted to show visitors his installations if he was at home and not out looking for more specimens. He continued to search for the antlers until the end of his life, and even after more than 65 years, he still confessed to an adrenaline hit when he found them on his hikes. Jim Phillips died suddenly at home at age 74, survived by his wife and three daughters and their families, who will maintain and preserve his *Horn House*.

THE HORN HOUSE ACCOMMODATES OVER 16,000 ANTLERS, ALL GATHERED BY HAND.

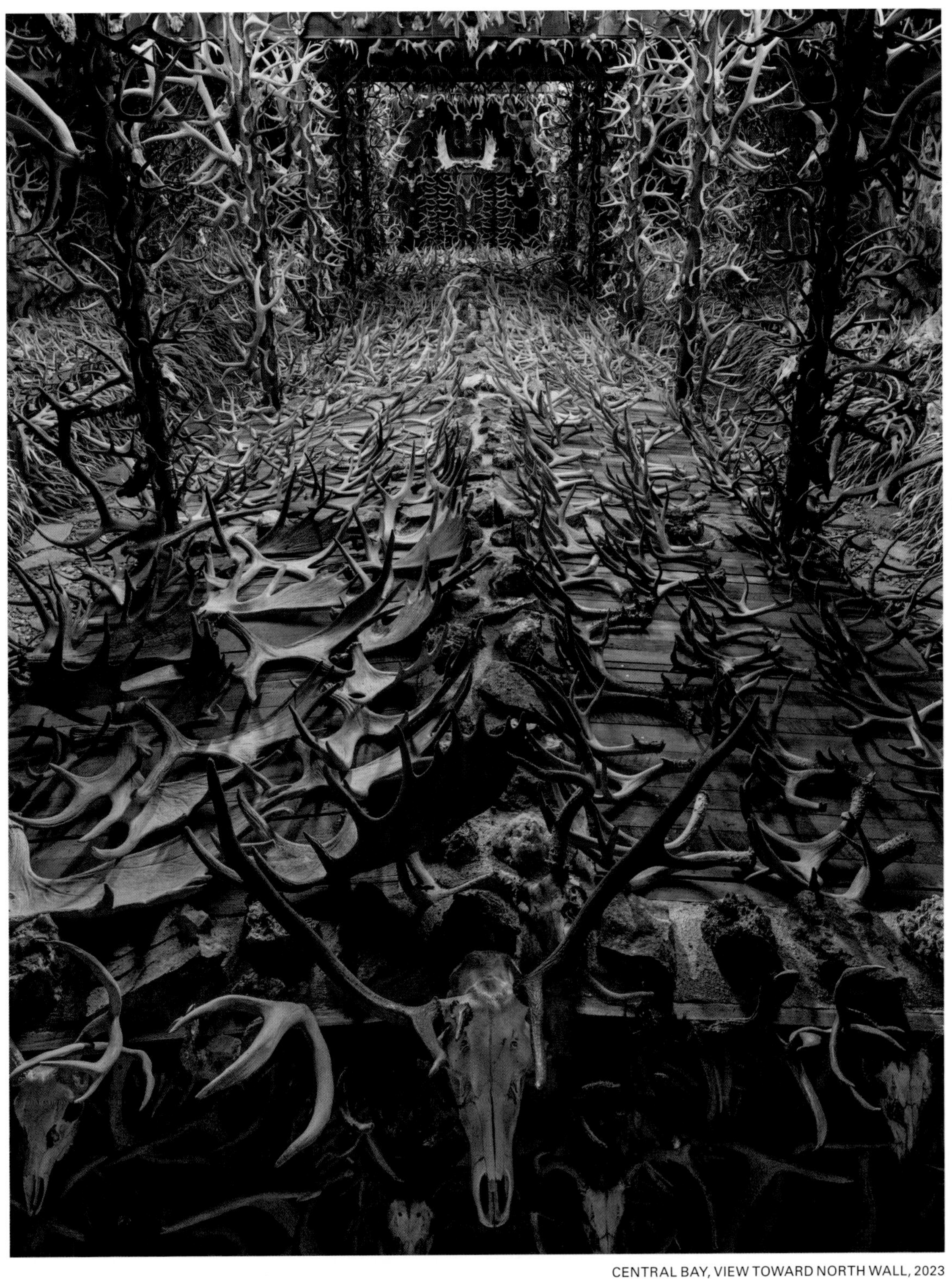

CENTRAL BAY, VIEW TOWARD NORTH WALL, 2023

TRESSA «GRANDMA» PRISBREY

—

BOTTLE VILLAGE

SIMI VALLEY, CALIFORNIA

Like Jim Phillips (see page 242), Prisbrey (1896–1988) originally sought to build what became her *Bottle Village* out of a desire to shelter her collections. In this case, it was thousands of pencils.

The youngest of eight children born in Easton, Minnesota, Thresie (Tressa) Luella Schafer moved with her impoverished family as they homesteaded near Minot, North Dakota. By age 15 she had married an elder sister's 52-year-old former fiancé (or ex-husband, according to some accounts) in what seems to have been an effort to achieve a modicum of security and keep regular food on the table, a welcome bargain in exchange for birthing and raising their seven children. After her husband's death, in the late 1930s she moved west, waitressing, working in factories, and taking other random jobs. By 1947 she was married to Al Prisbrey and living in their small mobile trailer on a ⅓-acre plot in what was then a rather barren, semirural area of southern California just downwind from a poultry farm. Legend holds that one day when her husband was out, she removed and hid the wheels of the trailer so that she would not have to move again.

Around 1956, wanting to build a retaining wall and storage shed but put off by the price of concrete blocks, she went to the local dump and loaded up her old Studebaker pickup truck with bottles and other discards, thinking that these could be used for construction. That "shed" became her *Pencil House*, and only the first of 15 separate buildings she would ultimately construct on this property. Before she realized it would be better to use a trowel, she mixed cement with her hands in a wheelbarrow borrowed from her sister, densely layering the bottles in horizontally, one by one. The subsequent buildings, named by their varied purposes, shapes, or contents—among them, the *Shell House*, the *School House*, the *Round House*, the *Rumpus Room*, *Cleopatre's* [*sic*] *Bed Room*, the *Shot House*, the *Thatched House*, and a *Meditation Room* graced with a secondhand piano—were visually linked by their scale, their proximity, and the use of bottles as primary building material.

The walls glowed like jewels with the sun's illumination and were enlivened by Prisbrey's careful attention to the patterns she could make with her glass color choices. And while she incorporated other materials as she found them—bricks, tiles, broken ceramic pots, auto headlights, and all kinds of random castoffs—the bottles were the essential connection among her constructions. She later recounted that she once took two days off to count them: 1,000,015 (this might have been partly magical thinking, because a later count tallied them at 90,000). Shrines and memorials to bring good luck (like wishing wells) and healing (like chapels) complemented the other buildings, perhaps a response to the death, as adults, of six of her seven children and her two husbands. (In between those marriages at least two serious boyfriends also passed away prematurely, leaving her, at that time, alone again.)

Prisbrey also linked the different structures through a series of decorative edgings, retaining walls, and multicolored mosaic and found-object walkways. The walkways included four discrete motifs in the form of a large heart, spade, diamond, and club laid directly on the dirt, memorializing the time she spent in Las Vegas during her travels. Some of the paths bordered such elements as her *Spring Garden*, a double-entendre installation of metal springs found at the dump that she recycled from bed frames, mattresses, and more robust mechanical coils and auto struts; another low border "wall" was assembled from television picture tubes. Every imaginable discard appears on-site—gardening tools, bullets, pens, toothbrushes, lipstick cartridges, flatware, scissors, toys, plastic flowers, golf tees, guns, license plates, lighters, locks, metal advertisements, and bottle caps—all used or damaged or marred in some way but interesting to Prisbrey for their form, their color, or the way their surfaces reflected the sun. As a girl who grew up without dolls or any other discretionary possession, she was amazed at the wealth and quantity of available castoff resources. They came to serve her both as building materials and to amplify her increasing collections. Nevertheless, she selected everything judiciously, each item critically and individually evaluated for whether and how it could be used.

As Prisbrey aged and her *Bottle Village* became more widely known, she started being known as "Grandma." She told jokes, expressed her impish sense of humor, played the piano, and sang bawdy songs to entertain increasing numbers of visitors as she gave "tours" through the property, pointing out significant elements or sections as she asserted that "it takes more than money to make something out of nothing." In addition to the pencils—17,000 of them, she estimated, many mounted in sunburst or other intricate displays onto recycled pieces of wood or cardboard—she collected roughly 600 dolls (and doll parts, including decapitated heads), innumerable perfume and miniature alcohol bottles, and countless keys and shot glasses. Although regularly grouping like objects together, she arranged everything improvisationally, without plans or drawings (or permits for the buildings), often layering smaller collection pieces onto larger objects: she dressed her dolls, for example, in outfits festooned with pop tops from aluminum cans.

In 1979 the nonprofit Preserve Bottle Village Committee (PBVC) was formed, and Prisbrey's site was honored as Ventura County Cultural Landmark #52. Two years later, it was among those 10 California art environments named as part of California Historical Landmark #939. In 1982, after a series of small strokes, she moved to San Francisco to live with her one remaining daughter, and then on to a nursing home, where she died in 1988. In 1994, a magnitude 6.7 earthquake caused severe structural damage to *Bottle Village*, but although federal emergency funds were allocated for repairs, a local official decried the use of taxpayer money to aid constructions made of "garbage" and refused the funds. Despite this setback, the site was added to the National Register for Historic Places in 1996, and in 2012 the PBVC initiated a restoration plan. Nevertheless, as of this writing the site has not yet been completely restored and much of it is decaying and in disrepair. In 2025 it was added to the list of Historic Artists' Homes and Studios maintained by the National Trust for Historic Preservation.

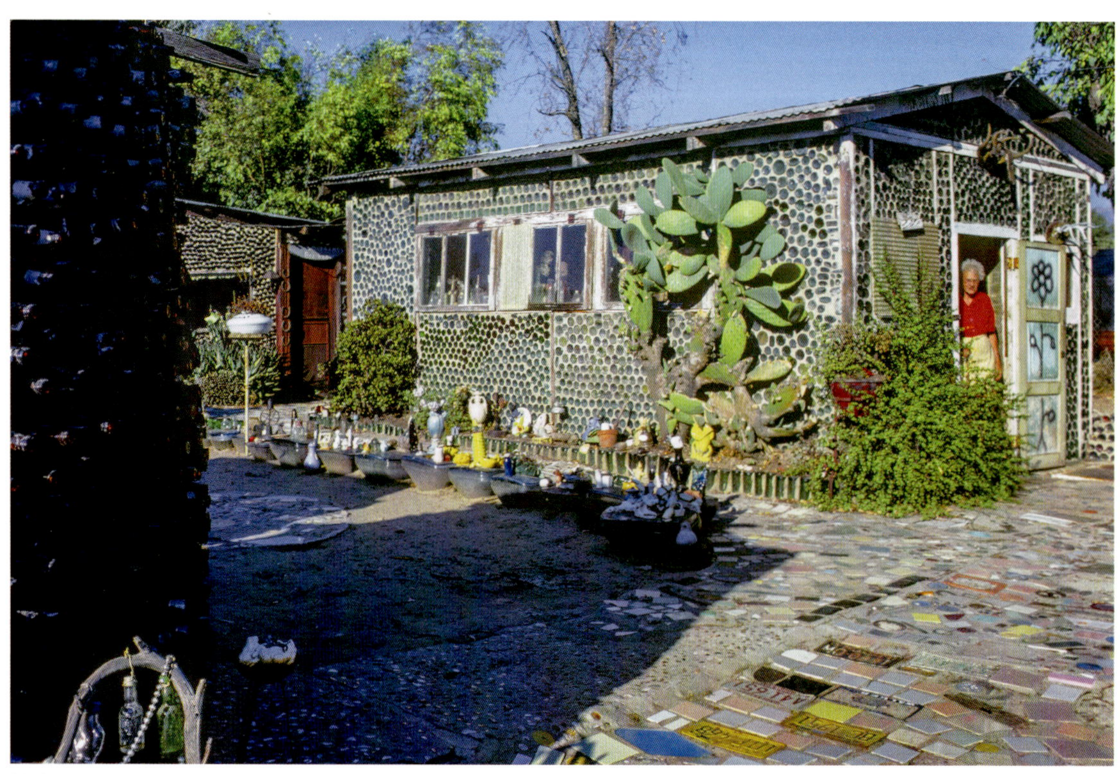

PRISBREY AT THE *BOTTLE HOUSE* DOOR, 1981. PHOTO: © ANDREA HASSIBA, COURTESY PRESERVE BOTTLE VILLAGE COMMITTEE

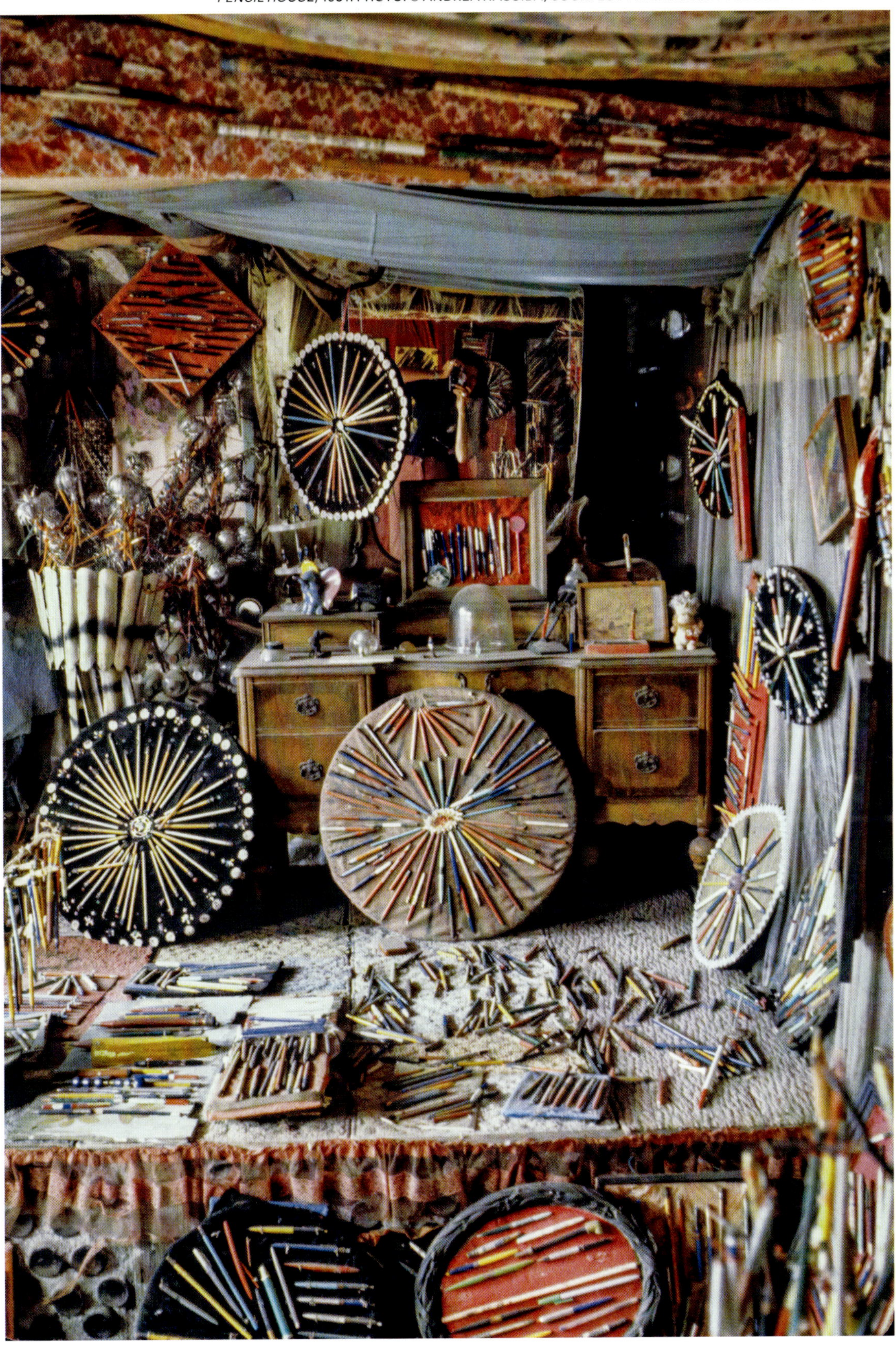

BOTTLE WALL, 2025

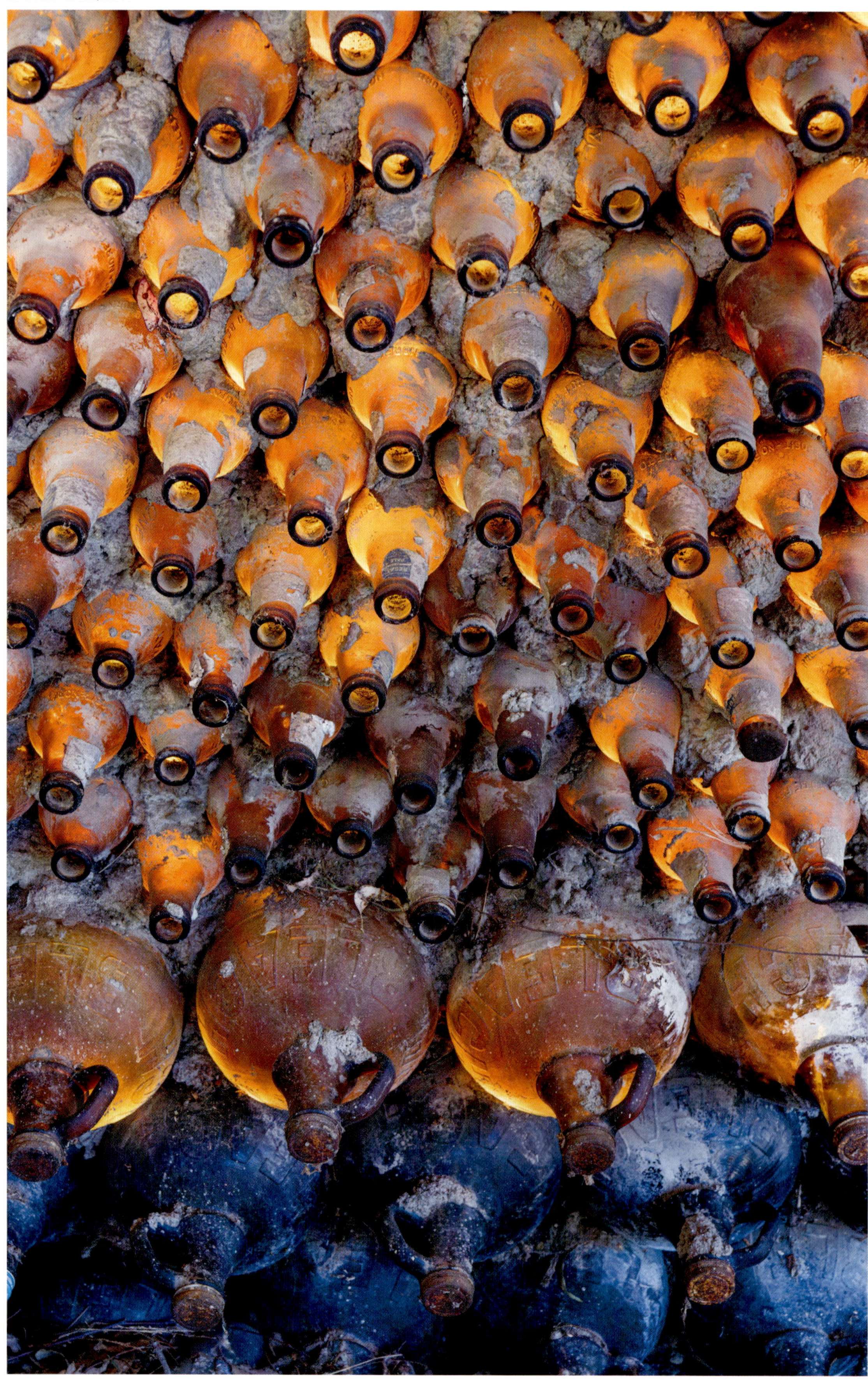

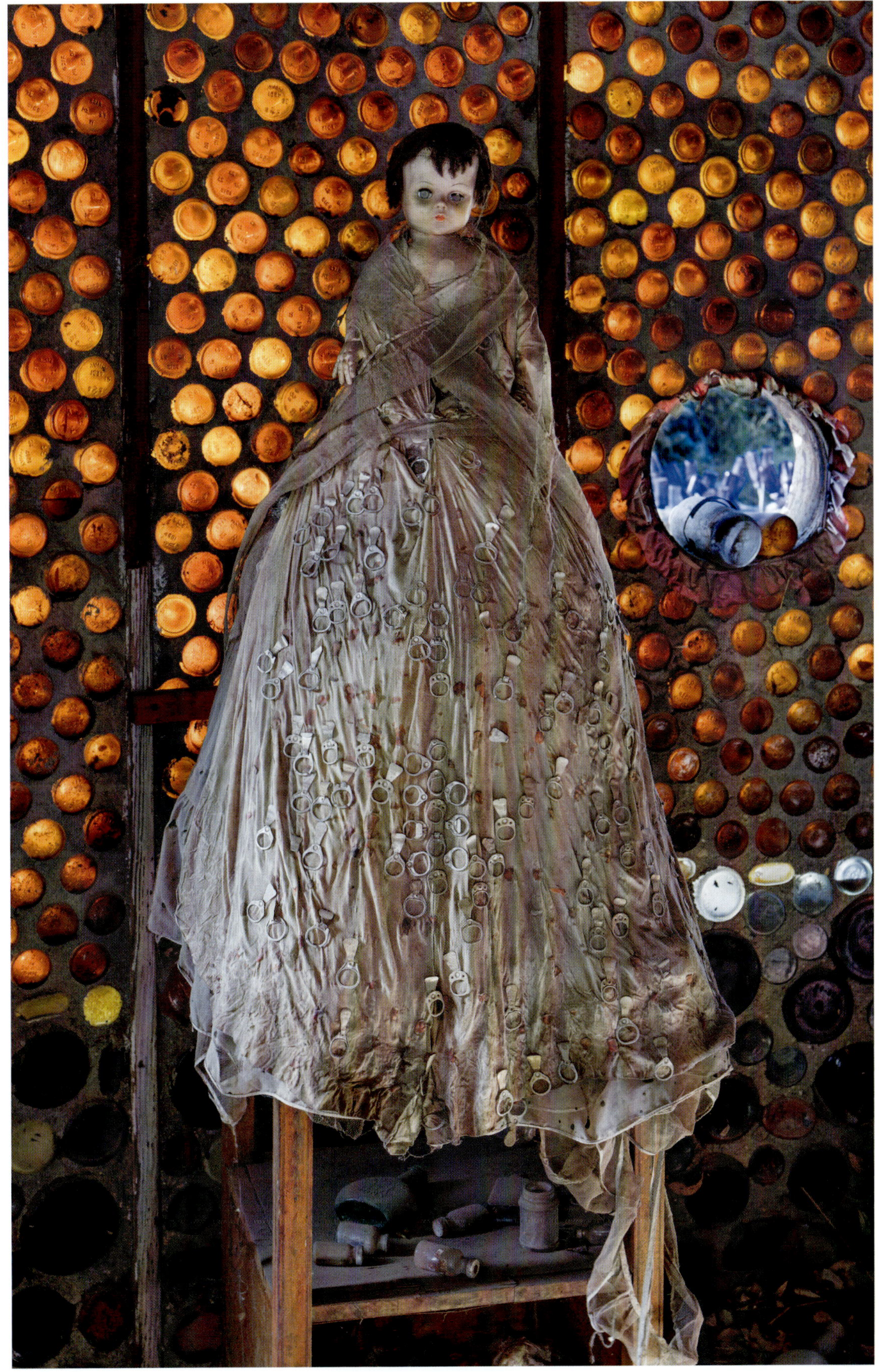

ROUND HOUSE INTERIOR (DETAIL), 2025

LINDSEY ALEXANDER

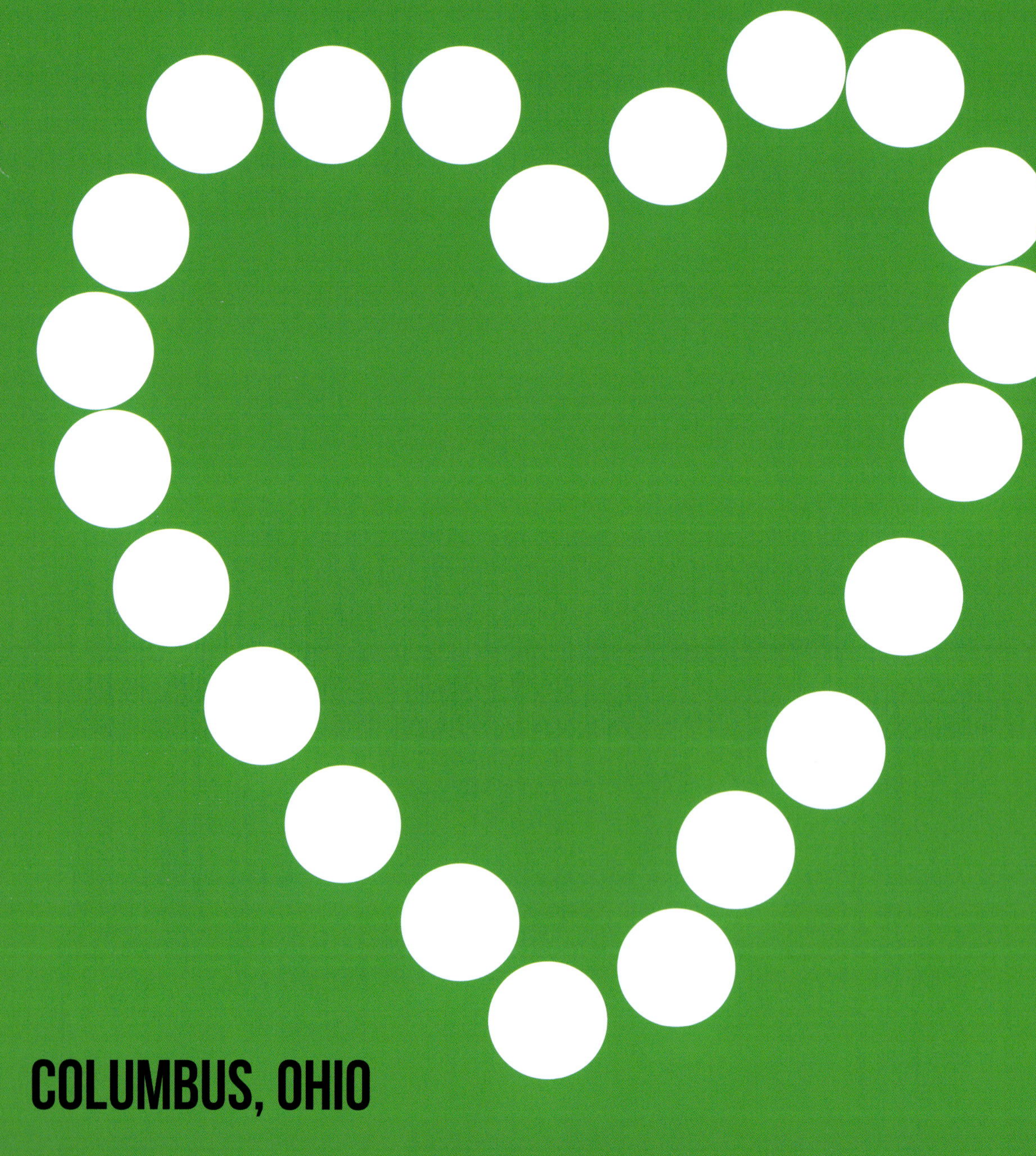

COLUMBUS, OHIO

Memory is often a crucial motivator in the creation of art environments, and its impact may be manifested in countless ways. Alexander (b. 1949), particularly stirred by recollections about her mother and the depth and beauty of mother/daughter relationships, has juxtaposed written reminiscences with inherited and created objects to fashion a charming and restorative area within her home. It is a place where she can simultaneously miss her mother, honor her, and celebrate the feminine gifts with which she herself has now become imbued and which she shares with her own daughters and granddaughters.

In 2000, wanting to downsize after their two daughters left home and happy to move to a brick, Arts and Crafts-style house in Columbus's German Village neighborhood with her husband, Steve Stout, Alexander would have been distressed to leave everything behind. She brought with her physical elements of previous homes, including the childhood house where her parents lived for 50 years and raised their five daughters, and the home in nearby Bexley where she and her husband had lived for 21 years prior to moving to Columbus. Remnants of built-in fixtures, plastered walls with layers of exposed paint and wallpaper, and even tiled floors that helped her to encapsulate her family's history were carefully transferred. (Although neither home was demolished, their interiors were gutted, so Alexander's targeted removals had no value for the new owners' remodel or any potential repurposing.) She also moved her years-long accumulation of meticulously stored resource materials, which she ultimately joined with a variety of constructed and found objects to form an intimate and compelling visual narrative.

Alexander had grown up in an artistic environment, as her mother had commissioned local artists and students to paint murals or furniture throughout their home. Curiously, however, although she had enjoyed those creative expressions, no one ever promoted her interest in art or encouraged her to study and involve herself further, and she never took art classes in high school. She studied elementary education in college, and diligently took one art class solely in order to fulfill the teaching requirement, but she never thought of herself as artistic.

Until the birth of her first daughter, Alexander worked as a fourth-grade teacher and then as a tutor for elementary-school students with disabilities. Taking time off afterward, she began a series of craft projects, making quilts as well as—after taking some classes—working with stained glass, ceramics, and watercolors. Considering a potential job as a part-time art teacher, she returned to college to get her art certification. Although the position never materialized, it motivated her to expand her interests, and she continued taking classes in a variety of sculptural media, learning the use of new tools and new techniques. For a time she worked as a substitute teacher for elementary and high schools in art and general studies, and she taught community and private art classes for children and adults until economic realities led her to work in a law office in order to gain retirement and health insurance benefits. Even so, she continued to make and show her art on the side.

Alexander belatedly came to realize that the process of taking objects apart and putting them back together had become a consistent technique in her work, as was converting forms or motifs to other media. This approach is particularly evident in the primary bathroom, which she began to ornament three years after their move to their house in Columbus. She has been drawn to ceramics, and in her work she augmented shards of porcelain tableware and figurines with handwritten letters and pages from her mother's diary that she transferred to ceramic tile. (To do so she enlarged the texts on a copier, laid the paper copies onto formed clay tiles, and cut through the paper to engrave the text forms into the clay. After firing the tiles, she rubbed black glaze into the carved lines and refired them with a clear overglaze.) A variety of trims—sequins, beads, buttons, and other glittering baubles—as well as a range of keepsakes and personal mementos inherited from her mother and grandmother or shared by family friends, found new homes on the walls and surfaces of the large bathroom. Prominent among them are her mother's collection of blue Estée Lauder "Youth Dew" perfume bottles, which she had saved for decades and urged Lindsey to make into art. Other images were memorialized by creating laser transfer decals that could be made permanent simply by baking them in

BATHROOM (DETAIL), 2018

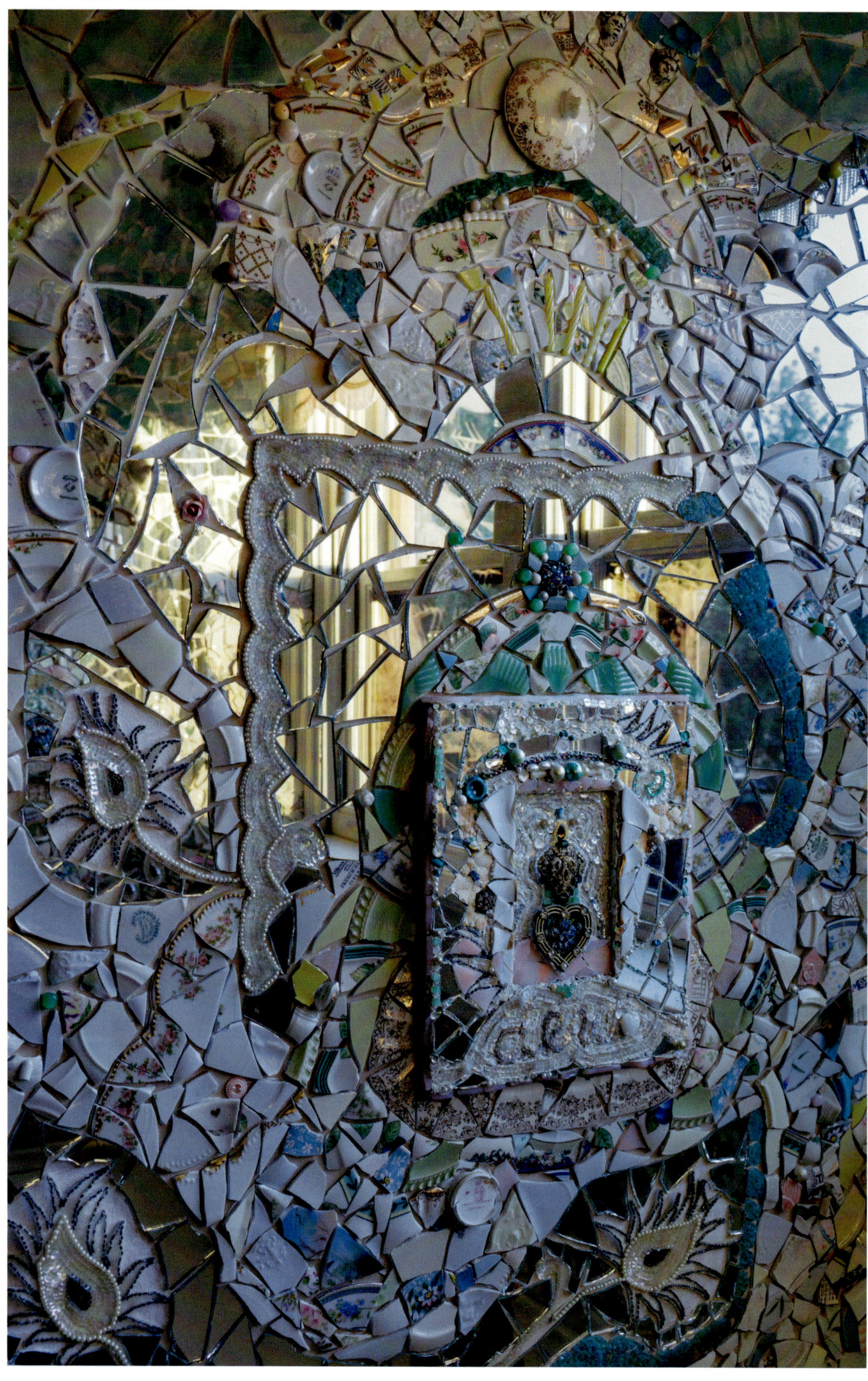

her kitchen oven. Alexander found that while the work was, in her words, heartbreaking, it was also immensely fulfilling: through the physical interaction with her mother's written words she was able to more profoundly feel the sensations of love, loss, longing, and the fleeting passage of time.

Mosaic fragments fill in spaces around and between the handwritten cursive lettering on the tiles as well as those sentences and phrases assembled directly on the wall surfaces. Separately framed-out motifs evoke the footprints of her young granddaughters, and others simultaneously honor and lament the growth and absence of family members: they "grew" and then "flew," she writes of her daughters. "I miss her" reads the mosaic remembering her mother. The durable ceramic tiles and fragments—eminently suitable for a bathroom—are incongruously paired with eggshells, media of the utmost fragility, in both an intriguing chandelier and on some of the room's wall surfaces. Through broader themes of home and femininity, this combination of strength and vulnerability also defines the five generations of women in her immediate family: her grandmother, her mother, Alexander and her four sisters, her two daughters, and two granddaughters.

While the bathroom is Alexander's most decorated and fully conceptualized ensemble, she has also expanded her mosaic and assemblage work elsewhere on the property. For example, a mosaic wall above the kitchen counter reiterates her father's vision that he and Lindsey's mother had wanted to stay in their home forever, her husband's uniform from his Vietnam service and letters home are grouped together in an assemblage that graces a wall on the first floor, understated low mosaic-covered walls adorn the street frontage just inside of an ornamental steel bar fence, and mosaic-covered garden borders, pathways, and columns complement the lush vegetation in the private backyard. (Some of these mosaic works were transferred from her previous homes, giving her a head start.) Occasional pieces of painted furniture complement the family heirlooms and antiques owned by her parents that dominate the home's interior.

For many years, Alexander accepted commissions for smaller works in ceramics, stained glass, and paintings, and she has both exhibited some pieces at a local gallery and hosted exhibitions by other artists in her own home. But as her work evolved, it has become more and more personal, and she is reluctant to involve herself with the demands of clients or to sell it—or even to price it. Instead, she emphasizes the "thread of history" that binds her to her past and, through her daughters and granddaughters, to the future. She is making art for herself, centered in her home, and engrossed in how her house is helping her expand her personal narrative, taking its place as both a link and a tribute to her family connections.

ALEXANDER CREATES RESTORATIVE SPACES THAT HONOR LOVE, LOSS, LONGING, AND THE FLEETING PASSAGE OF TIME.

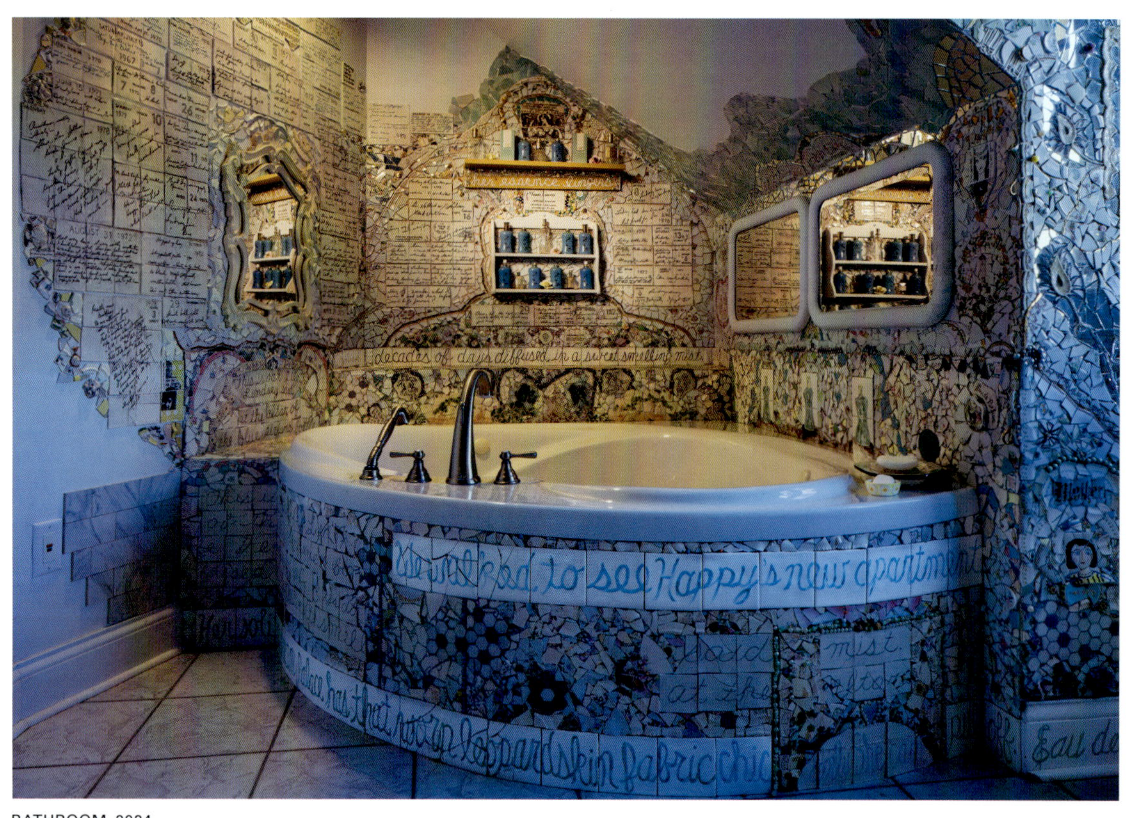

BATHROOM, 2024

BATHROOM (DETAIL), 2018

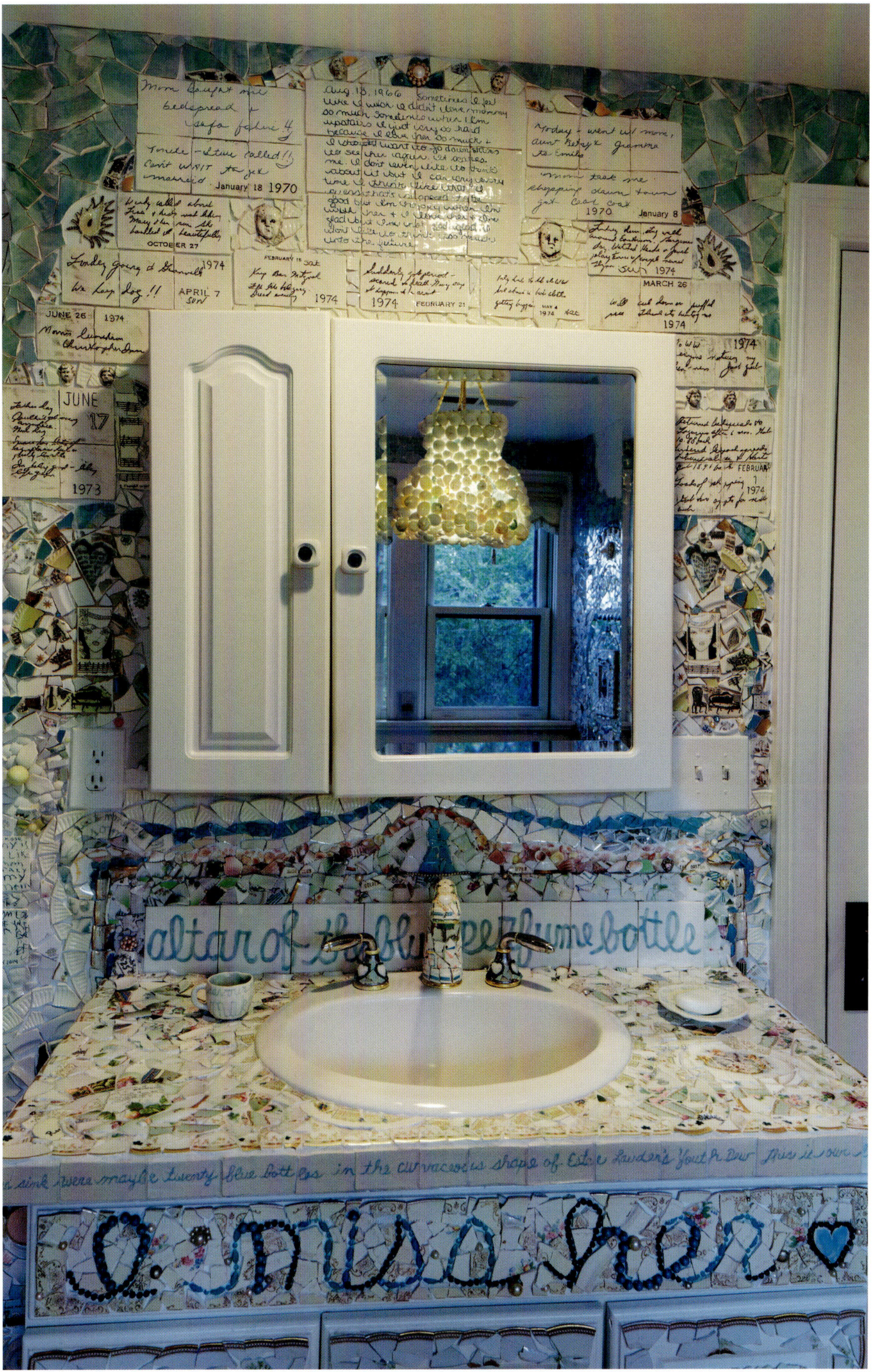

CHARLES WINCE

WINCEWORLD

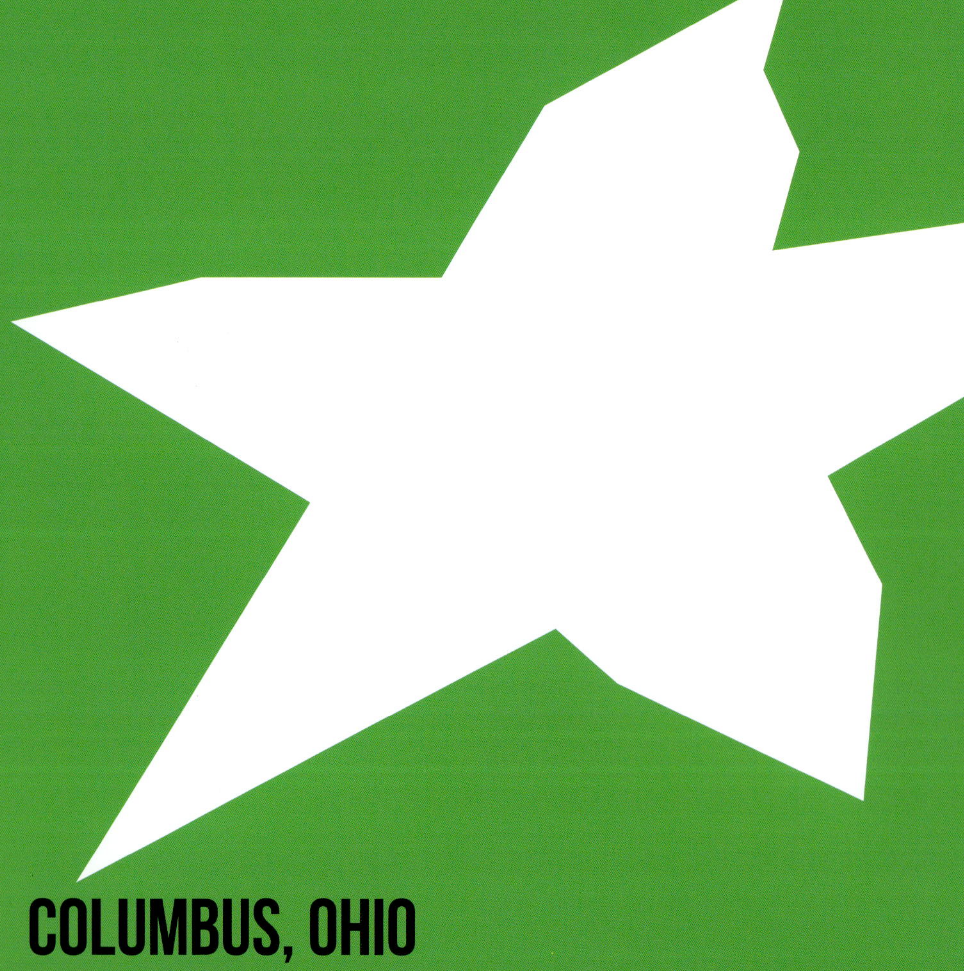

COLUMBUS, OHIO

When a flame lit by a school friend unexpectedly exploded a gasoline can as they were playing too close to it in his parents' garage, 10-year-old Wince (b. 1955) was rushed to the hospital with life-threatening burns over most of his body. He still carries the scars today. The adult Wince credits that near-fatal disaster with turning him away from a casual youthful delinquency born of poor impulse control and general lack of parental oversight, and toward a more introspective quest that led him to focus on artmaking. And the explosion continues to have long-lasting effects, as can be seen in its recurring reflection in themes he chooses for his paintings and in the jarring impact of those motifs on viewers.

Prior to the accident, he had enjoyed sketching simple comic-strip-like narratives to help him avoid the challenges of his learning disabilities (he was later diagnosed with dyslexia, ADHD, and dyscalculia), but storytelling through drawing grew in importance to become a lifeline for him during his convalescence, as he tried to come to grips not only with his life-changing trauma but with his family's general dysfunction. During this period and in subsequent years, he was misguidedly put on amphetamines by a doctor to help him catch up with his schoolwork (he never finished high school), and his art began to mimic the frantic, feverish moments of the explosion and its aftermath: more realistic images of normal life were overtaken by hallucinations that warp, fuse, and distort elements in each painting. And so, painting became Wince's revelatory means of expression: bold carnivalesque colors, hard edges, precise details, parodies of commercial products and pop culture, imaginary beasts, and, of course, unsettling images of flames and body parts and weapons. Much of the work reveals biographical elements that merge with social and political commentary, consumerist irony and greed, soft porn, dark humor, and graphic lettering. He taught himself to paint, and his technical proficiency is compelling.

Wince moved from rural Ohio to Columbus in 1982. In 1988, with income from working as a part-time mail carrier (a position he held for 23 years), he bought a rundown house in what was then the shabby Harrison West neighborhood, and he began to fill it with his paintings, assemblages, and explorations into other media. As he worked to renovate it on a budget, he learned to make his own ceramic tiles and also welcomed the work of students and friends to complement his own. This included interior modifications to the infrastructure and cosmetic treatments of the house, as well as designed furniture and contributions or commissions of other artwork. The resulting density, color, movement, and clash of imagery that frequently merged whimsy with pain has converted the house into a true environment, one that is even more notable now that the neighborhood has become gentrified. It is as if the Fun House at the county fair were incongruously surrounded by manicured chateaux.

Each section of *WinceWorld* impresses in a distinct manner. In his bedroom, for example, the monumental 12′ wide triptych *Mother Russia Meltdown* is given breathing space for viewers to appreciate the absurd yet technically sophisticated multilayered juxtapositions of imagery. Some of its motifs, such as the baby head with dollars coming out of its ears and Medusa-like hair whose twisted locks end in portraits of Stalin, are echoed on the headboard and other bedroom accoutrements. In contrast, the eclectic collages, paintings, posters, photographs, cutouts, and constructions on every surface in the bathroom ebb and flow together, enhancing and amplifying each other. The wildly varying motifs do not so much convey incompatibility as provocatively challenge viewers to understand the connections Wince suggests, both through their placement and through his backdrop-like painting directly on the room's floor, ceilings, and walls. Here, as in his collaborations with artist and designer friends in other areas of the house, neither his personal narrative nor his intensity are diminished. There are few, if any, sections of walls, floors, or furniture that have not been adorned or painted or tiled.

The interior of the house came together in a generally unpredictable manner, as he accumulated and posted the collected graphics, collaborated with pals on furniture, and developed his own rather improvisational yet methodical paintings (*Mother Russia Meltdown*, for example, has been continuously in process since 1994). In the meantime, although he has occasionally exhibited his work in off-site venues and it is still compelling no matter where it is seen, its impact is greatly amplified when surrounded by the contrasting colors, textures, and visual action of the central core of his expression, *WinceWorld*. To appreciate the whole is to begin to make the connection between the dark days of his past and how his artmaking has literally illuminated the ways those experiences helped him to

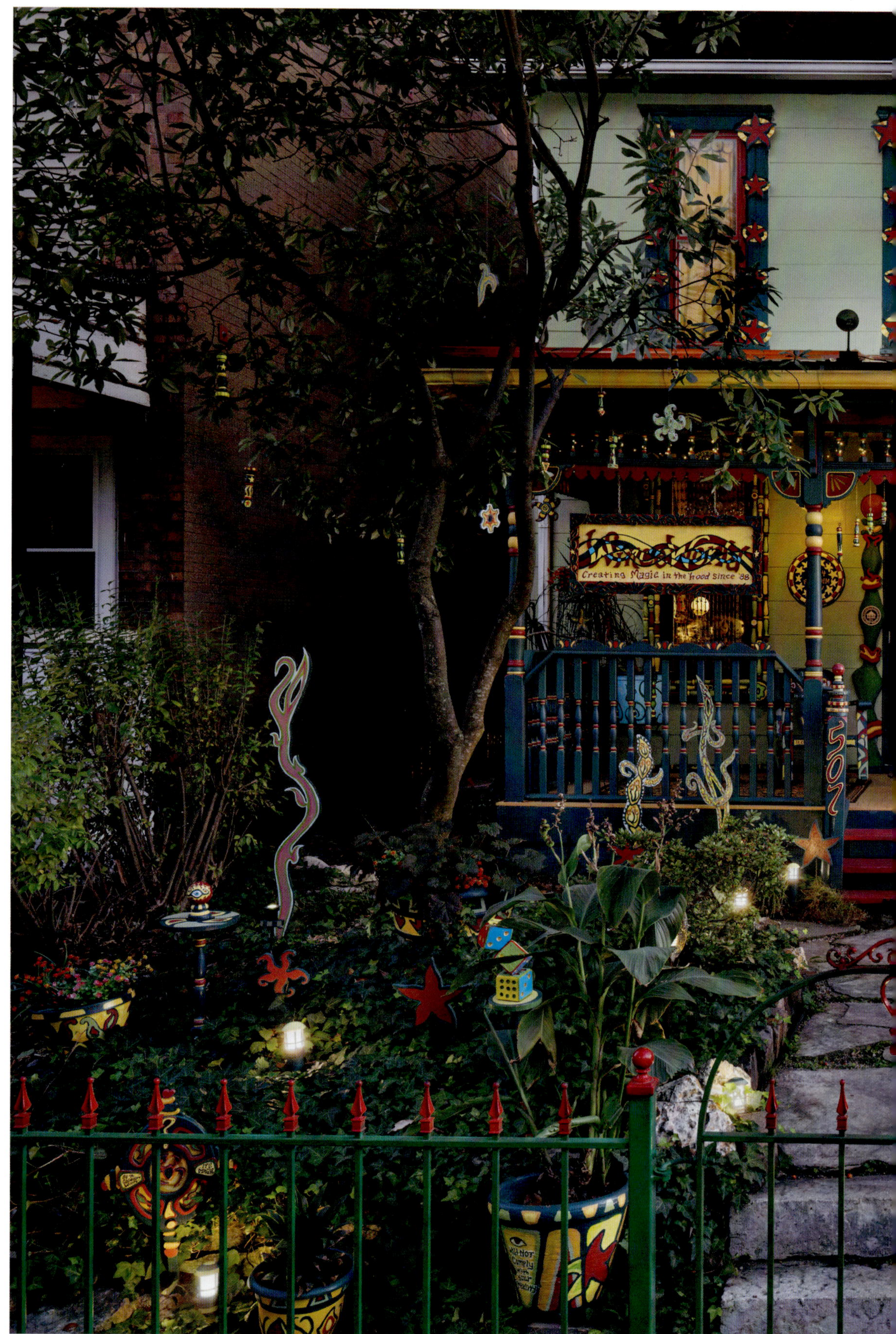

FRONT FAÇADE AND GROUNDS, 2024

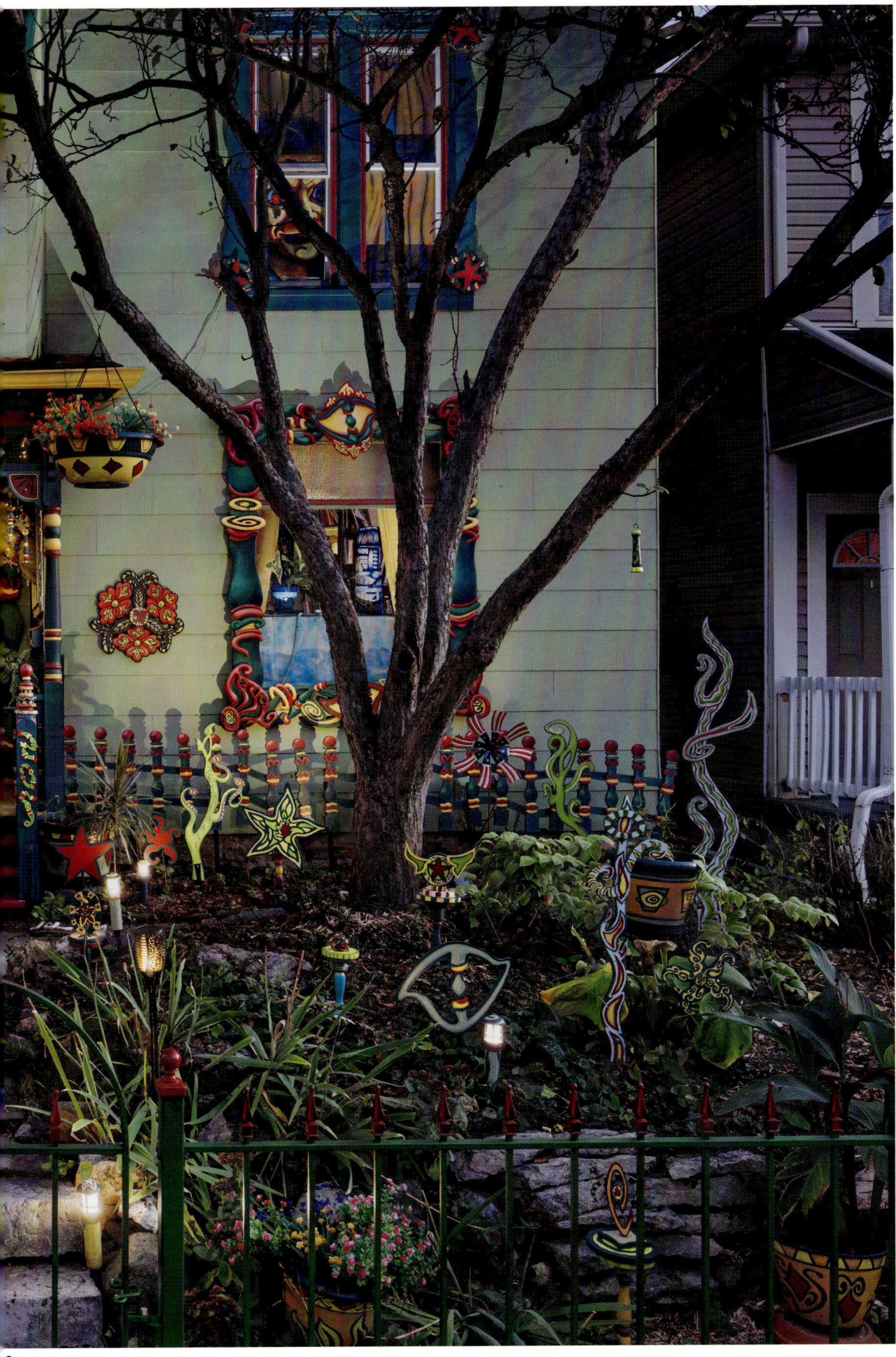

channel his creativity. Living in a singular fashion, ignoring conventional aesthetic and cultural norms while welcoming the insight born from passing through and superseding the emotional and physical distress of those earlier traumas, has brought depth, breadth, and greater visibility to *WinceWorld* and, perhaps at the same time, a degree of serenity for the artist.

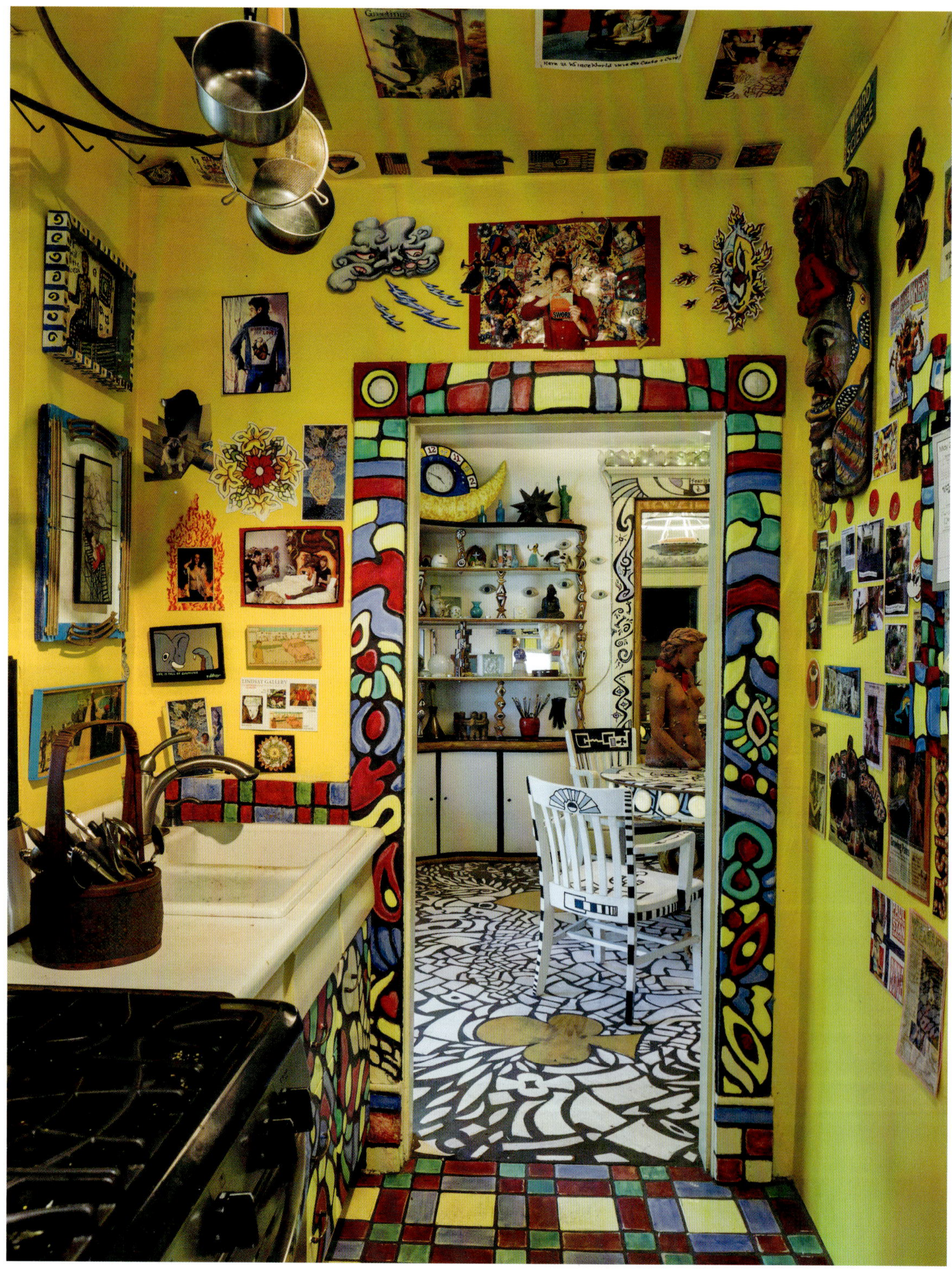

KITCHEN, 2015

BATHROOM, 2011

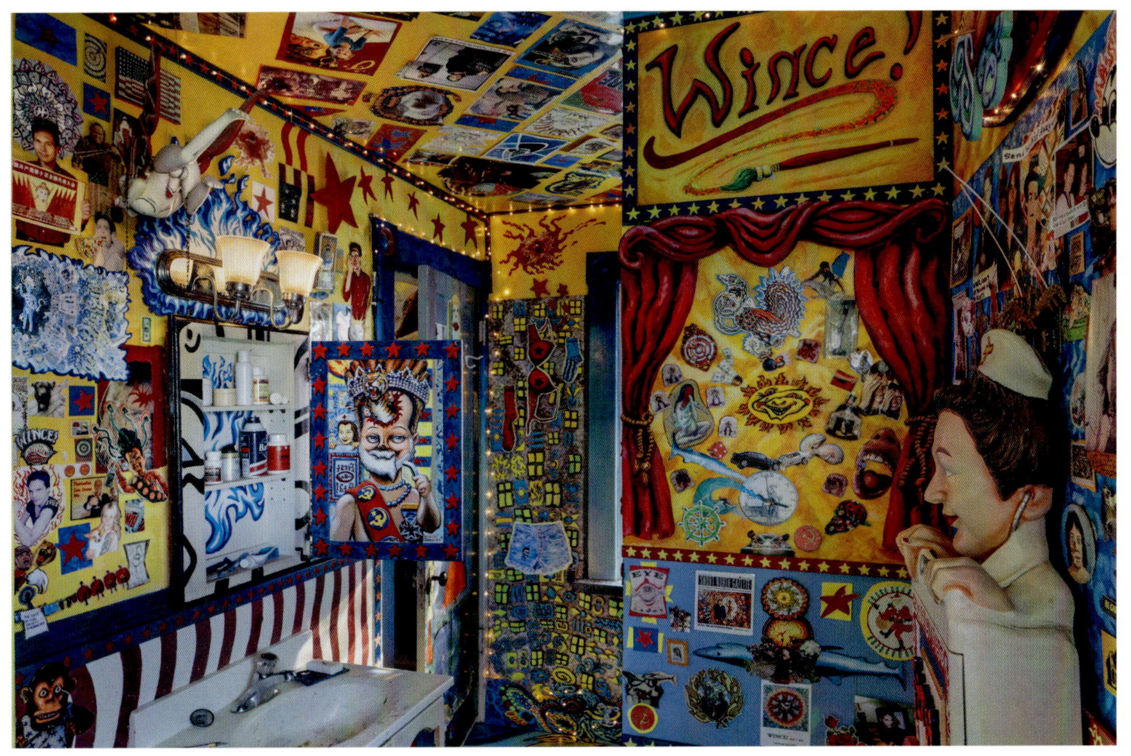

HIS WORK MERGES BIOGRAPHICAL ELEMENTS WITH SOCIO-POLITICAL COMMENTARY, CONSUMERIST IRONY AND GREED, SOFT PORN, AND DARK HUMOR.

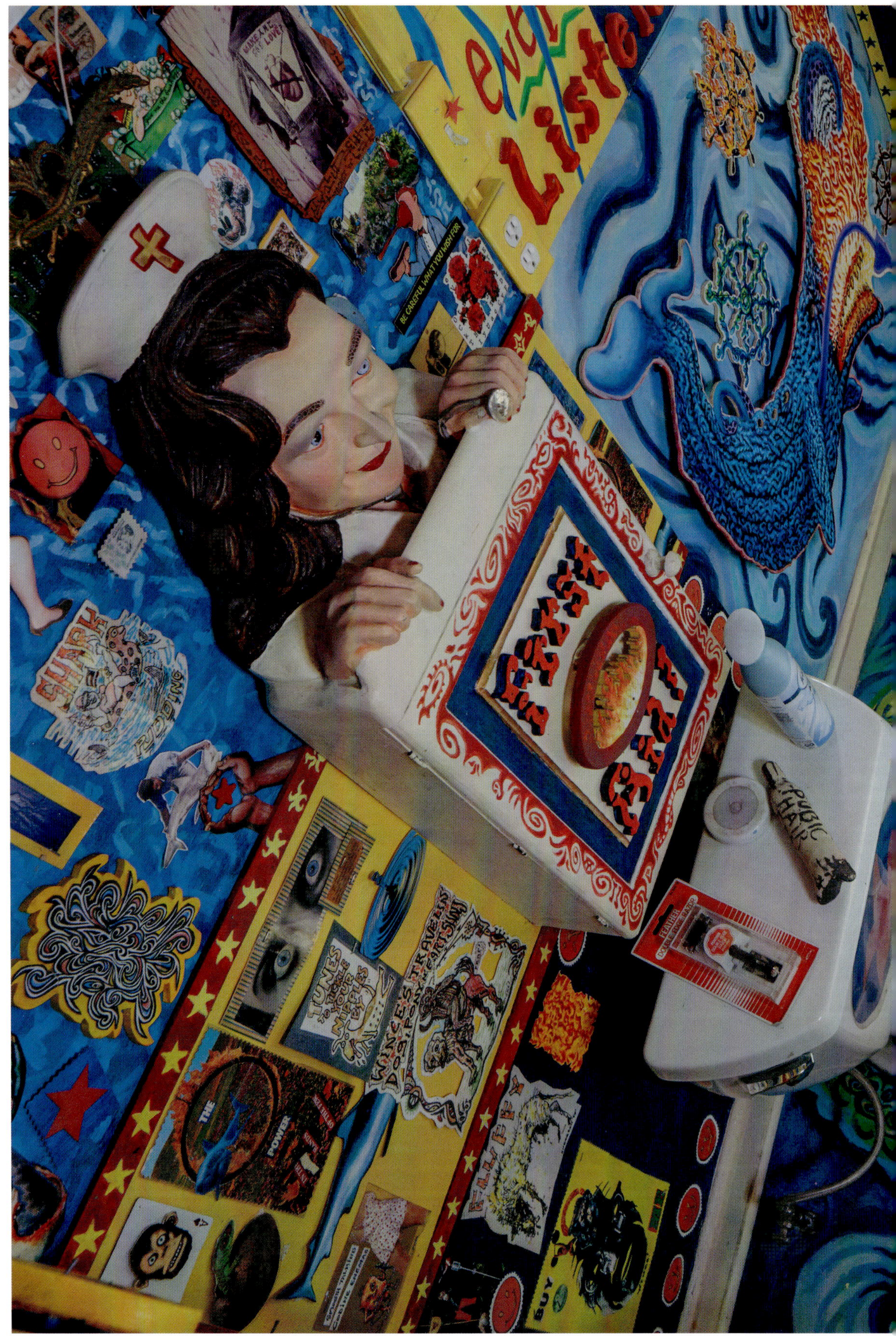

BATHROOM, 2019

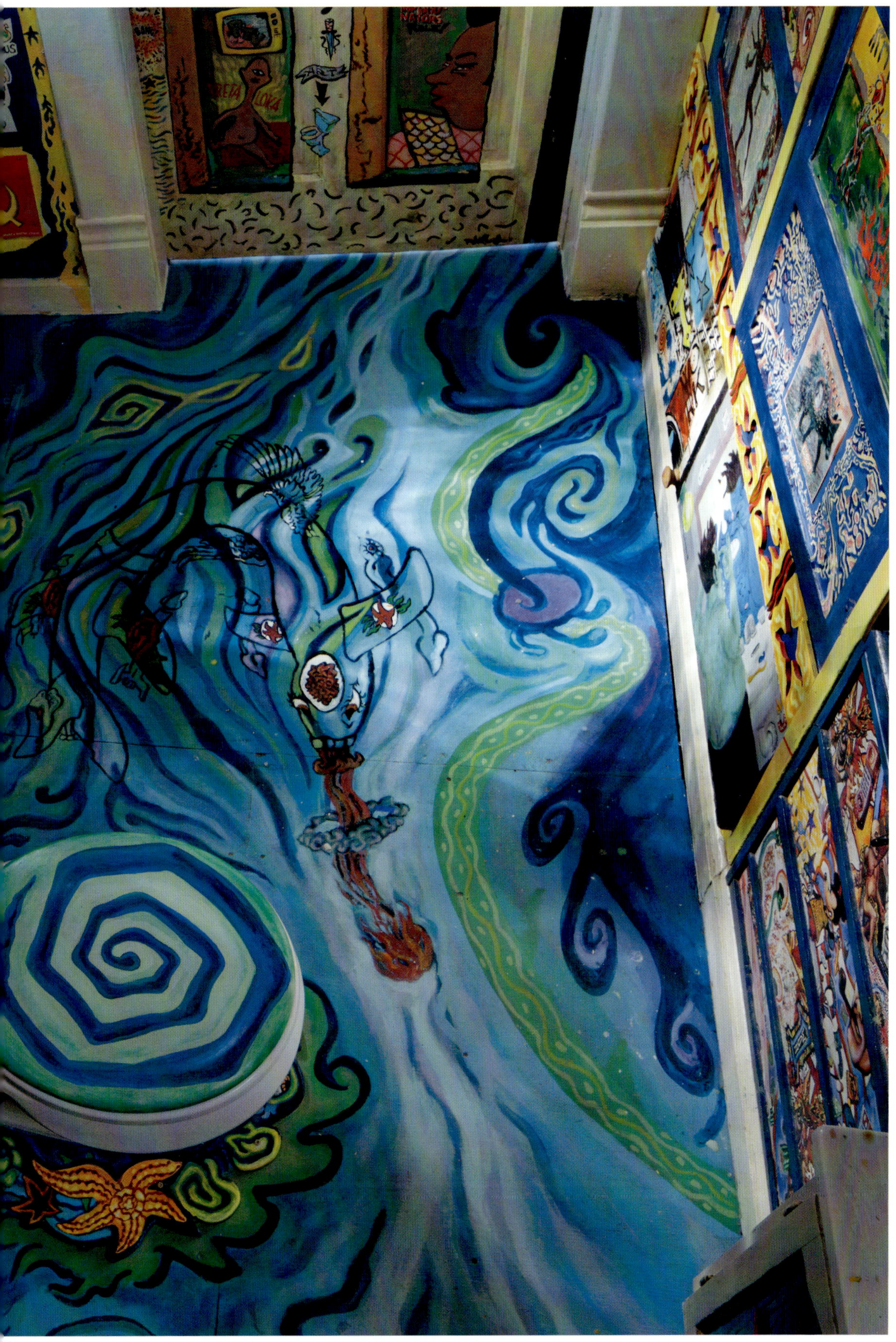

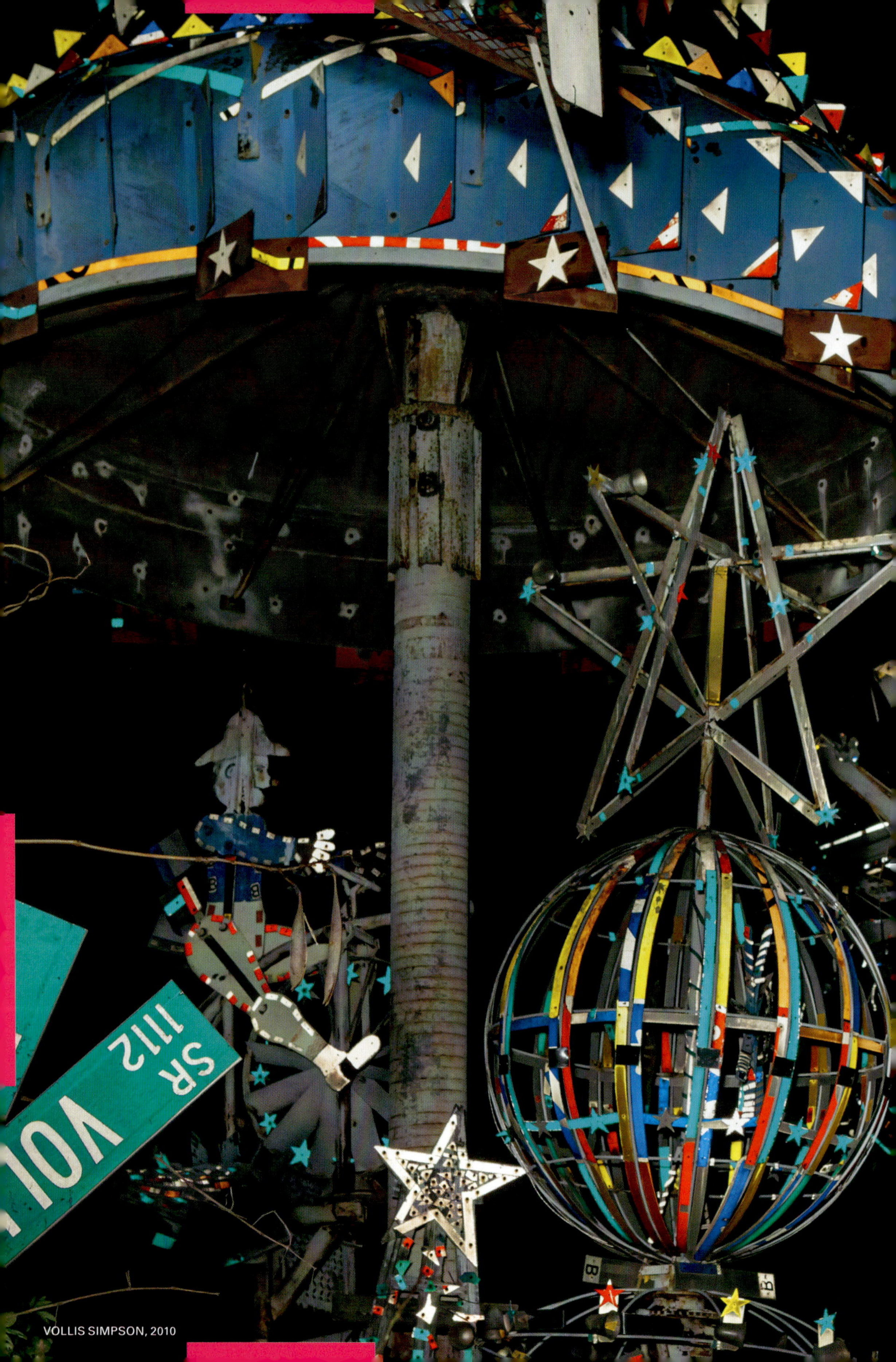

VOLLIS SIMPSON, 2010

CHAPTER 4

NO OCCUPANCY PERMIT REQUIRED

—

ARCHITECTURAL MONUMENTS

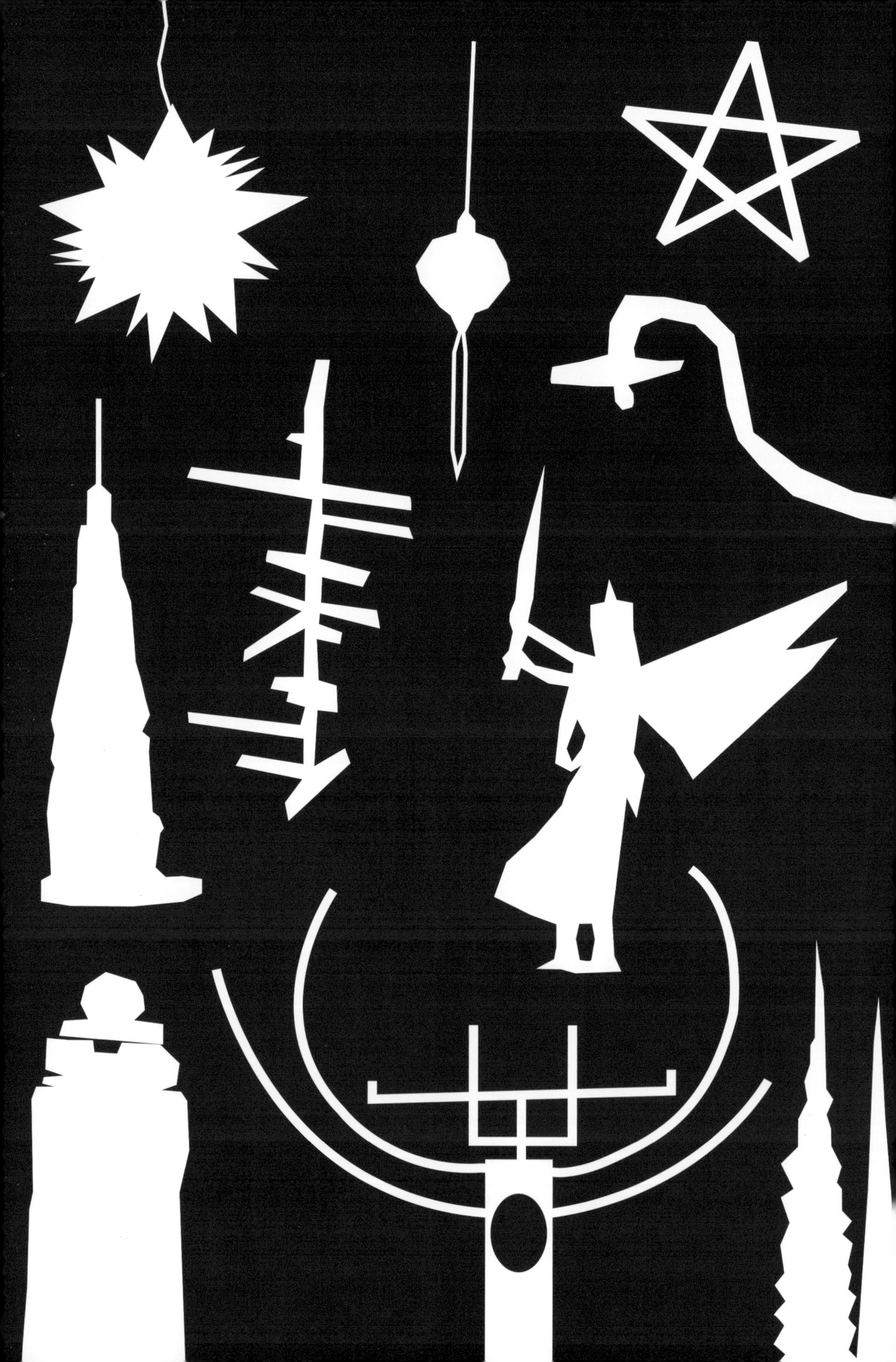

While not necessarily conceptualized as inhabitable structures, or even, in all cases, structures that would invite human interaction, this group of monuments is decidedly architectural. Sharing elements with bona fide buildings—towers and pinnacles, stairways and laddered treads, ground-level arches and beams strung high, even internal lighting and mechanics—these constructions can be considered in the tradition of architectural fantasies of the past.

In the eighteenth century, for example, the theory of *architecture parlante* (narrative architecture or, more literally, architecture that speaks) was the rage, practiced by such architects as Jean-Jacques Lequeu, who designed a cow-shaped stable for cows. These inventors posited that the shape of a building should provide the key to its function. Surely Tom Every's *Forevertron* (see page 304)—again, while not an actual building—can be linked to this tradition, with its form signaling its purpose of expediting otherworldly transportation.

It may also be useful to reference the two-dimensional caprices of visionaries—including Achilles G. Rizzoli (San Francisco, California) in the twentieth century and Alexander Brodsky (Moscow, Russia) and Olalekan Jeyifous (Lagos, Nigeria) in the twenty-first—who have or had no real expectation that their designs would ever be realized at scale. The imagination can run more freely if the drawn image is not intended to serve as a blueprint that crystallizes concepts into a buildable structure. And while advances in computer technology, engineering, and innovative materials have brought us to a stage where very few designs really remain physically unbuildable, the realities of urban codes or sociocultural expectations stand firm to impede fulfillment of most more radical concepts.

In a similar way, alt-stream builders, as we might call them, approach construction in an ad-hoc and improvisational manner, addressing physical and material challenges as they arise and ignoring the conventional rules of architecture. They tend to focus more on the process than on the appearance or scale of the finished product. Nevertheless, as with the more "building-like" sites in this book's other chapters, the expectation by the creator is that these monuments have to be experienced, not just seen. As such, they reveal an intention that parallels that of true architecture and leads viewers to an understanding of the maker's objectives, expressing themselves in singular ways to accomplish capricious and innovative works.

WILLIAM "BILLY" BLEVINS TRIPP

—

THE MINDFIELD CEMETERY

BROWNSVILLE, TENNESSEE

The monumental and still-developing architectural sculpture of Billy Tripp (b. 1955) reveals the collection of a lifetime's worth of memories and recycled metal components that are being assembled, like Tom Every's *Forevertron* (see page 304), into a single breathtaking creation.

The middle son of a Methodist minister, Tripp was born in Jackson, approximately 30 miles east of Brownsville, where he moved with his family when he was in third grade. After completing high school, he enrolled in a welding class, but only completed six weeks of the two-year course, long enough to learn the basics before he dropped out (he kept his textbook, however, which he still occasionally refers to). He later took a class in painting at a community college and then a couple of art history and sculpture classes at Memphis State University, where he was introduced to modern sculptors such as David Smith. But he again dropped out, preferring instead to study these subjects on his own. Nevertheless, even a passing familiarity with how metal has been assembled into nonfunctional forms by other artists might have influenced Tripp's opus. In fact, years later, he seamlessly incorporated some of his own early metal sculptures into what would become *The Mindfield Cemetery*.

From 1981 to 2020, a small commercial car wash provided Tripp's main source of income, but he also worked in his family's ham business, did odd jobs, and offered welding services to the public for a few years in the late 1980s and early 1990s. The modest returns he earned from these enterprises were augmented after his father's passing with a relatively significant financial and real property inheritance. This support has been instrumental in helping him to more generously fund purchases of materials and equipment.

Tripp's first in-depth explorations of his creativity, however, came through writing, a path perhaps kindled by his interest in reading biographies. In 1977, around the time of his mother's death, he began the first volume of a fictionalized and rather stream-of-consciousness autobiography, *The Mindfield Years (Billy Pyrene's Biography of Ned)*, which he self-published in 1996. This initial publication, about 725 pages long depending on the edition, concluded with the death of the protagonist's own mother and has been followed, as of this writing, by 11 additional volumes, each encapsulating one or two notebooks and memorializing Tripp's own experiences and activities. He published these books over a period of several years, and a metal representation of his first book, pages splayed open, now hangs from one of the high limbs of *The Mindfield Cemetery*. Notably, the books include entries recounting the construction of his singular monument in text and images.

While he was still involved in his early writings, around 1989 he began to build on a small parcel of land located near downtown Brownsville, and over time this three-dimensional structure became as autobiographical as his books: his story told in metal instead of words. The evolving architectural edifice is replete with specific references to his own life as well as broader and sometimes enigmatic ruminations about the universal human cycle of life and death. (These themes of birth, sex, marriage, and death were even more explicitly explored in the assemblage decoration on his motorcycle *Silvia*, alluding to the physical nature of the ride. He began that project in 2003, after his father's death the year before, although it has now been partially dismantled.) Already deep into his construction, Tripp came to conceptualize the monument as a "grave marker," and more specifically, as a cenotaph—a monument to persons buried elsewhere—to memorialize his parents, as he was unable to bury them underneath. (He has, however, received written permission from the city of Brownsville for his own interment there, when the time comes.)

Tripp also characterizes the *Mindfield* as a church- or cathedral-type building, distinguishing different sections that he perceives as the nave, sanctuary, and altar, and identifying the long vertical augers as steeples. At other times, he describes the whole as a ship. From different angles each of those associations are easy to see, although the various elements that make up these thematic markers are diverse and multilayered—and many are not easily decipherable without Tripp's annotated descriptions. Generally not weight-bearing, these motifs document his life journey, as they depict imagery that alludes to consequential experiences, events, and people, and memorialize what he describes as conversations he has with himself as he passes toward the next phase of existence. He describes the structural beams that have not yet been ornamented with images as "empty," a fitting signifier given that he is still living and working. Thus, the *Mindfield* is not only a commemorative articulation of his past but it will be his legacy after his death. He is cheered by this thought.

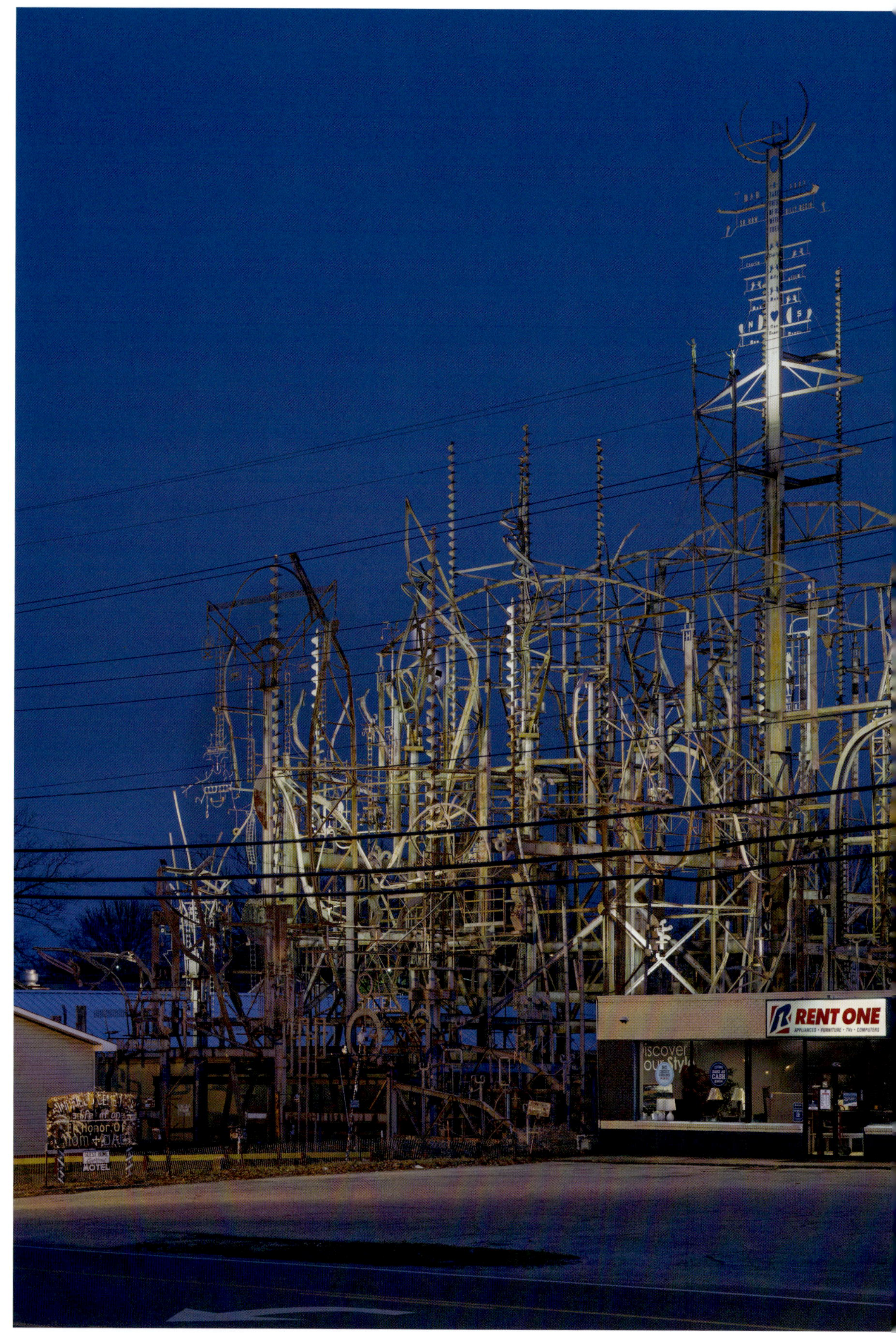

VIEW FROM NORTHWEST OF *MINDFIELD* AND NEIGHBORING BUSINESSES, 2024

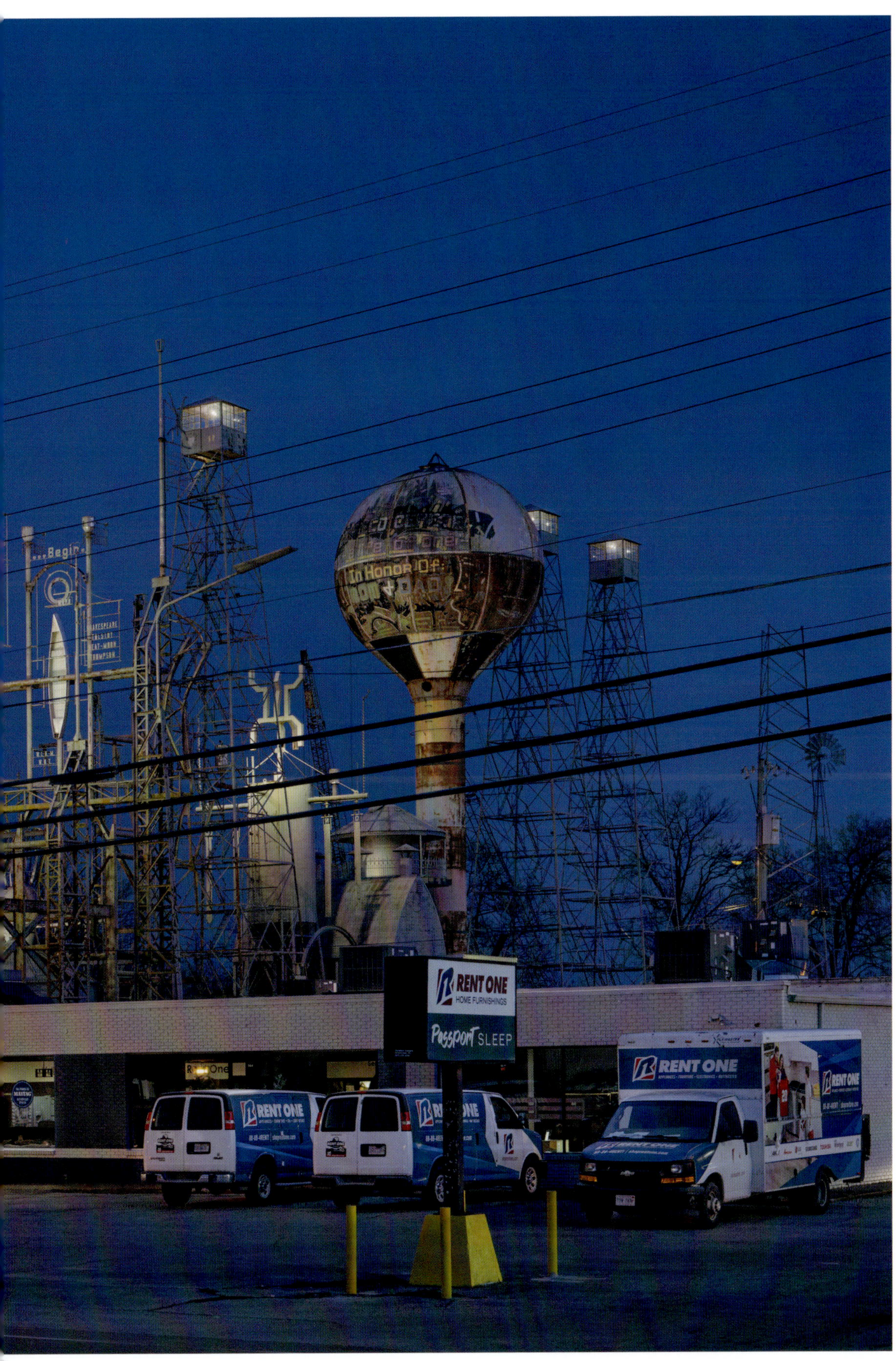
In Honor Of:
RENT ONE
HOME FURNISHINGS
Passport SLEEP
RENT ONE

Tripp's transition from writing to building began rather modestly, as he erected a small metal frame to hide an unsightly pile of concrete blocks. He enjoyed the construction process, so even after completing this task he continued, complementing his basic welding knowledge with on-the-job endeavors, learning by trial and error how to ensure the structural stability of his ever-growing yet uninhabitable architectural monument. In so doing, he became an expert welder. There is no single base or pad for the enormous monolith; rather, a series of concrete foundations with small footprints support the soaring verticals. (These pads were commissioned from a local building contractor after testing the soil and verifying that its composition could support the anticipated weight.) The more Tripp built, the more he began to consider the idea of the richness that would infuse his life if he were to dedicate himself to a singular long-term project. He was not interested in creating adjunct pieces that would not be part of the whole: he likes seeing all of his work in one place. Because this is a relatively small site and he was hemmed in on all sides, Tripp had nowhere to build but up.

Tripp utilizes a wide variety of salvaged steel girders and metal scraps of indeterminate function, as well as found objects that he sees as metaphors for his overall theme and which he incorporates into his art with virtually no change. For example, a tugboat, a canoe (the canoe a gift from one of his favorite authors), and even an all-metal 1968-era Cessna 150 airplane, may be seen as symbolic of the journey facilitating the departure for the next life, and a seed house could stand in for carrying nutrients that would be transplanted to nourish that new existence. He also added more personal items, many of which he fabricated himself: his brothers' negative and positive handprints cut from steel plate, a silhouette of his wife, posted cutout signs and sculptures that are markers of his experiences, and his childhood bed frame. Other components are those he modified, such as immense water, cell, and fire towers that he deconstructed, transported, reconstructed, mounted, and endowed with meaning. This was no easy feat: the water tank weighed 110,000 pounds when empty, and is 107 feet tall.

Some of the various cut-out or painted verbal fragments mounted on the structure are traces of what Tripp calls his "private language;" because he sometimes leaves out words that would make the phrases more comprehensible, they may be puzzling to viewers. There are also specific links to his writings, such as the word "Begin," the first and last word in his first autobiographical volume, which is posted more than once on the monument, perhaps an allusion to a perpetual cycle of life that blurs the boundaries between beginning and ending. But the public's understanding is not really his concern.

Literary clips range from the philosophical to the political. Examples of the philosophical callouts include "LIFE—No Key Needed" and "What I have to share be it through my work/What I have to make be it from what is here/My life for it lives knowingly for death/ Here I labor to live acceptingly trading." Political statements include "I support gay rights tho personally I like girls," which is painted on a fish form that alludes to the Christian religious symbol omnipresent on car bumpers in the 1970s and '80s, and "Defrock Tribalism." The texts underscore the link between Tripp's chosen media, and, indeed, the incorporation of so many scripts suggests a holistic approach to creativity that breaches the conventional genre boundaries of literature, architecture, and sculpture.

While some of the cutouts, signs, and found objects attract the eye with round or curving forms, the overwhelming impression is of a dense geometrically rectilinear assemblage that counterintuitively provides largely unobstructed views to the interior, inverting the generally accepted conventions of architectural construction. And this was Tripp's intention: he did not want to divorce the supportive framework from the lifeline markers he used to "dress" the structure.

Tripp's *Mindfield* can be viewed as a narrative work, but he equally insists on focusing attention on its formalistic aspects. For instance, he has enhanced the visual cohesion of all elements by painting both narrative and structural elements in a battleship-gray, rust-inhibitive paint that helps to dispel any association with their previous functions. Massive components—some "found" and others cheaply purchased—such as bridge trusses, an abandoned drive-in theater's A-frame supports, a cotton seed house, a silo, a sawmill's refuse burner, a church steeple, cell phone towers, and railroad tracks—form much of the weight-bearing framework and serve as an ever-changing scaffold. He has connected metal augers, chairs, chains, parts of fences, the bulbous vessels from cement mixing trucks, and even a bathtub to this

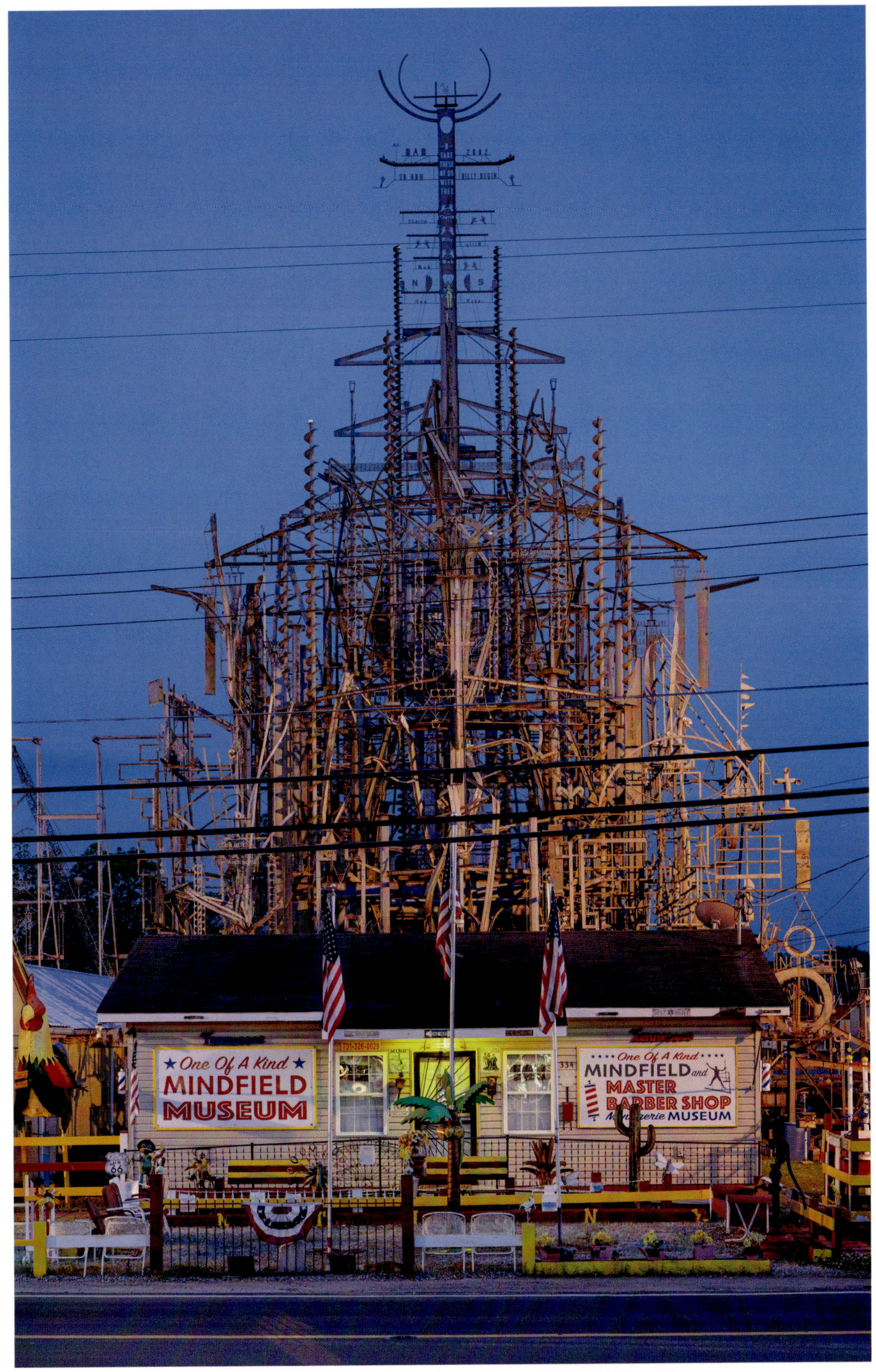

VIEW OF NORTH FACE OF *MINDFIELD* AND NO-LONGER-EXTANT MINDFIELD MUSEUM AND MASTER BARBER SHOP, 2023

SOUTHEASTERN SECTION OF *MINDFIELD* SITE WITH WATER AND FIRE TOWERS, CEMENT MIXER, AND SEED HOUSE, 2024

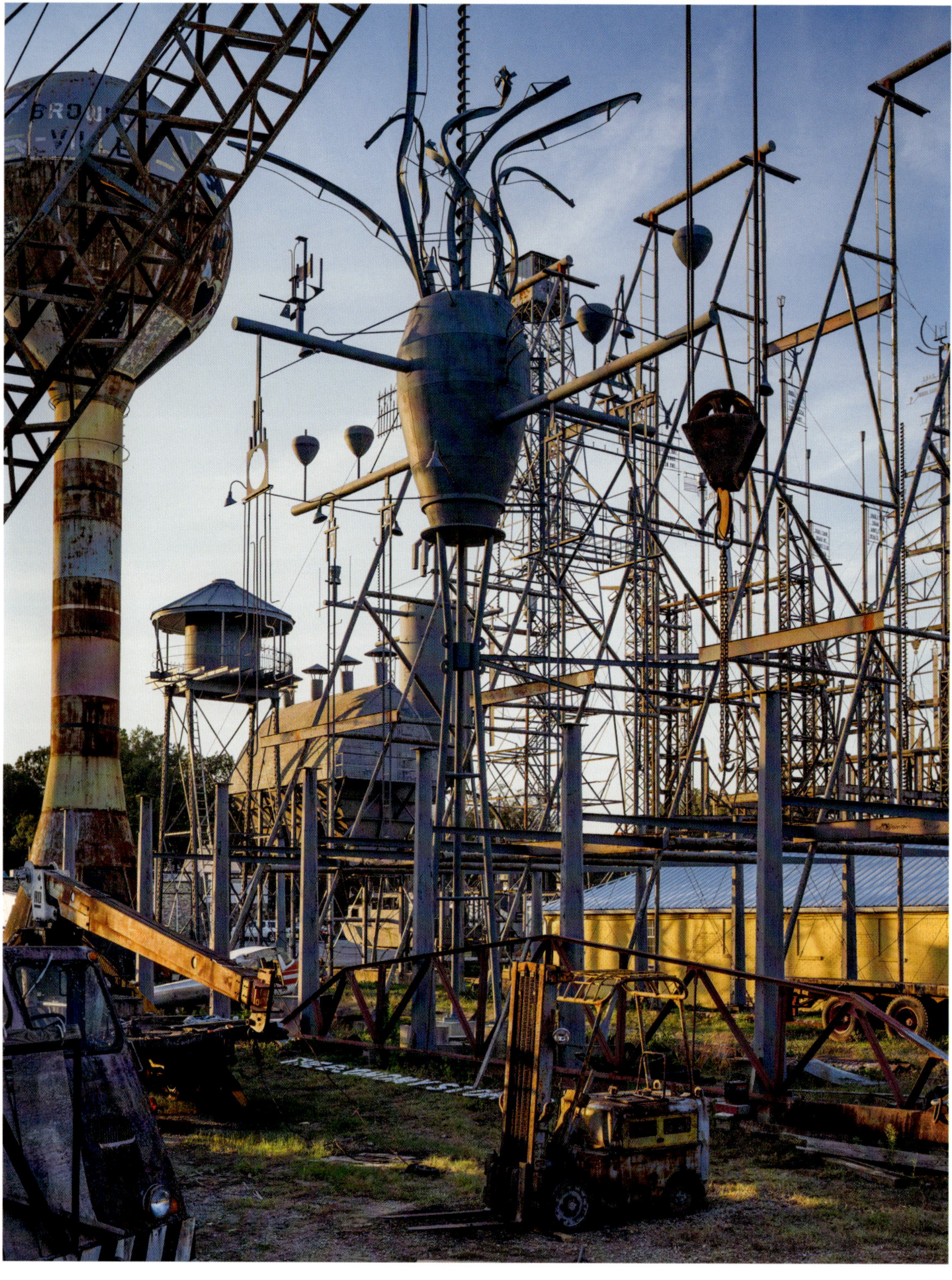

infrastructure in order to enrich his narrative and augment the density of the whole.

Much like Sabato Rodia (see page 332) climbed on the completed rungs of his *Towers* in Watts to add new treads as he built ever higher, Tripp, too, sure of foot, regularly uses existing components to support himself as he fearlessly scales the heights to weld or bolt new sections into place. All of his weight-bearing components function, at least occasionally, as permanent scaffolding, and he climbs with no additional personal support or security strapping. (Tripp has cut out and hung the initials "S" and "R" to pay homage to Rodia within the *Mindfield*; he had learned about this tour de force in a high school art class.) At ground level, he uses forklifts, winches, and cranes to facilitate his work.

Tripp thinks everything through before he begins—given the size of most of his resource materials, it could be a fatal mistake to be unprepared for eventualities. But although he may sketch out his ideas in his journals or in chalk on his shop tables or floor, or directly "draw" with the material as he lays pieces out, he works without detailed blueprints and elaborate sketches. This is generally true because the components come first: they are stored in his yard, and he knows their appearance and their size, so it is frequently more a question of verifying measurements to ascertain the necessary connections than hypothetically sketching designs to add pieces that do not yet exist. Spending most daylight hours on-site, he is constantly evaluating options for how and where to affix the elements he has, carefully considering placement and attachment options as he takes weight, stability, and wind shear into account. When he finally is ready to take his next step, there is no doubt that it will be successfully realized.

Tripp had originally considered, and then rejected, the idea of locating the as-yet not fully defined architectural sculpture on a more expansive piece of inherited family farmland outside of town. It is intriguing to suggest that by choosing the parcel closer to the urban center and the public eye, he perhaps unconsciously echoed Rodia's decision to build his *Towers* near train lines to be more eye-catchingly visible to the hundreds of commuters who passed each day. While reaction from out-of-towners to the *Mindfield* is overwhelmingly enthusiastic, local response has at times been ambivalent, particularly given some of the seemingly confrontational phrases Tripp has painted on different components—like the "In honor of Turd" painted on the side of the water tower, or the now-erased "Satan Saves" on the back of his pickup truck—provocative challenges in a town of fewer than 10,000 people served by around 100 churches. Others display a certain ambivalence, such as his description of Brownsville, which he asserts has been "good both to and for me," but hedges as being a "small town [with a] large mind, mostly, maybe." Nevertheless, he emphasizes that, like the content of his books, his building serves as a reflection of his personal ponderings: he is dimensionally articulating his own interests and feelings, and as far as he is concerned, he is the only critic of importance. While he now occasionally regrets that this intimate "conversation" is so visibly accessible, the fact that others can see it and react to it does not affect him. What it might mean to the public is not of interest to him.

One hundred twenty-seven feet high and originally located on a narrow ½-acre strip of land running north to south, Tripp began to expand the size of the *Mindfield* in recent years, not only extending it further south but also moving east, behind the next-door Sunrise Inn, into what used to be his salvage/storage yard. The structure now covers approximately 1¼ acres. But even before the recent expansions, *The Mindfield Cemetery* was clearly visible from behind a former barber shop, the motel, and an adjacent small retail strip—as, in the town's relatively flat landscape, it continues to be noticeable from many blocks away. Ever since an initial "stop work" order was issued back in 1990, when he was placing the first components—a prohibition that was lifted after he explained to the town officials that he was erecting a sculpture and not a commercial building—in general, they have supported his efforts. It is now included in the town's directional signs, featured on its website, and even celebrated in municipal murals: they take pride in the idea that it is putting Brownsville on the map. Tripp reiterates that he intends to continue to expand the work until he is unable to work any longer, after which he will return to concentrate more fully on his writing. He has made arrangements with the Kohler Foundation to assume ownership and provide for future long-term maintenance and care of his work, when he is ready.

TRIPP ADJUSTS ELEMENTS ON THE UPPER LEVELS OF THE *MINDFIELD*, 2017

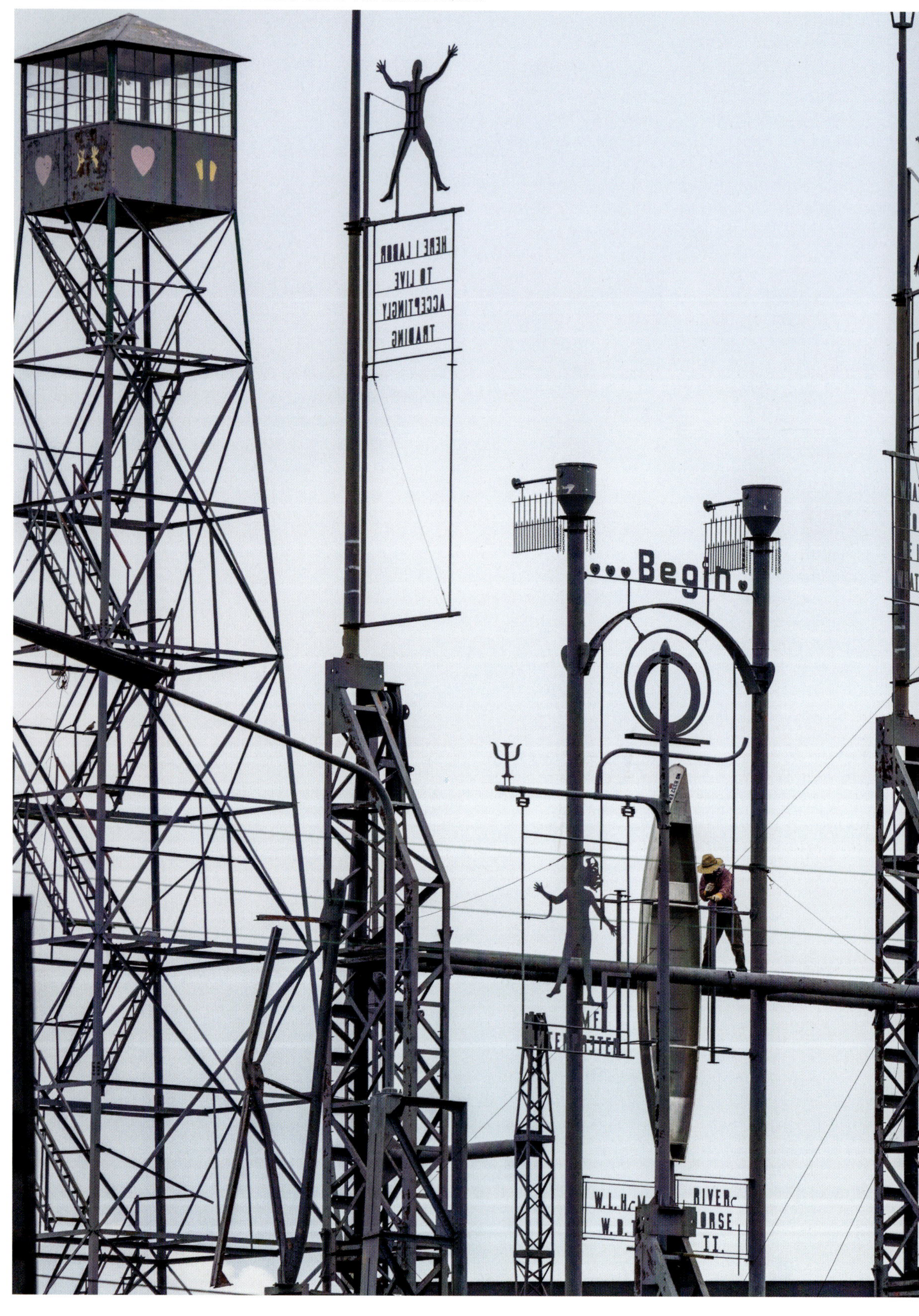

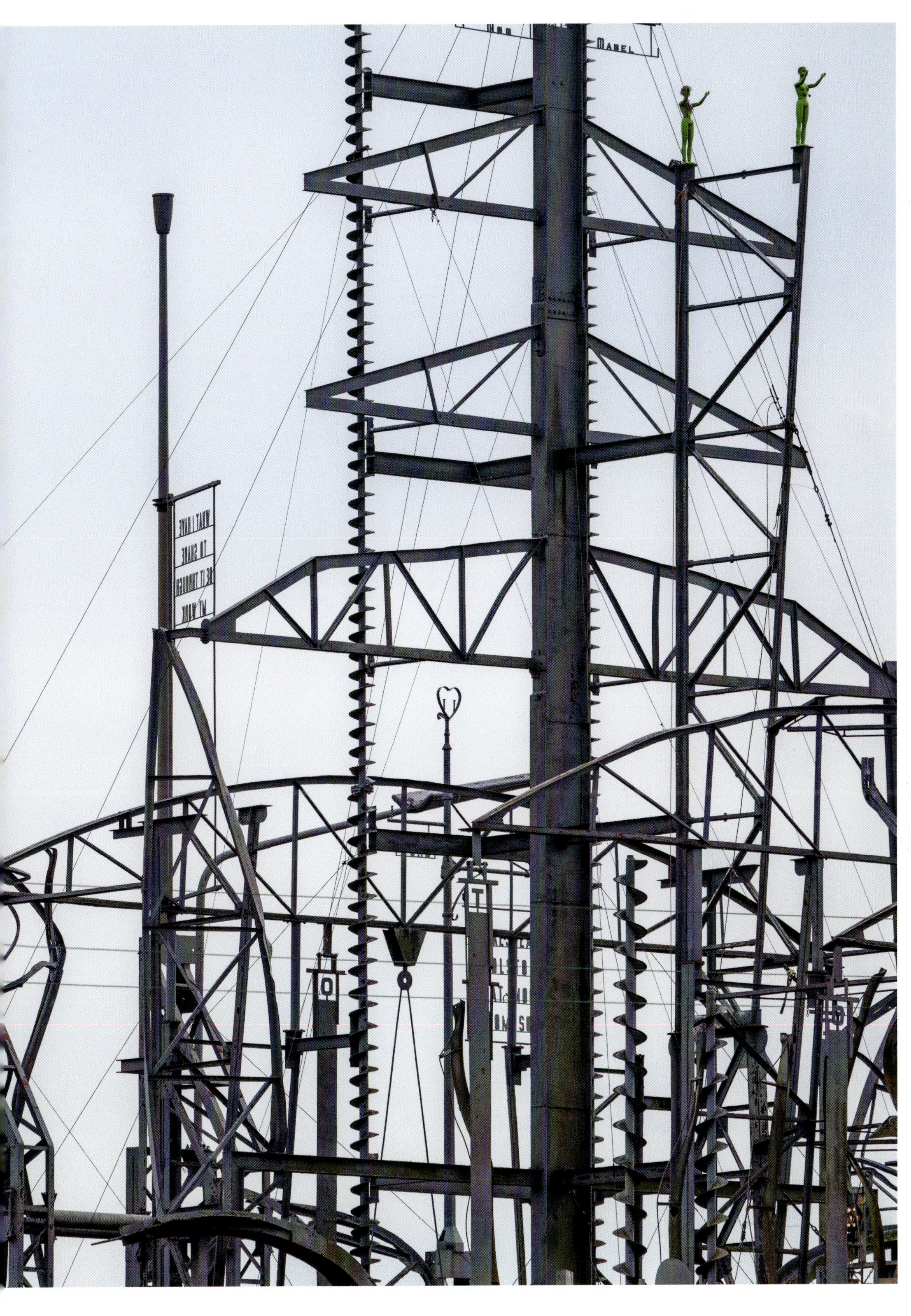
MABEL

JIM BOWSHER

TEMPLE OF TOLERANCE

WAPAKONETA, OHIO

As glaciers swept down from Canada to scour the American Midwest around 4.2 billion years ago, they left a chain of geological evidence, including massive boulders that had once been molten magma. Bowsher (1948–2024), driven by a vision of a monumental architectural construction that would welcome and be open to all, mapped the geographical lines where the glaciers had deposited the stones, and then hauled them from those areas to the backyard of his childhood home, which was located in the middle of a residential section of his small city. Over the years Bowsher pieced together several contiguous lots until he owned the equivalent of about two acres. Because he generally eschewed the use of labels or explanatory texts on or near his creations, he photographed each of the major rocks that he moved onto his property, documenting their provenance and history so that this information would be available when he was no longer around to recount their stories.

Without plans or even a design—but with his vision clearly in mind—he began building in 1981, and with the help of a vintage dump truck and a tractor with a backhoe, he ultimately dug out a cavity that he packed with 100 tons of blue clay and 50 tons of rocks. He used logs to roll many of the larger stones into place (he used cranes for others), and supplemented the natural forms with repurposed pavers, benches, gravestones, millstones, grinding stones, and quarried and cut slabs and steps. Bowsher created a 20-foot structure in the shape of a pyramid so as to assure its strength and equilibrium, working until he reached completion some 18 years later, when he installed the last of the 9,999 enormous rocks of basalt, granite, limestone, quartz, flint, and solidified magma at 9 p.m. on September 9, 1999. (Despite the sense of balance provided by these numbers, there are millions of elements contained within the monument, and he continued to tweak it with additions and modifications until his death.) He claimed that the largest boulder on-site weighed nine tons.

Born and raised in Lima, Ohio, after high school Bowsher studied at Kent State University but never graduated. He then spent some 15 years roaming around the country, supporting himself with odd jobs as he became a profound and sympathetic observer of the different people he met and how they lived their lives. After returning to Wapakoneta he combined his interests and became an amateur historian, collector, archeologist, anthropologist, historic preservationist, geologist, and storyteller. He often lived close to the poverty line, rejecting better-paid jobs in order to coordinate creative-writing programs in prisons and juvenile detention centers. His work with these incarcerated populations, however, led him to realize that developing the ability to forgive, to understand, and to empathize—particularly with people different from ourselves—was a way to create a better world and to become more tolerant of each other's differences.

Bowsher wrote profusely (often under a pseudonym) and regularly spoke to school and community groups in an effort to share his interpretation of humanity's footprints on this earth, promoting his vision of a present and future in which all would be treated equally and respected, and where each person could find peace. This was also the intention that motivated the *Temple of Tolerance*, a quiet place of refuge and safety that he especially targeted to the city's youth. He consciously built it to be visually and physically disorienting, believing that only by shedding all preconceived assumptions could these young people discover that behavior modification was the key to reaching their potential and more respectfully coexisting with others: he felt he needed to "readdict them to tranquility." All were welcomed to Bowsher's property, and the only rules were no drugs, no bullying, and no fighting. With an eye toward eliciting "the extraordinary out of ordinary people," he always took the time to share the stories of his constructions and his collections with his visitors. The decades worth of notes he received from those who had benefited from his efforts, after their lives stabilized, confirmed for him that his safe space had enabled them to not only survive, but to thrive.

The *Temple of Tolerance* is reached by threading a winding path through the extended backyard among Bowsher's collected and assembled treasures, low stone dividers, and salvaged wrought-iron fences. The central monument is encircled by a modest wall composed of small rectangular stone bricks that ring larger and more imposing boulders. This wall is interrupted by a stone-paved walkway fronted by high posts whose verticality is offset at ground level with rounded millstones. This walkway continues upward as it evolves into steps leading to the top of the structure.

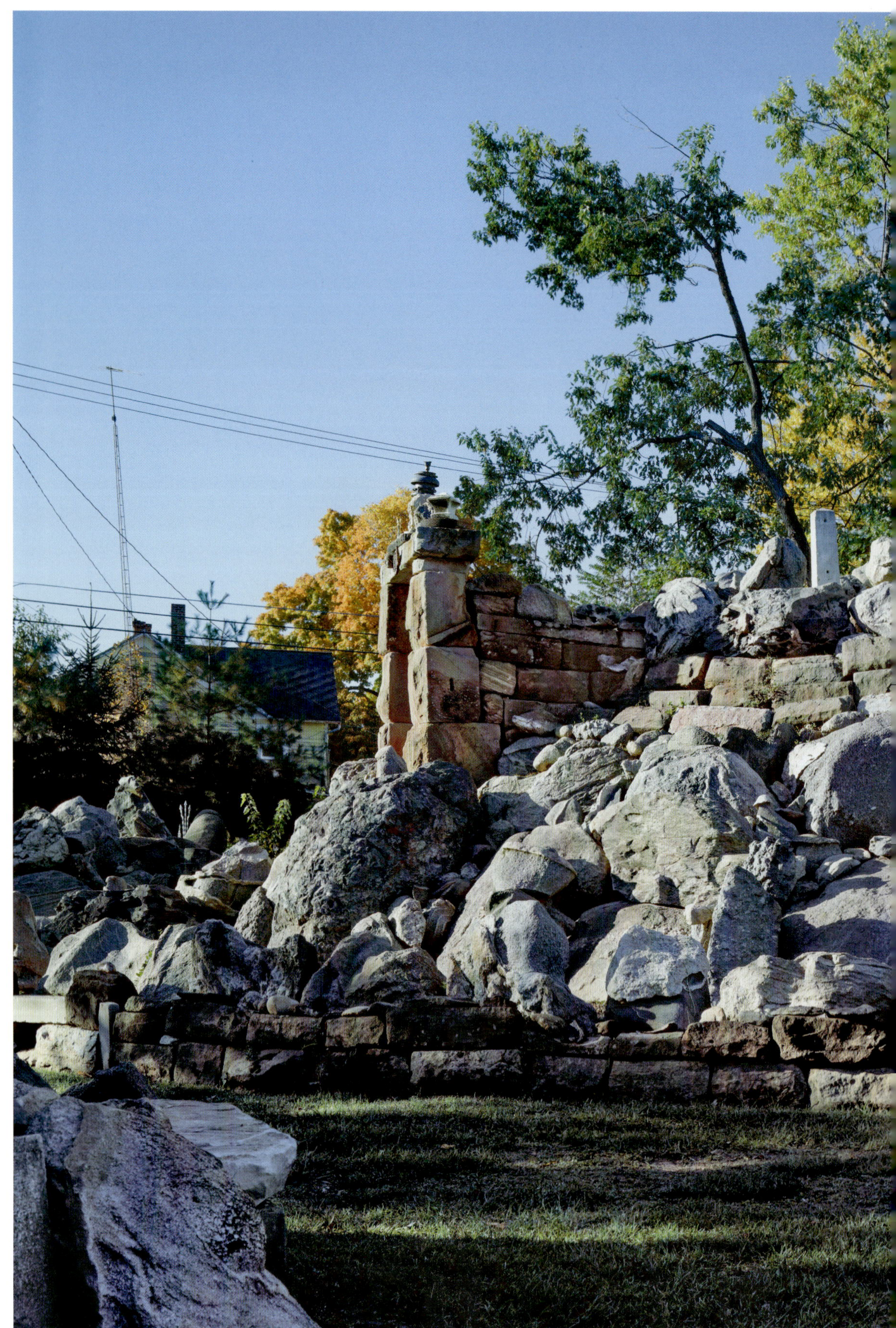

SIDE VIEW, 2005

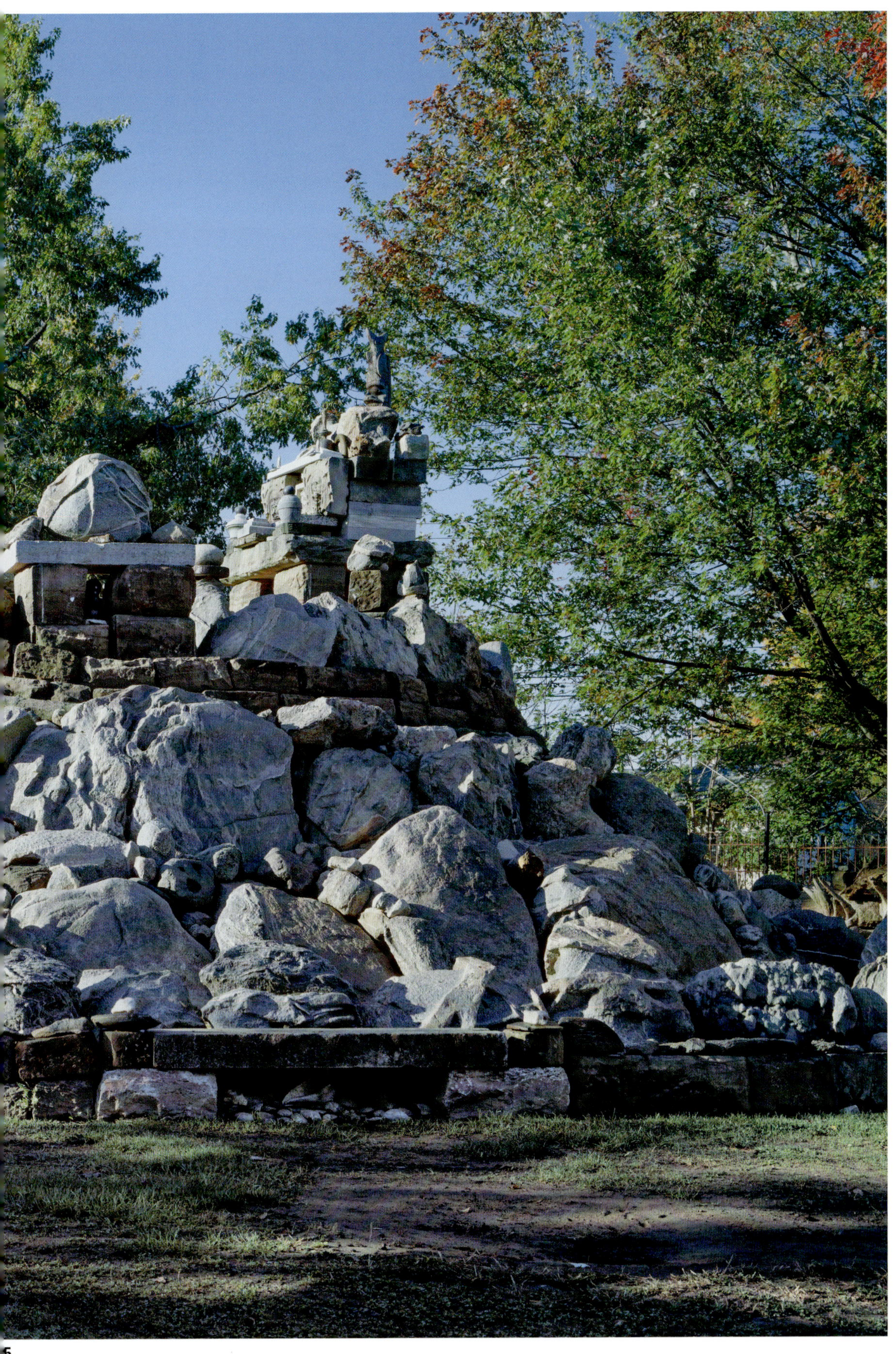

OVERVIEW OF *TEMPLE* AND SURROUNDING YARD INSTALLATIONS, 2018. PHOTO: SCOTT BRUNO

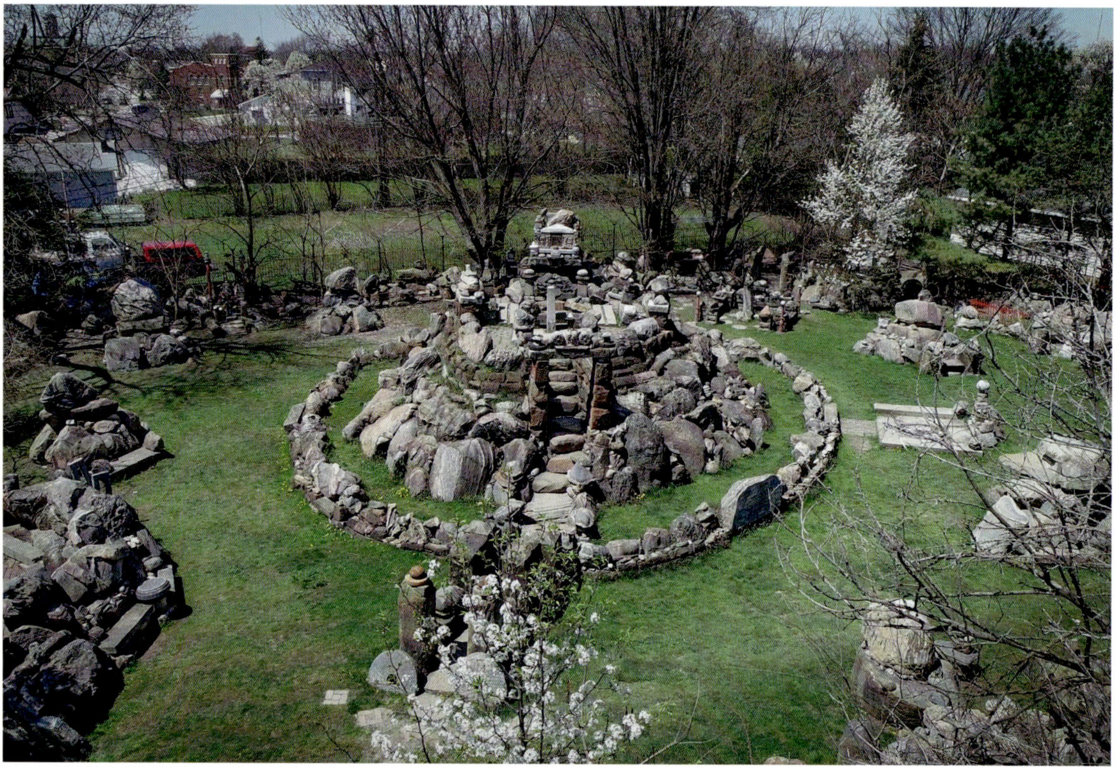

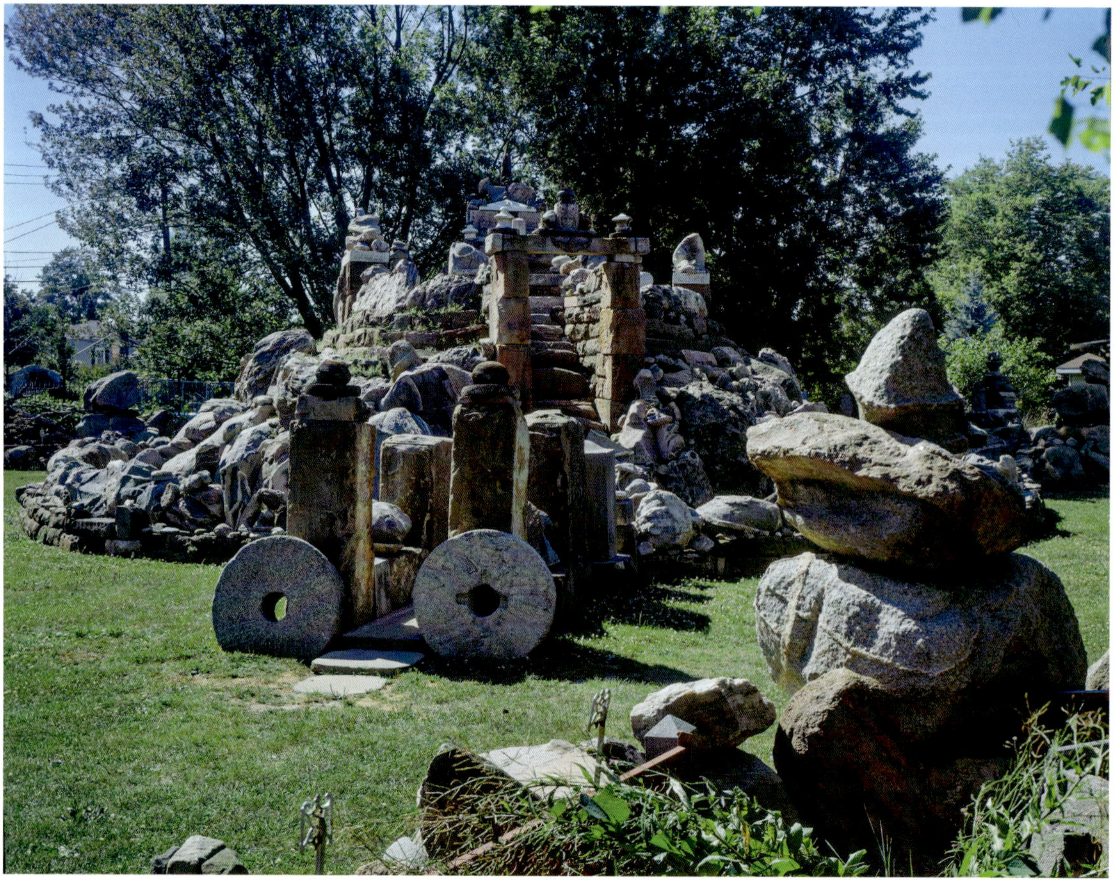

FRONT VIEW, 2005

To reach the summit, one must pass underneath a high rectangular arch surmounted with carved or cast-concrete angel heads and other found objects. The top of the pyramid is flattened with stone pavers, and two lateral benches flank a fire pit underlaid with dirt collected by Bowsher on his worldwide travels. Behind this is an altar-like construction with a square footprint, surmounted with assorted stones and what he calls "moon dog" visages: faces like the symbols for comedy and tragedy that alternate between smiling and grimacing with the shadows cast by moonlight. Also in this section is the only known extant stone boundary marker from the Hog Creek Shawnee reservation, land on which Wapakoneta now sits.

A bird's-eye view challenges the ground-level sensation that the boulders that form the *Temple* were tossed into place somewhat haphazardly by a giant hand, because the rounded footprint of the construction and its encircling wall is echoed elsewhere on-site with semicircular sectionals that provide space for viewing and contemplation. Too, the various discrete stone assemblages and shrines that complement the *Temple* grounds can be understood as accessory structures that serve to emphasize not only the prominence but the significance of the main attraction.

In addition to the *Temple of Tolerance*, various structures, stone outcroppings, and sculptures adorn the property. Among them are the *Memorial to Ohio War Dead*, which includes a tube filled with shell casings commemorating every fallen soldier since the War of 1812, a house in the shape of a barrel (once a rural speakeasy), and a rock described as a *Bully Eater*. Bowsher's wide-ranging collections are primarily kept within the house itself and feature a range of historical materials, many focusing on America's wars and issues of justice or injustice. Each has a story: how or when it was used or by whom, what purpose it served, or how he came to acquire it. He did not shy away from hard subjects, and he included objects that represent the ugly sides of the human character as well as those that show our decency and dignity. He presented selected objects from his collection as he spoke to school and community groups, always with the goal of promoting tolerance and fair-mindedness among people with different backgrounds.

While some stone and found-object works were installed in front of Bowsher's home, the monumentality of the nondenominational *Temple of Tolerance* only comes into view after walking around to the back, which is always open, free of charge, to anyone who would like to experience it. In fact, Bowsher conceptualized his privately-owned property as a public gathering space and, ultimately, a safe haven that would promote spiritual or emotional cleansing, built with the hope that the good in people will transcend the bad.

HIS VISION WAS TO CREATE A SAFE HAVEN ENCOURAGING TOLERANCE OF EACH OTHER'S DIFFERENCES.

NATHAN EDWARD "ED" GALLOWAY

TOTEM POLE PARK

FOYIL, OKLAHOMA

Significantly less monumental yet still conceived as a totality and, like Vollis Simpson's (see page 310), one that was created one discrete component at a time, is an art environment that has become known as the *Totem Pole Park*.

Galloway (1880–1962) was born near Springfield, Missouri, and informally developed his carving skills as a young boy. After eighth grade, he held a variety of low-level jobs, helping his father for a time in his blacksmithing forge, driving teams of packhorses to support his mining operations, and helping his uncle farm. He enlisted in the Army in 1901 and was sent to the Philippine Islands during the Philippine-American War. There, he became acquainted with the imagery and arts of Asia, an introduction that opened his eyes to the beauty and variety of global creativity. Once back home after his discharge, his memories of these works encouraged him to try his own hand at sculpting, primarily in wood. In the meantime, he married, and he and his new wife lived in several locations in southwestern Missouri and Oklahoma, finally moving more permanently to Oklahoma to be closer to her parents, who had relocated there.

After the founder of a new orphanage in Sand Springs saw one of Galloway's sculptures during a temporary display in a Tulsa drugstore, he hired him to teach woodworking and other manual arts to the resident boys. The job was low-paying but fulfilling, and Galloway held it for over 20 years. Responsible for building his own living quarters and workshop, as well as for furnishing and equipping them, he drew on his blacksmith training to make his own tools, and then used them to teach the boys how to fabricate a range of wooden furniture, sculpture, and decorative objects, including large works such as merry-go-round animals, a Ferris wheel, a pair of 10-ton sandstone lions that guarded the entrance to the Sand Springs Park, and a table with 9,999 odd-shaped parts, which he later gifted to the orphanage. Upon his retirement in 1937, Gallaway and his wife moved to rural acreage four miles east of Foyil, which they had purchased while he taught at Sand Springs.

After building a stone house to live in, this new property provided Galloway with room to explore his creativity. The largest and most emblematic work, what he called a "*Totem Pole*," rises over 70 feet and anchors the mostly level, park-like setting. Yet its premise is curious, given that none of Oklahoma's 39 tribal nations ever worked in this genre. It is said that Galloway ravenously perused copies of *National Geographic* magazine, however, so it is likely that he rather unreservedly riffed off of the images of Native Americans he found within its pages, notwithstanding their lack of connection to local indigenous peoples. Nevertheless, he did claim a small amount of Cherokee blood on his mother's side, and as he was born when Oklahoma was officially Indian Territory and was still a young man in 1907 when it gained statehood, his interest in paying homage to the people who had first lived on these lands with his *Monument to the American Indian* is understandable.

Galloway built up narrow scaffolding from salvaged lumber and slowly constructed his monuments with an infrastructure of local sandstone rocks set into mortar that he had reinforced with discarded guy wire from the railroads, along with steel rods and scraps; later, he sheathed the framework with concrete that he mixed using sand from a nearby creek. He subsequently embossed bas-relief designs on the surface by hand, shaping a variety of flora and fauna but also many profile heads and busts of Native Americans wearing (nonlocal) headdresses. The last step was painting the sculpted motifs in brightly fanciful colors that were not true to life; perhaps this was a function of his economic circumstances, which obliged him to use surplus house paint in random colors offered to him by his neighbors or to purchase half-cans cheaply at the hardware store that he then mixed himself. Among other whimsical treatments are a sky-blue turtle, bird figures with pink heads or wings, and a crustacean with a light green carapace.

The largest pole, its soaring sides aligned with the cardinal directions and its base in the shape of a turtle that he carved on top of an in-situ sandstone outcropping, is more conical than most traditional carved wooden poles. Furthermore, it is significantly more architectural, as it features an interior winding staircase that once provided access to its full seven stories, all of which branched off to small "rooms," each slightly smaller as one ascends. This is an innovation never seen in conventional totem pole carvings. The interior ground-floor walls have been smoothed with concrete, with an opening for a small triangular window and minimal bas-relief design ornamentation along its top edge. In contrast, the interior walls of the higher levels lack supplementary surface finishing, so the stone and mortar construction is clearly visible.

Galloway worked on this massive architectural sculpture for 11 years, reportedly using 28 tons of concrete, 6 tons of steel, and 100 tons of sand and rock. It features around 200 motifs that, given his chosen medium, are necessarily rather reductive and stylized. Around its 18-foot-diameter base are representations of tropical birds and vegetation, which may have been inspired by his years in the Philippines, and near the top are four, 9-foot-tall, almost fully three-dimensional figures that have been identified as Native American chiefs Quanah Parker, Sitting Bull, Geronimo, and Chief Joseph. Despite its cultural disassociation from true indigenous totem poles, this architectural colossus, completed in 1948, has been locally heralded as "The World's Largest Totem Pole."

After finishing this structure, Galloway erected four smaller concrete poles—more sculptural than architectural as they lack interior cavities allowing for human entry—as well as a *Fiddle House* with 11 sides. Twenty-six "totem poles" are interspersed around this building's walls as structural supports, each one anchoring a juncture, although—in another awkward example of cultural disconnection—its shape was inspired by the Navajo hogan. He used this jauntily decorated building as a studio and for the storage and display of his wooden carvings and handmade violins, many of which he ornamented with inlaid patterns after scraping them down with broken glass to smooth the surfaces. (His goal had been to carve a fiddle from every type of wood in the world; he completed over 300, although, Galloway being a carver and not a violinist, not all of them were playable.)

Another sculpture, this one tall and shaped like an arrowhead, is adorned with bas-relief busts said to represent the Five Tribes of Oklahoma. However, these motifs, as well as the additional 82 busts of Native men and two Native women on-site (69 on the large totem, 10 on the *Arrowhead*, 6 on the *Tree Totem* [which was originally built as a bird house] and 4 on the *Fiddle House*), seem to be general stereotypical illustrations rather than unambiguous likenesses linked to tribal groups that could be identified through careful portrayals of specialized regalia. There is also a gate featuring animal and bird forms: its central pole, with its interlocking designs, is more akin to Northwest Coast carvings than anything else on-site, and Galloway apparently told his son that he had based it on a postcard image from Ketchikan, Alaska. Public-friendly accoutrements such as picnic tables, a barbecue area, and bas-relief carvings of every U.S. president through John F. Kennedy rounded out the *Totem Pole Park's* offerings. Visitors were welcomed free of charge, and stopping by the 12 constructions on-site was popular with travelers, in part due to its location less than four miles from historic Route 66 on the road toward Grand Lake.

After Galloway's death, as the paint and concrete began to chip, exposing the interior steel elements within the substructure to rust and hastening further corrosion, the *Park* was closed to the public, although vandals continued to enter the property, tagging the poles with graffiti and leaving trash and litter. Although the family tried to care for the deteriorating site, in 1967 the house was broken into and many of the wooden carvings, including many of his fiddles, were stolen. They have never been recovered.

After the death of his son, surviving family members reached an agreement in 1989 to donate 1.45 acres to the local Rogers County Historical Society, and in 1992 this organization purchased just under nine additional acres in order to expand the parking and picnic areas, taking full ownership of the entirety. Seven years earlier a conservation project organized and led by the Kansas Grassroots Art Association focused on emergency repair and stabilization, and after significant research, a plan was developed for the repainting and longer-term renovation of the structures. In 1999, while this 16-year conservation project was underway, *Totem Pole Park* was added to the National Register of Historic Places.

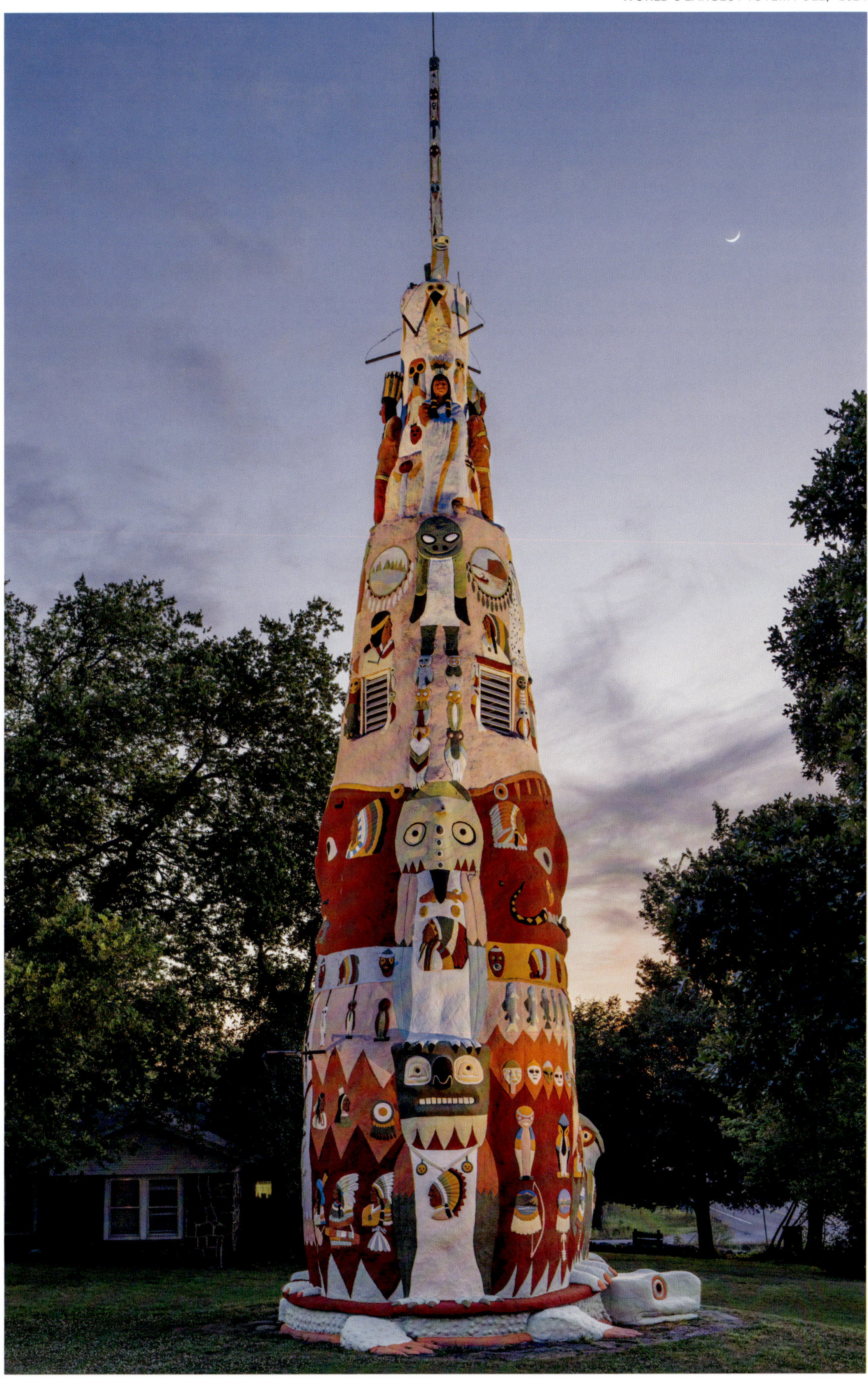

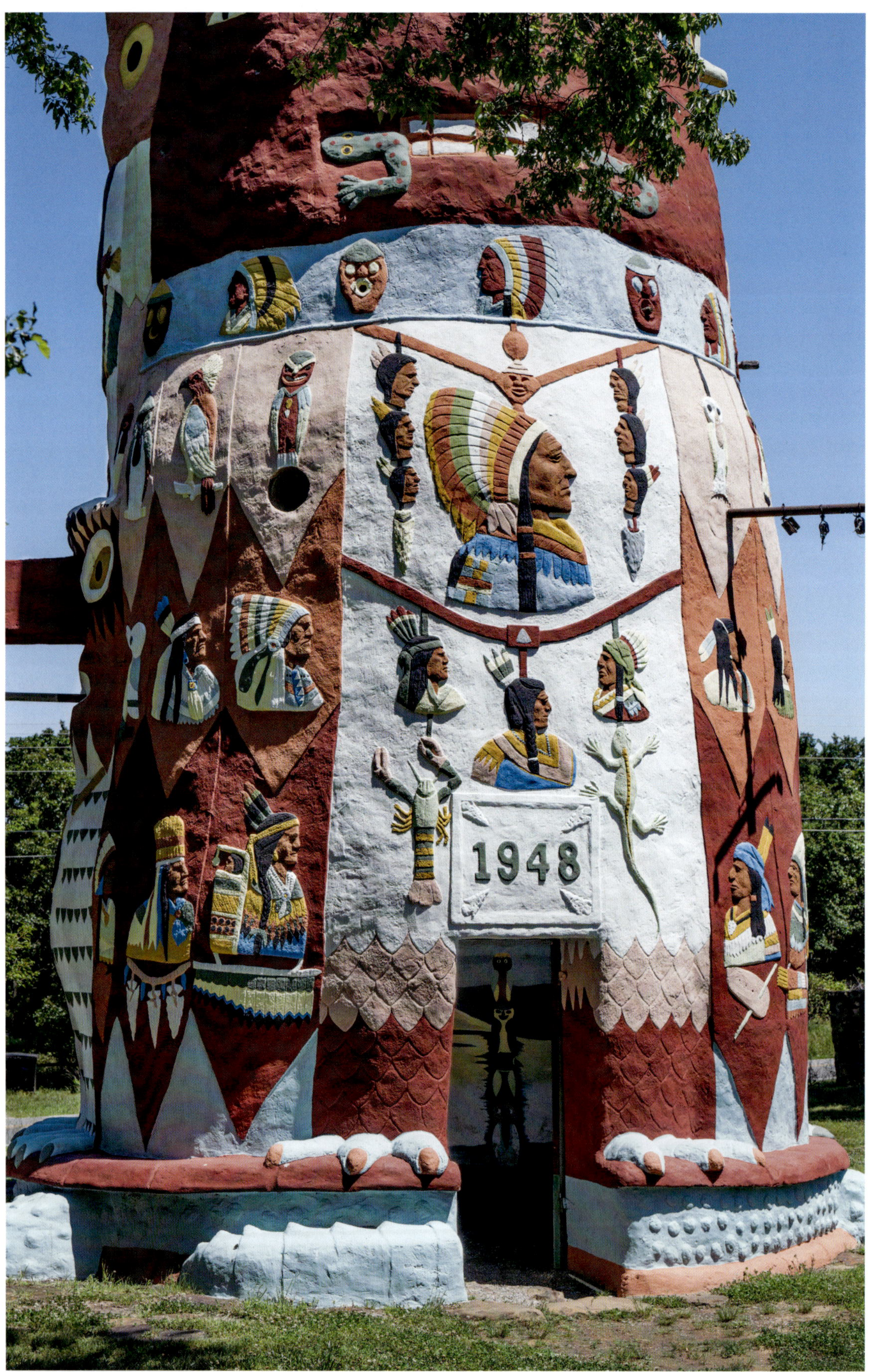

"WORLD'S LARGEST TOTEM POLE" (DETAIL), 2024

By 2009 the exterior painted concrete surfaces again manifested considerable decline, and a new conservation project was initiated in 2014–15. Thanks to the *Totem Pole Park's* ownership by the Historical Society, now with a heightened sensitivity to preservation, it is being more carefully monitored, with conservation and maintenance ongoing as funding permits, and it continues to receive relatively sizeable numbers of visitors each year. Plans are also underway to expand the site's narrative by more fully exploring the past and present history of cultural appropriation of Native themes within the context of how these groups are portrayed, not only in Oklahoma but more broadly around the United States. The goal is to better center Native perspectives at the same time that Galloway's intentions are more profoundly interpreted and analyzed.

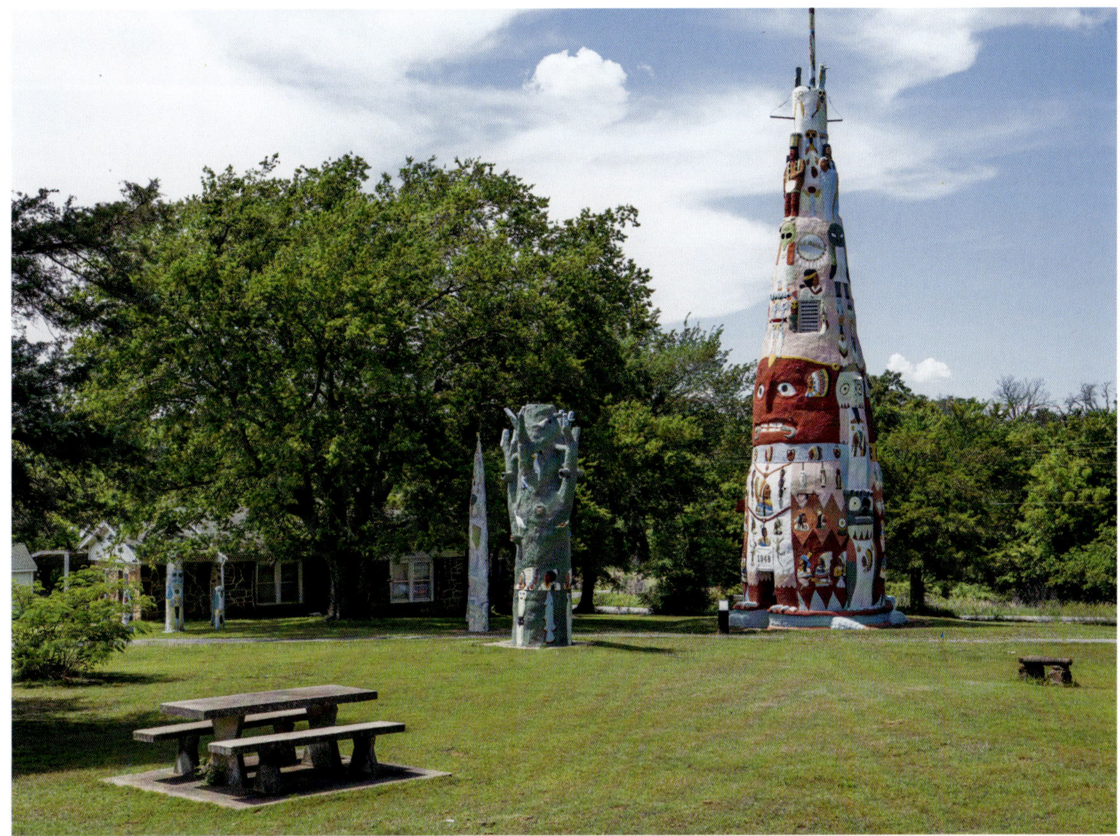

TREE TOTEM AND "*WORLD'S LARGEST TOTEM POLE*," 2024

SAMUEL P. DINSMOOR

—

STONE LOG CABIN MAUSOLEUM, GARDEN OF EDEN

LUCAS, KANSAS

Dinsmoor (1843–1932) is widely known among those interested in art environments because of the early time period of his production, his rather unique approach to his creations, and his sophisticated figurative exploration of themes of conflict: good versus evil, reality versus its artificial representation, Biblical versus modern motifs. The narratives are played out across the branches of 29 concrete trees that frame the west and north sides of his home, their interlacing limbs accentuating their relationships to each other. And they all also relate to Dinsmoor's philosophies, backed by 1890s-era populism and a social-political liberalism that contrasted with the literal and moralistic views of "God and Country" popular among nineteenth-century Plains settlers, as well as with the sometimes militant fundamentalism of the early years of the twentieth.

Born in Ohio, Dinsmoor served as a nurse in the Civil War; during his service he witnessed the Battle of Gettysburg and the surrender of General Robert E. Lee. Upon his discharge, he joined the Masonic Lodge, an organization that came to greatly influence his views, and in 1866 he moved to Illinois, where he farmed and taught school. He married in 1870, and he and his family moved several times between Illinois, Nebraska, and Kansas, finally settling on the outskirts of Lucas in 1888, where he continued to farm. Later they purchased a half-acre parcel in a residential area not far from Main Street, visible from the railroad tracks.

Before beginning the sculptures that have brought him renown, he constructed a "cabin"—actually, a three-story, 11-room home (the lowest story is below grade in the front). He assembled this dwelling not from wood but from locally sourced "post rock" limestone, a wry commentary on the area's scarcity of wood and a simultaneous reference to and parody of the stylistic and technical conventions of his Ohio upbringing, as he appropriated the building method of securing corner joints through dovetailing. He advanced this representation of wood in concrete a step further on the center post on the east porch, which he troweled into the shape of a log, even adding a fork and knots. Even at that time, it appears that he had conceptualized the house—with such eccentricities as no matching doors or windows—as a potential source of income, welcoming sightseers for a fee. (The site continues to be a visitor attraction, and entrance fees support maintenance and staff wages.)

After the house was complete, Dinsmoor embarked on a visual storyline that was similarly illustrated through reinforced-concrete elements sculpted to look like wood, realized via some 150 figures anchored by the concrete trees. Some of his motifs were more symbolic than realistic, such as the portrayal of God through a pointing hand and the "All-Seeing Eye" (a symbol associated with Freemasonry), but most of the sequential chronicles are decidedly recognizable. The western side focused on tales from the first few chapters of Genesis, embodying the *Garden of Eden* theme with a few modifications, while on the north and east he regaled his visitors with his view of modern civilization: Labor "crucified" by doctor, lawyer, preacher, and banker as citizens' rights are trampled by monopolistic interests. In contrast, another structure, the *Goddess of Liberty Tree*, is more optimistic, showing civilization as he thought it should unfold. Having addressed the past, with its Biblical stories, and the present, with its depictions of the conflict between capitalism and America's foundational ideals—perhaps portraying these virtues as a variant of the original paradise—he moved on to the future, building a mausoleum in the back yard for his final resting place.

While the *Stone Log Cabin Home*, completed in 1907, is notable for Dinsmoor's clever reinterpretation of the style of simple wooden buildings, the overall form continues to adhere to the vernacular common to the Kansas prairies. In contrast, his *Stone Log Cabin Mausoleum*, probably built in the mid-1910s, pushes technical, formal, stylistic, and conceptual parameters. Built over a six-foot-deep concrete foundation, it rises from a 14-foot-square base through three consecutively smaller levels, the geometrical starkness of that profile softened by limestone posts sheathed in troweled and rounded concrete that diagonally connect each corner, meeting at the top in a pyramidal shape. A concrete, painted, 4.5 x 7.5′ American flag once surmounted the entirety, but Dinsmoor had it taken down three years before his death, fearing it might fall in a storm. Still extant at the top of the third level is a horizontally installed "guardian angel" who waits to conduct him to heaven, if that will be his final destination (if not, he installed a two-gallon concrete jug at the foot of his coffin, just in case he is sent in the other direction: he wanted to be able to stay hydrated).

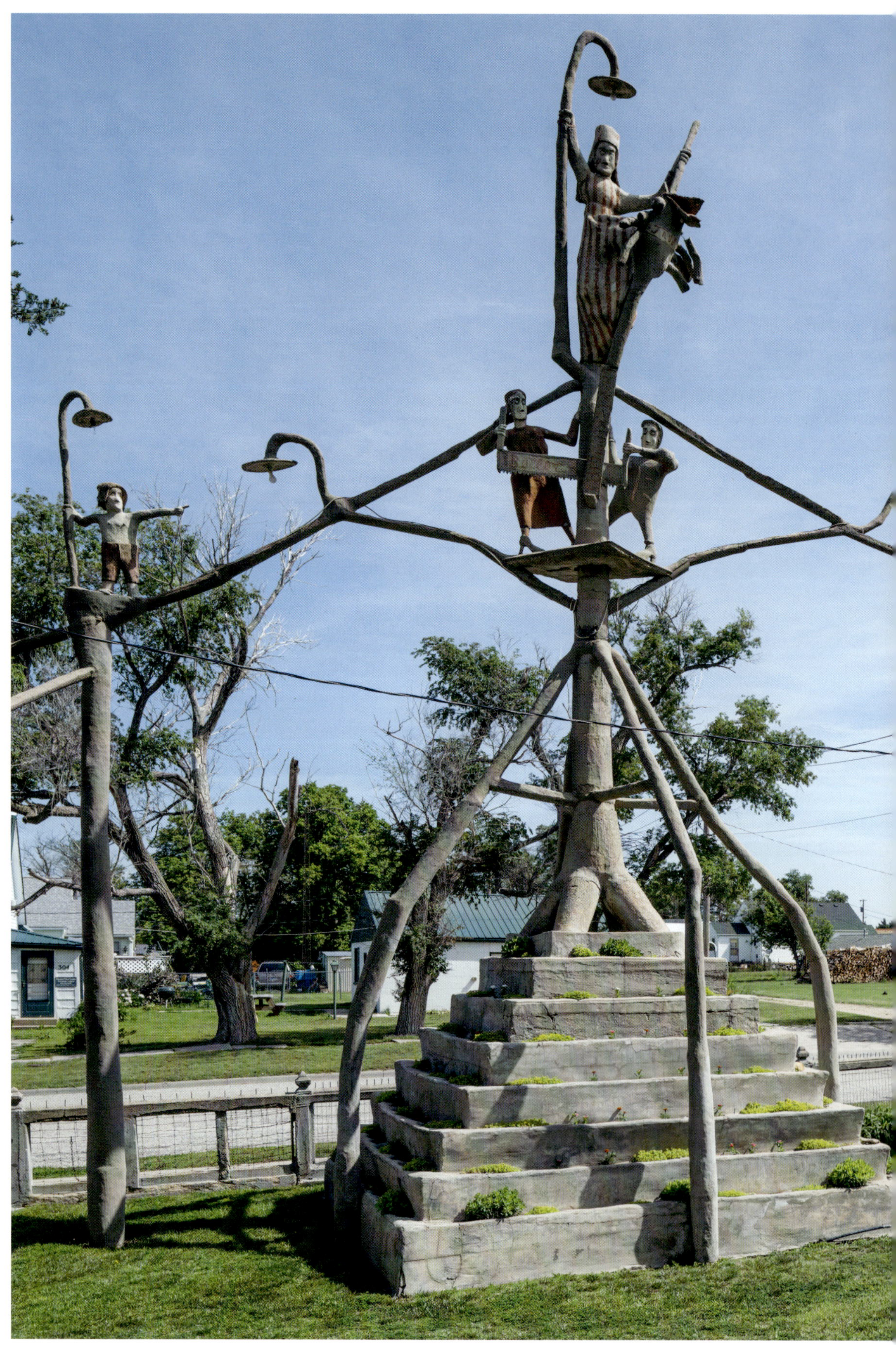

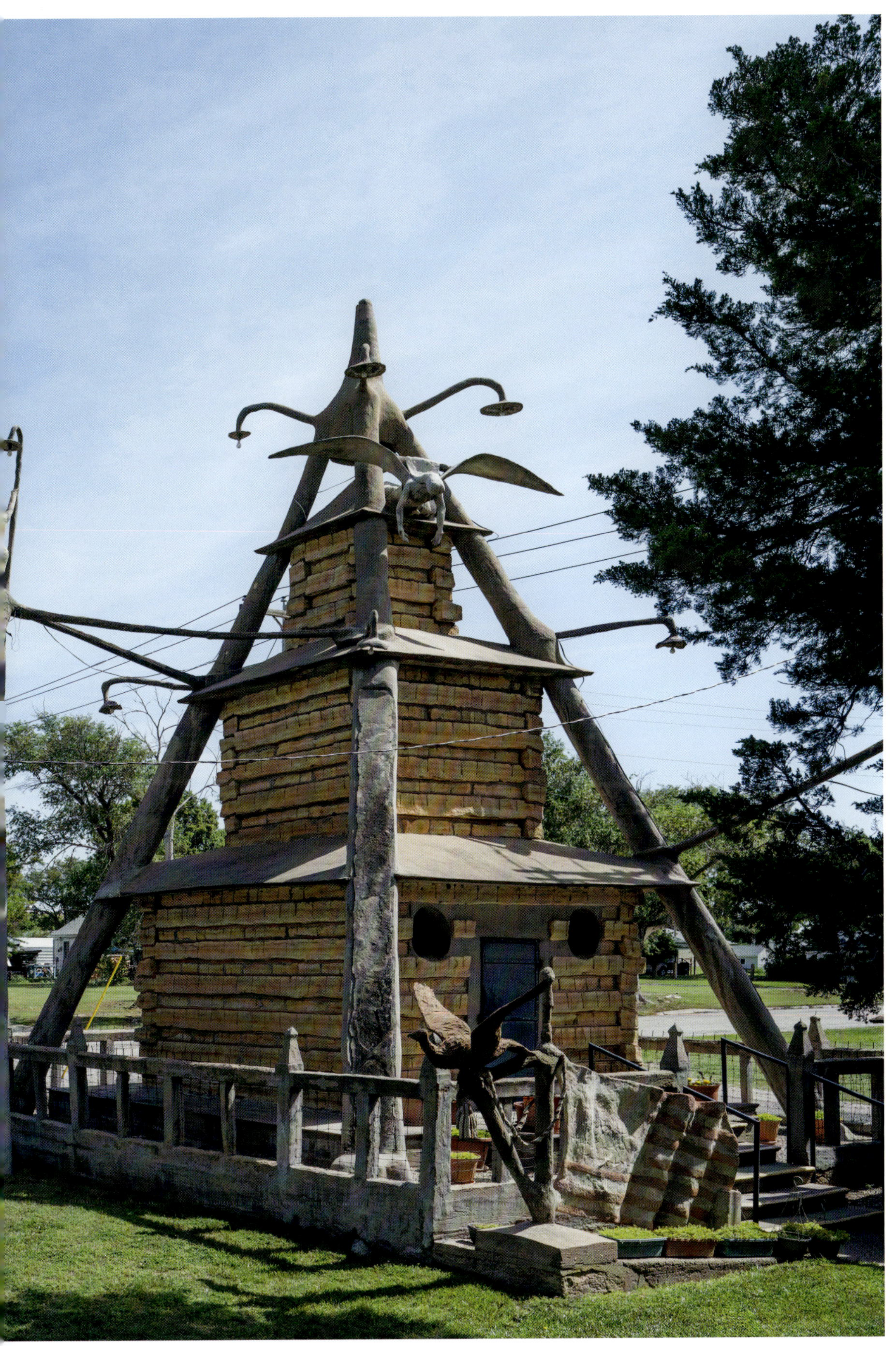

LIBERTY TREE AND *MAUSOLEUM*, 2024

STONE LOG CABIN HOME, WITH BIBLICAL SCULPTURES (RIGHT) AND "MODERN CIVILIZATION" (LEFT), 2024

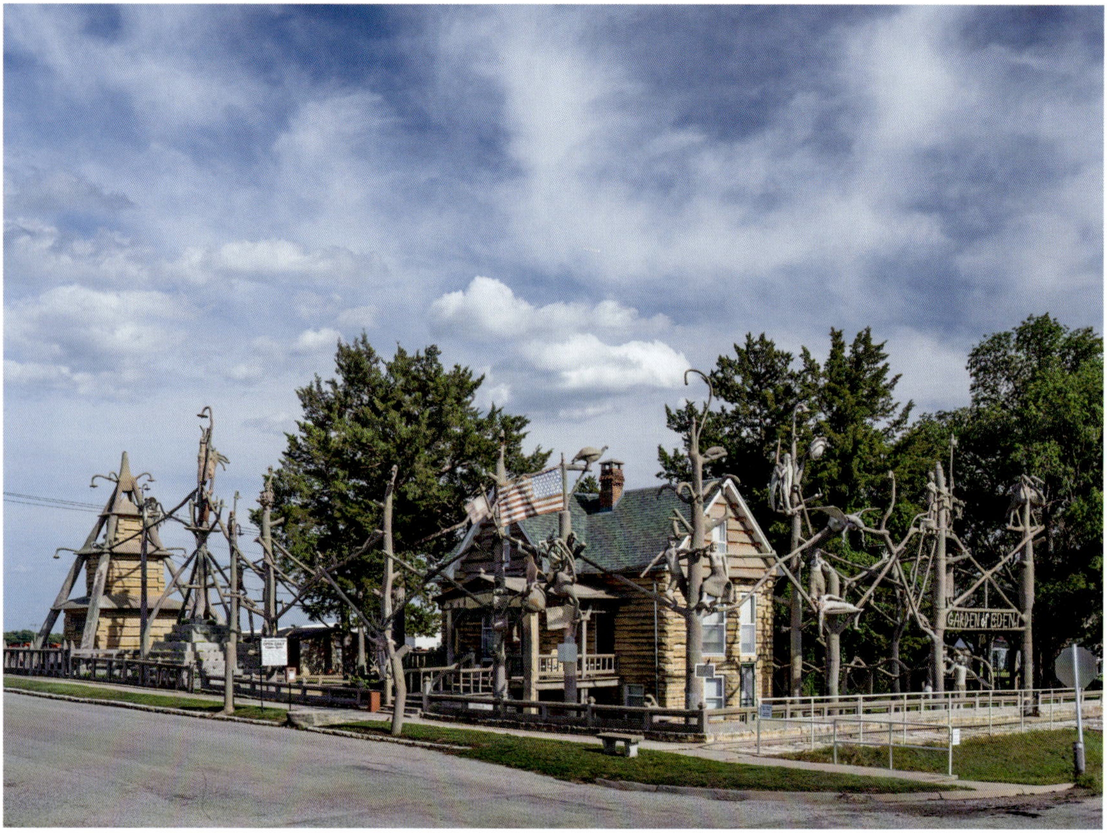

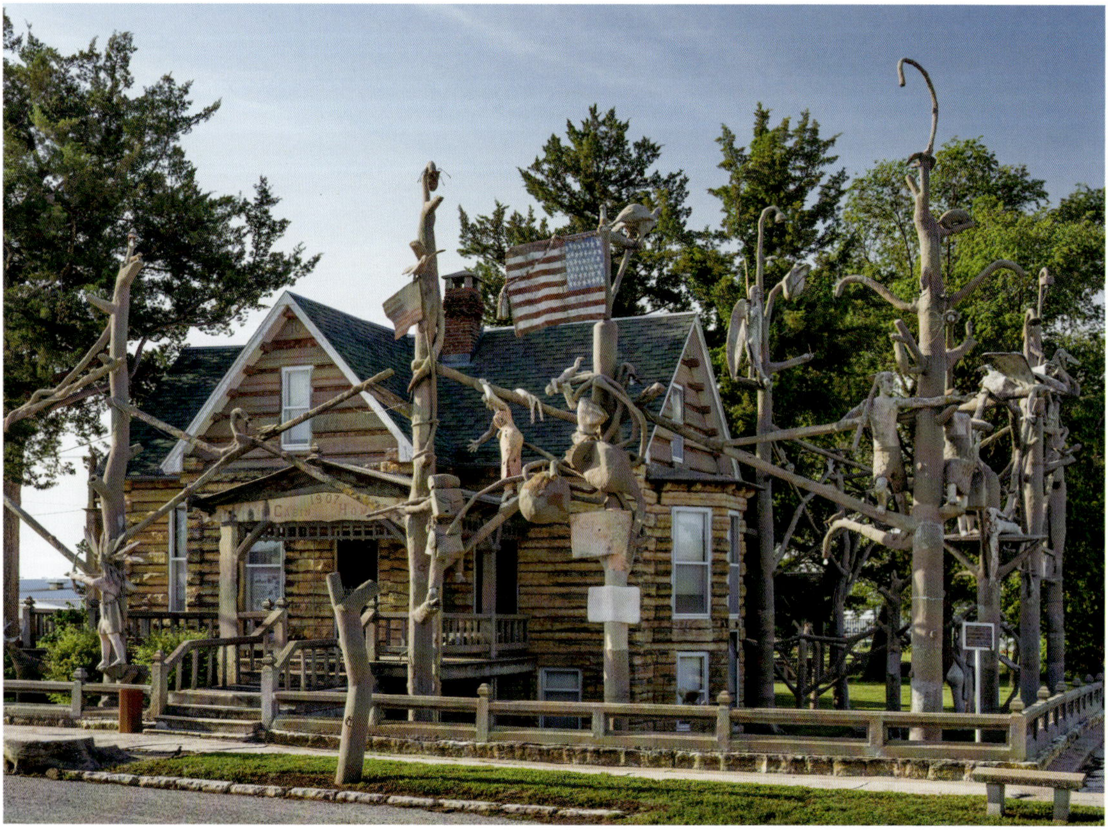

GARDEN OF EDEN, VIEW FROM NORTHWEST, 2024

The coffin is located in a 7 x 10′ room within the lowest level of the *Mausoleum*, behind a plate glass window that prohibits public access to the 3 x 2.5′ niche. His first wife is buried beneath him, not visible; Dinsmoor built his coffin out of reinforced concrete, and his head and upper body are clearly visible behind a glass pane. He flippantly wrote that this would enable him to watch visitors deposit a viewing fee, and when he saw that, he might give them a smile. Trying to anticipate all potentialities with this performative display, he reasoned that on "resurrection morn" his cement coffin would break apart, allowing him to ascend, in contrast to those in wood or steel coffins, who would either burn up or "fry." He ornamented his coffin lid with a bas-relief builder's square and compass, the Masonic symbols. (This motif is found elsewhere among his sculptures as well, including on the apron that Adam wears in the *Garden of Eden*.) The upper two levels of the *Mausoleum* have no publicly accessible interior chambers.

Dinsmoor worked for 22 years to ornament this property, using at least 113 tons of cement and many additional tons of limestone, financing it in part thanks to a clerical error through which he received two government pension checks every month instead of one. In 1976 the art environment was added to the National Register of Historic Places, and in 2025 it was added to the list of Historic Artists' Homes and Studios maintained by the National Trust for Historic Preservation. It is now managed and maintained by a nonprofit corporation. Here, 22 miles east of Paradise, Kansas, and 11 miles north of Hell Creek, visitors continue to be welcomed to the *Garden of Eden*.

HIS WORK REVEALS PHILOSOPHIES THAT CONTRASTED WITH THE LITERAL AND MORALISTIC VIEWS OF GOD AND COUNTRY COMMONLY HELD AT THE TIME.

EDDIE BOROS

THE TOY TOWER, A.K.A. THE GARBAGE CAN TOWER

NEW YORK, NEW YORK

New York–born Boros (1932–2007), the middle child of two Hungarian immigrants, lived his entire life in the East Village apartment in which he grew up, which happened to have a clear view of the rubble-strewn empty lot that later was transformed into the 6th and B Community Garden. Following their father's occupation, he and all of his brothers became union house painters. When he was drafted during the Korean War, Boros, a pacifist, was assigned to planting trees, and upon his return he became renowned as a local eccentric, often walking around barefoot and shirtless, sporting a string of pearls.

The 17,813-square-foot Community Garden was officially established in 1984, and each individual who asked was allocated a 4 x 8′ garden plot. Despite his gardening background, Boros chose instead to carve wooden sculptures, which he sometimes installed on his neighbors' plots; when some of them complained, he returned to his own, and he planted a few sunflowers in order to abide by the Garden's rules. Then he laid down a wooden plank and next, a high pole, around which he added what appeared to be rough scaffolding. He thought about erecting an open shed, but, inspired to keep building, he continued to expand. Squeezed by the plot's boundaries, he had nowhere to go but up.

Ultimately Boros's structure reached 65 feet high on a base that came to include six contiguous garden plots. He scavenged wood for the infrastructure from dumpsters, and began to ornament the limbs with discarded toys, mannequin parts, toy horses, religious statues, and stuffed animals, most of which he found on the streets. Perhaps he saw a link with the suspended children's toys on his growing tower and the children's garden and playground that were also located within the Community Garden. Reportedly beloved by the local children (he never married and had none of his own), he would give them toys or help them to ornament their bicycles even as many of their parents—and other gardeners—became increasingly frustrated by his construction. They claimed it was unstable and a potential danger; besides, it blocked sunlight from some of the other plots. Each year his fellow gardeners put its continued existence to a vote, and each year it survived by a narrow margin.

Boros continued to build for two decades, suspending more and more toys and other objects, and adding seasonal decorations as appropriate; it was said that he wanted to build his *Tower* so tall that he would be able to see the United Nations tower on East 45th Street, almost three miles away. With its vertical members not consistently plumb and diagonal buttresses sistered together in some sections and absent in others, the construction rose like a stepped building turned inside out, its interior framing easily visible from the exterior. The assembled ornaments, while interrupting the eye's sweep upward, did not break the rhythm of the work's constructivist geometry.

With the character of the Lower East Side changing as immigrant families moved out and artists—many from White, middle-class backgrounds—moved in, Boros's *Tower* became increasingly seen as an unofficial landmark of the East Village and a quintessentially New York eccentricity: its incorporation of the detritus of urban blight began to be appreciated as an aesthetic hallmark. It was featured in the credits for the television cop drama *NYPD Blue* and as part of the set design for the long-running Broadway musical *Rent*. But longer-time residents—and city officials—did not reverse their aversion to the monument, and the polarization continued.

Boros's strength was legendary, but in his early seventies he began to have circulatory problems in his legs, which he ignored until he had to have both legs amputated at the knee. However, the care that he received at the Veterans Hospital following his surgery was inadequate, and his relatives rushed him to another facility, but it was too late. The spring following his death, the city decided that the *Toy Tower* needed to be taken down, averring that elements were rotting and it was unsafe. It did, however, take Park Department workers several days, using a cherry picker and chainsaws, to bring it down, a testament to the complexity and robustness of its construction. After its demolition, many of its toys and other ornamentations were given away to community members as souvenirs.

A COMMUNITY GARDEN PLOT BECAME THE SITE FOR A SIX-STORY-HIGH STRUCTURE OF SCAVENGED WOOD ORNAMENTED WITH TOYS AND OTHER CASTOFFS.

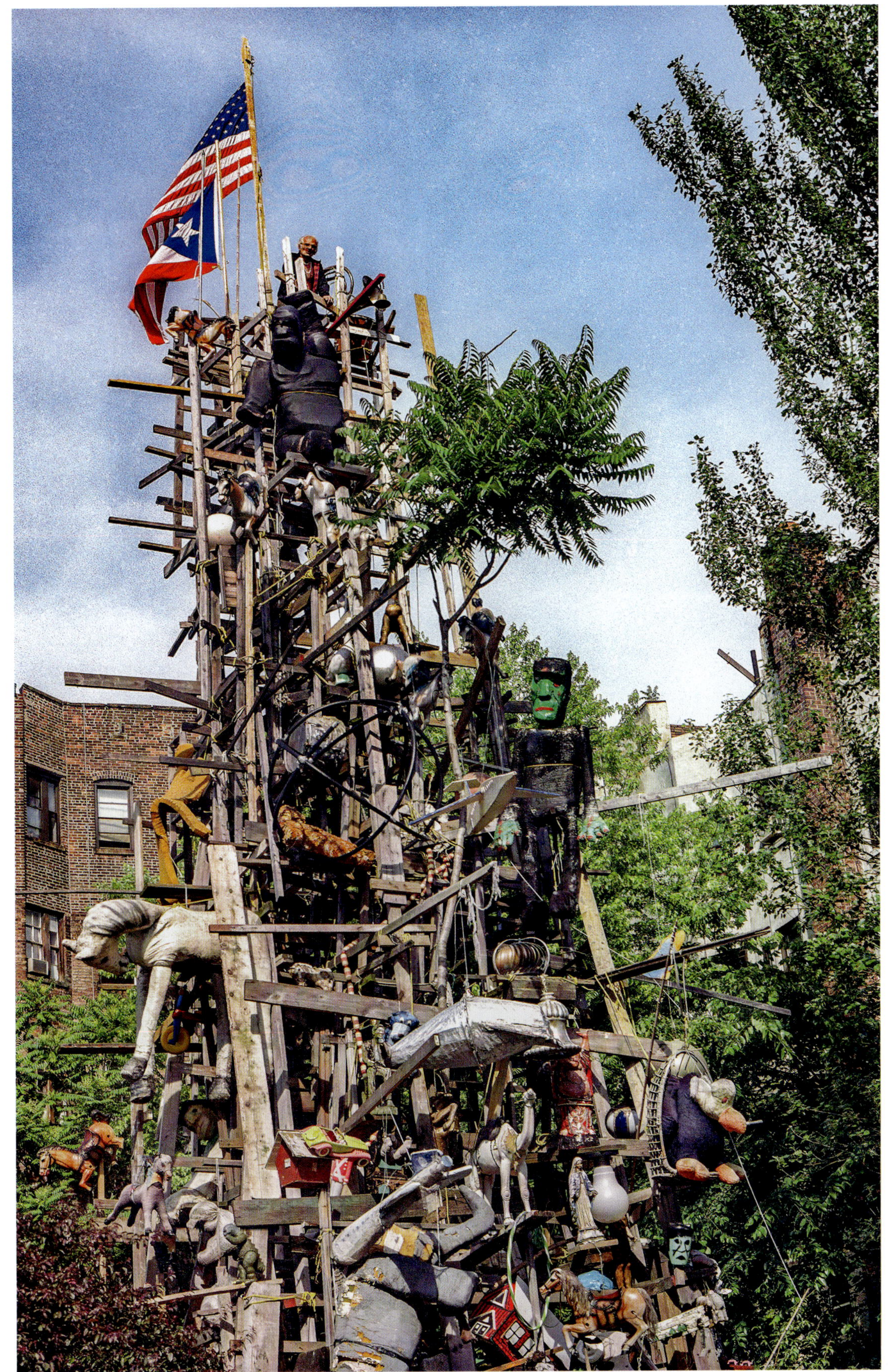

BOROS AT THE TOP OF HIS *TOWER*, 1998. PHOTO: TED DEGENER

TOM "DR. EVERMOR" EVERY

—

THE FOREVERTRON

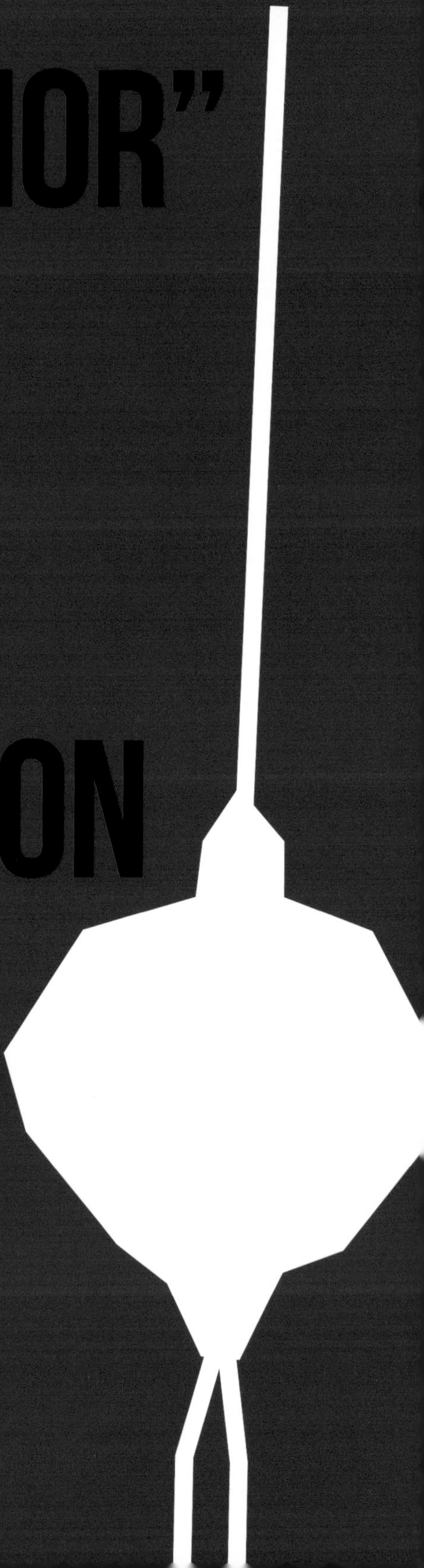

SUMPTER, WISCONSIN

Every's (1938–2020) immense architectural sculpture is one of this country's most extravagant and impressive monuments. Assembled on his rural property from an extensive variety of massive nineteenth- and early twentieth-century industrial relics, the resulting "machine" manifests a bygone aesthetic that amalgamates Steampunk, science fiction comics of the 1950s and '60s, and the kinds of space paraphernalia popularized in the Buck Rogers strips of the 1920s and '30s. The *Forevertron* was conceptualized as a tongue-in-cheek time machine intended to transport body and soul to another galactic realm.

Born in Brooklyn, Wisconsin, Every grew up on the family farm watching his parents contribute to the war effort by collecting scrap metal that could be melted down for armaments. He learned a range of skills and how to work with widely different materials, as most farm kids do, and even as a young boy he was also noted for his industriousness and initiative: he had organized his own salvage company by age 11.

This fledgling operation (which was shut down within six years because his "junkyard" was found to violate county ordinances) later evolved into the Wisconsin By-Products Corporation, a salvage venture through which Every oversaw the demolition of more than 350 once-flourishing industrial or commercial structures across the country, including mills, breweries, power plants, and railroads. While he sold off some of the metal scraps and remnants that he recovered, he retained literally tons of other pieces that he found particularly evocative or that he anticipated could be useful to him in his own future endeavors. After he retired in 1984, he took on the invented persona of the pith-helmet-wearing English scientist Dr. Evermor, and on his 10-acre site he began assembling his collected oddments into a variety of sculptures. The primary focus of his growing environment was the *Forevertron*; astonishingly, he completed most of the work on this architectural-scale monolith within two or three years.

Measuring roughly 120 feet wide, 60 feet deep, and 50 feet high, and estimated to weigh 300 tons, this massive assemblage, built with significant deliberation but without reference to drawings or models, includes among its constituent parts a decontamination chamber from the Apollo 11 moon mission, elements designed by Nikola Tesla that had been deaccessioned from the Henry Ford Museum, battery stacks from 1920s power stations, sections of railway engines and cargo ships, and two of Thomas Edison's original dipolar dynamos from the 1880s. There are steam compressors, irrigation and farm implements, transformers, lightning rods, a 32-foot "telescope," and, as the central element, a spherical glass ball that once advertised a hamburger stand in Green Bay, Wisconsin. Every encased this ball, for protection, in diagonally affixed copper bands that suggest a sense of movement, creating a more aerodynamic egg-shape form appropriate to its new "function" as a space capsule.

There are blades and cranks and switches and pipes and coils and cones and winches and bearings and spheres and tracks and scrap from the Army munitions plant located across the road, cleverly and smoothly joined together by Every's fabricated "blenders." Enamored of the decorative qualities of his chosen objects despite their intrinsically functional origin, he was careful to maintain the integrity of the original components: he sized them to fit, if necessary, and carefully welded or bolted them together into a lacy assemblage while endeavoring to maintain them as closely as possible to their original forms. He asserted that the energy inherent in those pieces was part of what would drive the force of the new assemblage in its reincarnated state, and that bonding discrete parts together with heat would further enhance the intrinsic energy retained by the salvaged objects. He professed that combining electrical energy and magnetic force would send him to the heavens on a "magnetic lightning force beam."

Every facetiously described how the *Forevertron* was actually a re-creation of a nineteenth-century invention by Dr. Evermor that was used for teletransportation. The sculpture became the core of an elaborate tale that required complementary components to ensure success and provide safe and comfortable accommodations during the voyage. Among these were the *Gravitron*, used to regulate and adjust the body's weight to that needed as the space-time continuum was breached; the *Celestial Listening Ear*, a microphone perpetually tuned to the landing site in order to receive contact information to ascertain that the vessel's voyage was correctly aligned to arrive on target; the *Overlord Master Control Tower* to track the trajectory of flight (its primary elements formerly having been used to control elevators); *Juicer Bugs* to generate electrical

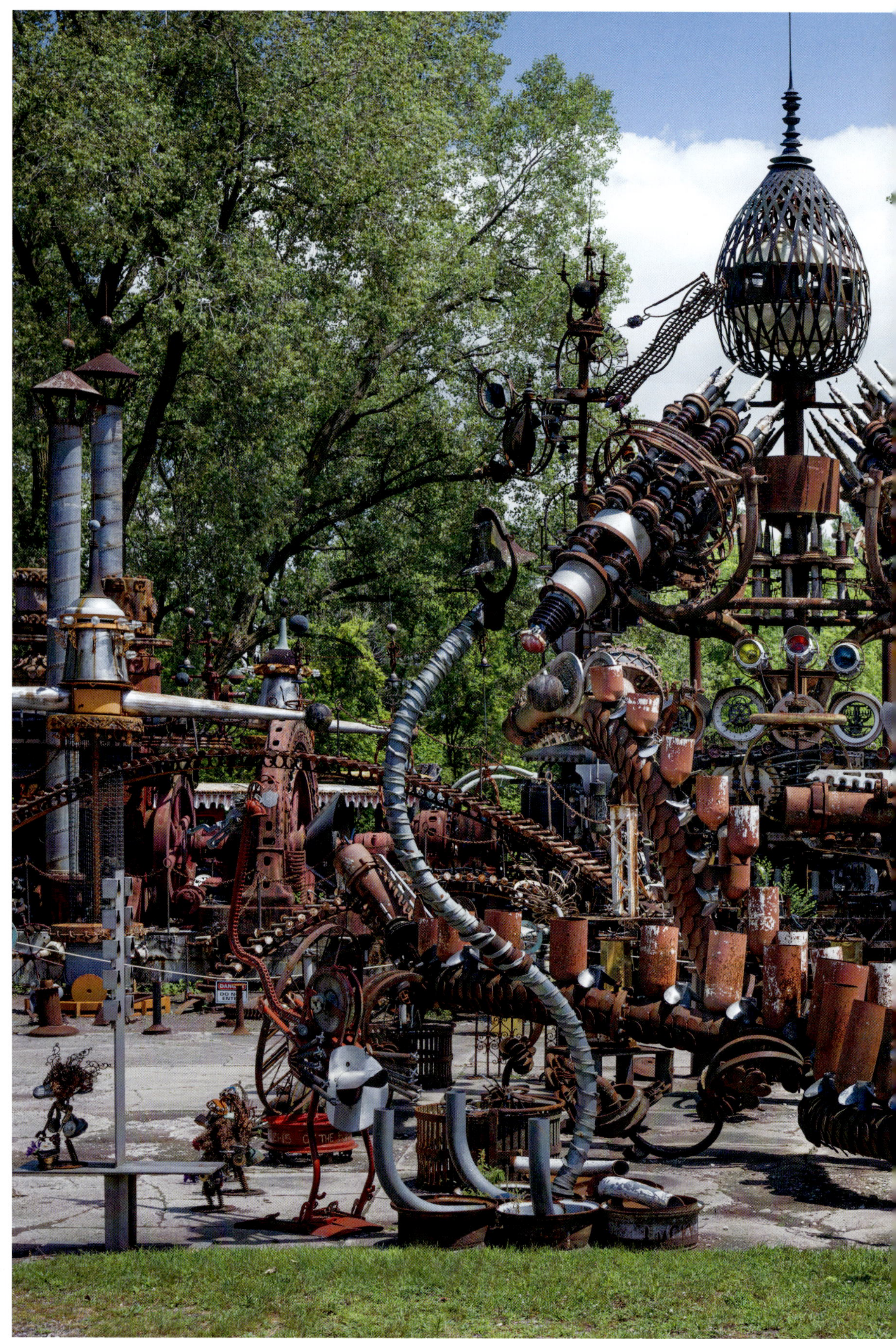

WESTERN VIEW, *FOREVERTRON* (DETAIL), 2024

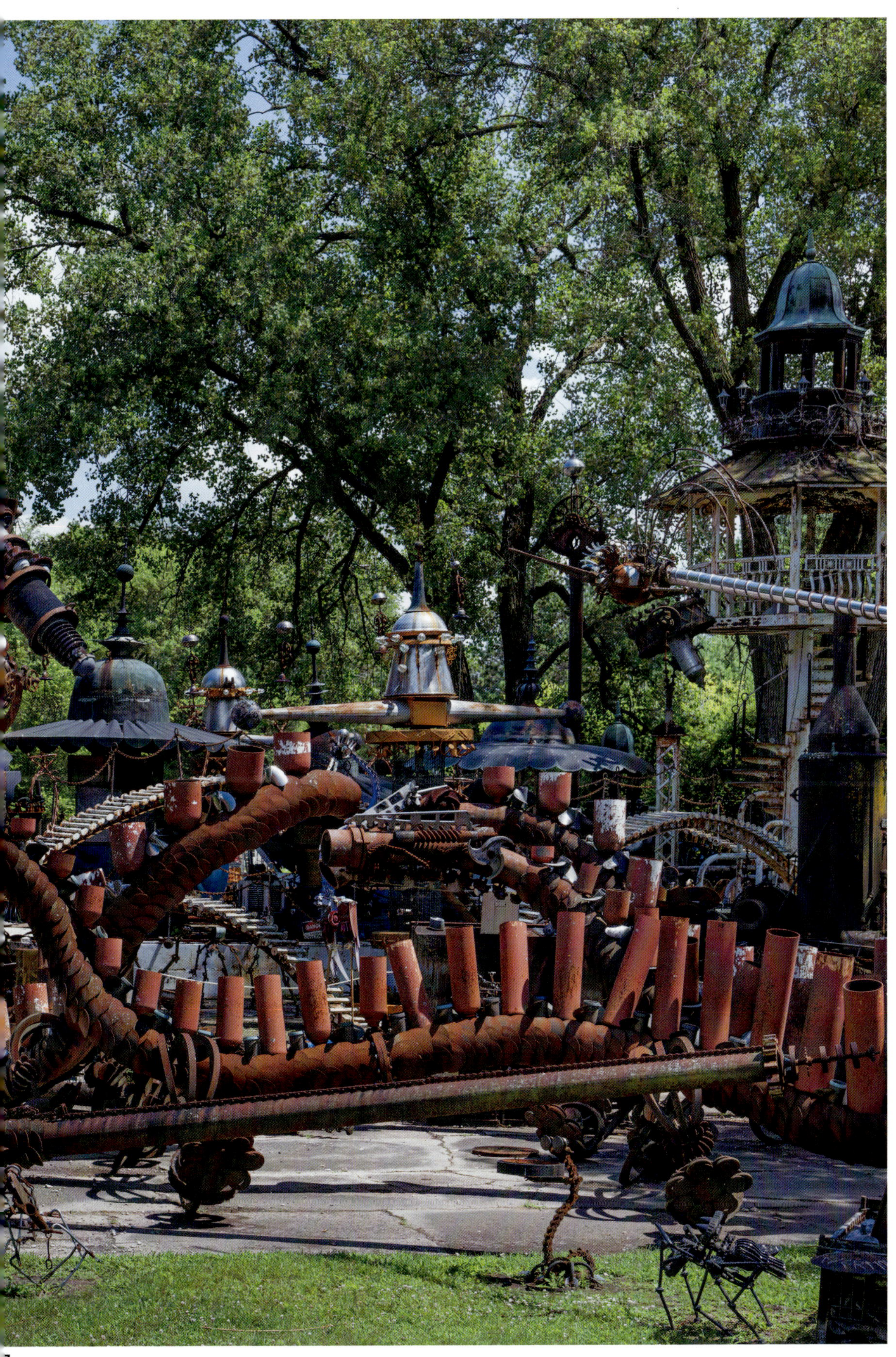

boosts as needed to dependably maintain the power of the speeding *Forevertron*; and the *Bird Band and Orchestra*, a series of around 70 metal bird-shaped forms to celebrate liftoff by playing triumphant music on instruments recovered from a thrift store. Understanding that watching all of this activity—the VIPs comfortably observing from the *Royal Gazebo*—would make sightseers hungry, the *Epicurean Grill* would provide sumptuous repasts. Every himself time-traveled as he toggled between an elaborately fabricated past and the authentic present, promoting a tale of forthcoming departure and transcendent rebirth for both his visitors and himself.

Visually and physically symmetrical and, according to Every, capable of being freestanding thanks to the care he took during fabrication to account for wind shear and the compression of the weight of individual components, the *Forevertron* includes parts that rotate or can be illuminated by flipping a switch. Although it rather counterintuitively looks somewhat delicate, almost filigree, it is complex and heavy, maintaining its balance through overbuilding and an almost impenetrable consolidation of forms. While designed with practical concerns in mind—not only the necessity of maintaining equilibrium but the theoretical objective of powering the ascent of the space capsule—his primary concern was formalist and aesthetic.

The central copper-clad glass capsule, artfully buoyed on a slender support as if poised for takeoff, is surrounded by four immense, diagonally installed assemblages that recall giant spark plugs and reference rocket thrusters, aimed at the capsule in order to fire its launch. Electromagnetic energies emanating from the earth would fuel their force, compounded by the power of the machine parts whose positioning was designed to capitalize on their inherent potency. Every's fusion of forms is much more hands-on, and its mechanics more clearly understandable, than the invisible digital ones and zeroes that power our world today. It is also a meaningful manifestation of the changes in our society and the probability of obsolescence—if not extinction— of today's materials and concerns as we face tomorrow.

In 1999 the nonprofit Evermor Foundation was established to help support Every's work in perpetuity, yet this is not assured, given that he had sold his half ownership of the property on which his work is sited to his original partner not long after its purchase in the 1970s. Although he was given the right to continue to work and store his collections on the land, and Every's widow is determined to have them stay there "forever," the long-term future of the sculptures is yet to be determined. While Every said that he had constructed the *Forevertron* so that it could be unbolted in sections and moved, he had not, by the time of his death, pinned down another location that could or would accept such a massive creation. While individual works, such as some of the bird band sculptures, have been sold or removed, long-term prospects for the immense *Forevertron* itself—identified in 1999 by the *Guinness Book of World Records* as the largest scrap-metal sculpture in the world—are still in doubt.

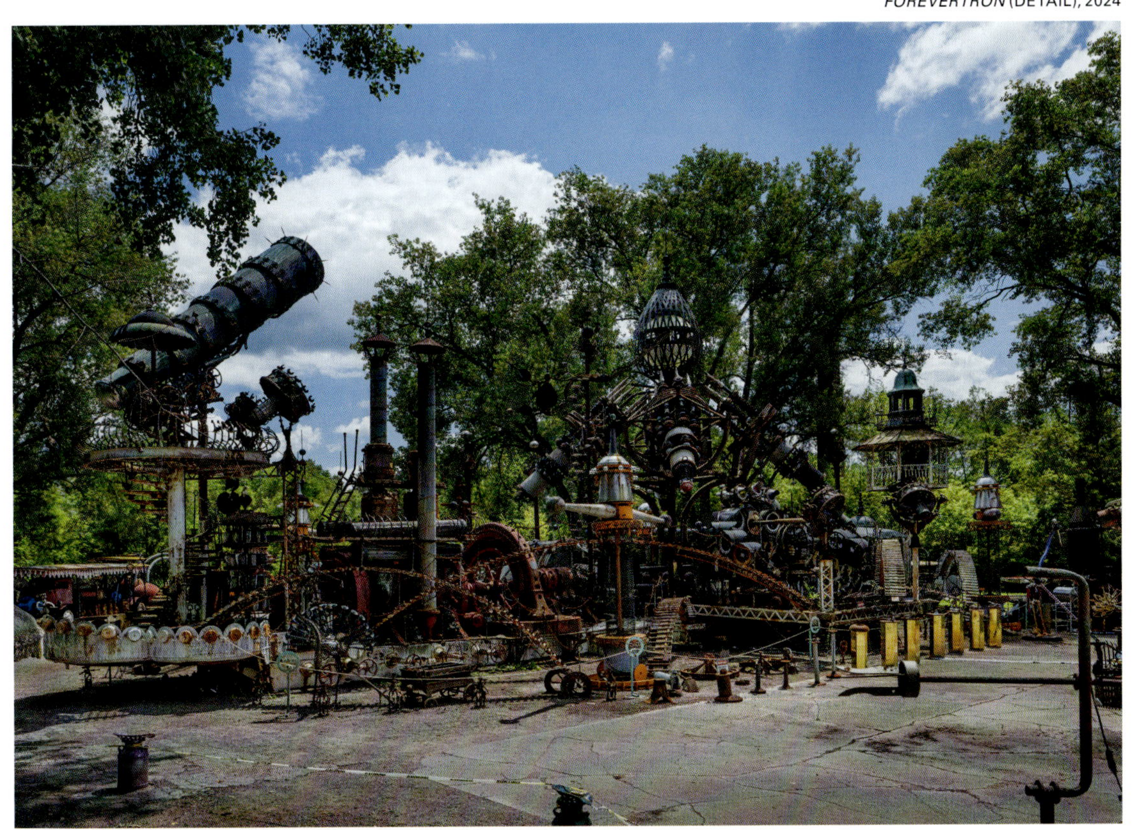

FOREVERTRON (DETAIL), 2024

THE FOREVERTRON WAS A TONGUE-IN-CHEEK TIME MACHINE INTENDED TO TRANSPORT BODY AND SOUL TO ANOTHER GALACTIC REALM.

VOLLIS SIMPSON

WHIRLIGIG PARK

WILSON, NORTH CAROLINA

Simpson's (1919–2013) occupations, like Tom Every's (see page 304), provided him with the resources and the expertise to manipulate and mount monumental components of steel and other recycled materials. But, in contrast to the Wisconsin artist's focus on otherworldly matters, Simpson's focus was closer to home: he celebrated the whimsical folk-art yard ornaments and the people and activities of the environs of his hometown hamlet of Lucama.

One of 12 children born to a farming family, Simpson completed the 11 grades his high school offered at that time and then helped around the farm, although he preferred repairing and maintaining the agricultural vehicles and implements to actual farming. He also assisted his father with his side business of moving houses and barns, using basic equipment like jacks and rollers to transport them by horsepower until automotive motors became more available and conventionally used. His work on the farm and relocating buildings provided the young Simpson with a range of skills, a facility in using numerous materials, and, not coincidentally, ease in addressing large-scale objects and complex projects. During his service in the Army Air Corps in World War II, for example, he fabricated a windmill-powered washing machine out of a defunct B-29 bomber, a contraption welcomed by his fellow troops stationed on the island of Saipan.

Upon his return, he opened a farm implement repair and welding shop with two of his brothers while he continued with his father's house-moving business, designing alternative devices or adapting existing ones to save time and energy, and absorbing the principles of balance and equilibrium. A tangential outcome from both of these lines of work was the gradual accumulation of miscellaneous parts—tools and mechanisms for machine repair and transportation as well as a variety of metal components and salvaged cogs, modules, propellers, fans, hubcaps, gears, chains, metal rims from headlights, and the still-useful workings from a wide range of vehicles and industrial equipment. Simpson maintained his interest in wind power and built at least one large windmill to heat his home that worked by blowing wood-heated air through the ducts in order to save on energy costs (it was decommissioned after his wife complained about how it made everything in the house smell smoky). After he retired, he relocated this windmill and began to assemble other recycled components into enormous whirligigs—nonfunctional wind-powered windmills—in close proximity to each other in his yard.

The defining characteristic of whirligigs is that the passage of wind through the blades results in movement, yet movement with aesthetic rather than functional purpose. Simpson engineered pieces that caused flat metal cutouts of lumberjacks to saw wood, dogs to wag their tails, horse-drawn carts to roll, bicyclists to pedal, musicians to strum their guitars, and geese to flap their wings: his motifs are homespun, related to his experiences as soldier, farmer, neighbor. Others, more formalist and nonfigurative, have multiple levels of rotating wheels, some powered by semispherical cup or can forms and others by numerous smaller fans, pinwheels, or vents mounted around a central wheel. All of these spinning, moving parts were interdependent, moving with precision in spite of his avowal that he did not measure them in advance. In some cases he hung chimes off of the main elements, so that with the wind—and the rotation of the whirligigs—they whirred and clanked and rang, a harmonizing polyphony that countered the groaning and creaking of the structures themselves: for all of Simpson's exact adjustments, the recycled bearings never produced silent movement. One presumes that this was simply never of importance for him.

Built from a veritable inventory of the kinds of mechanisms and structural components that had passed through Simpson's hands, the whirligigs—the largest of which reach 30 to 60 feet in height and weigh several tons—included fans and blades of all sizes, along with bicycle parts, plumbing supplies, steel and aluminum tubes and sheeting, pipes and rods, I-beams, gears, rollers from textile mills, ball bearings, wood strips, fiberglass, and a range of other random components. He supplemented these through his monthly circuit to the junkyard and visits to other local tradesmen, helping them out by removing the remnants they had no use for. He sank sturdy central steel pillars into a foundation of concrete, and used winches and cables to hoist the decorative components high into place. Each was unique and distinctive not only in subject but in shape and breadth, and as a display of how simple, similar technologies could be used to achieve notably different effects.

Simpson's property abutted the five-point intersection of narrow country roads, and he took advantage of this location by cutting up mirrors and reflective road signs so that moonlight or the beams from passing cars would illuminate the revolving whirligigs at night. This was a not-insignificant light show: one of the largest had some 2,000 painstakingly cut-out reflectors. He painted the different elements—with brushes or, more often, with spray paint—in bright, contrasting colors, and strung up supporting or decorative wires in conical, circular, spherical, or other geometric forms, festooning them with the little reflective cutouts so that, during the day, their colors would further enhance the gaiety of the kinetic kaleidoscopic display.

Thirty-one monumental whirligigs and dozens of smaller works ultimately adorned Simpson's property, arrayed around the small pond and field adjacent to his workshop. As needed, he would repaint peeling paint and grease the wheels and bearings, but as he aged it became progressively more difficult, and it was increasingly evident that major intervention was needed to maintain and preserve the rusting constructions. Concern was particularly raised at the community level, as the whirligigs had become the area's primary—if unofficial—tourist attraction, drawing regional, national, and even global visitors. Their visits contributed financially to the otherwise rather depressed local economy, once dependent upon tobacco.

A plan was developed to relocate the monumental whirligigs 11 miles from Simpson's property to a two-acre downtown public park in Wilson, the county seat, with the multiple objectives of enhancing the visibility of his work, offering local jobs in basic conservation, and benefiting Wilson's historic downtown area. Simpson and his family, gratified that the whirligigs would be maintained, agreed to the plan, and through a public-private partnership anchored by a significant National Endowment for the Arts award and several foundation grants, and supported by the North Carolina Arts Council—and later through an ownership transfer via the Kohler Foundation—the photography, inventory, assessment, conservation, and relocation took place, creating the core for an arts and cultural district that opened in 2017. (Countless numbers of Simpson's original parts, used and recycled to begin with, were so degraded that they needed to be replaced, but many were no longer easy to acquire. Conservators had to lease a milling machine and metal lathe in order to re-create or modify the parts needed to complete the project.) Anchored by Simpson's work, millions of dollars in private investment subsequently prompted the development of restaurants, residences, and other amenities near *Whirligig Park*, and an annual Whirligig Festival attracts some 40,000 visitors, as public engagement on all levels continues to grow. In 1996 five of his monumental works were installed in Atlanta as part of the international Olympic games, and in 2013 Vollis Simpson's *Whirligigs* were designated as the official folk art of North Carolina.

MAN ON TRICYCLE, 2010

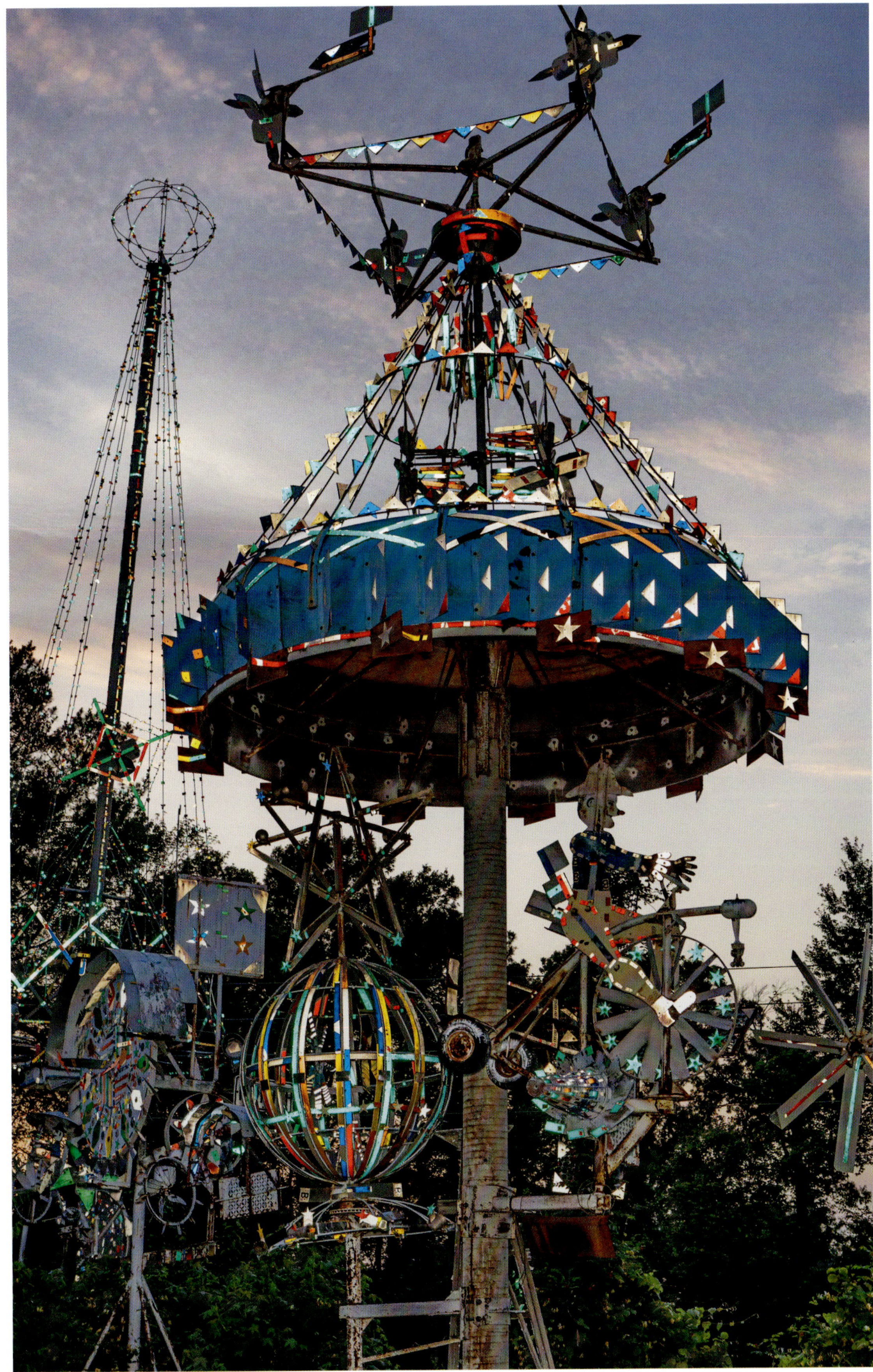

OVERVIEW OF GROUNDS, 2008

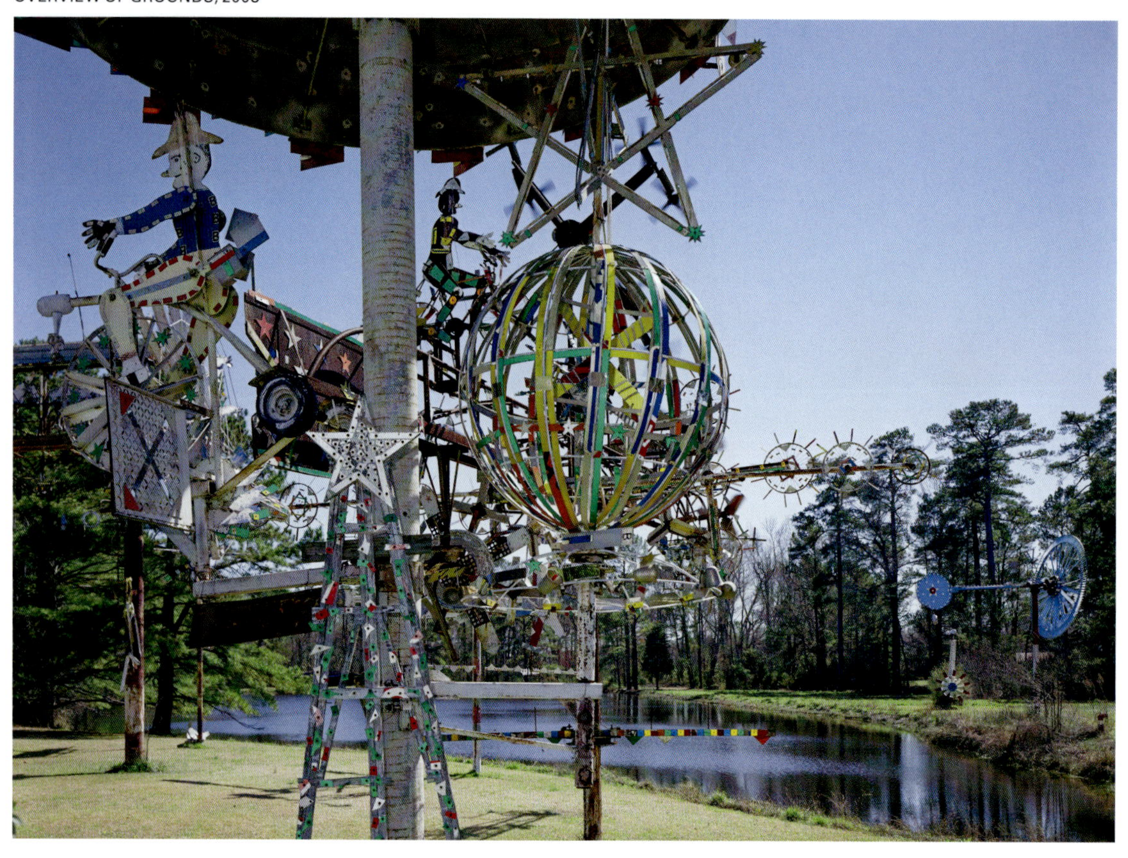

MONUMENTAL VERSIONS OF FOLK-ART YARD ORNAMENTS FEATURE THE PEOPLE AND ANIMALS OF THE ARTIST'S ENVIRONS.

OVERVIEW OF GROUNDS, 2011

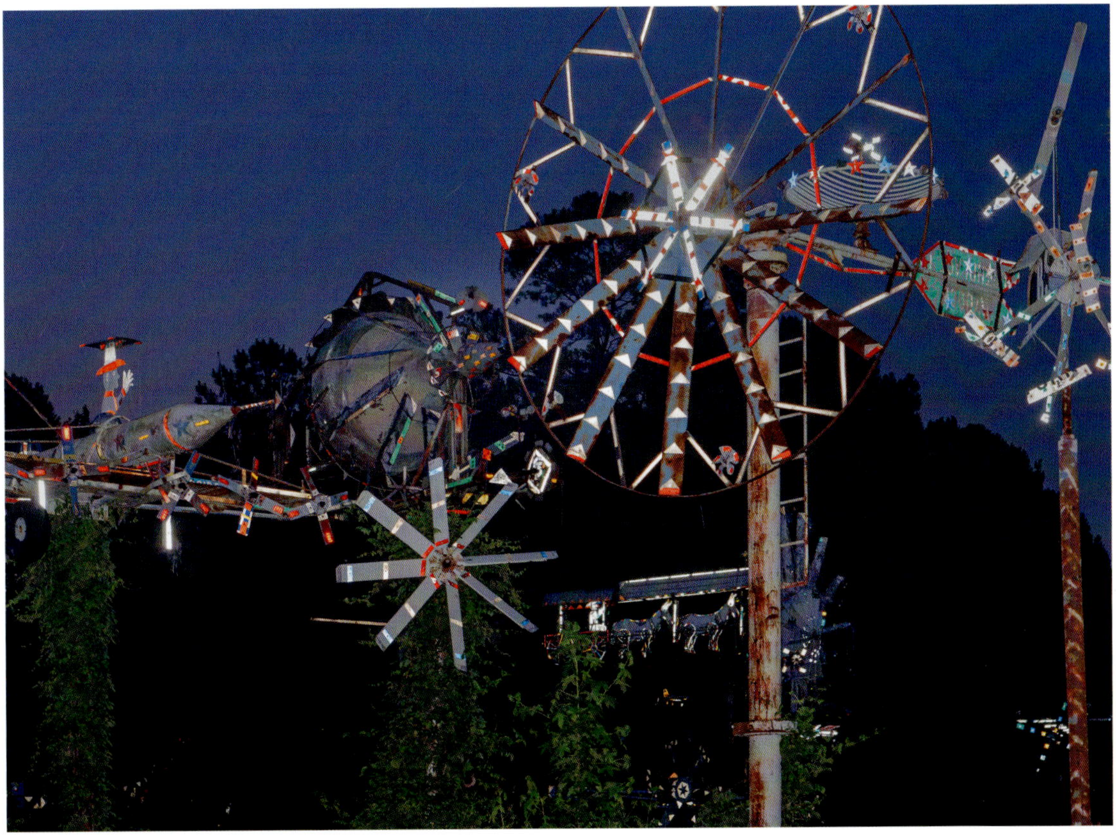

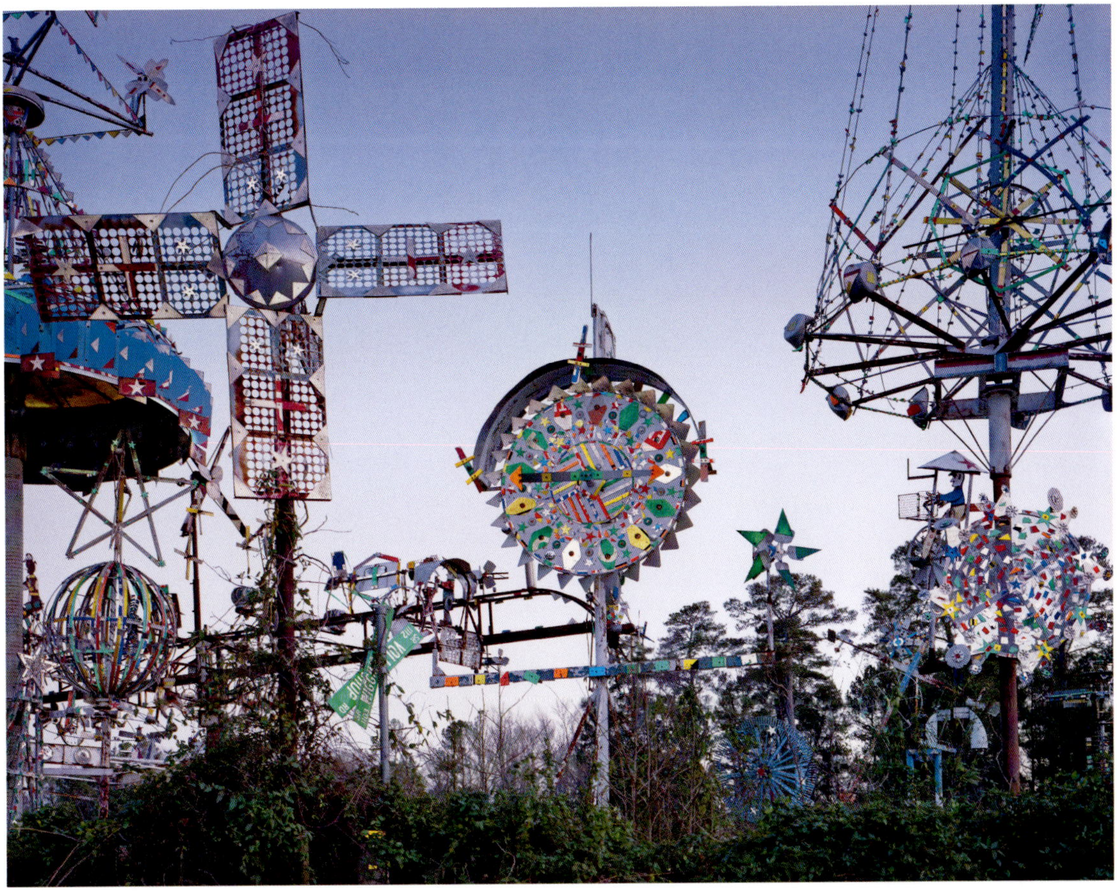

OVERVIEW OF GROUNDS, 2010

KENNY HILL

CHAUVIN SCULPTURE GARDEN

CHAUVIN, LOUISIANA

Hill (b. ca. 1950) is an artist whose backstory is rather enigmatic, as no currently available documentation confirms his birth date, location of birth, or even whether he is still alive. It is known that he was raised in Springfield, Louisiana, and became a mason and bricklayer, professional training that would later serve him well in his *Garden*. He married at age 20 and had three children, but he left his family in 1988 and made his way south to Chauvin, some 70 miles southeast of New Orleans. Here he squatted on 1⅓ acres of land lying alongside Bayou Petit Caillou until he was able to make arrangements with the landlord to pay a couple of hundred dollars a year to stay on the property.

As he spent many months each year on masonry jobs, sometimes out of the area or even out of state, he first lived only in a tent, but after building himself a small house (now demolished due to its state of disrepair and because it was not built to code), he branched out from his earlier creative expressions in two-dimensional paintings and human-scale wood carvings. Then, in 1990, he began to work in concrete to ornament the exterior of the site. Initially his work was not visible from the street, as the vegetation on that side was dense and overgrown, but it could be seen from boats on the bayou and from the far banks. He ultimately built approximately 100 sculptures and structures at this location.

The majority of Hill's sculptures are figurative and religious, with numerous self-portraits and an array of denizens of this world and a hoped-for alternative world. They include cowboys, winsome young women, animals such as horses, and birds, particularly eagles. But the largest group are angels, several of which are personalized, protecting and lifting up sinners, including the artist himself. A number of them, ministering in other ways to those who seek salvation, brandish swords or trumpets and harps to protect and herald, or cradle an hourglass to remind us of the passage of time. They are easily recognizable by their large wings and, for some, halos made of circular incandescent bulbs that float above their heads.

All of Hill's figures are thin, sized at human scale, and many were designed with outstretched arms, wings, or legs, an approach that required significant technical expertise and one that reveals his facility with tools and, even more, his impressive understanding of the limits of his media. He worked over a framework of steel rebar, piping, and wire mesh, sometimes supplemented with bricks and concrete chunks or blocks, and to do that, he developed a high-quality mortar to bind the elements and cover the infrastructure. Later, he often carved texture into the surface with simple tools like forks and spoons, and then brightly painted the whole, highlighting ornaments or accoutrements to communicate the structure's identity or purpose.

Even those works in the *Garden* that denote heavenly figures are grounded in our understanding of the everyday: an angel's face may be marked with tears or display blue eyes outlined with black eyeliner, or its flowing garments may reveal feather ornamentation. Female figures, once nude, had bathing suits painted on at a later time to mollify a neighbor's wife, and cowboys wear boots, vests, and hats, and carry guns in their holsters. In Hill's own self-portraits, he is often wearing torn jeans detailed with pockets and a characteristic belt buckle. Elsewhere he appears in different scenarios: on horseback, for example, or clutching at his bleeding heart, being lifted up by angels, seated and holding a large seashell to his ear and a horseshoe in his lap, or struggling as he carries a cross while following Christ (who, effortlessly hoisting his own cross, glances back as if to encourage him). Throughout the site, his self-representations appear interrelated as they suggest different states of belief, divine appraisal, and salvation. They create a complex and multilayered narrative that interweaves a dreamlike personal storyline with conventional, well-represented, and generally recognizable motifs from Christian iconography.

Hill complemented his figures with garden ornaments such as a trellis, a circular colonnade whose vertical supports are formed by the talons of eagles, and inscribed and colored concrete pathways anchored by circular discs. These ground-level ornaments, winding in and around the sculptures, sometimes display enigmatic symbols that generally mirror the layout of the *Garden* itself.

The 45-foot-high lighthouse-shaped tower is the most prominent architectural construction on the property and, given its monumentality, serves as the visual anchor for the entire site. This tower was mortared together from 7,000 bricks and built up over time into a slightly conical shape, as Hill was able to salvage bricks and mortar from his paying masonry jobs or make use of surplus materials donated to him by his neighbors. An arched doorway

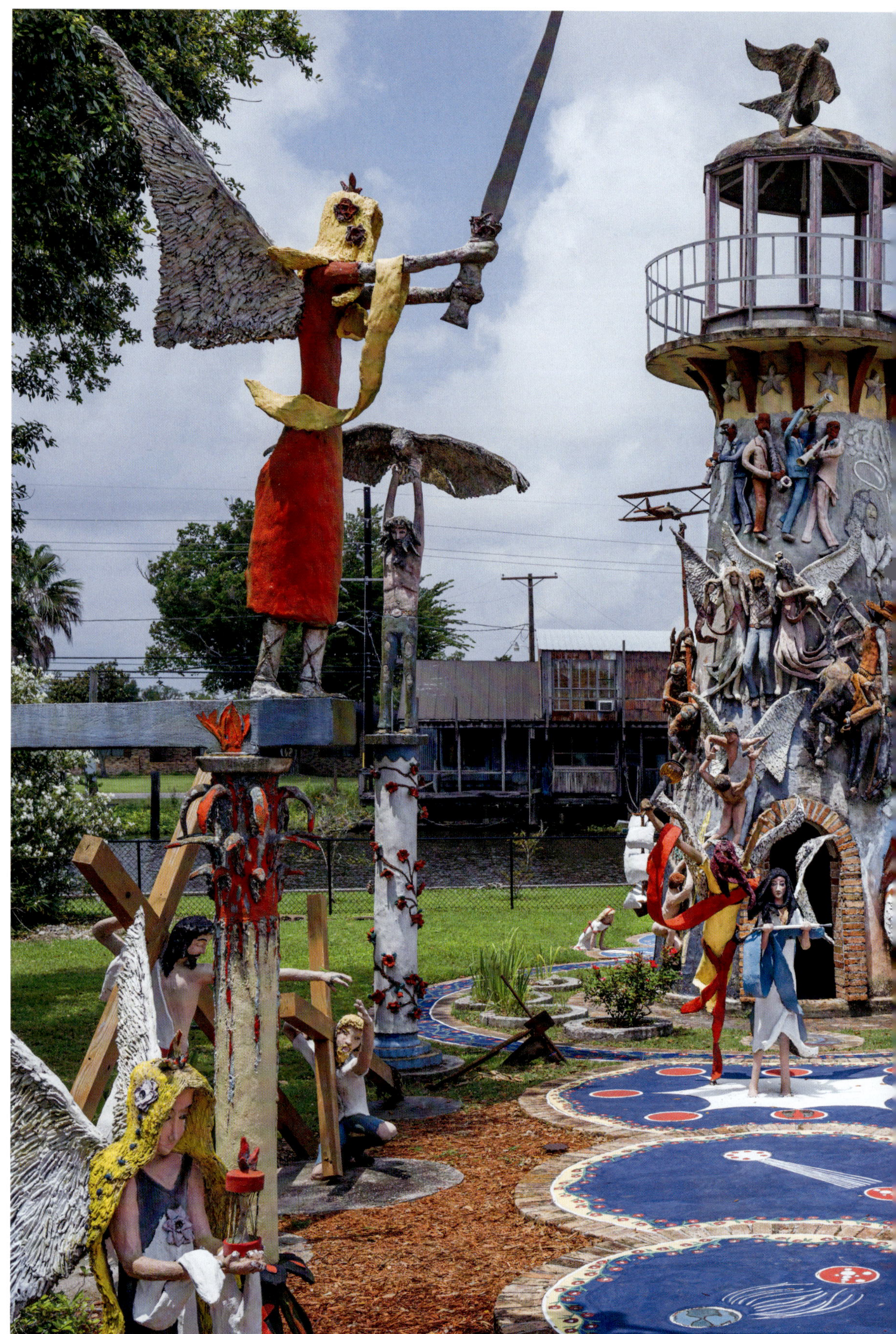

LIGHTHOUSE AND OVERVIEW OF *GARDEN*, 2024

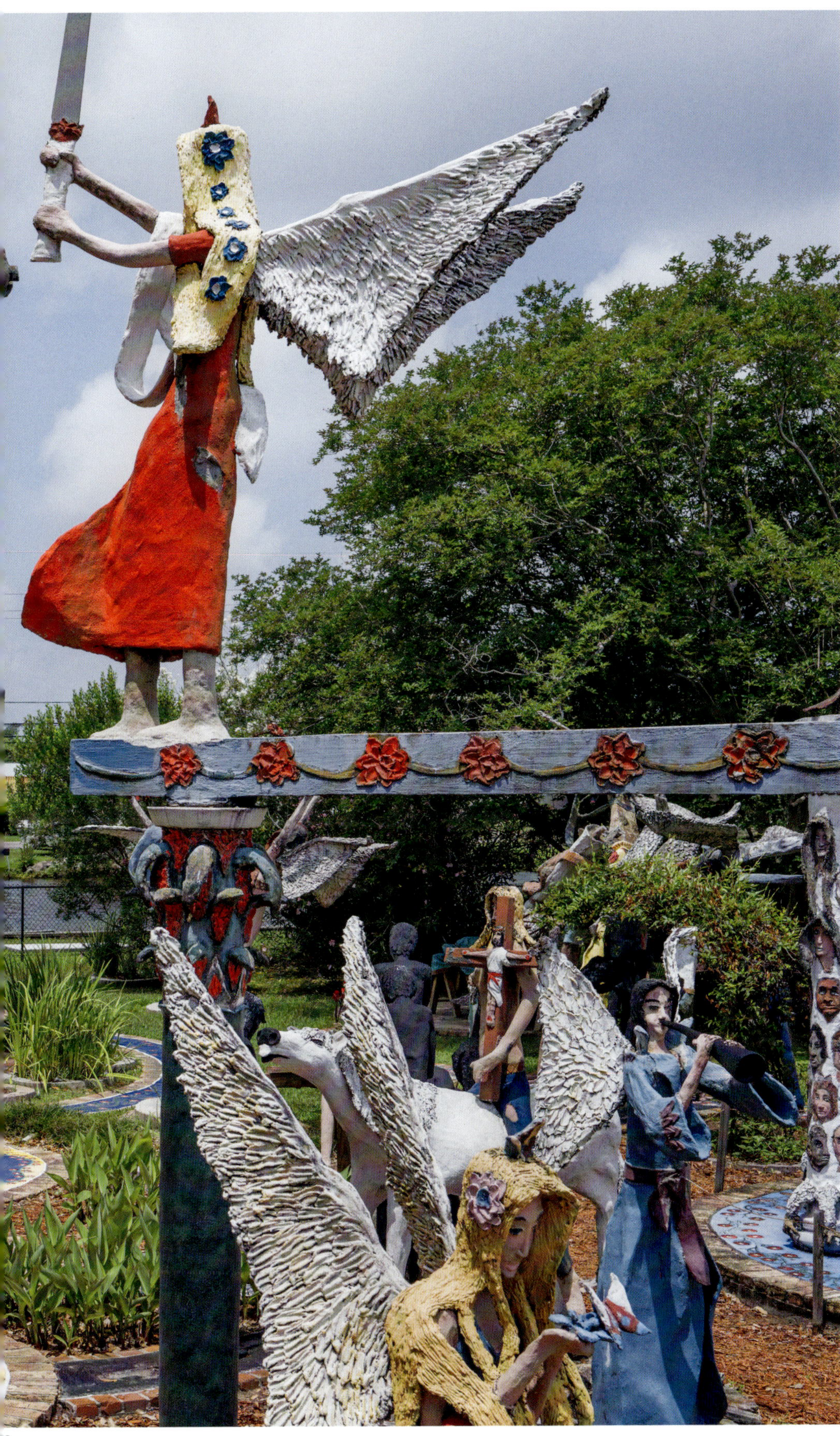

ARTIST RESCUED BY ANGEL AND *LIGHTHOUSE*, 2024

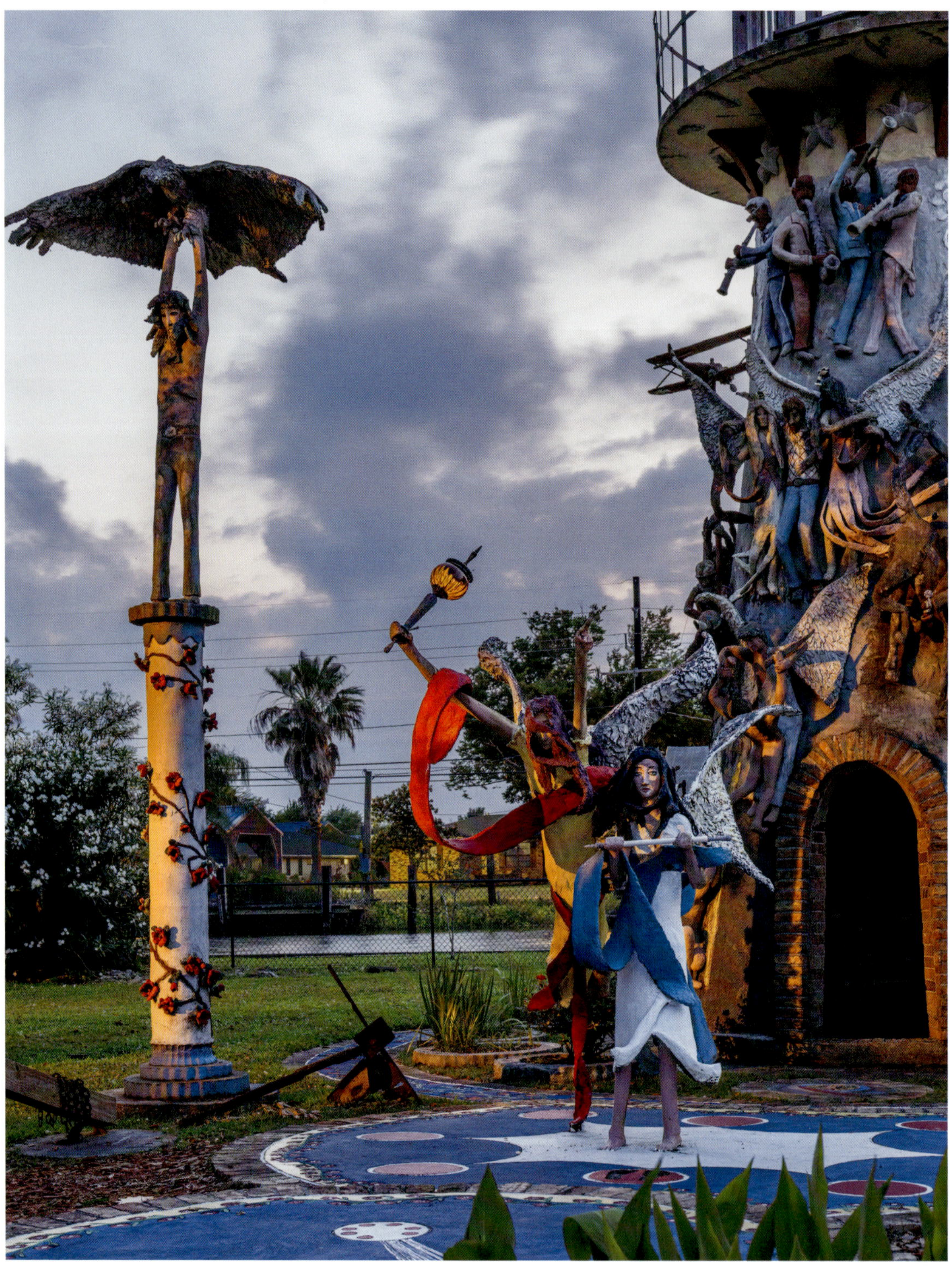

leads to the interior, and the exterior is encircled with a complex narrative of bas-relief and fully three-dimensional figures from history and mythology. Surface paintings—some with slight texture or depth—complement the sculpted chronicles with smaller-scale landscapes and motifs that imply perspective and a longer-range view behind the foregrounded dioramas.

Included among the dimensional motifs is a three-masted ship with billowing sails, portrayed at a significantly reduced scale in comparison to the figures on its shared wall space. Perhaps it is a patriotic reference to the *Mayflower* and the arrival of the European settlers, or perhaps it is linked more locally to the annual Blessing of the Fleet, where small boats pass down the adjacent bayou for a festive benediction. Figures on the exterior lighthouse walls showcase the soldiers who planted the American flag on Iwo Jima; a quartet of New Orleans-style jazz musicians; cowboys and their horses; a German World War I biplane; Native Americans in various poses, including one riding a pinto pony; God with luxuriant flowing hair; and helpful angels. In several instances figures are being pulled up toward the higher levels of the lighthouse: for example, an angel with bent arms strains to lift a naked sinner and a cowboy throws a lasso to another to drag him and his horse to safety. Perhaps this reflects Hill's belief that we need to place faith in both God and man to accept the help that will enable us to escape from our sins and troubles. Hill also rigged up a hose to the top of the lighthouse that could be connected in order to allow the tower to function as a fountain: the water cascading down the painted-blue side amplifies the sensation of a waterfall.

Flanking the lighthouse are two freestanding pillars, each topped with another three-dimensional self-portrait, arms upraised or outstretched, which appears to show Hill at the moment before he is lifted off by eagles. These birds are imbued with varying symbolism within Christian iconography, but they are often associated with Christ's resurrection, so perhaps here they presage Hill's hope for his own redemption. Another eagle, with outstretched wings, is mounted at the pinnacle of the slightly domed lighthouse roof. Just below the open platform balcony, the tower walls are ringed with bas-relief, five-pointed stars, perhaps conjoining the spiritual and patriotic nature of the eagle and star motifs, a not-uncommon theme among Southerners in general and art environment creators in particular.

Hill was reticent about interpreting his work, saying little more than it described what he had discovered about life and living, and he would toss inquiries back by asking visitors to determine on their own what they understood the different elements to mean. Numerous questions remain, such as whether a branched, flame-like form displayed alone within an expansive disc might refer to Moses's burning bush or to the flames of hell; this motif is frequently repeated in smaller scale as headdresses worn by his constructed angels. In conjunction with most of the other imagery on this site, this symbol seems to lend significant visual support to the idea of a journey from sin and transgression toward forgiveness and salvation on both communal and personal levels.

Some of Hill's self-portraits, such as the one showing his bleeding heart, might be seen as sacrilegious—they suggest that he took over Christ's suffering on behalf of humanity. This work, however, is mounted on top of a circular concrete pad that is inscribed "Enter In To My Heart...It is Em[p]ty;" perhaps in reference to his private grief and sense of loss. On the lighthouse itself, Hill's figure's face is painted half black and half white, and may refer to the good and evil found in every human. It is notable that both the vertical and horizontal pathways—the former encircling the lighthouse and the latter laid out in wavy paths between the sculptures as one wanders through the *Garden*—combine sacred and decidedly secular motifs. Perhaps Hill was using his creations as a way to assuage his personal struggles in the real world by referencing the more apocryphal battles described in Biblical texts.

In 2000, barely 10 years after he had begun to create his dense environment, the landlord who had sanctioned Hill's occupancy of the site passed away and Hill was served with a notice of eviction by the new owners as a result of his lack of care of the grounds and his failure to pay rent. In response, he simply walked away from the site, abandoning his work without providing guidance for either future upkeep or destruction, but not before first knocking the head off the sculpture of Christ as he left and scrawling "Hell is Here, Welcome" on his kitchen cabinets. Neighbors recall that he had seemed increasingly troubled in those later years and had come to repudiate his religion, despite its obvious earlier central importance to his life and his art. Since that time, although he had indicated to neighbors that he was going to see his brother in Missouri, his specific whereabouts have not been disclosed by his family, although they have indicated he is alive and well.

Prompted by local academicians, the Kohler Foundation purchased the site and worked with conservators, sculptors, and an architect to protect and restore Hill's work and to build, with the Army Corps of Engineers, a bulkhead to hold back the bayou waters to reduce erosion. (Additional conservation work was required after Hurricane Ida in 2021 significantly damaged the site; it had earlier been flooded by Hurricanes Katrina and Gustav.) The site was gifted by Kohler to nearby Nicholls State University, and it is now managed by the Art Department. Since 2002 it has been open to the public during daylight hours.

THE ARTIST FUSED THE RELIGIOUS WITH THE EVERYDAY, REVEALING HIS THOUGHTS ABOUT LIFE AND LIVING, FORGIVENESS AND SALVATION.

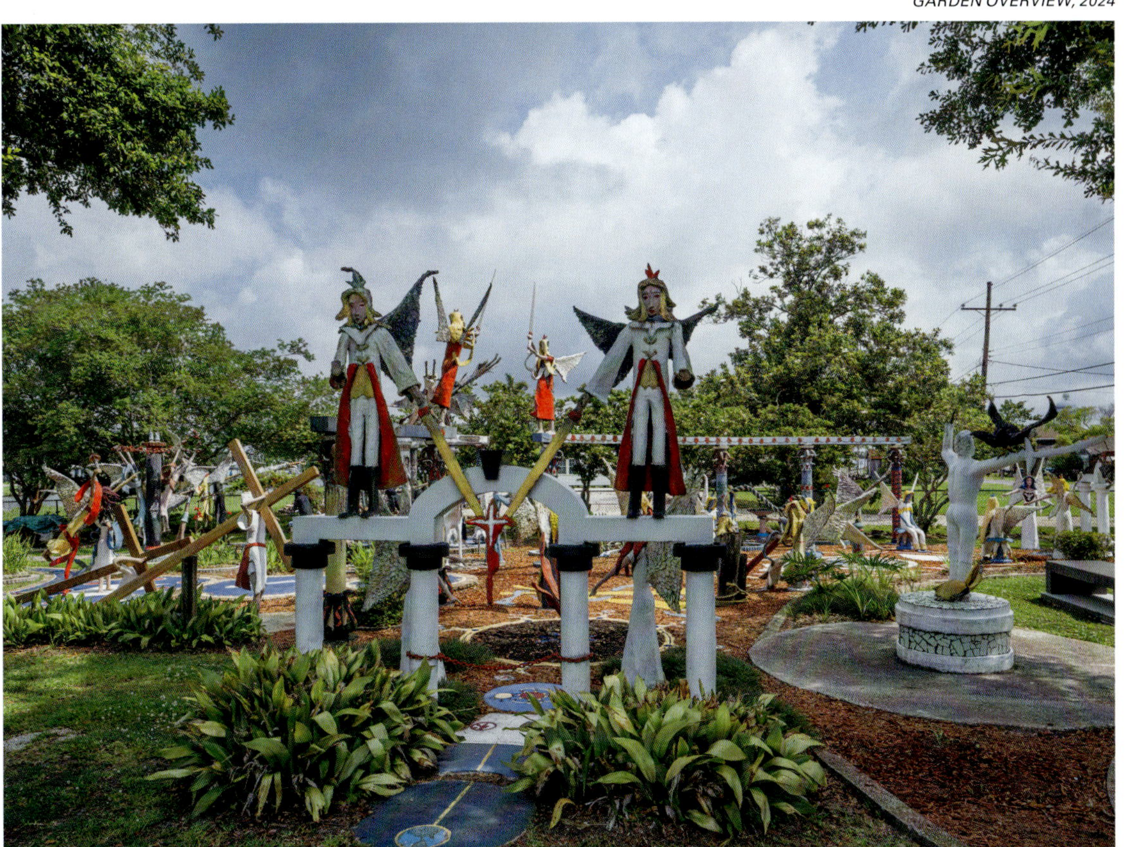

VINCE HANNEMANN

CATHEDRAL OF JUNK

AUSTIN, TEXAS

Hannemann (b. 1963) has been building site-specific, found-object assemblages since he was 16 years old. Born in Stuttgart, his German father was an architect who later managed the state museums in Baden-Wurttemberg. After he and his American mother—whose multiple careers included translator, English teacher, nurse, and acupuncturist—divorced when Vince was six years old, he and his brother and two sisters moved with her back to the Bronx to be near her parents. They kept on the move, traveling cross country more than once, until she settled in Santa Fe, New Mexico. It was here that Vince completed junior high and high school. After his mother remarried and moved with her new husband to Idaho, he accompanied them, repeating his last year of high school so that he could obtain residency and cheaply attend the University of Idaho. He spent a year taking classes with the intention of becoming an architect like his father, but he did not respond well to either the curriculum or the social scene, and he decided, first, that he would rather be an artist and, second, that he did not need to attend school to make that happen. He understood even then that the most important thing was to have the drive to follow through on his ideas and to leave himself open to the experiences, media, and techniques that would help him realize his visions.

After leaving the university, he moved back to Santa Fe and began working in the bronze foundry of a girlfriend's father, and although he only worked there for a year, he picked up valuable technical skills. By then his mother had moved on to Austin, and he followed her there in 1989, taking on a series of low-level jobs to make ends meet, from mowing lawns to working in health care as a certified nurse's aide. All along, he continued to make art in his spare time, primarily found-object sculptures assembled from various castoffs. He also began lining up hubcaps on the backyard fence of his small rental house, and soon started to incorporate his sculptures and an increasing number of found objects into a larger whole.

With no grand plan but concerned by the rampant consumerism of American society and intrigued by the possibilities inherent in repurposing, he worked for a time for an environmental nonprofit whose projects included the diversion of recyclable objects from landfills. This provided a means for personal scavenging and collecting of salvaged objects, and he began to use them as the basis for his work, assembling them in an improvisational manner as he found them. By 1992, he had christened the evolving work *Yardspace Eleven*.

Although his work is largely hidden from public view in his modest residential neighborhood (just a tip of the high tower is visible above and behind his home's rooftop from the street), as people learned of his efforts, they began bringing him donations of their own castoffs and discards, and it became, on many levels, a community-sourced architectural sculpture. Nevertheless, Hannemann does not accept everything that is offered, and retains sole control over what is welcomed and what is declined: he has to feel that he can actually use offered material in a way that will further his aesthetic objectives. (He also makes a clear distinction between "trash" that needs to be thrown out, and "junk," which still has life left in it and can be repurposed.) Over time, his needs change, depending upon what he lacks or, conversely, has too much of: the structure is always evolving.

Hannemann's varied background contributed to his ability to evaluate the placement of the wide variety of materials that came to form what his mother, in 1992, renamed the *Cathedral of Junk*. Ultimately, he piled an estimated 60 tons of recycled resources onto a hollow but secure infrastructure whose multiple levels rise 35 feet high. He compared its growth to that of a spiraling nautilus, developing and evolving into something that is always different despite the relatively consistent menu of supplies. Winding interior stairwells provide access to the upper levels, and slender pathways snake underneath arched tunnel-like passages that open up into various rooms and nooks. Within, platforms and chambers with domed ceilings reinforce the architectural experience, as benches and seating areas provide space to rest and to contemplate. It is a vertical maze, due in large part to the improvisational manner of its construction.

The components range from actual building materials like bricks and trusses to vehicle parts (cars, bicycles, lawnmowers), furniture, toys, dolls, mannequins, signs, televisions, porcelain toilets, beads, bowling balls, garden ornaments, CDs, musical instruments, circuit boards, telephones, ladders, crutches, and tires. In addition, certain functioning signs and electrical components can be plugged in, lit up, and turned on. As appropriate, items are wired together, stacked, welded, or—particularly for smaller items—set into concrete columns,

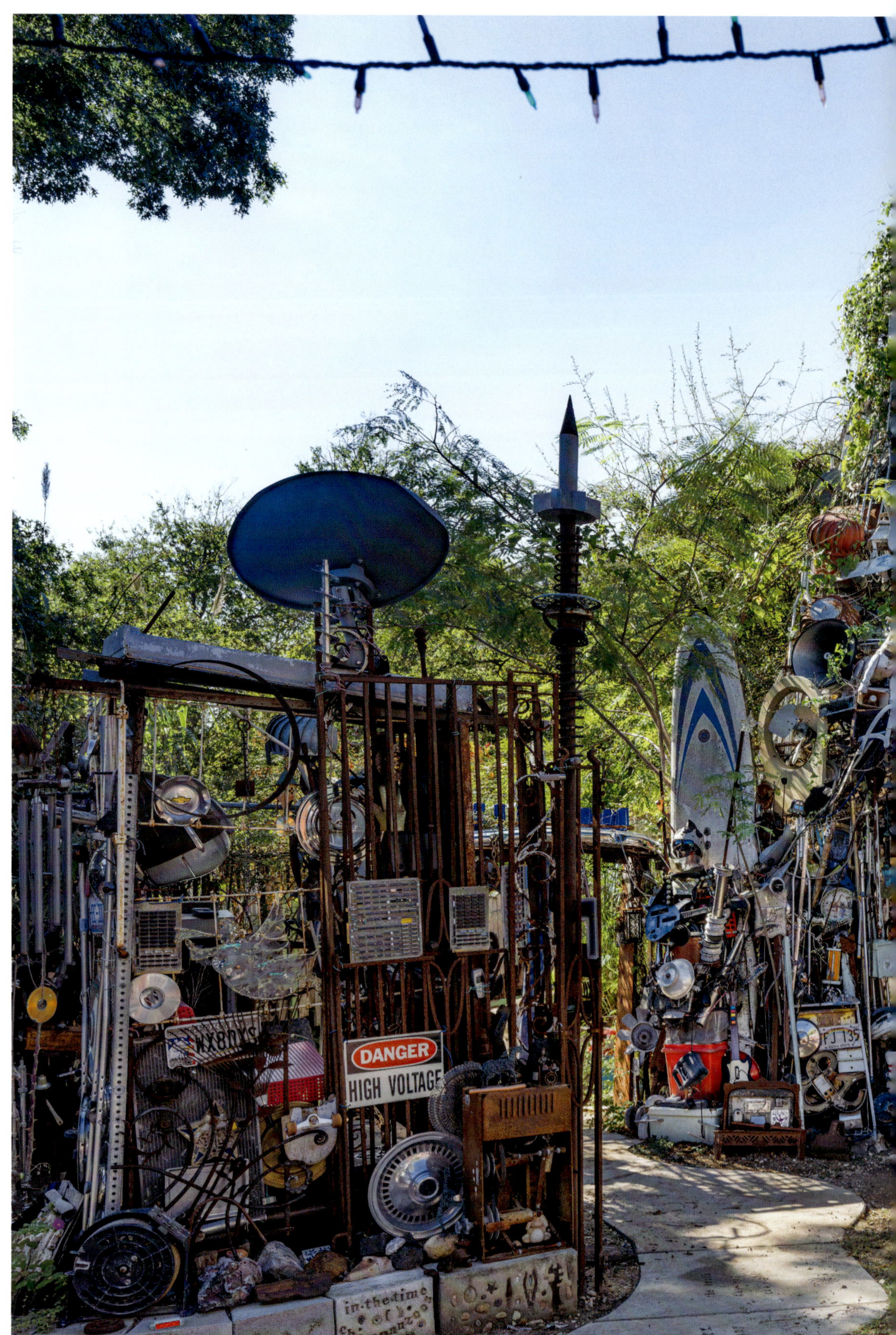
DANGER
HIGH VOLTAGE

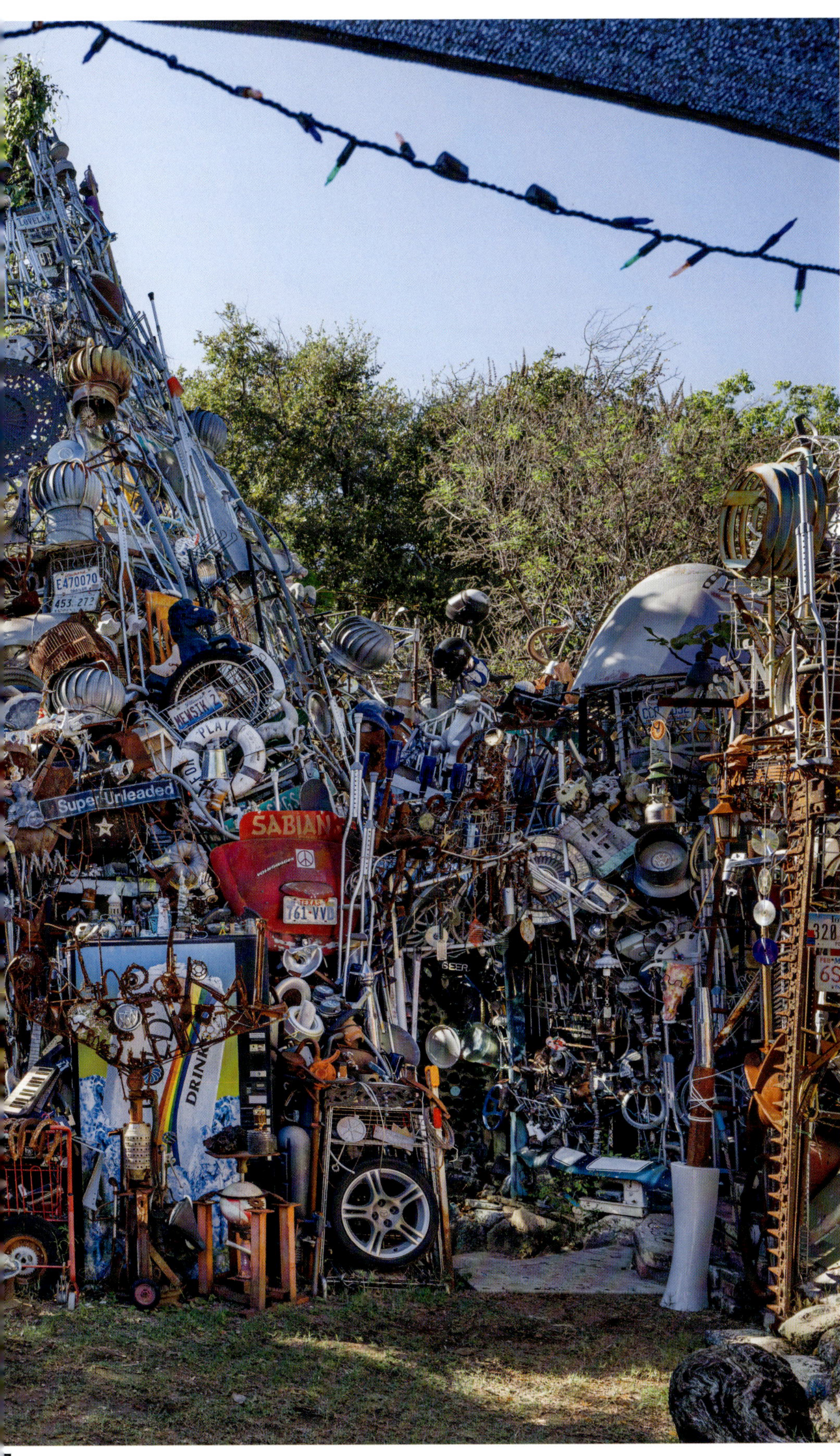
Super Unleaded
SABIAN
DRINK

stairs and risers, or walls. Care is taken to ensure that nothing is hollow, for otherwise the retention of rainwater would potentially compromise the stability of the whole. Over time, high winds and gravity naturally prod components to settle together, compacting them further and locking them into place.

Hannemann is thoughtful in how he arranges the different materials. The crutches, for example, are used in the highest tower to provide a visual exoskeleton in which he sees the ribs of Gothic arches, leading the eye up with consistent lines, color, and shapes. Hubcaps are used periodically as complementary interjections, their circular shapes and bas-relief indentations disrupting and softening the linearity of the crutches as they compel a more micro consideration of the whole. Looking up at this vaulted space from the interior, the various components lacily interweave in intricate patterns against the startlingly blue Texas sky, shaded, in some areas, by tendrils of creeping vegetation (he cuts the vines back each winter so that they do not overwhelm the construction). He has painted some sections to provide consistency of palette: one area may be all pink, while in another, red or yellow or blue may predominate. Appreciating their aesthetic transformations, the visual shapes of the assembled elements are foregrounded in a way that bypasses any focus on their prior functions or pre-established cultural implications.

Around the year 2000, Hannemann felt increasingly overwhelmed by his Frankensteinian creation and began to dismantle sections of the three-story tower. But he found he could not destroy what he had already spent 20 years creating, and he relocated those components to rebuild sections of the *Cathedral* in other areas. But as Austin became more gentrified, some neighbors alleged that the construction was a public safety hazard. In March 2010 it was found to be in violation of various zoning codes as an "unpermitted auxiliary structure," and Hannemann was given seven days to bring the *Cathedral* up to code. He could apply for an extension, but that would afford him only seven more days: for the entire seven-month process of trying to address their concerns, therefore, he went every week to file and be granted his extension.

Austin, like other cities, is threatened by technology, gentrification, and rapid development, and its bumper stickers and T-shirts had been imploring citizens to "Keep Austin Weird." So pro bono engineers, attorneys, and innumerable volunteers stepped up to assist. This process included complying with the requirements that Hannemann remove an estimated 40 tons of junk from the easement that had made up the front portion of the *Cathedral*, reduce the height to the 35-foot limit established by city ordinances, shrink the structure's footprint so that it maintained a five-foot setback from the property line, and calculate its weight-bearing capabilities in order to gauge the potential limits of human access. After meeting those terms and submitting drawings by a volunteer architect that codified the existing plans and elevation, the city provided a retroactive building permit and, after being deemed structurally safe by a city engineer, verified that the corpus of the structure could be preserved and sightseers could return.

While Hannemann laments the toll the process took, likening the trauma of demolishing and removing so much of the original structure to an amputation, he also believes that it was a good battle to fight. He knows that his work inspires young people, just like he himself was inspired by learning about Sabato Rodia's *Towers* (see page 332) by seeing an after-school special when he was young. Rodia gave him the conceptual permission to build the *Cathedral of Junk*, he asserts, and his work now offers permission to the next generation to spread their own wings. Young children are his biggest fans.

At times Hannemann insists that there was no weighty conceptualization underpinning the creation of the *Cathedral of Junk*—that it was just him having fun and building a "secret fort." Nevertheless, it is clear that it provides visual commentary about our society's emphasis on consumerism, even as he declines to conceptualize the monument as a didactic space or to overtly promote environmental activism: he prefers to let visitors draw their own conclusions.

EXTERIOR (DETAIL), 2021. PHOTO: VINCE HANNEMANN

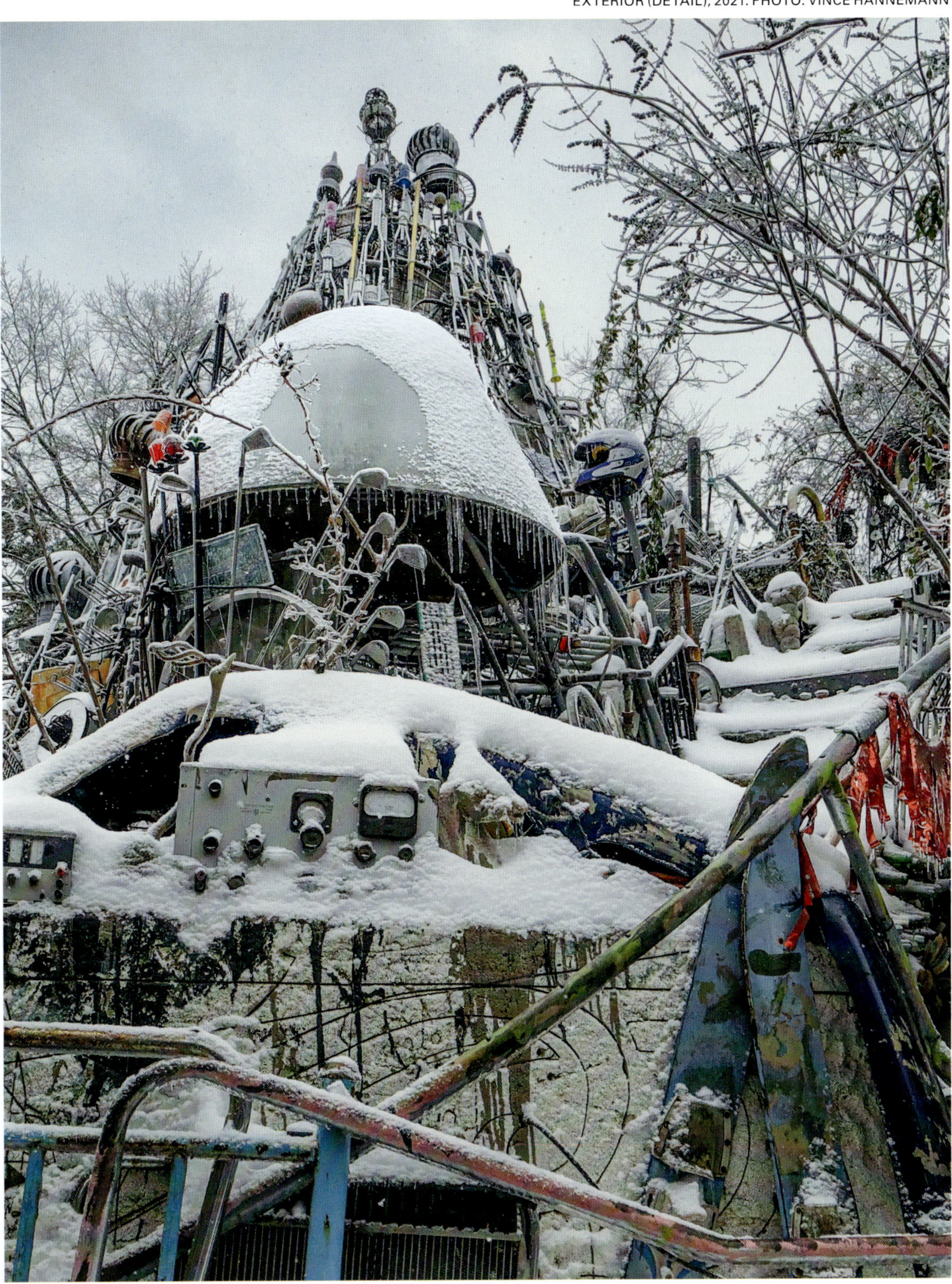

GROUND-LEVEL INTERIOR (DETAIL), 2024

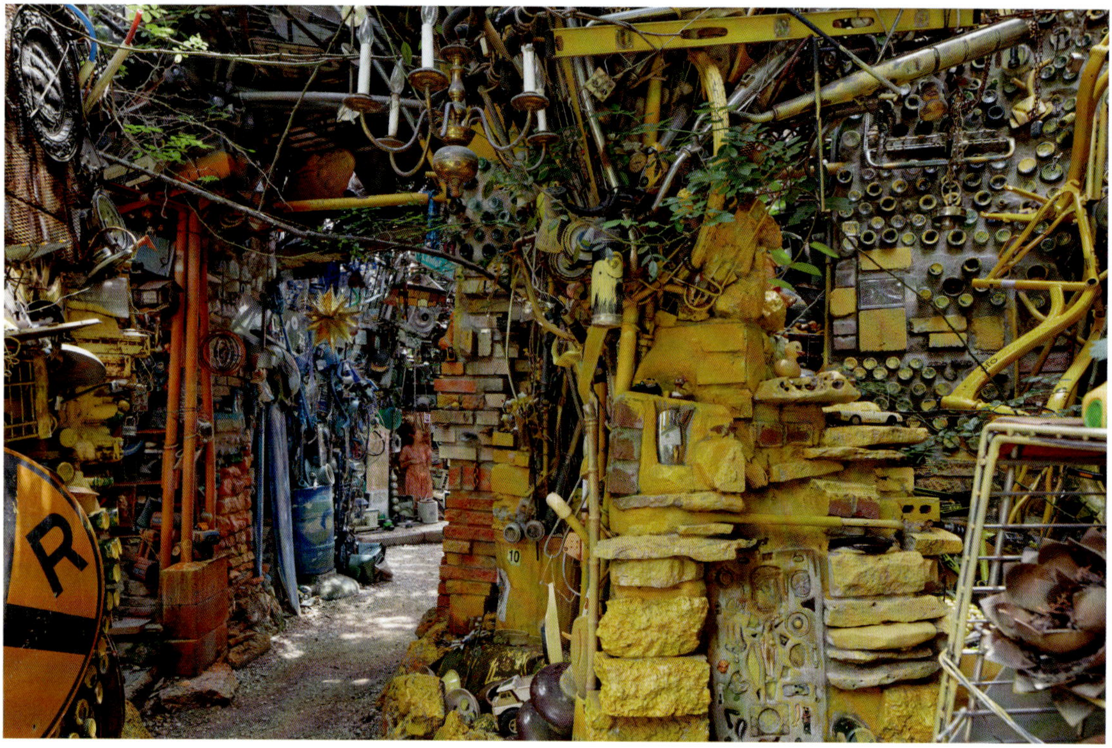

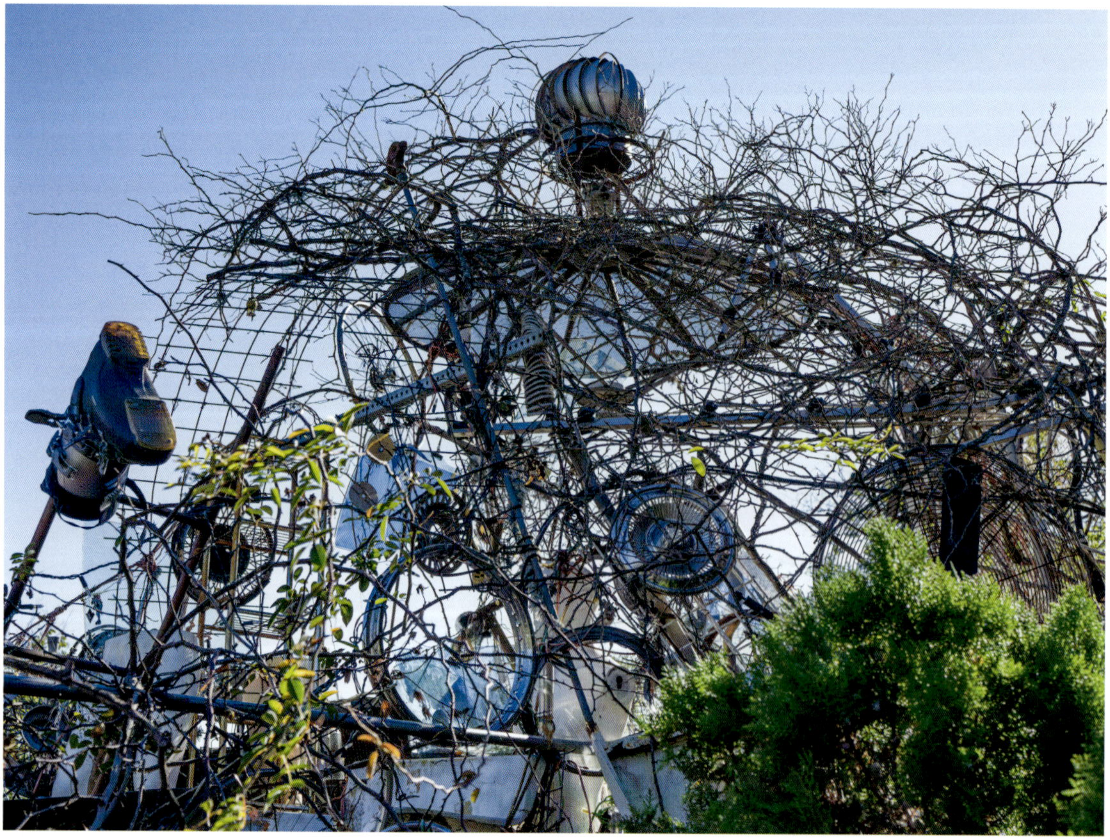

UPPER-LEVEL CROWN, 2024

But, when pressed, he shares a more profound observation. He has noted that time slows down for visitors when they approach and enter the *Cathedral*, as they take the time to experience personal connections with the assembled objects and sense the presence of the multilayered and multivalent reality that they envelop. And then later he sees how time speeds up again as they leave and return to their familiar circumstances and tasks. A trigger of forgotten memories or an opportunity to teach children about the kinds of objects their elders used is not just a superficial reflection; it collapses the time continuum and pushes us beyond three dimensions.

But this does not invalidate the joy of the experience: residents of and visitors to Austin have come to treat the site as a public space, celebrating weddings, birthdays, and bachelor parties there, showcasing it as the perfect "weird" stop for out-of-town guests, or scheduling an unusual field trip for homeschoolers. It has even been featured in music videos and a Hollywood film. It is an emphatic testament to the community's willingness to embrace the unique and celebrate creativity, and to preserve Hannemann's "happy mistakes," assembled over decades to provide a place of spirituality and play, both for his visitors and for himself.

HE BELIEVES THAT HIS WORK OFFERS A MODEL FOR THE NEXT GENERATION TO SPREAD THEIR OWN WINGS.

SABATO RODIA

—

TOWERS

LOS ANGELES, CALIFORNIA

The *Towers* in Watts are arguably the most renowned of U.S. art environments—indeed, they are one of the most recognizable of any of America's public art works in any genre. Yet their local fame, the international recognition that celebrates them, and the National Historic Landmark status that has honored them, mask a battle over their preservation—over their very worth—that has dragged on for almost 70 years.

Rodia (1879-1965), more commonly known as Simon or Sam rather than by his birth name Sabato, was born in the village of Ribottoli in Italy's southern Campania. Just before his 15th birthday, he followed an older brother to the United States. Little is known about his early years, except that after landing on the East Coast, he took various low-paying jobs in coal fields, quarries, railroads, and construction before making his way to the West Coast, passing through Seattle (where he married), the Bay Area (where it was said he helped to rebuild San Francisco after the 1906 earthquake and fire), and, finally, Southern California. In the process, he reformed his drinking habits and, outside a rented house in Long Beach, sculpted a gazebo and other garden ornaments, apparently his first artistic efforts. Between 1921 and 1923 he relocated to a small cottage on a 4,305-square-foot triangular site edging the Pacific Electric Railway Red Car tracks in Watts, an urban village annexed in 1926 to the City of Los Angeles.

The exact date of Rodia's initiation of his monumental endeavor is unknown, but starting in the early 1920s, he worked on them for over 30 years; when not employed in his day jobs, he was either constructing and decorating his *Towers* or amassing the materials necessary to do so. He combed the nearby railroad tracks for bits of glass and other discarded refuse that he could recycle into decorative surface treatment: green 7-Up and blue milk of magnesia bottles were especially attractive to him for their strong, saturated colors. He took the train to the beach to collect seashells and stones; broken pottery, tile, dishes, rocks, mirrors, and other found objects rounded out his palette.

Around his home a complex environment began taking shape, with fountains, niches, outdoor seating, a gazebo, "stalagmite" gardens, plazas, walkways, and the high conical towers, architectural in scale and impact. Every day Rodia added to what he had previously constructed: building, removing, rebuilding, transforming. He worked without scaffolding, forming the steel substructure by wedging the ends of metal beams under the railroad tracks, leaning over and pressing up, bending them to fit his need. A small, wiry man not even five feet tall, he slowly raised his *Towers* one short level at a time, using the structure itself as a ladder, a window-washer's belt around his waist, carrying a pail of wet concrete, his materials, and his simple tools. The *Towers* appear to have been built east to west, with each successive spire rising taller and showing greater economy of form and sophisticated construction methodology. He reinforced the vertical supports with horizontal bands circling the core, elegantly constricting the spokes as the spires rose in height, until the tallest tower, the westernmost, ascended to 99.5 feet, at that time the highest slender reinforced-concrete column in the world.

Alternating T-beams and angle irons, he spliced and overlapped their junctures, tying them together with chicken wire that he then tightly wrapped with wire mesh. The joints were not welded, bolted, or riveted together in any way, but many were configured in the most economically efficient structure possible: triangles developed into four-sided tetrahedrons, each tetrahedron having three triangles around each corner. These innovative "socket footing" connections have become known as the Rodia Joint.

He then covered the steel with a reinforced-concrete mortar, into which he pressed decorative glass and ceramic fragments that also served the important function of protecting the substructure from rain and moisture, a fitting crust for the essential simplicity and functional formalism of his aesthetic. This construction technique was a radical innovation and anticipated the thin-shelled ferro-cement structures of trained architects by at least five years. The light weight of this type of construction facilitates the building of tall structures, while successfully supporting tension and compression loads.

Rodia ultimately erected 17 separate structures on this site, all created in an additive manner. His works were by no means constructed haphazardly, but nevertheless, whenever he was asked (as he often was) why he never had anyone help him, his answer was always the same: he himself did not know what his next steps would be, so he could not possibly direct anyone else in the process. In addition to his ongoing modifications, after the 1933 Long Beach earthquake—which, at 6.3 on the Richter scale, damaged the foundation of the new Los Angeles City Hall, five miles further away from the epicenter, but had little impact on the *Towers*—Rodia made significant changes to strengthen his work. He added outside columns, intersecting rings, and decorative buttresses on the easternmost and center towers, and also widened and added weight to their bases in an intuitive understanding of the need for engineering redundancy.

As Rodia worked through the 1920s, '30s, and '40s, Watts was changing. From an ethnically diverse district of small Anglo, Mexican, and African-American homes alternating with larger Japanese truck farms, the Anglos moved on and the Japanese were interned, their farms turned into a higher-density, more homogenous residential district. During the Second World War, rumors swirled that the *Towers* were transmission stations sending classified information to the enemy Japanese (Tokyo Rose was believed to have been from Watts), and later they were alleged to be a source for passing secrets to the Communists. The aging Rodia, increasingly isolating himself from his neighbors, was angry at the world and what he saw as its disintegrating values. Contemporaries reported that he stopped expanding by the mid-1940s, spending the next decade finessing details and repairing damage that was already starting to appear. Local children, gleaning from their parents that he was a crazy old man—a characterization of which Rodia was well aware—threw rocks and climbed over the walls to smoke and drink. Treasure hunters unearthed sections and smashed crockery, convinced there was a fortune buried underneath. Debris and trash accumulated.

Finally, in 1954 Rodia packed up, deeded his property to a neighbor, filed his last will and testament with the City, and moved away. He never returned, and when asked what should be done with the *Towers*, he shrugged. The neighbor soon sold the property to another, and Rodia's cottage burned to the ground in 1955 or 1956, likely a result of arson, as the area within the ornamented walls continued to deteriorate.

In late 1958 or the spring of 1959, two film-industry creatives were visiting the neglected site when they met and proposed a sale to the neighbor for $20 down—all they had in their pockets at the time—plus a promise to pay a total of $3,000. They hoped to preserve the *Towers*; it was only later, when they applied for a permit to build an on-site caretaker's cottage, that they discovered that in 1957 the City had issued a demolition order, condemned the structures as "an unauthorized public hazard," and prohibited further development until the *Towers* were removed. They based this order on the lack of filed records indicating a "rational plan" that abided by generally accepted engineering and construction principles. As they believed repair was impossible, they mandated destruction.

The long history of grass-roots support to save the *Towers*, beginning with the 1959 "stress test" that proved its structural stability, continues to the present. There are many positives: this site was, in 1962, the first art environment to be the sole subject of a major museum exhibition; those who participated in the dramatic civil revolt in Watts in 1965 did not damage or even touch the *Towers*; building on earlier art classes and cultural programming, in 1970 the Watts Towers Art Center was opened and continues an active schedule of events and exhibitions; and its 1978 transfer of ownership to the State of California and its designations at municipal, state, and national levels (U.S. National Register of Historic Places, U.S. National Historic Landmark, California Historical Landmark, Simon Rodia State Historic Park, and Los Angeles Historic-Cultural Monument) have validated its importance. Sadly, this extraordinary recognition has not prevented deterioration or impeded corruption and exploitation from spoiling several different conservation campaigns.

Following successful lawsuits, it was not until 2011 that the Los Angeles County Museum of Art took responsibility for conservation. Approaching the problem scientifically, they connected sensors to monitor changes in heat, wind, and vibrations, and the resultant data suggested new treatment protocols to slow the deterioration caused by natural forces, including solar radiation, moisture seepage, and seismic stresses. This was aided by advances in the construction industry and building sciences and the development of new materials that helped to address and mitigate a variety of complications. To date, more than $6 million

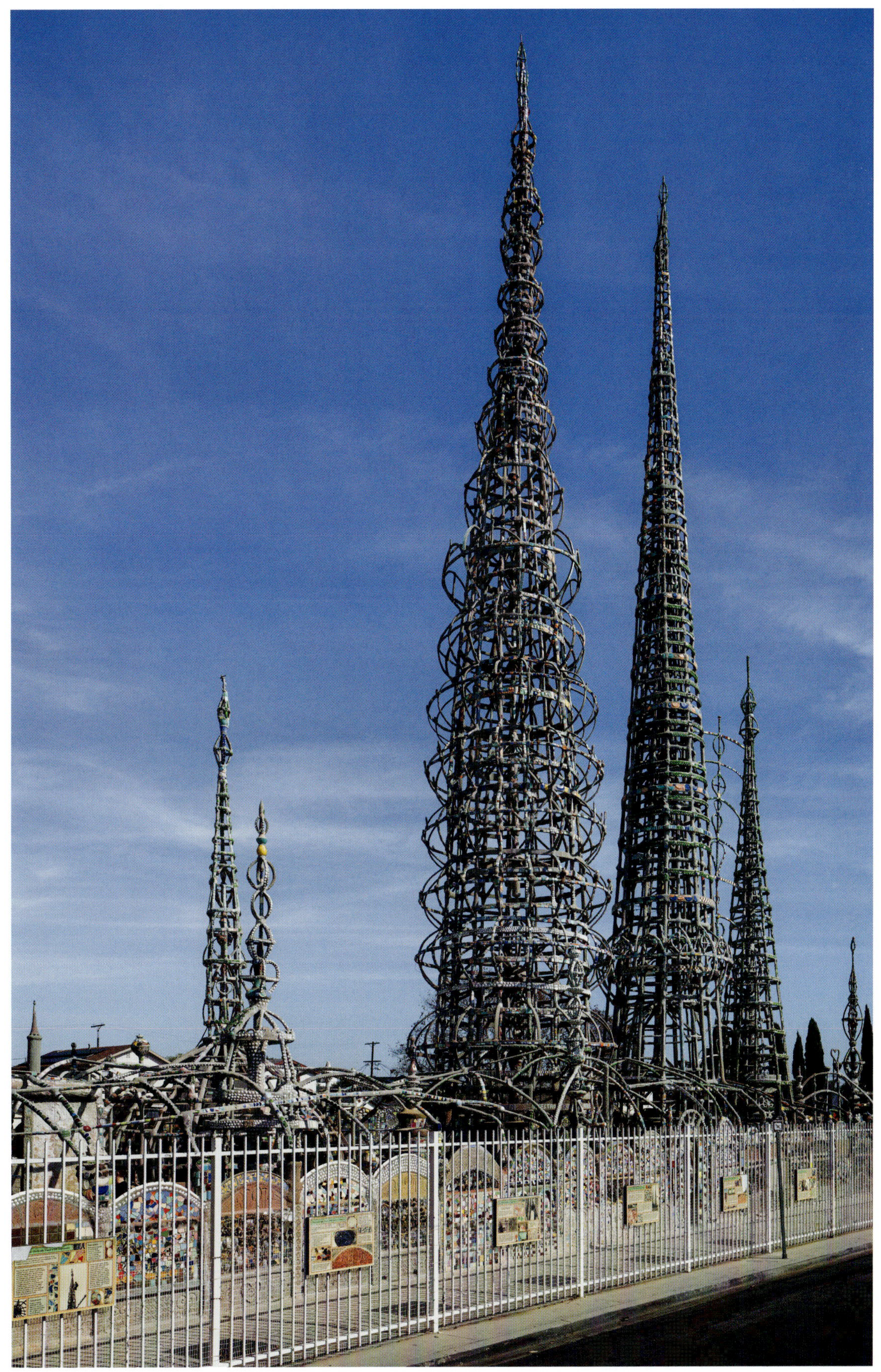

TOWERS, VIEW FROM THE WEST, 2025

WATTS COMMUNITY, CA. 1964. PHOTO: SEYMOUR ROSEN, © SPACES ARCHIVES, COURTESY JOHN MICHAEL KOHLER ARTS CENTER

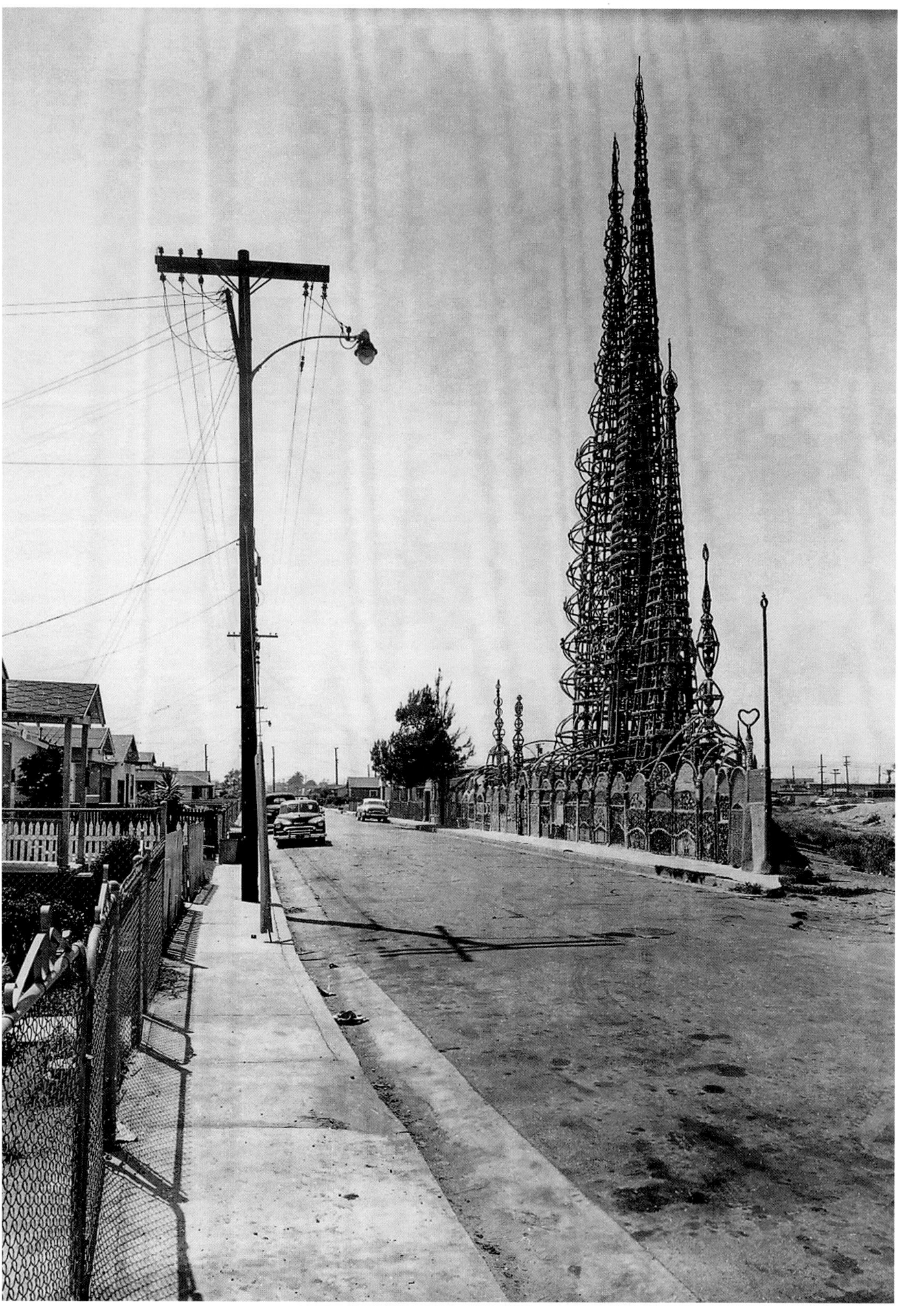

have been expended by federal, state, and municipal governments, private foundations, and hundreds of individual supporters, but the *Towers* are not yet secure and stabilized, nor are they immune from political grandstanding and proposals for misuse.

In other situations governmental ownership might be a good solution. But the bottom line, as we have seen here, is that because art and architectural works of this nature cannot be hermetically stored and protected, they need continued vigilance and a concerted, long-term effort from a broad base of local community members—backed up by art and preservation professionals internationally—to ensure their survival. Without this broad acceptance, we risk losing such marvels forever.

THE MOST RENOWNED U.S. ART ENVIRONMENT HAS BEEN AT THE CENTER OF PUBLIC CONTROVERSY FOR ALMOST 70 YEARS.

THE INNOVATIVE "RODIA JOINT:" TRIANGLES WIRED TOGETHER INTO TETRAHEDRONS WITHOUT NAILS, BOLTS, OR RIVETS, 1976. PHOTO: SEYMOUR ROSEN, © SPACES ARCHIVES, COURTESY JOHN MICHAEL KOHLER ARTS CENTER

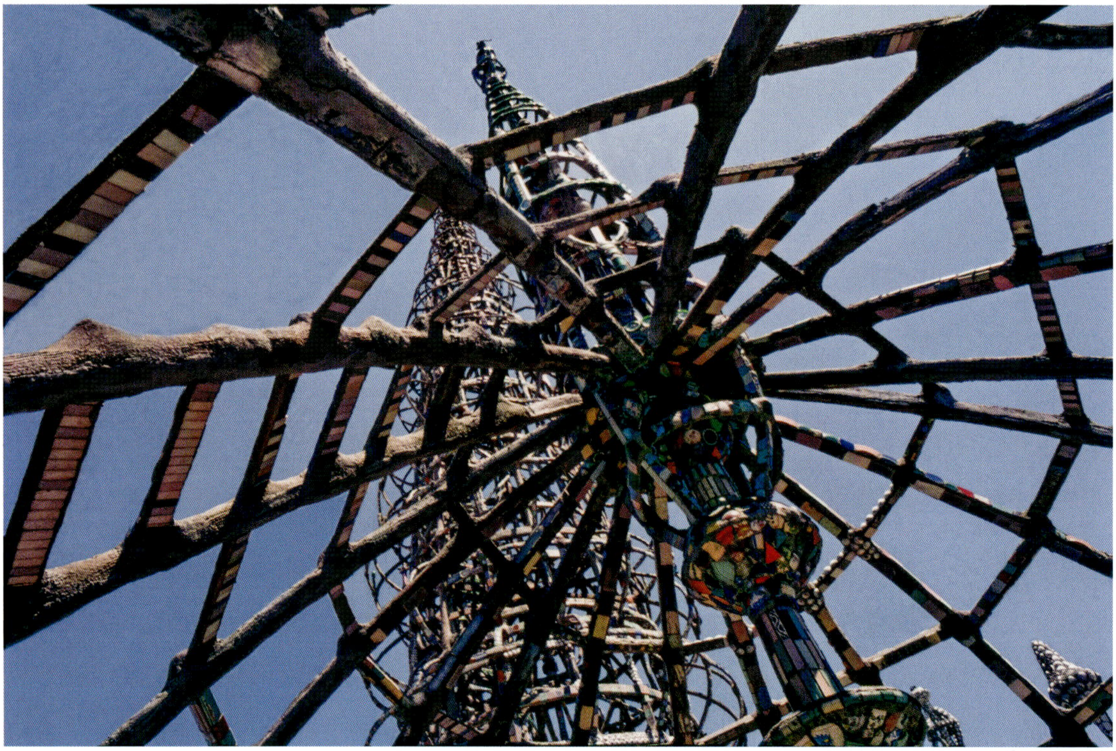

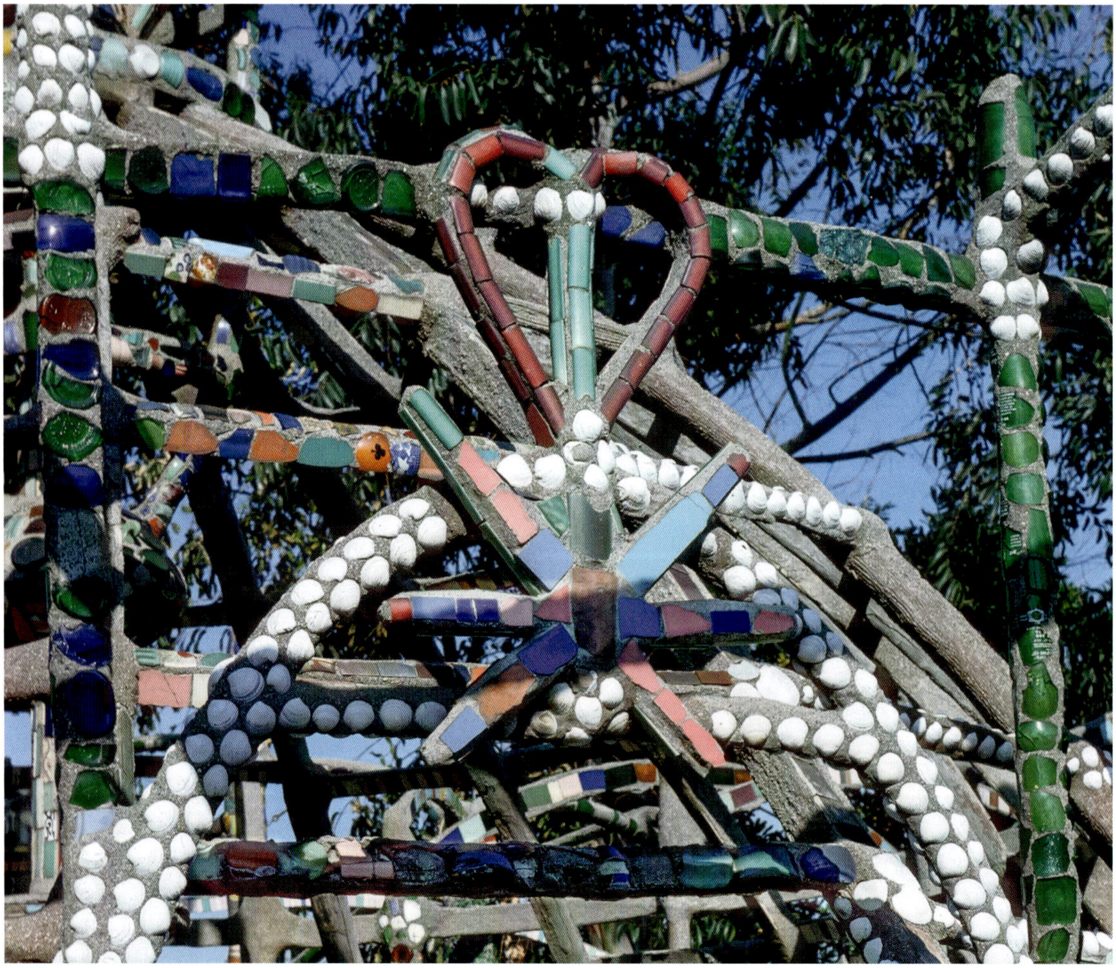

ARCHED ENTRY LEADING INTO INTERIOR GAZEBO, 1975. PHOTO: SAM HERNÁNDEZ

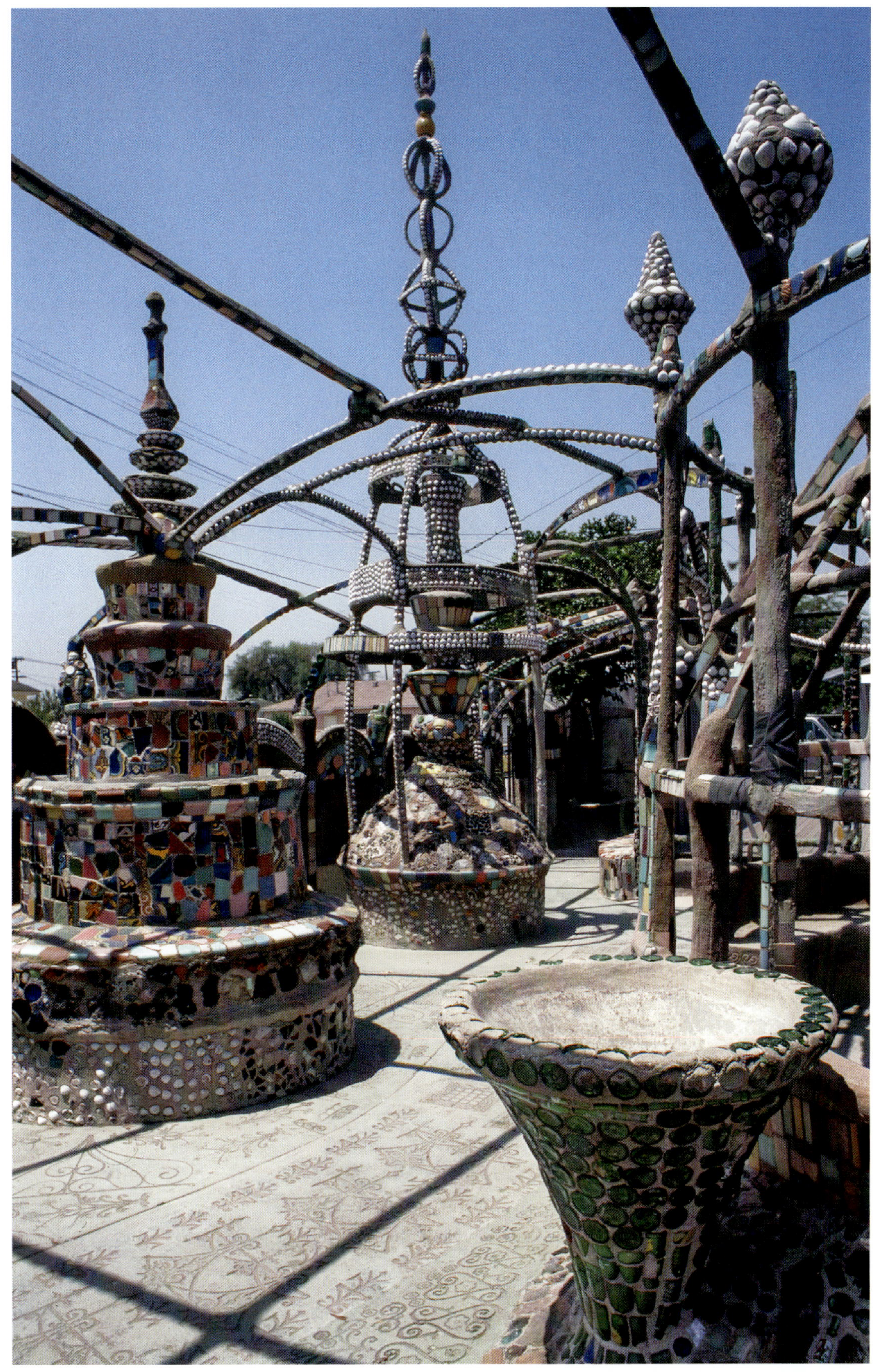

INTERIOR STRUCTURES WITHIN *TOWERS* COMPLEX, 1978.
PHOTO: SEYMOUR ROSEN © SPACES ARCHIVES, COURTESY JOHN MICHAEL KOHLER ARTS CENTER

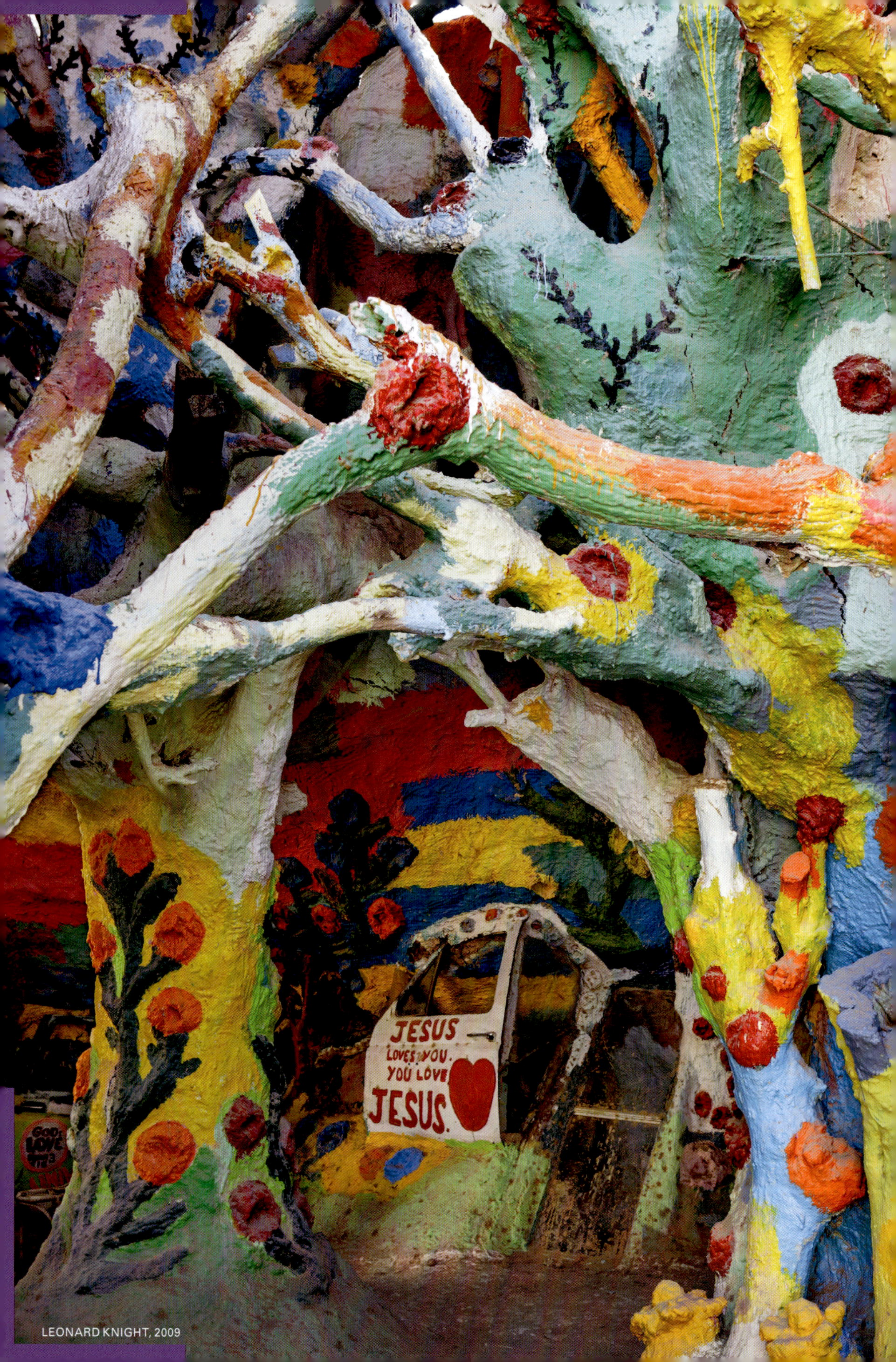

LEONARD KNIGHT, 2009

CHAPTER 5

A HIGHER CALLING

SITES OF HONOR, MEMORY, AND DEVOTION

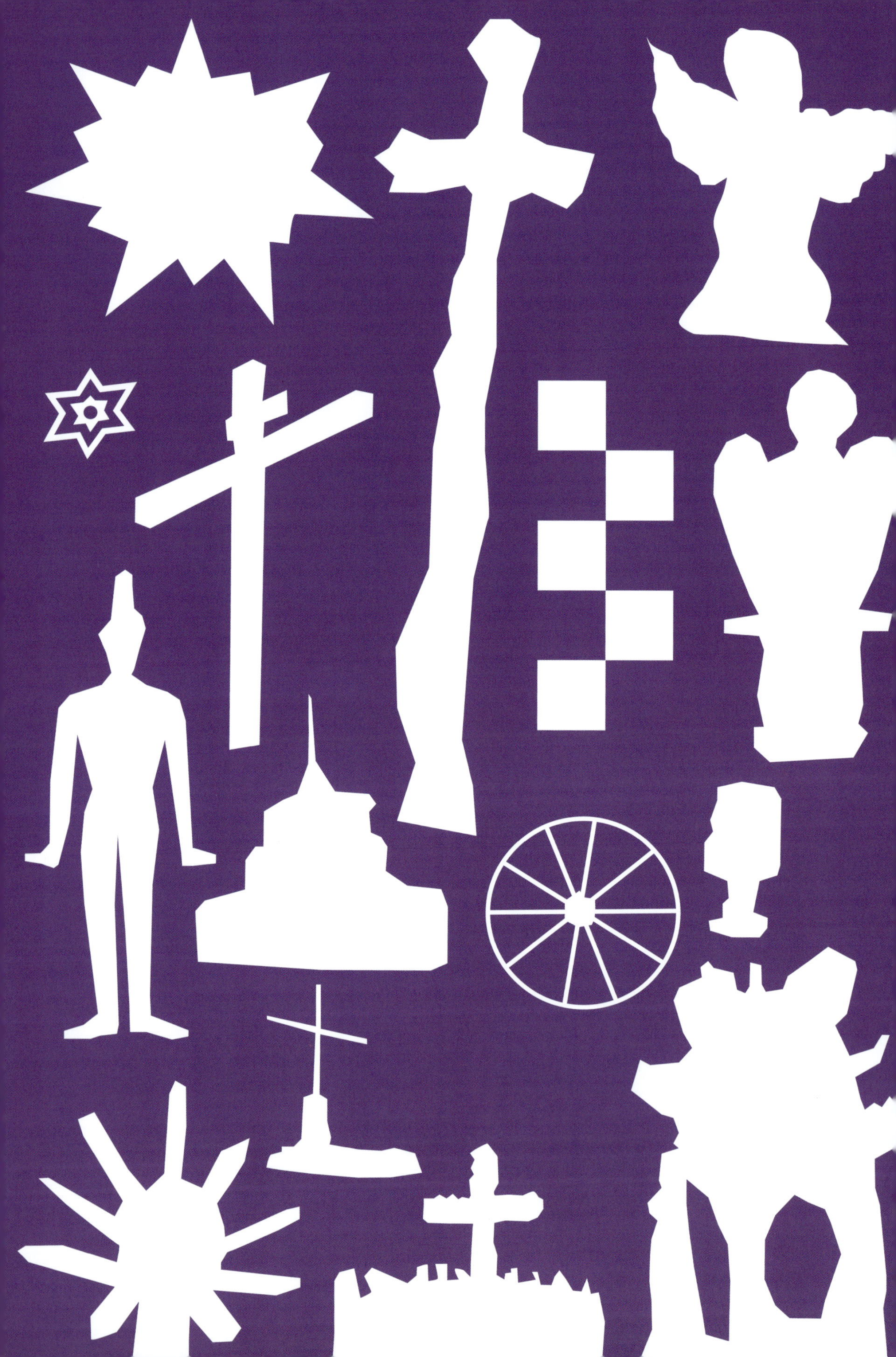

The preceding pages have shown how the sources of inspiration fueling the construction of art environments are many and diverse, but of all the different variants, it appears that the majority of U.S. sites are assembled out of a desire to pay homage to a concept larger than ourselves. The environments presented in this chapter interpret this category broadly: spiritual or religious devotion is the most significant component, but history and ethnicity are also important drivers, as are personal philosophies and tributes. Less loftily—and less often—we find constructions that symbolize a path to physical or emotional healing and comfort.

Like most others, these sites do not necessarily begin with a "grand plan" or fully fleshed-out idea of the objective the structure will fulfill. And, like others, over the course of creation they offer makers innovative avenues of self-expression and ways of engaging in paths of personal discovery that illuminate meaning. They also help the creator generate a sense of community, however that is defined, and by presenting their visual and dimensional interpretations to the public, they provide opportunities to solicit or foster human connections. As the makers work alone, a primary goal becomes the collective engagement of family, neighbors, community members, and even visitors from afar.

Because the majority of the U.S. sites that fall within this classification are associated with Christianity, one might expect that the expressions would be somewhat abbreviated, based on the assumption that most onlookers already understand the basis and arc of the narratives. This does not always appear to be true, however, as some of the older sites, which tend to be centered in Catholicism rather than in more evangelical branches, may be slightly more enigmatic to non-Christians because they may use certain motifs or even a single word to reference a broader concept. In contrast, many of the more recent creations are more literal and emphatic in their exhortations for visitors to follow this one way, as if there is no time to waste if one wants to be saved. As if, by persuading visitors and viewers to follow, the makers will themselves be saved.

Perhaps the great number of sites in this grouping also explains why so many of these environments now exist only in our memories or photographs: as so many were erected, there were so many more to lose. W.C. Rice's *Cross Garden* in Prattville, Alabama, and Mitchell Szewczyk's *House of Crosses* in Chicago are two that defiantly proclaimed their commitment to their belief systems, advocating rather strenuously, in visual terms, for others to heed the same path. Horace Burgess's *Treehouse* in Crossville, Tennessee, reflected a different aesthetic and manner but likewise was a serious place for people to rekindle their faith; David Westley "Nick" Connell's *East of Echo* cave in San Diego was reminiscent of the European grotto tradition; Mona Webb utilized part of her installations at *The Way House of Light* in Madison, Wisconsin, as a nondenominational shrine; and Osker Gilchrist's home and office in Nichols, South Carolina, reflected African healing traditions.

We did not have the space here to cover certain other U.S. sites that fall within this thematic category. In some cases, the installations did not reach a significantly monumental magnitude, such as Paul and Matilda Wegner's *Grotto* in Cataract, or Fred Zimmerman's *Garage* in New Glarus, both in Wisconsin; Madeline Buol's *Grotto*, originally in Dubuque, and E.O. Allen's *Mini Grotto* in Harris, both in Iowa; Claude Melton's *Christian Nativity Rock Museum* in Kearney, Missouri; Ramón Márquez's *Grotto* at Saint Mary's Parish in Gilroy, California; or Father Scheier's *St. Peter's Rock Grotto* in Farmer, South Dakota. Other sites were excluded because they were miniaturized versions of architectural structures; noteworthy examples are Brother Joseph Zoettl's *Ave Maria Grotto* in Cullman, Alabama; Catherine Bastian's *Ham Can Shrines* in Earlville, Iowa; and John Greco's *Holy Land USA* in Waterbury, Connecticut, which, at 18 acres, is the largest in the United States. Still others were more garden- or grotto-like than architectural, such as Father Phillip Ottavi's *Geode Grotto* in Jasper, Indiana; William H. Lightner's *Our Mother of Sorrows Grotto* in Cedar Rapids, Iowa; and Father Philip J. Wagner's *Rudolph Grotto* in Wisconsin. And, of course, there are also numerous other nonextant religious or devotional environments that cannot be considered architectural construction, including some whose components were relocated to museums. In general, perhaps more than the creators of most of the other built environments in this book, the makers featured in this chapter have not considered themselves to be artists or architects: their intentions and guiding stars—despite the materiality of their labors—were not tethered to mere earthly concerns.

PROPHET ISAIAH ROBERTSON

—

SECOND COMING HOUSE

NIAGARA FALLS, NEW YORK

Like Howard Finster (see page 424) and Juanita Leonard (see page 394), Robertson (1947–2020) came to his dual, complementary commitments to artwork and ministry later in life. Born in Jamaica, he developed a strong faith thanks to his mother, who died when he was only eight years old. Then, vowing to emulate Christ, he became a carpenter. He immigrated to the Toronto area at age 24, where he plied his trade, and in 2004 he moved to the border town of Niagara Falls, New York, obtaining his citizenship through marriage. There he continued his contract carpentry work while also buying, renovating, and reselling inexpensive houses around town.

Among other projects, he was hired by the Mount Erie Baptist Church, where he was a member of the congregation, to renovate its walls and ceiling. Rather than simply Sheetrocking and painting the broad expanses, however, Robertson felt this church was worthy of greater devotion, so he independently decided to sheath the surfaces in oak paneling. He cut the boards along grain patterns and laid them out in interlocking configurations, and, as he worked, he came to perceive Biblical motifs in these organic shapes. He also overlaid many sections of the paneling with familiar Christian forms—arches, crosses, stars, sunbursts, triangles, and divided circles—some of which he later repeated on the façade of his own home. The different woods and stains harmonize with each other in a rich-looking and sumptuously elegant composition. He believed that God had called him to ornament the Church in this way, and he identified this as his first prophecy.

This meditative process turned his thoughts to further faith-based action, and he came to believe that he had a mandate from God to decorate his own home, located nearby on a main street in a residential neighborhood. In 2006, he ringed his property with over 1,000 candles, and then, with no preparatory plans or sketches, began to assemble an elaborate and kaleidoscopic series of painted, mounted, and freestanding wooden motifs. He asserted that he was simply the vehicle for this creation, and God was working through his carpenter hands. He described this as his second prophecy, which foretold that the Second Coming of Christ would take place in 2014. In order to increase the number of people who would ascend to the heavens as part of the accompanying Rapture, Robertson amplified his artistic production in intensity and quantity, believing that if they were moved by his work they would be saved as surely as if they had accepted Christ's teachings in an established church.

The most compelling component of his extravagant installation was the monumental, 25-foot-high wooden *Healing Cross* that he erected at the head of the driveway adjacent to his home. Far from an austere linear form, it is festooned with a myriad brightly painted cutout forms—diamonds, stars, hearts, crosses, bells, arrows, circles, sunbursts, numbers—each of which, according to Robertson, was conscientiously placed and imbued with sacred or natural symbolism. (Some of this symbolism was conventionally comprehensible, but other designs needed to be personally decrypted by him.) Most of the elements are nailed together and layered directly on top of each other, but some of the forms, anchored with horizontal supports, float further out into three-dimensional space. Among these are representations of the nails used in the Crucifixion, which extend out from abstracted triangular shapes symbolizing Christ's hands.

While the *Second Coming House* is dedicated to Christ's prophesied return and the salvation possible if one accepts his teachings, the Old Testament also informs the complex composition, with Stars of David and motifs that Robertson described as representative of the Twelve Tribes of Israel. So too does Islam, symbolized by assorted crescent shapes.

Robertson filled in the negative spaces above and below the transverse arms of the cross, extending the structure across the width of the driveway with low angled latticework fences. He ultimately attached the construction to the house with a similarly adorned doorway, itself representing the heavenly Pearly Gates. The whole is frontally organized, emphasizing the view from the street; the back of the structure is generally not addressed or painted in other than a monochrome.

The house itself and the front yard are likewise adorned. While he used the same color palette as on the *Healing Cross*—generally high-gloss enamel house paint brushed straight out of the can—and many of the same symbols and motifs utilized on the *Cross* similarly appear on the house, there are also a smaller number of more narrative, albeit still abstracted, designs. These include Gabriel's Trumpets, crowns, lit candles, fish and bread "to feed the

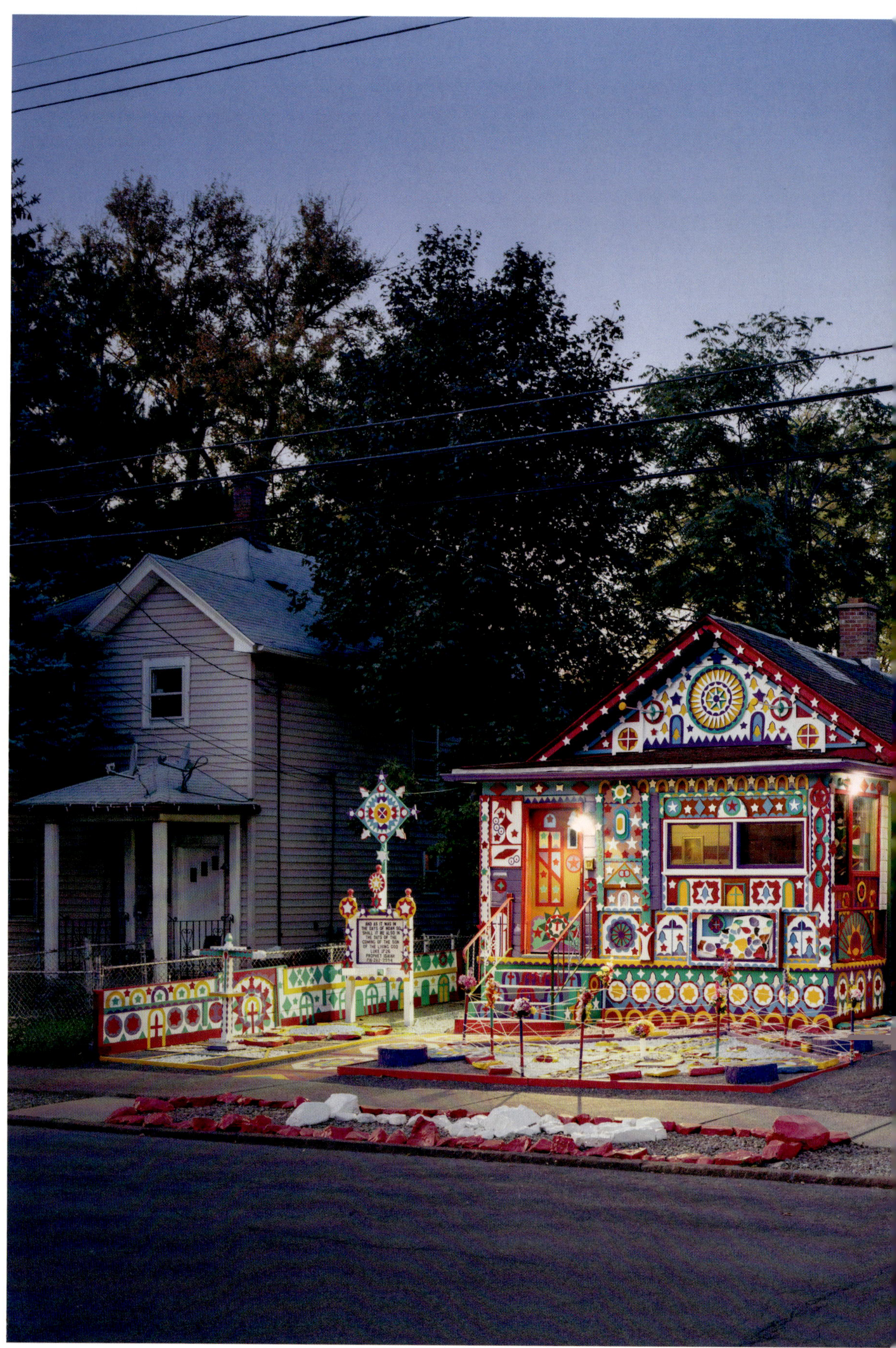

EXTERIOR OVERVIEW, 2011

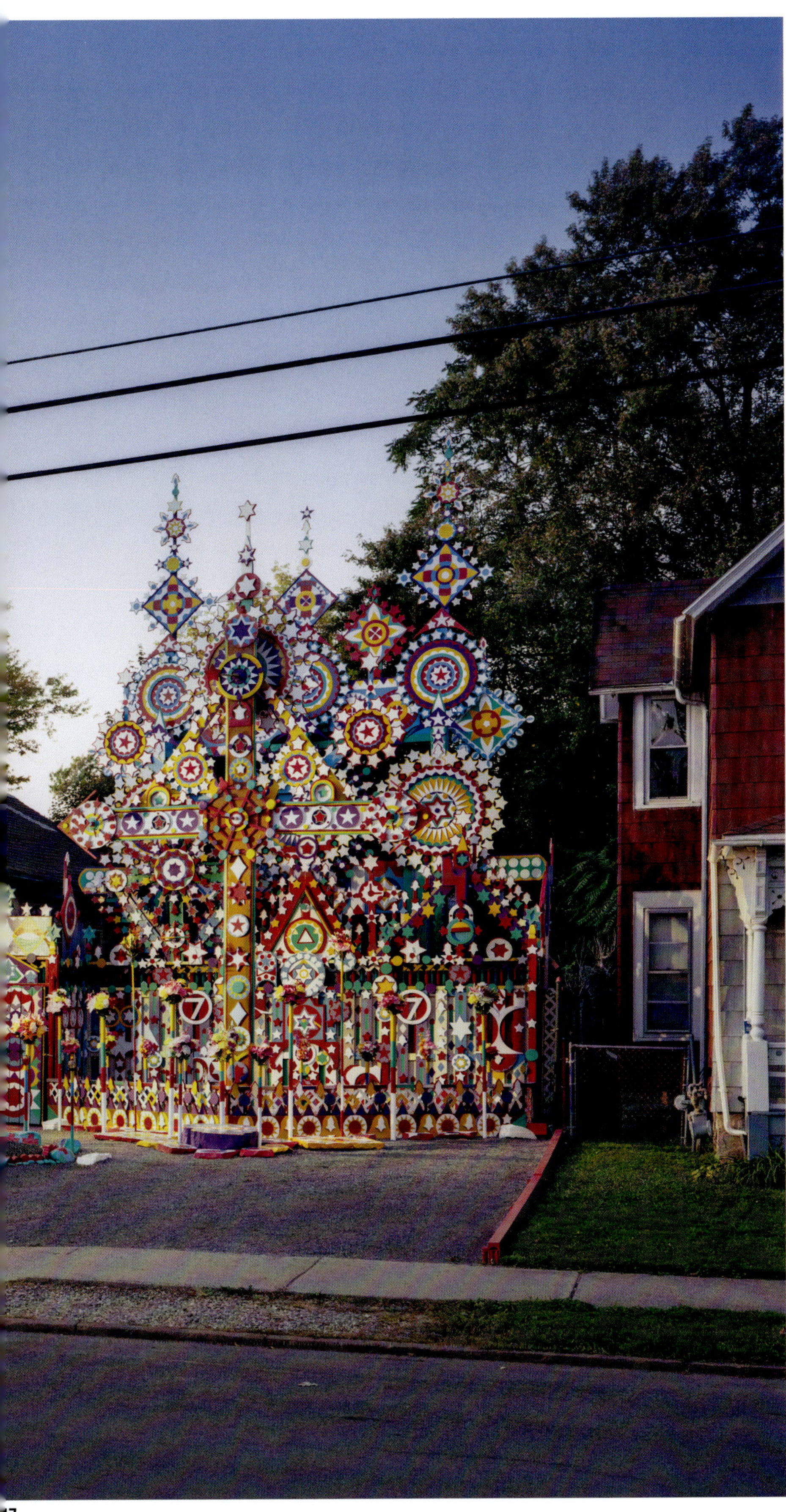

multitudes," the Ten Commandments, the Crucifixion, the figure of John of Patmos (the apostle understood to be the author of the Book of Revelation), bells, and chalices.

A low decorated fence on the west side delineates the property line, a freestanding vertical marquee features Biblical verses, and the ground of the front yard is replete with symbols, some painted and others marked by variously painted stones, such as the diamond-shaped *Resurrection Rock Garden*, which is ringed with multicolored posts to protect the assemblage. Elsewhere on the grounds are bas-relief motifs referencing the seven seals of the apocalypse from the Book of Revelation, Christ's 12 disciples, and the Ark of the Covenant, among others. On the small strip of land between the public sidewalk and the street, blindingly white painted boulders outline the body of a recumbent Christ as they symbolize his sepulcher; they are surrounded by red stones that represent his blood. (At times these white boulders were further adorned with other pigments, including purple, to reference the color of Christ's robe.) In every section, the motifs were painted precisely, with clean lines and fully saturated intensities.

The house interior also features painted or fabricated crosses and religious imagery on almost all walls, ceilings, and floors, most repeating the color palette and symbolism of the exterior; these hand-painted motifs are complemented with several framed commercial religious prints. Innumerable candles, plastic flowers, and multicolored iridescent glass beads map out a path to salvation and eternal life. In his *Holy Room*, in particular, the embellishments covering the floor make it difficult to even enter; dedicated exclusively to prophets, this room was often kept locked.

Robertson came to believe that the epicenter of the Second Coming and Judgment Day would be at nearby Niagara Falls; he believed the sacred power of this natural phenomenon was corroborated by the rainbow that is consistently viewable through the mist, which he associated with the rainbow described in the Book of Genesis as a sign of God's covenant with Noah. For that reason, although he had intended to return to Canada after he retired, he decided to remain in New York, so he could be closer to the Rapture and the end of time, when it came. After building the environment over 10 years, 5 months, and 19 days, as he waited for the Rapture he spent his later days retouching the paint and changing the color combinations as he saw fit in order to maintain the site in its full magnificence as inspiration for people's "last chance" to accept Christ. He thus served as a spiritual advisor to members of the community, who were in no doubt that he was, indeed, a prophet.

As he aged, however, his maintenance of the site became less attentive, and its condition deteriorated as a result of continuous exposure to the region's brutal cold and damp. Almost two years after Robertson's death, the Kohler Foundation agreed to undertake a preservation project that would address not only repainting but also replacement of structural losses with replicated elements. The entire construction was dismantled and moved off-site for the necessary work, and the decision was made to substitute nonorganic faux-wood PVC materials for most of the wooden components in order to maximize their lifespan, instead of trying to conserve the originals. (This was of particular concern because Robertson had used a significant amount of scrap material as he built. The original *Cross* was also conserved and transferred to the Kohler's Art Preserve in Sheboygan, Wisconsin.) The conservators adhered to precise color and shape matching in their work, and were able to position the thousands of pieces according to a grid mapped out by drone prior to dismantling, aided by thousands of Fred Scruton's photographs from over the years. The house itself has also been improved, with a new roof, windows, and rear ramp for enhanced access.

The entire structure reopened to the public on August 10, 2024, and is now being maintained under the auspices of the Niagara Falls National Heritage Center. It will function as a small community space for events and programs, and will be made available for viewing through limited public tours. In 2025 the *Second Coming House* was added to the list of Historic Artists' Homes and Studios maintained by the National Trust for Historic Preservation.

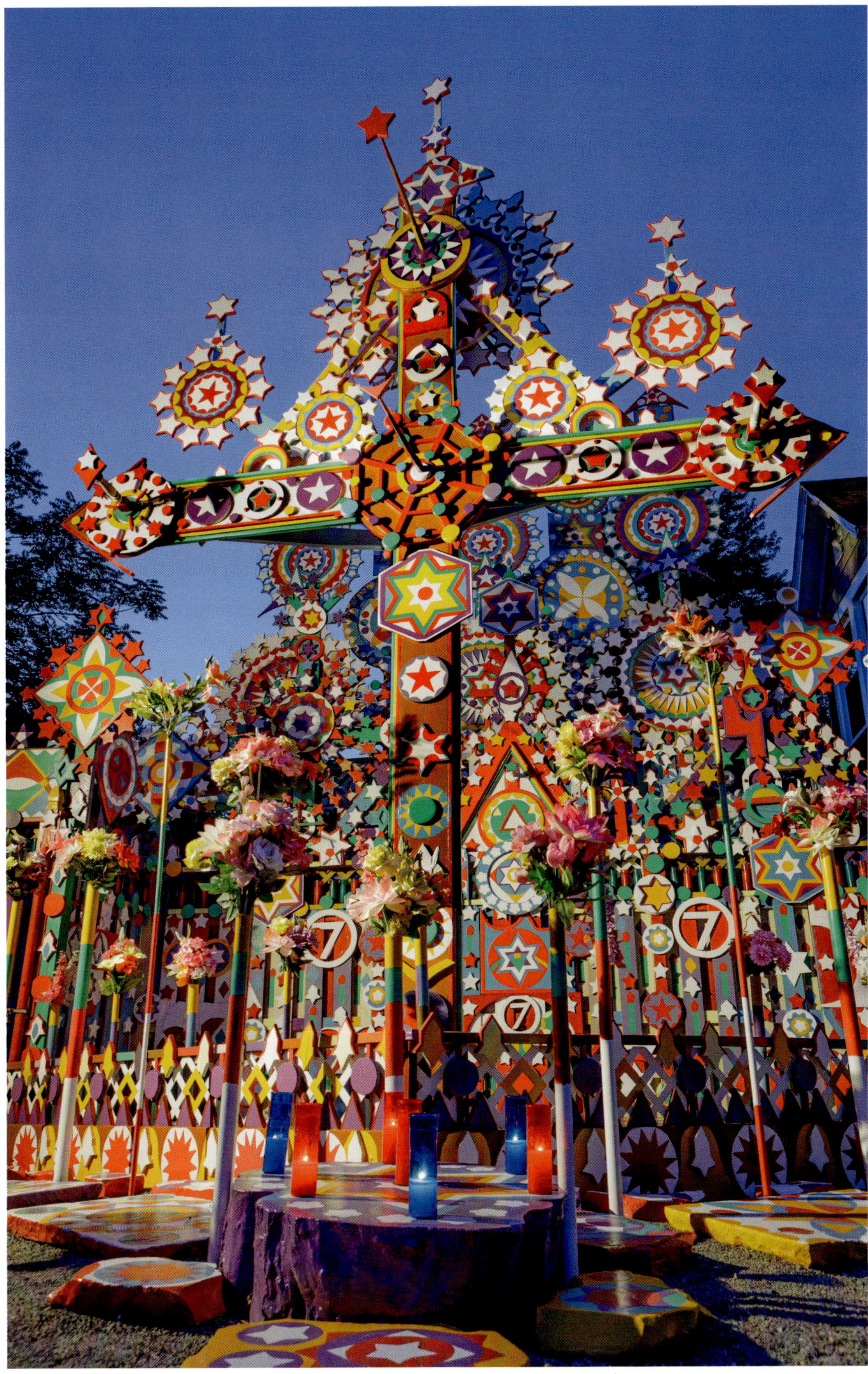

LIVING ROOM, 2016

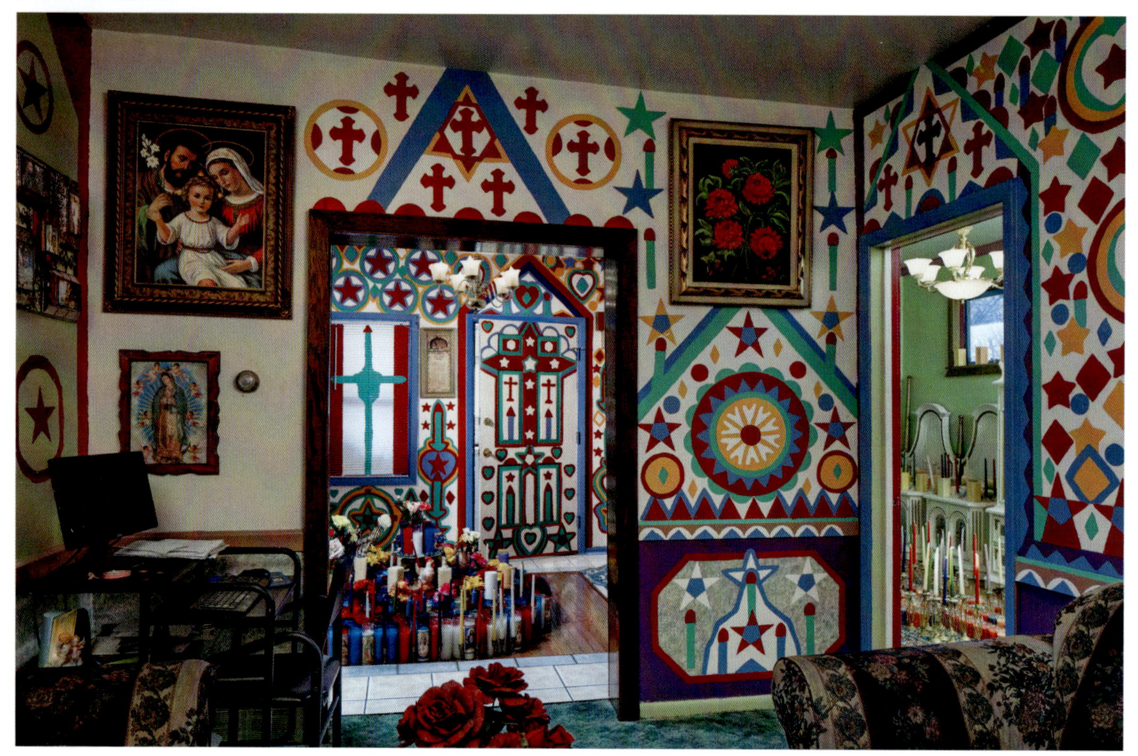

HE ASSERTED THAT HIS HOUSE DECORATION WAS MADE POSSIBLE BY GOD, WORKING THROUGH HIS CARPENTER HANDS.

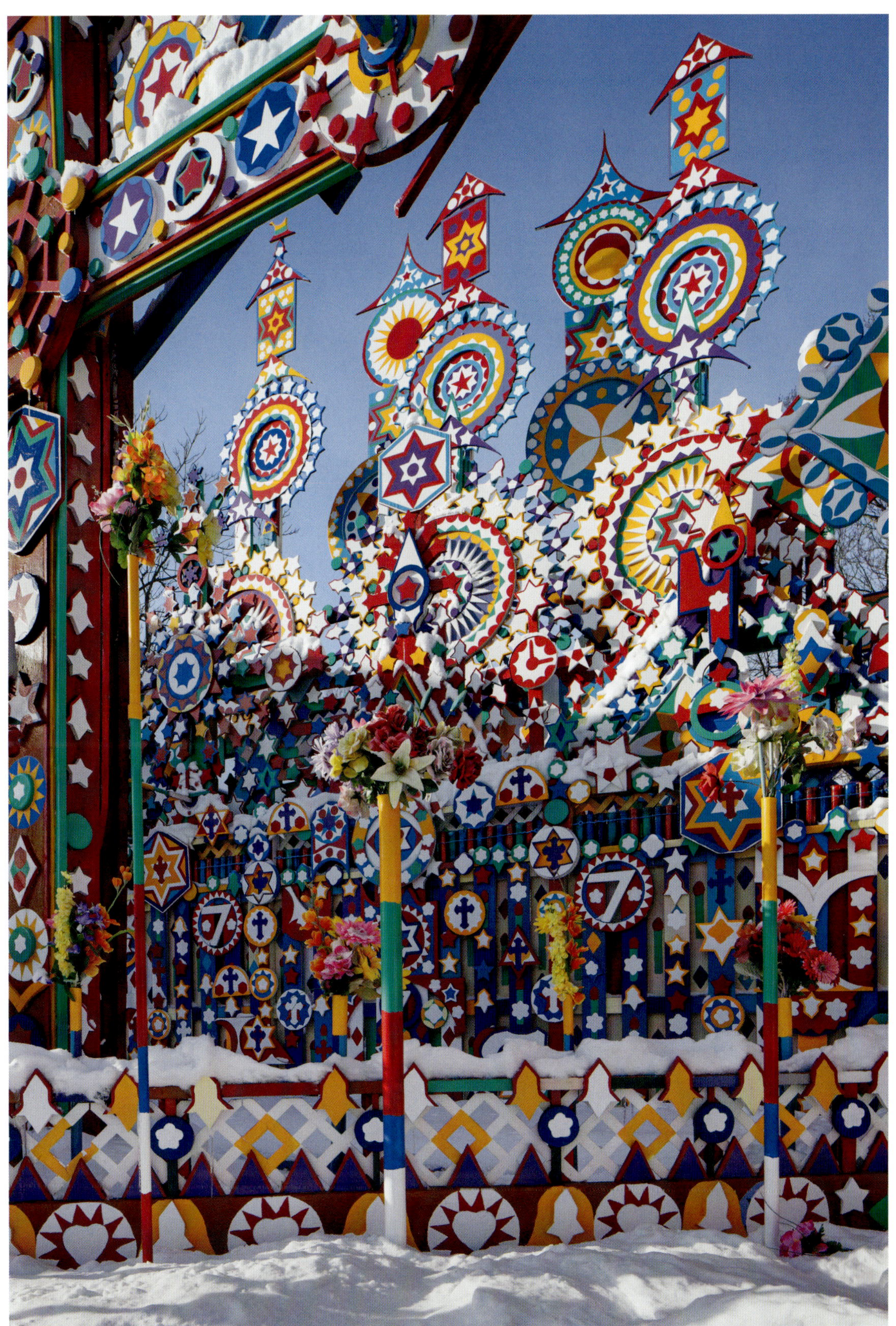

EXTERIOR ORNAMENT WITH SYMBOLIC REPRESENTATIONS OF THE UNIVERSE, 2014

DIONICIO RODRÍGUEZ

CRYSTAL SHRINE GROTTO

MEMPHIS, TENNESSEE

Practically alone among the creator-builders featured in this book, Rodríguez (1891–1955) did not work on his own property or on property with which he had a personal connection. Instead, he designed and crafted a varied series of primarily functional constructions commissioned by different patrons, largely located across the southern and southwestern United States. These included bridges, fountains, cemetery and park structures, fences, gates, and gazebos.

Born in Toluca, the capital of the State of Mexico, Rodríguez moved with his family to Mexico City when he was young and, as soon as he was able, began working alongside his father and brother as a bricklayer. In the early 1920s he moved to Monterrey, Mexico, and in 1924, apparently to escape the political upheaval of his homeland, he again moved, first to Laredo, Texas, and then, later that same year, on to San Antonio. In both Mexico and Texas he worked for cement companies and with artisans who fashioned concrete decorations for architectural structures, a genre that had been established in Texas as early as the mid-nineteenth century. He was not the first to work in a rustic mode—examples exist in France from the eighteenth century and pattern books were already being published in England and Europe by the early nineteenth century. He was, however, clearly more skillful than most, and he became renowned for the accuracy and creativity of his *faux bois* (fake wood) technique, sculpting concrete into realistic-looking branches, logs, stones, and other natural forms.

This technique—known in Mexico as *trabajo rústico* (rustic work)—featured iron rebar supplemented with rubble, if necessary, for larger pieces. Rodríguez lashed this infrastructure together with wire, mesh, and screen (other practitioners may have welded the interior components instead). Then, by hand, he infilled the forms with a rough concrete mortar. After it dried, he sheathed the whole in a smooth finish coat of undiluted Portland cement before using handmade tools, combs, and kitchen utensils to score and carve the surface. Rodríguez modeled these forms with such attention to realism that his mock wood included peeling bark, lichen, fallen branches, artificial knots, and wormholes. The last step was to brush the concrete surface with a proprietary "secret" tinting formula that he protectively guarded, working in private and destroying any remaining product after he had finished each piece. He securely anchored the larger works with concrete footings.

Reviewing the *faux bois* constructions that Rodríguez erected in eight states, several of which have been honored with inclusion on the National Register of Historic Places, it is generally agreed that his most comprehensive and innovative work was created at the *Memorial Park* in Memphis between 1935 and 1943. This park's built, rolling landscape circumvented the visual interruption of vertical tombstones by mandating flat grave markers, imitating the design of Forest Lawn Cemetery in Los Angeles. Here, Rodríguez worked with patron E. Clovis Hinds (1868–1949), a successful life insurance company owner, to help him fulfill his vision for a cemetery that would be designed to attract not only those who came to mourn their dead but those who wanted to enjoy its serene lake-studded landscape and park-like setting.

In 1924, Hinds sold his insurance business to purchase the property for the *Memorial Park.* He assembled a small team of designers and artisans: John Noyes of the George Kessler landscape architecture firm designed the original 54-acre site, and the idea of adding sculpture was inspired by Paris's Père Lachaise Cemetery, although, in this case, the commissioned works were not linked to individual graves, and they were broadly spaced out to permit longer vistas. Rodríguez, hired in 1935, was responsible for designing and creating the architectural and sculptural eccentricities, and while a linear grouping consisting of *Abraham's Oak*, the *Fountain of Youth*, the *Broken Tree Bench*, the *Cave of Machpelah*, a *Wishing Chair*, the *Pool of Hebron*, and a series of *faux bois* footbridges also grace the site, Rodríguez's *Crystal Shrine Grotto* was the physical and spiritual center of *Memorial Park*.

The most elaborate structure on-site, the *Grotto*—like the other works, inspired by Biblical narratives and developed without preliminary sketches—took several years to complete, and is equally compelling from the interior and exterior. A tall and organically textured spire marks the entrance to the obscurity of the cavern, but once inside, the walls and ceilings sparkle, embedded with five tons of crystals and glass, many of which were sourced from the Diamond Cave in Jasper, Arkansas. Some of these were inserted into ducts that pierced the enclosure all the way to the exterior, so that sunlight could illuminate them with greater potency. Artificial stalactites punctuate the ceiling, with two larger elements serving as columns to support the roof.

CRYSTAL SHRINE GROTTO EXTERIOR, 2025

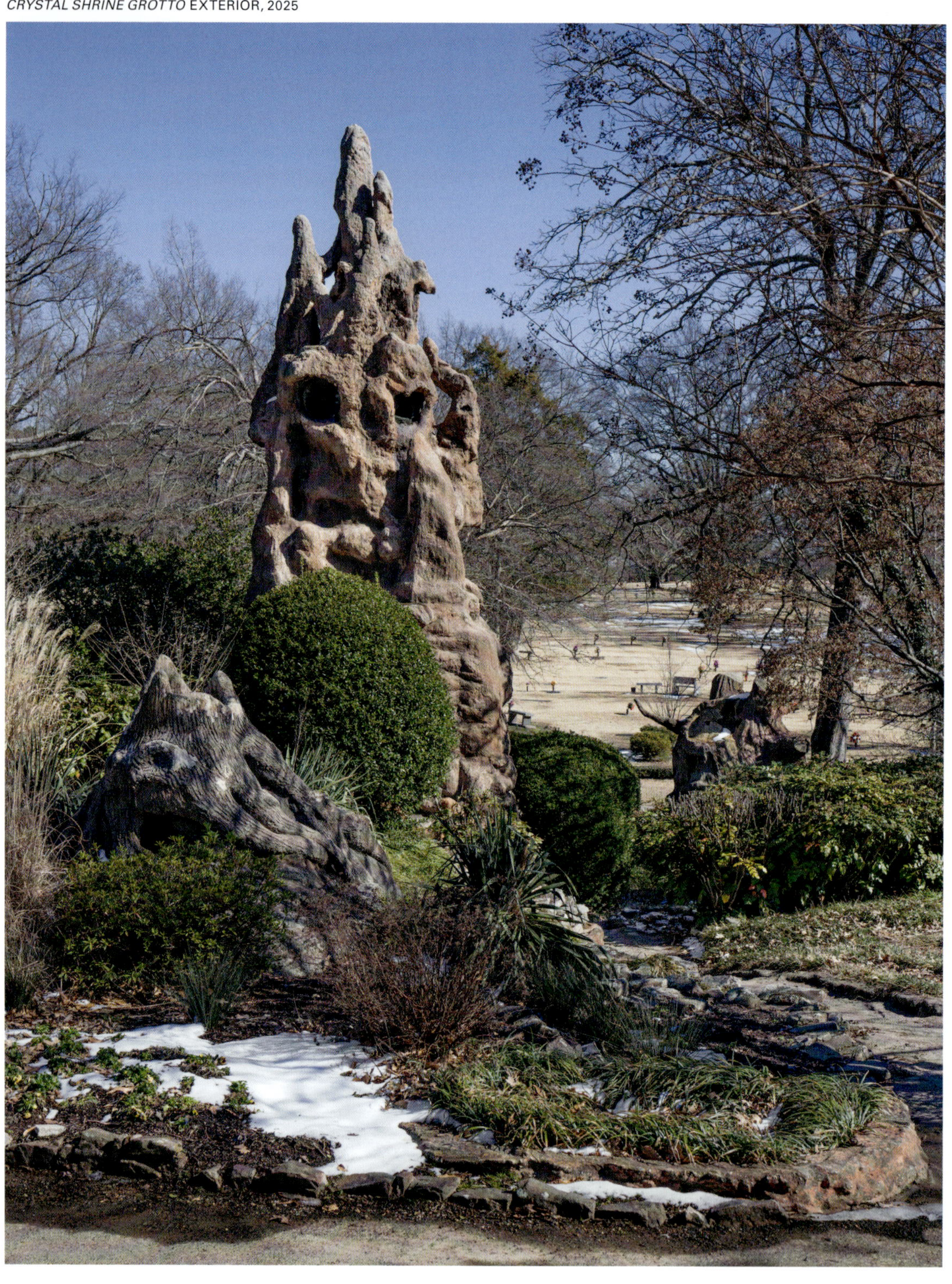

The cavern is ornamented with 10 niches, each with a miniature diorama depicting a scene of Christ's life, from birth to resurrection. Given that the cave is largely—albeit artificially—subterranean as it is carved 59 feet into a constructed hill, it is easy to become immersed in the story and cross a threshold of belief into a spiritual realm, as was intended. Some of these tableaux are set against backdrops painted by Rodríguez—the only extant examples of his paintings—while others are embellished with wood and stone sculptures carved by Memphis artists. Hinds paid Rodríguez $75 weekly for his work; this salary covered his fee and expenses as well as those of an assistant laborer.

Following the completion of the conical *Crystal Shrine Grotto* in 1943, vaunted as the only manmade crystal cave in the world, Rodríguez returned to San Antonio. He became increasingly ill with diabetes, and it is not clear how many additional commissions he was able to complete prior to his death eight years later. The *Memphis Memorial Park* was added to the National Register of Historic Places in 1991.

HE WAS RENOWNED FOR THE REALISTIC MEANS BY WHICH HE SCULPTED CONCRETE TO LOOK LIKE WOOD, COMPLETE WITH LICHEN, PEELING BARK, AND WORMHOLES.

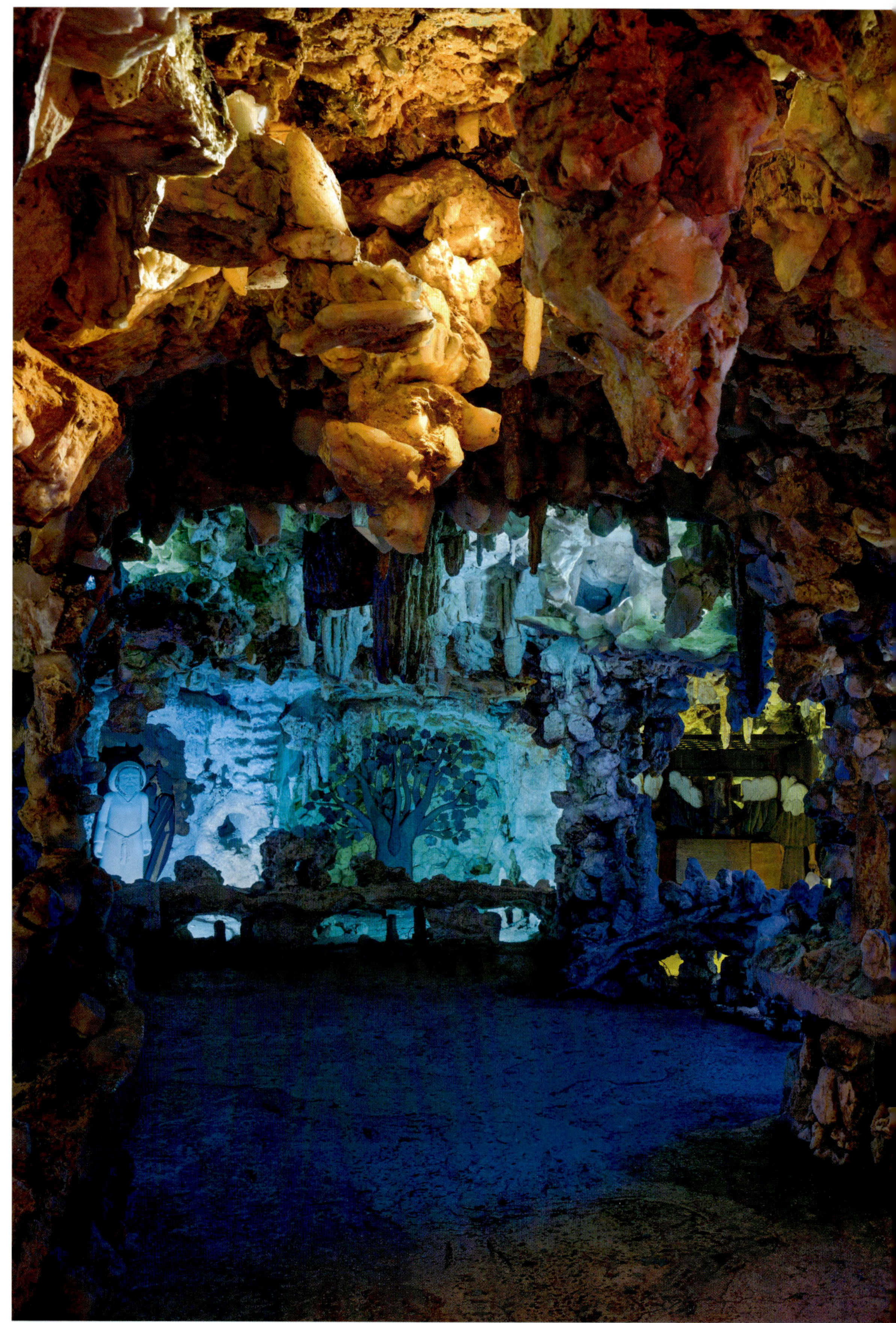

GROTTO INTERIOR, 2025

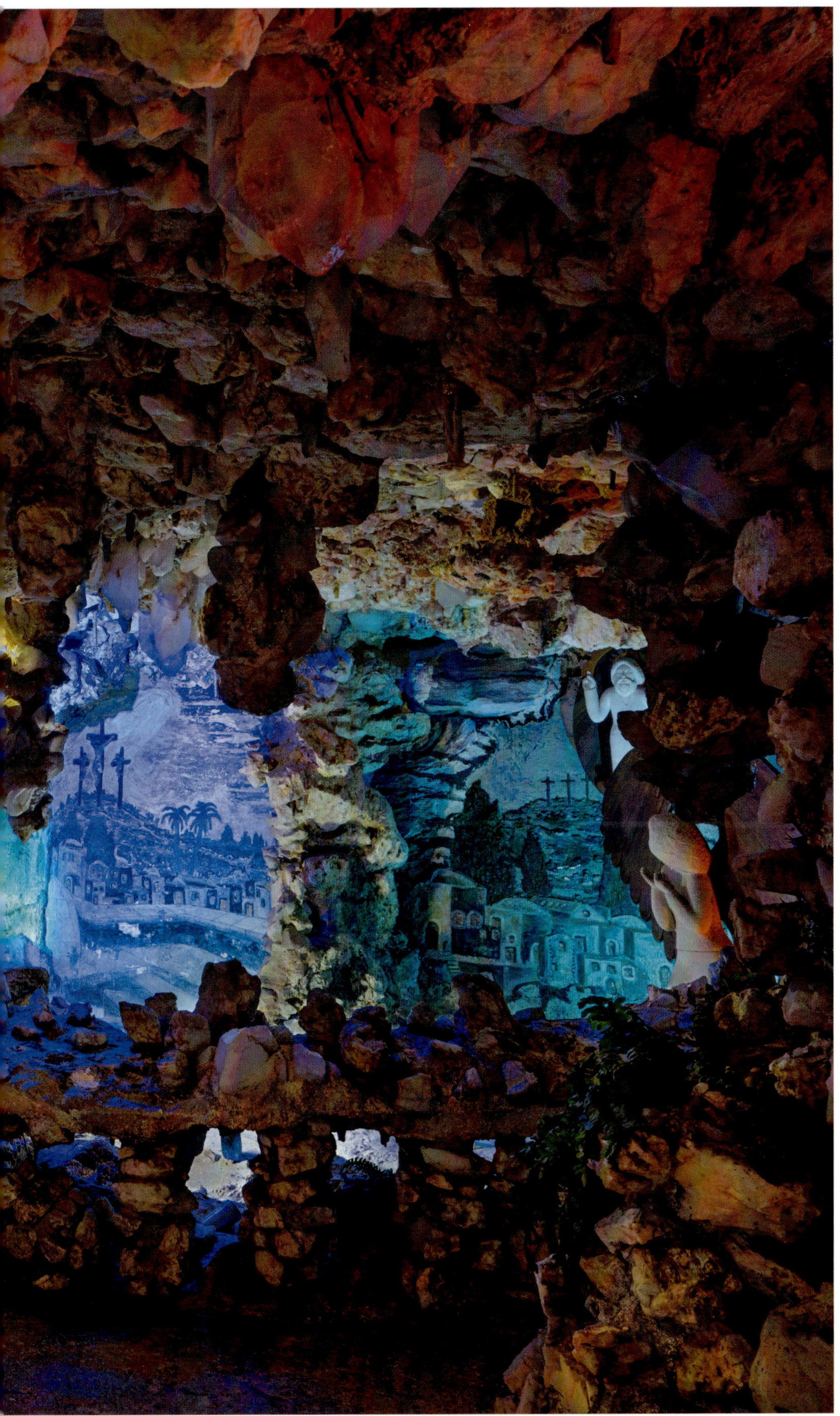

REVEREND HERMAN DON "H.D." DENNIS AND MARGARET ROGERS DENNIS

—

MARGARET'S GROCERY AND MARKET

VICKSBURG, MISSISSIPPI

This low profile, relatively nondescript frame structure on the outskirts of Vicksburg once housed a grocery run by Margaret Rogers (1916–2009). Rogers was one of the first Black female business owners in the entire state, and her market was the only one owned and managed by a Black woman on the length of historic Highway 61, the old road that winds from New Orleans all the way north to Minnesota. She opened the grocery in the 1950s; it provided essentials (and likely served as a juke joint) and was the only store in the community, a semi-rural hamlet of primarily Black residents that has since been annexed by Vicksburg.

After her husband of 39 years was killed during a robbery, she met and was wooed by H.D. Dennis (1916–2012), a preacher who had been evangelizing since he was a teenager and who had been ordained in 1936 in Columbus, Georgia, in the Missionary Baptist Church. He promised he would turn Margaret's modest country establishment into a castle if she would marry him, and after they wed in 1984, united by their shared faith, he almost immediately began working to make that happen. In the process he transformed the site into one of the most notable art environments in the South, a monument both to his love for Margaret and to his religious beliefs.

Dennis had learned some basic bricklaying skills during his Army service in World War II, when he served as a prison guard supervising captured German forces, and upon his return he took advantage of the G.I. Bill to study more advanced masonry techniques. Although born in Mississippi, he had grown up in Georgia and then moved north to Detroit, where he spent 23 years building Chrysler automobiles. Back in Vicksburg, he was confident that his varied skills in masonry, carpentry, and working with metals would enable him to build Margaret a "castle" that would attract visitors from around the world. He conceived of this castle—and its attendant structures—as a material extension of his ministry.

Dennis mounted hand-painted signs with Biblical passages and his own exhortations (religious admonitions as well as prosaic notices about, for example, where to park), and he painted the building's surfaces with alternating blocks of glossy red, white, and blue—to which Margaret herself added yellow as well as pink, her favorite color. They explained the exuberant color palette on the formerly drab grocery building, now enhanced and expanded, by comparing it to the different colors of flowers in a bouquet, diverse yet complementary, like the different skin colors of "God's children." But they also recognized that the eye-catching colors might cause passersby to stop and explore further, and the Reverend would then have the opportunity to share words of his faith with them. "Welcome Jews and Gentiles—This Church Open 24 Hours a Day" read a prominent sign, a condensed marker of his belief urging people to respect one another and live in harmony.

Dennis used cinder blocks and wooden lattice to build up almost a dozen high towers in front of and around the *Grocery* building, many of which were paired with corresponding structures of similar height, palette, and decoration. The *Ten Commandments of God Tower* rose close to three stories high and contained a seating area on the second level outfitted with a Bible so that people could contemplate God's word in a more private space. He also erected stepped chimney-like shrines, sculptures, gates, monuments, and an arched formal entrance to the complex that was more symmetrical than most of his constructions. It, too, was built from cinder blocks and bricks and topped with an ornamental double-headed eagle. (A member of the Masonic Lodge, Dennis identified this motif as providing protection from both east and west, but it is also the 32nd degree of the Scottish Rite.) Lower-scale walkways and walls linked the various structures, some of which were physically joined to the original building. Balanced by shape and scale, accented by improvisation, and coordinated by color palette, found objects, and cut-out forms, the embellished architectural and sculptural constructions expanded both the elevation and the breadth of Margaret's original market as they simultaneously amplified the impact of Dennis's work and his spiritual message.

Relatively early during his work on-site, he received a yellow school bus from the city of Vicksburg, which he parked on the side of the property when he was not driving his neighbors around so they could visit their relatives (a task that afforded him the opportunity to preach to them as he drove). By the mid- to late 1980s he removed the steering mechanisms and driver's seat and proceeded to ornament the interior with Christmas lights, glittering Mardi Gras beads, tinsel, plastic flowers, hubcaps, and other found objects, and he used the seats as pews as he preached from the front. This became his primary chapel, but he also sermonized

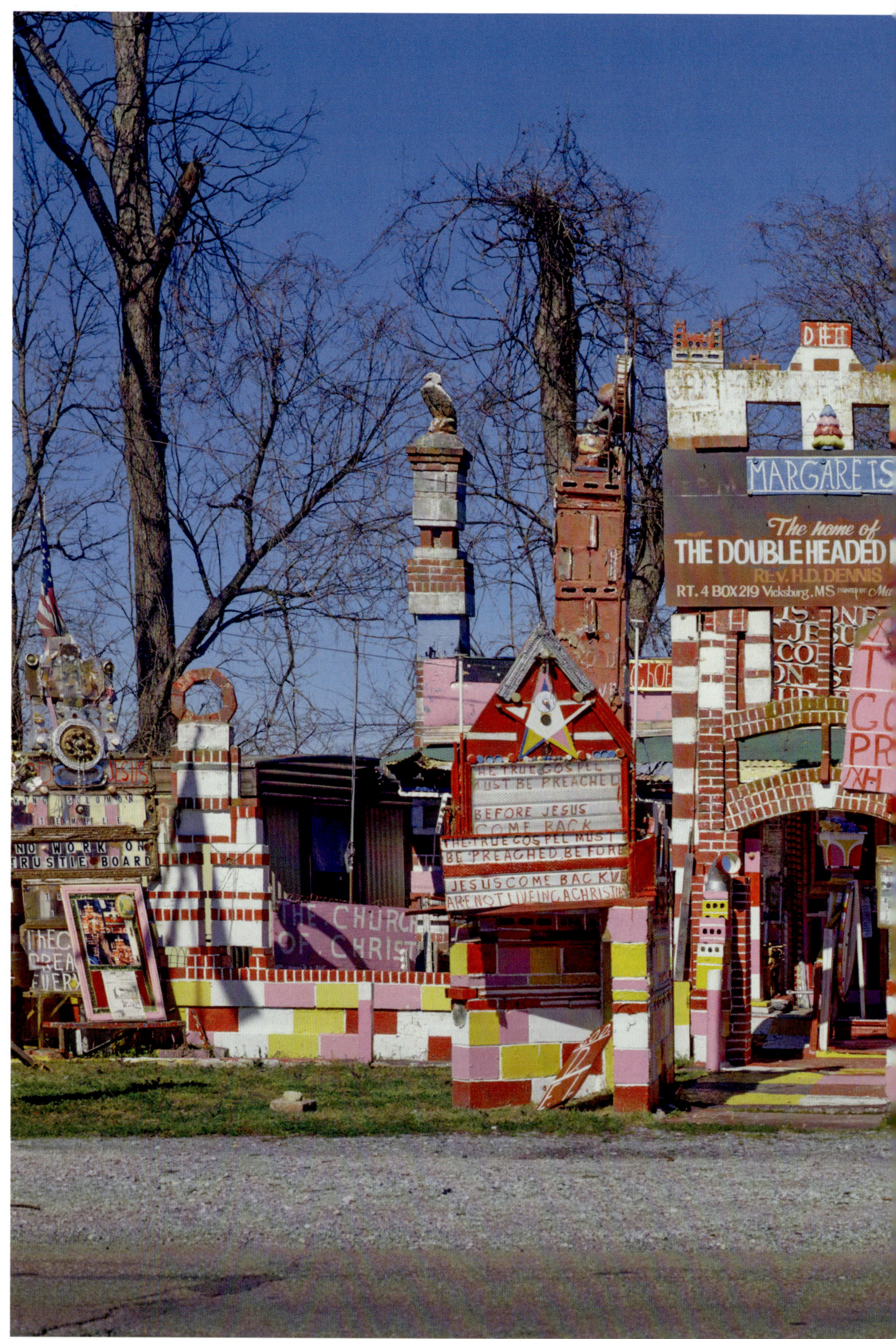

FRONT FAÇADE, 2005

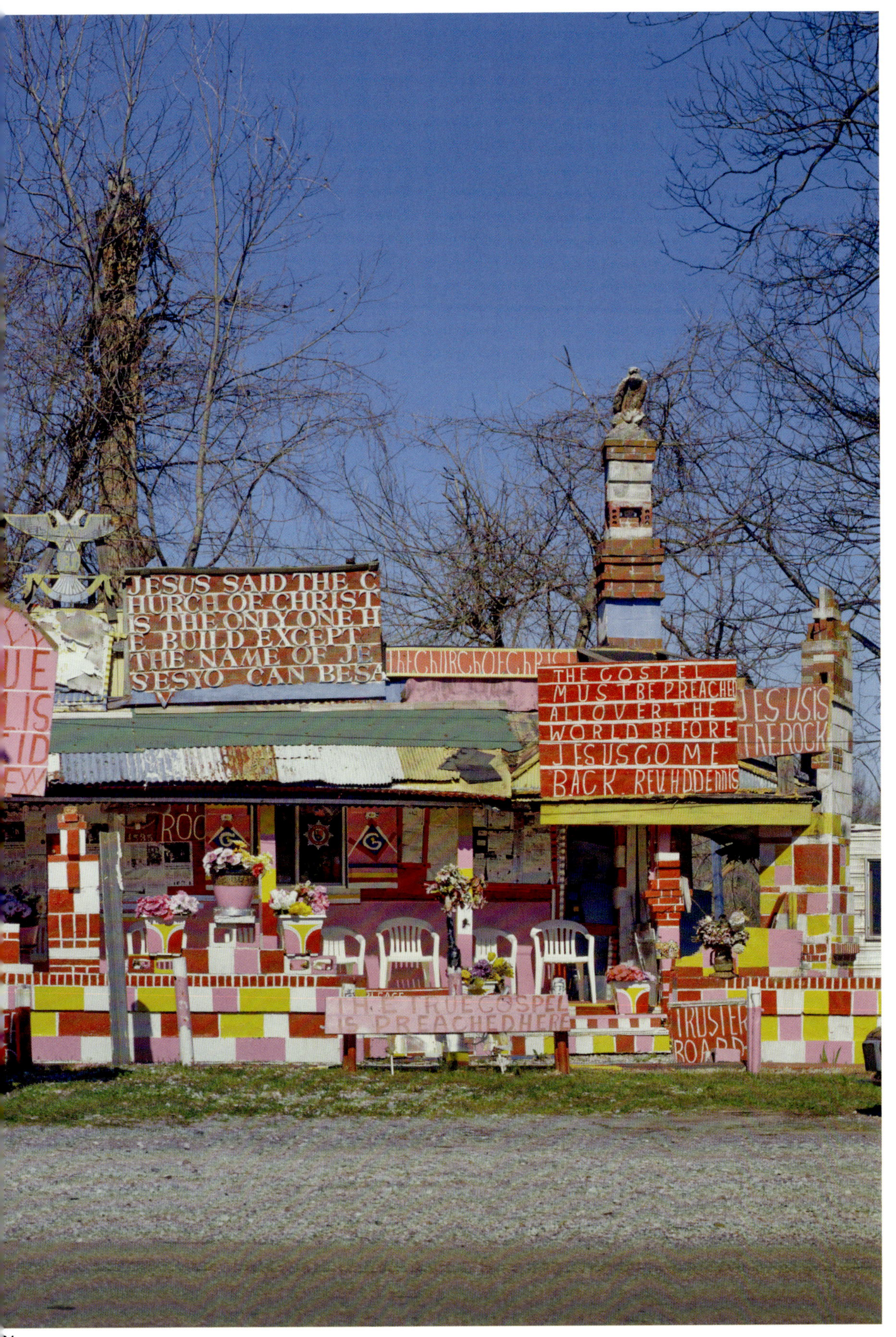
JESUS SAID THE C
HURCH OF CHRIST
IS THE ONLY ONE H
E BUILD EXCEPT
THE NAME OF JE
SESYO CAN BESA
THE GOSPEL
MUST BE PREACHED
ALL OVER THE
WORLD BEFORE
JESUS COME
BACK REV H D DENNIS
JESUS IS
THE ROCK
THE TRUE GOSPEL
IS PREACHED HERE
TRUSTER
BOARD

SCHOOL BUS *CHAPEL*, 2005

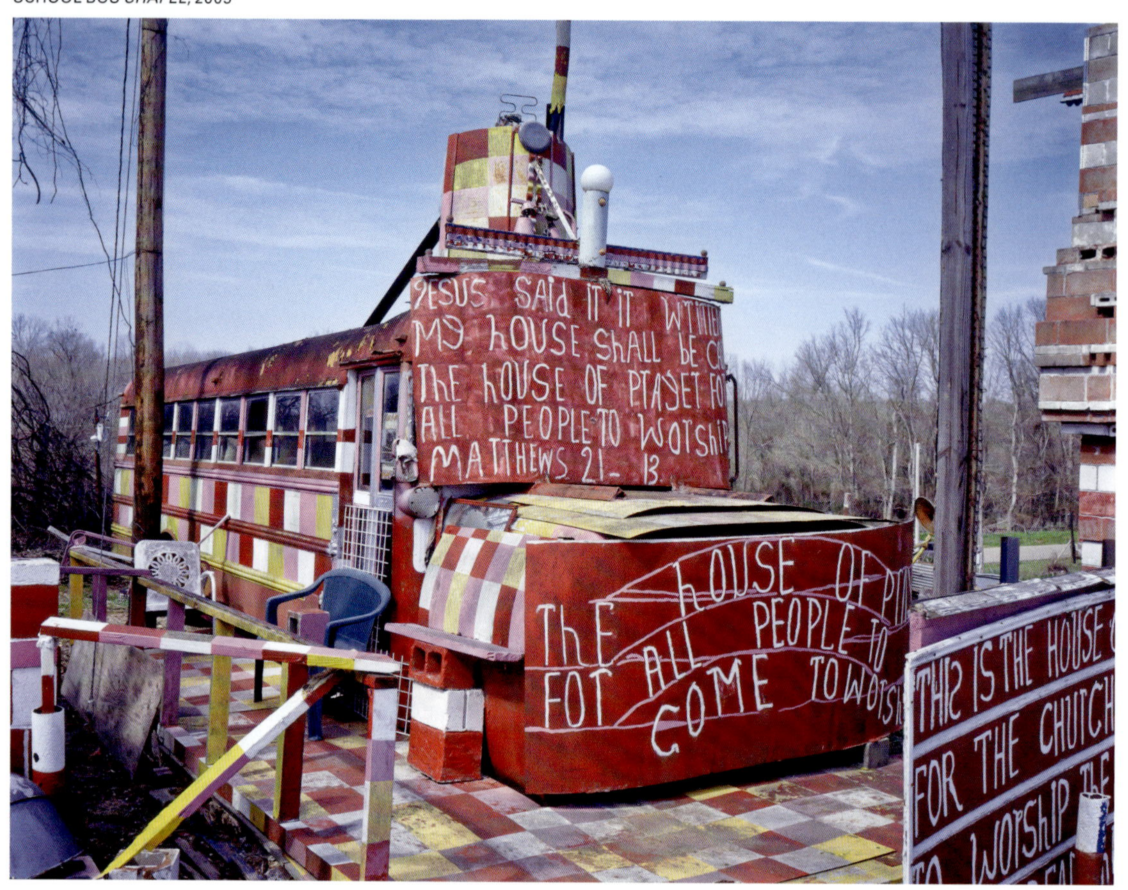

HE PROMISED THAT HE WOULD MAKE MARGARET'S GROCERY STORE INTO A CASTLE IF SHE WOULD MARRY HIM.

from anywhere else on the property, demanding, in righteous fervor, that all visitors and worshippers repent for their sins.

The entire site served as a "nondenominational" (but decidedly Christian) religious center. Little by little the groceries were replaced with ornamentation, and the market's secular function was overtaken with religious imagery that spread throughout the walls, ceilings, and floor space of its six rooms. The images included an elaborately festooned and gold-painted *Ark of the Covenant* repurposed from a steamer trunk, numerous discrete assemblages of colorful and sparkling found objects, Masonic emblems, photographs, framed sermons, religious prints, clippings, and often enigmatic symbolic letters and motifs. The density of the ornamentation on-site and its theatrical impact was—albeit to a much lesser degree—echoed by Reverend Dennis's own sartorial choices: sparkling crowns and wreaths of bead necklaces were standard accoutrements of his personal style.

After some two decades of construction, modifications, additions, painting, and repainting, in the mid- to late 2000s first Margaret and then H.D. were moved to an assisted living facility. Vacant, the site fell into disrepair: the colorful paint began to peel and the towers toppled, a result of weather-driven deterioration as well as rodent and insect infestation, vandalism, and theft. Dennis's inclusion of materials such as Styrofoam, plastics, untreated wood, and plywood in weight-bearing locations had also weakened the structure and increased the possibility of its collapse.

About a year after the Preacher's death, the nonprofit Mississippi Folk Art Foundation was incorporated in order to be able to receive grant funding and solicit individual donations to preserve *Margaret's Grocery*. While many of the smaller or movable components—including the school bus—have been temporarily relocated off-site for safekeeping, fundraising and conservation efforts continue. Although the art environment is not yet completely stable nor secure, progress is ongoing, and as funding becomes available, the ultimate goal is to preserve the site, returning it to its colorful and potent resplendence.

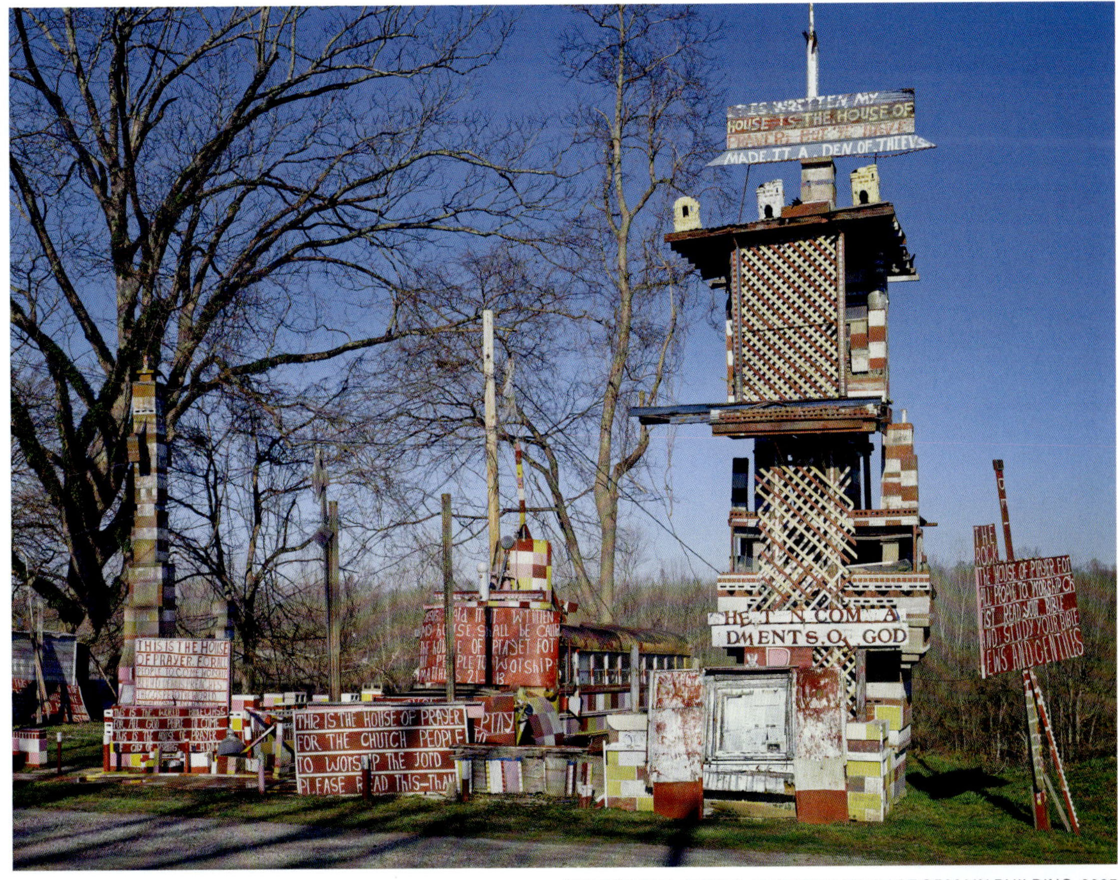

TOWERS AND INSTALLATIONS NORTHEAST OF MAIN BUILDING, 2005

RALPHAEL PLESCIA

CHRISTIAN SCHOOL

SALT LAKE CITY, UTAH

Among all of the art environments in the United States that focus on the maker's religious beliefs, most are meant to proselytize, to bring the viewer around to a conventional or widely held point of view. They do this in many ways, often recounting New Testament narratives of the birth, life, death, and resurrection of Jesus Christ, or excerpting Biblical verses and passages that are thought to convincingly lay out a righteous path for nonbelievers. But Plescia's (1937–2022) somewhat unnerving site concentrated, instead, on a graphic and self-described educational depiction of "untold" and rather unorthodox stories of creation based on his own rather eccentric interpretation, with striking images that simultaneously foretold of heaven while warning of the fires and watery depths of hell.

One of four children born to a Mormon family in Salt Lake City, Plescia was good with his hands and interested in making art from an early age. In his spare time he explored the nearby *Gilgal Sculpture Garden* art environment and watched as owner Thomas Child produced a series of sculptures manifesting his Mormon faith. He helped his father, who used a wheelchair as a result of wounds sustained in World War I, by stocking parts and doing simple repairs in his auto parts store. But Plescia's father also believed his children needed to gain a broader understanding of commerce, so his son took jobs in a mortuary and later in a music store where he repaired broken instruments. Over the years he also taught himself construction, mechanical engineering, restoration, painting, and sculpting.

The elder Plescia willed the auto parts building to his son for use during his lifetime only, and named the local Shriners Children's Hospital as the ultimate beneficiary. When the younger man's parents, sister, and youngest daughter died in a 1970 car accident (a grandmother who had been instrumental in raising him had died five months earlier) Plescia became the building's new owner, at least temporarily. He was precluded from passing it on as an inheritance.

The trauma of those violent deaths (as well as the 2009 death of another daughter due to a cerebral aneurism) caused him to increasingly and obsessively turn to religion, albeit on an idiosyncratic path, as he did not profess association with any specific denomination or church. Over time, Plescia authored an illustrated book, *The Theory of Creation*, which he carefully painted on large wooden panels, and he drew a series of calendars that charted the busy week of creation from God's perspective. He inscribed other plaques with his unconventional understanding of various Biblical narratives, in roman letters ornamented with curly-cue serifs.

Plescia also began the process of modifying the two-story commercial space into his private museum to express his beliefs and serve as a "school." While the front exterior façade drew attention with high-relief and fully three-dimensional plaques, paintings, sculptures, crosses, and carvings of religious motifs and commentary, the interior was even more compelling. He produced a series of thin, elongated figures, all left in the natural gray of the concrete that he used for their fabrication, in contrast with the pale but more colorful palette of his series of paintings with religious themes. In both two and three dimensions, his main focus was a visual recitation to remind visitors that they had a heavenly mother—whom he named "Lady Wisdom"—as well as a heavenly father: the Godhead, in his view, included each member of the entire nuclear family.

Basing his work on his studies of passage 12 from the New Testament's Book of Revelation, he depicted the sacred mother as a buxom nude—clothed only "with the rays of the sun"—and visibly pregnant, looking to flee from Satan and a seven-headed red dragon that threatened to drag her to hell before her child could be born. In order to escape, she crawled inside a lion's mouth that symbolized wilderness. Plescia used his art to sequentially depict this narrative in explicit detail, and although he readily acknowledged that not everyone would agree with his interpretation, he felt that he was "defending" the Bible as written. While standalone pieces existed, much of the work was permanently attached to or embedded in the building's ceiling, foundation, and walls. And many of the pieces were larger than life.

ENTRANCE TO THE UNDERWORLD, 2023. PHOTO: KIRK HUFFAKER

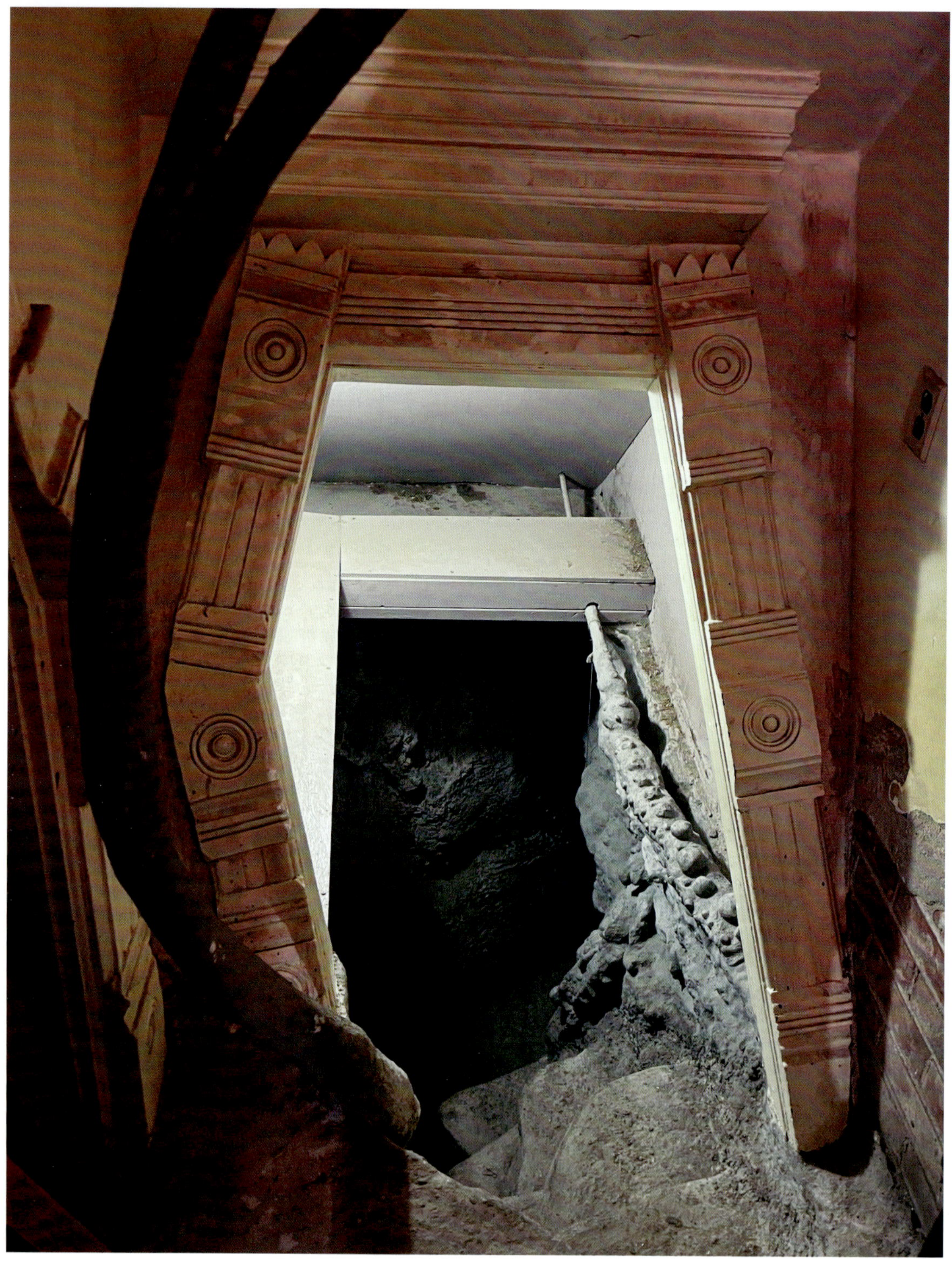

Dissatisfied with the size of his existing space, Plescia added another level to the building by digging out the basement by hand, removing the earth one five-gallon bucket at a time, and excavating underground tunnels until he unexpectedly reached ground water that pooled into a pond. Thinking creatively, he built narrow pathways and bridges to cross this watery underworld, which he turned into a metaphor for Hell. To emphasize the terror of this section, he added desperate half-submerged souls, fabricated from concrete, who reached up through the dim light to plead for deliverance from their torture. A winding tunnel ended with a pivot to the Old Testament and the Garden of Eden, as Eve, the Serpent, and the Tree of Knowledge exploded up to the building's ground floor.

In contrast, the top level was airy and bright, with a vaulted ceiling painted with a mural backlit by a large skylight of Plescia's own design, featuring God in heaven as well as portraits of family members who had passed away. Around the walls were a series of nine-foot-tall paintings with religious subjects. While he called his art environment the *Christian School*, with the exception of some of the main characters, his educational museum could not be mistaken for a conventional Christian narrative or point of view: it functioned instead to visually communicate his personal beliefs and interpretations.

Plescia's stated intent was to dispense knowledge through his *School*, and he was never interested in making money, so he was consequently rightly skeptical that his art environment would survive his death. The building was located on a shabby commercial strip at the side of an urban section of national Highway 89 that was slated for redevelopment, and after his death, with the building passing to the Shriners, they exercised their new ownership rights and demanded that all artwork be removed. By accepting the bid of another buyer, they dashed the hopes of a local arts organization that had wanted to purchase the building, offer public access, and preserve it as a monument to Plescia's 50-year intervention.

While the site suffered some theft and vandalism during the negotiations, some of the artwork was, despite overwhelming legal and physical challenges, extricated and moved to the family home; over the course of the three-month period of the move, the family was forced to rent back the building to have time to sort through Plescia's belongings. Other works were taken to the Utah Art Alliance's *Art Castle*, despite the difficulty and cost of the task, given that so many of the larger works were implanted in the structure and their removal risked causing irreparable damage.

Ultimately, all of Plescia's modifications on the unreinforced building triggered many code violations, so it will remain vacant until such time as the new owners can be guaranteed financing, permits, and zoning allowances to enable the structure to be demolished and the site repurposed. But Plescia had declared that he was content because, when he looked back, he knew he had tried to do what he thought was right. The *Christian School* is no longer extant.

THE "HEAVENLY MOTHER" TRIES TO ESCAPE FROM THE DRAGON, BASEMENT LEVEL, 2023. PHOTO: KIRK HUFFAKER

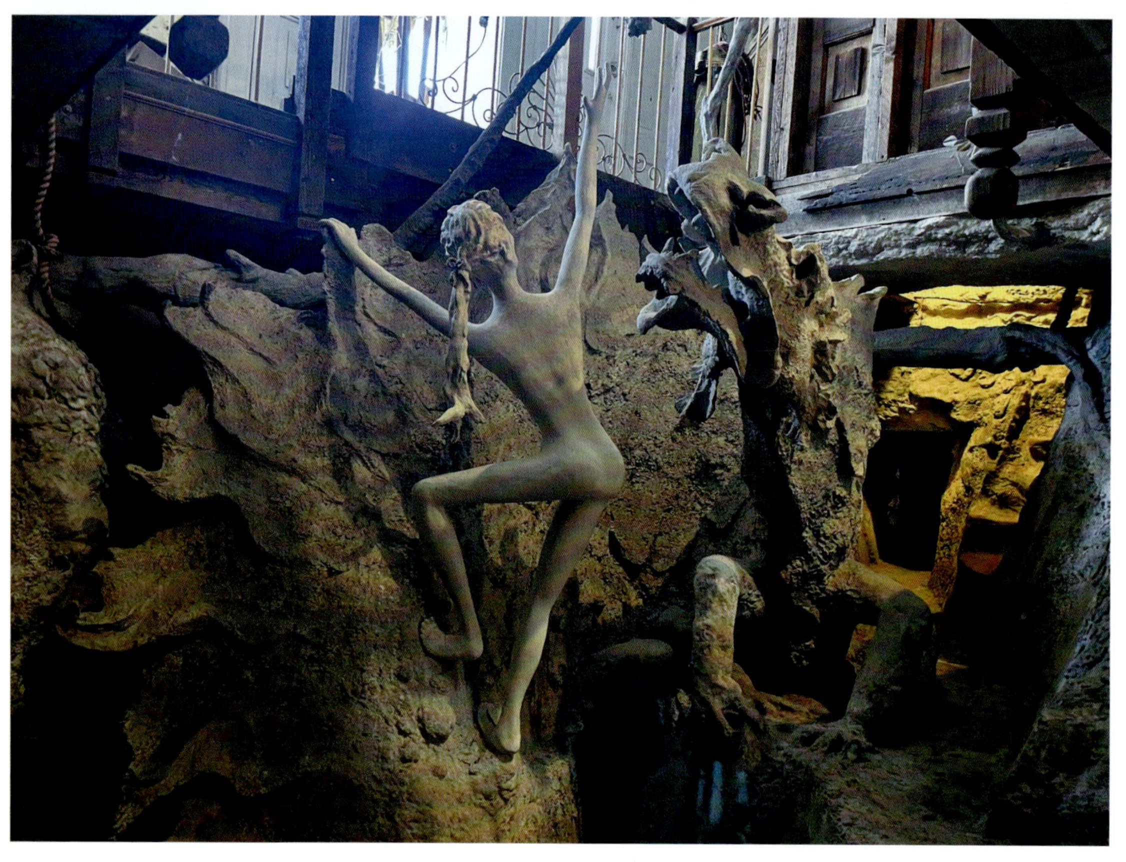

HE DEPICTED THE "UNTOLD" STORIES OF CREATION, BASED ON HIS OWN UNIQUE INTERPRETATION.

TORTURED SOULS TRY TO ESCAPE FROM THE WATERY DEPTHS OF HELL, BASEMENT LEVEL, 2023. PHOTO: KIRK HUFFAKER

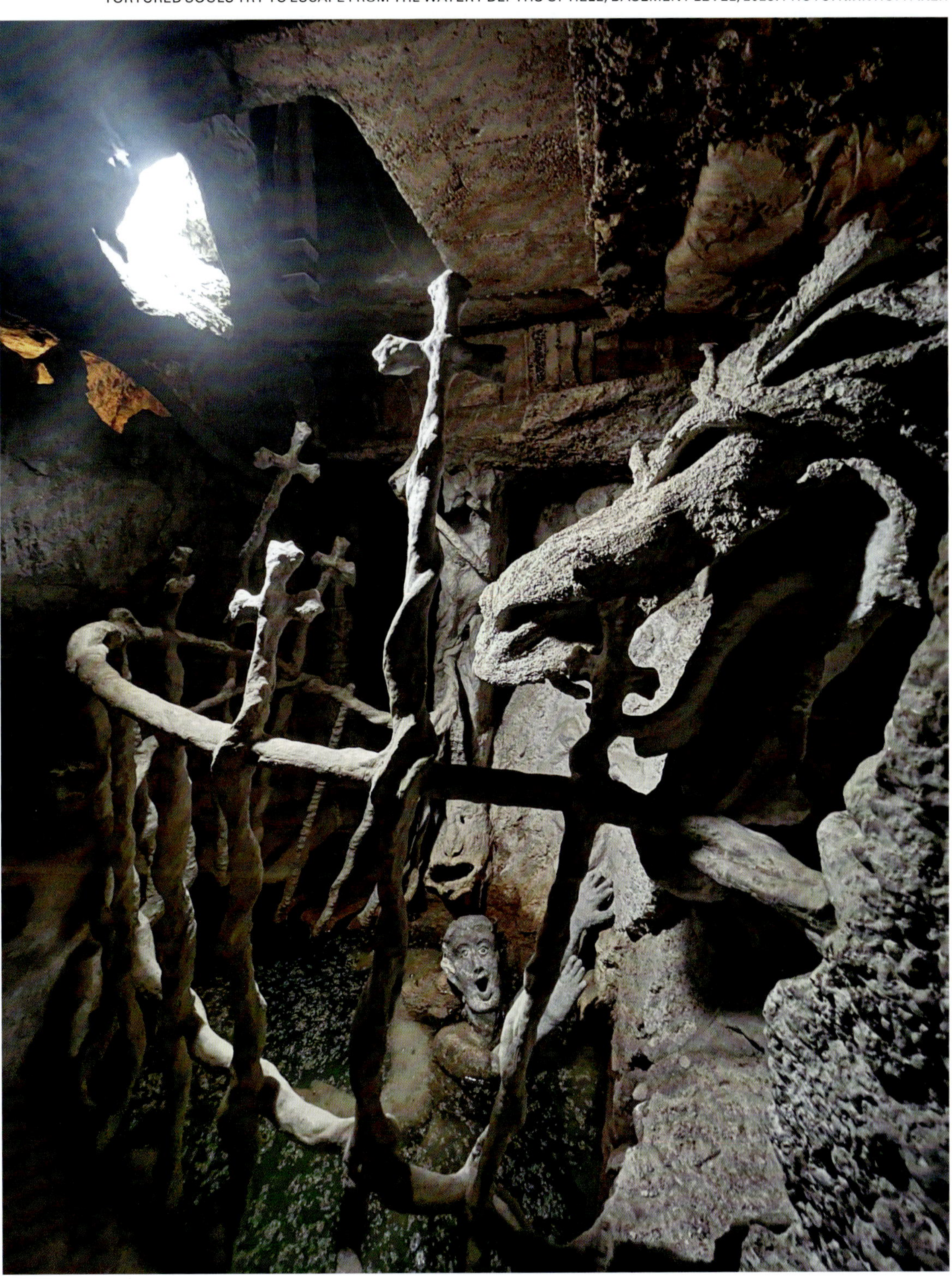

RUFINO LOYA RIVAS

LA CASA DE AZÚCAR (THE HOUSE OF SUGAR)

EL PASO, TEXAS

Born in Ciudad Juárez, Mexico, Loya (1933–2022) was a radio technician who immigrated just across the U.S. border to the adjacent West Texas city of El Paso in the early 1960s, where he found employment as a black-and-white television repair technician. He was offered a job in California but found the cost of living higher there, so he returned to El Paso in 1963 and spent the rest of his career in two local textile manufacturing plants, including that of Levi Strauss & Co. Although the work was steady, the wages were relatively low, and he was unable to afford the purchase of a large home in an elegant neighborhood for his wife and growing family. The best he could provide was a corner lot with a modest bungalow located next to a busy freeway in a district where the streets were not yet paved, but in 1973, after they moved in, he vowed that he would transform this "ugly" one-story home into something special that would make his wife proud.

With no art, architecture, or engineering training, yet with considerable visual memory of the elaborate Catholic churches of Mexico, Loya's work reflected that Baroque aesthetic from the very beginning. While he had been particularly attracted by the carved devotional stonework, he acknowledged that he had neither the skills to work with this difficult medium nor the funds to purchase those materials. Consequently, he turned to the use of rocks and Portland cement as his primary building supplies, and after work, on evenings and weekends, he taught himself similar techniques through trial and error. Energized as he laid brick and poured concrete to develop ever more intricate decorations, he patiently molded countless simple concave forms within cups or bowls, grouping or stacking them with others to create flower-like modules that he attached with masonry glue to constructed pedestals, pillars, and supports. In this way he produced fences, archways, columns, and elaborate flowerpots (some of which held real flowers while others contained fabricated metal or concrete varietals), expanding the hardscape to the curb in each direction, and supplementing his built construction with precisely planted and pruned vegetation.

Although Loya's inspired channeling of the imagery, symbolism, and dense visual detailing of Mexico's opulent churches was of significantly reduced scale and fabricated from significantly more base materials, it does not necessarily suffer in comparison. Each component is not only lavishly adorned with concrete or found-object ornaments, but the whole has been precisely painted in white, light blue, and pastel colors of rose and terra cotta, giving the impression of a sugary confection. Members of the public started colloquially referring to the environment as the *Casa de Azúcar/House of Sugar*, and Loya, bemused, installed a small plaque on-site to identify it by this name.

The appliquéd ornaments, colorful eave and window treatments, and floating archways that adorn the house are replicated at even greater scale and intensity in a series of monuments and grottoes that have overtaken much of the yard. Freestanding shrines and memorials reveal his beliefs—above all in his fervent Catholicism, particularly lauding Saint Francis of Assisi and the Franciscan order's explorers who opened up the pass between Juárez and El Paso—but also his dedication to his adopted country, with constructed roses expressing his deep sorrow on behalf of the victims of the September 11, 2001 terrorist attacks.

The most elaborate work is a multileveled altar exalting the Sacred Heart of Jesus, which is densely adorned with angels and cherubs and surmounted by a large painted sculpture of Christ. Another, dedicated to the Virgin of Guadalupe and featuring a painted polychrome portrait of this aspect of Mary—who is always represented with semi-indigenous features and is revered as Mexico's most popular symbol of religious devotion—is similarly extravagant. Each of these two shrines took hundreds of hours of work to complete. Loya's fabricated modules form the predominant mass of the structures, but they are complemented with commercially produced religious statues, which he painted and repainted over the years; other smaller components in the environment site also feature these manufactured elements. In each case, elaborate finials cap ornate symmetrical detailing and enhance both visual balance and aesthetic consistency, enlivening the impact of the various motifs.

Throughout the site are small hand-painted plaques—mostly in Spanish but a few also translated into English—that reflect Loya's religious piety and sense of humility in the face of his sumptuous extended environment, while others offer homespun adages to promote living an ethical life. They also reflect his deep affection for and lifelong association with the land of his birth: "*Esta casa es un pedacito de México*/This house is a little piece of Mexico" reads one painted sign, and another describes the environment

OVERVIEW OF SITE, 2018

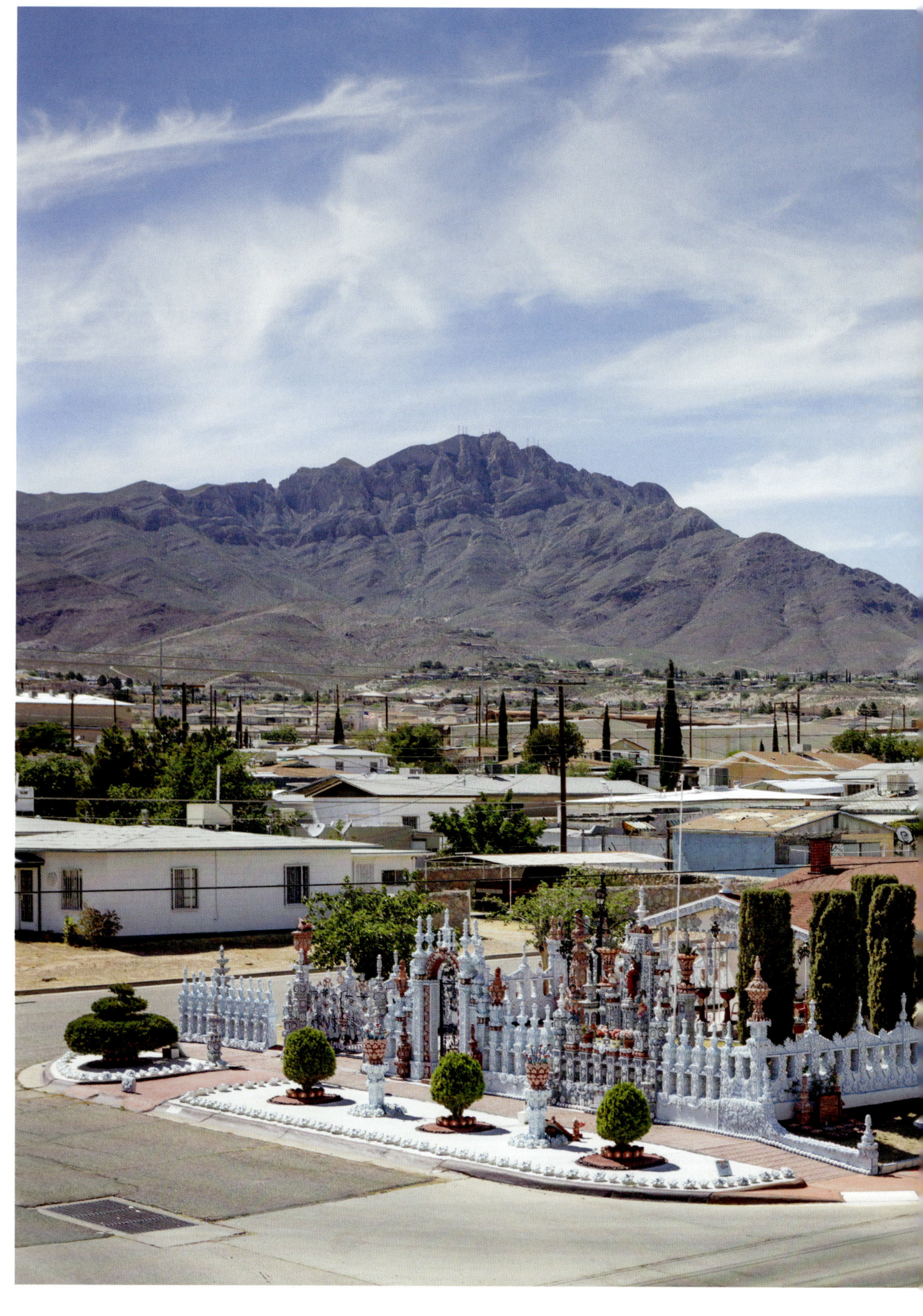

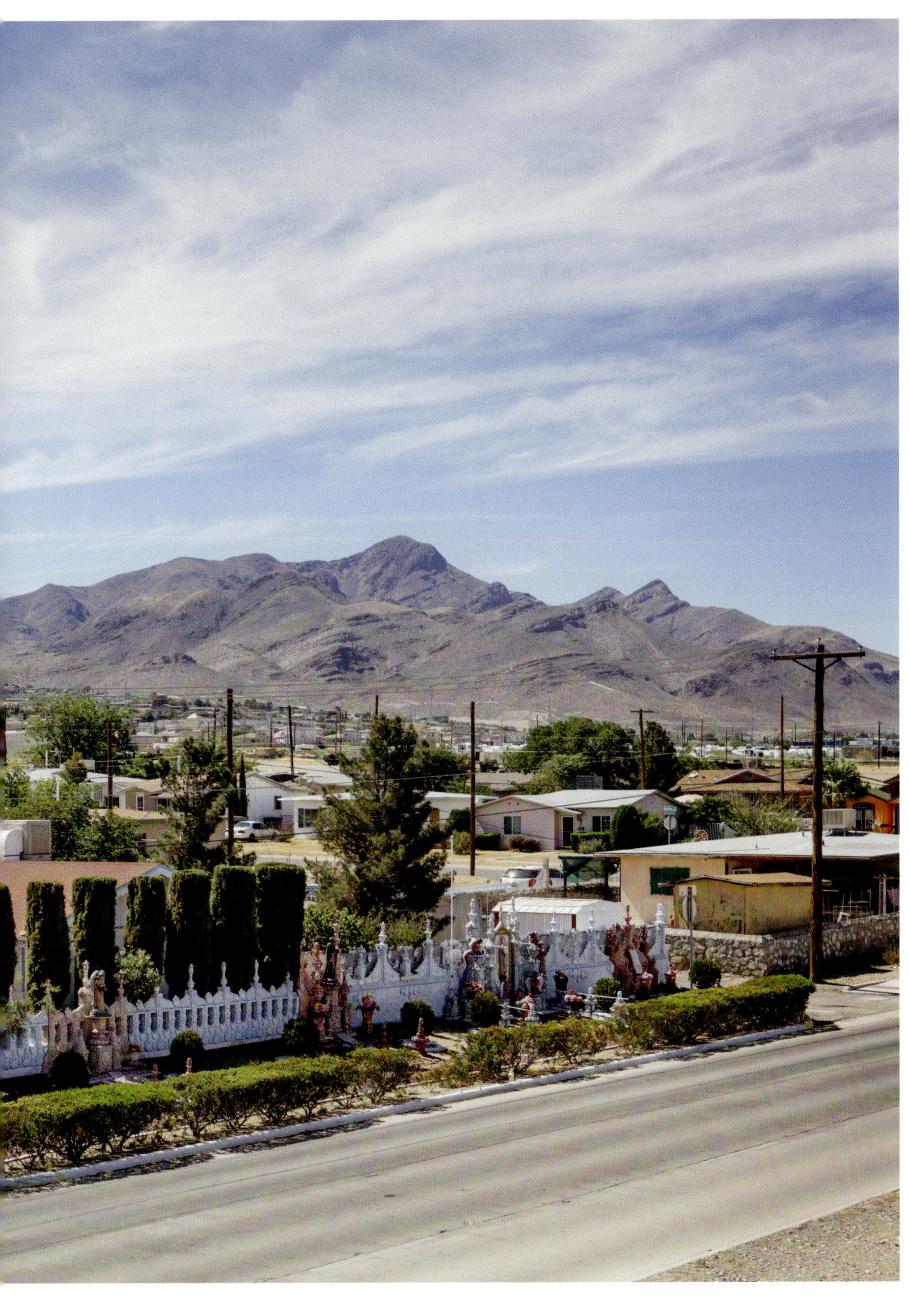

as the display of "Mexican Art Works" created in homage to the city of El Paso.

One more sign, embellished with the imprint of his two hands and those of his wife, reports that the site was created between 1973 and 1998, yet Loya actually continued to repaint and repair in the years until his death in order to preserve and maintain the appeal of his architectural confection. While acknowledging that even nonreligious visitors found it alluring, he was clear that his intent was to manifest his deep Catholic faith: his belief led him to the path to delight his wife and family and also to enthrall the residents of his adopted city of El Paso and the country to which he immigrated, where he so clearly thrived. Someone told him, he said, that if a person does not do art during their life, then they have not lived.

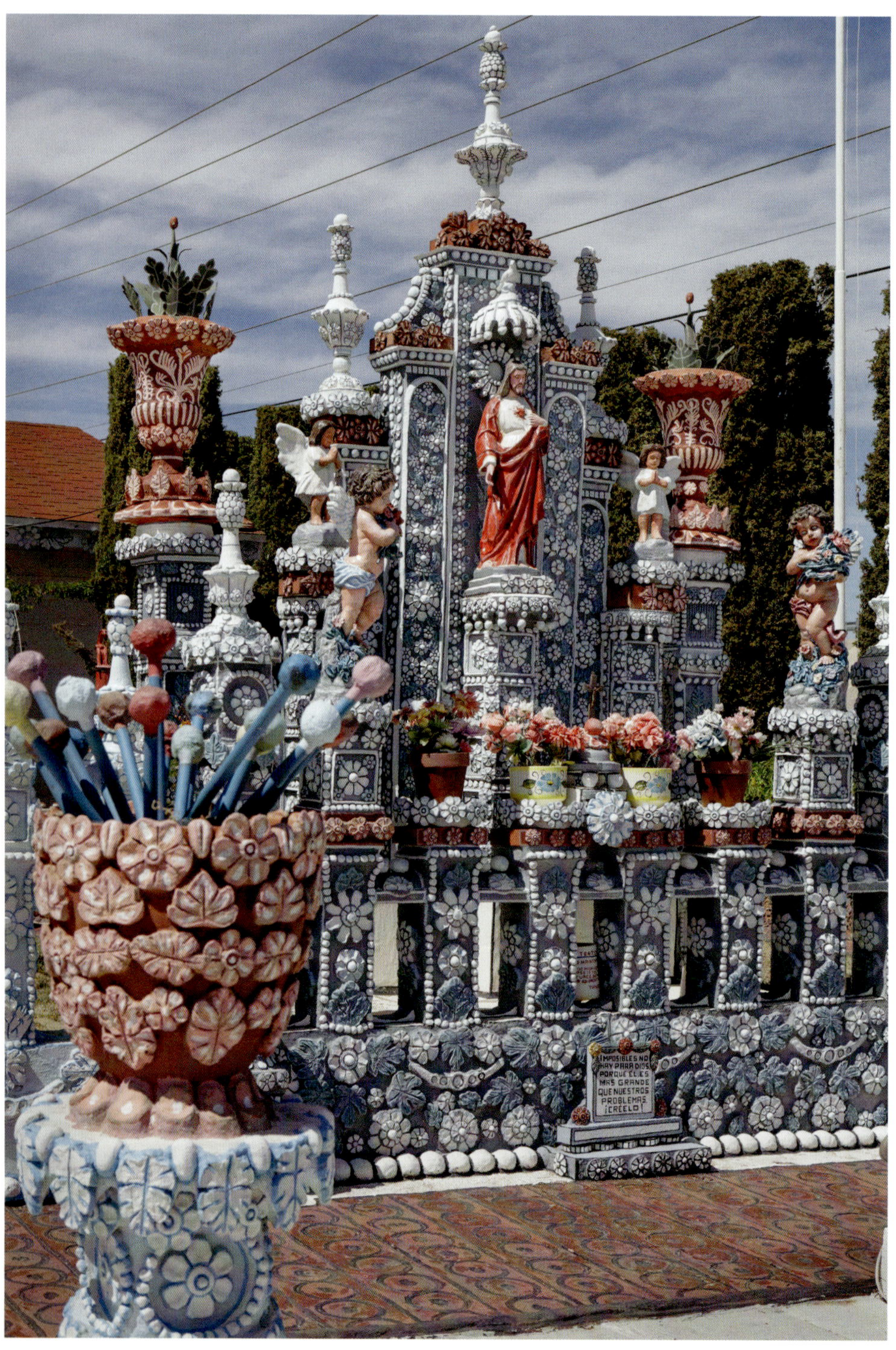

SHRINE OF THE SACRED HEART (DETAIL), 2018

FRONT (SOUTH) FAÇADE, 2018

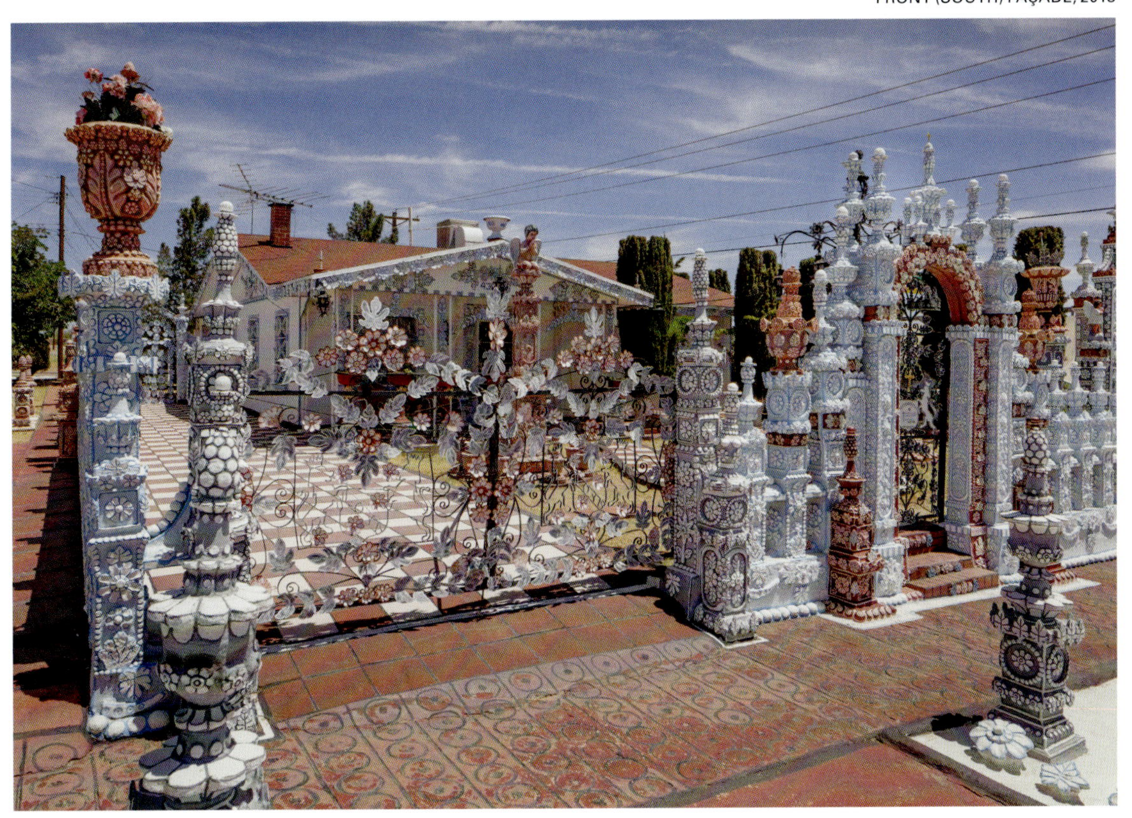

HE REFLECTED THE BAROQUE AESTHETIC OF MEXICO'S OPULENT CATHOLIC CHURCHES AT HIS MODEST HOME BY THE SIDE OF A TEXAS HIGHWAY.

JAMES HAMPTON, JR.

—

THRONE OF THE THIRD HEAVEN OF THE NATIONS' MILLENNIUM GENERAL ASSEMBLY

WASHINGTON, D.C.

During the last 14 years of his life, Hampton (1909–1964) created a spectacular devotional monument to respond to the imperatives of his religious visions. Secreted in the dingy interior of a rented garage in an African-American neighborhood, it was not until after his death that this elaborate assemblage was discovered. Immediately recognized as extraordinary, the *Throne of the Third Heaven of the Nations' Millennium General Assembly* may have been the first notable artist-built environment accepted into a major public collection, and it remains on permanent display today at the Smithsonian American Art Museum.

Elloree, South Carolina, the town of Hampton's birth, was primarily populated by African-American sharecroppers and tenant farmers. His father was a self-ordained Southern Baptist minister, but the elder Hampton's commitment to heavenly salvation apparently took precedence over the reality of his earth-bound existence, as he abandoned his wife and four children to follow his calling, wandering and preaching on an itinerant basis to small groups of believers. In his absence, his wife and community members took care of the children's spiritual needs by raising them according to strict fundamentalist tenets, in counterpoint to the daily work as fieldhands that generated the subsistence living necessary to support their needs on earth.

Hampton followed an older brother to Washington D.C. in 1939 at age 19, and took jobs as a short-order cook. This kind of repetitive work did not interfere with the holy visions that, beginning as early as 1931, he had begun to experience and, occasionally, record. He was drafted in 1942 and sent to the Pacific Islands as part of a segregated noncombatant squadron tasked with maintaining the Army's airstrips. Upon his return in 1945, after receiving an honorable discharge and a Bronze Star, he was hired by the General Services Administration as a night custodian in federal office buildings, a job he held until his death. This employment, and his older brother, who died suddenly in 1948, were the two aspects of his daily reality that were not involved in the complex spiritual life in which he was increasingly absorbed.

While he was in Guam in 1945, Hampton assembled at least one small altar that he brought home and later incorporated as part of his *Throne*. But it was not until 1950 that he had the wherewithal to rent that small unheated garage, an expense necessary to give him the physical space to focus his free time on carrying out his visions. Given his janitorial job, this typically did not begin until after midnight. These images coalesced around his belief in the Second Coming of Christ in the end times, where Christ would sit at God's side and judge the living and the dead. It was self-evident to Hampton that Christ would need a throne on which to rest, a monument worthy of His return and suitable for His everlasting rule of heaven on earth. Although Hampton was a modest and soft-spoken man who had few friends and never married, as the inspired architect of this precious, indispensable construction he privately began identifying himself as St. James and as Director, Special Projects for the State of Eternity.

Hampton pieced together discards and detritus that he salvaged from his janitorial job at the federal buildings, scavenged off the street, or purchased cheaply at second-hand shops. Among these items were wood planks and cardboard tubes, beat-up furniture, fiber acoustic and insulation boards, burned-out light bulbs, construction paper, plastic, bottles and vases, electrical conduit, and used-up or unwanted office supplies. He also covered 180 separate objects with purple paper and silver- and gold-colored metallic foil, punctuating them with bits of glass and mirrors chosen for their reflective qualities. Befitting its purpose, the *Throne* was meant to evoke a sensation of majesty, of magnificence, of glory.

At the rear of the garage, Hampton built risers to support and elevate some of the constructions. Others were arranged in front on the floor, and on several of the larger components he attached iron casters so that he could roll them to their precise and proper locations. He used nails, upholstery tacks, pins, and glues to meticulously affix everything together, sawing legs off tables, upending drawers, or extending planks to enhance scale and prominence as he built up the multiple levels that became so essential to the impact of the whole. The central focal point of the assemblage is a seven-foot-high, second-hand chair with plush cushions, its appended projections alluding to angel wings, and its elongated back, with a complex arched form topped with the encouragement "Fear Not," presumably referring to the "tribulation" expected to accompany the end of days.

To each side are symmetrical elements that, on the left, are associated with Moses and the Old Testament and, to the right, Christ

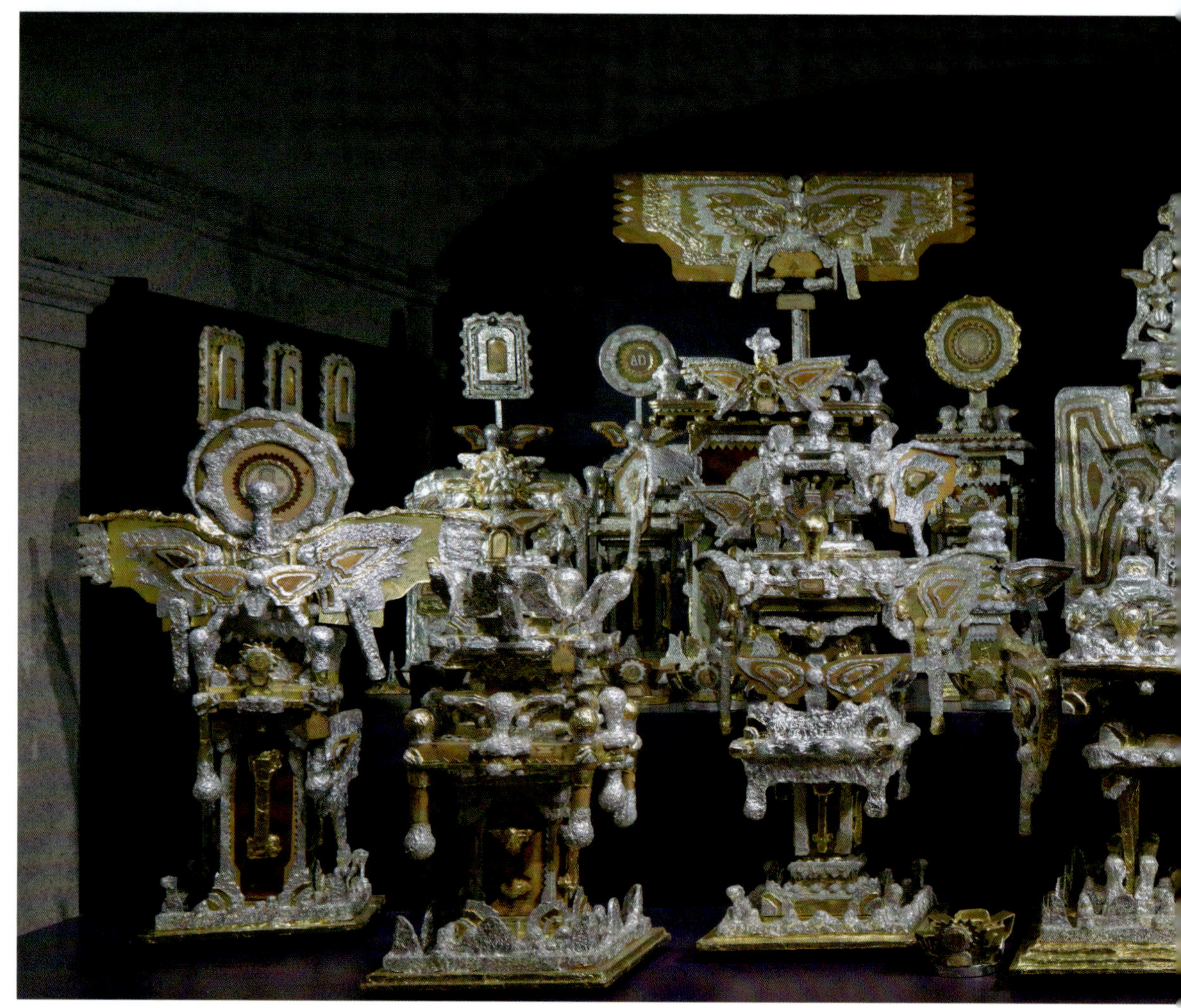

THE THRONE OF THE THIRD HEAVEN OF THE NATIONS' MILLENNIUM GENERAL ASSEMBLY, CA. 1950-1964, MIXED MEDIA, DIMENSIONS VARIABLE. SMITHSONIAN AMERICAN ART MUSEUM, GIFT OF ANONYMOUS DONORS, 1970.353.1-.116. PHOTO: COURTESY SMITHSONIAN AMERICAN ART MUSEUM

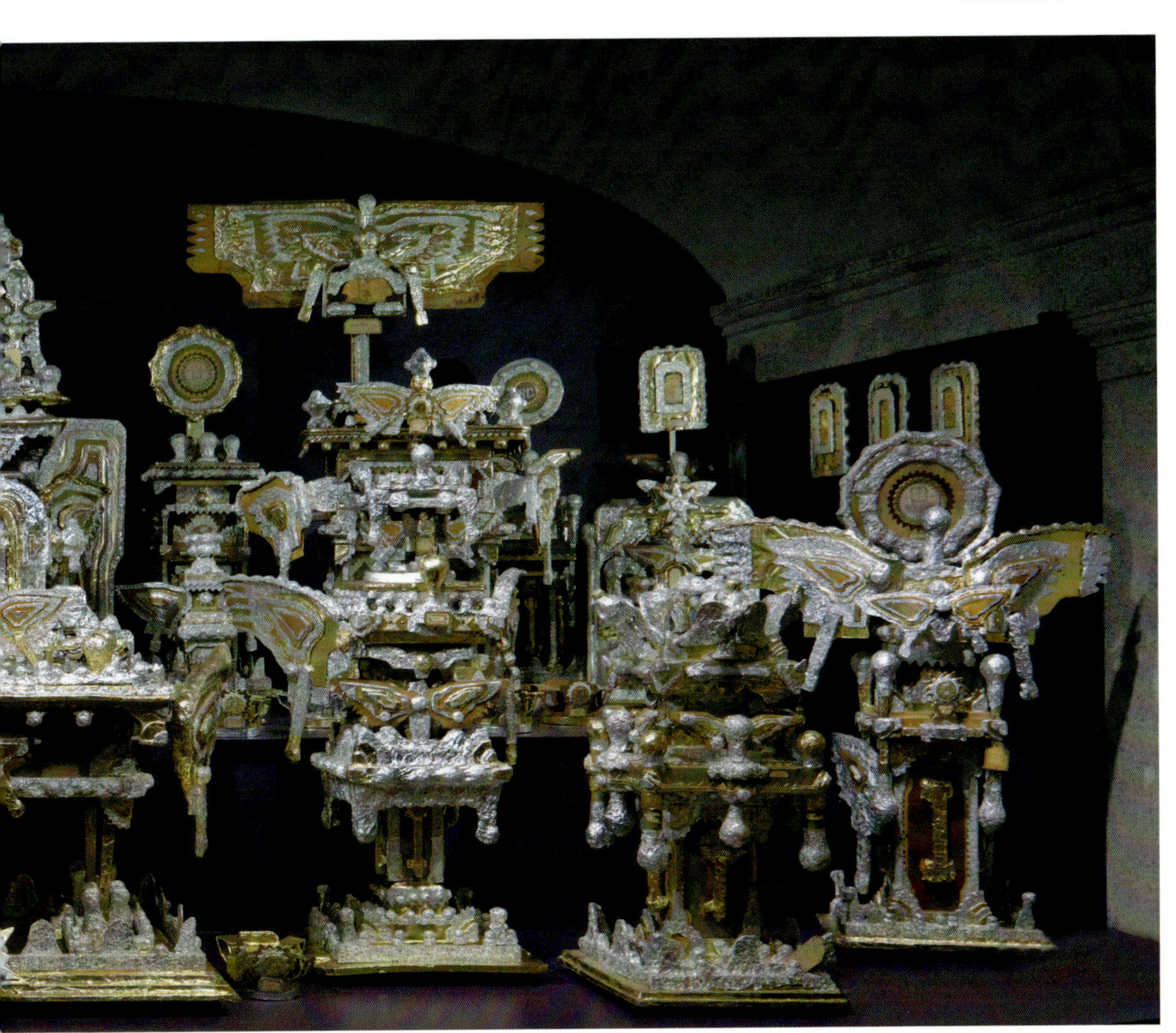

and the New Testament; some are captioned with quotes from the Book of Revelation. Pulpit-like structures provide the opportunity for multiple preachers to simultaneously address an audience that Hampton expected would be rapturously attentive. Each component is intricately constructed, with layered surfaces and bas- and high-relief components that look like stars, scepters, altars, crowns, and chalices, all appointments that would not be incongruous in a traditional church. Rows of foil-covered light bulbs—perhaps metaphorically referencing Christ as the light of the world—reinforce the almost baroque visual sophistication with which Hampton balanced faith and opulence. The luminous installation helped him to overcome his penurious and lonely existence in a lavish display of celestial grandeur.

Hampton died from stomach cancer at age 53, and it seems likely that he would have continued to work and expand his installation if he had had more time. He left behind a journal, *The Book of the 7 Dispensations by St. James*, written in an inscrutable symbolic script that has not yet been deciphered; perhaps someday its secrets—the word of God as he understood it, or possibly his thoughts as he constructed his masterpiece—will be revealed, although after some decryption analysis, scholars have suggested that it may be the written equivalent of speaking in tongues. He rarely spoke of his spectacular *Throne* to others, and although he had hoped to utilize it as the keystone of a storefront ministry, this plan never came to fruition.

It was not until the landlord, wondering why the rent payment was in arrears, broke open the door after his death that Hampton's glittering, sparkling radiance was discovered. Not quite knowing what to do, he called a newspaper reporter who, in December 1964, penned the first public account of the *Throne's* existence; as a result, several mainstream painters and sculptors came to see it, as did a curator at the National Collection of Fine Arts (now the Smithsonian American Art Museum). The curator paid the back-due rent and took possession of the installation so that its pieces could be carefully moved and brought into the collection. Hampton's relocated *Throne of the Third Heaven of the Nations' Millennium General Assembly* is now praised as America's finest and most illustrious work of visionary religious art.

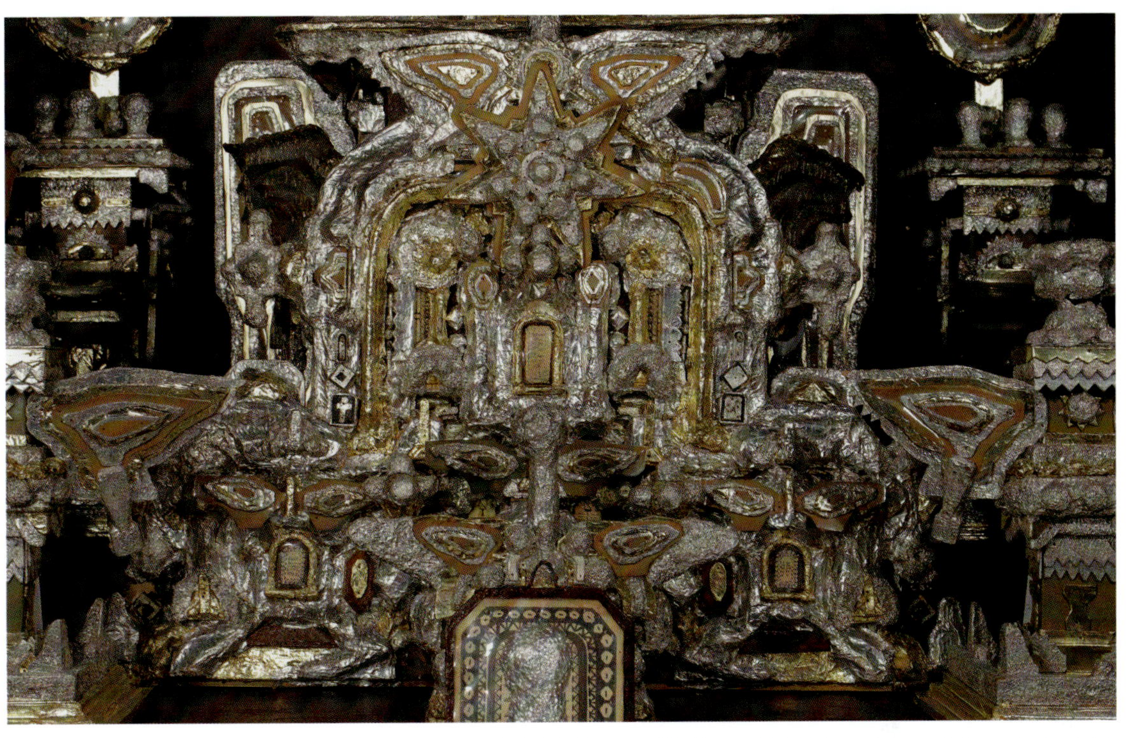

THE THRONE OF THE THIRD HEAVEN OF THE NATIONS' MILLENNIUM GENERAL ASSEMBLY (DETAIL), CA. 1950-1964, MIXED MEDIA, DIMENSIONS VARIABLE. SMITHSONIAN AMERICAN ART MUSEUM, GIFT OF ANONYMOUS DONORS, 1970.353.1-.116. PHOTO: COURTESY SMITHSONIAN AMERICAN ART MUSEUM

THE DARK INTERIOR OF A RENTED GARAGE HID A GLITTERING DEVOTIONAL MONUMENT FOR A PRIVATE CHURCH THAT WAS NEVER OPENED.

FATHER PAUL MATTHIAS DOBBERSTEIN

—

GROTTO OF THE REDEMPTION

WEST BEND, IOWA

The dark interior of Hampton's projected garage ministry is a truly singular expression, glowing with the radiance of his foil-wrapped *Throne* (see page 376) and alluding to the mysteries of religious illumination. More common—in the United States as well as in European antecedents—is the sanctified grotto, originally an actual cave or cavern but later a modified or even a newly constructed architectural structure meant to evoke the same sensation one might experience in a natural setting. Dobberstein (1872–1954) created grottos that came to embody the archetype of this kind of devotional architecture not only through his initial construction in West Bend and in several subsequent commissioned grottos in Iowa, Wisconsin, and South Dakota, but also through the influence his work had on other grotto designers and builders, such as Father Mathias Wernerus in Wisconsin (see page 388) and Madeline Buol in Iowa.

Dobberstein was born and raised in Germany, and, as a university student, he learned six languages and studied a range of other subjects, including geology and minerology. In 1893 he immigrated to the United States, where, while attending seminary near Milwaukee, Wisconsin, and shortly before he took his vows, he was stricken with pneumonia. Praying for health, he promised to erect a shrine to the Virgin Mary should he recover and successfully be ordained. While the small cave-like *Our Lady of Lourdes* grotto at the seminary, dedicated in 1894, is attributed to Dobberstein, he had greater ambitions, and after he was assigned to the Church of Saints Peter and Paul in West Bend, he lost little time making his mark. He built a parochial school, and purchasing a house adjacent to the church for use as a rectory, he excavated the marsh on that property to form a lake. Then, despite this farmland region's marked scarcity of rock, he began stockpiling fieldstones and rocks with help from children, neighbors, and parishioners. They next dug 20-foot-deep holes for the foundation, outlining the scale of the grotto he planned to build in fulfillment of his promise. This promise became the beginning of a lifetime of work.

Knowledgeable about European grotto traditions and encouraged by the new availability of concrete for nonindustrial use, Dobberstein began to construct the complex that would become the *Grotto of the Redemption* in 1912. But he soon realized that the materials he and community members had been able to gather would not be nearly sufficient. Moreover, his university-level familiarity with rocks and minerals—as well as his vision of the grandeur of the construction—motivated him to search out ever more distinctive resources. A hands-on spelunker and minerologist, he was driven to collect exceptional semiprecious stones, crystals, ores, and stalactites and stalagmites from caves and specialized geological sites throughout the area. Executing his ambitious vision took precedence over the kind of environmental concern that we might express today regarding the removal of at least 100 loads of materials carried on trucks and train cars away from sensitive areas.

The ostensible purpose of the *Grotto* was to shelter and showcase recognizable religious figures and provide an intimate space for the Biblical narrative to spark spiritual contemplation. Consequently, the purchased Carrara marble statues in their iconic poses would have been expected to be the focus of this environment. But, in truth, Dobberstein's constructions became the essential draw. Following his example, the technique of encasing excavated rocks and minerals in concrete became the default building method for such devotional architecture in the Upper Midwest, as this additive form of building was a means of making use of geometrically irregular materials and being able to improvisationally accommodate them as they became available. In addition, while the project's essence was the simulated sacred cave secreted within an artificial mountain, his technique allowed for a range of architectural styles and the installation of supplemental components such as towers, pillars, exterior niches and alcoves, planters, parapets, and pedestals. The consistent use of similar materials helped to ease any stylistic incongruity.

The first building, the 35-foot-tall *Grotto of the Trinity*, features a large Roman arch at the entrance and three interior recessed apses with a central dome, but it was not the only attraction. Ultimately, nine contiguous grottos on this site came to illustrate the journey from the original sin in the Garden of Eden, at the north, through a series of canopied *Stations of the Cross* formations that ended, at the south, with the Crucifixion. To the west of the central pathway is the 40-foot-high *Grotto of Gethsemane* and the grottos of the *Entombment* and the *Resurrection*, this latter similarly designed with three apses, its entrance flanked by columns capped with rock crystal. The visitor is encouraged to stroll among the components to understand the dramatic, albeit condensed, Biblical

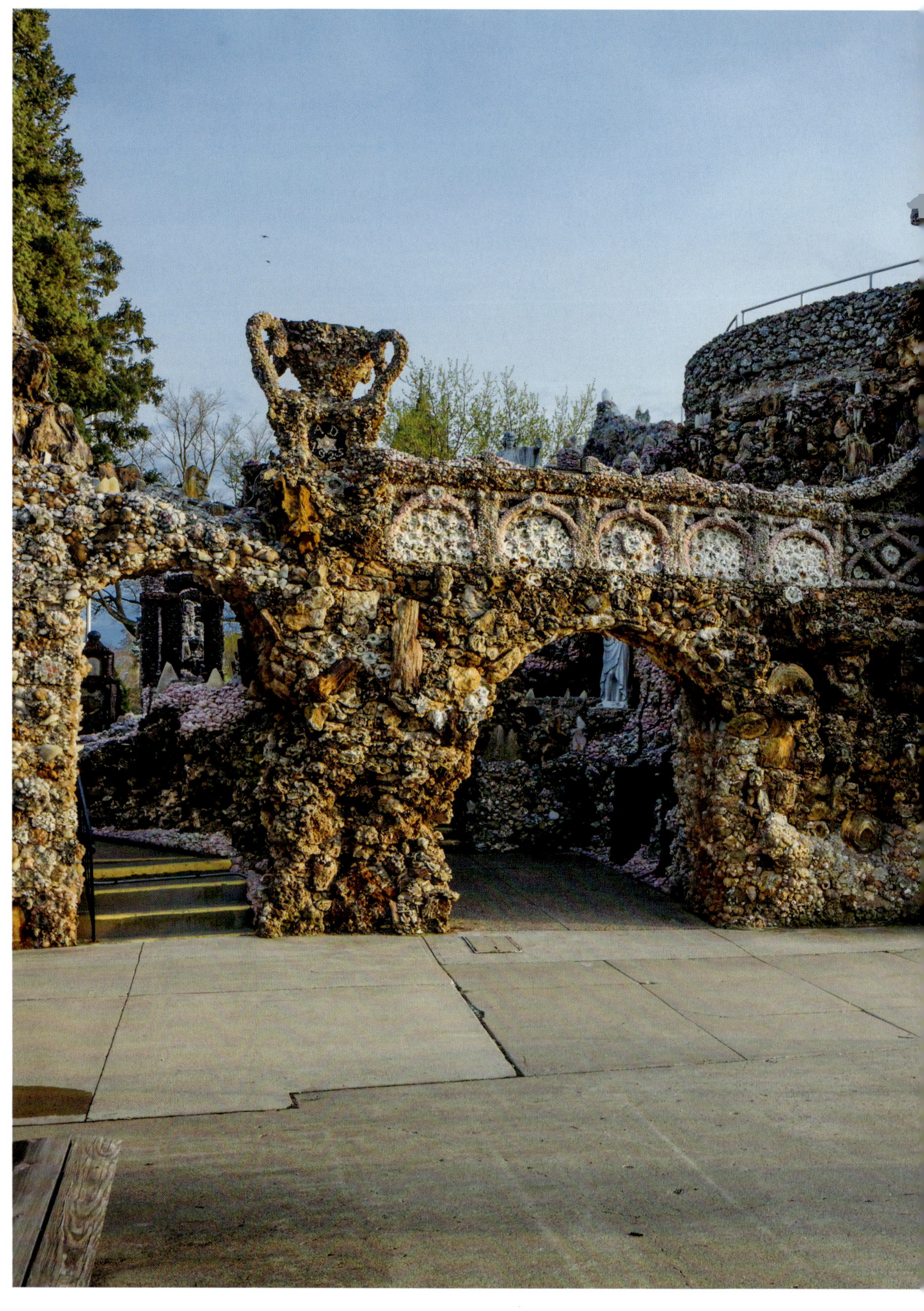

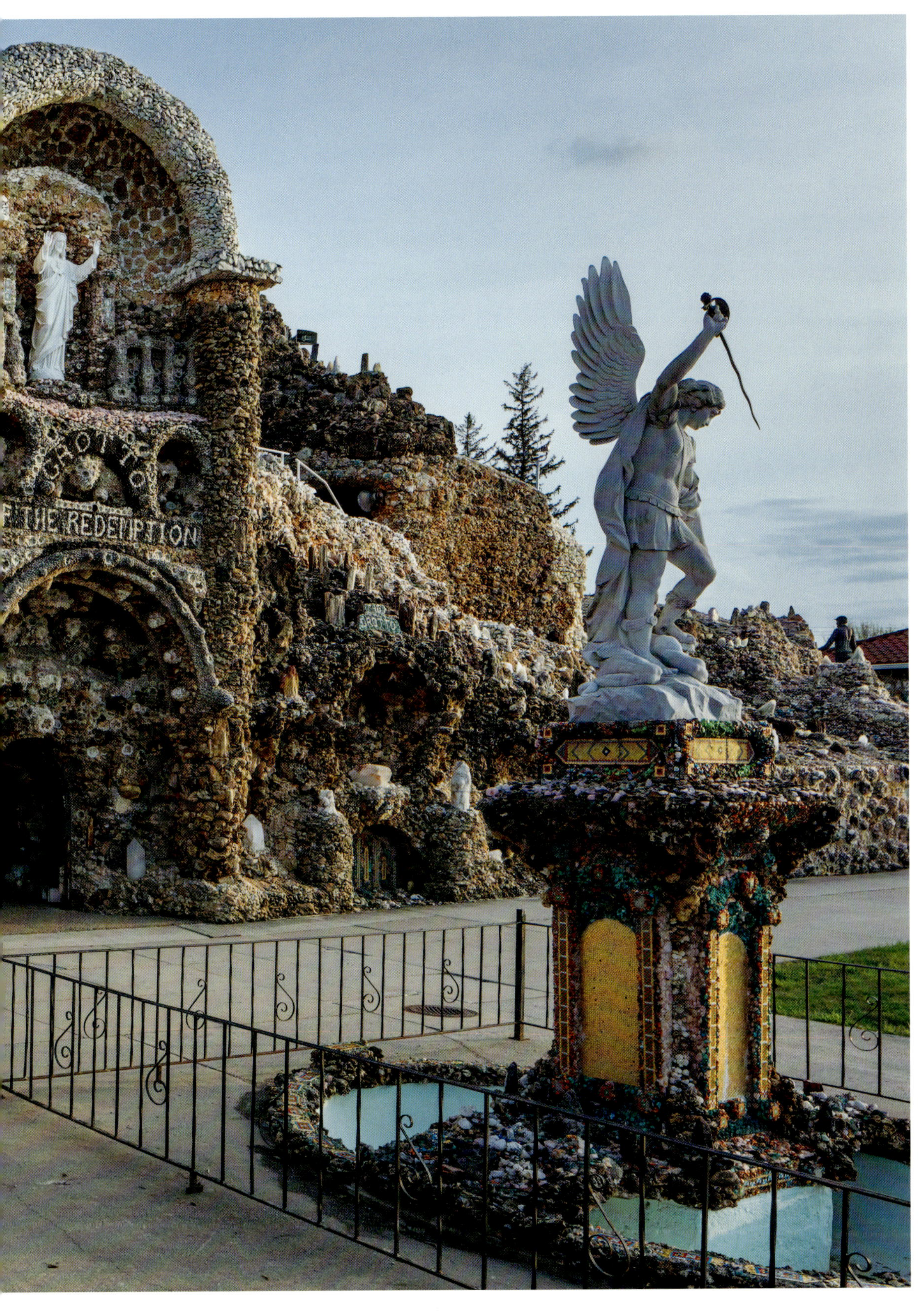
GROTTO
THE REDEMPTION

narrative, and to increase receptivity for a personal spiritual experience.

Plantings were added to reference the naturally occurring caverns that had originally inspired this kind of built construction, and the embellishment of exotic shells, colored stones, geodes, quartz, mica, fossils, corals, petrified wood, and geological formations was intended to recall Biblical assurances of the beauty of the promised paradise, heightening the likelihood of a spiritual awakening (if not a religious conversion). Nor were secular concerns forgotten: the pond attracted swimmers, fishermen, picnickers, and all kinds of community activities during the summer, with ice-skating and snowman-building in the winter. Dobberstein, reportedly a showman possessed of a robust ego, organized other spectacles (including, for a while, a zoo) to attract less religiously inclined visitors as well.

He spent 42 years working on the West Bend *Grotto*, but during this time Dobberstein also accepted commissions for the construction of several other sacred and secular projects, including other religious grottos. He always asked that the sponsoring church or municipality pay materials expenses and the wages of his helper, but he donated his own time and efforts. Because he prefabricated certain components back in West Bend and then shipped them to the satellite sites, most share a similar aesthetic: inspirational marble statues in the style of classical Christian iconography, varieties of rocks and stones, and a small and darker interior sacred space surrounded by embellished and robustly textural exteriors meant to reference naturally occurring outcroppings and settings.

For six more years after Dobberstein's death, his decades-long assistant, Matt Szerensce, continued to work up until his own retirement on the *Grotto of the Redemption*. So did Dobberstein's replacement, Father Louis Greving, who added a museum and souvenir shop to the expanded *Grotto* and modified some of the original components by, for example, altering the original entry with the addition of an encrusted arch. Believed to be the largest manmade grotto in the world, this environment was listed on the National Register of Historic Places in 2001. It is an appropriate honor for an immigrant priest who can be credited with reimagining the European grotto tradition and successfully melding architecture, sculpture, and the natural environment into a hybrid that came to serve as an iconic inspiration for a range of other art environments throughout the Midwest.

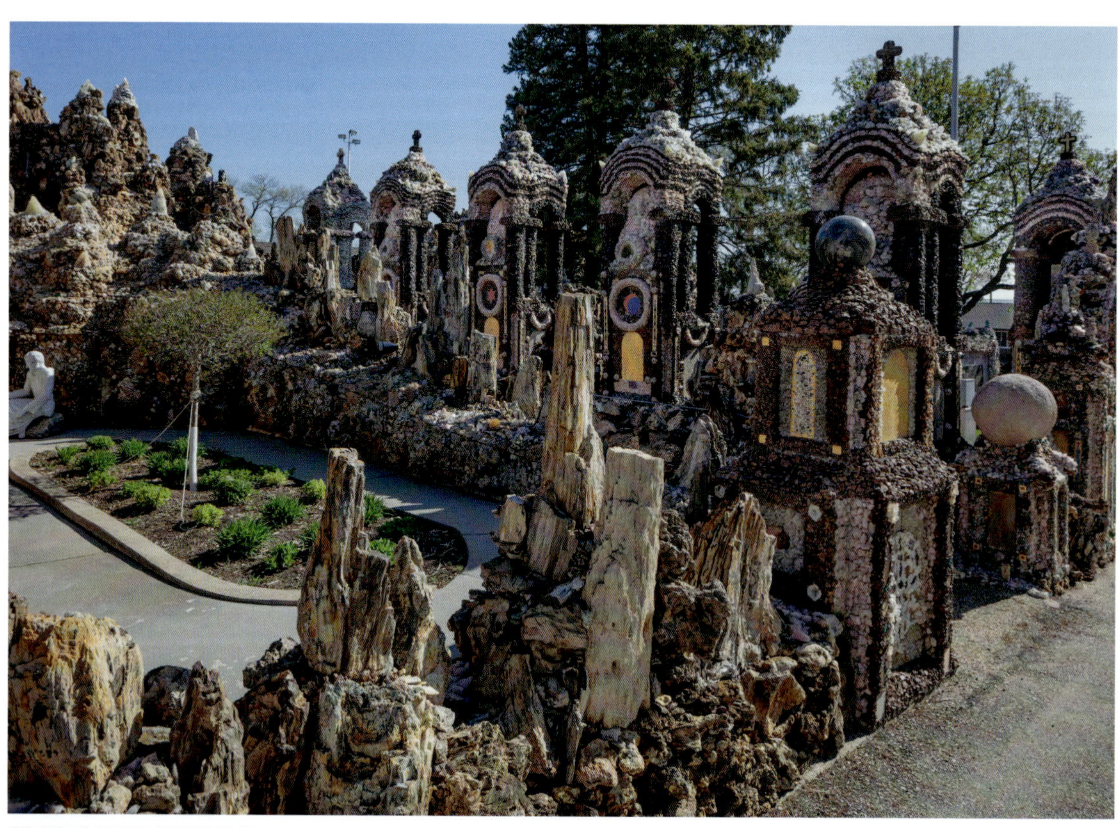

STATIONS OF THE CROSS, 2019

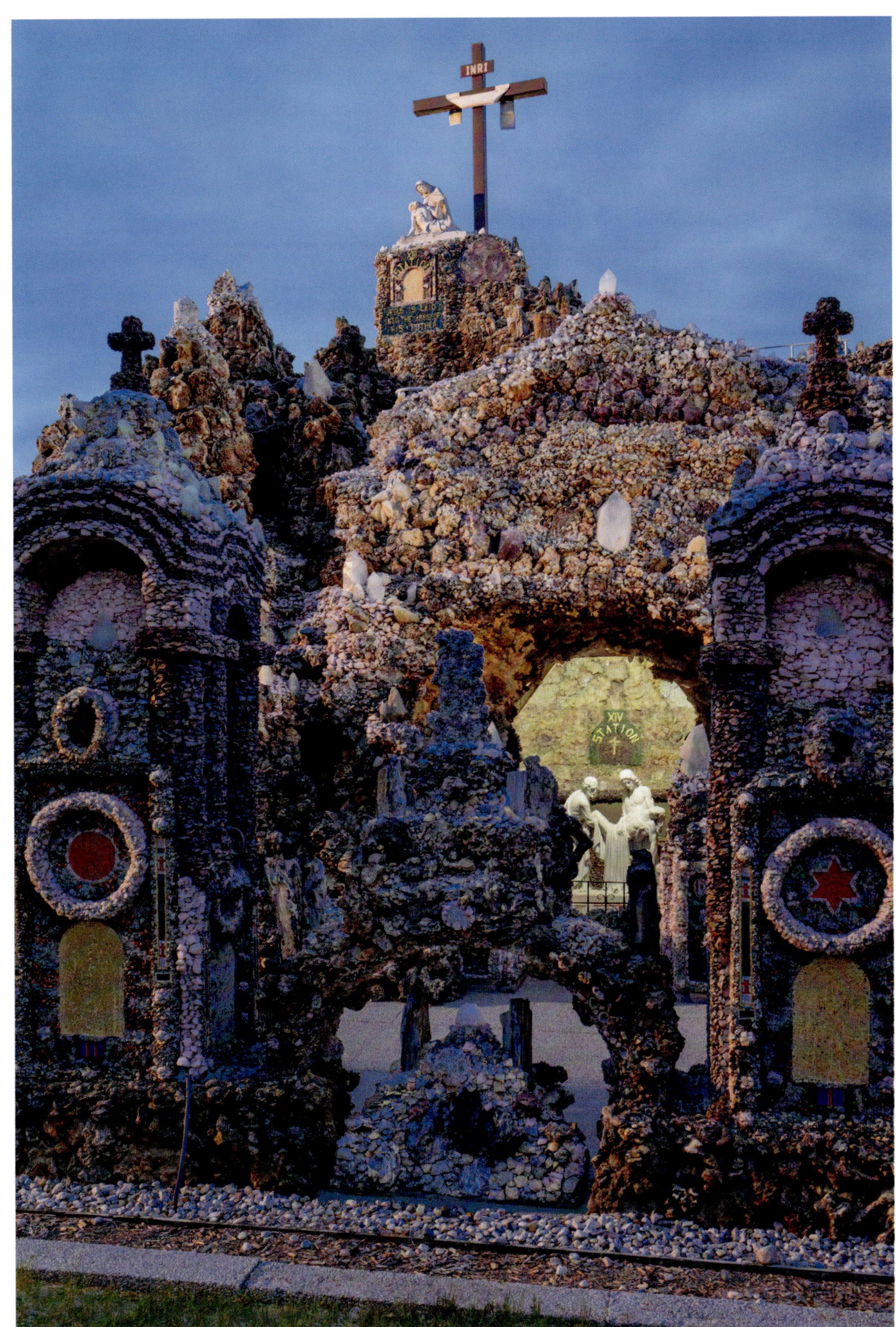

STATIONS OF THE CROSS (DETAIL) AND MARY HOLDING CHRIST AFTER THE CRUCIFIXION ON MOUNT CALVARY (CENTER REAR), 2019

FATHER MATHIAS WERNERUS

HOLY GHOST PARK, A.K.A. DICKEYVILLE GROTTO

DICKEYVILLE, WISCONSIN

Dickeyville is about 250 miles due east of West Bend, Iowa. The priests of their two Catholic parishes, both of German origin, were born only a year apart, and after immigrating to the United States, they attended the same seminary in Wisconsin, so Wernerus must have been aware of the small grotto Dobberstein built there. That Wernerus was influenced by Dobberstein's work (see page 382) is hardly surprising, given the overlapping dates of the construction of Dobberstein's *Grotto of the Redemption* (which evolved from 1912 through 1954) and Wernerus's *Holy Ghost Park* (constructed between 1926 and 1930), and by the facts that they both drew inspiration from the same European grotto genre, that they used similar production techniques and choice of media, and even that the location of one of Dobberstein's satellite sites was close to Dickeyville. To underscore the connection, Dobberstein's successor recalled that Wernerus had traveled to West Bend and worked with the older priest for "a week or two" as he learned techniques and processes. Both also similarly impacted the character and history of their small Midwestern farming communities in ways that may have been unanticipated.

Wernerus (1873–1931) was born in Kettenis, Germany, served his required three-year Army stint, and then began his studies for the priesthood in Belgium. He immigrated to the United States in 1904 and completed his education at St. Francis Seminary, where he was ordained in 1907. After serving in several parishes, in 1918 he was assigned a permanent position at the Holy Ghost Catholic Church in Dickeyville.

Along with his regular priestly duties, Wernerus began to develop ideas for the beautification of the parish properties. One of his first projects was a memorial to the three young men from the parish who had died in the First World War. Wernerus's contribution to the tableau, which was primarily composed of purchased elements, was to encrust two marble urns that flanked the base of a conventional Crucifixion scene. Limited funding for this project caused him to use readily available materials, which he gathered from nearby rock quarries and from bluffs along the Mississippi River. Shortly thereafter, he constructed two "flowerpots" that he planted with porcelain and glass flowers and then set into ornamented concrete bases. He subsequently built a square but richly ornamented *Grotto of the Holy Eucharist* near the cemetery.

These projects apparently inspired Wernerus to broaden his concept about what "beautification" of the church grounds might entail. After a parishioner gifted a statue of the Virgin and Child in gratitude for surviving an illness, Wernerus began his first major construction, the *Grotto of the Blessed Mother*. Located between the church and the rectory, it is reported to have the equivalent amount of rock and concrete below the surface as that which rises above. Recognizing that a project of this size would need community support on a variety of levels, Wernerus availed himself of the work of parishioners to help dig the massive foundation and gather stones and rocks. It is even said that he would dismiss children from parochial school classes if he needed extra hands. Like Dobberstein, he became a spelunker to facilitate his search for special stones and stalactites and stalagmites, but unlike the Iowan, who refused to use common glass or ceramics unless no other option were available, Wernerus was happy to accept gifts of a variety of manufactured as well as natural objects to adorn his growing building.

The most frequently used rock was petrified moss, but rose quartz, petrified sequoia and cedar wood, lava, seashells, coral, fossils, and a variety of geological formations also amplified the decoration. Tiles and broken glass were purchased by the barrel from kilns in Kokomo, Indiana, and Wernerus set up a brazier to melt down broken pieces of glass into colorful swirls. Minerals, marble, ores, crystal, and coal were inserted along with dishware and utensils of all kinds, porcelain figurines, printer's plates, arrowheads, pipestone, and a diverse selection of personal objects, many donated by parishioners. The substructure was concrete poured into wooden armatures reinforced with chicken wire, and after the decorative materials were pressed into the wet surface and the mortar had hardened, the framework was removed and the panels were affixed in their intended places. This is the same technique Dobberstein used.

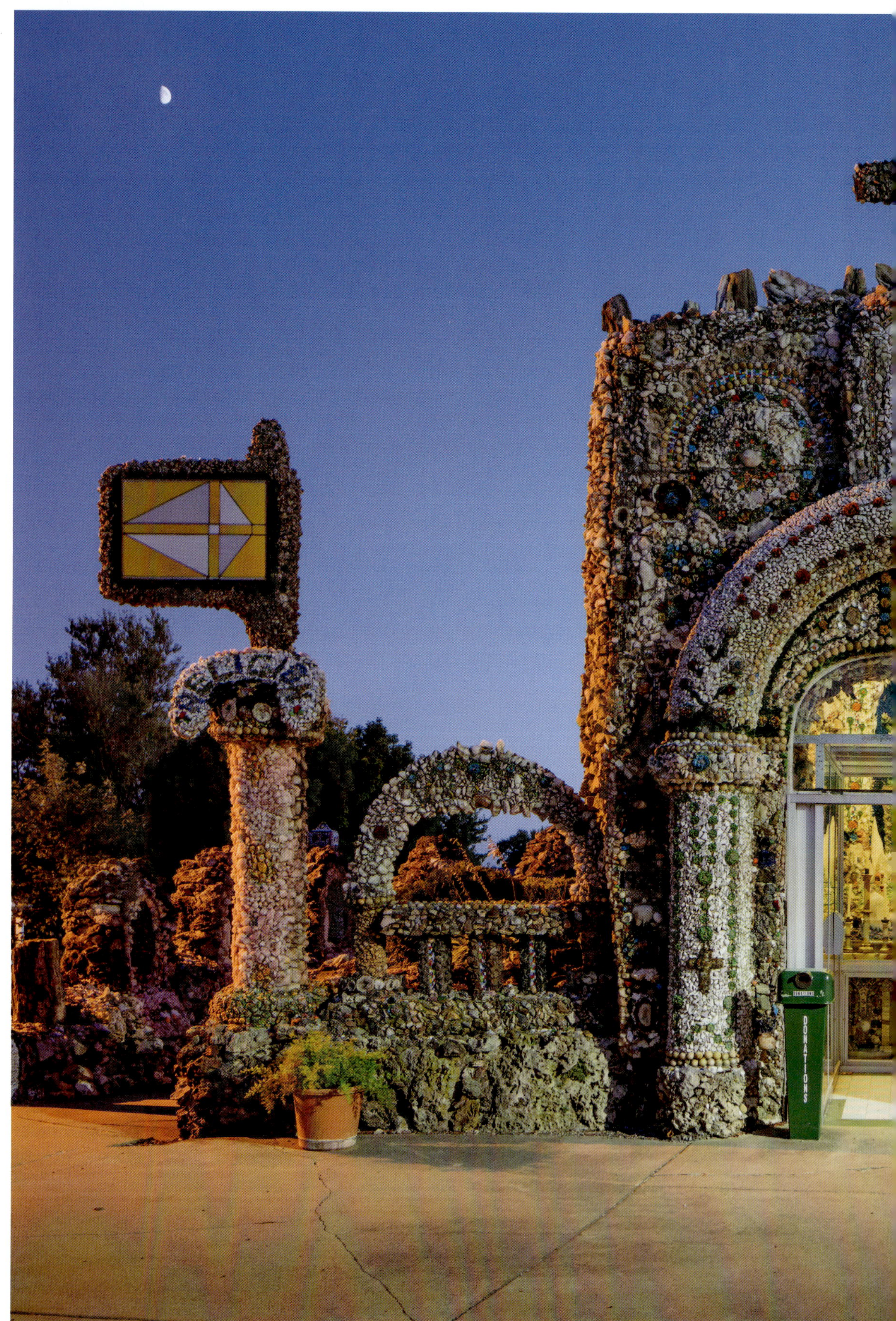

FRONT FAÇADE, *GROTTO OF THE BLESSED MOTHER*, 2017

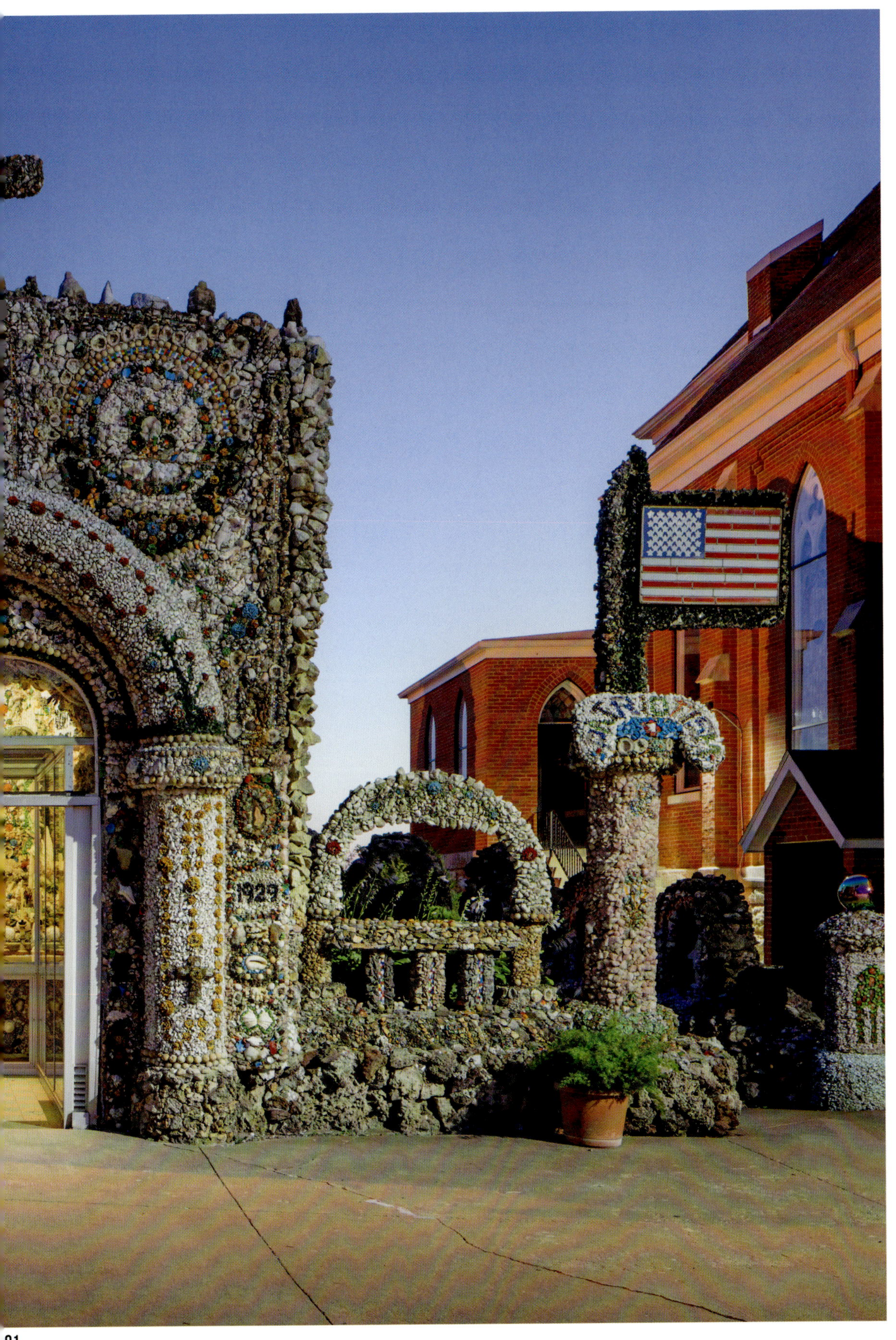
1929

The attention Wernerus gave to the inlaid decoration on the *Grotto* was extraordinary, as he fit together flourishes of mosaic texts and a broad range of objects, all united by symbolic color choices and motifs. The number of inlaid pieces doubles, triples, or even quadruples those gracing the works of other makers in this genre: the ornaments are inserted so tightly that no mortar remains visible between them.

The *Grotto of the Blessed Mother* (like the expansive *Patriotic Shrine*, the other major installation on-site) was designed to be viewed from the front, despite the complex ornamentation of its sides. Broadly visible from streetside, two round motifs grace the upper right and left sections of the almost square façade—shapes that, in certain light, appear like eyes—and a Roman arch, upon which glass flowers with hundreds of colored glass petals represent rosary beads, encircles the darkened and compressed interior where the Carrara marble statue is displayed. Yet while the *Grotto* was ostensibly constructed to protect and glorify the statue, the Virgin is dwarfed within the intimate and intricate niche by the overpowering edifice that envelops her.

Two rose quartz columns flank the *Grotto* building. On top of the left pillar is a concrete papal flag and, on the right, is the U.S. flag, the two encapsulating the religious/patriotic theme of the entire *Park*. (The American flag may also be a gesture acknowledging the need to downplay the influence of Rome among Catholics and to offset the anti-Catholic sentiment of those postwar years.) The rounded side walls of the exterior contain seven niches, each devoted to one of the seven Gifts of the Holy Spirit, and a tree whose trunk was constructed from petrified wood graces the rear, its many branches formed by glass and stone inscriptions of the Twelve Fruits of the Holy Spirit. It is symbolically topped by a dove.

Behind the *Grotto* building and linked to it by a narrow pathway is a semicircular wall crowned by niches that gradually increase in scale, erected in honor of the Twelve Apostles and St. Joseph. At the center is a statue of Christ, set within a 27-foot-high niche whose walls are abundantly ornamented with rose quartz, petrified wood, and a stalactite. This complex was constructed between 1926 and 1929, and was dedicated in 1930 with great fanfare, accompanied by a speech from Wisconsin's governor.

Several other units are enclosed in the *Holy Ghost Park* setting, joined to each other by shrub-lined paths bordered by decorated, low, concrete fences. Among the formal garden beds are smaller statues, concrete animals, a wishing well, and birdhouses, efforts to add "human touches" and enhance a sensation of well-being. Although the elements appear to have been developed in a semi-improvisational manner, they all generally reflect the same themes of religion and patriotism. The *Sacred Heart Grotto* is a replica of the altar used at the 1926 Eucharistic Congress in Chicago, itself a copy of the main altar of St. Paul's Outside the Walls Church in Rome, and it displays certain architectural characteristics. The *Grotto of the Blessed Mother*, however, is the only true architectural work on-site.

Wernerus died unexpectedly in early 1931 after a short illness brought on by a pastoral visit to administer the last rites. His death halted further construction and explains why the Dickeyville site is so much less developed than Dobberstein's *Grotto of the Redemption* in West Bend. Nevertheless, the site is well maintained by the church and is popular with tourists and religious pilgrims: local boosters claim that it changed Dickeyville from a small hamlet of 250 residents to "the most famous village in Wisconsin." Yet despite the billboards on nearby highways and the gift shop with *Grotto* T-shirts and paperweights, the overall effect is decorous and respectable, befitting the gardens and park of the Holy Ghost Catholic Church.

VIRGIN MARY STATUE WITHIN THE *GROTTO OF THE BLESSED MOTHER*, 2017

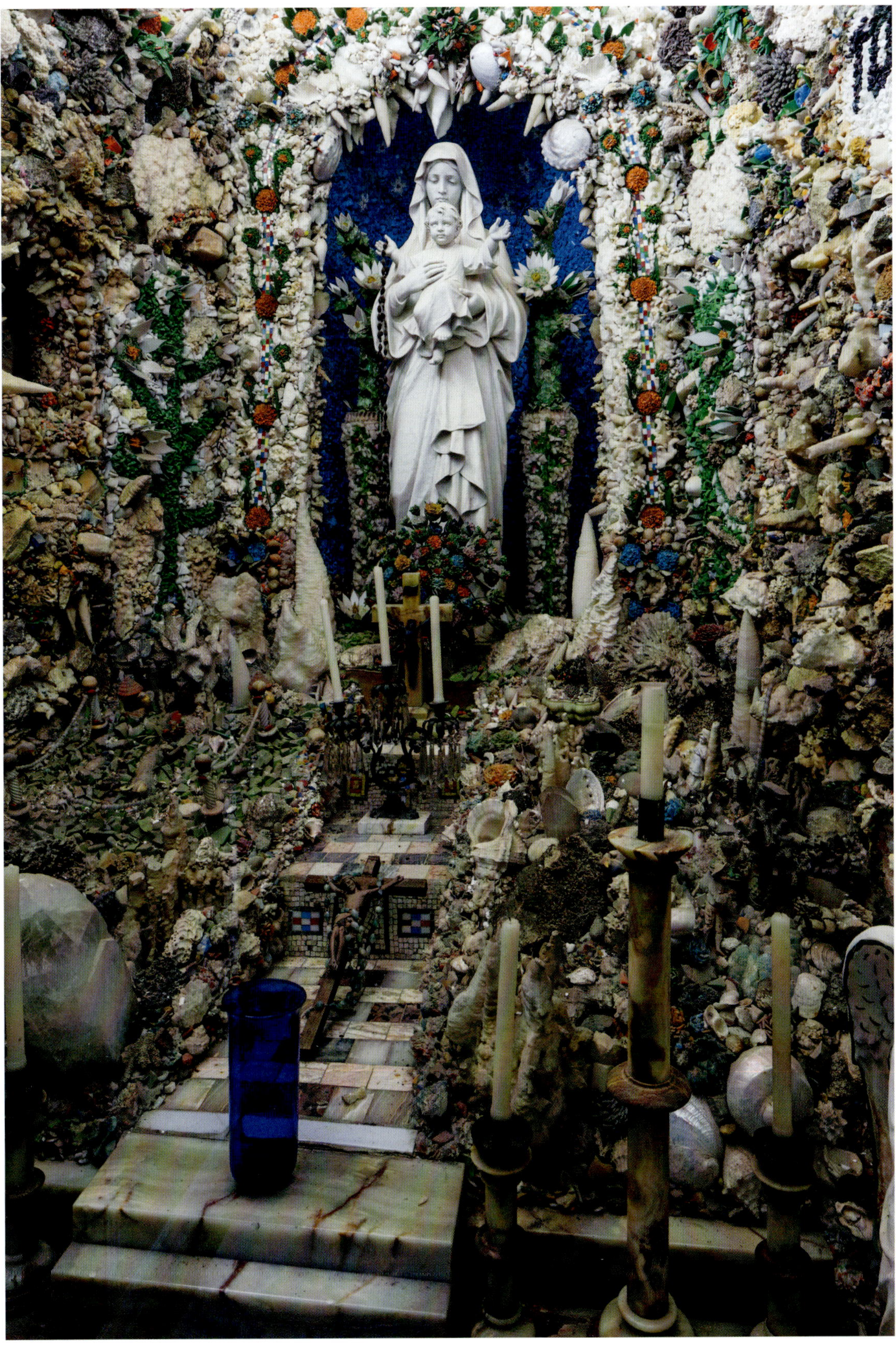

JUANITA LEONARD

HELPING HANDS MINISTRY, HOLY LAND

MONTGOMERY, LOUISIANA

Leonard (b. 1960) has lived in northcentral Louisiana her entire life. Born to a family with 13 children, her mother picked cotton and her father was a Baptist preacher and fieldhand who died when Juanita was young, so all of the siblings helped to raise each other. With neither art education nor a high school diploma, decorating her mother's car at age 17 was Leonard's first foray into painting; meeting with approval, she next began to use her brush directly on the interior walls and cabinets of their home. But it was not until more than 20 years later, in the year 2000, that she began seriously to paint, instructed by a call that she believed came directly from Jesus.

She fused the mission to paint with a call to ministry. Although she initially had reservations about doing so, feeling that she was unworthy, after a compelling night vision she began preaching to neighbors and friends, and in 2004 she designated one of her self-modified mobile homes on her rural property near Montgomery (population approximately 730) as a church. She assembled the church and outfitted it with scavenged materials, teaching herself construction techniques as she worked, salvaging wood and metal where she could, and welcoming discards dropped off by community members.

The elaborate interior and exterior decorations on floors, ceilings, walls, and furniture, always somewhat in flux, cannot be separated from her deep-seated faith. Leonard asks all visitors to join her in the chapel to hold hands and agree to open themselves up to prayer before viewing her work (she is always hopeful that even those who profess greater interest in her art than in her faith may ultimately undergo a spiritual experience). While welcoming everyone, the 20-odd members of her regular congregation sit in distinctively painted pews surrounded by the painted decorations of "God's House," the figurative motifs surrounded by brushed- or drawn-on maxims, Biblical verses, and words of thanks, guidance, or encouragement. She was formally ordained a minister in 2004.

Leonard's earliest paintings were in the style of memory-painter Clementine Hunter, who used paints left behind by a visitor to adorn the interior walls of outbuildings on Melrose Plantation, where she worked and lived and achieved a significant measure of local fame. The motifs of both women focused on the daily lives of African Americans, although as visualized reminiscences the focus tended to be on a rural lifestyle that had largely passed. In Leonard's case, she added recurrent images of the chickens that would run all over the yard, and of her mother picking cotton or smoking a pipe, perhaps wearing a Sioux-like headdress to reference her partial Native American lineage. Her figures are stylized and often expressionless, even lacking clear facial features, but her colors are strong and bright, and the entire effect is uplifting and compelling.

As Leonard continued to creatively express her faith, she amplified her imagery as she likewise expanded from two to three dimensions, using her self-taught construction skills, tools, and media to build a variety of sculptures. A series of these sculptures are mounted or lean against both the interior and exterior of the church, and although angels are prioritized, chickens, roosters, and other creatures of land and sea are also widely featured, as are self-portraits and further references to Native American cultural heritage. She is innovative in her use of materials: for example, she cut out her six- to eight-foot-tall angels from corrugated metal, and then affixed more dimensional painted concrete faces and clasped prayerful hands to those shallow figures. Corrugated metal additionally serves as the infrastructure for slender posts in the yard, painted with stacked figures reminiscent of the layout of Northwest Coast totem poles. Some of these manifest rather formulaic Native American motifs and are similar to her Hopi kachina-like two-dimensional painted wooden and mixed media constructions.

Leonard has also constructed sacred figures out of bent wires covered with plaster or concrete-dipped sheets to round out the forms, a treatment that recalls the carved folds of classical statues, although her constructed bodies tend to lack the articulation of elbows, wrists, and even backbones. Built on or from infrastructures of older recycled materials that she often did not obtain until they were already well-used or damaged, she understands that ongoing maintenance is crucial, and she regularly works to care for her works and keep them in good condition. On the interior, paintings and sculptures are often adorned with plastic ivy and flowers, shimmering fabrics, ribbons, and tiny Christmas-style lights.

Leonard does create discrete works, most of which are paintings on recycled boards or roofing tin, although she also forms "spirit dolls" from clay she digs up in her yard, which she offers for sale on eBay or

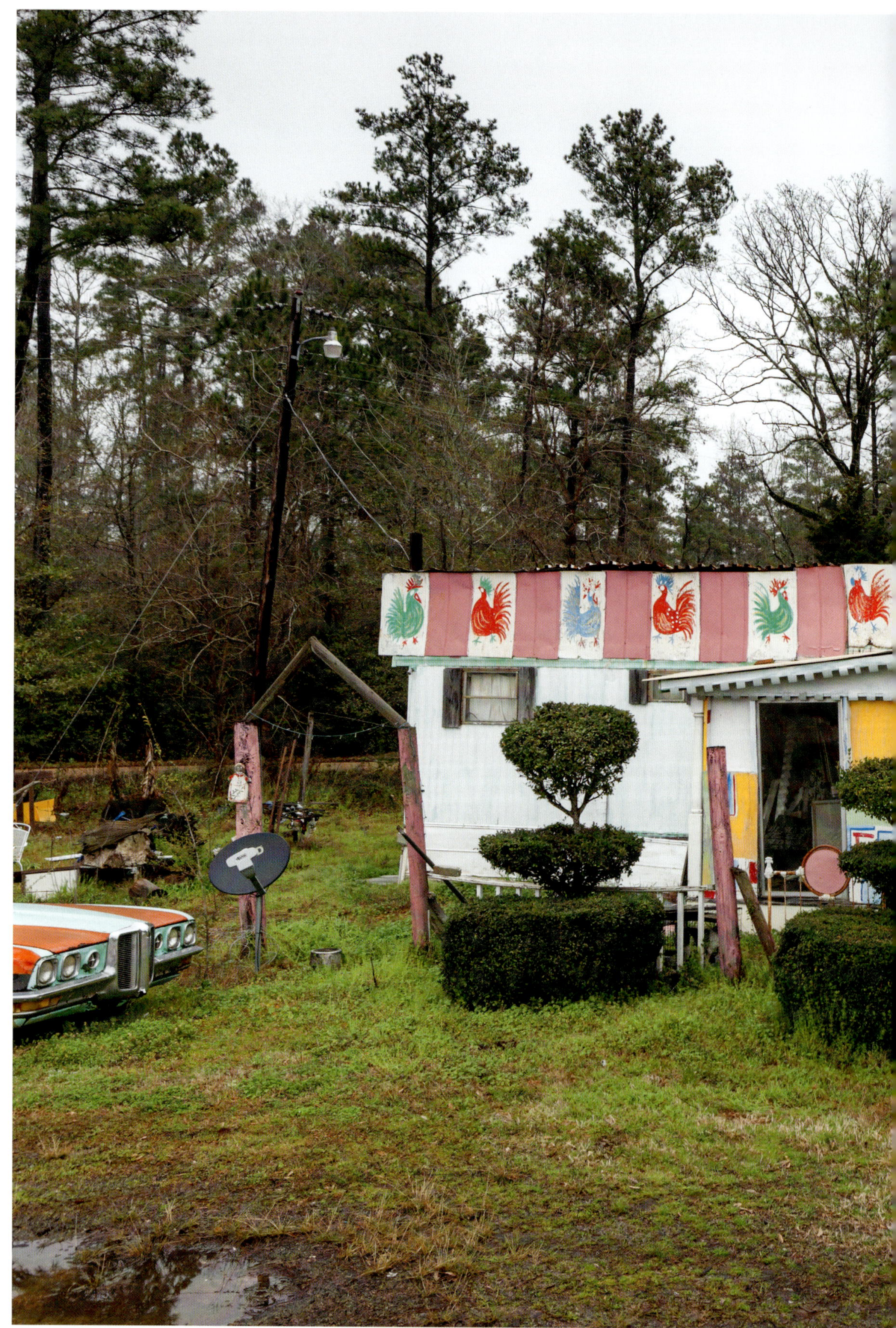

LEONARD'S HOME, 2015

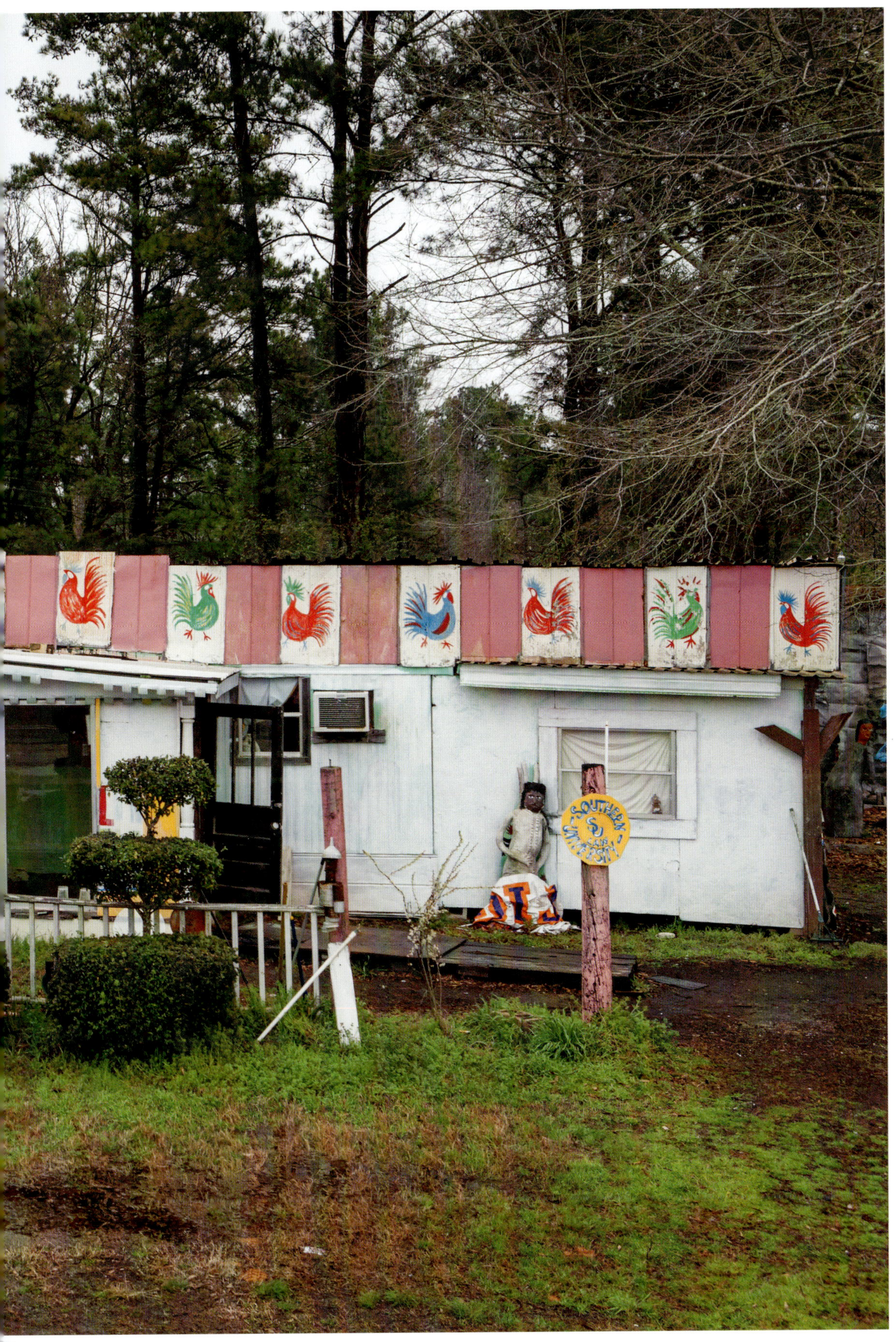
SOUTHERN
SU
LAW
UNIVERSITY

AUXILIARY BUILDING EXTERIOR, 2015

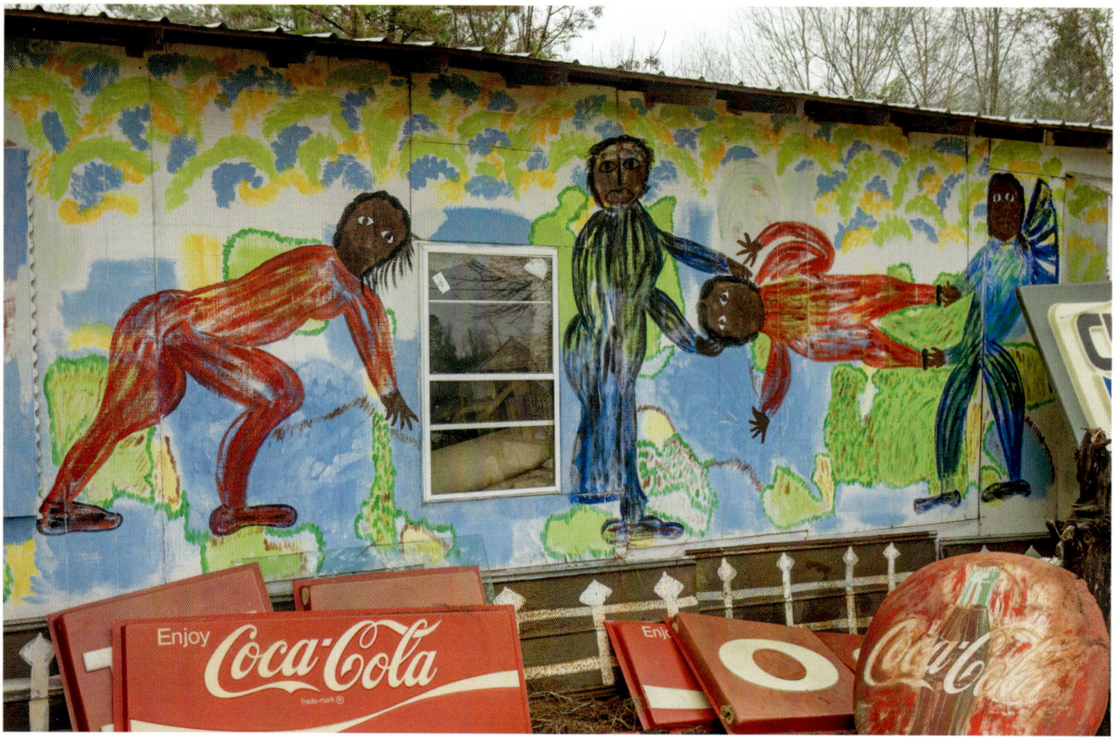

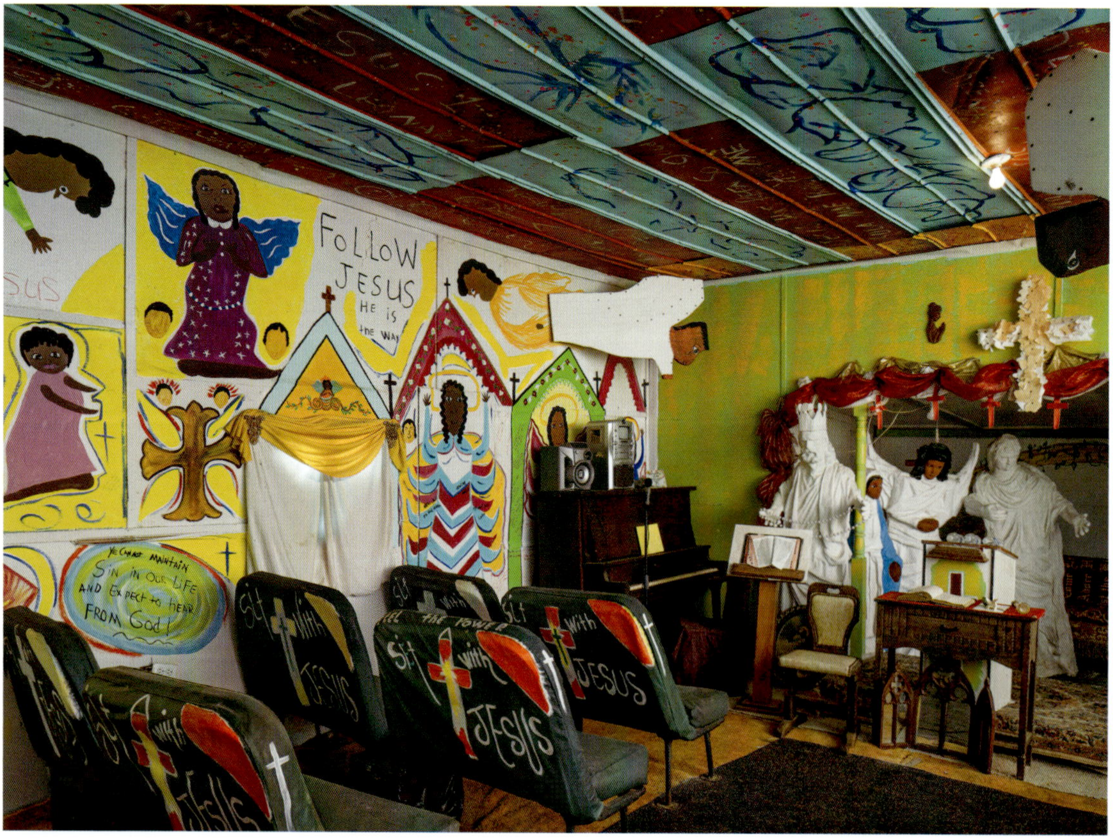

CHURCH INTERIOR, 2024

to visitors. Nevertheless, the two mobile homes, constructed house, and two churches, along with assorted freestanding sculptures, crosses, and text-based signage that make up her roadside art environment take precedence. Confidently linking the deep power of her faith with her family's mainly tranquil experience of rural Louisiana life, and combining them into a holistic vision, she continues to labor every day to attract visitors and neighbors to share in the blessings she so deeply feels.

HER DESIRE TO PAINT IS FUSED WITH HER CALL TO MINISTRY.

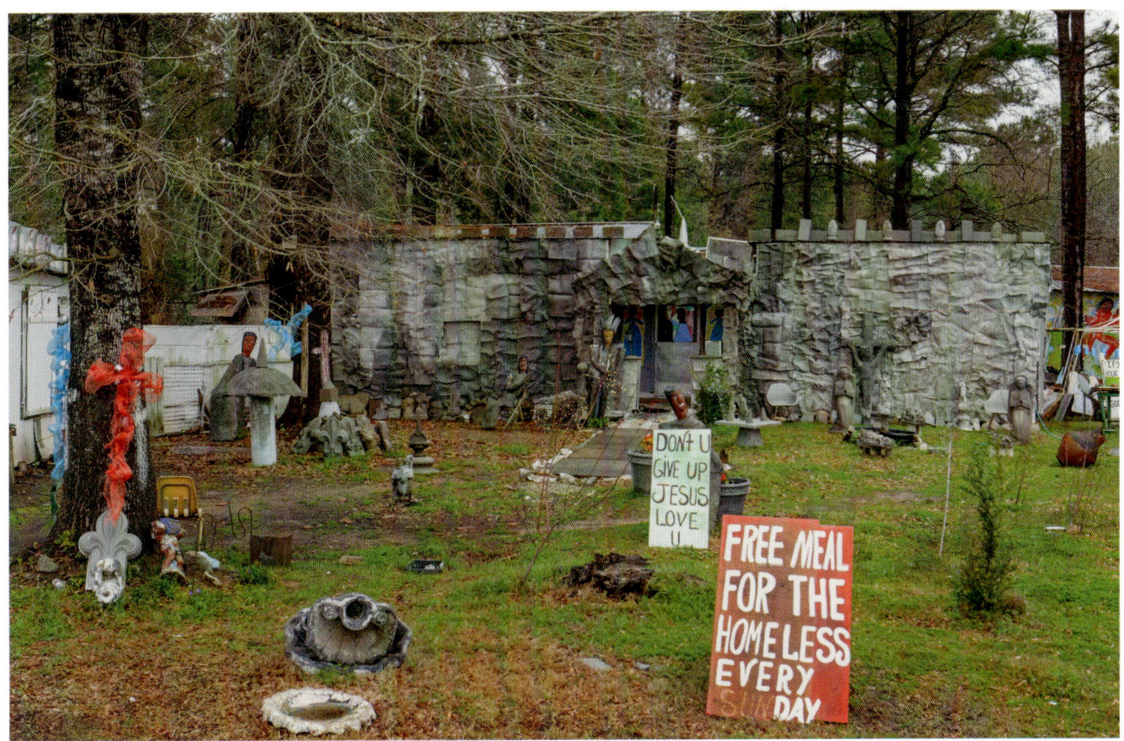

CHURCH EXTERIOR AND YARD INSTALLATIONS, 2015

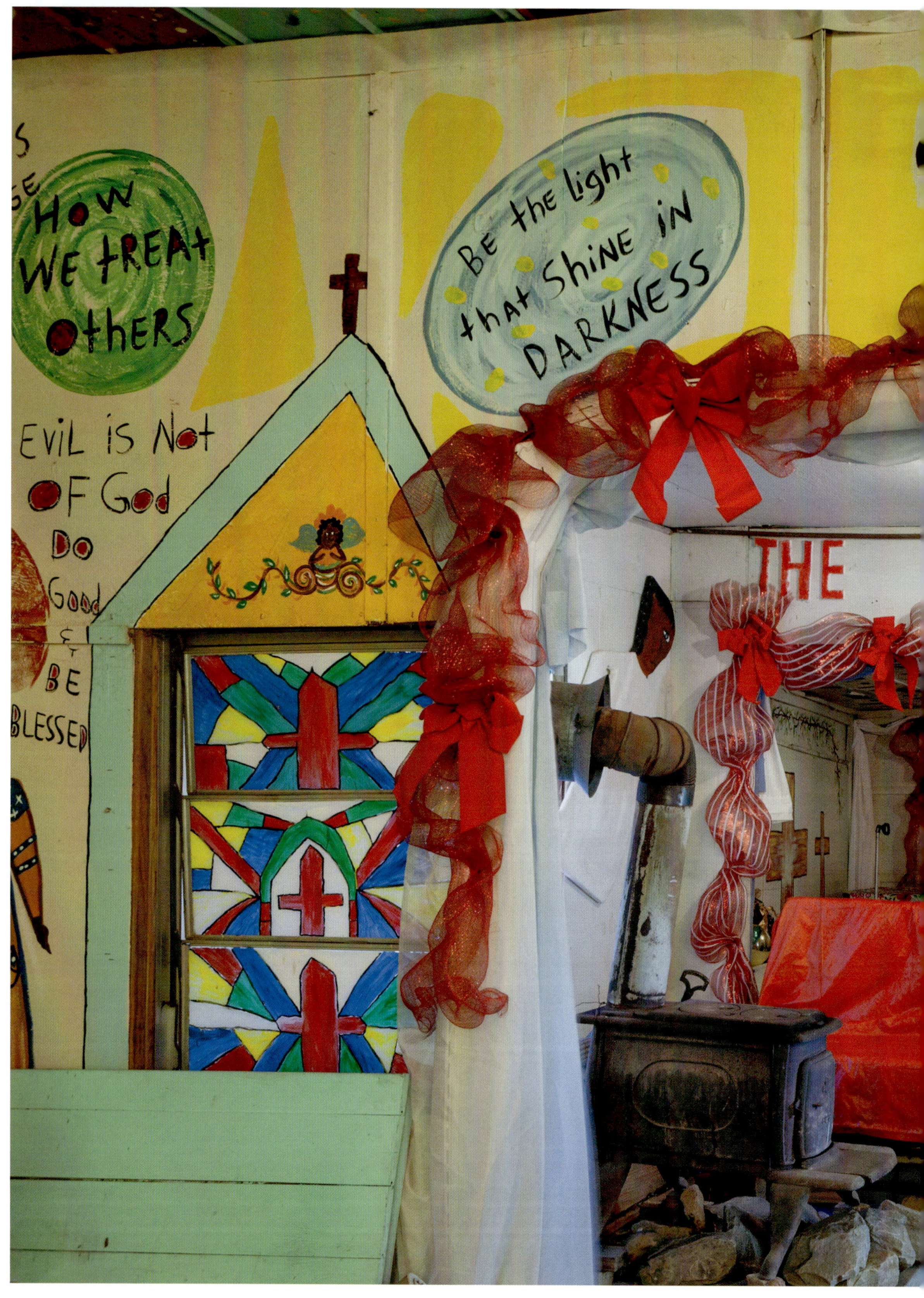
How
We treat
others
EVIL IS Not
OF God
Do
Good
&
BE
BLESSED
Be the light
that Shine in
DARKNESS
THE

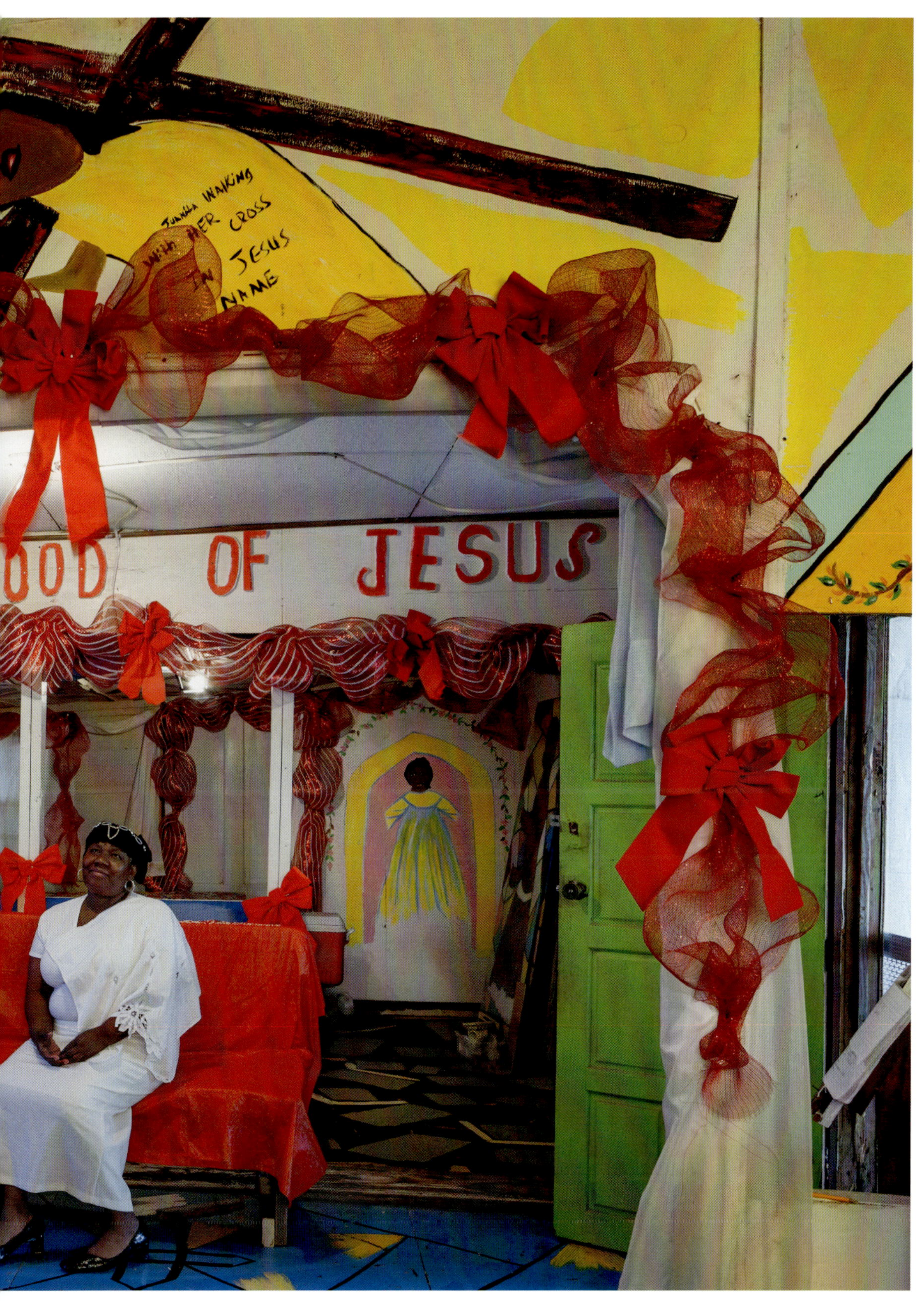
WAKING
WITH HER CROSS
IN JESUS
NAME
OOD OF JESUS

EDDIE OWENS MARTIN

PASAQUAN

BUENA VISTA, GEORGIA

The four-acre complex known as *Pasaquan* is a striking illustration of an art environment that pushes boundaries and categories. On the one hand, it could fall into the category of "modified existing structures" because its extraordinary forms and colors owe their beginnings to a modest home and outbuildings. And yet the compound ultimately evolved into a variety of eye-catching pagodas, shrines, totems, temples, and a worship/dance circle—clearly also a vibrant example of a religious or devotional site. Because its spiritual nature is so overwhelmingly manifest, it has been included in this chapter on sites that celebrate sacred and secular inspiration, although, in contrast to the many environments linked to mainstream religious practice, Martin (1908–1986) was this religion's only priest and its only practitioner. As such, he ultimately took on the moniker of St. EOM: the "E" is silent, so his ecclesiastical name, derived from his initials, is pronounced like the Hindu invocation, *om*.

In 1935, during a severe illness, Martin had a vision that opened this path for him. At that time he was living in New York City, surviving as a young street hustler, card shark, drug dealer, and fortune-teller, a subsistence that, while precarious, was apparently preferable to living in a poor sharecropper's family home in western Georgia with an abusive father and surrounded by a repressive environment that prevented him from expressing his sexuality. After his father died, he returned home periodically to help his mother harvest the crops, but it was not until 1957 that he moved back permanently, after inheriting the house and surrounding acreage. (He was bequeathed approximately 60 acres, but his brothers were ready to fight him for it, so he surrendered that extra portion of his inheritance with no resistance.) He continued to tell fortunes for his Georgia neighbors, and he began to ornament the low-profile vernacular home and outbuildings, using basic construction skills he had learned while growing up.

In due course, Martin's conception of the compound as a kind of sacred space began to unfurl in a manner befitting the universal birthplace and sole location of *Pasaquoyanism*. While the name came to him fully formed, it was not until later that he conjectured that it must have derived from the Spanish word *pasa* (pass) and what he described as an "Oriental" word, *quoyan*, which he thought referred to the melding of past and future. Martin knew little Spanish and no Asian languages.

The site also functioned, on a certain level, as a fortress to shut out the world. It was defended by big German shepherd dogs, and the perimeter of the property, ringed with fences, bamboo, and cane, served as a shield for his art and architecture, and offered privacy for his sacred dance performances, which had attracted local hooligans intent on harassment because he staged the dances while wearing elaborate drag regalia. As a whole, it provided a safeguard for his bodily security.

Martin augmented his basic construction skills by trial and error, replacing and continually enhancing components as he unspooled the forms and images that illustrated his religion and its color palette, behaviors, and precepts. In 1967 he had traveled solo to Mexico in search of inspiration because he had come to believe that *Pasaquoyanism* had "Indian" roots, and he felt that the experience of visiting that country "converted" him, in body and spirit, to the "Indian way of life," although he disavowed specific links to any images, costumes, or artwork. He described the colors and bas-relief motifs he began to build on the fences, paint on his house interior, or frame as discrete works as referential to Native American, Asian, and African cultures, as well as to creative manifestations of the fictional worlds of Mu and Atlantis. He adapted and transformed them all for their new purpose.

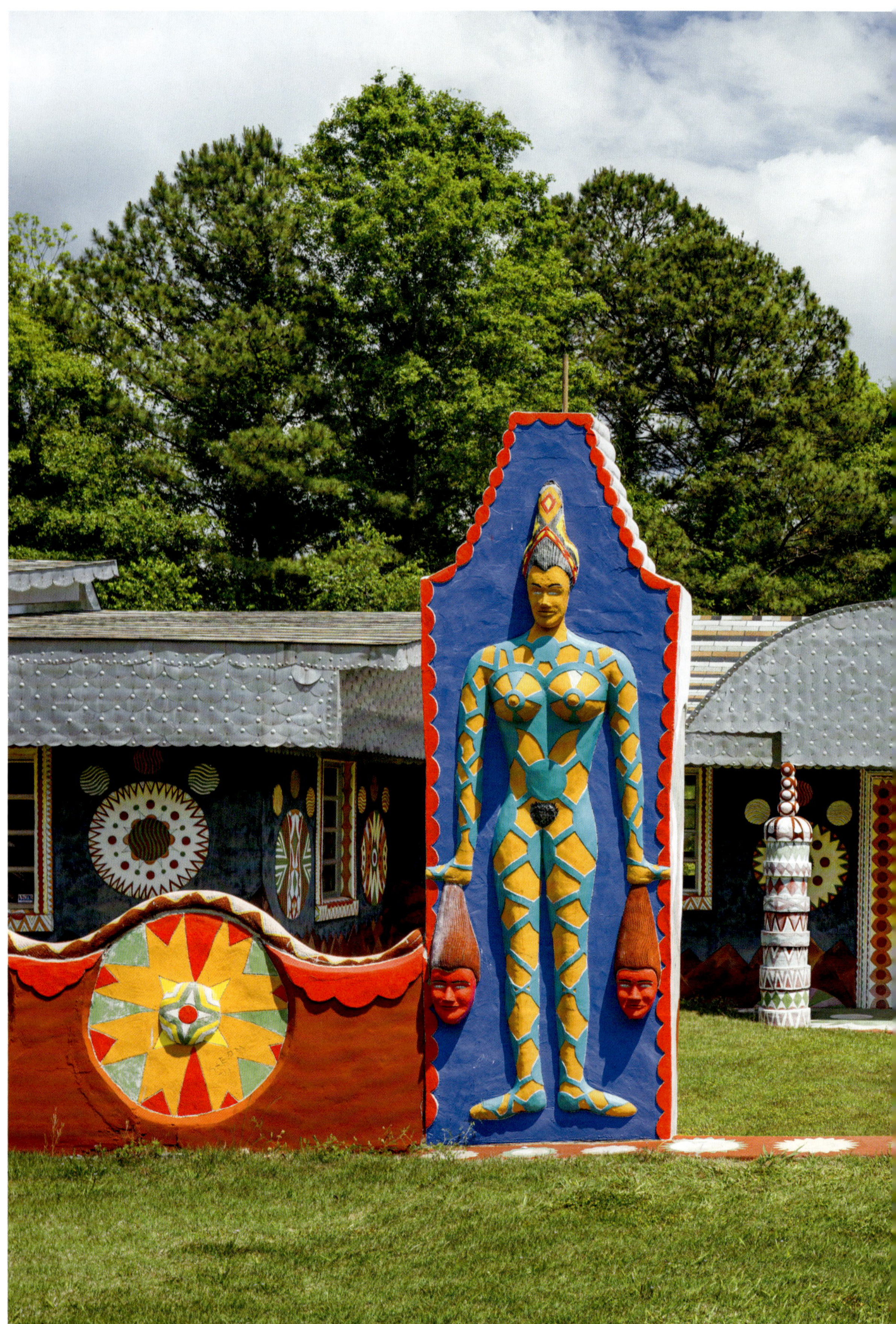

SIDE GATEWAY FLANKED BY PASAQUOYAN DANCERS, 2024

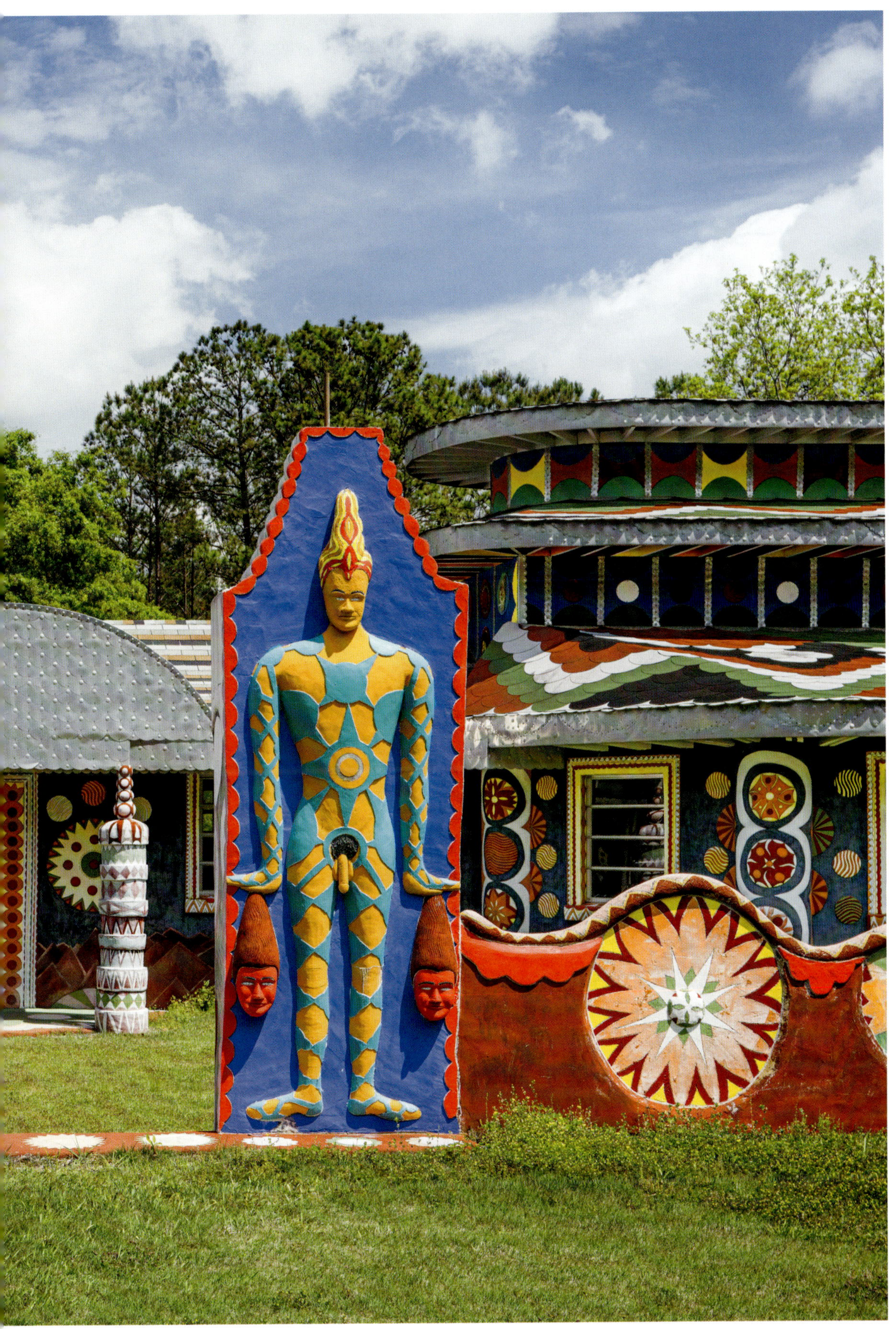

The two brightly painted concrete pillars flanking the front entranceway were meant to depict proud Pasaquoyans wearing elaborate regalia. They appear elsewhere on the compound as well, while other images were variously representative of people he knew, magnetic fields, floral forms, astral elements, deities, images from a previous life or prescriptions for how to live and dress in this one, and the "unknown." The tenets of his personal sanctuary were illuminated by representations of whirling mandalas; male genitalia; masked faces; ornamented nudes; heads with beards and long hair pulled up to indicate the proper, "natural" way to care for oneself; not-yet-invented elastic suits that would give humans the power to resist gravity through levitation; and by many geometric and organic abstractions, some of which had been derived from cosmological bodies and others that were pure configurations of patterns.

Coated with house paint straight out of the can, the bright, colorful structures contrast strongly with the flat, low-cut lawn and perimeter pines. Existing interior rooms were repurposed and repainted to accommodate areas for reading fortunes; crafting "lucky" trinkets, jewelry, and regalia; dance, music, poetry, and drama performances; and meditation. On the grounds, the ornamented concrete walls, with their emblems and symbols dramatically standing out against a stark white background or linear abstraction and periodically interrupted by columnar totems depicting Pasaquoyans, cut across the lawn in angular or curvilinear slices. They connect to the one- or two-level architectural structures that are themselves adorned with similar colors, motifs, and patterns.

Some eaves, rooftops, and portions of exterior façades were overlaid with embossed aluminum shingles, a more subtle surface treatment than that of most of Martin's work in terms of color as well as pattern, albeit one that, depending on the sun's path, caused them to shine and glow. Stepped and lozenge-shaped roofs appear on structures such as the *Well House* and the *Inner Sanctum*; as neither of these forms are standard among examples of local vernacular architecture, they provide yet another layer of aesthetic interest. And even those structures that remained relatively true to their architectural roots—such as, notably, the original family home, or the carport—were sufficiently adorned, inside and out, so that they are neither discordant nor do they detract from the harmonious impression of the whole. Indeed, they help to ground the environment with links to its origin.

Pasaquan was the product of a visionary effort to create a safe space where Martin could practice his art and his faith and where, as the self-identified spiritual leader and thus the one who set all parameters, he could avoid the pressures and tension that he suffered as a result of trying to make his way in the larger world. It let him "prove" to himself and to others that he had worthy qualities, abilities, and imagination. But, depressed, aging, and ill by the mid-1980s, he took his own life. *Pasaquan* was added to the National Register of Historic Places in 2008; it has since been restored and operates in conjunction with Columbus State University.

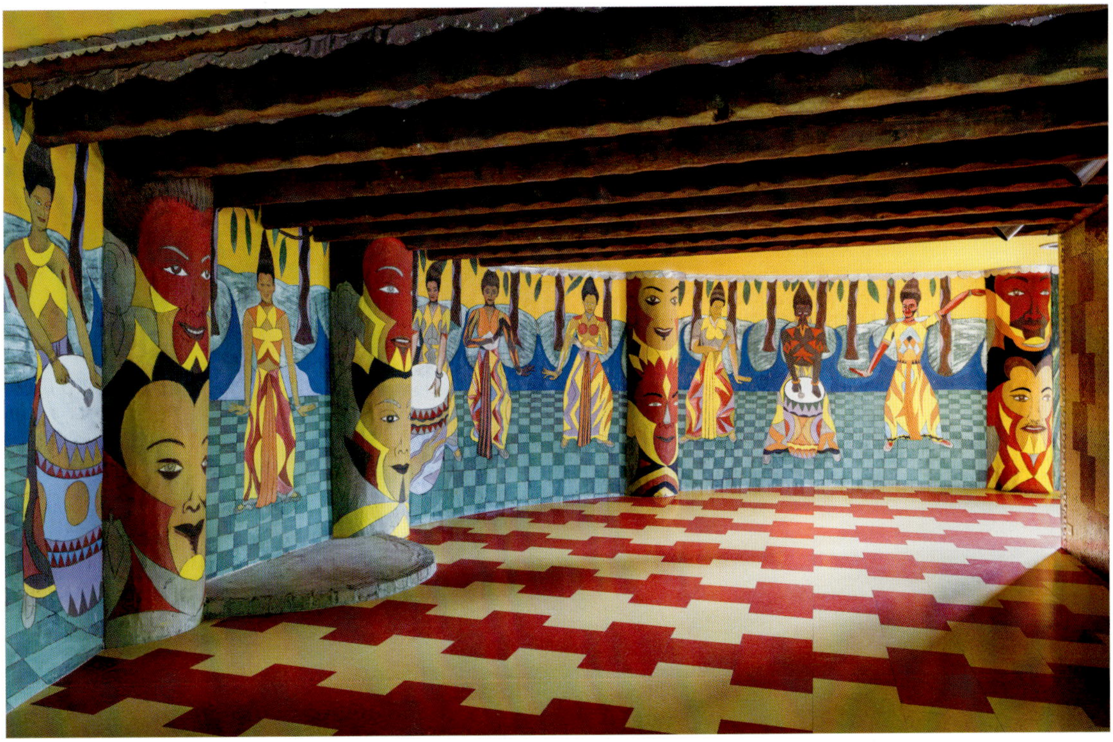

"ORATORY" INNER SANCTUM, 2024

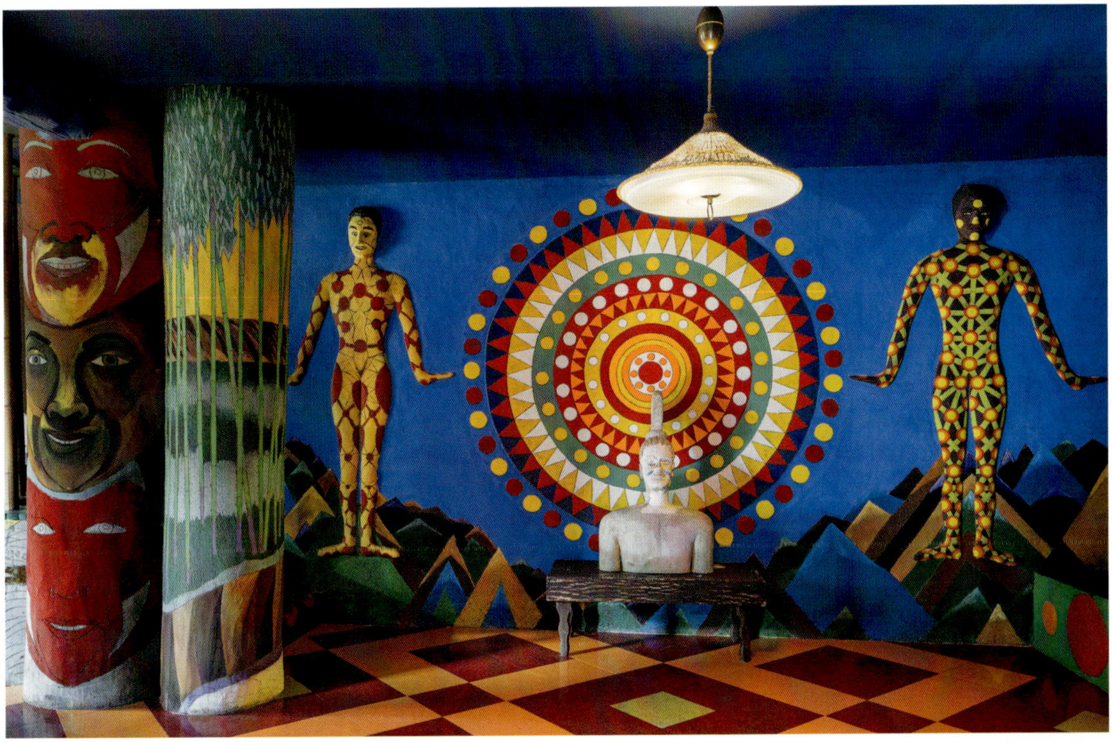

MUSIC ROOM WITH *MANDALA*, 2024

WELL HOUSE, STAIRS, AND DECORATIVE WALLS, 2024

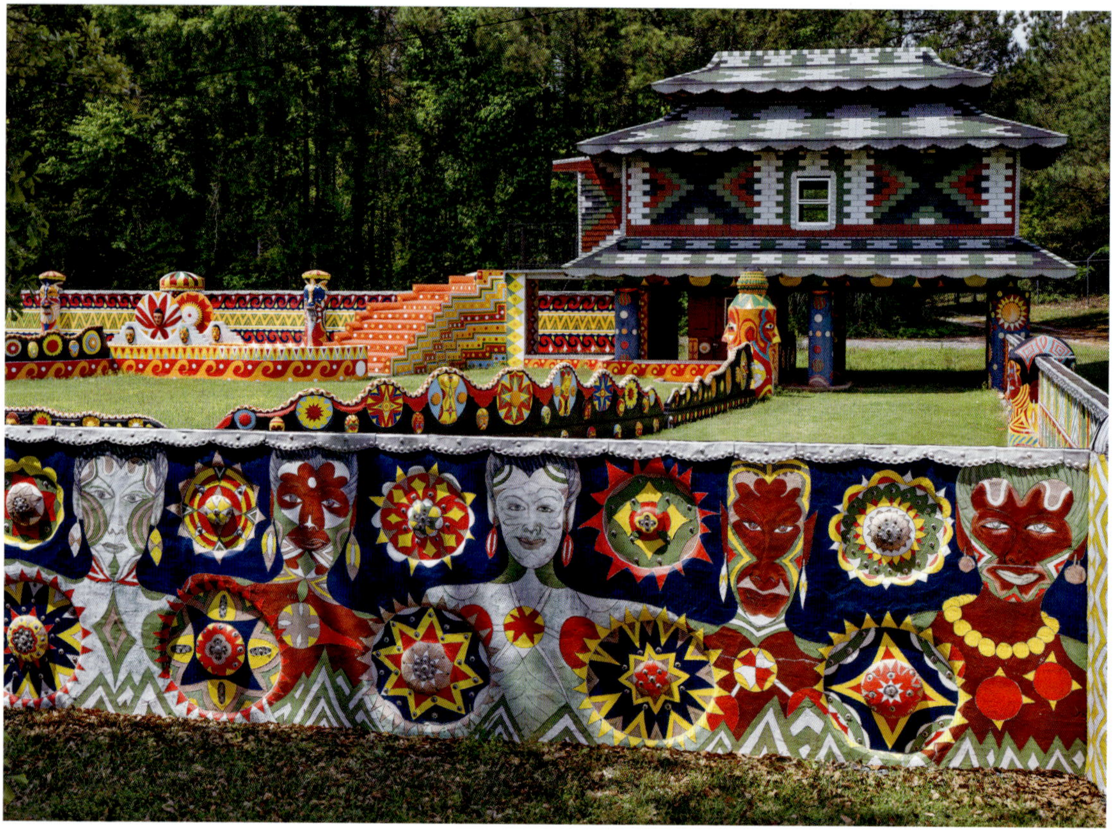

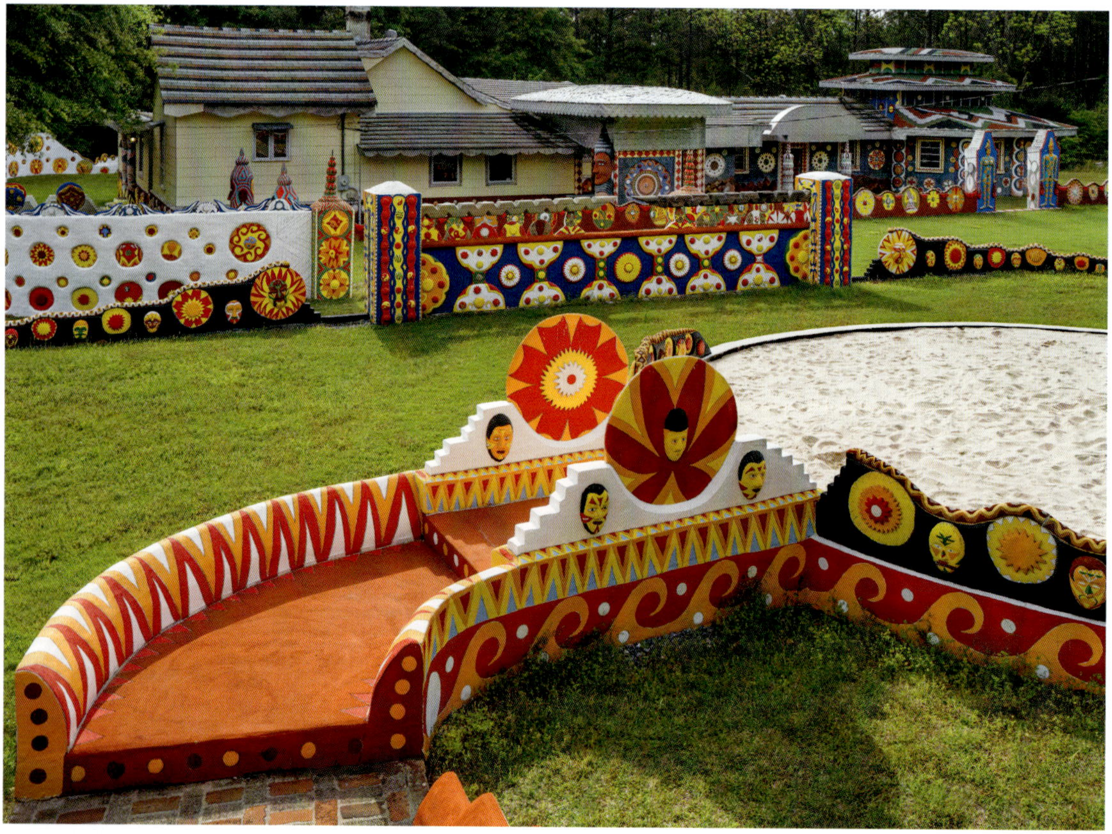

WALKWAY FROM *WELL HOUSE* TO *DANCE CIRCLE*, WITH ORIGINAL MODIFIED AND EXPANDED HOME VISIBLE AT REAR, 2024

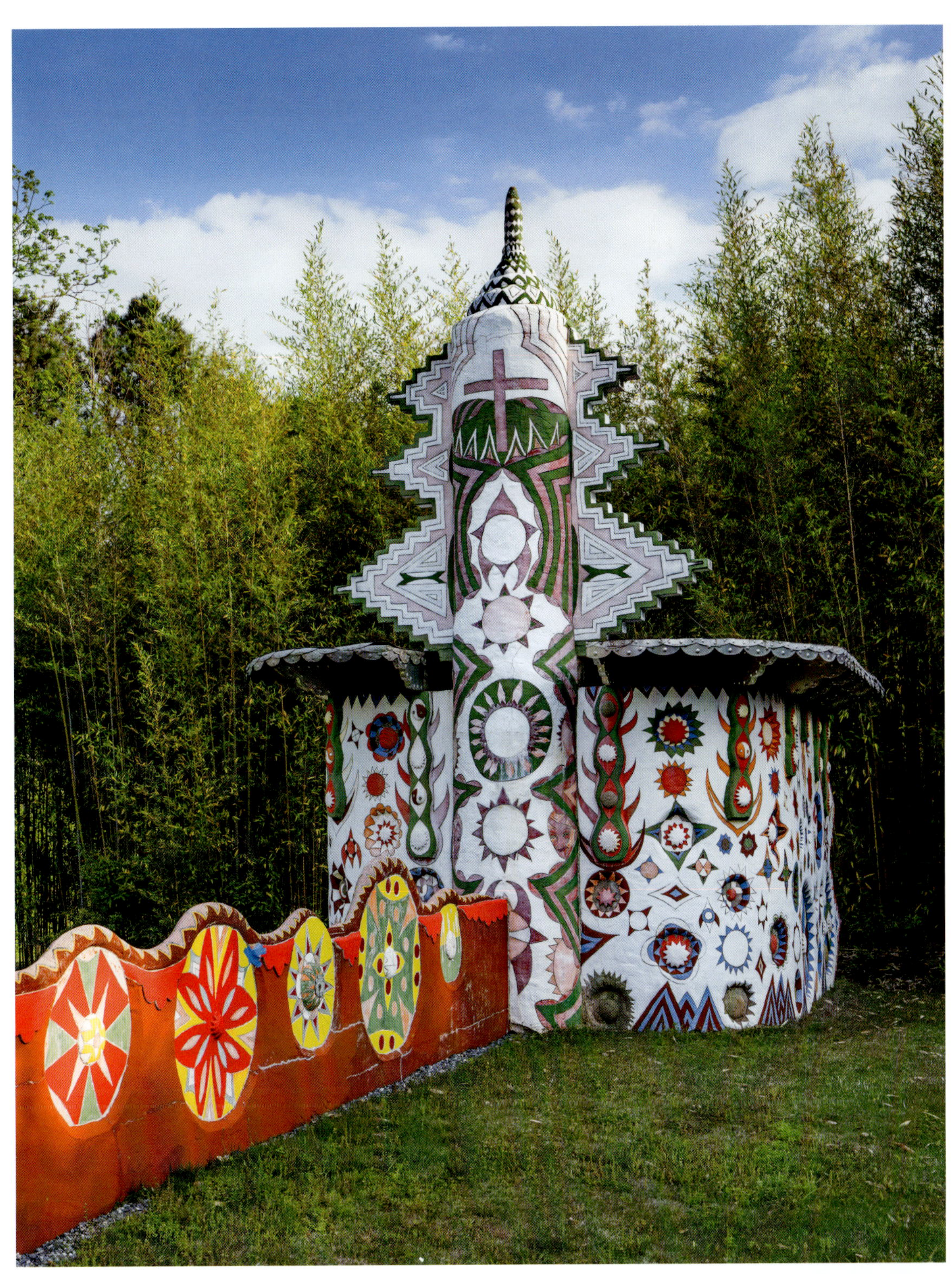

PROPANE SHED WITH *EFFIGY* COLUMN, 2024

DR. CHARLES SMITH

AFRICAN-AMERICAN HERITAGE MUSEUM AND BLACK VETERANS ARCHIVE

AURORA, ILLINOIS, AND HAMMOND, LOUISIANA

Smith (b. 1940) consecutively developed two different art environments: the original, in Aurora, Illinois, was superseded by the current one, in Hammond, Louisiana, but both displayed dense and impactful imagery that focuses on the Black experience in America. He has used his work to simultaneously try to teach about the collective realities of systemic racism and to personally heal from the anger, frustration, and pain that has resulted from his own experiences with bigotry and marginalization. And while Smith is better known for his three-dimensional figural sculptures than his architectural work, he approached the two small wooden homes located on those two properties with an equal intensity, radically modifying their modest vernacular bearings with a concomitantly defiant and wistful confidence that cuts through prevailing attempts to dodge hard questions.

Smith's father was purposefully drowned in what was likely a random Southern racist attack; the artist, age 14 at the time, scoffs at the official account of this tragedy as an accident. His mother moved the family from New Orleans to Chicago within the year, joining the Great Migration of Black families northward, undertaken to evade the pervasive battering of White Southern aggression. Shortly thereafter she brought the family to the open-casket funeral of Emmett Till, who was roughly Smith's age and who had been brutally murdered because he allegedly whistled at a White woman. These killings profoundly affected the young boy and the man he would become.

In 1966 Smith was drafted. Enrolled in the Marine Corps, he was sent to Vietnam, another searing experience that compounded the rage and resentment he had experienced while young, as racism did not seem to make sense when he saw the blood of combatants of all races mingling together on the ground. After his honorable discharge in 1968, he went through many difficult years, struggling with post-traumatic stress disorder, taking drugs, and having difficulties holding a job. It was not until 1986 that he moved to a dilapidated property in Aurora Township, Illinois, where he felt directed by God to explore creative expression. Here he was able to find his footing.

He spent the next 14 years transforming the house and property into the *African-American Heritage Museum and Black Veterans Archive*, a visual stream-of-consciousness representation of Black life in America, beginning with the Middle Passage and the forced removal of Africans to American shores, and extending across the centuries to his own life. He began referring to himself as "Dr." Smith, an honorific meant to represent the wisdom he had gained over the course of his life experiences.

Mirroring the ongoing and multitiered narrative of Black history in America, Smith's growing and constantly changing sculptural environment manifested innumerable material and conceptual layers. Relying to a great extent on repurposed found objects to create framework, accoutrements, and surfaces for both bas-relief and three-dimensional figures, he fleshed them out with wood, plaster, concrete, textiles, rocks, and more found objects before coating them with enamel paint. Anonymous figures and busts were interspersed with portraits of famous historical personages—heroes and artists, spiritual leaders and athletes, musicians and prisoners—as well as of his friends, neighbors, and comrades in arms. He adorned the simple gabled house on every surface (including the roof) with plaques, busts, signs, stones, and fully formed figures. Set back at the rear of the property, the building, depending on vantage point, almost disappeared behind the mass of sculptures crowding the yard. Yet up close it was clear that Smith considered the building as yet another sculpture: concrete and found objects thickened its footprint, and faces modeled directly into the walls seemed to be ghostly reminders of the suffering of unnamed ancestors.

After Smith began to realize that his "weatherization" process—leaving the works outside—was pushing them to a point beyond stability, he asked the Kohler Foundation to intervene. They purchased, removed, and conserved over 400 works, ultimately gifting them to the John Michael Kohler Arts Center in Sheboygan, Wisconsin, and to numerous other museums so they could be protected inside. Relieved that what he then considered his life's work was going to be preserved, he left the Aurora site and headed back to New Orleans to be closer to his mother.

HOUSE AND GROUNDS, WITH "*UNNAMED SLAVE BOY*" OF HAMMOND, LA'S FOUNDING FAMILY AT RIGHT, 2016

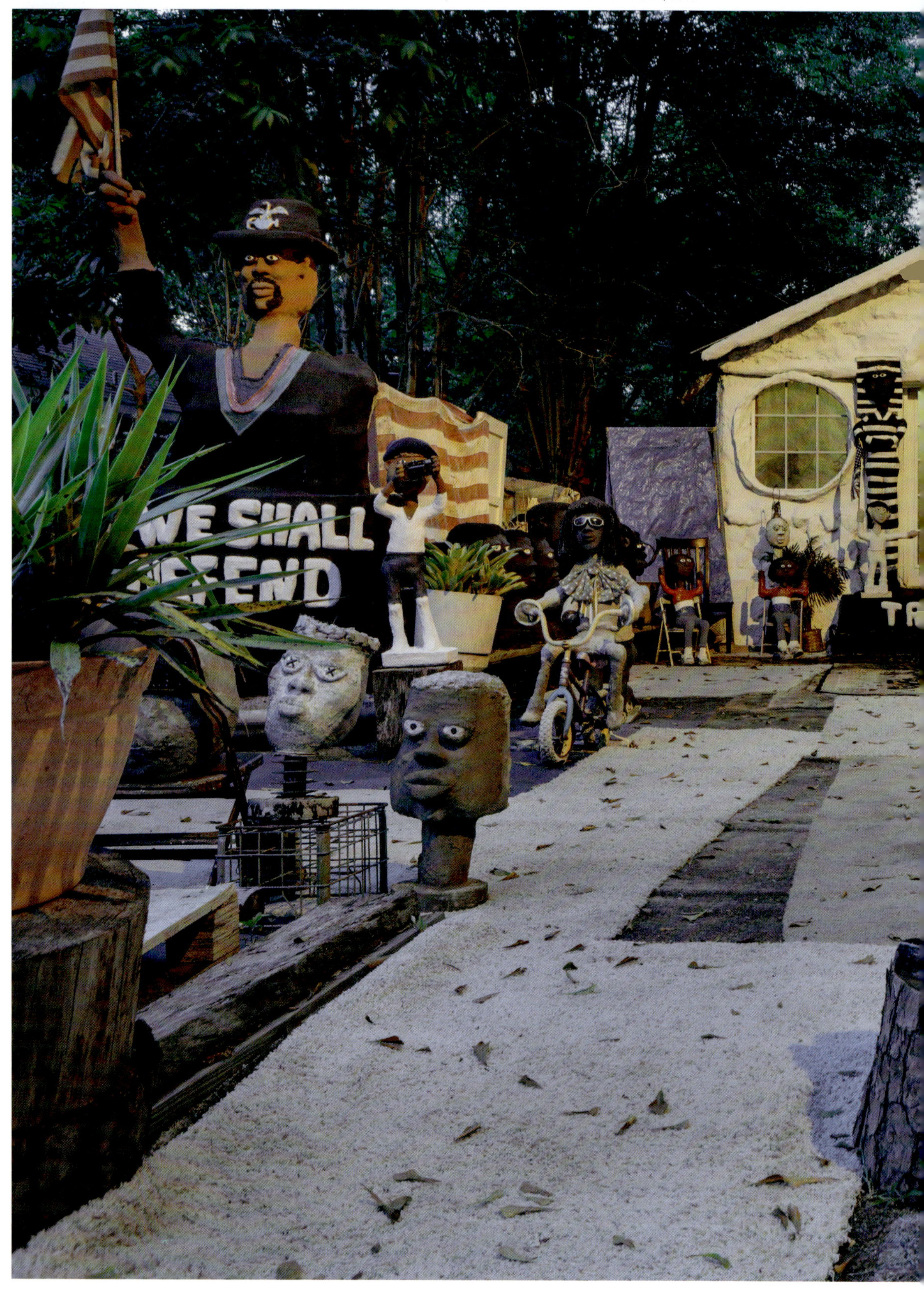

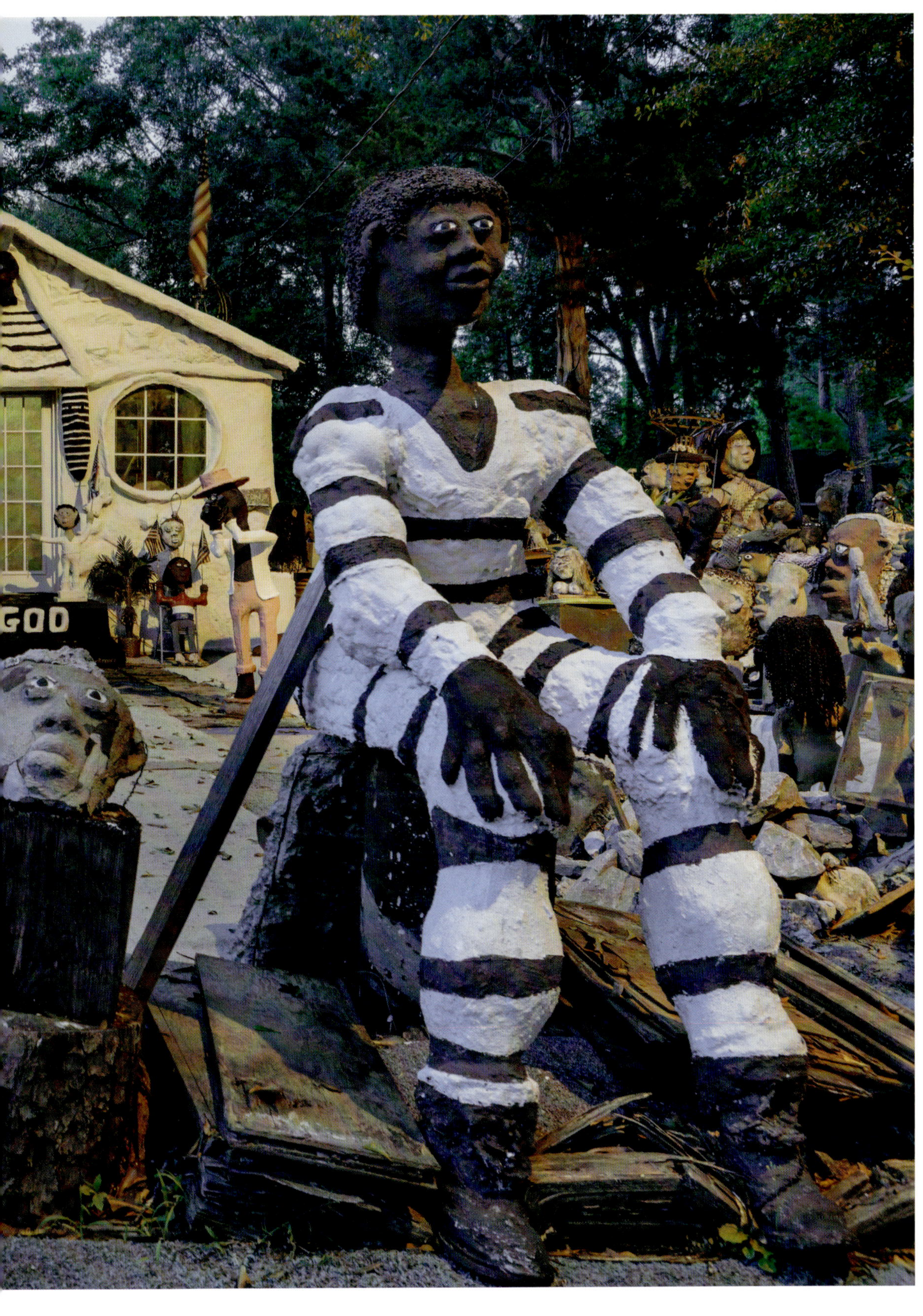
GOD

On the way, he passed Hammond, Louisiana, and he decided to check out the home of the family who gave the town its name. He was shocked to read the bronze historical marker that memorialized them, along with "a favorite slave boy," whose nearby grave was marked as an "Unnamed Slave Boy." Smith was wrenchingly affected by the casual worthlessness that this anonymity represented, and immediately recognized that the area was sorely in need of education. He purchased a home and embarked on the second iteration of the *African-American Heritage Museum and Black Veterans Archive*, an environment comparable in aesthetic, intention, and media with the no-longer-extant Aurora site.

Without delay, Smith began to expand and amplify the frame house in Hammond (originally similar to the small vernacular Aurora building), adding a front extension and reinforcing the porch and walls with stones set into mortar. He opened four large round windows in the front and sides, and offset the line of the front gable with a high-relief triangle enclosing the bust of a prototypical African ancestor. The black-and-white stripes below the head and the geometry of the sculpted enclosure bring to mind the headdresses of the Egyptian pharaohs, a fitting allusion to an archetypical royal progenitor whose offspring spread to other continents. The triangle's broad base is meant to embrace the multitude of Africans dragged from their homes en route to centuries of slavery as it likewise, on a more micro scale, symbolizes the Great Migration of families such as his own, who left the broad geographic spread of the South and headed for the North, represented by the vertex of the sculpted triangle and the star at the roof ridge.

Smith is particularly adept at diminishing the distances of time and space. The base of the triangle is flanked on the left by a black-and-white striped figure representing Americans who fought for civil rights during the twentieth century, while on the right is a similarly striped "mask of faith," and the painted black steps leading to the front door are emblazoned with the appeal to "TRUST GOD." The eastern wall brings the narrative to the twenty-first century, with rows of sculpted wraithlike heads memorializing victims of Hurricane Katrina in 2005. The highest row of heads reaches the level of the high-water mark in New Orleans and recalls how victims hammered through their ceilings and rooftops to try to reach safety.

The environment continues to evolve as Smith is spurred by recent events—such as the 2012 massacre of children at Sandy Hook school in Connecticut—while, at the same time, he reaches back into history to resurrect people or characters that serve as symbols for historical markers, such as the racist Black "lawn jockey" ornaments installed in the yards of White property owners and the "silent butlers" obsequiously offering ashtrays, manufactured at reduced scale to emphasize their lack of worth and status. He has memorialized the nine falsely accused Scottsboro Boys of 1931 Alabama, the lifesaving efforts of doctors in Africa working to control the Ebola virus, and a Sankofa figure with two back-to-back faces symbolizing the importance of reflecting on the past in order to move toward a more successful future.

Dr. Smith continues to intersperse figures and animals from across time and space, breaking down boundaries between architecture and sculpture, legend and history, individual and collective. Naming the unnamed, he weaves together a reality meant to be simultaneously didactic, critical, heartbreaking, and restorative.

BUST OF PROTOTYPICAL AFRICAN ANCESTOR ON HAMMOND HOME'S FRONT GABLE. THE TRIANGLE'S BROAD BASE REPRESENTS BOTH THE ENORMOUS NUMBER OF AFRICANS TORN FROM THEIR HOMES AND SOLD INTO SLAVERY AND THE NUMBER OF BLACK AMERICANS WHO MIGRATED NORTH DURING THE GREAT MIGRATION; THE NORTH STAR SURMOUNTS THE PEAK AS IT REPRESENTS THE WAY TO FREEDOM FOR SOUTHERN AFRICAN AMERICANS, 2014

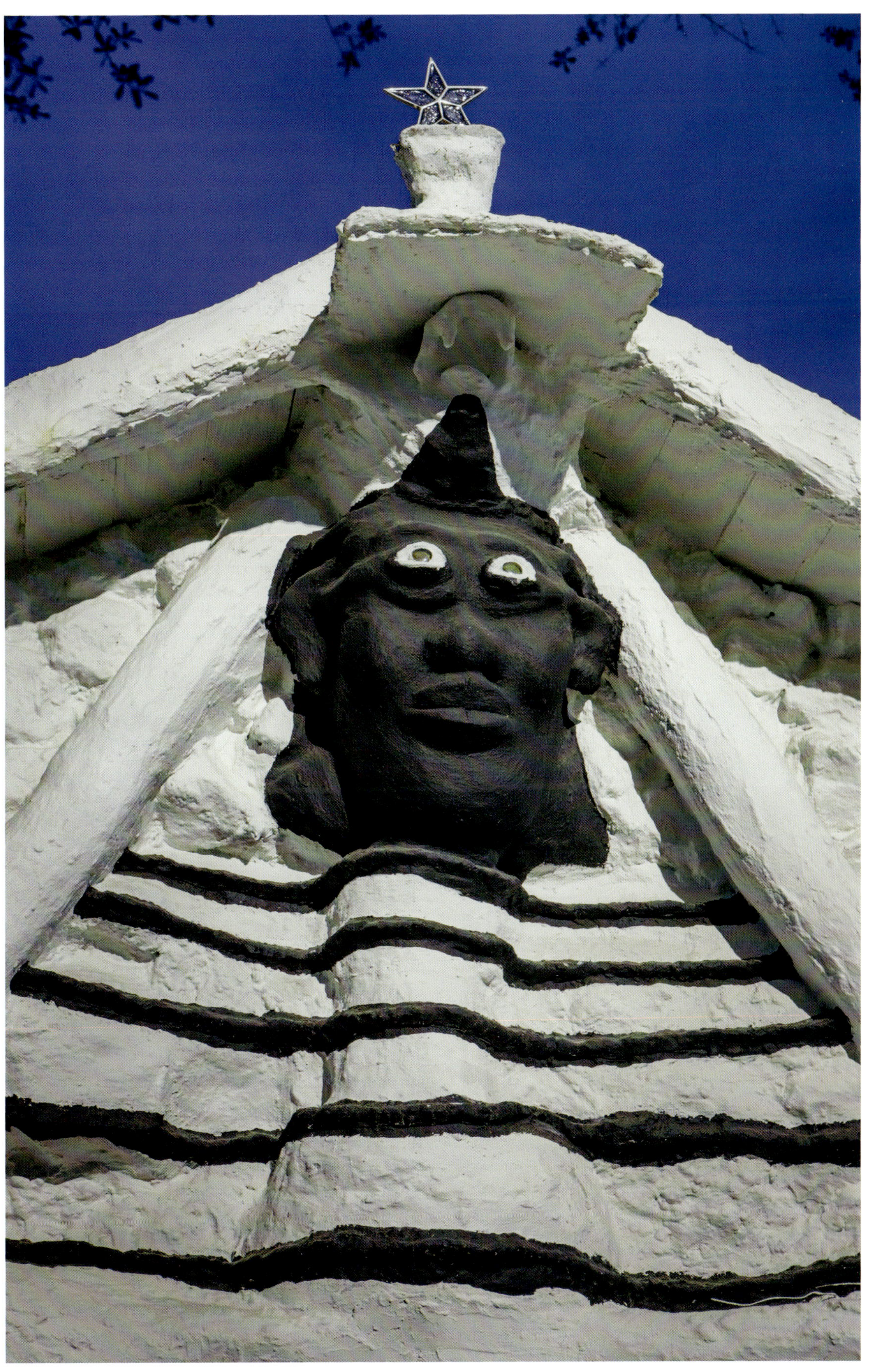

NO-LONGER-EXTANT HOME AND YARD INSTALLATIONS, AURORA, IL, 2000. PHOTO: SUSAN MORAN

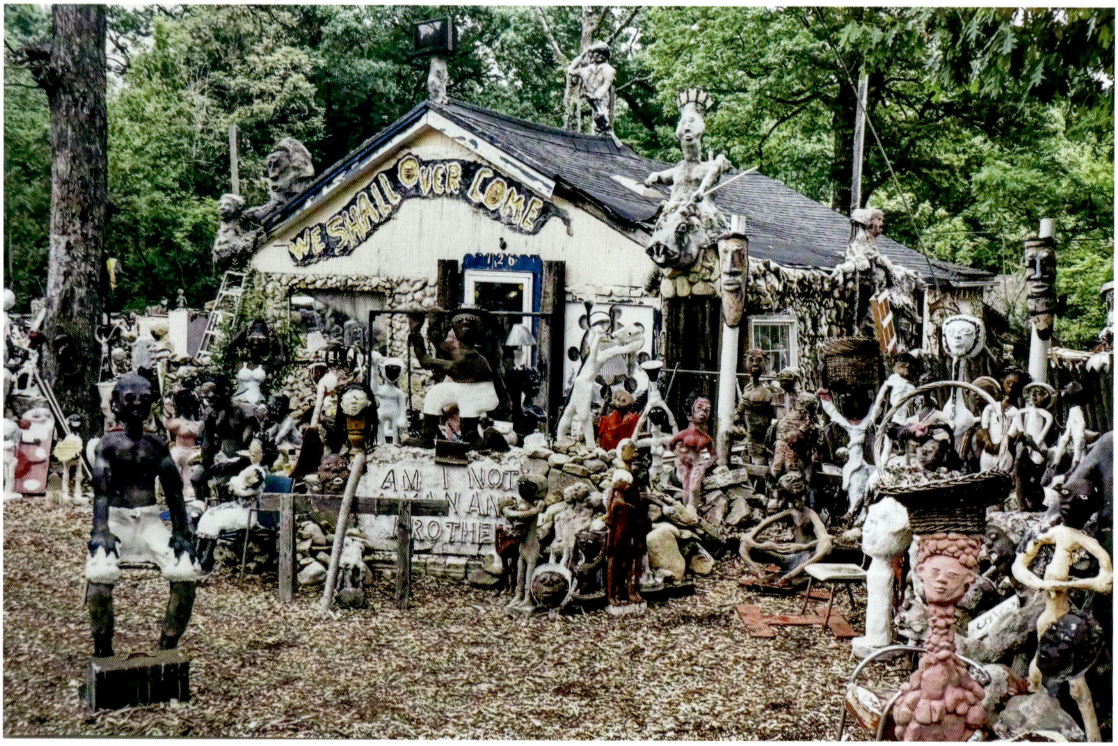

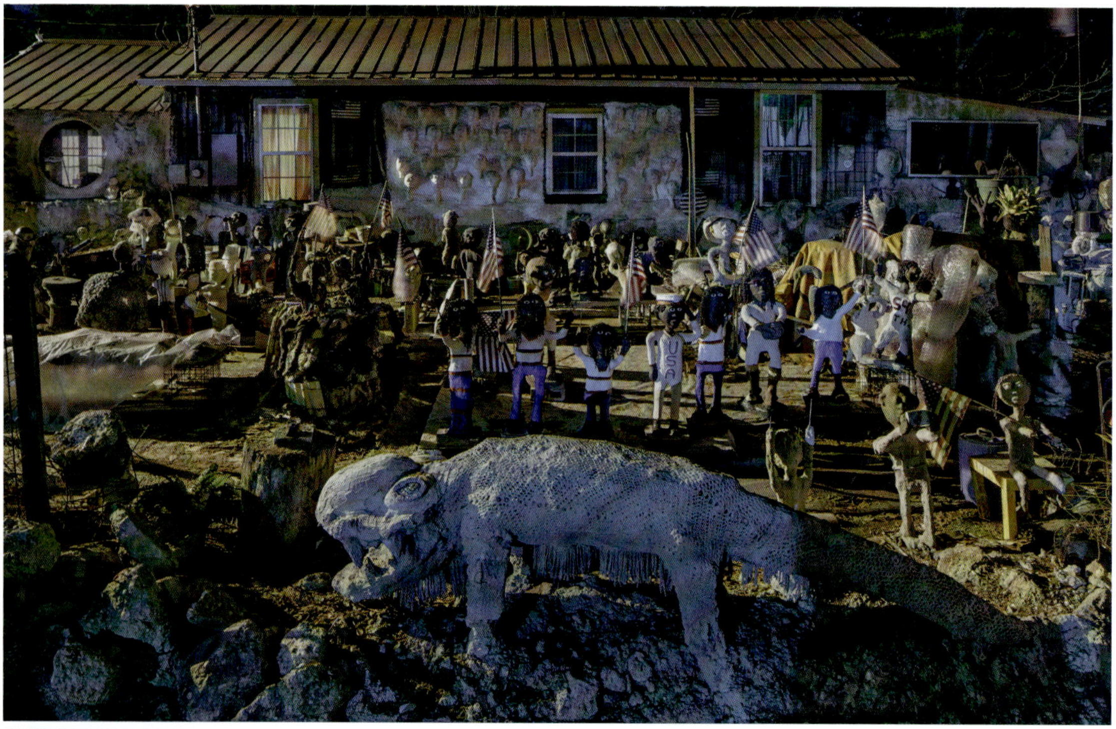

OVERVIEW OF EAST YARD, HAMMOND, LA., WITH WATER MONSTER IN FOREGROUND AND HEADS MEMORIALIZING HURRICANE KATRINA'S VICTIMS MODELED ONTO HOME'S EASTERN WALL, 2014

HIS WORK TEACHES ABOUT THE COLLECTIVE REALITIES OF SYSTEMIC RACISM AS IT HELPS HIM PROCESS AND HEAL FROM HIS OWN EXPERIENCES WITH BIGOTRY AND MARGINALIZATION.

SILVIO BARILE

ITALIAN AMERICAN HISTORICAL ARTISTIC MUSEUM AND GALLERIA BELLE ARTI CULTURAL CENTER

REDFORD TOWNSHIP, MICHIGAN

Many immigrants retain an almost visceral affection for their homeland, often perpetuating that attachment through cultural expressions, preparation and consumption of traditional foods, and using names for their children that have been passed down for generations. World War II refugee Barile (1938–2019), born in the central Italian town and comune of Ausonia, manifested his love for his native land more creatively than most, assembling a dense three-dimensional environment to celebrate the country of his birth while also honoring his adopted home.

After settling in Michigan in 1960, six years after his family's arrival in the United States, Barile apprenticed at a local bakery, and once on his own, he decided to open a shop that would focus on the breads and pastries of Italy. Opening up Silvio's Rita Pizzeria in a municipality about 16 miles west of Detroit, the bakery flourished as he promoted his Italian heritage. Yet he felt that he needed to do more to advance understanding and appreciation of his homeland among his American clientele.

When he was young, Barile had created small toys and trucks from local, naturally occurring clay. At this time, perhaps intuitively channeling Italy's illustrious cultural and aesthetic history, he began to adorn the bakery's interior walls with painted murals, photographs, and postcards featuring some of Italy's best-known subjects, which he often annotated with admiring commentaries. He crafted his own reduced-scale sculptures of Julius Caesar and Michelangelo's *Pietà*, images of the Roman Coliseum, reproductions of well-known paintings such as the *Mona Lisa*, and pictures of bucolic landscapes. He added commercial religious images, toy Italian sports cars, beads, and plastic flowers until the embellishments threatened to overtake the shop's stock of baked goods and groceries. Then he branched out into three dimensions with larger-scale and mostly figurative works celebrating notable Italian characters of myth (e.g., Venus, Romulus and Remus), legend (renowned saints), history (Caesar, Amerigo Vespucci), religion (several popes), and culture (the TV character Columbo, Luciano Pavarotti). But he included motifs important in American narratives as well, such as the Statue of Liberty, the Alamo, and an homage to the Detroit Tigers.

As the pizzeria's adornments grew denser, he expanded into the back patio and, ultimately, the wooded acre behind the building. With more room in these exterior locations, the scale of his work also increased, with narrative groupings of three or more figures that he distinguished by their accessories. Barile constructed the majority of his sculptures out of unpainted concrete layered over an infrastructure of steel rods, identifying them with labels and dense notations in roman capital letters inscribed into the modeled clothing or on accompanying concrete plaques, in order to ensure that his American audience understood their import. He emphasized details with small ceramic tile fragments, marbles, pebbles, and other durable ornaments as well as, occasionally, brightly painted elements to which he wanted to draw attention. Most were meant to be viewed frontally, and often decoration on the back side was minimal or even absent.

Barile's pizzeria was shut down in 2002 for health code violations. By that time, however, he had begun receiving Social Security payments, and he was no longer compelled to spend all his hours working. He was able to continue to sell packaged liquor and other goods, but the focus of his efforts shifted almost completely to his elaborate paean to Italy. Some of the shrine-like memorials rose to 25 feet in height, reiterating the cultural and historical glories that had so informed his life and work. But although his concentration was on his motherland, he asserted that his complex series of creations was also meant to make America better—to inspire native-born Americans through Italian narratives, but perhaps also to thank his new country for providing economic opportunities to immigrants such as himself. He inscribed his name and the name of his birthplace of Ausonia on many of the concrete sculptures, centering his own personal narrative within the broader scope of global history and culture.

After Barile's death at age 80, his family demolished the site. The Kohler Foundation was able to acquire several pieces, which they gifted to the Kohler Art Preserve, and other samples of his work may have found their way into private hands, but the environment is no longer extant.

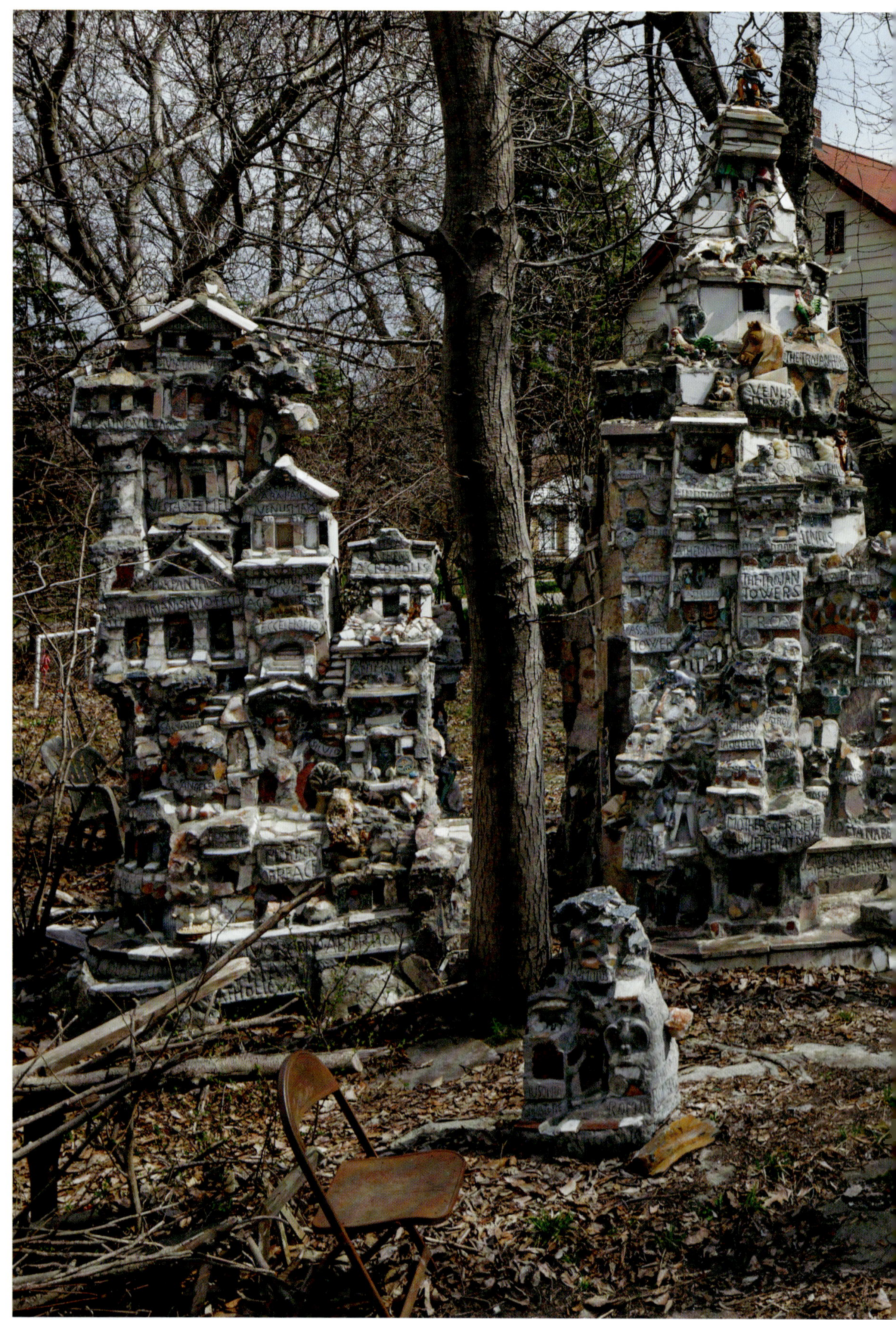

EXTERIOR INSTALLATION (DETAIL) WITH BARILE HOME, 2018

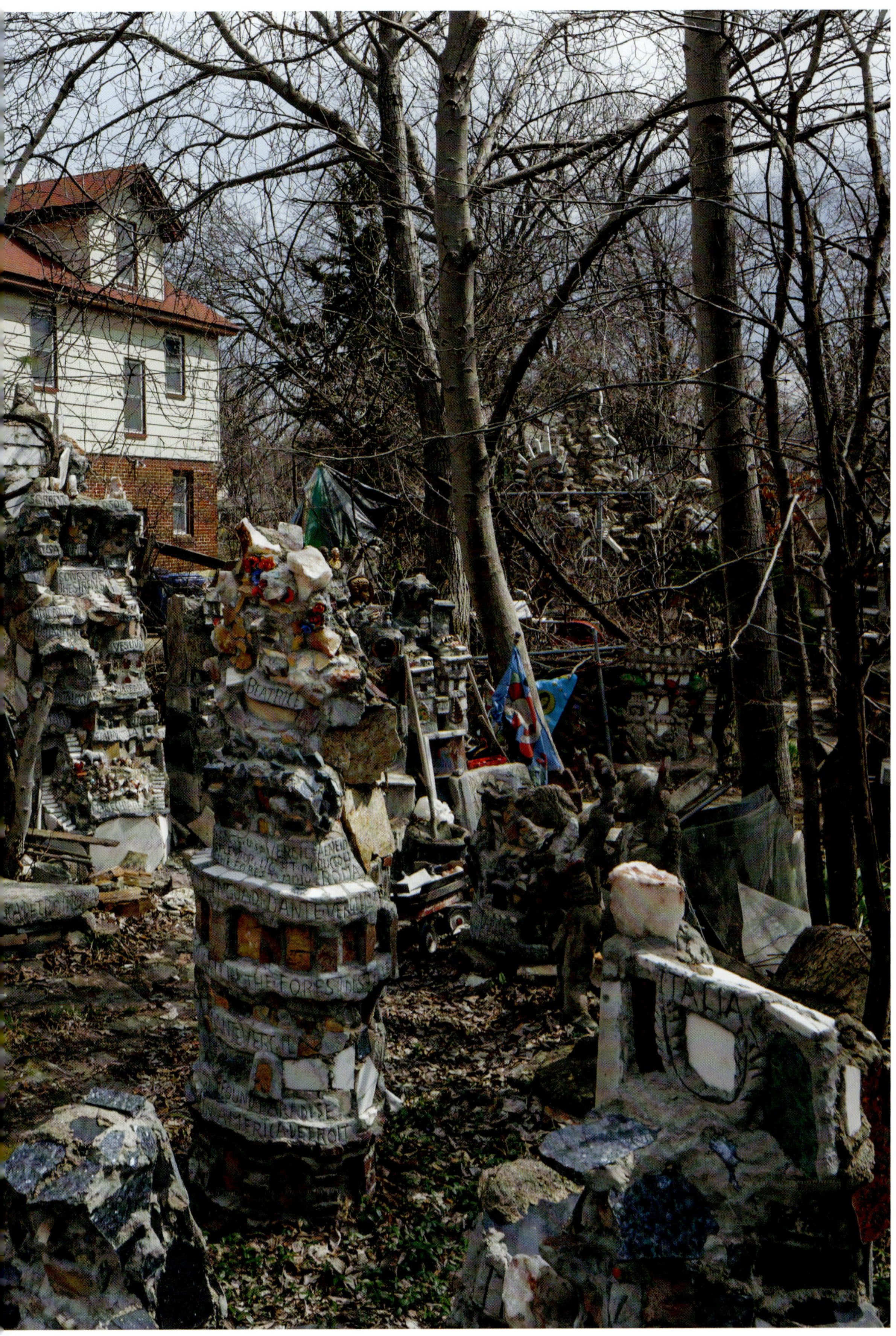
BEATRICE
ROMA
DANTE
THE FOREST
PARADISE
AMERICA DETROIT
ITALIA

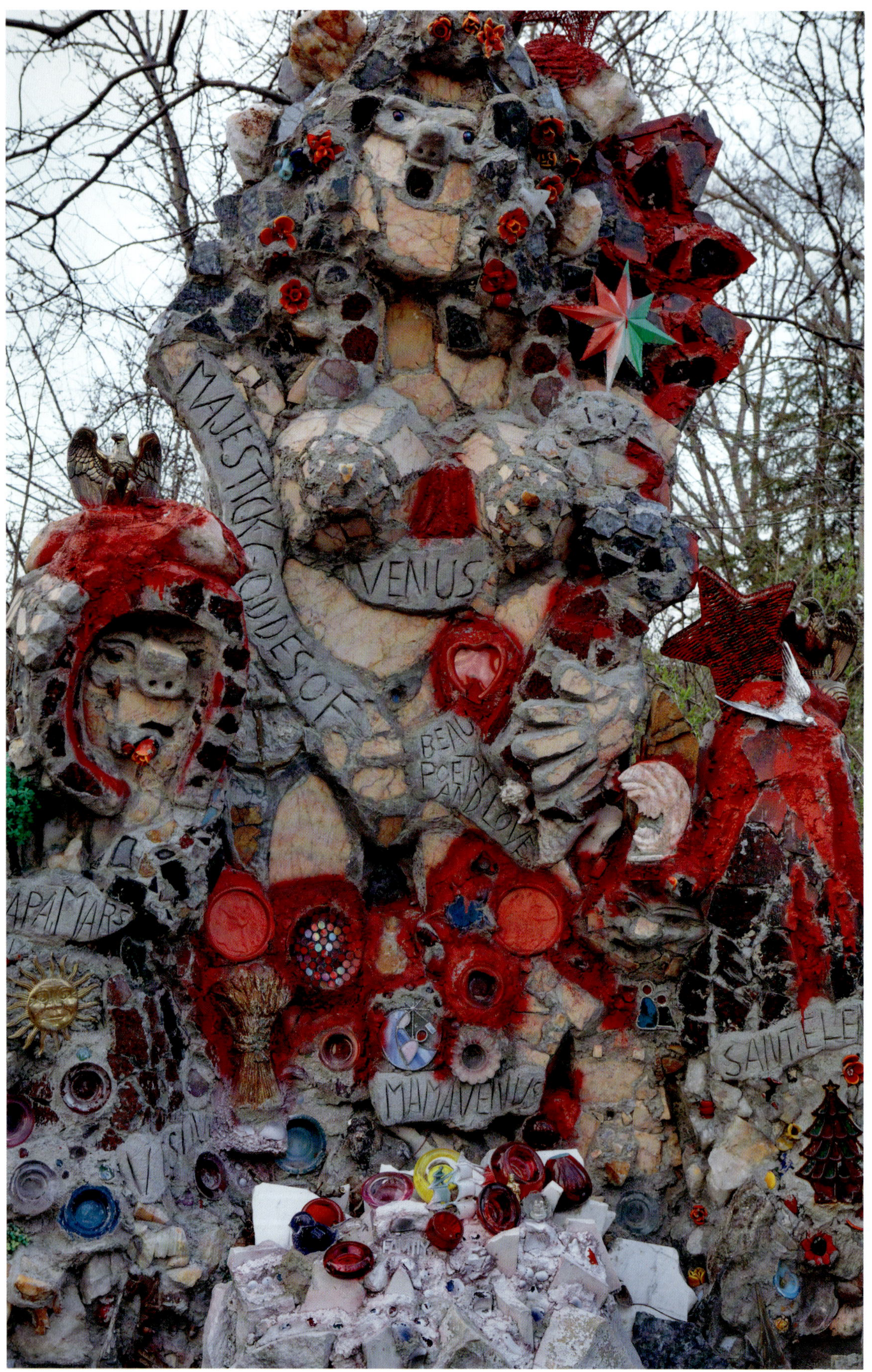

VENUS (DETAIL), 2018

INTERIOR INSTALLATION (DETAIL), 2018

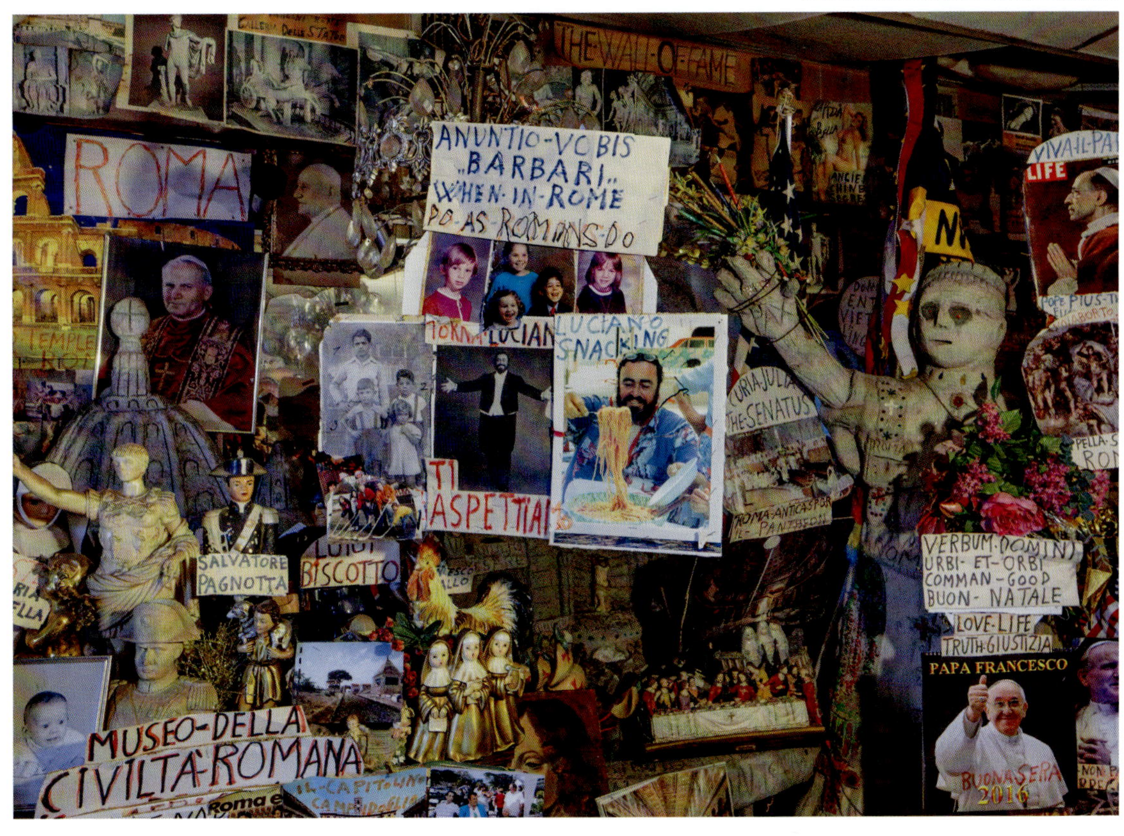

HE CELEBRATED THE COUNTRY OF HIS BIRTH WHILE ALSO HONORING HIS ADOPTED AMERICAN HOME.

HOWARD FINSTER

WORLD'S FOLK ART CHURCH, PARADISE GARDEN

PENNVILLE, GEORGIA

With roots in the fundamentalist religious traditions of the South, Finster (1916–2001), a self-ordained minister and pastor, felt called to use his considerable talent for public speaking to lead others to salvation and to further supplement those skills with visual cues in both two and three dimensions. He substantiated this by noting that one day he had asked members of his congregation to recall the theme of that morning's sermon but they had forgotten. By building his *Garden,* he believed it would be easier for them to remember his message.

Finster was one of 13 children born to a self-sufficient farm couple in a remote corner of DeKalb County, Alabama. Although his parents did not attend church regularly, the young boy experienced his first "vision" at three years old, was "saved" by age 13, and despite having only a sixth-grade education, began preaching two years later. He pastored several small rural churches over some 40 years, supplementing his pastoral income by working variously as a janitor, repairman, mill hand, mechanic—and almost 20 other trades.

In his spare time, he made little ornamental sculptures and miniature architectural environments with twigs and rocks, but by 1945, when he and his family had moved to Trion, Georgia, he had expanded his range, creating a variety of miniature and full-scale buildings as well as animal enclosures, ponds and signs. He also began collecting found objects (his goal at that time had been to collect an example of every human invention ever developed). In its totality, he described this site, located behind his hand-built home/grocery store, with its roof shingled in flattened quart motor-oil cans, as a "museum park."

But he felt hemmed in by the size of the Trion property, and after about a decade of work, in 1961, he relocated slightly south to nearby Pennville, a small, unincorporated hamlet between Trion and Summerville. Filling the larger, two-acre, swampy, cobbled-together site with monuments, bottle houses, found-object constructions, ornamented paths, ponds, and a wide variety of plants, some of which he had transferred from Trion, he was driven by visions that he saw as a visual extension of his preaching. After a 1975 article in *Esquire* magazine dubbed this new site a "Garden of Paradise," Finster himself started calling his *Plant Farm Museum* by a new name, *Paradise Garden*.

An oft-repeated legend explaining Finster's explosive production of two-dimensional works recounts that at the same time that he noticed that a spot of paint on his finger looked like a face, he heard a voice that told him to "paint sacred art." These new works were expansive in subject matter: the expected Biblical figures and illustrations of scriptural passages certainly appeared, but so did personages such as Elvis, George Washington, Hank Williams, and Santa Claus. Spaceships, dinosaurs, camels, Coca-Cola bottles, and the Statue of Liberty were also frequently represented. The number of sermonizing cartoon- or comic book-style paintings that he subsequently created numbered over 46,000, most of which he annotated with religious texts, accounts of his history or visions, or encouragement to seek salvation. He believed—identifying himself as a visitor from another planet reincarnated on earth—that his visions were specific mandates from God, and that through his artwork he was serving as an essential instrument to spread the Holy Word. He considered his two vocations of artist and preacher to be indivisible.

Apart from this output, which has garnered him the most publicity among collectors, rock musicians, politicians, television personalities, students, and art historians, are his architectural creations. He created some of these structures from the ground up, erecting amalgamations of recycled found objects such as bottles or hubcaps or bicycles—as noted on a sign posted in the *Garden*, "I TOOK THE PIECES YOU THREW AWAY/AND PUT THEM TOGATHER [*sic*] BY NIGHT AND DAY...." Others were modified existing buildings, adapted to serve Finster's—meaning God's—purpose. Another sign reads "I BUILT THIS PARK OF BROKEN PIECES TO TRY TO MEND A BROKEN WORLD OF PEOPLE WHO ARE TRAVELING THEIR LAST ROAD."

The *Pump House* (a shed built with Coca-Cola bottles), the *Mirror House*, and the *Bible House* were among the buildings Finster erected at the Pennville site, but the foremost architectural attraction became the *World's Folk Art Church*. That building was originally a modest board-and-batten chapel located at the northern end of his *Garden* that had been built "crooked" by the then-owner in the 1960s. When the property was put up for sale, Finster pooled his funds, including a $5,000 grant from the National Endowment for the Arts. After purchasing it, he decided to radically modify the existing vernacular architecture, and in the early 1980s he began

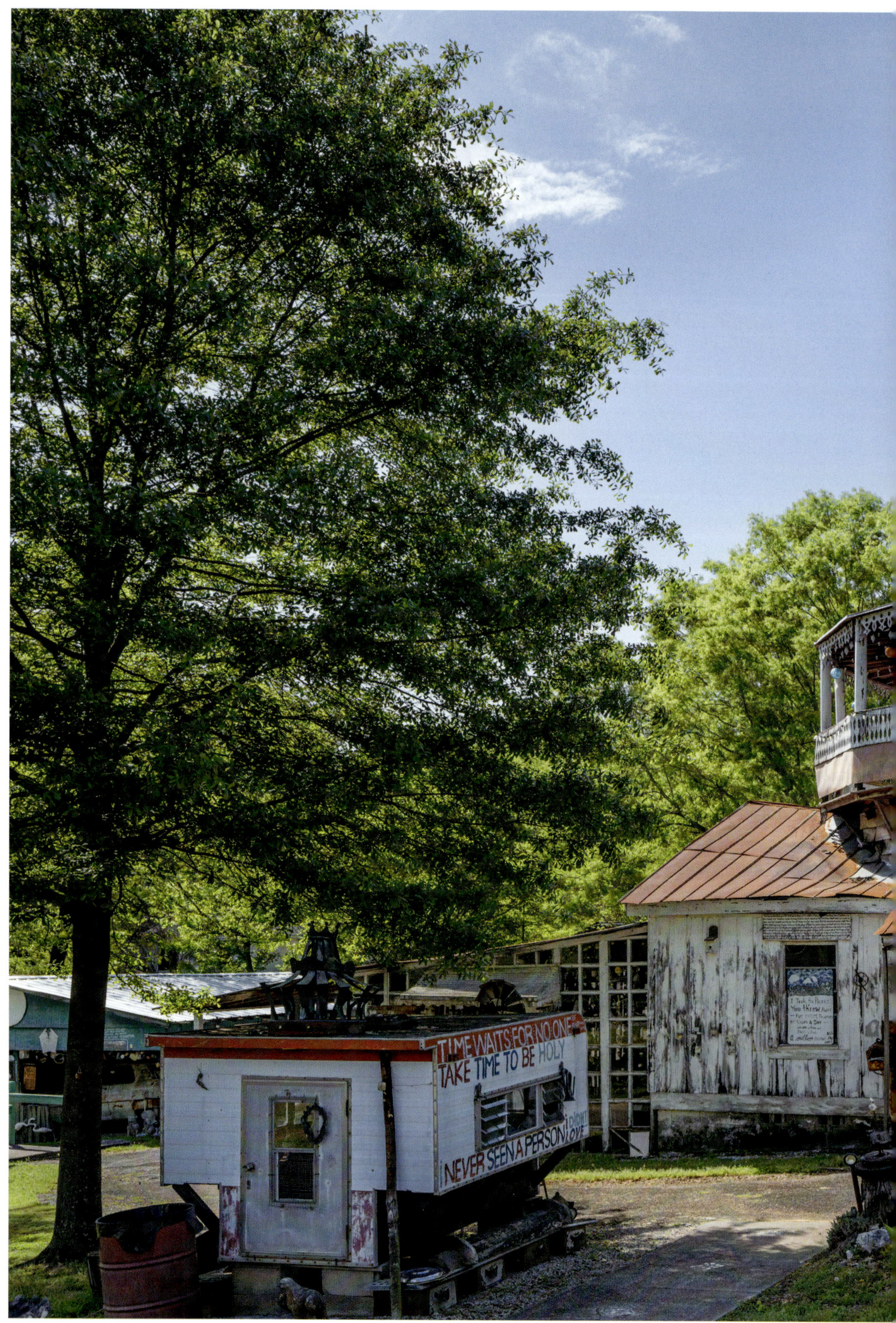

WORLD'S FOLK ART CHURCH, 2024

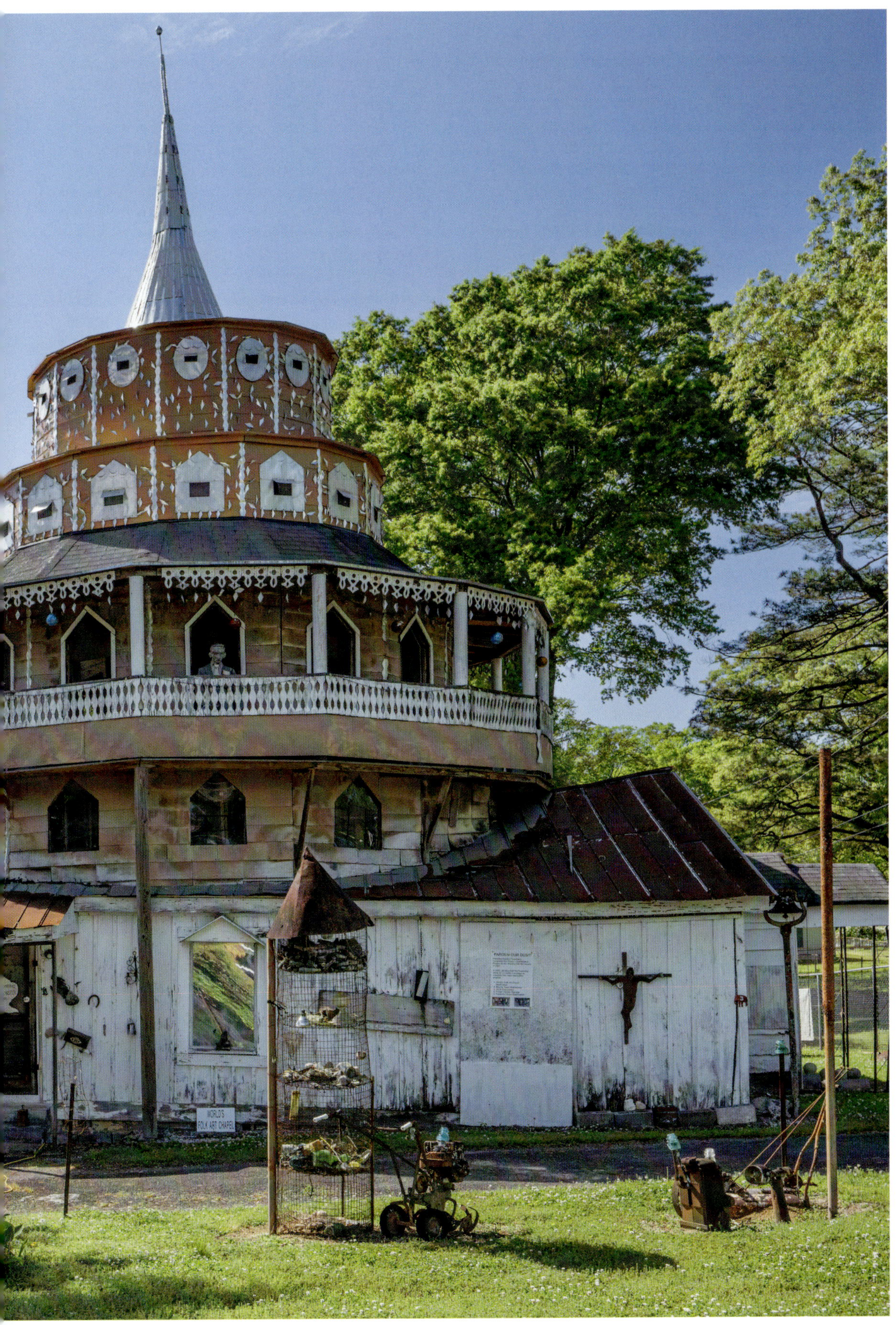
WORLD'S
FOLK ART CHAPEL

a two-year conversion project to add a four-level "round" tower (actually, a multi-angled polyhedron) above the existing single-story structure. The *World's Folk Art Church* is topped with a shiny tapering metal steeple and looks like an elaborate wedding cake. Built without plans or even, Finster claimed, a tape measure, it was both reminiscent of and inspiration for the heavenly mansions he envisioned and illustrated in his paintings. The *Church* is pierced with windows in the shape of elongated pentangles on the lower levels and circles on the top, with elaborate railings along the exterior pathways that encircle the structure and lacy ornamentation that hangs below the eaves. The title of this building equally emphasizes the global reach of his proselytizing and his acknowledgment that his primary ministry had become his art (when he was first gaining visibility among the public, he had been introduced as a "folk artist"). He finished the *Church* in July 1987 and filled it with art, artifacts, and tools, having never planned to celebrate Sunday services there—the architecture in and of itself was the focal point of his evangelization.

Finster's increasing fame—a spot on *The Johnny Carson Show*, articles in *People* and *Time* magazines, album covers for Talking Heads and R.E.M.—motivated him to concentrate on his two-dimensional work during his last years, although he always spoke about returning to work on the *Garden*. In the meantime, some of his relatives started to produce work in Finster's own style even as he himself regularly resorted to copying older compositions, and the expanded compound took on the impact of a cottage industry. Without constant upkeep, the humid climate and swampy landscape took a toll on the wooden buildings, and Finster closed public access to the Church two years before his death. It did not officially re-open to the public until June 2025. Now the entire site is a public park, owned by Chattooga County and leased, through its Development Authority, to the nonprofit Paradise Garden Foundation. The Foundation manages the site and organizes projects to help fundraise for future conservation efforts not only to preserve Finster's work but to serve as an economic engine for Chattooga County.

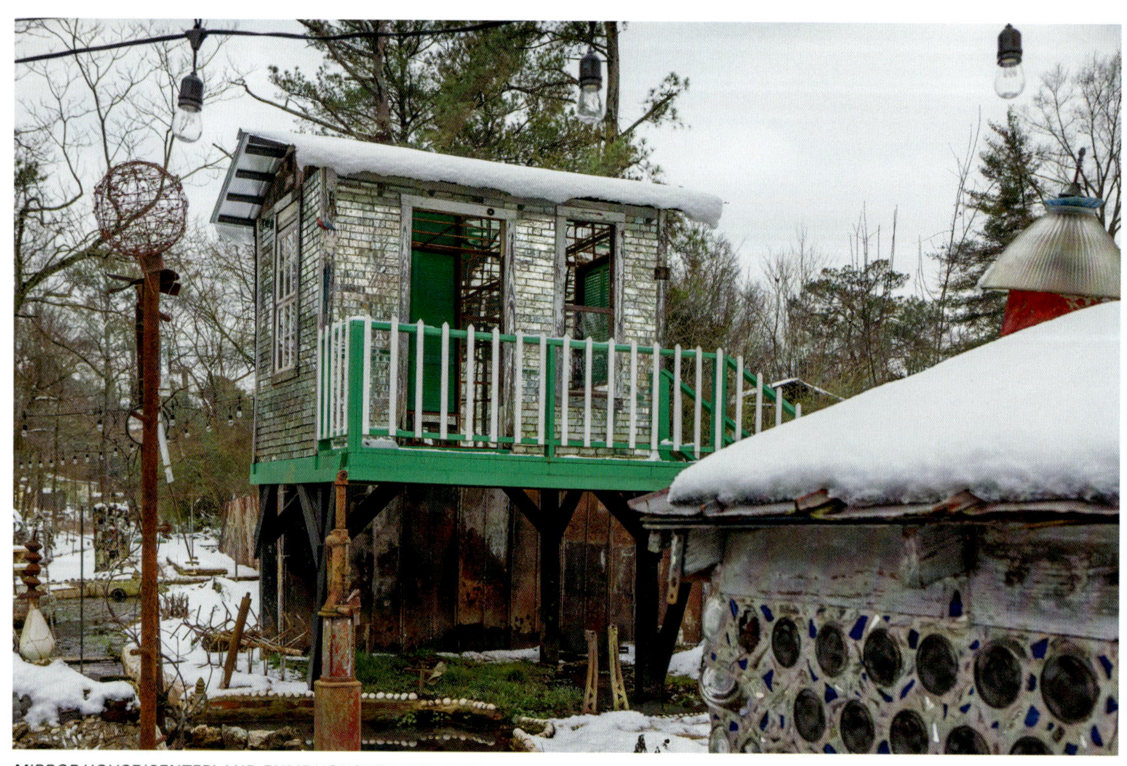

MIRROR HOUSE (CENTER) AND *PUMP HOUSE* (RIGHT), 2015.

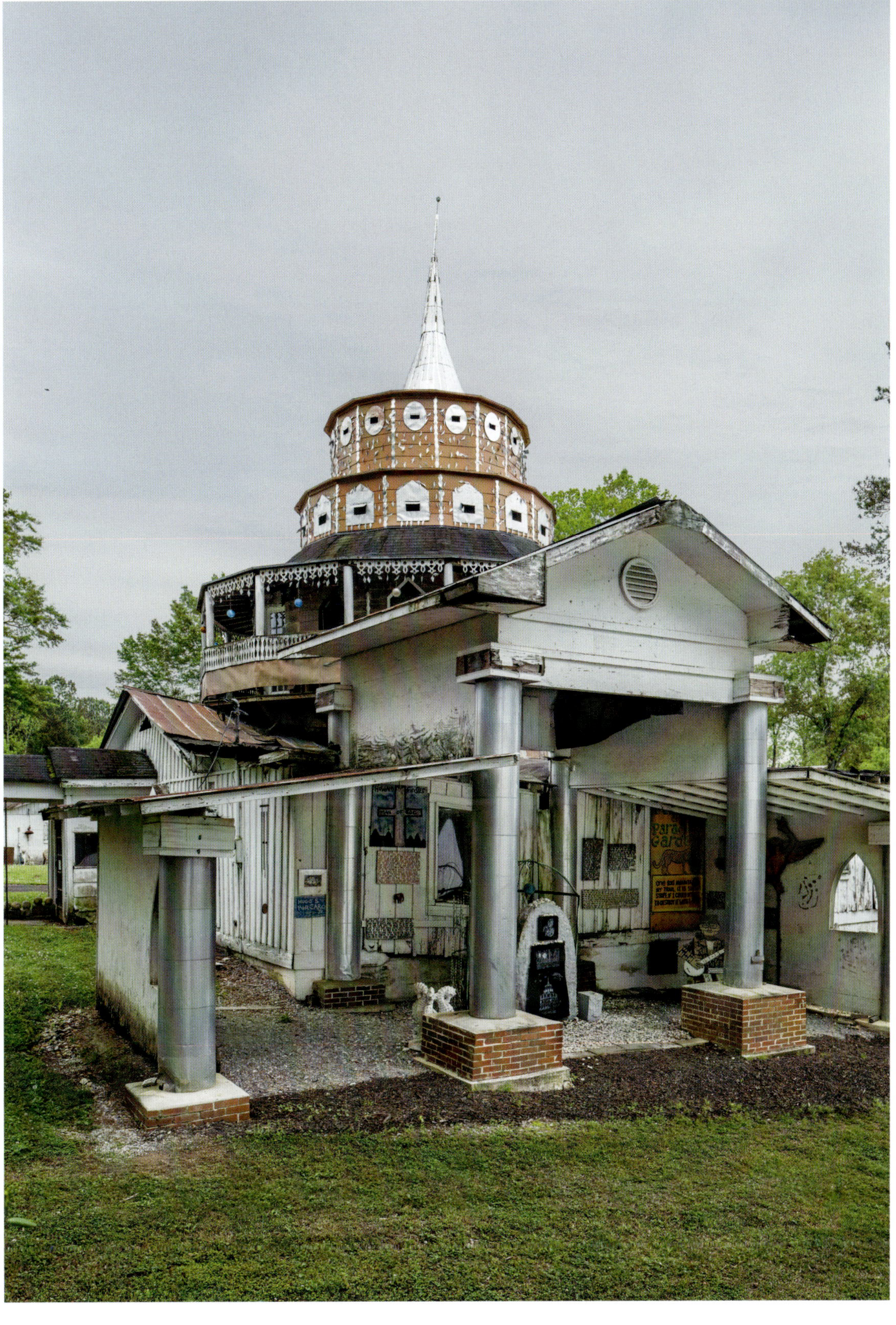

JEFFERSON DAVIS MCKISSACK, JR.

THE ORANGE SHOW

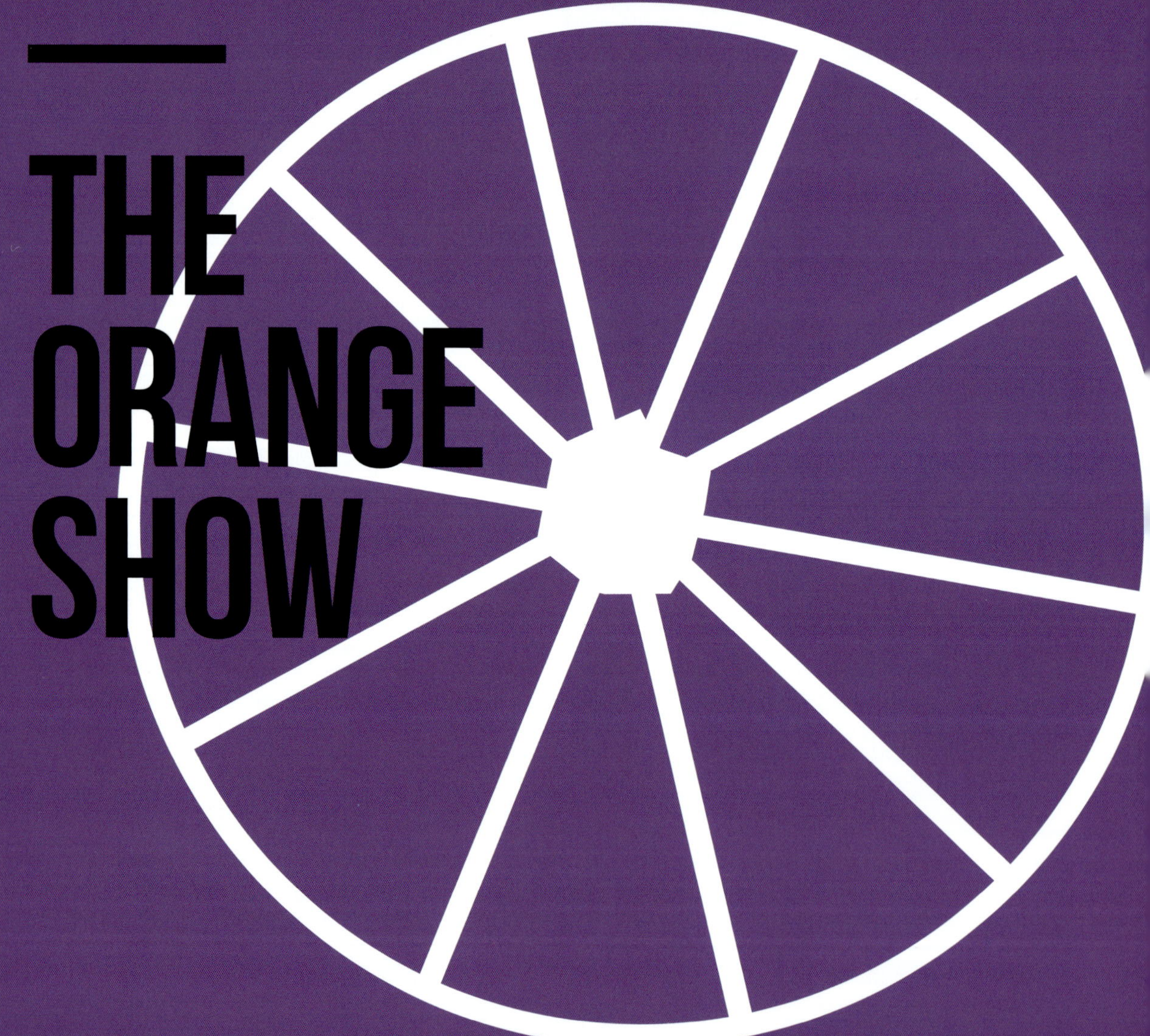

HOUSTON, TEXAS

Alone among U.S. art environments, McKissack's site, full of pomp and pageantry, focuses its homage not on a religious movement, an ethnic or cultural connection, or a tribute to historical figures or events, but on his favorite fruit, the orange. Crediting it as the key to a long and healthy life, he linked the orange to utopian concepts of self-reliance, respect, hard work, maintaining a positive attitude, virtue, and steam power (this latter perhaps a somewhat controversial inclination in this city largely built on the back of the fossil fuel industry). Steam is like the orange, he said: both produce energy.

McKissack (1902–1980) was born in Fort Gaines, Georgia, to a family of seven children and parents who were so proud of the South's Civil War legacy that they named their son after the president of the Confederacy. They ran a general store, and he had what he considered an idyllic childhood near the Chattahoochee River, watching the steamboats as they churned back and forth between his hometown and the ports of Columbus, Georgia; Eufaula, Alabama; and Apalachicola, Florida. He enjoyed school and earned a degree in commerce at Mercer College in Macon, Georgia, after which he moved to New York to work at a bank and enroll in graduate school at Columbia University. But he soured on academia and left after only one year, coming to believe that life as a tradesman was a better avenue to success.

By 1930, he had migrated to California, and living in the town of Signal Hill, he would likely have been aware of San Bernardino's municipal showcase for the citrus industry, the National Orange Show. Only an hour away from his home, this 100,000-square-foot exposition reportedly attracted 300,000 annual visitors to marvel at the extravagant programs, events, pageants, and architectural models that celebrated the orange.

After McKissack moved back to Georgia, he opened a series of businesses, but success eluded him, and during the Depression he was reduced to trucking oranges from Florida across the South. He subsequently continued a rather marginalized existence picking vegetables, and then, despite his age, did a brief stint in the Air Force during World War II. He later learned to weld in a further attempt to support the war effort, plying his trade at a ship-building company, experience that would later serve him well. But after his mother's death in 1948, he experienced what his siblings considered a mental breakdown, and they committed him to an institution for evaluation. Following his release in 1951, and wanting a fresh start, he moved to Houston.

He purchased a plot of land in the East End on which he built a concrete block home and then, buoyed by the steady income he received from his postal carrier job, purchased two contiguous parcels cattycorner across the street, a total of 3,000 square feet. He considered opening a beauty salon (possibly in order to meet women, as he thought of himself as a ladies' man) but then pivoted to establish a tree nursery and worm ranch on the property. Neither was profitable. But in 1968 he hit on the idea of what would become *The Orange Show*.

This was a booming period in Houston, and developers were enthusiastically ripping down historic downtown buildings in order to erect modern behemoths more suited, they thought, to this growing metropolis. McKissack took note, unobtrusively salvaging bricks, fences, gears, tile, metal umbrellas and awnings, and even fire escapes, which he hauled back home in his mail truck with the intention of repurposing them for his new enterprise. He supplemented these finds with garden ornaments and antiques, and began assembling his bounty into a multileveled architectural maze. He sold his car and pinched pennies so that he could direct all available funds to support this increasingly extravagant project, and when the nursery folded, he transitioned all the rest of his assets to help form *The Orange Show*.

Presumably still motivated and inspired by his knowledge of the multimedia National Orange Show back in California (although he never acknowledged it as a precursor or inspiration), McKissack included on his site a variety of exhibits extolling how eating oranges and engaging in productive labor would promote a long and healthy life. He added platforms, walkways, statues, didactic displays, water fountains, a museum of curiosities, and cymbal-playing battery-powered monkeys. Viewing areas with vividly painted tractor seats could accommodate 250 spectators overlooking a "steamboat" pond whose constructed miniature "boat" traveled in circles and, according to an identifying sign, pretended to call at the same four ports where the Chattahoochee River steamboats had docked during his childhood. Multicolored wagon wheels, their spokes resembling the sections of an orange, delineated different sections of the site; metal figures welded from scrap displayed signs to encourage visitors to abide by his counsel; and a wishing well was expected to satisfy everyone's fondest desires. Rippling flags, swiveling weathervanes, and spinning whirligigs and windmills added to the sensory overload, which was visually united by the color orange. "Love Oranges and Live," read one sign.

McKissack had been certain that thousands of people would attend the inauguration of the 3,000-square-foot site on May 9, 1979, but only about 150 visitors—mostly members of Houston's art community—stopped by, and over the subsequent months attendance dropped precipitously. He was perplexed, having spent over 10 years doggedly creating an amusement park that he expected to both entertain and educate a national audience. He was also deflated, and while he continued to tinker with and maintain the different exhibits, the life goal that had energized his previous decade dissipated. And McKissack turned out not to be the perfect embodiment of the lifestyle epitomized by the orange after all: despite writing a tract in which he predicted that enthusiasts who followed his advice would live to be 100 years old, he suffered a stroke in late December and never recovered, dying two days shy of his seventy-eighth birthday.

McKissack had left his property to a nephew, but a note on his desk indicated that Marilyn Oshman, former chair of the board of Houston's Contemporary Art Museum and a wealthy philanthropist, should be contacted in case something happened to him. Oshman organized a fundraising campaign and formed a nonprofit organization to purchase the site in order to preserve it. Although they undertook some basic maintenance and stabilization prior to the public reopening in 1982, there remained significant physical and logistical challenges: while McKissack may have been able to weld, his construction skills were much less polished.

Conservation, however, was not the nonprofit's only goal: its broader objective was to amplify the visibility of the site and integrate it into Houston's more expansive cultural landscape. Supporters established a multifaceted series of programs, forming a critical mass of offbeat exhibits and events with their acquisition of the *Beer Can House* (see page 214), the development of the now world-famous Art Car Parade, and, just south of *The Orange Show*, with the establishment of the linear Smither Park, where 300 artists encrusted every component in mosaic.

McKissack's original site was renamed the *Orange Show Center for Visionary Art*, and it has become a truly vibrant hub and major Houston attraction, with support from varied sources and an active schedule of exhibits, events, performances, concerts, films, classes, tours, and festivals. It was added to the National Register of Historic Places in 2006. A major capital campaign is in process to restore and conserve McKissack's original site while refurbishing an adjacent five-acre commercial property that was purchased in 2017, forming an expanded campus to support and present a wide range of creative programming. *The Orange Show* and its new components are projected to reopen to the public in 2026.

AMPHITHEATRE SEATING AND "STEAMBOAT" STAGE, 2024

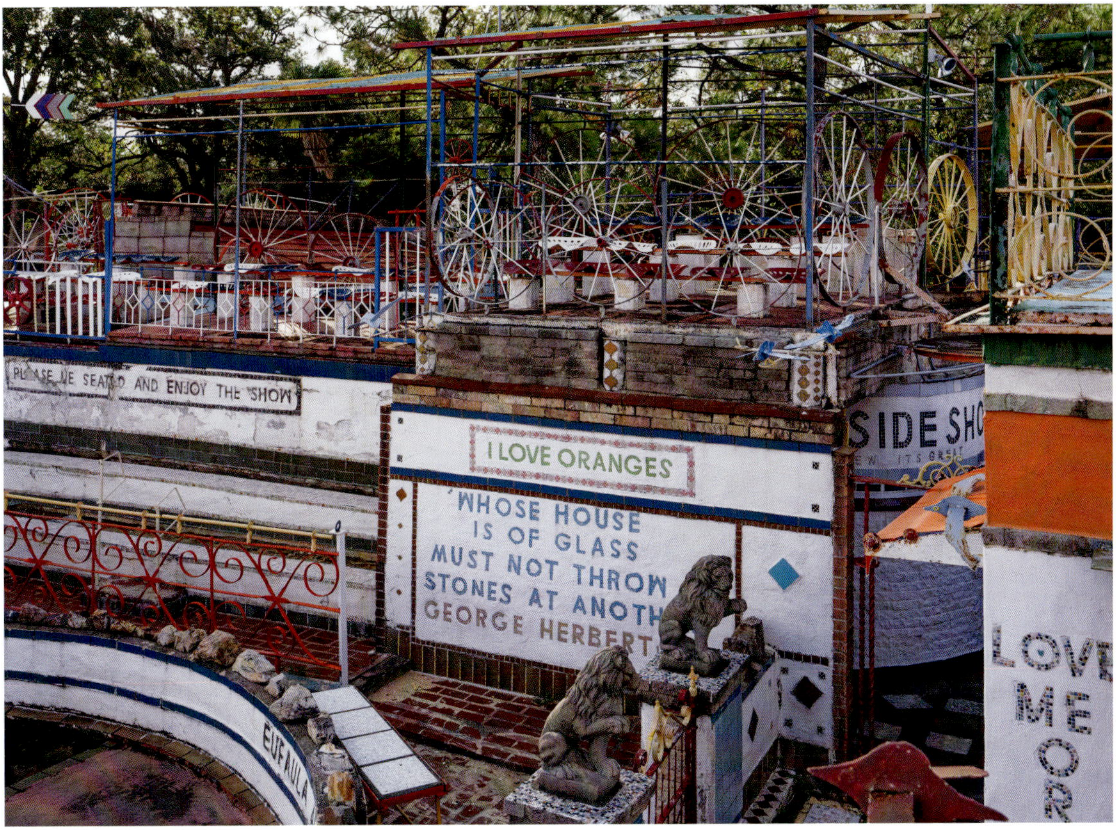

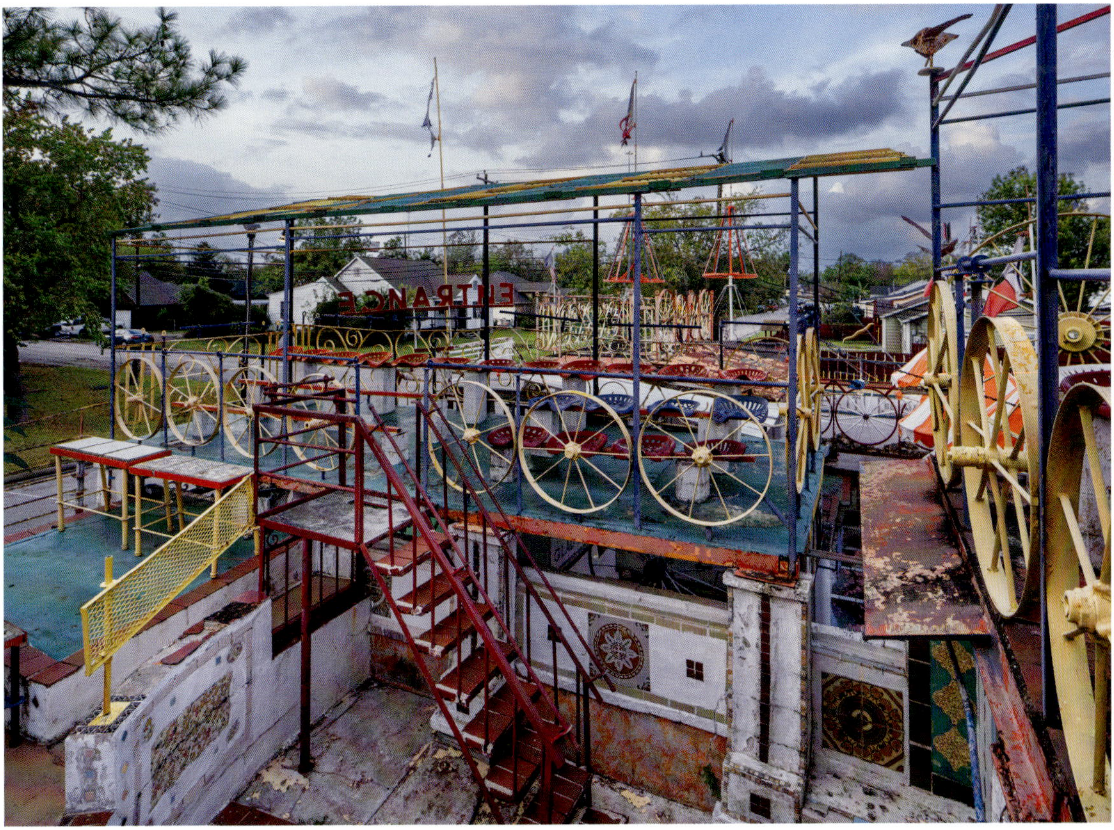

AMPHITHEATRE SEATING, 2024

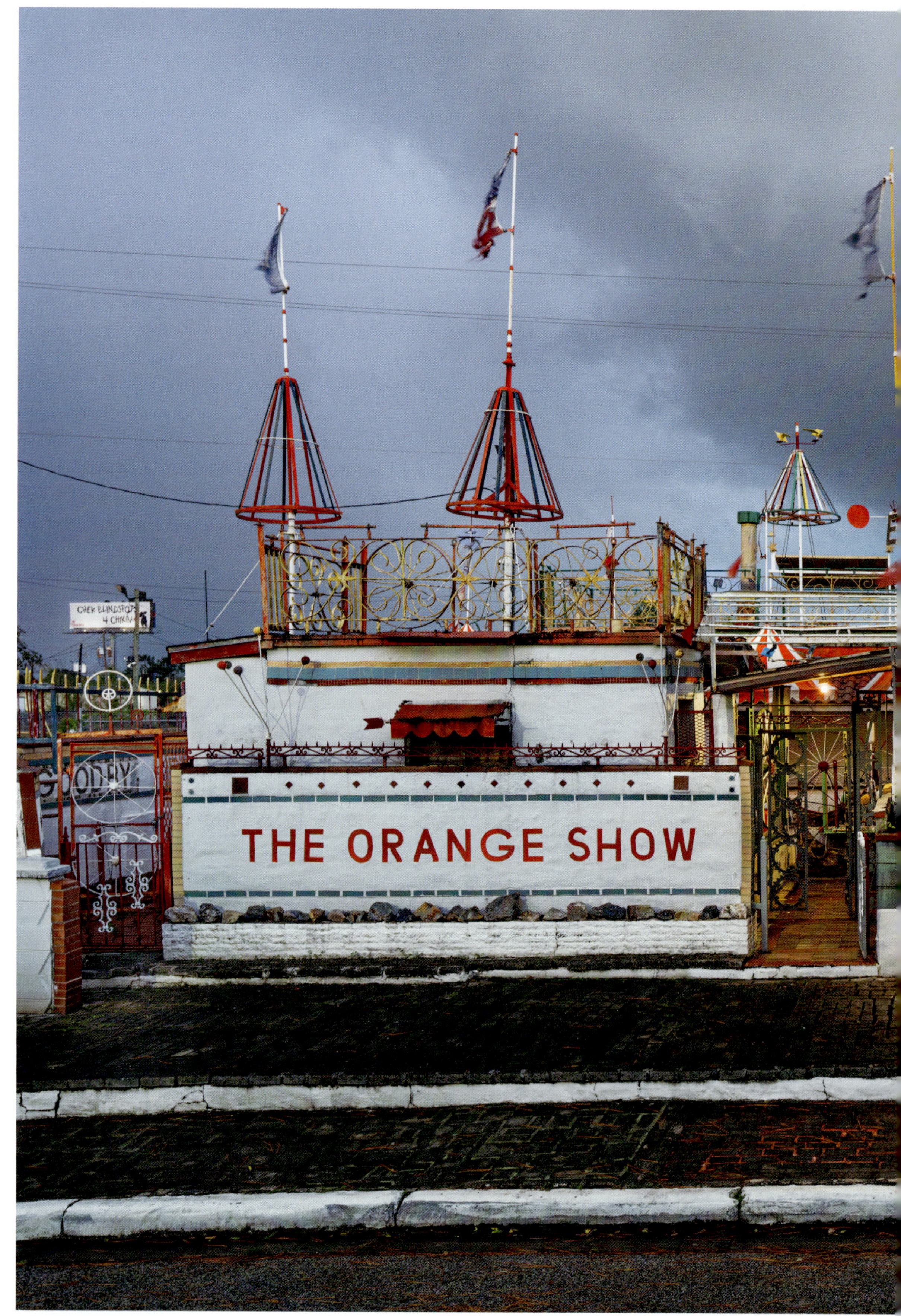

FRONT FAÇADE AND ENTRANCE, 2024

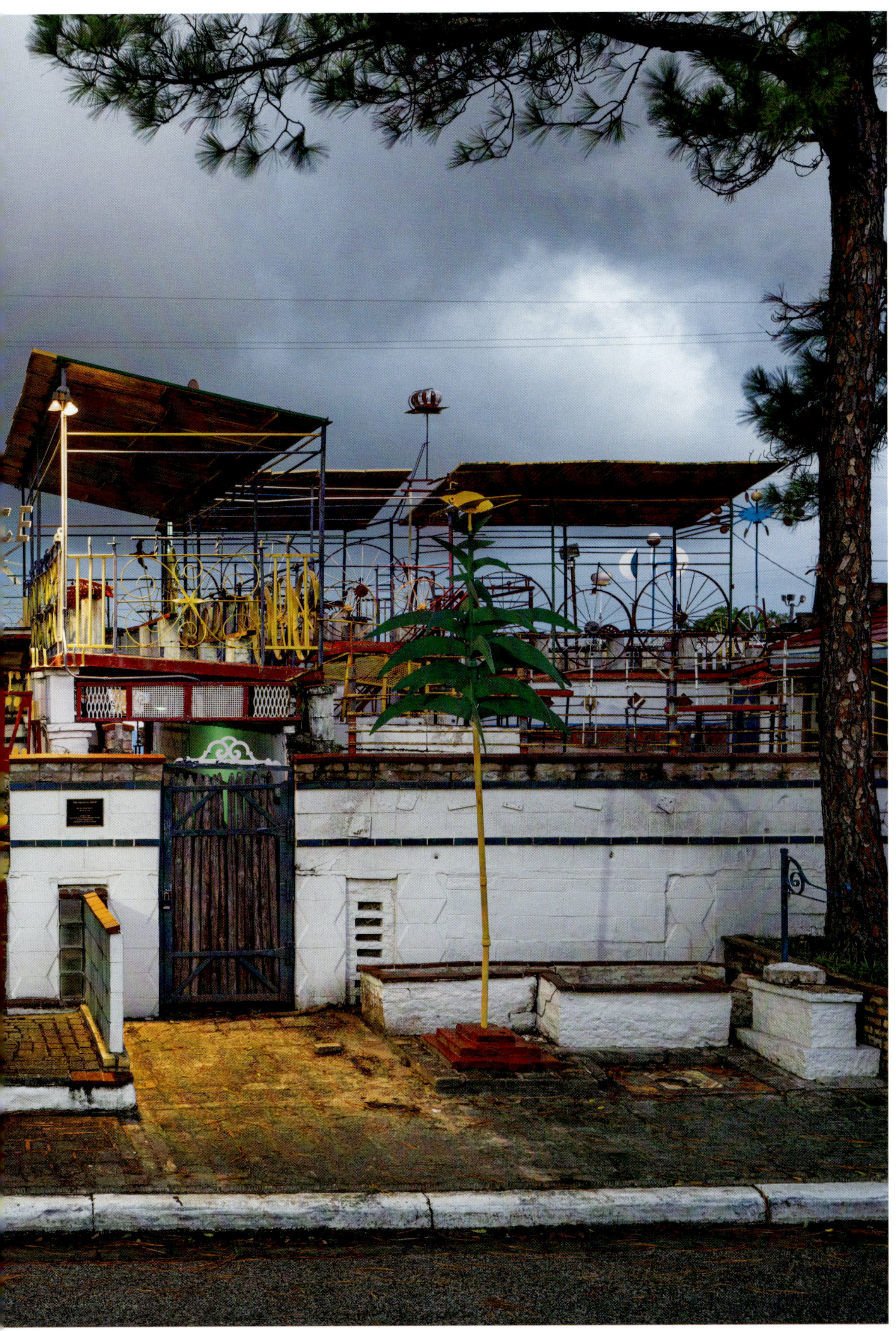

GROUND FLOOR "SIDE SHOW," 2024. PHOTO: JO FARB HERNÁNDEZ

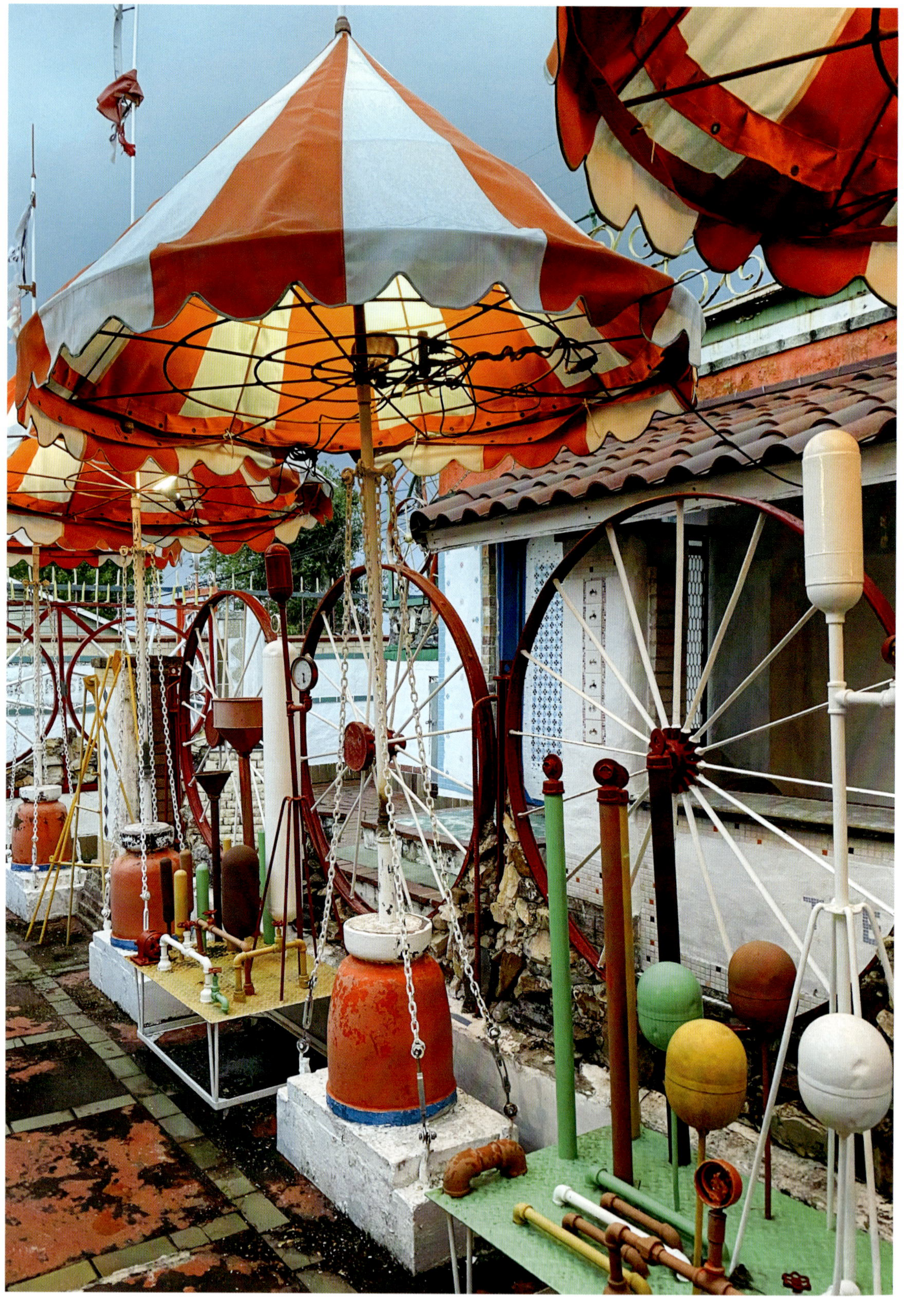

"STEAMBOAT" STAGE AND SITE OVERVIEW, 2011. PHOTO: © PETE GERSHON, COURTESY ORANGE SHOW CENTER FOR VISIONARY ART

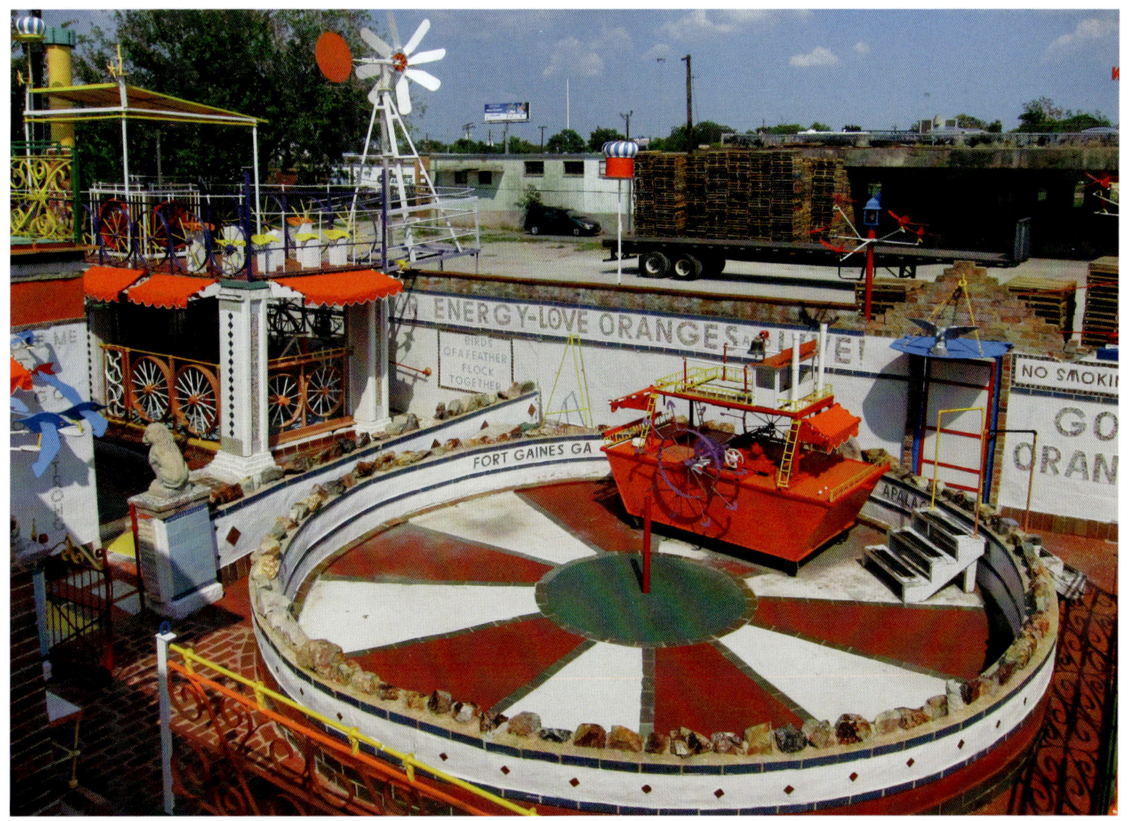

THIS HOMAGE TO THE ORANGE LINKS THE ARTIST'S FAVORITE FRUIT TO CONCEPTS OF SELF-RELIANCE, HARD WORK, RESPECT, AND VIRTUE.

LEONARD KNIGHT

SALVATION MOUNTAIN

NILAND, CALIFORNIA

Knight (1931–2014) was the fourth of six children born to a rural Vermont family. He attended a one-room school until high school but dropped out after his sophomore year, uncomfortable with the larger student body and his inability to fit in. He worked in the factory where his father was a foreman, then was drafted and served in the Korean War (albeit briefly, as the war ended 10 days following his arrival). He took a variety of jobs as he moved rather randomly back and forth across the country—painting cars, giving guitar lessons, picking apples, cutting wood—until 1967, when, visiting his sister in San Diego, California, he had a religious experience and "accepted Jesus into [his] heart." From that time he attempted to gently proselytize in any way he could, sharing his intense belief in the simplicity of religion: "God Is Love." At first he tried to interest the clerics of various denominations in his approach but was rebuffed, and, concluding that churches only complicate the relationship between individual and God with their emphasis on materialism and their oft-manifest corruption and hypocrisy, he declined to attend church or link himself to any congregation for the rest of his life.

In a further attempt to broadcast his beliefs, he next tried to sew a hot-air balloon emblazoned with his message of universal love, which he dreamed of launching over the populace. But after 14 years of buying small amounts of fabric with the paltry sums accumulated from his various low-paying jobs, he finally gave up as one section after another of the fabric rotted. The enormous pieced balloon did not fly.

By this time he was living on the outskirts of Niland, a poor desert hamlet with a declining population, and he had decided that after his most recent failure he would move on. But before he did, he set about erecting a small monument to memorialize his efforts and promote his beliefs, using a half bag of cement and ornamenting the formation with found objects. This building project inspired him anew, and, acquiring more cement, he kept working, climbing higher and higher on his new manmade hill, which he tucked into the side of a natural desert ridge. He used an unwieldy proportion of sand to stretch the mortar mixture, and he integrated discarded appliances and other objects he found at the dump or on the desert floor to expand and enhance his design. But after a few years it all collapsed: despite his range of earlier experiences, he had gained no real construction skills.

Knight was nothing if not tenacious, however: he had not known the first thing about sewing before he started fabricating his balloon. Rather than give up, he thanked God for showing him that his mountain was unsafe before someone got hurt, and he vowed that henceforth he would hand over the responsibility of construction. From this time forward, Knight would only serve as God's channel and physical instrument, and would no longer describe himself as an "architect." He abandoned the use of cement and switched to the desert's native adobe mixed with straw as his primary raw material, learning as he worked how to mix, apply, and sculpt the mixture. This time, he succeeded.

Knight continued for almost 30 years to apply his adobe/straw mixture to the five-story hillside that became known as *Salvation Mountain*, using it as an idiosyncratic billboard to disseminate his "simple" religious message. He also enveloped various found objects and vehicles in adobe, which he transformed from its natural hue into candy-colored representations of flowers, pine trees, waterfalls, rivers, a "yellow brick road," and flying birds, the motifs coming to life thanks to hundreds of thousands of gallons of paint donated by friends and supporters. Over time his monument blossomed into a complex, vivid, and compelling masterpiece of worldwide importance. And as he built and recounted the story of his life again and again to a steady stream of visitors, Knight frequently came to be regarded as belonging to the tradition of desert prophets who gained wisdom as a result of their asceticism and solitude. He tested his faith and overcame his tribulations in the kind of location where holy men of both the Old and New Testaments encountered God and created sacred spaces.

Knight considered his spiritual and personal interactions an experiential cycle based on giving. Beyond the initial gift of Christ giving his life for humanity, God then gave Knight the gift of being able to create the *Mountain*, and in turn Knight gave the *Mountain* to the public. The cycle continued as art and religious pilgrims alike gifted him paint and paintbrushes, food and funds, and he, in return, gifted them the wisdom he had gained by living how and where he did (as well as with such handmade mementos as concrete painted flowers). Through their presence, his audience bore witness to Knight's message as they gave him their time and attention.

OVERVIEW, *SALVATION MOUNTAIN*, 2012. PHOTO: JO FARB HERNÁNDEZ

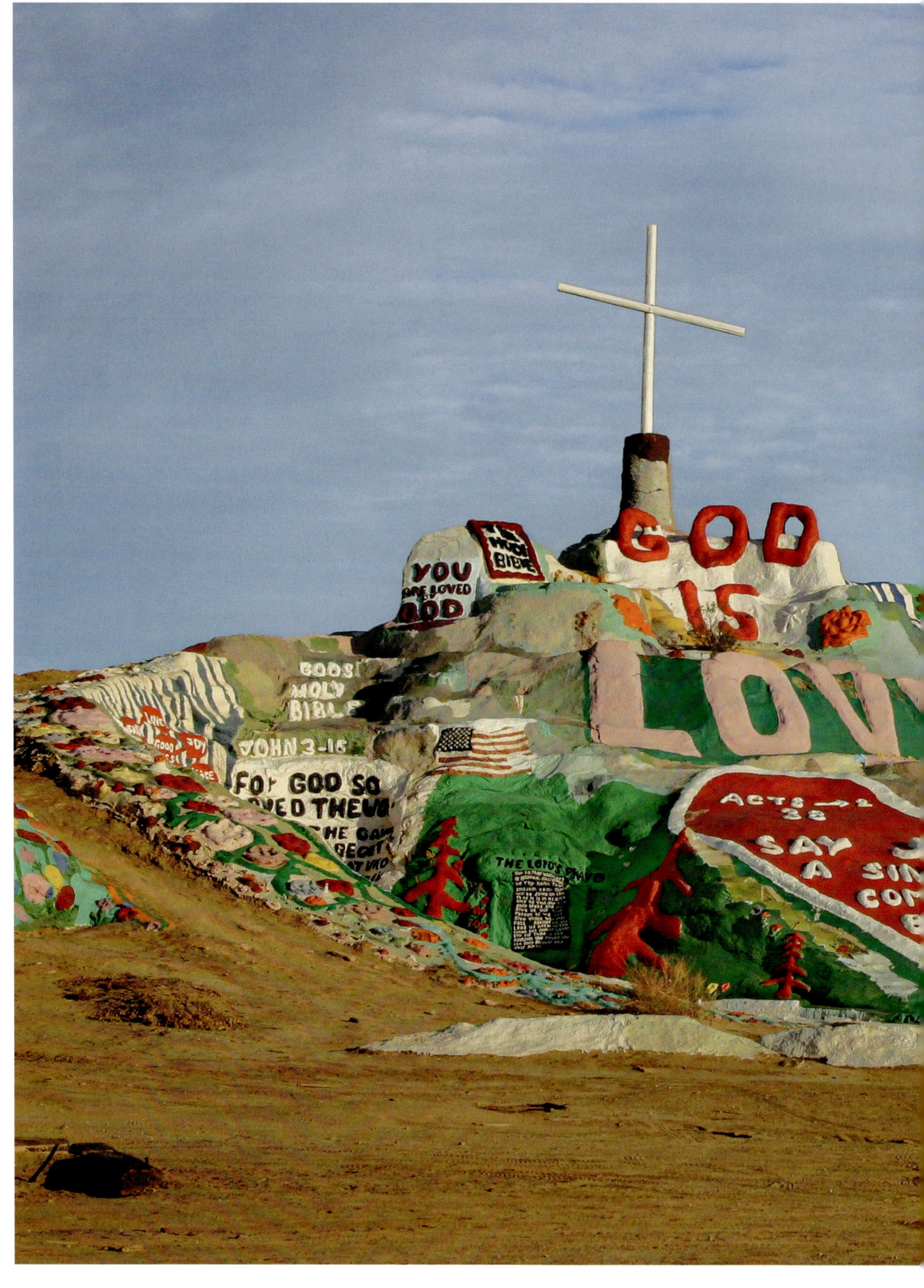

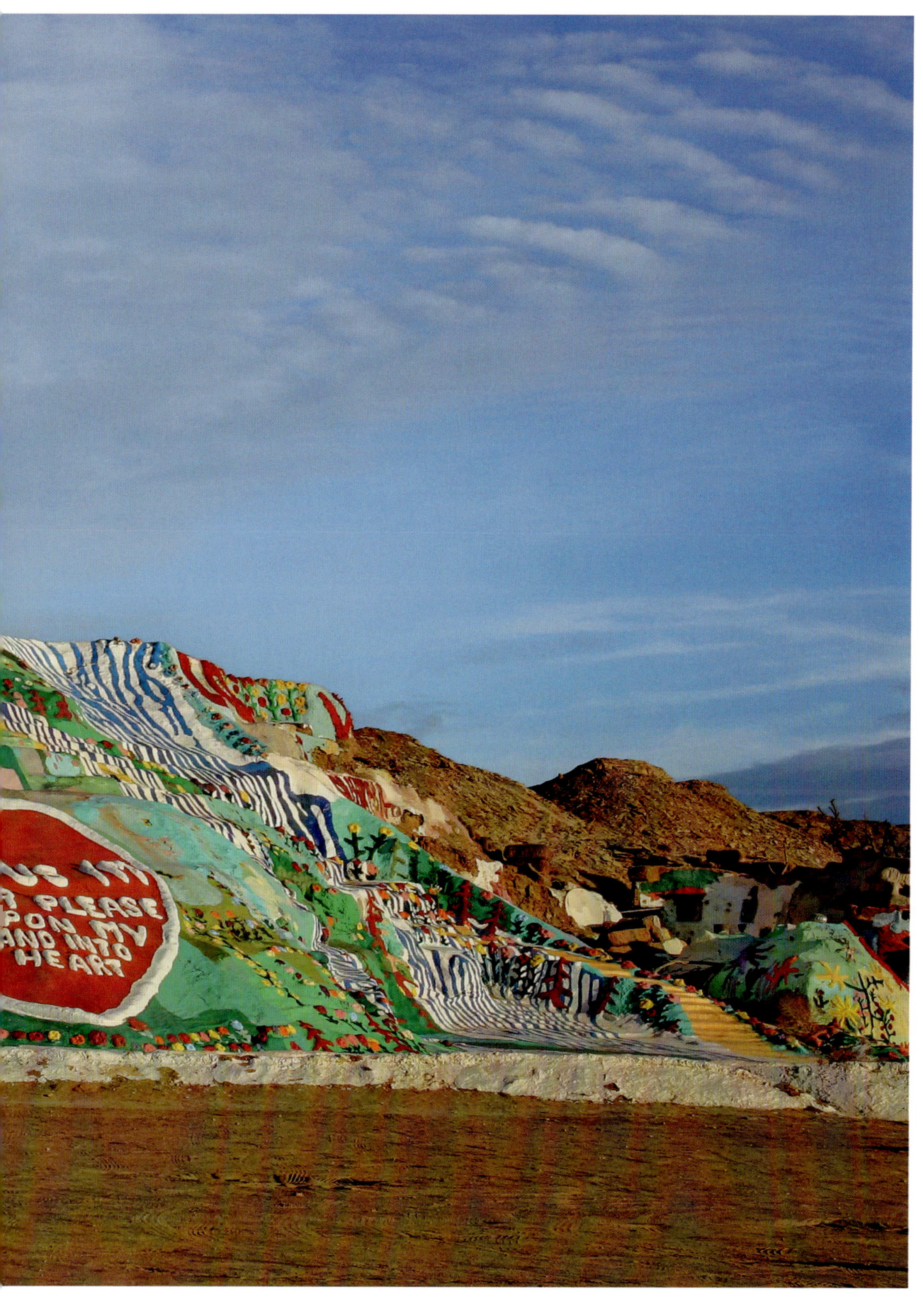
PLEASE
MY
INTO
HEART

Despite his trust in this gifting cycle, Knight was also sensitive to the ecological and economic ravages linked to the nearby inland Salton Sea and the checkered history of its development, and he hoped that his *Mountain* would become a tourist attraction sufficient to bring "millions of dollars" to this isolated corner of the desert, as Imperial County is one of the poorest in the state. Nevertheless, Knight never tried to monetize or commercialize his work, in contrast, for example, to creators such as Howard Finster (see page 424).

While the *Mountain* itself—roughly 150 feet wide at its base—has drawn the most interest, for the purposes of this book, we focus our attention on its adjacent constructions: a sequence of concave, domed, lofty interior and semi-interior spaces created through the geometries of stacked hay bales. The exterior visual impression is not unlike a multicolored version of Israeli-Canadian architect Moshe Safdie's *Habitat 67* complex, built for the 1967 Montreal World's Fair; nevertheless, it is certain that Knight came to this aesthetic on his own.

In 1998, his initial idea for the first section of this architectural space led him to create a Navajo-style hogan. He never moved in, however, and instead he continued to live on-site in his truck, despite the presumed attraction of the significant insulating qualities of the hay bale construction, which neutralized the extremes of the desert's weather fluctuations. He intermittently interrupted the stacks of hay bales with apertures, sealing them with secondhand glass windshields and windows that amplified the building's function as a shelter while allowing light to pass into the interior (there is no electricity or running water on-site). He heightened the durability of the hay bales by coating interior- and exterior-facing surfaces with adobe and straw, later painting them in his characteristic multicolored patterns. He also used this mixture to build up decorative motifs on the interior walls: flowers, hearts, birds, and reiterations of his all-consuming belief that "GOD IS LOVE." He further covered the interior surface with a myriad of photographs, clippings, artifacts, and sculpted Biblical and natural references that helped to chronicle the history of the site, and he was pleased when visitors added to the adornments with their own gifts and mementos.

To the side, he continued to expand into additional domed rooms, supporting the hay bale construction with the tangled limbs of dead trees (not particularly abundant in this desert region), which he inserted into pillars of stacked recycled tires that he filled and covered with adobe and painted in bright and contrasting colors like those of the *Mountain's* exterior. He started to think of this somewhat-labyrinthine architectural interior as a museum, and its interior rotundity a tribute to the failed balloon project from decades earlier.

Salvation Mountain has constantly been beset with ongoing maintenance concerns and legal challenges over the almost 40 years of its existence. Certainly weather patterns have been an unending problem, as the extreme heat and cold, coupled at different times of the year with either high winds blowing abrasive sand or monsoon rains, incrementally advance the surface fracturing that leads to deeper ruptures. But these natural difficulties were compounded in 1994 by Imperial County claims that the *Mountain* was toxic and an environmental hazard. Without substantiation, they assumed the paints were leaching lead into the soil, so officials advocated tearing the entire structure down and carting the residue off to a toxic waste disposal site.

Thanks to a network of supporters who publicized the threat, that particular assessment was disputed and resolved, as alternate testing samples were submitted that impartially determined that the level of contaminants in the soil did not reach unacceptable levels. But continual conservation needs persist, as, since Knight's death, do questions regarding who has the right to address these challenges. The nonprofit organization that was formed with the goal of preserving the site has variously had to contend with new artists who want to move on-site and reform the *Mountain* to their own taste, fervent religious believers who misrepresent Knight's message, untrained volunteers whose efforts may do more harm than good and whose handiwork is a mismatch with Knight's unified vision, and with the thousands of annual visitors who climb the formations and inadvertently scrape and scratch the surfaces with their shoes and the studs on their jeans. Significant security and stability challenges remain, as do ownership issues. As of this writing, the site remains owned by the California State Lands Commission and, while the nonprofit has pursued trying to purchase

HOGAN INTERIOR, 2006. PHOTO: JO FARB HERNÁNDEZ

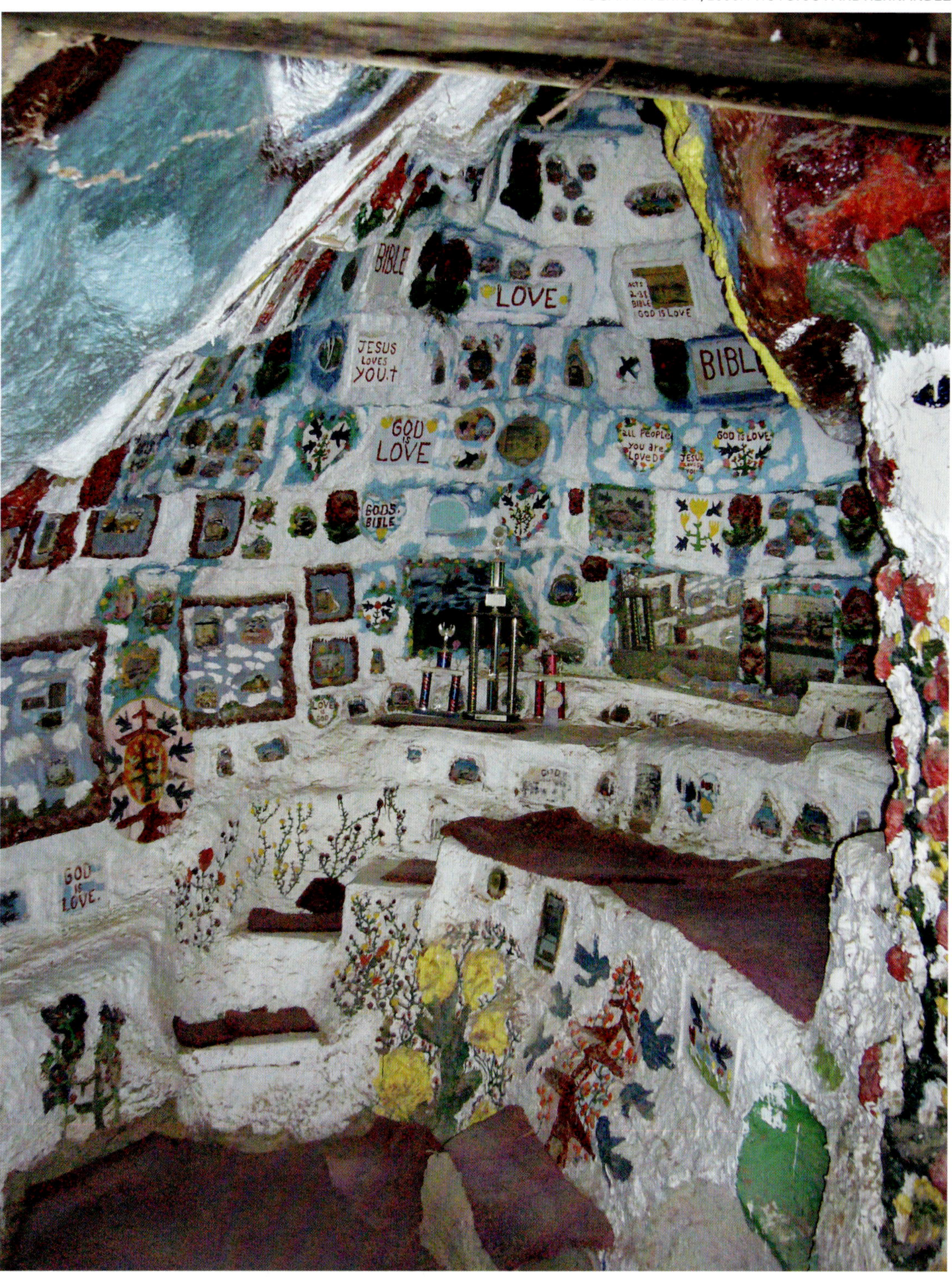

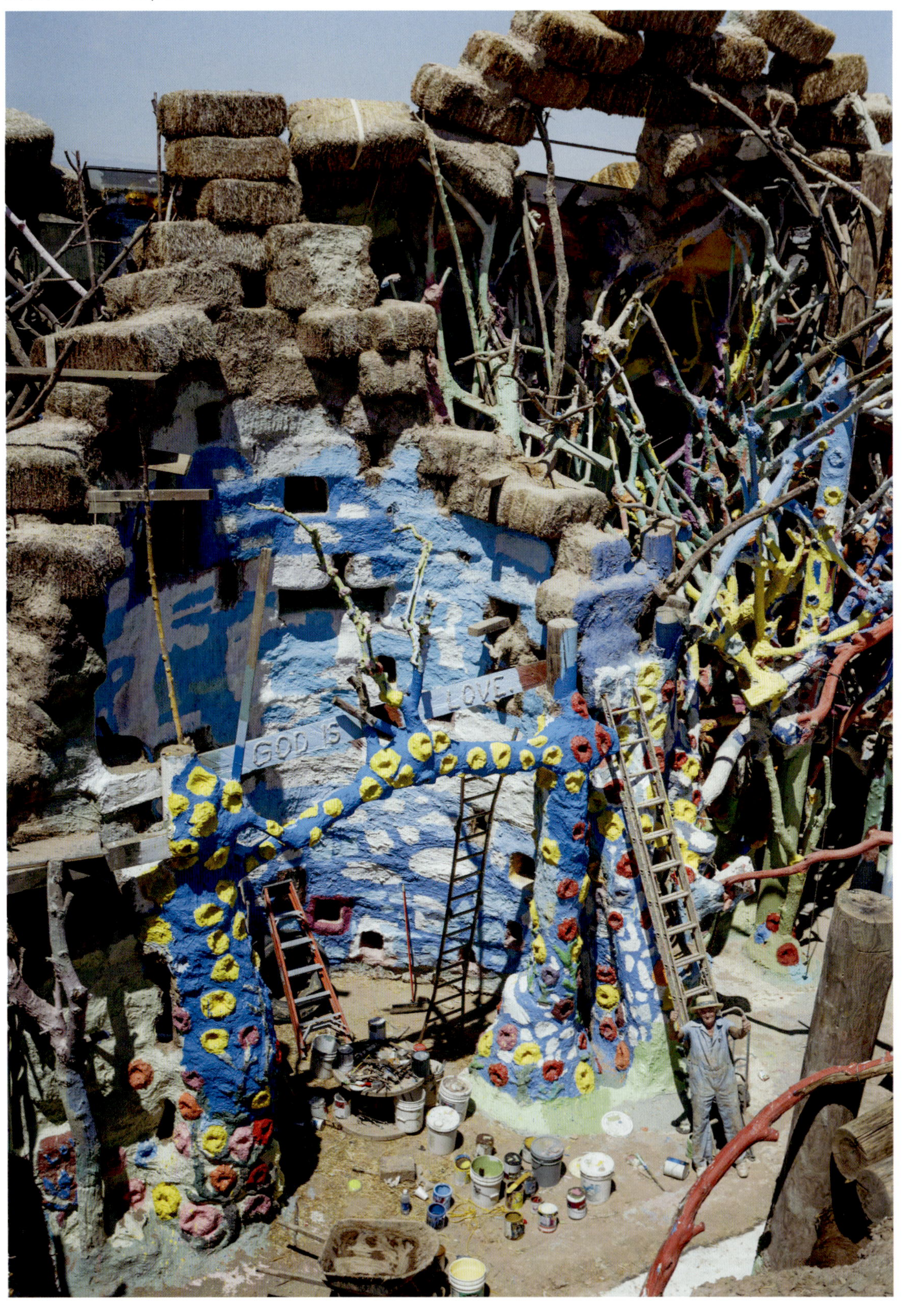
GOD IS
LOVE

the property for over a decade, many issues are yet unresolved. Nevertheless, while some sections of the environment are regularly closed to public access due to damage or in-process or precautionary conservation measures, *Salvation Mountain* is still extant and available for viewing from sunup to sundown.

Once decried as an environmental hazard and unauthorized use of state land, in 2002 the site was entered into the Congressional Record as a National Treasure, and even Imperial County, in 2024, designated it as a "historically significant property." Albeit contested, it remains a sacred space: no one who has been to *Salvation Mountain* has remained untouched or unchanged by its intensity and its beauty, whether they are attracted by or indifferent to its religious message. Believers and nonbelievers alike can find inspiration here.

HE CAME TO BE SEEN AS BELONGING TO THE ANCIENT TRADITION OF DESERT PROPHETS WHO GAINED WISDOM AS A RESULT OF THEIR ASCETICISM AND SOLITUDE.

OVERVIEW, *SALVATION MOUNTAIN* AND *MUSEUM*, 2009

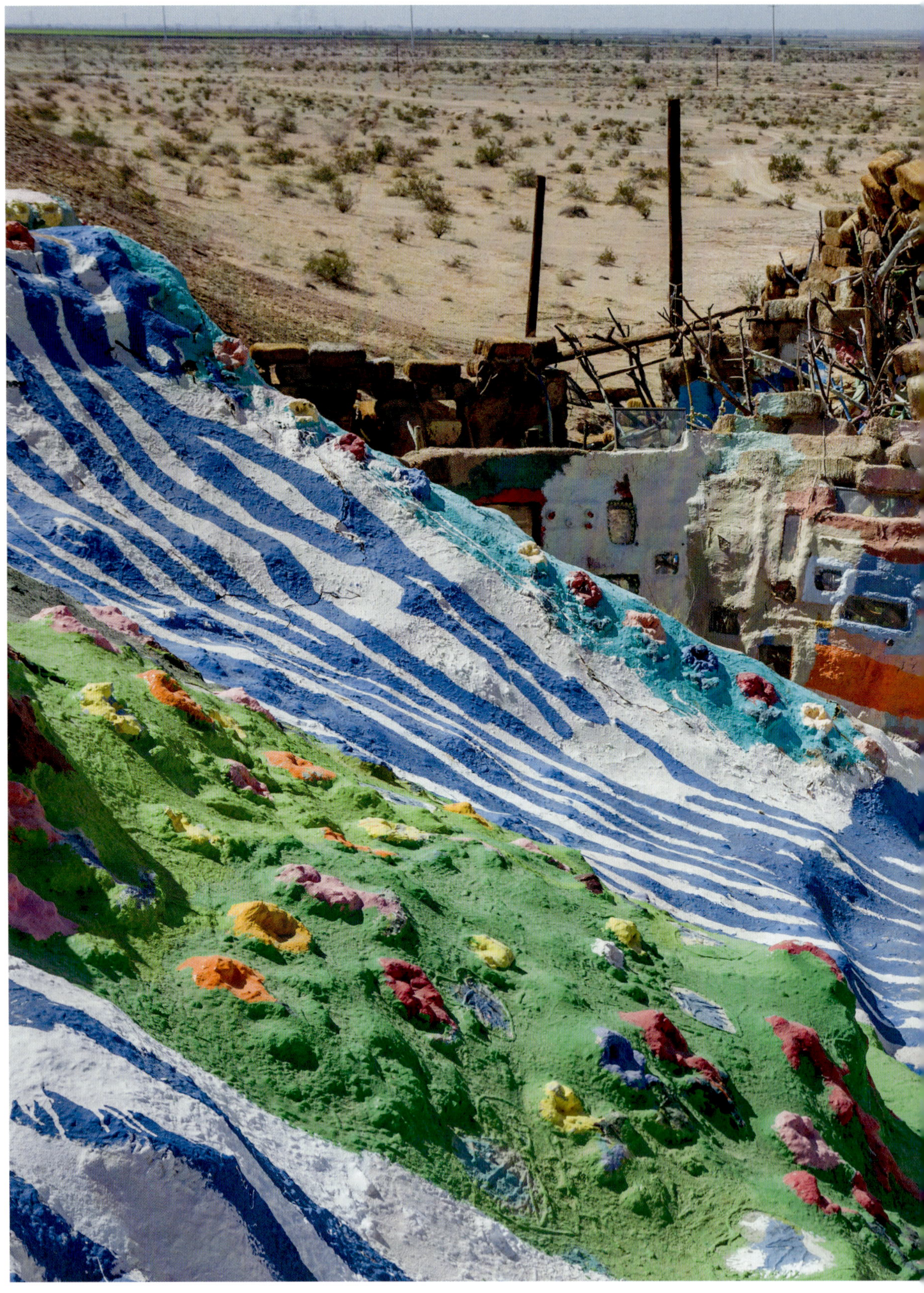

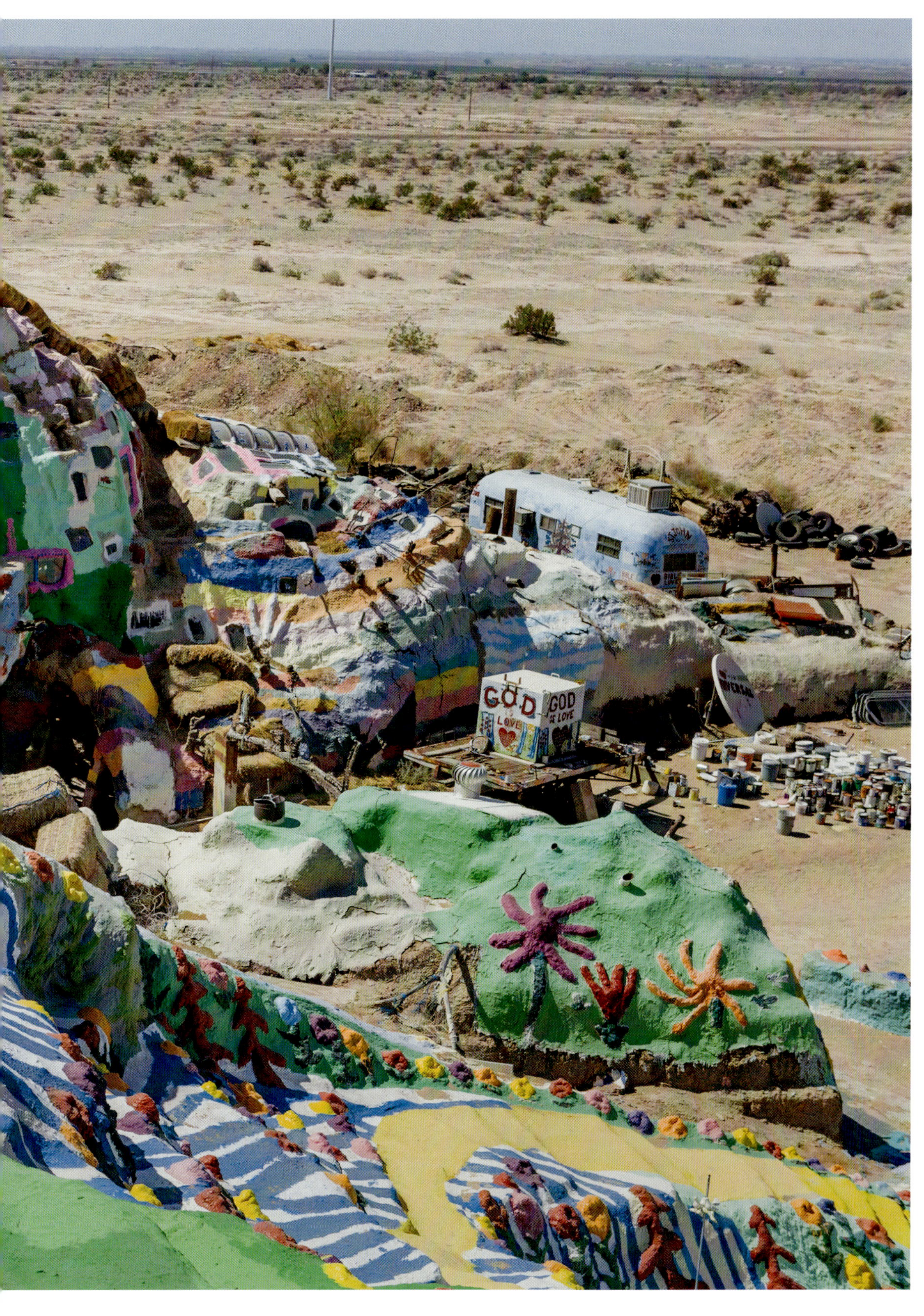
GOD
LOVE
GOD
IS LOVE

«IT'S IMPOR

TO LEAVE A

A RECORD O

TIME ON TH

EARTH.»

ANT

FOOTPRINT...

OUR

S

—BILLY TRIPP

WORKS CONSULTED

Adeane, Ant, dir. *The Angels of the Bayou*. BBC Radio 4, July 25, 2019. https://www.bbc.co.uk/sounds/play/m00070my.

Albright, Alex. "Vollis and his Fun Machine." *Vollis Simpson, 1919–2013*. Originally published 2021. https://alexalbright.works/research/local-history/vollis-simpson/.

Allamel, Frédéric. "An Architectural Riddle: Billy Tripp's Mindfield." *Study the South*, October 31, 2022. https://southernstudies.olemiss.edu/study-the-south/an-architectural-riddle/.

_____. "From Builders to Town Dreamers: Some Ethical Considerations in Self-Taught Architecture." *Southern Quarterly* 39:1-2 (Fall/Winter 2000–01): 5–15.

Allen, David. "How Martín Sanchez's Art Made Tios Tacos a Riverside Landmark." *Press Enterprise*, August 29, 2021. https://www.pressenterprise.com/2021/08/29/how-martin-sanchezs-art-made-tios-tacos-a-riverside-landmark/.

Allen, Margaret Day. "The Inspired Art of Juanita Leonard." *Folk Art Messenger* 21:2 (Fall/Winter 2009), https://folkart.org/juanita-leonard/.

Anderson, Lincoln. "A Force of Nature Leaves a Tower in Avenue B Garden." *The Villager* 76:49 (May 2–8, 2007). https://web.archive.org/web/20080921133941/http://www.thevillager.com/villager_209/aforceofnatureleaves.html.

Arnett, William and Paul Arnett, eds., *Souls Grown Deep: African American Vernacular Art*. 2 vols. Atlanta, GA: Tinwood Books, 2000–01.

Art Spark Texas. "Vince Hannemann Interview–Cathedral of Junk." *YouTube*, January 8, 2021. https://www.youtube.com/watch?v=MyYT6oI4-Il.

Atlas Obscura. "Ohio's Whimsical Temple of Tolerance." *YouTube*, June 25, 2019. https://www.youtube.com/watch?v=5Uu0ooJk2lo.

Ballacchino, Katia. "Spires and Towers Between Tangible, Intangible, and Contested Transnational Cultural Heritage." In *Sabato Rodia's Towers in Watts: Art, Migrations, Development*, edited by Luisa Del Giudice, 289–305. New York: Fordham University Press, 2014.

Banks, Floyd Jr., and Fred Scruton. *Fortress of Faith*. Self-published, 2024.

Beach, Charlotte. "Cheri and Gonzalo of the Mosaic Tile House Express Their Love for Each Other One Tile at a Time." *Print Magazine*, March 15, 2023. https://www.printmag.com/designer-interviews/mosaic-tile-house/.

Beardsley, John. *Gardens of Revelation: Environments of Visionary Artists*. New York: Abbeville Press, 1995.

Beddingfield, Duante. "African Bead Museum Founder Olayami Dabls Named 2022 Kresge Eminent Artist." *Detroit Free Press*, January 27, 2022. https://www.freep.com/story/entertainment/2022/01/27/african-bead-museum-founder-olayami-dabls-named-kresge-eminent-artist/9230887002/.

Bedford, Clarke. *Vanadu Art House*. https://www.vanaduarthouse.org.

Bilek, Carl. "A Castle of Cans Holds Special Connection For Its Creator." *CPR News*, September 3, 2021. https://www.cpr.org/show-segment/a-castle-of-cans-holds-special-connection-for-its-creator/.

Bishop Castle. https://www.bishopcastle.org.

Blasdel, Gregg. "The Grassroots Artist." *Art in America* 56 (September–October 1968): 24–41.

_____. "The House of Mirrors." *Raw Vision* 56 (Autumn 2006): 24–31.

Borderzine Reporting across fronteras. "Casa 'de Azúcar' en El Paso." *YouTube*, April 13, 2017. https://www.youtube.com/watch?v=qTVKymaQfRY.

Boscarino, Ricky. www.lunaparc.com.

Boster, Seth. "Jim Bishop's Castle: A Towering Legacy Forged Through Sickness and Tragedy." *The Gazette* (Colorado Springs, CO), November 22, 2024. https://gazette.com/life/jim-bishop-was-the-complicated-king-of-a-stunning-colorado-castle/article_60059798-a844-11ef-aa2e-774a672d0ef0.html?fbclid=IwY2xjawGx8nhleHRuA2FlbQIxMQABHacTlvvUWgQ1nW6mYrGQ6EP4jC-QKyR72cB3Px4_f1Rtpp2LxM_XoXzlZg_aem_w5DYm-IFWa3X1OF1ZAwVqQ.

_____. "Meet the Man Behind Bishop Castle, Whose Colorado Creation Is a Source of Public Envy and Private Ruin." *The Gazette* (Colorado Springs, CO), August 28, 2016. https://gazette.com/life/meet-the-man-behind-bishop-castle-whose-colorado-creation-is-a-source-of-public-envy/article_bfec0eac-68fe-5e63-85b6-7736110a6c2d.html.

Bottoms, Greg. *Spiritual American Trash*. Berkeley, CA: Counterpart Press, 2013.

Bowsher, Jim. https://jimbowsher.com/the-temple-of-tolerance/.

Brackman, Barbara, and Cathy Dwigans, eds. *Backyard Visionaries: Grassroots Art in the Midwest*. Lawrence, KS: University Press of Kansas, 1999.

Burns, Evan. "The Junk King." *Colossal*, September 20, 2012. https://www.thisiscolossal.com/2012/09/an-austin-man-builds-a-cathedral-of-junk/.

Cardinal, Roger. "The Vulnerability of Outsider Architecture." *Southern Quarterly* 39:1-2 (Fall/Winter 2000–01): 169–86.

Carraher, Ronald. *Artists in Spite of Art*. New York: Van Nostrand Reinhold, 1970.

Carter, Theodore. "Clarke Bedford on Art Cars, Humor in Visual Art, and Comfort in Nonconformity." *Theodore Carter*, August 19, 2015. https://theodorecarter.com/clarke-bedford-on-art-cars-humor-in-visual-art-and-comfort-in-nonconformity/.

CBS Sunday Morning. "Cave-digging artist finds inspiration underground." *YouTube*, May 18, 2014. https://www.youtube.com/watch?app=desktop&v=oxcftjJ39BU&.

Cibelli, Deborah H. "Expression of Faith and Fear: The Chauvin Sculpture Garden by Kenny Hill." *National Center for Preservation Technology and Training*, September 8, 2018. https://www.nps.gov/media/video/view.htm%3Fid%3DAF4DAD8E-1DD8-B71B-0B66DD8E8C010785.

_____. "Kenny Hill's Revelatory Environment in Louisiana Bayou Country." *Raw Vision* 53 (Winter 2005): 58–63.

Cicala, John Allan, and Anthony Julian Tamburri. "A Moralizing Landscape as Scenography: Silvio Barile's 'Italian American Historical Artistic Museum.'" In *New Italian Migrations to the United States: Vol. 2: Art and Culture since 1945*, edited by Laura E. Ruberto and Joseph Sciorra, 93–116. Champaign, IL: University of Illinois Press, 2017.

"Connecting the World, One Bead at a Time." *School of Information, University of Michigan*, September 11, 2023. https://www.si.umich.edu/about-umsi/news/connecting-world-one-bead-time.

Conrads, Ulrich, and Hans G. Sperlich. *The Architecture of Fantasy*. New York: Frederick A. Praeger, 1962.

Cook, Katie. "African History Told Through Beads and Art at Detroit Museum." *WKAR Public Media*, September 19, 2016. https://www.wkar.org/arts-culture/2016-09-19/african-history-told-through-beads-and-art-at-detroit-museum.

Coral Castle Museum. https://coralcastle.com/.

Corso, Greg, and Molly Hunker. "No Rhyme or Reason: The Whimsicality of Folk Art Environments." *Shaping New Knowledge*. Conference Proceedings 104, Association of Collegiate Schools of Architecture (2016): 480–484.

Crown, Carol. "Paradise Revisited: The Desecration and Reclamation of Howard Finster's Paradise Garden." *Number 39* 15:1 (2001): 28–33.

Crown, Carol, and Charles Russell, eds. *Sacred and Profane: Voice and Vision in Southern Self-Taught Art.* Jackson, MS: University Press of Mississippi, 2007.

Dabls Mbad African Bead Museum. https://www.mbad.org.

D'Ambrosio, Brian. "Forevertron: The Mythic Obsession of Dr. Evermore's [*sic*] Kinetic Architecture." *Uncharted 101*, November 14, 2014. https://www.uncharted101.com/forevertron-the-mythic-obsession-of-dr-evermores-kinetic-architecture/.

Danchin, Laurent, and Pascale Marini-Jeanneret, *Architecture,* Lausanne: Collection de l'Art Brut, and Milan: 5 Continents Editions, 2015.

Darson, Steve. "More than Materialismo: Silvio Barile." *Raw Vision* 56 (Fall 2006): 42–47.

Décimo, Marc, and Sandra Persuy. "Megalometallic Hero-Making; or The Ordinary in the Life of Billy Tripp." *Southern Quarterly* 39:1-2 (Fall/Winter 2000–2001): 136–51.

Del Giudice, Luisa, ed. *Sabato Rodia's Towers in Watts: Art, Migrations, Development.* New York: Fordham University Press, 2014.

Delio, Michelle. "An Artist's Junkyard of Dreams." *Wired*, October 2004. https://www.wired.com/2004/10/an-artists-junkyard-of-dreams/.

Dickson, Bruce. "Tio's Tacos: Riverside's Folk Art Wonderland." *Artbound–KCET*, June 20, 2012. https://www.youtube.com/watch?v=FdK50RTArss.

Dinsmoor, Samuel P. *Pictorial History of the Cabin Home in Garden of Eden.* Lucas, KS: privately printed. Undated reprint of 1927 pamphlet.

"Dionicio Rodríguez." *The Cultural Landscape Foundation.* https://www.tclf.org/pioneer/dionicio-rodriguez.

"Do It Yourself 'Skyscraper.'" *Ebony* XVIII:5 (March 1963): 75–78.

Ellis, William L. "Billy Tripp's Mindfield." *Folk Art Messenger* 26:2 (Spring/Summer 2015): 9–13.

Esri. "Pasaquan." *ArcGIS*, 2016. https://www.arcgis.com/home/webmap/viewer.html?webmap=159f18cc0f164547a3cf188dd5ae969b&extent=-84.5832,32.3449,-84.5792,32.3472

Evans, Christopher. "Flower House Decorations Create Controversy in Cleveland Neighborhood: What's the Real Issue?" *Cleveland Sun*, April 13, 2016. https://www.cleveland.com/metro/2016/04/flower_house_decorations_create_controversy_in_cleveland_neighborhood_whats_the_real_issue.html.

Fallstead, Cheryl. "New Mexico Cavedigger–Ra Paulette." *Santa Fe*, September 29, 2020. https://santafe.com/ra-paulette-cavedigger/.

Farr, Jory. "On Fire: The Art of Charles Wince." *Shortnorth*, March/April 2013. https://www.shortnorth.com/WinceOnFire.html.

Fenoli, Marc. *Le Palais Idéal du facteur Cheval.* Grenoble: Éditions Glénat, 1991.

Ferguson, Wes. "For Years, an East Texas Carpenter Has Been Building a Gothic Contraption of Decks and Spikes in a Historic Square." *Texas Monthly*, June 2020. https://www.texasmonthly.com/arts-entertainment/east-texas-carpenter-gothic-contraption-decks-spikes-historic-square/.

Finster, Howard, with Tom Patterson. *Stranger from Another World: Man of Visions Now on This Earth.* New York: Abbeville Press, 1989.

Flynn, Annalise. "Vernacular Sanctuary in the American South." *Southern Cultures* 28:2 (2022). https://www.southerncultures.org/article/world-building-for-one/.

Fortraiture. "Tio's Taco The Most Unique Restaurant in America." *YouTube*, October 30, 2022. https://www.youtube.com/watch?v=ADYIh7z_P8Q.

Foster, M. Ruth. *The Cathedral of Junk: Cultural Critique Through Yard Art.* Master's thesis in history, University of Memphis, 2013.

Friedman, Martin, et.al. *Naives and Visionaries.* New York: E.P. Dutton and Co, 1974.

Friends of S.P. Dinsmoor's Garden of Eden, Inc. https://www.gardenofedenlucas.org, 2020.

Gavon, Lisa. "Rolling Mountain Thunder Aspired to a Radiant Heart." *Nevada Humanities*, May 9, 2024. https://www.nevadahumanities.org/blog/2024/5/6/rolling-mountain-thunder-aspired-to-a-radiant-heart.

_____. *The Nevada Monument of Rolling Mountain Thunder.* Self-published, 2024.

Gerloff, Scott. "National Register of Historic Places Inventory/Nomination: Lemmon Petrified Park." *National Park Service*, December 1975. https://npgallery.nps.gov/NRHP/GetAsset/NRHP/77001254_text.

Germain, Jacqui. "Iron, Wood, Rock and Mirrors: The Evolution of the MBad African Bead Museum." *Alive* 18:3 (December 2, 2019). https://www.alivemagarchives.com/our-stories/iron-wood-rock-and-mirrors-the-evolution-of-the-mbad-african-bead-museum.

Gershon, Pete. *Painting the Town Orange.* Charleston, NC: The History Press, 2014.

_____. "The Beer Can House." *Raw Vision* 110 (Spring 2022): 12–17.

Gilbert, David. "Cano's Castle, a Southern Colorado Folk Art Landmark, Is Heavily Damaged in Fire." *The Colorado Sun*, January 13, 2022. https://coloradosun.com/2022/01/13/canos-castle-fire-damage/.

Gili Galfetti, Gustau. *Mi Casa, Mi Paraíso.* Barcelona: Editorial Gustavo Gili, S.A., 1999.

Glassie, Henry H. *Vernacular Architecture.* Bloomington, IN: Indiana University Press and Philadelphia, PA: Material Culture, 2000.

Glendora Historical Society. *National Register of Historic Places Registration Form: Rubel Castle Historic District.* https://glendorahistoricalsociety.org/rubel_castle_historic_district.pdf.

_____. "Rubel Castle." https://www.glendorahistoricalsociety.org/castle/.

Godshall, Zack, dir. *God's Architects.* Film. 2009. https://www.zackgodshall.com/god-s-architects.

Gould, Steven Jay. "James Hampton's Throne and the Dual Nature of Time," *Smithsonian Studies in American Art* I:1 (Spring 1987): 46–57.

Griffiths, Alyn. "Cavedigger: Inside Ra Paulette's Luminous Subterranean World." *CNN*, December 15, 2015. https://www.cnn.com/style/article/cavedigger-new-mexico/index.html.

Groves, Martha. "A Mosaic-Loving Family's Journey of Many Tiles." *Los Angeles Times*, January 27, 2014. https://www.latimes.com/local/la-me-c1-tile-house-20140127-dto-htmlstory.html.

_____. "Let There Be Color." *Los Angeles Times*, February 19, 2003. https://www.latimes.com/archives/la-xpm-2003-feb-19-et-groves19-story.html.

Gundaker, Grey, ed. *Keep your Head to the Sky/Interpreting African American Home Ground.* Charlottesville, VA: University Press of Virginia, 1998.

Hapner, Breck. "Moment Of Explosion: Interview With Artist Charles Wince." *Medium*, March 6, 2022. https://medium.com/@breckjhapner/moment-of-explosion-interview-with-artist-charles-wince-fffae8f19ff7.

Harbison, Robert. *Eccentric Spaces.* Cambridge and London: MIT Press, 2000. Originally published in 1977 by Alfred A. Knopf.

Harlow, Elizabeth. “Dabls Honored for Unique Museum.” *Michigan Public*, February 14, 2022. https://www.michiganpublic.org/show/stateside/2022-02-14/one-city-block-and-thousands-of-beads-olayami-dabls-honored-for-unique-museum.

Hayes, Jeffrey R. “Dr. Evermor’s Forevertron.” *Folk Art Messenger* 11:1 (Winter 1988): 8–10.

_____. “Dr. Evermor’s Machine on the Prairie: Art, History, and the Mirror Eye.” *Southern Quarterly* 39:1-2 (Fall/Winter 2000–01): 112–35.

Headley, Gwyn. *Architectural Follies in America*. New York: John Wiley & Sons, Inc., 1996.

Headley, Gwyn, and Wim Meulenkamp. *Follies, Grottoes and Garden Buildings*. London: Aurum Press, 2003.

Heidelberg Project. www.heidelberg.org.

Hernández, Jo Farb. “A.G. Rizzoli: Master Architect.” *The Outsider* XII:2 (Fall 2007): 11–16.

_____ (as Joanne Farb). “Concrete Assemblage: Sculptural Fantasy as Folk Art.” Master’s thesis in Folklore and Mythology, University of California, Los Angeles, 1975.

_____. “Le torri di Sabato Rodia a Watts: Una Lunga Lotta e un’incerta Vittoria,” *Osservatorio Outsider Art* 21 (Spring 2021): 48–73.

_____. “Local Art, Global Issues: Tales of Survival and Demise Among Contemporary Art Environments.” In Luisa Del Giudice, ed., *Sabato Rodia’s Towers in Watts: Art, Migrations, Development*. New York: Fordham University Press, 2014: 29-67.

_____. “Singular Spaces/Authentic Visions.” In *Nonconformers*, edited by Lisa Slominski, 217–221. New Haven, CT, and London: Yale University Press, 2022.

_____. *Singular Spaces: From the Eccentric to the Extraordinary in Spanish Art Environments*. Watford, U.K.: Raw Vision; San José, CA: Natalie and James Thompson Art Gallery; Aptos, CA: SPACES, 2013.

_____. *Singular Spaces II: From the Eccentric to the Extraordinary in Spanish Art Environments*. Milan: 5 Continents Editions, 2023.

_____. “Taking It With You When You Go: The Monumentality of Death and Everlasting Life in Artist-built Environments.” *Eternal Sadness: Representations of Death in Visual Culture from Antiquity to the Present Time*, edited by Luis Vives-Ferrándiz Sánchez, *Eikón Imago* 10 (2021): 129–144.

_____. “Taya Doro Mitchell: Art for Healing.” *Raw Vision* 71 (Winter 2010/2011): 40–45.

_____. “Watts Towers.” *Raw Vision* 37 (December 2001): 32–39.

Hernández, Jo Farb, Roger Cardinal, and John Beardsley. *A.G. Rizzoli: Architect of Magnificent Visions*. New York: Harry N. Abrams, Inc., 1997.

Hinton, Marks. “Visitor’s Guide to the Beer Can House.” *The Orange Show Center for Visionary Art*, 2008. https://www.full.orangeshow.org/beer-can-house.

Hird, Kevin, and Jennifer Van Rite. “A. Clarke Bedford.” *University of Maryland–Art History*, April 2016. https://sites.google.com/terpmail.umd.edu/umd-art-history-museum-world/artists/a-clarke-beford.

Ho Peché, Linda. “El Paso’s Pride: La Casa de Azúcar, The House of Sugar.” *Texas Folklife Resources*, 2007. https://www.academia.edu/4247626/_El_Paso_s_Pride_La_Casa_de_Azucar_The_House_of_Sugar_?auto=download.

Holmes, Meghan. “Roadside Attraction: Juanita Leonard blends folk art with religious ministry.” *Country Roads Magazine*, October 25, 2018. https://countryroadsmagazine.com/art-and-culture/visual-performing-arts/roadside-attraction/.

Hooks, Margaret. *Surreal Eden: Edward James and Las Pozas*. New York: Princeton Architectural Press, 2006.

Huber, Leslie. “The Forevertron.” *Forevertron.org*, n.d. https://www.forevertron.org/frvt/.

Hunt, Ted. “Florida, Once Upon a Time: The Improbable History behind Florida’s ‘Stonehenge.’” *Citrus County Chronicle*, February 22, 2023. https://www.chronicleonline.com/florida-once-upon-a-time-the-improbable-history-behind-florida-s-stonehenge/article_ef301efc-865e-5807-8e0f-bb438d8d0f51.html.

Ingalls, Helen. “James Hampton’s Throne of the Third Heaven of the Nations’ Millennium General Assembly.” *National Park Service*, October 13, 2020. https://www.nps.gov/media/video/view.htm%3Fid%3DB0139FD5-1DD8-B71B-0B87F9C578ECA54B.

Jameson, Jennifer Joy. “Southern Voices: Rhinestone Man.” *Southern Cultures* 23:3 (Fall 2017): 79–90.

Karoff, Jeffrey. “Cave Digger.” *YouTube*, October 14, 2019. https://www.youtube.com/watch?v=9n_bHcZaGJs.

“Kea’s Improbable Art.” *Chicago Tribune*, April 22, 1987. https://www.chicagotribune.com/1987/04/22/keas-improbable-ark/.

Kendrick, Randall. “The Steel Garden.” *YouTube*, March 9, 2024. https://www.youtube.com/watch?v=r9-O3gJEhVA.

Kiaralinda Studio. http://www.kiaralinda.com/.

Kloos, Maarten. *Le paradis terrestre de Picassiette*. Paris: Éditions Encre, 1979.

Knights of the Golden Trail. *Loveland Castle*. https://lovelandcastle.com/.

Konvicka, Michael. *The House with the Face on the Chimney: Gene Dillard and His Vision*. Durham, NC: Self-published, 2023.

Kottler, Tya. *World of Dr. Evermor*. https://www.worldofdrevermor.com/.

Krasovic, Mark. “Have You Seen This Ark?” *Gallery Aferro*, 2016. https://aferro.org/wp-content/uploads/2013/11/2keasark_blue.pdf.

Krause, Sandy. “Rubel Castle.” *SPACES Archives*, n.d. https://spacesarchives.org/explore/search-the-online-collection/michael-clarke-rubel-castle/.

Kuhlman, Jerry, and Peralta Projects. “Roy Smith Documentary.” *YouTube*, November 25, 2018. https://www.youtube.com/watch?v=GRz-_D5GLGs.

Labrum, Chloe. “Ralphael Plescia’s Christian School.” *Bingham Prospector*, February 8, 2023. https://binghamprospector.org/arts-and-entertainment/2023/02/08/ralphael-plescias-christian-school/.

Landes, Tim. “Restoring Ed Galloway’s Totem Pole Park: A Q&A with Erin Turner about Her August Workshops and Lecture Series.” *Tulsa People*, July 5, 2023. https://www.tulsapeople.com/about-town/restoring-ed-galloways-totem-pole-park-a-q-a-with-erin-turner-about-her-august/article_5523a7ca-1b46-11ee-b8e3-5757121c90aa.html.

Langnser, Jules. “Sam of Watts.” *Arts and Architecture* 68:7 (July 1951): 23–25.

Latus, Janine. “Vollis Simpson’s Moving Art.” *Saturday Evening Post*, April 10, 2023. https://www.saturdayeveningpost.com/2023/04/vollis-simpsons-moving-art/.

“Les dèries d’una arquitectura imaginària.” *L’Avui*, October 12, 2006. https://www.monistrolde montserrat.cat/default.php?idcanal=3&idcategory=22&idsubcategory=0&idgroup=34&idevent=3122&hist=1.

Lidz, Franz. “Studying Dad’s Favorite Topic: Himself.” *New York Times*, August 13, 2009. https://www.nytimes.com/2009/08/16/arts/television/16lidz.html.

Light, Allie, and Irving Saraf. *Visions of Paradise. Grandma’s Bottle Village: The Art of Tressa Prisbrey*. Film. San Francisco, CA: Light-Saraf Films, 1982.

Light, Patsy Pittman. *Capturing Nature: The Cement Sculpture of Dionicio Rodríguez*. College Station, TX: Texas A&M University Press, 2008.

Lipke, William C., and Gregg Blasdel. *Clarence Schmidt*. Burlington, VT: Robert Hull Fleming Museum, University of Vermont, 1975.

Lombardi, Sarah. "The Exhibition *Richard Greaves Anarchitect.*" In *Taking the Road Less Traveled: Built Environments of Vernacular Artists,* 49–54. Sheboygan, WI: John Michael Kohler Arts Center and Kohler Foundation, Inc., 2007.

Lombardi, Sarah, and Valérie Rousseau. *Richard Greaves: Anarchitecte/Anarchitect*. Milan: 5 Continents Editions, and Montréal: Société des arts indisciplinés, 2005.

Long Island Craft Guild. "A tour of Luna Parc with Ricky Boscarino." *YouTube*, May 20, 2022. https://www.youtube.com/watch?v=lJNosJZJG78.

Low, Travis, Torben Bernhard, and Marissa Lila. "The Gospel According to Ralphael." *OHO Media*, 2016. https://vimeo.com/171180640.

Magliozzi, Marielle. *Art Brut, Architectures Marginales: Un art du bricolage*. Orléans, Fr.: L'Ecarlate/L'Harmattan, 2008.

Manley, Roger. *Signs and Wonders*. Raleigh, NC: North Carolina Museum of Art, 1989.

Manley, Roger, and Mark Sloan. *Self-Made Worlds: Visionary Folk Art Environments.* New York: Aperture, 1997.

Manno, Silvio. *The Forestiere Underground Gardens*. Fresno, CA: Ionian Publications, 2006.

McBride, Danielle. "Clarke Bedford's Vanadu Art House." *YouTube*, September 14, 2021. https://www.youtube.com/watch?v=_topJDpe4Cc.

McClure, Rusty, and Jack Heffron. *Coral Castle: The Mystery of Ed Leedskalnin and His American Stonehenge*. Dublin, OH: Ternary Publishing, 2009.

McGay, Maddie. "Once dilapidated, now a whimsical piece of art." *USA Today/North Jersey Media Group*, October 17, 2025: 7H.

"Meet The Cave Sculptor Creating Dreamy Subterranean Worlds Inside New Mexico's Hills." *Something Curated*, February 1, 2022. https://somethingcurated.com/2022/02/01/meet-the-cave-sculptor-creating-dreamy-subterranean-worlds-inside-new-mexicos-hills/.

Meier, Allison. "A Visit to an Overlooked Folk Art Cave of Crystals." *Hyperallergic*, October 23, 2013. https://hyperallergic.com/89785/a-visit-to-an-overlooked-folk-art-cave-of-crystals/.

Mendoza, Martha. "Artist Carves Shrine Into Sandstone Cliff." *Los Angeles Times*, September 1, 1996. https://www.latimes.com/archives/la-xpm-1996-09-01-me-39768-story.html.

Menzies, Richard. "A Monumental Undertaking." *Thunder Mountain Monument*, n.d. http://thundermountainmonument.com/background.htm.

Meyer, Norma. "Tio's Tacos Masters the Art of Recycling." *The San Diego Union-Tribune*, January 31, 2013. https://www.sandiegouniontribune.com/lifestyle/travel/sdut-tios-tacos-art-recycling-2013jan31-htmlstory.html.

Miller, M.H. "Tyree Guyton Turned a Detroit Street Into a Museum. Why Is He Taking It Down?" *New York Times*, May 9, 2019. https://www.nytimes.com/2019/05/09/magazine/tyree-guyton-art-detroit.html.

Miller, Naomi. *Heavenly Caves: Reflections on the Garden Grotto.* London: George Allen & Unwin, 1982.

Mina, Gabriele. *Costruttori de babele*. Milan: Elèuthera, 2011.

Mirandé, Mano. "'El Tio de Riverside': The Artistic Universe of Martín Sanchez." *The Riversider Magazine* 3:6 (December 2023): 28–33.

Mississippi Department of Archives & History. "History Is Lunch: Suzi Altman, 'Saving a Folk Art Icon: Margaret's Grocery.'" *YouTube*, August 25, 2021. https://www.youtube.com/watch?v=UBppOYCmSik.

Modiano, Sarah Anne. "Magical Mosaics: Preserving Isaiah Zagar's Philadelphia Art Environment." Master's thesis, Columbia University, 2011.

Montpied, Bruno. *Éloge des Jardins Anarchiques*. Montreuil, Fr.: L'insomniaque, 2011.

_____. *Le Gazouillis des Éléphants*. Saint-Loup-de-Naud, Fr.: Éditions du Sandre, 2017.

Morgan, Jeanne. "Rodia's Towers: Nuestro Pueblo, A Gift to the World." In *Personal Places: Perspectives on Informal Art Environments*, edited by Daniel Franklin Ward, 72–82. Bowling Green, OH: Bowling Green State University Popular Press, 1984.

Morton, Amy. "The Secret Sandstone Caves of New Mexico." *Tales of a Telecommuter*, March 24, 2013. https://talesofatelecommuter.blogspot.com/2013/03/the-secret-sandstone-caves-of-new-mexico.html.

Ngo, Audrey. "Tio's Tacos in Riverside Hides a Vast Outdoor Sculpture Museum." *Laist*, February 6, 2019. https://laist.com/news/food/tios-tacos-sculpture-museum-recycled-art-riverside.

Nicholls State University. *Chauvin Sculpture Garden*. https://www.nicholls.edu/folkartcenter/park.html.

Niles, Susan A. *Dickeyville Grotto: The Vision of Father Mathias Wernerus*. Jackson, MS: University Press of Mississippi, 1997.

Pann, Cheri, and Gonzalo Durán. *The Mosaic Tile House*. https://www.mosaictilehouse.com/.

Paradise Garden Foundation. https://paradisegardenfoundation.org/.

Parker, Mitchell. "First Comes Love, Then Comes a Wildly Colorful Mosaic House." *Houzz*, January 26, 2016. https://www.houzz.com/houzz-tv/houzz-tv-first-comes-love-then-comes-a-wildly-colorful-mosaic-home-stshtvvw-vt~60424172?sscid=51k8_5l9u3&utm_source=ShareASale&utm_medium=Affiliate&utm_campaign=314743&utm_term=1755841&vm=list.

Patterson, Sara M. *Middle of Nowhere: Religion, Art and Pop Culture at Salvation Mountain*. Albuquerque, NM: University of New Mexico Press, 2016.

Patterson, Tom. *St. EOM in the Land of Pasaquan*. Winston-Salem, NC: Jargon Society, 1987.

Peacock, Robert, and Annibel Jenkins. *Paradise Garden: A Trip Through Howard Finster's Visionary World*. San Francisco, CA: Chronicle Books, 1996.

Perkins, Jonas. https://www.jonasperkins.com/.

Philadelphia's Magic Gardens. https://www.phillymagicgardens.org.

Phillips, Jim. *Antler Collection*. https://www.antlerman.com/.

Picone, Kiri. "The Enigma of Coral Castle, The 2.2-Million-Pound Monument Made by a Single Man." *All That's Interesting*, October 4, 2021. https://allthatsinteresting.com/coral-castle.

Preserve Bottle Village Committee. *Bottle Village*. https://bottlevillage.weebly.com/.

Prévost, Claude, and Clovis Prévost. *Les Bâtisseurs de l'imaginaire*. Jarville-La Malgrange, Fr.: Éditions de l'Est, 1990.

Radford, Benjamin. "Mystery of the Coral Castle Explained." *Live Science*, June 1, 2018. https://www.livescience.com/41075-coral-castle.html.

Rappaz, Pauline. "Architectures Singulières." *Tracés* (Écublens, Switz.), January 29, 2016: 19–20.

Roadtrippers. "Eclectic Folk Art, a Beer Bottle Chapel, and Enchiladas with a Twist at Tio's Tacos." *Roadtrippers*, April 16, 2021. https://roadtrippers.com/magazine/tios-tacos-riverside-eclectic-art/.

Rosen, Seymour. *In Celebration of Ourselves*. San Francisco, CA: California Living Books, 1979.

Rosen, Seymour, and Paul LaPorte. *Simon Rodia's Towers in Watts*. Los Angeles, CA: Los Angeles County Museum of Art, 1962.

Rubio, Clara, and Edurne Rubio. "Arquitectura espontánea." *Historias Gemelas*. http://www.historiasgemelas.org/site/spip.php?article58.

Rubio, Elías. "Castillos para el siglo XXI." *Diario de Burgos* (October 31, 1993): 14–15.

Rudofsky, Bernard. *Architecture without Architects*. New York: Doubleday, 1964.

Rush, Katie, and Jerry Johnston, producers. *Emery Blagdon and His Healing Machine*. Film. *NET Television*, 2013. https://www.pbs.org/video/pbs-emery-blagdon-and-his-healing-machine/.

Salvation Mountain. https://www.salvationmountain.us/, 2004.

Salvation Mountain, Inc. https://salvationmountain.org/.

Sargent, Antwaun. "This Artist Took Over an Entire City Block to Build an African Bead Museum." *Vice*, March 20, 2018. https://www.vice.com/en/article/evqg7m/this-artist-took-over-an-entire-city-block-to-build-an-african-bead-museum.

Schrank, Sarah. "Picturing the Watts Towers: The Art and Politics of an Urban Landmark." In *Reading California: Art, Image, and Identity, 1900–2000*, edited by Stephanie Barron, Sheri Bernstein, and Ilene Susan Fort, 373–386. Berkeley, CA: University of California Press, 2000.

Schuyt, Michael, Joost Elffers, and George Roseborough Collins. *Fantastic Architecture: Personal and Eccentric Visions*. New York: Harry N. Abrams, 1980.

Sciorra, Joseph. *Built with Faith: Italian American Imagination and Catholic Material Culture in New York City*. Knoxville, TN: University of Tennessee Press, 2015.

_____. "'Why a Man Makes the Shoes?': Italian American Art and Philosophy in Sabato Rodia's Watts Towers." In *Sabato Rodia's Towers in Watts: Art, Migrations, Development*, edited by Luisa Del Giudice, 183–203. New York: Fordham University Press, 2014.

_____. "Yard Shrines and Sidewalk Altars of New York's Italian–Americans." In *Perspectives in Vernacular Architecture* III, edited by Tom Carter and Bernard Herman, 185–198. Columbia, MO: University of Missouri Press, 1989.

Scruton, Fred. "Billy Tripp: Navigating the Mindfield." *Raw Vision* 82 (Summer 2014): 32–37.

_____. "Dominic Espinoza: Pure of Heart." *Raw Vision* 86 (Summer 2015): 34–39.

_____. "Dr. Charles Smith." *Raw Vision* 92 (Winter 2016/2017): 40–47.

_____. "Floyd Banks' COVID message." *YouTube*, February 13, 2021. https://www.youtube.com/watch?si=FH5ztn8-PQXSESjG&v=pCDgPdxHIC8&feature=youtu.be.

_____. "Floyd 'Junior' Banks, Fortress of Faith Castle." 2019. *Vimeo*, February 13, 2021. https://vimeo.com/512087041.

_____. *Messages from the Interior*. Summit, NJ: Visual Arts Center of New Jersey, 2018.

_____. "Ms Juanita's Church." *Raw Vision* 90 (Summer 2016): 38–45.

_____. "Proof at the Greenback Castle that we are not alone in the universe." *YouTube*. https://www.youtube.com/watch?v=pCDgPdxHIC8.

_____. "Prophet Isaiah Robertson: Apocalypse at Niagara Falls." *Raw Vision* 80 (2013): 34–39.

_____. *Rivers of Fire and Redemption: The Niagara Falls Prophecy of Isaiah Robertson*. Film. 2014. www.fredscruton.com.

_____. "The Second Coming of the Second Coming House: Restoration of Prophet Isaiah Robertson's Second Coming House." *Folk Art Messenger* 33:3 (Winter/Spring 2024): 14–17.

_____. "WinceWorld." *Raw Vision* 107 (Summer 2021): 18–23.

Shaffer, Cory. "'Premeditated savagery': Couple Gets Life Sentences in Christmas Day Home-Invasion Murder of Lakewood Hairdresser." *Cleveland.com*, November 21, 2023. https://www.cleveland.com/court-justice/2023/11/premeditated-savagery-couple-gets-life-sentences-in-christmas-day-home-invasion-murder-of-lakewood-hairdresser.html.

Shane, Scott. "Junkyard Poet of Whirligigs and Windmills." *New York Times*, April 5, 2010. https://www.nytimes.com/2010/04/06/arts/design/06vollis.html.

Slagter, Lauren. "Partner Profile: Dabls Mbad African Bead Museum." *Michigan News*, September 28, 2022. https://detroit.umich.edu/news-stories/partner-profile-dabls-mbad-african-bead-museum/.

Slominski, Lisa, ed. *Nonconformers*. New Haven, CT, and London: Yale University Press, 2022.

Soler Sasera, Eva. "El delirio en construcción." *Levante Posdata* XVII:689 (November 20, 2009): 2–3.

Stansfield, William. "The Enigma of Coral Castle." *Skeptic* 12:2, 2006. https://www.bibliotecapleyades.net/ciencia/ciencia_modernmegalithsus02a.htm.

Stone, Lisa, and Jim Zanzi. "Grotto Follies in the Heartland." *The Follies Journal: Grottoes and Other Follies* 11 (Winter 2011): 1–17.

_____. *Sacred Spaces and Other Places: A Guide to Grottos and Sculptural Environments in the Upper Midwest*. Chicago, IL: School of the Art Institute of Chicago, 1993.

Stone, Lisa, Jim Zanzi, and Earl Iversen. "In Imitation of Nature: Father P.M. Dobberstein's Grottoes in Iowa and Wisconsin." In *Backyard Visionaries: Grassroots Art in the Midwest*, edited by Barbara Brackman and Cathy Dwigans, 50–69. Lawrence, KS: University Press of Kansas, 1999.

Stryker, Mark. "The End, and a New Beginning, for Detroit's Iconic Heidelberg Project." *Detroit Free Press*, August 14, 2016. https://www.freep.com/story/entertainment/arts/2016/08/14/heidelberg-project-guyton-dismantle/88626738/.

"The Heidelberg Project." *The Cultural Landscape Foundation*, 2014. https://www.tclf.org/sites/default/files/microsites/art-landscape/heidelberg-project.html.

"'The Incuriosity Bedroom' Is a Traffic Stopper." *Lodi News-Sentinel*, June 17, 1953, n.p.

The Orange Show Center for Visionary Art. "The Beer Can House." *The Orange Show*. https://www.full.orangeshow.org/beer-can-house.

The Shrine of the Grotto of the Redemption. https://www.westbendgrotto.com/.

Thieken Moore, Lindsey. "At Home: It's Wince's World, and We're Just Living In it." *Columbus Underground*, September 12, 2023. https://columbusunderground.com/at-home-its-winces-world-and-were-just-living-in-it-lt1/.

"Thunder Mountain Park." *Roadside America*, 1988. https://www.roadsideamerica.com/story/7813.

Townsend, Eileen. "The Secrets of Crystal Shrine Grotto." *Memphis Magazine*, December 1, 2015. https://memphismagazine.com/culture/the-secrets-of-crystal-shrine-grotto/.

Trillin, Calvin. "I Know I Want to Do Something." *The New Yorker* (May 29, 1965): 72–120.

Turner, Erin P. "Restoration of Ed Galloway's Totem Pole Park." Conference proceedings, *Are We There Yet? Preserving Roadside Architecture and Attractions*, April 10–12, 2018, Tulsa, OK. https://www.nps.gov/articles/000/restoration-of-ed-galloway-s-totem-pole-park.htm.

"Two Houses." *Progressive Architecture* (May 1968): 101–103.